Table of Contents

Fix-It and Enjoy-It!® Diabetic Cookbook

Fix-It and Enjoy-It!® Diabetic Cookbook

Stove-Top and Oven Recipes – for Everyone!

By *The New York Times* bestselling author

Phyllis Pellman Good

with

American Diabetes Association®

Cure • Care • Commitment®

Good 🌳 Books®

Intercourse, PA 17534
800/762-7171
www.GoodBooks.com

Although the analysts and editors have attempted full accuracy in the nutritional data and analyses included in this cookbook, many variables (including variations related to particular brands, to the refinement of products, and to the exact amounts of ingredients, as well as whether they are cooked or raw) could result in the analyses being approximate.

Because many factors influence your health, please check with your health-care expert before making substantial changes in what you eat.

Cover design and illustrations by Cheryl Benner
Design by Cliff Snyder

FIX-IT AND ENJOY-IT!® DIABETIC COOKBOOK
Copyright © 2007 by Good Books, Intercourse, PA 17534

International Standard Book Number: 978-1-56148-579-6 (paperback edition)
International Standard Book Number: 978-1-56148-581-9 (hardcover gift edition)
International Standard Book Number: 978-1-56148-580-2 (comb-bound paperback edition)
Library of Congress Catalog Card Number: 2007021593

Library of Congress Cataloging-in-Publication Data
Good, Phyllis Pellman, 1948-
Fix-it and enjoy-it diabetic cookbook : stove-top and oven recipes-for everyone! / Phyllis Pellman Good.
    p. cm.
Includes index.
ISBN-13: 978-1-56148-579-6 (pbk.), ISBN-13: 978-1-56148-580-2 (plastic comb binding)
ISBN-13: 978-1-56148-581-9 (hardcover) 1. Diabetes--Diet therapy--Recipes. I. Title.
RC662.G599 2007
641.5'6314--dc22   2007021593

About *Fix-It and Enjoy-It Diabetic Cookbook*

The recipes in this collection are for everyone! No more isolating persons with diabetes at mealtime. In fact, these delicious recipes offer both great taste and nutritional value—and easy preparation—the *Fix-It and Enjoy-It* trademark.

The American Diabetes Association joined us in this cookbook, using their know-how to adapt the recipes and analyze them so they fit into meal plans. Each recipe is followed by its Exchange List Values and its Basic Nutritional Values. Persons with diabetes need this information so they can manage their calories, and their carb, fat, and sodium counts.

Do you wish you knew more about diabetes?

Don't miss the basic information given in our introduction, "Healthy Choices When You Have Diabetes" (pages 5-6) and, after the recipes, "10 Most Asked Questions About Diabetes" (pages 270-271). If you want to learn more, see the "Recommended Reading List" on page 283.

Would you like a little more help to manage your own or your loved one's eating? The American Diabetes Association provides a Week of Menus on pages 255-270, using one or two recipes from this cookbook each day.

Calculating the Nutritional Analyses

If the number of servings is given as a range, we used the higher number to do the nutritional analyses calculations.

The nutritional analysis for each recipe includes all ingredients except those labeled "optional," those listed as "to taste," or those calling for a "dash." If an ingredient is listed with a second choice, the first choice was used in the analysis. If a range is given for the amount of an ingredient, the first number was used. Foods listed as "serve with" at the end of a recipe, or accompanying foods listed without an amount, were not included in the recipe's analysis. In recipes calling for cooked rice, pasta, or other grains, the analysis is based on the starch being prepared without added salt or fat, unless indicated otherwise in the recipe.

Please note, too, that the nutritional analyses do not cover the ingredients included in the Tips and Variations which follow some of the recipes.

The analyses were done assuming that meats were trimmed of all visible fat, and that skin was removed from poultry, before being cooked.

Relax and enjoy these recipes!

Mealtimes should be refreshing. Now you can relax and enjoy these recipes because you know the content of what you're preparing and how that will affect a meal plan.

These easy-to-prepare recipes take so little time and attention, they'll help you stick to your food goals.

Diabetes need not keep us from all gathering around the table together, eating tasty, wholesome food.

After all, a diet that's healthy for persons with diabetes is healthy for everyone. And everyone can eat and enjoy it when you use recipes from *Fix-It and Enjoy-It Diabetic Cookbook: Stove-Top and Oven Recipes—for Everyone*!

— *Phyllis Pellman Good*

Healthy Choices When You Have Diabetes

Popular nutrition suggestions seem to change on a weekly basis. Fad diets become popular, "cure" diets for diseases blanket the news, and a new nutrition revolution is proclaimed. Then, months later, these claims fade away as it becomes apparent that the unrealistic assertions and hard-to-believe results were, in fact, too good to be true.

No matter what the latest diet fad promises, the recommendations for people with diabetes remain relatively the same—*count carbohydrates, avoid saturated fat, eat moderate portions, and focus on fruits, vegetables, and whole grains.* Choosing the right foods, exercising every day (such as walking), and taking diabetes medications are the three things you can do to balance your blood sugar levels and stay healthy.

Carbohydrates and Diabetes

All carbohydrates raise blood glucose levels for those who have diabetes. Because of this, it has been suggested that people with diabetes should simply not eat carbohydrates. In theory, this sounds like a pretty good idea. Unfortunately, it's more complicated than that. Not only would it be difficult for a person to go his or her entire life without eating bread, milk, pasta, or starchy vegetables, it would also be very unhealthy.

Whole-grain breads and pastas are actually quite good for you, and vegetables are veritable nutrition powerhouses, packed with vitamins and minerals.

And let's not forget that these foods contain a lot of fiber, which slows down digestion of your food, which in turn slows down the rise in your blood sugar. Eating foods with fiber keeps your body working well. Cutting out all of these foods, as some diets suggest, is simply bad for you.

However, there are some carbohydrate-containing foods that are best avoided. Sugary foods and drinks, and highly processed snack foods made from white flour, are filled with carbohydrates, calories, and not much else. These foods generally have very little nutritional value, and, because they don't have fiber, these carbs are digested quickly, raising blood sugar more quickly, too.

Chips, cookies, and desserts are carb foods that also contain fat. Fat slows down digestion, so it helps to balance the blood-sugar spike caused by white flour and white sugar. But some fats are better for you than others. Most processed foods contain fats called trans fats that are found in the "hydrogenated vegetable oil" listed on the ingredients label. We are learning that trans fats may be the worst of the saturated fats, and as you've probably seen or heard in the news, many restaurants, manufacturers, and even entire cities are eliminating trans fats from their foods.

Good Fats

Research shows that we all need to eat some fat every day. Our bodies just don't work right without fats. So which fats are best for your health?

Stay away from saturated fats and trans fats, which are often found in solid form, such as margarine, butter, marbled meat, or cheese. Vegetable oils are better, and olive oil and canola oil are the best oils because they contain balanced amounts of omega-6 and omega-3 fats. These fats are important for your heart and blood vessels (which is why you should eat more fish and soy).

Other good fats include nuts, avocados, olives, nut butters, olive oil, canola oils, sesame seeds, and sunflower seeds. In fact, you might try a handful or two of raw almonds as a part of your daily "bread."

Moderate Portions and Physical Activity

It's becoming more and more obvious that much of the weight gain and related illness in our culture is coming not necessarily from what we eat, but from *how much* we eat. When this is coupled with our increasingly sedentary lifestyle, you get the current obesity epidemic. Choosing moderate portions, avoiding the super-sized meals found in restaurants, and getting at least some physical activity are often the easiest steps to losing weight and improving health.

Remember:

- **Good carb choices:** whole grains, fruits, and vegetables.
- **Good fat choices:** olive oil, avocados, fish, nuts, and seeds.
- **Good lifestyle choices:** moderate portions and physical activity.

Cure • Care • Commitment®

Appetizers and Snacks

Hot Virginia Dip

Sue Suter
Millersville, PA

*Makes 4 cups, or 32 servings
Serving size is 2 Tbsp.*

**Prep Time: 20-30 minutes
Baking Time: 20-25 minutes**

1 cup chopped pecans
2 Tbsp. butter
2 8-oz. pkgs. fat-free cream
  cheese, softened
4 Tbsp. fat-free milk
5 ozs. dried beef, chopped
1 tsp. garlic powder
1 cup fat-free sour cream
4 tsp. chopped onion

1. In skillet, saute pecans in butter. Set aside.
2. Combine remaining ingredients. Spread in greased baking dish.
3. Sprinkle sauted pecans over top.
4. Bake at 350° for 20-25 minutes.

Exchange List Values:
Very Lean Meat 1.0, Fat 0.5

Basic Nutritional Values:
Calories 60 (Calories from Fat 31),
Total Fat 3 gm (Saturated Fat 0.7
gm, Trans Fat 0.0 gm, Polyunsat
Fat 0.7 gm, Monounsat Fat 1.8 gm,
Cholesterol 6 mg), Sodium 263 mg,
Total Carbohydrate 2 gm, Dietary
Fiber 0 gm, Sugars 1 gm, Protein 4 gm

Ham Dip

John D. Allen
Rye, CO

*Makes 4 cups, or 32 servings
Serving size is 2 Tbsp.*

**Prep Time: 15 minutes
Chilling Time: 8 hours,
  or overnight**

8 ozs. finely chopped,
  extra-lean, low-sodium,
  cooked ham
1½ cups fat-free mayonnaise
1⅓ cups fat-free sour cream
2 Tbsp. chopped onion

2 Tbsp. chopped fresh
  parsley
2 tsp. dill seed
2 tsp. Beau Monde
  Seasoning

1. Combine all ingredients thoroughly.
2. Refrigerate for 8 hours.
3. Serve with crackers, chips, or cocktail rye bread.

Exchange List Values:
Fat 0.5

Basic Nutritional Values:
Calories 23 (Calories from Fat 1),
Total Fat 0 gm (Saturated Fat 0.1
gm, Trans Fat 0.0 gm, Polyunsat
Fat 0.0 gm, Monounsat Fat 0.1 gm,
Cholesterol 4 mg), Sodium 179 mg,
Total Carbohydrate 2 gm, Dietary
Fiber 0 gm, Sugars 1 gm, Protein 2 gm

Sausage Bean Dip

Sherlyn Hess
Millersville, PA

Makes 6 cups, or 48 servings
Serving size is 2 Tbsp.

Prep Time: 30 minutes
Cooking Time:
15 minutes on stove-top,
or 3 hours in slow cooker

½ lb. bulk sausage
½ lb. hot sausage,
    squeezed out of casing
⅔ cup chopped onions
2 16-oz. cans B&B beans
1 cup barbecue sauce
3 Tbsp. brown sugar

1. Brown sausage and onions in skillet. Drain.
2. Combine all ingredients in food processor or blender. Blend until smooth.
3. Heat in slow cooker for 3 hours on low, or in a saucepan on the stove for 15 minutes.
4. Serve warm with crackers, nachos, or tortilla chips.

Exchange List Values:
Carb 0.5, Fat 0.5

Basic Nutritional Values:
Calories 49 (Calories from Fat 16), Total Fat 2 gm (Saturated Fat 0.7 gm, Trans Fat 0.0 gm, Polyunsat Fat 0.2 gm, Monounsat Fat 0.8 gm, Cholesterol 6 mg), Sodium 202 mg, Total Carbohydrate 7 gm, Dietary Fiber 1 gm, Sugars 3 gm, Protein 2 gm

Baked Clam Dip

Barbara Lukan
Ridgewood, New York

Makes 1 cup, or 8 servings
Serving size is 2 Tbsp.

Prep Time: 5-8 minutes
Baking Time: 30 minutes

6.5-oz. can minced clams
¼ cup bread crumbs
1 tsp. garlic powder
1 tsp. parsley
⅛ tsp. dried oregano
⅛ tsp. salt
1 tsp. chopped onion
2 Tbsp. oil
Parmesan cheese
crackers

1. Combine all but Parmesan cheese and crackers. Pour into small greased baking dish. Sprinkle with cheese.
2. Bake at 275° for 25-30 minutes.
3. Serve with crackers.

Exchange List Values:
Carb 0.5, Very Lean Meat 1.0, Fat 0.5

Basic Nutritional Values:
Calories 82 (Calories from Fat 38), Total Fat 4 gm (Saturated Fat 0.4 gm, Trans Fat 0.0 gm, Polyunsat Fat 1.3 gm, Monounsat Fat 2.1 gm, Cholesterol 15 mg), Sodium 88 mg, Total Carbohydrate 4 gm, Dietary Fiber 0 gm, Sugars 2 gm, Protein 6 gm

Dilly Crab Dip

Joyce M Shackelford
Green Bay, Wisconsin

Makes 1½ cups, or 12 servings
Serving size is 2 Tbsp.

Prep Time: 30 minutes
Chilling Time: 2-8 hours

½ cup reduced-fat
    mayonnaise *or* salad
    dressing
½ cup reduced-fat sour
    cream
1 cup flaked crabmeat,
    divided
1 tsp. dried dill weed
2 tsp. finely chopped onion
    or scallion
½ tsp. finely shredded
    lime peel
1 tsp. lime juice
dash of bottled hot pepper
    sauce
dash ground red pepper,
    optional
salt and pepper to taste

1. Stir together mayonnaise, sour cream, ⅔ cup crabmeat, dill weed, onion, lime peel, lime juice, hot pepper sauce, and red pepper. Season with salt and pepper to taste.
2. Refrigerate for 2 hours, or overnight.
3. Just before serving, sprinkle with reserved crabmeat.
4. Serve with warm or chilled artichokes or crackers.

Exchange List Values:
Fat 1.0

Basic Nutritional Values:
Calories 57 (Calories from Fat 39),
Total Fat 4 gm (Saturated Fat 1.2
gm, Trans Fat 0.0 gm, Polyunsat
Fat 1.9 gm, Monounsat Fat 1.0 gm,
Cholesterol 16 mg), Sodium 122 mg,
Total Carbohydrate 2 gm, Dietary
Fiber 0 gm, Sugars 1 gm, Protein 3 gm

*Tip: Canned or frozen crab
meat may be used.*

Cheese and Shrimp Strudel

D. Fern Ruth
Chalfont, PA

*Makes 18 slices
Serving size is 1 slice*

*Prep Time: 20 minutes
Baking Time: 20-25 minutes
Cooling Time: 20 minutes*

half a 17.25-oz. pkg.
 (1 sheet) frozen puff
 pastry, thawed
¾ cup (3 ozs.) shredded,
 reduced-fat Swiss cheese
½ cup fat-free sour cream
¼ cup thinly sliced green
 onion
1 cup (4 ozs.) cooked
 shrimp, chopped, *or*
 4.5-oz. can shrimp,
 rinsed, drained, and
 chopped
1 egg, beaten

1. On a lightly floured
surface, roll the thawed puff
pastry to a 10 x 18 rectangle.

2. Place rectangle of pastry
on lightly greased, large
baking sheet.

3. In a medium-sized bowl,
stir together cheese, sour
cream, onion, shrimp, and
half the beaten egg (about 2
Tbsp.).

4. Spread the mixture
lengthwise down half of the
rectangle. Brush edges of
pastry (using pastry brush)
with some of the remaining
beaten egg.

5. Carefully fold dough
over the filling and seal edges
with the tines of a fork. Brush
top and sides of strudel with
remaining egg.

6. Bake at 400° for 20-25
minutes, or until golden.

7. Remove from oven
and cool 20 minutes before
slicing.

8. With a very sharp knife,
slice slightly on the diagonal.

Exchange List Values:
Starch 0.5, Lean Meat 1.0

Basic Nutritional Values:
Calories 84 (Calories from Fat 41),
Total Fat 5 gm (Saturated Fat 1.4
gm, Trans Fat 1.3 gm, Polyunsat
Fat 0.4 gm, Monounsat Fat 1.3 gm,
Cholesterol 26 mg), Sodium 110 mg,
Total Carbohydrate 5 gm, Dietary
Fiber 0 gm, Sugars 1 gm, Protein 5 gm

*Tip: You can also make this
with crabmeat, or a combination of shrimp and crab.*

*This is part of our late-
evening meal of oyster stew and
varied appetizers and desserts
at our family homestead, following Christmas Eve services at
church.*

Salmon Spread

Erma Brubaker
Harrisonburg, VA

*Makes 1½ cups, or 12 servings
Serving size is 2 Tbsp.*

Prep Time: 5 minutes

2 6-oz. cans salmon
 (without bones or black
 skin)
8 ozs. light cream cheese
1 Tbsp. dried onion
1 Tbsp. light hickory
 smoke
1 Tbsp. Worcestershire
 sauce
1 Tbsp. lemon juice
1 Tbsp. horseradish

1. In mixing bowl, mix
together salmon, cream
cheese, onion, hickory smoke,
Worcestershire sauce, lemon
juice, and horseradish.

2. Beat together for 2
minutes or until smooth.

3. Serve with your favorite
crackers.

Exchange List Values:
Lean Meat 1.0, Fat 0.5

Basic Nutritional Values:
Calories 86 (Calories from Fat 51),
Total Fat 6 gm (Saturated Fat 3.0
gm, Trans Fat 0.0 gm, Polyunsat
Fat 0.6 gm, Monounsat Fat 2.0 gm,
Cholesterol 23 mg), Sodium 227 mg,
Total Carbohydrate 1 gm, Dietary
Fiber 0 gm, Sugars 1 gm, Protein 7 gm

Hot Cheese Dip
Renee D. Groff
Manheim, PA

Makes 7 cups, or 56 servings
Serving size is 2 Tbsp.

Prep Time: 10 minutes
Baking Time: 25 minutes

2 cups shredded reduced-
  fat mozzarella cheese
2 cups shredded reduced-
  fat cheddar cheese
2 cups fat-free mayonnaise
1 medium-sized onion,
  chopped
4-oz. can chopped green
  chilies, drained
1½ ozs. sliced
  turkey pepperoni
½ cup sliced black olives

1. Combine cheeses, mayonnaise, onion, and green chilies.
2. Pour into greased 8 x 12
baking dish or 9" or 10" pie
pan.
3. Top with pepperoni and
black olives.
4. Bake at 325° for 25
minutes.
5. Serve warm with crack-
ers and/or corn chips.

Exchange List Values:
Fat 0.5

Basic Nutritional Values:
Calories 32 (Calories from Fat 15),
Total Fat 2 gm (Saturated Fat 0.9
gm, Trans Fat 0.0 gm, Polyunsat
Fat 0.1 gm, Monounsat Fat 0.5 gm,
Cholesterol 6 mg), Sodium 153 mg,
Total Carbohydrate 2 gm, Dietary
Fiber 0 gm, Sugars 1 gm, Protein 2 gm

Spinach Dip
Karen Stoltzfus
Alto, MI

Makes 4½ cups, or 36 servings
Serving size is 2 Tbsp.

Prep Time: 10-15 minutes

1 envelope dry vegetable
  soup mix
8 ozs. reduced-fat sour
  cream
1 cup reduced-fat
  mayonnaise
10-oz. pkg. frozen chopped
  spinach, thawed and
  squeezed dry
8-oz. can water chestnuts,
  drained and chopped

1. Combine all ingredients.
2. Serve with crackers.

Exchange List Values:
Fat 1.0

Basic Nutritional Values:
Calories 42 (Calories from Fat 26),
Total Fat 3 gm (Saturated Fat 0.9
gm, Trans Fat 0.0 gm, Polyunsat
Fat 1.2 gm, Monounsat Fat 0.7 gm,
Cholesterol 5 mg), Sodium 203 mg,
Total Carbohydrate 3 gm, Dietary
Fiber 0 gm, Sugars 1 gm, Protein 1 gm

Healthy Hummus
Barbara Forrester Landis
Lititz, PA

Makes 1½ cups, or 12 servings
Serving size is 2 Tbsp.

Prep Time: 15 minutes

1½ cups drained canned
  Great Northern beans
¼ red onion, chopped
1 tsp. fresh minced garlic
1 tsp. fresh rosemary,
  finely chopped
1 tsp. Kosher salt, or to taste
1 tsp. black pepper, or to taste
½ cup extra-virgin olive oil

1. In a food processor, puree
beans until they are halfway
between chunky and smooth.
2. Add onion, garlic,
rosemary, salt, and pepper.
3. Puree while drizzling in
olive oil.
4. Add more or less olive
oil, salt, and pepper to taste.
5. Serve with crackers
or pita chips. Or spread in
tortilla wraps with roasted
vegetables, or with cheese
and salsa.

Exchange List Values:
Starch 0.5, Fat 1.5

Basic Nutritional Values:
Calories 105 (Calories from Fat 82),
Total Fat 9 gm (Saturated Fat 1.2
gm, Trans Fat 0.0 gm, Polyunsat
Fat 0.9 gm, Monounsat Fat 6.7 gm,
Cholesterol 0 mg), Sodium 35 mg,
Total Carbohydrate 5 gm, Dietary
Fiber 1 gm, Sugars 1 gm, Protein 2 gm

*Note: The hummus should be
spreadable.*

Fruit Dip
Wanda Marshall
Massillon, OH

Makes 2 cups, or 16 servings
Serving size is 2 Tbsp.

Prep Time: 10-15 minutes

1 pint fat-free sour cream
¼ cup brown sugar
   substitute
6 ⅔-oz. macaroon cookies
   crushed or broken

1. If the cookies are hard, crush with a rolling pin. If softer, break into small pieces.
2. Mix together sour cream and brown sugar substitute. If using hard cookies, stir in small pieces and allow to stand for 5 hours or longer. If using soft cookies, stir in cookie pieces just before serving.
3. Serve as a dipping sauce for bite-sized chunks of pineapple, cantaloupe, kiwi, and watermelon.

Exchange List Values:
Carb 0.5, Fat 0.5

Basic Nutritional Values:
Calories 63 (Calories from Fat 14), Total Fat 2 gm (Saturated Fat 1.3 gm, Trans Fat 0.0 gm, Polyunsat Fat 0.0 gm, Monounsat Fat 0.1 gm, Cholesterol 3 mg), Sodium 28 mg, Total Carbohydrate 7 gm, Dietary Fiber 0 gm, Sugars 6 gm, Protein 2 gm

Cranberry Appetizer
Christie Detamore-Hunsberger
Harrisonburg, VA

Makes 8 servings
Serving size is 2½ Tbsp.

Prep Time: 5-10 minutes
Cooking Time: 20 minutes
Cooling Time: 1 hour

1 cup water
½ cup sugar blend for
   baking (Splenda)
8- *or* 12-oz. pkg. fresh
   cranberries
½ cup low-sugar apricot
   preserves
2 Tbsp. lemon juice
⅓ cup toasted slivered
   almonds
8-oz. pkg. fat-free cream
   cheese

1. In saucepan over medium heat, bring sugar blend and water to a boil without stirring. Boil 5 minutes.
2. Add cranberries and cook until the berries pop, about 10 minutes. Remove from heat.
3. Add preserves, lemon juice, and almonds. Cool.
4. Place cream cheese block on a serving dish. Pour cranberry mixture over cheese. Serve with crackers.

Exchange List Values:
Carb 1.0

Basic Nutritional Values:
Calories 83 (Calories from Fat 13), Total Fat 1 gm (Saturated Fat 0.1 gm, Trans Fat 0.0 gm, Polyunsat

Fat 0.3 gm, Monounsat Fat 0.9 gm, Cholesterol 2 mg), Sodium 115 mg, Total Carbohydrate 14 gm, Dietary Fiber 1 gm, Sugars 12 gm, Protein 3 gm

Peanut-Buttery Fresh Fruit Dip
Mary Jane Musser
Manheim, PA

Makes 3 cups, or 24 servings
Serving size is 2 Tbsp.

Prep Time: 5 minutes

1 cup peanut butter
8-oz. pkg. fat-free cream
   cheese, softened
½ cup brown sugar blend
   (Splenda)
¼ cup milk

1. Mix all ingredients together until well blended. Chill.
2. Serve with sliced apples.

Exchange List Values:
Carb 0.5, Fat 1.0

Basic Nutritional Values:
Calories 95 (Calories from Fat 51), Total Fat 6 gm (Saturated Fat 1.1 gm, Trans Fat 0.0 gm, Polyunsat Fat 1.6 gm, Monounsat Fat 2.7 gm, Cholesterol 1 mg), Sodium 122 mg, Total Carbohydrate 7 gm, Dietary Fiber 1 gm, Sugars 5 gm, Protein 4 gm

Zingy Cheese Spread

Lois Gae E. Kuh
Penfield, NY

Makes 2 cups, or 16 servings
Serving size is 2 Tbsp.

Prep Time: 5-7 minutes

10-oz. jar low-sugar
  pineapple marmalade
10-oz. jar sugar-free
  applesauce
5½-6-oz. jar white
  horseradish
3 Tbsp. dry mustard
2 8-oz. pkgs. fat-free cream
  cheese

1. Combine marmalade,
applesauce, horseradish,
and dry mustard until well
mixed.
2. Place blocks of cheese
on a serving plate. Pour zingy
mixture over cream cheese.
3. Refrigerate until ready
to serve.
4. Serve with cut-up fresh
vegetables or a variety of
snack crackers.

Exchange List Values:
Carb 1.0

Basic Nutritional Values:
Calories 73 (Calories from Fat 4),
Total Fat 0 gm (Saturated Fat 0.0
gm, Trans Fat 0.0 gm, Polyunsat
Fat 0.0 gm, Monounsat Fat 0.0 gm,
Cholesterol 3 mg), Sodium 231 mg,
Total Carbohydrate 12 gm, Dietary
Fiber 1 gm, Sugars 9 gm, Protein 4 gm

Artichoke Appetizer

Joyce Bowman
Lady Lake, FL

Makes 10 servings
Serving size is 3 pieces

Prep Time: 30 minutes
Baking Time: 8-10 minutes

14-oz. can artichokes,
  drained
¾ cup fat-free mayonnaise
¾ cup Parmesan cheese
1 tube refrigerated
  biscuits, 10-biscuit size

1. Cut artichokes in pieces.
Set aside.
2. Mix mayonnaise and
Parmesan cheese together. Set
aside.
3. Snip or cut each biscuit
in thirds and press each
lightly into a square shape.
Spread mayonnaise mixture
on each biscuit piece. Top
each with a piece of artichoke.
4. Place on lightly greased
baking sheet.
5. Bake at 400° for 8-10
minutes. Watch carefully so
they don't burn.

Exchange List Values:
Carb 1.0, Fat 0.5

Basic Nutritional Values:
Calories 100 (Calories from Fat 27),
Total Fat 3 gm (Saturated Fat 1.4
gm, Trans Fat 0.0 gm, Polyunsat
Fat 0.3 gm, Monounsat Fat 0.7 gm,
Cholesterol 6 mg), Sodium 430 mg,
Total Carbohydrate 14 gm, Dietary
Fiber 1 gm, Sugars 3 gm, Protein 5 gm

*Note: After the biscuits have
been baked, you can cool them
and then place them in freezer
bags and store them in the
freezer until you need them.
To serve, heat them in the
microwave.*

Crab-Stuffed Mushrooms

Kim Stoll
Abbeville, SC

Makes 6 servings
Serving size is 2 mushrooms

Prep Time: 30 minutes
Baking Time: 15 minutes

12 large, fresh mushrooms
vegetable spray
½ cup crabmeat, chopped
  fine
¼ cup fat-free cream cheese,
  at room temperature
½ cup reduced-fat Monterey
  Jack cheese, grated
dash of pepper
½ tsp. garlic powder

1. Clean mushrooms and
remove stems.
2. Spray mushroom tops
lightly with vegetable spray
and place each one in a muffin tin cup, bottom-side up.
3. Mix remaining ingredi-
ents together in a bowl.
4. Fill mushrooms with
crab-cheese mixture.
5. Bake at 400° for
15 minutes.

Basic Nutritional Values:
Calories 59 (Calories from Fat 21),
Total Fat 2 gm (Saturated Fat 1.2
gm, Trans Fat 0.0 gm, Polyunsat
Fat 0.1 gm, Monounsat Fat 0.5 gm,
Cholesterol 14 mg), Sodium 187 mg,
Total Carbohydrate 4 gm, Dietary
Fiber 1 gm, Sugars 1 gm, Protein 7 gm

Variations:
1. You can substitute other cheese for the Monterey Jack, such as Colby or mozzarella.
2. Instead of using mushroom caps, cut slices of bread into quarters, dip in the melted butter, and push down into the individual cups in a mini-muffin pan. Fill the center of each bread cup with the crab mixture. Bake according to directions above.

Stuffed Mushrooms
Hannah D. Burkholder
Bridgewater, VA

Makes 21 mushrooms, or 7 servings
Serving size is 3 mushrooms

Prep Time: 30 minutes
Cooking Time: 5 minutes

2 ozs. (about ½ cup) reduced-fat Swiss cheese, shredded
1 hard-cooked egg, finely chopped
3 Tbsp. fine bread crumbs
½ clove garlic, finely chopped

2 Tbsp. 65% vegetable oil stick margarine, softened
21 medium-sized mushrooms, stems removed
vegetable spray

1. In mixing bowl, combine cheese, egg, bread crumbs, garlic, and softened margarine. Blend thoroughly.
2. Spray tops of mushrooms lightly with vegetable spray; then fill each with cheese mixture. Place in long baking pan, stuffed side up.
3. Broil for 5 minutes or until the caps sizzle.

Basic Nutritional Values:
Calories 79 (Calories from Fat 42),
Total Fat 5 gm (Saturated Fat 1.4
gm, Trans Fat 0.4 gm, Polyunsat
Fat 1.1 gm, Monounsat Fat 1.3 gm,
Cholesterol 33 mg), Sodium 102 mg,
Total Carbohydrate 5 gm, Dietary
Fiber 1 gm, Sugars 1 gm, Protein 5 gm

A Tip —
Sensible, healthy snacks between meals are a great way to keep from overeating at lunch and dinner. Just be sure your meals are smaller to account for the snacks!

Hot Buffalo Wing Dip
Barbara Kuhns
Millersburg, OH

Makes about 8 cups
Servings size is 2 Tbsp.

Prep Time: 15 minutes
Baking Time: 45 minutes

8-oz. pkg. reduced-fat cream cheese, at room temperature
8-oz. pkg. fat-free cream cheese, at room temperature
8 ozs. fat-free Ranch dressing
12 ozs. hot wing sauce
3 cups grilled chicken, cubed
2 cups reduced-fat cheddar cheese, shredded

1. Combine cream cheese, Ranch dressing, and hot wing sauce. Mix well.
2. Add chicken and cheddar cheese. Pour into greased baking dish.
3. Bake at 350° for 45 minutes.
4. Serve warm with tortilla chips or celery.

Basic Nutritional Values:
Calories 41 (Calories from Fat 19),
Total Fat 2 gm (Saturated Fat 1.1
gm, Trans Fat 0.0 gm, Polyunsat
Fat 0.2 gm, Monounsat Fat 0.6 gm,
Cholesterol 12 mg), Sodium 238 mg,
Total Carbohydrate 1 gm, Dietary
Fiber 0 gm, Sugars 1 gm, Protein 4 gm

Chicken Wraps

Marlene Fonken, Upland, CA

Makes 30 wraps, or 15 servings
Serving size is 2 wraps

Prep Time: *30 minutes*
Chilling Time: *2 hours*

Wraps:
4 boneless, skinless
  chicken breast halves
  (about 1 lb.)
1¾ cups chicken broth
¼ cup light soy sauce
1 Tbsp. Worcestershire
  sauce
30 large leaves of fresh
  spinach

Dip:
1 cup reduced-fat sour
  cream
2 tsp. toasted sesame seeds
½ tsp. ground ginger
4 tsp. light soy sauce
2 tsp. Worcestershire sauce

1. To make the wraps,
combine chicken, broth,
¼ cup soy sauce, and 1 Tbsp.
Worcestershire sauce in a skillet or saucepan. Simmer until
chicken is just cooked. Cool
and cut meat into chunks.
  2. Wash spinach. Pour
boiling water over the leaves.
Immediately drain and cool.
  3. Place a chunk of chicken
on stem end of spinach leaf.
Roll leaf over. Fold ends in
and continue to roll. Secure
with toothpick and chill.
  4. To make dip, mix
together all dip ingredients
and chill.

5. Serve stuffed leaves with
dip.

Exchange List Values:
Very Lean Meat 1.0, Fat 0.5

Basic Nutritional Values:
Calories 67 (Calories from Fat 21),
Total Fat 2 gm (Saturated Fat 1.3
gm, Trans Fat 0.0 gm, Polyunsat
Fat 0.4 gm, Monounsat Fat 0.5 gm,
Cholesterol 24 mg), Sodium 162 mg,
Total Carbohydrate 3 gm, Dietary
Fiber 1 gm, Sugars 2 gm, Protein 9 gm

---

*Tip: To toast sesame seeds,
spread in a single layer on a
cookie sheet. Bake at 350° for
15 minutes.*

---

*Variation: If you prefer less
Worcestershire sauce, reduce
the amount in the wraps to
1 tsp., and in the dip to 1 tsp.*

Feta Bruschetta

Lena Sheaffer, Port Matilda, PA

Makes 10 servings
Serving size is 1 bruschetta

Prep Time: *15 minutes*
Baking Time: *20 minutes*

---

3 Tbsp. soft-tub margarine
3 Tbsp. olive *or* vegetable oil
10 slices French bread, cut
  1" thick (about 1 oz. each)
4-oz. pkg. crumbled fat-free
  feta cheese
2-3 garlic cloves, minced
1 Tbsp. chopped fresh
  basil, *or* 1 tsp. dried basil
1 large tomato, seeded and
  chopped

1. Combine butter and oil.
Brush on both sides of bread.
Place on baking sheet.
  2. Bake at 350° for 8-10 minutes, or until lightly browned.
  3. Combine feta cheese,
garlic, and basil. Sprinkle
over toast. Top with tomato.
  4. Bake 8-10 minutes
longer, or until heated
through. Serve warm.

Exchange List Values:
Starch 1.0, Fat 1.5

Basic Nutritional Values:
Calories 151 (Calories from Fat 66),
Total Fat 7 gm (Saturated Fat 1.2
gm, Trans Fat 0.0 gm, Polyunsat
Fat 1.8 gm, Monounsat Fat 3.9 gm,
Cholesterol 0 mg), Sodium 376 mg,
Total Carbohydrate 16 gm, Dietary
Fiber 1 gm, Sugars 1 gm, Protein 5 gm

---

*Variation: Mix chopped red
pepper into Step 3, along with
any other of your favorite herbs.*

Garlic Bread

Barbara Yoder
Christiana, PA

Makes 20 servings
Serving size is ½ slice

Prep Time: 15-20 minutes
Baking Time: 40 minutes

1 16-oz. loaf Italian bread
  cut into 10 slices
7 ¾-oz. slices of reduced-fat
  Colby, cheddar, Swiss, *or*
  Monterey Jack cheese
1 tsp. minced garlic
½ tsp. seasoning salt
½ tsp. lemon juice
1½ tsp. poppy seeds
3 Tbsp. soft-tub margarine
1 cup chopped
  mushrooms, *optional*
1 small onion finely
  chopped

1. With a very sharp knife, cut down diagonally through the loaf, making slices approximately 1" apart. Do not cut through the bottom of the loaf. Then cut slits on the diagonal in the opposite direction, also about 1" apart, also without cutting completely through the bottom of the loaf.

2. Place loaf on large piece of foil. Place slices of cheese in grooves going the one direction.

3. Place remaining ingredients in microwave-safe bowl. Stir until well mixed. Cover and microwave on high for 2 minutes.

4. Spoon evenly over bread.

5. Wrap loaf in foil, pinching closed so no ingredients ooze out while baking. Place on a cookie sheet to catch any drippings. Bake at 350° for 40 minutes.

Exchange List Values:
Starch 1.0, Fat 0.5

Basic Nutritional Values:
Calories 96 (Calories from Fat 31), Total Fat 3 gm (Saturated Fat 1.3 gm, Trans Fat 0.0 gm, Polyunsat Fat 1.0 gm, Monounsat Fat 0.8 gm, Cholesterol 4 mg), Sodium 242 mg, Total Carbohydrate 12 gm, Dietary Fiber 1 gm, Sugars 1 gm, Protein 4 gm

Ham and Cheese Sticky Buns

Rosanne Weiler
Myerstown, PA

Makes 24 servings
Serving size is 1 bun

Prep Time: 10 minutes
Baking Time: 20 minutes

24 party-size potato rolls
6½ ozs. sliced, reduced-fat
  Swiss cheese
½ lb. sliced extra-lean low-
  salt ham
½ cup soft-tub margarine
2½ Tbsp. brown sugar blend
  (Splenda)
2 Tbsp. Worcestershire
  sauce
2 Tbsp. prepared mustard
2 Tbsp. poppy seeds

1. Slice rolls in half and place bottoms in 9 x 13 pan.

2. Layer on cheese and ham, and top with roll tops.

3. Melt butter and add brown sugar, Worcestershire sauce, mustard, and poppy seeds. Bring to boil and let boil 2 minutes.

4. Immediately pour over rolls and bake at 350° for 20 minutes.

Exchange List Values:
Starch 1.0, Lean Meat 1.0

Basic Nutritional Values:
Calories 134 (Calories from Fat 47), Total Fat 5 gm (Saturated Fat 1.4 gm, Trans Fat 0.0 gm, Polyunsat Fat 2.1 gm, Monounsat Fat 1.3 gm, Cholesterol 7 mg), Sodium 287 mg, Total Carbohydrate 14 gm, Dietary Fiber 1 gm, Sugars 4 gm, Protein 7 gm

Tip: These can be made ahead and heated when ready to serve.
  When I serve these as an appetizer, everyone comes back for seconds!

A Tip —

  If you find yourself snacking more and more in the evening, get moving! Your eating could be a result of boredom.

Breakfast and Brunch Dishes

Cinnamon Coffee Cake

Janice Burkholder
Richfield, PA

Makes 16 servings
Serving size is 1 slice

Prep Time: 15 minutes
Baking Time: 70 minutes

½ cup canola oil
1¼ cups sugar blend for
  baking (Splenda), *divided*
2 tsp. vanilla
4 eggs
3 cups flour
2 tsp. baking powder
1 tsp. baking soda
1 tsp. salt
2 cups (16 ozs.) fat-free
  sour cream
2 Tbsp. cinnamon
½ cup chopped walnuts

1. In a large mixing bowl,
cream butter ¾ cup sugar
blend together with a mixer
until fluffy. Blend in vanilla.

2. Add eggs one at a time,
beating well after each
addition.
3. Combine flour, baking
powder, soda, and salt in a
separate bowl and add to egg
mixture, alternating with
sour cream.
4. Spoon ⅓ of the batter
into a greased 10″ tube or
bundt pan.
5. Combine cinnamon,
nuts, and remaining ½ cup
sugar blend. Layer ⅓ of this
mixture over batter. Repeat
layers two more times.
6. Bake at 350° for 70
minutes, or until toothpick
inserted in center of cake
comes out clean.
7. Remove from pan and
cool on a wire rack.

Exchange List Values:
Carb 2.5, Fat 2.0

Basic Nutritional Values:
Calories 276 (Calories from Fat 97),
Total Fat 11 gm (Saturated Fat 1.1
gm, Trans Fat 0.0 gm, Polyunsat
Fat 4.1 gm, Monounsat Fat 4.8 gm,
Cholesterol 56 mg), Sodium 304 mg,
Total Carbohydrate 35 gm, Dietary
Fiber 1 gm, Sugars 17 gm, Protein 7 gm

Rhubarb Coffee Cake

Mary Lou Mahar
Williamsfield, IL

Makes 12 servings
Serving size is 3¼″ x 3″ slice

Prep Time: 10 minutes
Baking Time: 40 minutes

1½ Tbsp. butter *or* margarine, at room temperature
2½ Tbsp. canola oil
1 cup sweetener/brown
  sugar blend (Splenda),
  divided
1 egg
1 tsp. vanilla
2 cups flour
1 tsp. baking soda
pinch of salt
1 cup fat-free milk
2 cups chopped rhubarb
½ tsp. cinnamon

1. With an electric mixer,
cream together butter, oil and
¾ cup brown sugar blend.

Add egg and vanilla and mix thoroughly.

2. In a separate mixing bowl, stir together flour, baking soda, and salt.

3. Add dry ingredients to creamed ingredients alternately with milk.

4. When well blended, mix in rhubarb by hand. Pour batter into greased 9 x 13 glass baking pan.

5. Sprinkle with ¼ cup reserved brown sugar blend and cinnamon.

6. Bake at 350° for 40 minutes.

Exchange List Values:
Carb 2.5, Fat 0.5

Basic Nutritional Values:
Calories 213 (Calories from Fat 45), Total Fat 5 gm (Saturated Fat 1.3 gm, Trans Fat 0.0 gm, Polyunsat Fat 1.1 gm, Monounsat Fat 2.3 gm, Cholesterol 22 mg), Sodium 134 mg, Total Carbohydrate 34 gm, Dietary Fiber 1 gm, Sugars 18 gm, Protein 4 gm

---

A Tip —

Don't skip morning meals. Studies have shown that people who eat breakfast lose weight and have better glucose control.

Raspberry Custard Kuchen
Tabitha Schmidt
Baltic, OH

Makes 10-12 servings
Serving size is 3¼" x 3" slice

Prep Time: 30 minutes
Baking Time: 40-45 minutes

1½ cups flour, *divided*
½ tsp. salt
1½ Tbsp. cold butter *or* margarine
1 Tbsp. canola oil
2 Tbsp. fat-free evaporated milk
3 Tbsp. sugar blend for baking (Splenda)
3 cups fresh raspberries, *or* 2 pints frozen raspberries, thawed and drained

Topping:
½ cup sugar blend for baking (Splenda)
2 Tbsp. flour
2 eggs, beaten
1 cup fat free evaporated milk
1 tsp. vanilla

1. In a medium-sized bowl, combine 1 cup flour, salt and oil. Cut in butter with pastry cutter until coarse crumbs form. Stir in evaporated milk.

2. Pat into a greased 9 x 13 baking pan.

3. Combine sugar blend and remaining flour (½ cup) and sprinkle over crust. Arrange raspberries over crust.

4. For topping, combine sugar blend and flour in a mixing bowl. Stir in eggs, evaporated milk, and vanilla. Pour gently over berries, being careful not to scatter them.

5. Bake at 375° for 40-45 minutes, or until lightly browned. Serve warm or chilled. Store any leftovers in refrigerator.

Exchange List Values:
Carb 2.0, Fat 0.5

Basic Nutritional Values:
Calories 176 (Calories from Fat 34), Total Fat 4 gm (Saturated Fat 1.3 gm, Trans Fat 0.0 gm, Polyunsat Fat 0.7 gm, Monounsat Fat 1.4 gm, Cholesterol 40 mg), Sodium 147 mg, Total Carbohydrate 30 gm, Dietary Fiber 3 gm, Sugars 16 gm, Protein 5 gm

Variation: Substitute whipping cream for evaporated milk.

Note: This is great for breakfast, or served with ice cream for a dessert.

Peach Cobbler Coffee Cake

Jean Butzer
Batavia, NY

Makes 20 servings
Serving size is 2⅔" x 2¼" rectangle,
or ¹⁄₂₀ of recipe

Prep Time: 20 minutes
Baking Time: 60-70 minutes
Cooling Time: 30 minutes

21-oz. can peach pie filling
16-oz. can sliced peaches,
  drained well
½ cup sweetener/brown
  sugar blend (Splenda)
4 cups flour, *divided*
½ cup dry quick oats
⅓ cup 65%-vegetable-oil
  stick margarine,
  softened (Blue Bonnet)
¾ cup canola oil
¾ cup sugar blend for
  baking (Splenda)
1¼ cups fat-free sour cream
2 eggs, slightly beaten
1 Tbsp. vanilla
1 tsp. baking powder
1 tsp. baking soda
½ tsp. salt
1 cup confectioners sugar
1-2 Tbsp. fat-free milk

1. In a medium-sized mixing bowl, stir together pie filling and sliced peaches. Set aside.
2. In another mixing bowl, mix together brown sugar blend, 1 cup flour, and oats. Cut in vegetable oil stick margarine with a pastry cutter until mixture resembles coarse crumbs. Set aside to use as topping.
3. In a large electric mixer bowl, beat together canola oil and sugar blend for baking until creamy. Add sour cream, eggs, and vanilla. Beat until well mixed.
4. Reduce speed to low and gradually add 3 cups flour, baking powder, baking soda, and salt. Beat until well mixed.
5. Spread half the batter into a greased 9 x 13 deep baking pan. Spoon peach filling evenly over batter. Drop spoonfuls of remaining batter over filling. (Do not spread.)
6. Sprinkle with topping. Bake at 350° for 60-70 minutes, or until toothpick comes out clean.
7. Cool 30 minutes. Meanwhile, stir together confectioners sugar and enough milk to make glaze. Drizzle over cooled coffee cake.

Exchange List Values:
Carb 3.0, Fat 2.0

Basic Nutritional Values:
Calories 312 (Calories from Fat 103), Total Fat 11 gm (Saturated Fat 1.3 gm, Trans Fat 0.4 gm, Polyunsat Fat 3.4 gm, Monounsat Fat 5.7 gm, Cholesterol 23 mg), Sodium 199 mg, Total Carbohydrate 45 gm, Dietary Fiber 1 gm, Sugars 21 gm, Protein 5 gm

Tips:
1. You may use any fruit (pie filling and canned fruit) of your choice. Just be sure the sliced fruit is well drained.
2. Use a deep pan (at least 2¼") since this recipe fills it right to the top.

Apple Coffee Cake

Tabitha Schmidt
Baltic, OH

Makes 18 servings
Serving size is 3¼" x 2¼" rectangle

Prep Time: 40 minutes
Baking Time: 35-40 minutes

1 cup sugar blend for
  baking (Splenda)
2 eggs, beaten
½ cup canola oil
1 tsp. vanilla
2½ cups flour
2 tsp. baking powder
1 tsp. baking soda
1 tsp. salt
1 tsp. cinnamon
4 cups apples, peeled and
  finely diced
1½ cups chopped nuts,
  optional

Topping:
¼ cup brown sugar blend
  (Splenda)
½ cup chopped nuts,
  optional
½ tsp. cinnamon
¼ tsp. nutmeg

1. Combine sugar blend for baking, beaten eggs, oil, and vanilla in a large mixing bowl. Mix until creamy.
2. In a separate bowl, combine flour, baking powder, baking soda, salt, and cinnamon. Add to sugar-egg mixture and mix well. Batter will be crumbly.
3. Fold in apples, and nuts, if desired. Pour into a greased and floured 9 x 13 baking pan.

4. In the mixing bowl, mix topping ingredients together well, and sprinkle over batter.

5. Bake at 350° for 35-40 minutes, or until tooth pick inserted into center comes out clean.

Exchange List Values:
Carb 2.5, Fat 1.0

Basic Nutritional Values:
Calories 223 (Calories from Fat 70), Total Fat 8 gm (Saturated Fat 0.7 gm, Trans Fat 0.0 gm, Polyunsat Fat 2.2 gm, Monounsat Fat 4.3 gm, Cholesterol 26 mg), Sodium 279 mg, Total Carbohydrate 35 gm, Dietary Fiber 1 gm, Sugars 19 gm, Protein 3 gm

Tips:

1. Granny Smith, or other crisp, apples are especially good in this cake.

2. Skip peeling the apples, and save time and add fiber to your diet!

3. Chopped pecans are a tasty nut to use here.

Maple Twists
Marcella Heatwole
North Lawrence, OH

Makes 18 servings
Serving size is 1 twist

Prep Time: 2 hours
Rising Time: 2½-3 hours
Baking Time: 18-22 minutes

Dough:
¾ cup fat-free milk
¼ cup canola oil
2¾-3 cups flour, *divided*
3 Tbsp. sugar

½ tsp. salt
1 pkg. yeast
1 tsp. maple extract
1 egg
6 Tbsp. 65%-vegetable-oil stick margarine, *divided*

Filling:
¼ cup brown sugar blend (Splenda)
⅓ cup nuts
1 tsp. cinnamon
1 tsp. maple extract

Glaze:
2 Tbsp. 65%-vegetable-oil stick margarine, melted
1 Tbsp. fat-free milk
½ tsp. maple extract
1 cup confectioners sugar

1. In small pan, heat milk and oil until it just reaches the boiling point.

2. In large electric mixer bowl, blend warm liquid, 1 cup flour, 3 Tbsp. sugar, salt, yeast, 1 tsp. maple extract, and egg at low speed until moistened. Beat 2 minutes at medium speed.

3. By hand, add remaining flour to form soft dough.

4. Place on floured surface and knead until smooth and elastic. Place dough in greased bowl. Cover and let rise until double, about 1½-2 hours.

5. Grease 12″ pizza pan. Divide dough into 3 balls. Roll out 1 ball of dough to cover pan. Brush with 2 Tbsp. 65%-vegetable-oil stick margarine, melted.

6. Sprinkle with ⅓ of filling, made by combining brown sugar blend, nuts, cinnamon and 1 tsp. maple extract in a small bowl.

7. Repeat two more layers:

rolled-out dough, melted stick margarine, and filling. (Press last layer of filling down into dough to prevent it from falling off during Step 8.)

8. With scissors, mark 16 or 18 evenly spaced wedges in the circle. Cut from outside edge of circle into wedges. Carefully twist each wedge 5 times.

9. Lay twists on a jelly roll pan. Cover. Let rise for 45-60 minutes, or until almost double in size.

10. Bake at 375° for 18-22 minutes.

11. Cool to room temperature. Drizzle with glaze made by combining 2 Tbsp. melted stick margarine, milk, ½ tsp. maple extract, and powdered sugar. Add 1 Tbsp. more milk if needed to make of pouring consistency.

Exchange List Values:
Carb 2.0, Fat 1.5

Basic Nutritional Values:
Calories 220 (Calories from Fat 83), Total Fat 9 gm (Saturated Fat 1.4 gm, Trans Fat 0.7 gm, Polyunsat Fat 3.4 gm, Monounsat Fat 3.4 gm, Cholesterol 12 mg), Sodium 126 mg, Total Carbohydrate 29 gm, Dietary Fiber 2 gm, Sugars 12 gm, Protein 5 gm

Apple Nut Ring

Naomi Cunningham
Arlington, KS

Makes 10 servings
Serving size is 2 biscuits

Prep Time: 10 minutes
Baking Time: 25-30 minutes

2 7.5-oz. pkgs. refrigerated,
   low-fat buttermilk biscuits
¼ cup corn-oil stick
   margarine, melted
⅔ cup sugar
2 Tbsp. ground cinnamon
3-4 medium-sized apples
⅓ cup nuts, chopped

1. Separate biscuits.
2. In a saucepan, melt the butter or margarine.
3. Combine sugar and cinnamon in a small bowl.
4. Dip biscuits in butter, and then roll in sugar mixture. Arrange biscuits, so that they overlap, around the edge and into the center of a greased 9 x 13 baking pan.
5. Peel, core, and slice the apples. Cut slices in half crosswise. Place an apple slice between each biscuit and around the outer edge of the baking dish.
6. Mix the nuts with any remaining sugar mixture. Sprinkle over top of biscuits and apples.
7. Bake at 400° for 25-30 minutes, or until biscuits are a deep golden brown.

Exchange List Values:
Carb 2.5, Fat 1.5

Basic Nutritional Values:
Calories 241 (Calories from Fat 77), Total Fat 9 gm (Saturated Fat 1.3 gm, Trans Fat 0.8 gm, Polyunsat Fat 3.6 gm, Monounsat Fat 2.2 gm, Cholesterol 0 mg), Sodium 426 mg, Total Carbohydrate 40 gm, Dietary Fiber 2 gm, Sugars 21 gm, Protein 3 gm

Country Brunch

Esther J. Mast, Lancaster, PA
Barbara Yoder, Christiana, PA
Ruth Ann Gingrich
New Holland, PA
Lafaye Musser, Denver, PA

Makes 15 servings
Serving size is 3" x 3⅓" rectangle

Prep Time: 30 minutes
Chilling Time: 8 hours, or
   overnight
Baking Time: 45-60 minutes
Standing Time: 10-15 minutes

16 slices firm white bread
12 ozs. (2½ cups) cubed,
   extra-lean, low-sodium
   ham, drained
6 ozs. (1½ cups) reduced-fat,
   shredded cheddar cheese
4 ozs. (1 cup) reduced-fat,
   shredded mozzarella
   cheese
2 cups egg substitute
3½ cups fat-free milk
½ tsp. dry mustard
¼ tsp. onion powder
½ tsp. seasoning salt
1 Tbsp. parsley

Topping:
3 cups uncrushed cornflakes

1. Trim crusts from bread and cut slices in half.
2. Grease a 10 x 15 baking dish.
3. Layer ingredients in this order: cover bottom of pan with half the bread, top with half the ham, then half the cheddar cheese, and then half the mozzarella cheese.
4. Repeat layers once more.
5. In large mixing bowl, combine egg substitue, milk, dry mustard, onion powder, seasoning salt, and parsley. Mix well and pour over layers.
6. Cover and refrigerate for 8 hours, or overnight.
7. Remove from refrigerator 30 minutes before baking.
8. Sprinkle cornflakes over casserole.
9. Cover loosely with foil to prevent over-browning. Bake at 375° for 45 minutes.
10. Remove from oven and let stand 10-15 minutes before cutting into squares.

Exchange List Values:
Starch 1.0, Lean Meat 2.0

Basic Nutritional Values:
Calories 183 (Calories from Fat 42), Total Fat 5 gm (Saturated Fat 2.4 gm, Trans Fat 0.0 gm, Polyunsat Fat 0.6 gm, Monounsat Fat 1.2 gm, Cholesterol 24 mg), Sodium 566 mg, Total Carbohydrate 19 gm, Dietary Fiber 1 gm, Sugars 5 gm, Protein 16 gm

A Tip —

See a registered dietitian (RD) as soon as you're diagnosed with diabetes.

Overnight Breakfast Casserole

Hannah D. Burkholder
Bridgewater, VA
Esther S. Martin
Ephrata, PA

Makes 12 servings
Serving size is 3″ x 3¼″ rectangle

Prep Time: 45 minutes
Chilling Time: 8 hours, or
* overnight*
Baking Time: 1 hour

½ lb. fresh bulk sausage
4 cups cubed day-old bread
1 cup shredded reduced-fat,
  sharp cheddar cheese
1 tsp. dry mustard
2½ cups egg substitute
4 cups fat-free milk
1 tsp. salt
freshly ground pepper to
  taste
¼ cup chopped or grated
  onion
½ cup peeled, chopped
  tomatoes
½ cup diced green and red
  peppers
½ cup sliced fresh
  mushrooms

1. Cook the sausage in a skillet until browned. Drain and break up the meat into small pieces. Set aside.
2. Place bread in buttered 9 x 13 baking dish. Sprinkle with cheese.
3. Combine the next 6 ingredients. Pour evenly over the bread and cheese.
4. Sprinkle cooked sausage and chopped tomatoes, peppers, and mushrooms over the top.
5. Cover and chill in refrigerator for 8 hours, or over-night.
6. Preheat over to 325°. Bake uncovered for 1 hour. Tent with foil if top begins to brown too quickly.

Exchange List Values:
Starch 0.5, Fat-Free Milk 0.5,
Lean Meat 1.0

Basic Nutritional Values:
Calories 149 (Calories from Fat 48), Total Fat 5 gm (Saturated Fat 2.3 gm, Trans Fat 0.0 gm, Polyunsat Fat 0.7 gm, Monounsat Fat 1.9 gm, Cholesterol 16 mg), Sodium 582 mg, Total Carbohydrate 12 gm, Dietary Fiber 1 gm, Sugars 6 gm, Protein 13 gm

Breakfast Pizza

Jessica Hontz
Coatesville, PA

Makes 8 servings
Serving size is 1 slice

Prep Time: 10 minutes
Baking Time: 20-25 minutes

10-oz. refrigerated pizza
  crust
2 cups egg substitute
¼ cup fat-free milk
2 slices bacon, cooked
  crisp and crumbled
⅔ cup shredded reduced-fat
  cheddar, or Monterey
  Jack, cheese

1. Unroll pizza crust onto baking sheet.
2. Bake at 425° for 10 minutes.
3. Whisk together egg substitute and milk in a large mixing bowl.
4. Cook in skillet until eggs start to congeal, about 3-4 minutes. Spoon onto crust.
5. Top with bacon and cheese.
6. Bake an additional 10 minutes until eggs are set and crust is golden brown.

Exchange List Values:
Starch 1.0, Lean Meat 1.0

Basic Nutritional Values:
Calories 148 (Calories from Fat 29), Total Fat 3 gm (Saturated Fat 1.4 gm, Trans Fat 0.0 gm, Polyunsat Fat 0.7 gm, Monounsat Fat 0.7 gm, Cholesterol 7 mg), Sodium 468 mg, Total Carbohydrate 18 gm, Dietary Fiber 0 gm, Sugars 3 gm, Protein 11 gm

Eggs California

Vonda Ebersole
Mt. Pleasant Mills, PA
Judy Gonzales
Fishers, IN
Esther Gingerich
Parnell, IA

Makes 12 servings
Serving size is 3" x 3¼" rectangle

Prep Time: 20 minutes
Baking Time: 40-45 minutes

2½ cups egg substitute
2 cups cottage cheese
½ cup flour
1 tsp. baking powder
¼ tsp. salt
2 Tbsp. canola oil
3½ ozs. grated reduced-fat
   cheddar, Swiss, *or*
   Monterey Jack cheese
1 or 2 4-oz. cans chopped
   green chilies, depending
   upon your taste
   preference

1. In a mixing bowl, beat
together eggs substitute,
cottage cheese, flour, baking
powder, salt, and canola oil.
2. Stir in cheese and green
chilies.
3. Pour into a greased 9 x 13
baking dish.
4. Bake at 350° for 40 to
45 minutes, or until set.

Exchange List Values:
Carb 0.5, Lean Meat 1.0,
Fat 0.5

Basic Nutritional Values:
Calories 117 (Calories from Fat 41),
Total Fat 5 gm (Saturated Fat 1.4
gm, Trans Fat 0.0 gm, Polyunsat
Fat 0.8 gm, Monounsat Fat 2.0 gm,

Cholesterol 7 mg), Sodium 437 mg,
Total Carbohydrate 6 gm, Dietary
Fiber 0 gm, Sugars 2 gm, Protein 12 gm

Tips:
*1. Garnish with chopped
avocado, sour cream, or salsa.*
*2. Add steamed and cut-up
shrimp, fried and crumbled
bacon, or fully cooked, cubed or
chipped ham to Step 2.*

Greek Eggs

Mrs. Rosanne Hankins
Stevensville, MD

Makes 4 servings
Serving size is ¼ recipe or ¾ cup

Prep Time: 15 minutes
Cooking Time: 20 minutes

2 garlic cloves, sliced
¼ cup sliced white onion
1 Tbsp. oil
10-oz. pkg. frozen chopped
   spinach, thawed and
   squeezed as dry as
   possible
16 ozs. eggbeaters or 8 eggs,
   beaten
½-1 tsp. dried oregano,
   according to your taste
   preference
3 ozs. reduced-fat feta
   cheese

1. In large skillet, saute
garlic and onion in oil for 3-4
minutes.
2. Stir in spinach.
3. Pour eggs and oregano
into hot skillet.
4. Cook, turning 2-3 times
until eggs are lightly cooked,
about 5 minutes.
5. Turn off heat, crumble
cheese over top of spinach-
egg mixture. Cover and let set
for 2 minutes, or until cheese
melts into eggs.

Exchange List Values:
Vegetable 2.0, Lean Meat 2.0

Basic Nutritional Values:
Calories 159 (Calories from Fat 60),
Total Fat 7 gm (Saturated Fat 2.2
gm, Trans Fat 0.0 gm, Polyunsat
Fat 1.3 gm, Monounsat Fat 2.9 gm,
Cholesterol 6 mg), Sodium 577 mg,
Total Carbohydrate 7 gm, Dietary
Fiber 3 gm, Sugars 2 gm, Protein 19 gm

Variations:
*1. For added color and flavor,
stir half a sweet red bell pepper,
chopped, into Step 1.*
*2. For additional flavor, add
¼ tsp. black or white pepper
and ⅛ tsp. salt in Step 3.*

Mushroom Oven Omelet

Elaine Patton
West Middletown, PA

Makes 8 servings
Serving size is 2" x 4" rectangle

Prep Time: 20 minutes
Baking Time: 20 minutes

½ lb. fresh mushrooms, cleaned and sliced
1 Tbsp. canola oil
2 Tbsp. flour
1½ cups egg substitute
⅓ cup fat-free milk
⅛ tsp. pepper
¼ cup chopped onions, *optional*
¼ cup chopped green pepper, *optional*
½ cups shredded reduced-fat cheddar cheese, *divided*
2 Tbsp. real bacon bits

1. In a small skillet, saute mushrooms in oil until tender. Drain. Set aside.
2. In a bowl, combine flour, egg substitute, milk, and pepper until smooth. Add chopped vegetables if you wish.
3. Stir in 6 Tbsp. cheese, bacon, and mushrooms.
4. Pour into a greased 8"-square baking dish.
5. Baked uncovered at 375° for 18-20 minutes, or until eggs are completely set.
6. Sprinkle with remaining cheese, return to warm oven for 1 minute, and then serve.

Exchange List Values:
Lean Meat 1.0, Fat 0.5

Basic Nutritional Values:
Calories 84 (Calories from Fat 34), Total Fat 4 gm (Saturated Fat 1.3 gm, Trans Fat 0.0 gm, Polyunsat Fat 0.6 gm, Monounsat Fat 1.6 gm, Cholesterol 6 mg), Sodium 212 mg, Total Carbohydrate 4 gm, Dietary Fiber 0 gm, Sugars 1 gm, Protein 8 gm

Eggs ala Shrimp

Willard E. Roth
Elkhart, IN

Makes 8 servings
Serving size is ¾ cup, or ⅛ recipe

Prep Time: 10 minutes
Baking Time: 20 minutes

2 Tbsp. canola oil *or* butter
3 cups egg substitute
¼ cup fat-free evaporated milk
1 onion, chopped fine
½ cup celery leaves
4 ozs. precooked shrimp (can be frozen)
3 Tbsp. white wine
4 ozs. frozen peas
seasoning to taste

1. Preheat electric skillet to 375° and melt butter in it.
2. While skillet with oil is heating, toss eggs with milk in a mixing bowl. Set aside.
3. When oil has heated, saute onion and celery leaves in it.
4. Add shrimp and wine to skillet. Cover and cook for 2 minutes.

5. Pour egg substitute-milk mixture into skillet and stir in frozen peas.
6. Turn the skillet down to 325°, and stir contents gently as they cook.
7. When eggs are set, but not hard, serve on warm platter.

Exchange List Values:
Carb 0.5, Very Lean Meat 2.0

Basic Nutritional Values:
Calories 117 (Calories from Fat 34), Total Fat 4 gm (Saturated Fat 0.3 gm, Trans Fat 0.0 gm, Polyunsat Fat 1.1 gm, Monounsat Fat 2.1 gm, Cholesterol 28 mg), Sodium 231 mg, Total Carbohydrate 6 gm, Dietary Fiber 1 gm, Sugars 3 gm, Protein 13 gm

I developed this recipe to share with my first formal cooking classmates at Patchwork Quilt Country Inn in 1976.

A Tip —

Avoid trans fats in your foods. These fats raise your bad cholesterol (LDL) and lower your good cholesterol (HDL).

Breakfast Burritos

Arleta Petersheim
Haven, KS

Makes 8 servings
Serving size is 1 tortilla

Prep Time: 35-40 minutes
Baking Time: 15 minutes

¼ lb. bulk sausage
1 Tbsp. canola oil
2 large potatoes, peeled
  and grated
1 green pepper, chopped
½ cup chopped onion
2 cups egg substitute
½ tsp. salt
¼ tsp. pepper
8 6-inch flour tortillas
½ cup shredded reduced-fat
  cheddar cheese
salsa, *optional*

1. Brown sausage in skillet over low heat. Drain all sausage drippings. Set sausage aside.

2. Heat 1 Tbsp. canola oil and cook potatoes, chopped pepper, and onions in skillet over medium heat, stirring occasionally.

3. When potatoes are soft, add egg substitute, salt, and pepper. Continue cooking until eggs are set. Add sausage.

4. Divide meat/egg mixture onto individual tortillas and roll up. Place in lightly greased 9 x 13 pan. Cover tightly with foil.

5. Bake at 375° for 10 minutes. Sprinkle with cheese. Cover again and bake 5 more minutes.

6. Serve with salsa if you wish.

Exchange List Values:
Starch 1.0, Lean Meat 1.0

Basic Nutritional Values:
Calories 242 (Calories from Fat 82), Total Fat 9 gm (Saturated Fat 2.2 gm, Trans Fat 0.0 gm, Polyunsat Fat 1.8 gm, Monounsat Fat 4.5 gm, Cholesterol 9 mg), Sodium 584 mg, Total Carbohydrate 28 gm, Dietary Fiber 2 gm, Sugars 3 gm, Protein 12 gm

These burritos are a great main dish for brunch. I usually make them a day ahead and refrigerate them (covered) overnight so I can just pop them in the oven the next morning. They will need to bake 10 minutes longer if you put them in the oven cold.

A Tip —

Be active! Regular activity keeps HDL levels normal, reduces blood pressure, helps control stress, helps control body weight, gives your heart muscle a good workout, and improves glucose control.

Scrambled Egg Muffins

Julia Horst, Gordonville, PA
Mary Kay Nolt
Newmanstown, PA

Makes 12 servings
Serving size is 1 muffin

Prep Time: 20 minutes
Baking Time: 20-30 minutes

⅓ lb. bulk sausage
3 cups egg substitute
½ cup chopped onion
¼ cup chopped green pepper
½ tsp. salt
¼ tsp. pepper
¼ tsp. garlic powder
½ cup shredded reduced-fat
  cheddar cheese

1. In a skillet, brown sausage. Drain.

2. In a bowl, pour the egg substitute.

3. Add onion, green pepper, salt, pepper, and garlic powder to the egg substitute and blend well. Stir in sausage.

4. Spoon by ⅓-cupfuls into greased muffin cups.

5. Bake at 350° for 20-30 minutes, or until knife inserted near centers comes out clean.

Exchange List Values:
Lean Meat 1.0, Fat 0.5

Basic Nutritional Values:
Calories 69 (Calories from Fat 26), Total Fat 3 gm (Saturated Fat 1.2 gm, Trans Fat 0.0 gm, Polyunsat Fat 0.3 gm, Monounsat Fat 1.1 gm, Cholesterol 8 mg), Sodium 327 mg, Total Carbohydrate 2 gm, Dietary Fiber 0 gm, Sugars 1 gm, Protein 8 gm

Asparagus Quiche

Moreen Weaver
Bath, NY

Makes 9 servings
Serving size is 1 slice

Prep Time: 10-15 minutes
Baking Time: 40-50 minutes
Standing Time: 10 minutes

2-3 cups asparagus, cut in
  small pieces, depending
  upon how much you love
  asparagus
½ cup reduced-fat sharp
  cheddar cheese, shredded
1 cup fat-free mayonnaise
2 tsp. lemon juice
9″ unbaked pie crust

1. In a mixing bowl,
combine asparagus, cheese,
mayonnaise, and lemon juice.
Mix thoroughly.
2. Spoon into pie crust.
3. Bake at 350° for 40-50
minutes.
4. Let stand 10 minutes.
Serve warm.

Exchange List Values:
Carb 1.0, Fat 1.0

Basic Nutritional Values:
Calories 118 (Calories from Fat 46),
Total Fat 5 gm (Saturated Fat 1.4
gm, Trans Fat 0.3 gm, Polyunsat
Fat 0.9 gm, Monounsat Fat 2.1 gm,
Cholesterol 4 mg), Sodium 284 mg,
Total Carbohydrate 15 gm, Dietary
Fiber 1 gm, Sugars 3 gm, Protein 4 gm

Baked Peach French Toast

Lynette Nisly
Lancaster, PA

Makes 6 servings
Serving size is 4½″ x 4⅓″ rectangle

Prep Time: 20-30 minutes
Baking Time: 15-25 minutes

10 slices, 1″-thick (about
  1 oz.) French *or* Italian
  bread
4 ozs. light cream cheese
  spread
15-oz. can peach slices,
  drained
½-¾ cup chopped pecans,
  optional
¾ cup egg substitute
¼ cup fat-free milk
⅓ cup maple syrup
1 Tbsp. 65%-vegetable-oil
  stick margarine, melted
1 Tbsp. sugar
1 tsp. cinnamon
1 tsp. vanilla

1. Spread cream cheese on
both sides of bread slices.
2. Place bread in a greased
9 x 13 baking pan. Prick each
bread slice 3-4 times with a
fork.
3. Top bread with peach
slices and sprinkle chopped
pecans over peaches, if
desired.
4. In mixing bowl, pour
egg substitute and combine
with milk, maple syrup,
margarine, sugar, cinnamon,
and vanilla. Whisk together.
Pour egg mixture over bread.

5. Bake at 400° for 15-25
minutes, or until egg mixture
is set.
6. Serve with syrup, if you
wish.

Exchange List Values:
Carb 3.0, Fat 1.0

Basic Nutritional Values:
Calories 280 (Calories from Fat 51),
Total Fat 6 gm (Saturated Fat 2.4
gm, Trans Fat 0.3 gm, Polyunsat
Fat 1.0 gm, Monounsat Fat 2.0 gm,
Cholesterol 9 mg), Sodium 476 mg,
Total Carbohydrate 47 gm, Dietary
Fiber 2 gm, Sugars 19 gm, Protein 10 gm

*Tip: You can prepare this the
night before you want to serve
it. Cover and refrigerate it
overnight. If you put it in the
oven cold, be sure to uncover it
and bake it for 35 minutes, or
until brown, and until a knife
inserted in the center comes out
clean.*

Baked French Toast

Susan Wenger, Lebanon, PA
Nancy Funk, North Newton, KS

Makes 8 servings
Serving size is 1 slice of bread

Prep Time: 20 minutes
Chilling Time: 4 hours, or
overnight
Baking Time: 35-45 minutes

¼ cup corn-oil stick
  margarine
½ cup brown sugar blend
  (Splenda)
2 tsp. molasses
8 slices sturdy white bread
peanut butter, *optional*
1¼ cups egg substitute
1½ cups fat-free milk
1 tsp. cinnamon

1. In a saucepan, heat
margarine, brown sugar blend,
and molasses together until
sugar is dissolved and margarine is melted. Stir occasionally to prevent sticking. When
melted and blended together,
pour into a 9 x 13 baking pan.
2. If you wish, spread
peanut butter on one side of
each slice of bread and then
lay the bread on the syrup,
peanut-butter side down. If you
don't include peanut butter,
simply lay the bread in a single
layer on top of the syrup.
3. In a mixing bowl, mix
egg substitute, milk, and
cinnamon together, and then
pour on top of bread.
4. Cover and refrigerate for
at least 4 hours, or overnight.

5. Bake at 350° for 35-45
minutes, or until browned.

Exchange List Values:
Carb 2.0, Fat 1.5

Basic Nutritional Values:
Calories 216 (Calories from Fat 58),
Total Fat 6 gm (Saturated Fat 1.2
gm, Trans Fat 1.0 gm, Polyunsat
Fat 2.2 gm, Monounsat Fat 1.7 gm,
Cholesterol 1 mg), Sodium 287 mg,
Total Carbohydrate 29 gm, Dietary
Fiber 1 gm, Sugars 17 gm, Protein 7 gm

Variations:
1. Instead of ½ cup brown
sugar blend and 2 tsp. molasses,
use ¼ cup brown sugar blend
and ¼ cup pure maple syrup.
2. Immediately after Step
1, sprinkle ½-1 cup coarsely
chopped pecans over the syrup.
(Drop the peanut butter in Step 2.)
3. Instead of milk, use
fat-free half-and-half. And add
1 tsp. vanilla to Step 3.
—Esther Nafziger,
  Bluffton, OH

Variation: After Step 1, add a
layer of the following mixture,
tossed lightly together: 3 tart
apples, peeled, cored, and thinly
sliced; ½ cup raisins; 2 tsp.
cinnamon. Continue with Step 2,
without the peanut butter.
—Diann J. Dunham,
  State College, PA

Light Buttermilk Pancakes

Mary Lynn Miller
Reinholds, PA

Makes 4 servings, or 8 pancakes
Serving size is 2 pancakes

Prep Time: 10 minutes
Cooking Time: 10-15 minutes

1 cup flour
1 Tbsp. sugar
1½ tsp. baking powder
⅛ tsp. salt
½ tsp. baking soda
1 Tbsp. oil
1 cup low-fat buttermilk*
1 egg, beaten

1. Combine dry ingredients
in mixing bowl.
2. Combine oil, buttermilk,
and egg in a separate bowl.
Add to dry ingredients, stirring just until flour mixture
is moistened.
3. Using about ¼ cup batter
for each pancake, fry on griddle
until bubbly on top. Flip and
continue cooking until bottom
is lightly browned.

Exchange List Values:
Starch 2.0, Fat 1.0

Basic Nutritional Values:
Calories 201 (Calories from Fat 50),
Total Fat 6 gm (Saturated Fat 0.9
gm, Trans Fat 0.0 gm, Polyunsat
Fat 1.4 gm, Monounsat Fat 2.7 gm,
Cholesterol 55 mg), Sodium 451 mg,
Total Carbohydrate 30 gm, Dietary
Fiber 1 gm, Sugars 7 gm, Protein 7 gm

* *If you don't have buttermilk,*
make your own by placing

1 Tbsp. lemon juice in a one-cup measure. Fill cup with low-fat milk. Mix well.
—**Linda E. Wilcox**
Blythewood, SC

Mom's Oatmeal Pancakes
Donna Treloar, Hartford City, IN

Makes 12 servings, or 24 pancakes
Serving size is 2 pancakes

Prep Time: 15 minutes
Cooking Time: 3-5 minutes
per skillet- or griddle-full

1½ cups low-fat buttermilk
1 cup quick *or* regular oats,
    uncooked
¼ cup brown sugar
¼ cup corn-oil stick
    margarine, melted
2 eggs, slightly beaten
1 cup flour
1 tsp. baking soda
1 tsp. salt
⅓ cup applesauce
¼ tsp. cinnamon, *optional*

1. In a medium-sized mixing bowl, place oats in buttermilk and let stand for several minutes.
2. Stir in brown sugar.
3. In a separate bowl, add melted margarine into eggs and then stir into oat mixture.
4. In the now-empty butter-egg bowl, mix together flour, baking soda, and salt. Add to oat mixture, stirring just until blended.
5. Gently stir in applesauce,

and cinnamon if you wish.
6. Spoon batter onto lightly greased skillet or griddle. Cook until golden brown.
7. Top with butter and your favorite syrup.

Exchange List Values:
Starch 1.0, Fat 1.0

Basic Nutritional Values:
Calories 142 (Calories from Fat 48), Total Fat 5 gm (Saturated Fat 1.1 gm, Trans Fat 0.7 gm, Polyunsat Fat 1.5 gm, Monounsat Fat 1.5 gm, Cholesterol 36 mg), Sodium 383 mg, Total Carbohydrate 19 gm, Dietary Fiber 1 gm, Sugars 7 gm, Protein 4 gm

Tip: Store leftover pancakes in a resealable plastic bag and refrigerate. When ready to serve, pop in the toaster.

Pumpkin Pancakes
Stacy Schmucker Stoltzfus
Enola, PA

Makes 8 servings, or 16 pancakes
Servings size is 2 pancakes

Prep Time: 5-10 minutes
Cooking Time: 4 minutes per batch

2 heaping cups flour
3½ tsp. baking powder
1 tsp. cinnamon
1 tsp. nutmeg
3 eggs, beaten
½ cup sugar blend for
    baking (Splenda)
1 cup fat-free milk
⅓ cup canola oil
1 tsp. vanilla
1¼ cups canned pumpkin
1 cup coconut, *optional*

1. Whisk together flour, baking powder, cinnamon, and nutmeg in a small bowl.
2. In a large bowl, beat together eggs, sugar blend, milk, canola oil, vanilla, and pumpkin.
3. Add dry ingredients and coconut to pumpkin mixture, stirring just until moistened. A few lumps are okay.
4. Preheat oven to Warm (150-200°). Preheat large skillet or griddle pan over medium-high heat.
5. Pour desired amount of batter onto hot griddle and turn heat down to medium. Cook until edges are dry and pancake is bubbly. Flip over and cook 1-2 minutes more.
6. Place pancake in warm oven* and continue making remaining pancakes. (*This keeps the pancakes warm, but will not dry them out, unless you forget they're there!)
7. Serve hot with maple syrup, vanilla yogurt, and/or toasted pecans.

Exchange List Values:
Starch 3.0, Fat 1.5

Basic Nutritional Values:
Calories 304 (Calories from Fat 103), Total Fat 11 gm (Saturated Fat 1.4 gm, Trans Fat 0.0 gm, Polyunsat Fat 3.1 gm, Monounsat Fat 6.1 gm, Cholesterol 80 mg), Sodium 201 mg, Total Carbohydrate 43 gm, Dietary Fiber 2 gm, Sugars 16 gm, Protein 7 gm

Variations:
1. Use half whole wheat flour; half all-purpose flour.
2. Use ¼ cup brown sugar blend; ¼ cup sugar blend for baking.

Strawberry Pancakes

Becky Frey
Lebanon, PA

Makes 8 servings, or 16 pancakes
Serving size is 2 pancakes

Prep Time: 10-15 minutes
Cooking Time: 10 minutes

2 eggs
1 cup low-fat buttermilk
1 cup crushed strawberries*
¼ cup oil
1 tsp. almond extract
2 cups whole wheat
(or white) flour
2 Tbsp. brown sugar
2 tsp. baking powder
1 tsp. baking soda

1. In large mixing bowl beat eggs until fluffy.
2. Stir buttermilk, strawberries, oil, and almond extract into eggs.
3. In a separate bowl, combine flour, brown sugar, baking powder, and baking soda. Add to wet ingredients. Beat together with whisk just until smooth.
4. Heat skillet or griddle until a few drops of water sizzle when sprinkled on top. Fry pancakes until bubbly on top. Flip and continue cooking until browned. Strawberries can scorch, so keep checking to make sure they're not burning. Turn the heat lower if necessary.

Exchange List Values:
Starch 2.0, Fat 1.5

Basic Nutritional Values:
Calories 216 (Calories from Fat 81), Total Fat 9 gm (Saturated Fat 1.1 gm, Trans Fat 0.0 gm, Polyunsat Fat 2.5 gm, Monounsat Fat 4.6 gm, Cholesterol 54 mg), Sodium 301 mg, Total Carbohydrate 29 gm, Dietary Fiber 4 gm, Sugars 6 gm, Protein 7 gm

---

* You can use fresh or frozen berries. If frozen, thaw them and drain them well before mixing into batter.

Notes:
1. I have a tough time getting small pancakes to turn out nicely. I make one "plate-size" pancake at a time. It can easily be cut into wedges to serve to those with smaller appetites.
2. Top finished pancakes with vanilla yogurt and fruit sauce and serve for breakfast, brunch, a light lunch or supper, or as a dessert.

Chocolate Pancakes

Cassandra Ly, Carlisle, PA

Makes 15 servings, or 30 pancakes
Serving size is 2 3" in diameter pancakes

Prep Time: 5-7 minutes
Cooking Time: 5 minutes
per batch

2 cups whole chocolate milk
2 eggs, slightly beaten
2 cups flour
1 tsp. baking soda
1 tsp. baking powder
1 Tbsp. sugar

2 Tbsp. corn-oil margarine, melted
60 mini M&Ms
syrup, optional
vanilla *or* plain yogurt, *optional*

1. Mix all ingredients together in a large mixing bowl, except M&Ms and optional ingredients.
2. Pour by ¼-cupfuls onto a hot non-stick griddle to make pancakes 3 inches in diameter. Place 2 mini M&Ms on each pancake.
3. Flip pancakes when bubbles formed on their tops begin to break. Remove pancakes from griddle when the bottoms are golden brown.
4. Serve with syrup or yogurt.

Exchange List Values:
Carb 1.0, Fat 1.0

Basic Nutritional Values:
Calories 122 (Calories from Fat 29), Total Fat 3 gm (Saturated Fat 1.4 gm, Trans Fat 0.0 gm, Polyunsat Fat 0.5 gm, Monounsat Fat 0.9 gm, Cholesterol 33 mg), Sodium 149 mg, Total Carbohydrate 19 gm, Dietary Fiber 1 gm, Sugars 5 gm, Protein 4 gm

Apple Puff Pancake

Wilma Stoltzfus
Honey Brook, PA

Makes 8 servings
Serving size is 3¼" x 4¼" rectangle

Prep Time: 20 minutes
Baking Time: 50 minutes

4 Tbsp. 65%-vegetable-oil
  stick margarine
2 large apples, peeled and
  thinly sliced
3 Tbsp. brown sugar
1 tsp. cinnamon
1½ cups egg substitute
1½ cups milk
1 cup flour
3 Tbsp. sugar
1 tsp. vanilla extract
½ tsp. salt
½ tsp. cinnamon
confectioners sugar
syrup, *optional*

1. Melt margarine in a 9 x 13 pan. Arrange apples over butter. Mix brown sugar and cinnamon in small bowl and sprinkle over apples.
2. Bake at 375° about 10 minutes, or until apples soften.
3. Combine in blender, egg substitute, milk, flour, sugar, vanilla, salt, and cinnamon. Blend thoroughly and pour over apples.
4. Return to oven and bake 40 minutes.
5. Sprinkle with confectioners sugar and serve immediately. Serve with syrup if you like.

Exchange List Values:
Carb 2.0, Fat 1.0

Basic Nutritional Values:
Calories 200 (Calories from Fat 44), Total Fat 5 gm (Saturated Fat 1.1 gm, Trans Fat 0.8 gm, Polyunsat Fat 1.6 gm, Monounsat Fat 1.3 gm, Cholesterol 1 mg), Sodium 309 mg, Total Carbohydrate 32 gm, Dietary Fiber 1 gm, Sugars 18 gm, Protein 8 gm

Fluffy Waffles and Cider Syrup

Jan McDowell
New Holland, PA
Phyllis Peachey Friesen
Harrisonburg, VA

Makes 14 waffles
Serving size is 1 waffle

Prep Time: 15 minutes
Cooking Time: 5-6 minutes
* per waffle*

Waffles:
2 cups flour
3 tsp. baking powder
1 Tbsp. sugar
1 tsp. salt
2 eggs, separated
1⅔ cups fat-free milk
6 Tbsp. canola oil

Syrup:
½ cup sugar blend for
  baking (Splenda)
2 Tbsp. cornstarch
¼ tsp. cinnamon
¼ tsp. nutmeg
2 cups apple cider
2 Tbsp. lemon juice
4 Tbsp. 65%-vegetable-oil
  stick margarine

1. To make waffles, mix flour, baking powder, sugar, and salt together in a medium-sized bowl.
2. In a separate bowl, beat together egg yolks, milk, and oil. Add to dry ingredients and mix well.
3. In a third bowl, beat egg whites until stiff. Gently fold into above mixture.
4. Bake in waffle iron.
5. To make syrup, mix sugar blend, cornstarch, cinnamon, and nutmeg in saucepan.
6. Stir in cider and lemon juice.
7. Heat to boiling, stirring constantly. Boil 1 minute or until slightly thickened.
8. Blend in margarine and serve warm.

Exchange List Values:
Carb 2.0, Fat 1.5

Basic Nutritional Values:
Calories 214 (Calories from Fat 86), Total Fat 10 gm (Saturated Fat 1.3 gm, Trans Fat 0.4 gm, Polyunsat Fat 2.8 gm, Monounsat Fat 4.6 gm, Cholesterol 31 mg), Sodium 300 mg, Total Carbohydrate 29 gm, Dietary Fiber 1 gm, Sugars 13 gm, Protein 4 gm

My mother used to make these waffles for our Sunday night supper.
—Jan McDowell

Tip: Vanilla pudding, vanilla yogurt, and fresh or canned fruit are all good toppings for these waffles at any time of the day. Or cover them with chicken or sausage gravy and serve them for lunch or dinner.
—Phyllis Peachey Friesen

Oatmeal Breakfast Scones

Suzanne Nobrega, Duxbury, MA

Makes 12 servings
Serving size is ½ wedge

Prep Time: 15 minutes
Baking Time: 10-15 minutes

1¼ cups flour
¼ cup sugar
2 tsp. baking powder
¼ tsp. salt
6 Tbsp. cold 65%-vegetable-oil stick margarine
1 cup regular *or* quick dry oats
¼ cup dried fruit, i.e. raisins, craisins, cherries, etc., *optional*
1 egg, lightly beaten
¼-⅓ cup fat-free milk
1 egg beaten with 1 Tbsp. water
confectioners sugar

1. Sift flour, sugar, baking powder, and salt into large bowl. Stir well.
2. Divide cold margarine into ¼" cubes and mix into flour mixture with pastry blender or fingers until mixture becomes coarse crumbs.
3. Stir in the oats and the dried fruit, if you wish.
4. Beat together 1 egg and milk and add to dry ingredients, mixing until just moistened.
5. Turn dough onto lightly floured surface and knead 4-5 times into a ball.
6. Gently roll out to a 6-7 inch circle and cut into six pie shaped wedges.
7. Place slightly apart on parchment-lined cookie sheet. Brush tops with egg/water mixture. Sprinkle with confectioners sugar, if desired.
8. Bake at 400° for 10-15 minutes or until lightly browned.
9. Serve warm with raspberry, or your favorite, jam.

Exchange List Values:
Starch 1.0, Fat 1.0

Basic Nutritional Values:
Calories 144 (Calories from Fat 53), Total Fat 6 gm (Saturated Fat 1.4 gm, Trans Fat 0.8 gm, Polyunsat Fat 1.8 gm, Monounsat Fat 1.7 gm, Cholesterol 35 mg), Sodium 275 mg, Total Carbohydrate 19 gm, Dietary Fiber 1 gm, Sugars 5 gm, Protein 4 gm

Tip: This can be used for breakfast, brunch, or an afternoon tea.

Baked Oatmeal

Lena Sheaffer, Port Matilda, PA
Susie Nissley, Millersburg, OH
Esther Nafziger, Bluffton, OH
Katie Stoltzfus, Leola, PA
Martha Hershey, Ronks, PA
Evie Hershey, Atglen, PA

Makes 6 servings
Serving size is 4" x 2⅔" rectangle

Prep Time: 10 minutes
Baking Time: 30 minutes

½ cup unsweetened applesauce
¼ cup brown sugar blend (Splenda)
1 egg
3 cups rolled *or* quick oatmeal, uncooked
2 tsp. baking powder
1 cup fat-free milk
½ tsp. cinnamon *or* nutmeg, *optional*
¼ cup raisins, *or* other fruit*

1. Combine applesauce, brown sugar blend, and egg in a large mixing bowl.
2. Add dry oatmeal, baking powder, and milk. Mix well.
3. Add spices, if you wish, and nuts and/or fruit. Mix well.
4. Pour into a greased 8" square baking pan.
5. Bake at 350° for 30 minutes.
6. Serve hot, cold, or at room temperature with milk.

Exchange List Values:
Carb 3.0, Fat 0.5

Basic Nutritional Values:
Calories 249 (Calories from Fat 31), Total Fat 3 gm (Saturated Fat 0.8 gm, Trans Fat 0.0 gm, Polyunsat Fat 1.1 gm, Monounsat Fat 1.1 gm, Cholesterol 36 mg), Sodium 155 mg, Total Carbohydrate 45 gm, Dietary Fiber 4 gm, Sugars 16 gm, Protein 9 gm

* *Add any these instead of rasins: ¼ cup dried cherries, ¼ cup dried cranberries, ¼ cup cut-up apricots, ¼ cup apples.*
  —Annabelle Unternahrer
  Shipshewana, IN

A Tip —

Visit www.eatright.org to find a dietitian in your area.

Peach Baked Oatmeal
Bertha Burkholder, Hillsville, VA

Makes 10 servings
Serving size is 4½″ x 2⅔″ rectangle

Prep Time: 10 minutes
Baking Time: 35 minutes

½ cup canola oil
1 cup egg substitute
¾ cup sugar blend for
  baking (Splenda)
3 cups dry quick oats
4 tsp. baking powder
2 tsp. salt
2 tsp. vanilla
1 pint juice-pack, canned
  peaches, chopped
  (reserve liquid)
2 cups fat-free milk

1. In large mixing bowl, combine oil, egg substitute, and sugar blend. Add dry quick oats, baking powder, salt, and vanilla.
2. Drain peaches, reserving juice. Add water to peach juice to make 2 cups.
3. Add chopped peaches, peach juice, and milk to oatmeal mixture.
4. Pour into a greased 9 x 13 pan. Bake at 350° for 35 minutes. Serve warm with milk.

Exchange List Values:
Carb 2.5, Fat 2.5

Basic Nutritional Values:
Calories 301 (Calories from Fat 112), Total Fat 12 gm (Saturated Fat 1.1 gm, Trans Fat 0.0 gm, Polyunsat Fat 3.8 gm, Monounsat Fat 6.9 gm,

Cholesterol 1 mg), Sodium 448 mg, Total Carbohydrate 40 gm, Dietary Fiber 3 gm, Sugars 23 gm, Protein 8 gm

Overnight Oatmeal
Barbara Forrester Landis
Lititz, PA

Makes 11 servings
Serving size is ¾ cup

Prep Time: 5 minutes
Baking Time: 6-7 hours

1 cup dry steel-cut oats
1 cup dried cranberries
1 cup chopped, dried
  apricots
3 cups water
1½ cups fat-free milk

1. In a slow cooker, combine all ingredients and set on low.
2. Cover and cook for 6-7 hours.

Exchange List Values:
Carb 1.5

Basic Nutritional Values:
Calories 108 (Calories from Fat 7), Total Fat 1 gm (Saturated Fat 0.1 gm, Trans Fat 0.00 gm, Polyunsat Fat 0.3 gm, Monounsat Fat 0.2 gm, Cholesterol 1 mg), Sodium 19 mg, Total Carbohydrate 24 gm, Dietary Fiber 2 gm, Sugars 17 gm, Protein 3 gm

Tips:
1. Make this before you go to bed, and it will be ready in the morning.
2. Serve topped with vanilla or plain yogurt.
3. Heat any leftovers in the microwave before eating.

Grits Casserole
Sue Williams
Gulfport, MS

Makes 6 servings
Serving size is ¾ cup

Prep Time: 15 minutes
Baking Time: 15-20 minutes

1 cup quick-cooking grits
4 cups water
¾ tsp. salt
2 Tbsp. corn-oil stick
  margarine
½ cup reduced-fat sharp
  cheddar cheese, grated
½ cup egg substitute

1. Cook grits in boiling, salted, water for 5 minutes. Add margarine and cheese. Stir until well mixed. Cool.
2. Add egg substitute and mix thoroughly.
3. Pour mixture into a greased pan or casserole dish.
4. Bake at 400° for 15-20 minutes, or until lightly browned.
5. Serve hot.

Exchange List Values:
Starch 1.5, Fat 1.0

Basic Nutritional Values:
Calories 165 (Calories from Fat 54), Total Fat 6 gm (Saturated Fat 1.9 gm, Trans Fat 0.7 gm, Polyunsat Fat 1.4 gm, Monounsat Fat 1.7 gm, Cholesterol 7 mg), Sodium 448 mg, Total Carbohydrate 21 gm, Dietary Fiber 0 gm, Sugars 0 gm, Protein 7 gm

Breads

French Bread

Martha Ann Auker
Landisburg, PA
Joan Miller
Wayland, IA

Makes 3 12-slice loaves
Serving size is 1 slice

Prep Time: 30 minutes
Standing/Rising Time:
  60-75 minutes
Baking time: 20 minutes

2 pkgs. dry yeast
¾ Tbsp. sugar
¾ cup warm (120-130°)
  water
2 cups boiling water
2 Tbsp. shortening
2 Tbsp. sugar
2 tsp. salt
6-6½ cups flour
1 egg white
1 tsp. sesame seeds

1. Dissolve 2 pkgs. yeast and ¾ Tbsp. sugar in ½ cup warm water. Set aside.

2. In large mixing bowl, mix together boiling water, shortening, 2 Tbsp. sugar, and salt. Stir and let cool.

3. When cooled to room temperature, add yeast mixture. Add as much flour as you can by hand, mixing well. Let stand 10 minutes.

4. Place dough on floured surface and knead in remaining flour. Cover dough on floured surface and allow to stand for 10 minutes.

5. Knead again for 5 minutes, until dough becomes smooth and elastic. Repeat standing/kneading 3 more times.

6. After the final kneading, cut the dough into 3 pieces. Roll out each piece and then roll each one up into a long roll. Shape each into a long French-bread-shaped loaf.

A Tip —

While a daily vitamin never hurts, it's better to get your vitamins and minerals directly from healthy foods.

Place on 1 or 2 greased cookie sheets, with at least 4 inches between the loaves.

7. Cover and let rise 10-15 minutes. Cut diagonal marks ¼" deep, spaced every 2 inches across the top of each loaf.

8. Brush tops with egg white and sprinkle with sesame seeds.

9. Bake at 400° for 20 minutes, or until lightly golden.

Exchange List Values:
Starch 1.0

Basic Nutritional Values:
Calories 88 (Calories from Fat 8), Total Fat 1 gm (Saturated Fat 0.2 gm, Trans Fat 0.0 gm, Polyunsat Fat 0.3 gm, Monounsat Fat 0.3 gm, Cholesterol 0 mg), Sodium 132 mg, Total Carbohydrate 17 gm, Dietary Fiber 1 gm, Sugars 1 gm, Protein 2 gm

Sunflower Oatmeal Bread

Orpha Herr
Andover, NY

Makes 1 12-slice loaf
Serving size is 1 slice

Preparation time: 30 minutes
Rising time: 2-3 hours
Baking time: 30 minutes

2¼ tsp. dry yeast
1 cup, plus 2 Tbsp., warm
   (120-130°) water
¼ cup honey
2 Tbsp. butter *or*
   margarine
1½ tsp. salt
½ cup dry quick-cooking
   oats
3 cups flour
2 Tbsp. dry milk powder
½ cup roasted sunflower
   seeds

1. In small bowl, dissolve yeast in warm water. When thoroughly mixed, add honey.
2. In a large mixing bowl, combine remaining ingredients. Add yeast mixture and blend thoroughly.
3. Knead with bread hook for 8 minutes.
4. Put dough in greased bowl, turning once to grease both sides. Cover and let rise until double, about 1-1½ hours.
5. Punch down. Shape into loaf. Place in greased 9 x 5 bread pan. Cover and let rise until double, about 1-1½ hours.
6. Bake at 350° for 30 minutes, or until lightly browned.
7. After removing from oven let stand 5 minutes. Remove from pan and cool on cooling rack.

Exchange List Values:
Starch 2.0, Fat 0.5

Basic Nutritional Values:
Calories 172 (Calories from Fat 40), Total Fat 4 gm (Saturated Fat 1.4 gm, Trans Fat 0.0 gm, Polyunsat Fat 1.7 gm, Monounsat Fat 1.0 gm, Cholesterol 4 mg), Sodium 266 mg, Total Carbohydrate 29 gm, Dietary Fiber 2 gm, Sugars 6 gm, Protein 5 gm

Barb's Multi-Grain Bread

Dawn Ranck
Lansdale, PA

Makes 2 12-slice loaves
Serving size is 1 slice

Prep Time: 35 minutes
Rising/Resting time: 70 minutes
Baking time: 30-35 minutes

2-2½ cups flour, *divided*
2⅓-3 cups whole-grain
   wheat flour, *divided*
½ cup dry rolled oats
½ cup flaxseed
½ cup dry wheat bran
½ cup instant dry fat-free
   powdered milk
1 Tbsp. dry yeast
2½ cups water
¼ cup honey
2 tsp. salt
3 Tbsp. butter *or*
   margarine

1. In large electric mixer bowl, combine 1 cup flour, 1½ cups whole wheat flour, oats, flaxseed, wheat bran, dry milk, and yeast.
2. In a saucepan, heat together water, honey, salt, and butter until just warm (115-120°), stirring constantly to melt butter.
3. Add to dry mixture. Beat with electric mixer on low speed for 30 seconds, scraping sides of bowl constantly. Then beat 3 minutes on high speed.
4. By hand, stir in enough of remaining flours to make a moderately stiff dough.
5. Turn dough onto lightly floured surface. Knead until smooth (5-7 minutes), kneading in as much remaining flour as you can.
6. Place dough in large greased bowl. Turn once to grease surface of dough. Cover and let rise until double, about an hour.
7. Punch down. Divide dough in half. Cover and let rest 10 minutes.
8. Shape each portion into a loaf. Place in 2 greased 9 x 5 loaf pans.
9. Bake at 400° for 30-35 minutes.
10. Remove from pans. Cool on wire racks.

Exchange List Values:
Starch 1.5

Basic Nutritional Values:
Calories 127 (Calories from Fat 24), Total Fat 3 gm (Saturated Fat 1.1 gm, Trans Fat 0.0 gm, Polyunsat Fat 0.7 gm, Monounsat Fat 0.6 gm, Cholesterol 4 mg), Sodium 214 mg, Total Carbohydrate 23 gm, Dietary Fiber 3 gm, Sugars 4 gm, Protein 4 gm

Whole Wheat Walnut Bread

Kathy Hertzler
Lancaster, PA

Makes 3 12-slice loaves
Serving size is 1 slice

Prep Time: 20-30 minutes
Rising and Standing Time:
1 hour and 50 minutes
Baking Time: 40-45 minutes

3 cups warm (120-130°)
    water
2 scant Tbsp. dry yeast
¾ cup honey
¼ cup zero-trans-fat
    shortening, melted
4 cups whole wheat flour,
    stone-ground if possible
5-6 cups bread flour,
    divided
1¼ tsp. salt
2 cups walnuts, coarsely
    chopped
1 Tbsp. butter, melted

1. Place 3 cups warm water in large electric mixer bowl. Whisk in yeast by hand. Let stand 5 minutes.
2. Add honey and melted shortening.
3. Add whole wheat flour and one cup bread flour. Mix with dough hook.
4. Stir in salt and walnuts. Mix well.
5. Add remaining flour. Mix with dough hook for 5 minutes.
6. Place dough on lightly floured surface. Knead for a few strokes by hand, adding a few tablespoons of flour if

dough is very sticky.
7. Place dough in greased bowl. Rotate dough to grease it all over. Cover bowl and let dough rise for about 60 minutes, or until double.
8. Cut dough in thirds. Form into loaves. Place in greased 8 x 5 loaf pans.
9. Allow to rise until the dough just reaches the top of the pans, about 45 minutes.
10. Bake at 350° for 40-45 minutes, or until crusty and golden brown.
11. Remove loaves from oven and brush tops with butter.

Exchange List Values:
Starch 2.0, Fat 1.0

Basic Nutritional Values:
Calories 196 (Calories from Fat 59), Total Fat 7 gm (Saturated Fat 1.0 gm, Trans Fat 0.0 gm, Polyunsat Fat 3.8 gm, Monounsat Fat 1.3 gm, Cholesterol 1 mg), Sodium 86 mg, Total Carbohydrate 30 gm, Dietary Fiber 3 gm, Sugars 6 gm, Protein 5 gm

Note: Using a dough hook cuts the kneading time in half. You can also knead the bread by hand for 8-10 minutes.

Variation: Substitute maple syrup for the honey, and pecans for the walnuts.

Bread Machine Challah

Sheila Raim
Oxford, IA

Makes 1 12-slice loaf
Serving size is 1 slice

Preparation Time: 10 minutes,
*   plus 1½ hours knead cycle*
Rising Time: 1-1½ hours
Baking Time: 20 minutes for
*   loaves; 45 minutes for the braid*

1¼ cups water
¼ cup oil
¼ cup honey
1½ tsp. salt
2½ cups whole wheat flour
2 cups flour
1½ Tbsp. quick-rising dry
    yeast
1 Tbsp. gluten
1 egg white, for braid only
2 Tbsp. sesame seeds, for
    braid only

1. Measure ingredients into bread pan in order listed. Use dough setting. Adjust flour as needed so dough cleans the side of the pan as it kneads.
2. At the end of the dough cycle, form dough into two loaves. Place in lightly greased 9 x 5 loaf pans and cover. Let rise until double, about 1-1½ hours.
3. Bake for 20 minutes at 350°, or until golden brown.

Basic Nutritional Values:
Calories 115 (Calories from Fat 24),
Total Fat 3 gm (Saturated Fat 0.2
gm, Trans Fat 0.0 gm, Polyunsat
Fat 0.8 gm, Monounsat Fat 1.4 gm,
Cholesterol 0 mg), Sodium 147 mg,
Total Carbohydrate 20 gm, Dietary
Fiber 2 gm, Sugars 3 gm, Protein 3 gm

*Variation: To form the dough
into braids, break off half of
dough after the dough cycle
ends and form into 3 8"-long
ropes. Braid and seal ends.*

*Divide the rest of the dough
into 3 equal parts. Form into
14"-long ropes and braid,
sealing ends.*

*Place long braid on lightly
greased baking sheet. Lay short
braid on top of long braid. Press
down gently to make braids
adhere to each other.*

*Cover, and let rise until
double, about 1-1½ hours.*

*Brush with egg white and
sprinkle with sesame seeds
before baking. Bake at 325° for
45 minutes.*

A Tip —

Keep a food record of
what you eat. Writing
down this information
makes it easier to
positively change your
eating habits.

Italian Bread
Tabitha Schmidt
Baltic, OH

Makes 9 servings
Serving size is 1 wedge

Prep Time: 25 minutes
Rising Time: 20 minutes
Baking Time: 15 minutes

2½ cups flour
1 tsp. salt
1 tsp. sugar
1 Tbsp. dry yeast
1 cup warm (120-130°)
  water
1 Tbsp. oil

Topping:
¼-⅓ cup fat-free Italian
  salad dressing
¼ tsp. garlic powder
¼ tsp. dried oregano
¼ tsp. dried thyme,
  optional
dash of pepper
1 Tbsp. grated Parmesan
  cheese
½ cup grated reduced-fat
  mozzarella cheese

1. In a large mixing bowl,
combine flour, salt, sugar, and
yeast.
2. In a separate bowl, mix
water and oil together. Add to
flour mixture.
3. Stir well. Add more
flour, if needed, to form soft
dough.

4. Place dough on lightly
floured surface, and knead
for 1-2 minutes, or until
smooth. Place in a greased
bowl. Cover and let rise for
20 minutes.
5. Knead dough down.
Then place on a 12" pizza
pan. Roll or pat into a 12"
circle.
6. Brush with salad
dressing.
7. Combine seasonings and
sprinkle over top. Sprinkle
with cheeses.
8. Bake at 450° for 15 minutes, or until golden brown.
9. Cover with foil tent to
prevent over-browning if
necessary.
10. Cut into narrow wedges
and serve warm.

Basic Nutritional Values:
Calories 183 (Calories from Fat 35),
Total Fat 4 gm (Saturated Fat 1.4
gm, Trans Fat 0.0 gm, Polyunsat
Fat 0.8 gm, Monounsat Fat 1.4 gm,
Cholesterol 7 mg), Sodium 423 mg,
Total Carbohydrate 28 gm, Dietary
Fiber 1 gm, Sugars 2 gm, Protein 8 gm

A Tip —

If you take insulin,
a small snack before
bedtime can help prevent
low blood glucose levels
while you sleep.

Cheese-Filled Ring

Gwendolyn Chapman
Gwinn, MI

Makes 14 servings
Serving size is 1 roll

Prep Time: 30-40 minutes
Rising Time: 60-70 minutes
Baking Time: 30-35 minutes

16-oz. pkg. hot roll mix
¾ cup warm (120-130°)
  water
1 tsp. dried oregano
1 tsp. dried basil
1 large egg, slightly beaten
1 cup coarsely shredded
  sharp, reduced-fat
  cheddar cheese
4 Tbsp. grated Parmesan
  cheese, *divided*
2 tsp. parsley flakes
⅛ tsp. paprika
1 egg yolk, beaten
2 tsp. fat-free milk

1. In a mixing bowl,
dissolve yeast from hot roll
mix in ¾ cup warm water.
2. Add herbs, whole egg,
and flour mixture (from hot
roll mix).
3. Turn onto slightly
floured board and knead until
smooth.
4. Place dough back in
cleaned and slightly greased
mixing bowl. Cover and let
rise 30 minutes.
5. Turn onto floured
board and knead again until
smooth.
6. Roll into 10 x 15 rectangle.

7. Sprinkle with cheddar
cheese, 2 Tbsp. Parmesan
cheese, parsley flakes, and
paprika.
8. Starting along the 15"
side, roll the dough tightly to
form a log.
9. Place on a greased
baking sheet, seam down.
Shape into a 7"-diameter
ring, pinching ends securely
together.
10. Cut ½"-deep slashes at
2" intervals along the top of
the roll.
11. Cover and let rise 30-40
minutes.
12. In a small mixing bowl,
combine egg yolk and milk
or cream. Brush over dough
ring.
13. Sprinkle with 2 Tbsp.
Parmesan cheese.
14. Bake at 350° for 30-35
minutes. (Tent with foil if the
top begins to get too brown
before end of baking time.)
15. Remove from oven and
cool slightly before slicing
and serving.

Exchange List Values:
Starch 1.5, Fat 1.0

Basic Nutritional Values:
Calories 148 (Calories from Fat 34),
Total Fat 4 gm (Saturated Fat 1.4
gm, Trans Fat 0.0 gm, Polyunsat
Fat 0.4 gm, Monounsat Fat 1.3 gm,
Cholesterol 35 mg), Sodium 280 mg,
Total Carbohydrate 23 gm, Dietary
Fiber 1 gm, Sugars 2 gm, Protein 7 gm

Tomato Bread

Betty Hostetler
Allensville, PA

Makes 2 12-slice loaves
Serving size is 1 slice

Prep Time: 35-40 minutes
Rising Time: 70-100 minutes
Baking Time: 20-25 minutes

2 cups tomato juice
2 Tbsp. butter
3 Tbsp. sugar
1 tsp. salt
½ tsp. dried basil
½ tsp. dried oregano
¼ cup ketchup
¼ cup grated cheese
1 pkg. dry granulated yeast
¼ cup warm water (110-115°)
7 cups bread flour, sifted

1. In saucepan, heat tomato
juice and butter together until
butter is melted.
2. Stir in sugar, salt, herbs,
ketchup, and cheese. Cool to
lukewarm.
3. In a large electric mixer
bowl, sprinkle yeast on warm
water. Stir to dissolve.
4. Add tomato mixture and
3 cups flour to yeast. Beat at
medium speed for 2 minutes
or until smooth.
5. Gradually add enough
remaining flour to make soft
dough that leaves the sides of
the bowl.
6. Turn onto slightly
floured board. Knead for 8-10
minutes, until elastic and
smooth.

7. Place in lightly greased bowl, turning once. Cover and let rise in warm place until double, about 1-1½ hours.

8. Punch down. Divide in half. Cover and let rest 10 minutes.

9. Shape into loaves. Place in greased loaf pans. Cover and let rise until doubled, about 1 hour.

10. Bake at 375° for 15 minutes. Cover with foil and bake an additional 10 minutes.

Exchange List Values:
Starch 2.0

Basic Nutritional Values:
Calories 171 (Calories from Fat 19), Total Fat 2 gm (Saturated Fat 0.9 gm, Trans Fat 0.0 gm, Polyunsat Fat 0.3 gm, Monounsat Fat 0.4 gm, Cholesterol 4 mg), Sodium 215 mg, Total Carbohydrate 32 gm, Dietary Fiber 1 gm, Sugars 3 gm, Protein 5 gm

Easy Nut Bread
Betty B. Dennison
Grove City, PA

Makes 3 10-slice loaves
Serving size is 1 slice

Prep Time: 45 minutes
Rising Time: 5-10 hours
Baking Time: 25-30 minutes

2 pkgs. dry yeast
1 cup non-fat milk, warmed to 120-130°
¾ cups sugar
½ tsp. salt
4 eggs, separated
¾ cup canola oil
4 cups flour
4 cups ground nuts, any kind
maple or walnut flavoring
½ cup sugar blend for baking (Splenda)
1 egg, beaten

1. In small mixing bowl, stir yeast into warm milk until dissolved.

2. Add ¾ cup sugar and salt to yeast mixture. Let cool.

3. In a large bowl, beat egg yolks (reserve whites). Add canola oil, cooled yeast mixture, and 2 cups flour. Stir until well blended.

4. Place dough on floured surface and knead in as much of the remaining flour as needed to make a soft dough. Cover and place in refrigerator at least 3 hours, or overnight.

5. Meanwhile, beat the egg whites until stiff. Set aside.

6. Make the filling in a large bowl by mixing together ground nuts, ½ cup sugar blend, stiffly beaten egg whites, and flavoring.

7. When dough is thoroughly chilled, divide into 3 balls. Roll out one at a time into circles, each about 12" in diameter.

8. Spread each circle with ⅓ of the filling, then roll each into a long loaf.

9. Place all 3 loaves on 1 or 2 slightly greased cookie sheets. Let stand for 2 hours in a warm place.

10. Brush tops with 1 egg beaten well.

11. Bake at 350° for 25-30 minutes.

12. When cooled, slice and serve.

Exchange List Values:
Starch 1.0, Carb 0.5, Fat 2.5

Basic Nutritional Values:
Calories 227 (Calories from Fat 121), Total Fat 13 gm (Saturated Fat 1.3 gm, Trans Fat 0.0 gm, Polyunsat Fat 6.8 gm, Monounsat Fat 4.5 gm, Cholesterol 35 mg), Sodium 55 mg, Total Carbohydrate 23 gm, Dietary Fiber 1 gm, Sugars 9 gm, Protein 5 gm

A Tip —

While there are weight-loss drugs on the market, there is no "magic pill." Diet medication is meant to be used in conjunction with healthy eating and exercise.

60-Minute Dinner Rolls

Dolores Horst
Hinton, VA

Makes 24 rolls
Serving size is 1 roll

Prep Time: 12-15 minutes
Rising Time: 30-35 minutes
Baking Time: 20 minutes

2 pkgs. dry yeast
¼ cup sugar
1½ cups warm (120-130°)
  fat-free milk
1 tsp. salt
¼ cup butter, melted
4 cups flour

1. In a large mixing bowl, add yeast and sugar to warm milk. Stir to dissolve. Let stand 15 minutes.
2. Stir in remaining ingredients. Mix well.
3. Cover and let stand in warm place for 15-20 minutes, or until double in size.
4. Form 24 rolls, each the size of an egg. Place on greased cookie sheets.
5. Bake at 375° for 20 minutes.

Exchange List Values:
Starch 1.0, Fat 0.5

Basic Nutritional Values:
Calories 108 (Calories from Fat 19), Total Fat 2 gm (Saturated Fat 1.3 gm, Trans Fat 0.0 gm, Polyunsat Fat 0.2 gm, Monounsat Fat 0.5 gm, Cholesterol 5 mg), Sodium 118 mg, Total Carbohydrate 19 gm, Dietary Fiber 1 gm, Sugars 3 gm, Protein 3 gm

Refrigerator Butterhorns

Becky Frey
Lebanon, PA

Makes 48 rolls
Serving size is 1 roll

Prep Time: 15-20 minutes
Rising Time: 7-9 hours
Baking Time: 10-12 minutes

1 Tbsp., *or* 1 pkg., fast-rise,
  dry yeast
½ cup sugar
1 tsp. salt
6 cups flour
6 Tbsp. butter, cut in pieces,
  at room temperature
6 Tbsp. canola oil
2 cups warm (120-130°)
  non-fat milk
1 egg, beaten
2 Tbsp. water

1. In a large mixing bowl, combine yeast, sugar, salt, and flour.
2. In a separate bowl, add butter and canola oil to warm milk. Stir until butter melts. Beat in egg and water.
3. Pour liquid into flour mixture. Mix well, but do not knead. Dough will be sticky.
4. Cover with well-greased waxed paper. Refrigerate 4-5 hours.
5. Divide dough into three parts. Roll each into a 9"-10" circle on a lightly floured counter.
6. Cut each circle into 16 wedges. Roll each wedge up, beginning with the point and rolling toward the wide end, as you would to make a butterhorn. Place on greased cookie sheets, about 2 inches apart from each other.
7. Cover with waxed paper. Let rise 3-4 hours, or until double in size.
8. Bake at 375° for 10-12 minutes, or until golden brown.

Exchange List Values:
Starch 1.0, Fat 0.5

Basic Nutritional Values:
Calories 99 (Calories from Fat 31), Total Fat 3 gm (Saturated Fat 1.1 gm, Trans Fat 0.0 gm, Polyunsat Fat 0.7 gm, Monounsat Fat 1.5 gm, Cholesterol 8 mg), Sodium 65 mg, Total Carbohydrate 15 gm, Dietary Fiber 0 gm, Sugars 3 gm, Protein 2 gm

Variations:
1. For whole wheat rolls: Replace flour with whole wheat flour. Add 1 Tbsp. wheat gluten to dry ingredients (in Step 1). Add 1 Tbsp. liquid soy lecithin to wet ingredients (in Step 2).
2. For part-whole wheat rolls: Use 3 cups white flour and 3 cups whole wheat flour.

Note: You do not have to refrigerate the dough. I'm usually in a hurry for them. Just let the dough rise until double. Roll out and shape. Let rise again until double and bake. The rising times are much shorter when the dough is warm.

A Tip —

When a recipes calls for oil, use canola oil or olive oil. These are brimming with good monounsaturated fats.

Oatmeal Dinner Rolls

Martha Bender, New Paris, IN

Makes 20 rolls
Serving size is 1 roll

Prep Time: 30-35 minutes
Rising and Resting Time:
about 2 hours
Baking Time: 20-25 minutes

2 cups water
1 cup dry quick oats
3 Tbsp. butter *or* margarine
1 pkg. dry yeast
⅓ cup warm (120-130°)
    water
⅓ cup packed brown sugar
1 Tbsp. sugar
1 tsp. salt
4¾-5¼ cups flour

1. In a saucepan bring 2 cups water to boil. Add oats and butter. Cook and stir 1 minute. Remove from heat. Cool to lukewarm.

2. In a large mixing bowl, dissolve yeast in ⅓ cup warm water. Add cooled oats mixture, sugars, salt, and 4 cups flour. Beat until smooth. Add enough remaining flour to form a soft dough.

3. Turn onto floured board and knead 6-8 minutes, kneading in more flour, until smooth and elastic.

4. Place in greased bowl, turning once to grease top. Cover and let rise in warm place until doubled, about 1 hour.

5. Punch down. Allow to rest 10 minutes.

6. Shape into 20 balls. Place in greased 9″ round baking pan. Cover. Let rise until double, about 45 minutes.

7. Bake at 350° for 20-25 minutes until golden brown. Remove from pan to wire racks to cool.

Exchange List Values:
Starch 2.0

Basic Nutritional Values:
Calories 156 (Calories from Fat 21), Total Fat 2 gm (Saturated Fat 1.2 gm, Trans Fat 0.0 gm, Polyunsat Fat 0.3 gm, Monounsat Fat 0.6 gm, Cholesterol 5 mg), Sodium 132 mg, Total Carbohydrate 30 gm, Dietary Fiber 1 gm, Sugars 5 gm, Protein 4 gm

Bread Machine All-Bran Rolls

Sheila Raim, Oxford, IA

Makes 16 servings
Serving size is 1 roll

Preparation Time: 10 minutes,
plus 1½ hour dough cycle
Rising Time: 1 hour
Baking Time: 15 minutes

1 cup warm (120-130°) water
½ cup dry All-Bran cereal
¼ cup oil
¼ cup honey
¾ tsp. salt
1 egg
1½ cups whole wheat flour
2-2¼ cups unbleached
    flour
2 tsp. dry fast-rising yeast
1 Tbsp. wheat gluten
2 Tbsp. butter, melted

1. Add all ingredients except 3 Tbsp. butter to bread pan in order listed. Allow All-Bran to soak in the water until it is soft before beginning the dough cycle.

2. Adjust the amount of flour as needed so that the dough cleans the sides of the bread pan as it kneads. Use the dough setting on the bread machine.

3. At the end of the cycle, divide the dough in half. Roll out each half into a 10″ circle.

4. Spread the circles with a thin coat of melted butter. Then cut each circle into 8 pie-shaped wedges.

5. Roll up each wedge, starting from the wide edge.

6. Place wedges on baking sheets, about 2 inches apart, and let rise until double, about an hour.

7. Bake at 350° for 15 minutes, or until golden brown.

Exchange List Values:
Starch 1.5, Fat 1.0

Basic Nutritional Values:
Calories 168 (Calories from Fat 51), Total Fat 6 gm (Saturated Fat 1.3 gm, Trans Fat 0.0 gm, Polyunsat Fat 1.3 gm, Monounsat Fat 2.6 gm, Cholesterol 17 mg), Sodium 131 mg, Total Carbohydrate 26 gm, Dietary Fiber 3 gm, Sugars 5 gm, Protein 5 gm

A Tip —

Fiber is power food. Eat as many fiber-rich foods as possible.

Whole Wheat Cottage Cheese Rolls

Janelle Myers-Benner
Harrisonburg, VA

Makes 2 dozen rolls
Serving size is 1 roll

Prep Time: 20-30 minutes
Rising Time: 2-3 hours
Baking Time: 12-15 minutes

3½–4 cups whole wheat
   flour, *divided*
2 Tbsp. dry yeast
½ tsp. baking soda
1½ cups low-fat (1% fat)
   cottage cheese
½ cup water
¼ cup brown sugar
2 Tbsp. oil
2 tsp. salt
2 eggs

1. In large electric mixer bowl, stir together 2 cups whole wheat flour, yeast, and baking soda.
2. In a saucepan, heat together cottage cheese, water, sugar, oil, and salt until very warm (130°).
3. Add wet ingredients to dry mixture, along with eggs.
4. Beat vigorously for 3-4 minutes with electric mixer—½ minute on low, and 3 minutes on high.
5. Stir in enough remaining flour to make a stiff dough. Knead dough on lightly floured surface for 8-10 minutes.
6. Place in a greased bowl turning once to grease all sides.

7. Cover and let rise until double (1-1½ hours).
8. Shape into 24 rolls. Place in lightly greased muffin tins, or on a lightly greased cookie sheet.
9. Let rise until nearly double (1-1½ hours).
10. Bake at 350° for 12-15 minutes.

Exchange List Values:
Starch 1.0, Fat 0.5

Basic Nutritional Values:
Calories 97 (Calories from Fat 19), Total Fat 2 gm (Saturated Fat 0.4 gm, Trans Fat 0.0 gm, Polyunsat Fat 0.5 gm, Monounsat Fat 0.9 gm, Cholesterol 18 mg), Sodium 286 mg, Total Carbohydrate 16 gm, Dietary Fiber 2 gm, Sugars 3 gm, Protein 5 gm

Tips:
   1. This recipe is a great way to use up cottage cheese that may have soured. It won't hurt the rolls!
   2. This recipe works well with Bronze Chef flour, a high protein flavorful flour.
   3. Try a different presentation and form each roll by first making 3 small balls. Put all 3 into one muffin tin and you'll have a 3-leaf clover roll.

A Tip —

   Skip croissants, muffins, and biscuits. These foods are surprisingly high in calories and fat.

Bread Sticks

Janice Burkholder, Richfield, PA

Makes 30 sticks
Serving size is 1 stick

Prep Time: 15 minutes
Rising Time: 1-1½ hours
Baking Time: 10-15 minutes

1½ cups warm (120-130°)
   water
1 Tbsp. dry yeast
1 Tbsp. oil
1 Tbsp. salt
1 Tbsp. sugar
3 cups whole wheat flour
1 cup flour
¼ cup butter, melted
3 Tbsp. vegetable *or* olive oil
3 Tbsp. Parmesan cheese
1 tsp. garlic powder
2 Tbsp. dried parsley
1 tsp. dried oregano

1. In large mixing bowl, dissolve yeast in warm water.
2. Add oil, salt, and sugar.
3. In separate bowl mix flours together.
4. Stir flour into wet ingredients until dough becomes stiff.
5. Place dough on lightly floured surface and knead in flour, if some remains, for several minutes until smooth and elastic.
6. Place dough in greased bowl. Turn dough to grease all over, and then cover. Allow to rise until double in size, about 1-1½ hours.
7. On a flat, lightly floured surface, roll dough out into a 15" square.
8. Cut in half with a pizza

cutter, and then cut each half into 1" strips. Lay strips on a lightly greased cookie sheet.

9. In a small bowl, combine butter, oil, Parmesan cheese, garlic powder, parsley, and oregano. Brush strips of dough with the mixture.

10. Bake at 400° for 10-15 minutes or until golden brown.

11. Serve as is or with warm pizza sauce.

Exchange List Values:
Starch 1.0, Fat 0.5

Basic Nutritional Values:
Calories 92 (Calories from Fat 35), Total Fat 4 gm (Saturated Fat 1.3 gm, Trans Fat 0.0 gm, Polyunsat Fat 0.7 gm, Monounsat Fat 1.6 gm, Cholesterol 5 mg), Sodium 250 mg, Total Carbohydrate 13 gm, Dietary Fiber 2 gm, Sugars 1 gm, Protein 2 gm

Butter-Dipped Bread Sticks

Lori Newswanger, Lancaster, PA

Makes 32 sticks
Serving size is 1 stick

Prep Time: 15-20 minutes
Baking Time: 12-15 minutes

⅓ cup butter *or* margarine
2½ cups flour
1 Tbsp. sugar
3½ tsp. baking powder
1½ tsp. salt
½–1 cup grated reduced-fat cheese
1 cup milk

Toppings: sesame seeds, garlic powder, celery seed, your favorite herbs

1. In a saucepan, or in the microwave, melt butter. Set aside.

2. In a mixing bowl, combine flour, sugar, baking powder, salt, and cheese.

3. Add milk and stir slowly with a fork. When dough clings together, turn onto a well-floured board. Roll dough to coat with flour. Knead gently 10 times.

4. Roll dough into a 12 x 8 rectangle, ½" thick. Cut dough in half to form 2 12 x 4 rectangles. Cut each rectangle into 16 ¾"-wide strips.

5. Dip strips in melted butter. Lay in rows in lightly greased 9 x 13 baking pan. Sprinkle with your choice of toppings.

6. Bake at 450° for 12-15 minutes. Serve immediately.

Exchange List Values:
Starch 0.5, Fat 0.5

Basic Nutritional Values:
Calories 61 (Calories from Fat 21), Total Fat 2 gm (Saturated Fat 1.4 gm, Trans Fat 0.0 gm, Polyunsat Fat 0.1 gm, Monounsat Fat 0.6 gm, Cholesterol 6 mg), Sodium 177 mg, Total Carbohydrate 8 gm, Dietary Fiber 0 gm, Sugars 1 gm, Protein 2 gm

Cheesy Flat Bread

Clarice Williams, Fairbank, IA

Makes 8 slices
Serving size is 1 slice

Thawing Time: 8 hours, or overnight
Prep Time: 10 minutes

Rising Time: 30 minutes
Baking Time: 20-25 minutes

1 1-lb. loaf frozen bread dough
butter-flavored spray (Pam)
2-3 tsp. paprika
½ tsp. dried oregano
½ tsp. dried basil
½ tsp. garlic powder
¾ cup shredded reduced-fat mozzarella cheese

1. Allow frozen dough to thaw in the fridge for 8 hours, or overnight.

2. Pat thawed bread dough onto bottom and up the sides of a greased 14" pizza pan or 15" baking pan, forming a crust.

3. Spray lightly with butter flavored spray and sprinkle with herbs.

4. Prick the crust; then sprinkle with cheese.

5. Cover and let rise in warm place for 30 minutes.

6. Bake at 375° for 20-25 minutes, or until golden.

7. Top with your favorite pizza sauce and toppings, and bake until heated through. Or serve as is for dipping into soup or spaghetti sauce.

Exchange List Values:
Starch 2.0, Fat 0.5

Basic Nutritional Values:
Calories 181 (Calories from Fat 32), Total Fat 4 gm (Saturated Fat 1.4 gm, Trans Fat 0.0 gm, Polyunsat Fat 0.9 gm, Monounsat Fat 0.7 gm, Cholesterol 6 mg), Sodium 404 mg, Total Carbohydrate 29 gm, Dietary Fiber 2 gm, Sugars 3 gm, Protein 8 gm

Harvest Quick Bread

Lorraine Pflederer
Goshen, IN

Makes 1 12-slice loaf
Serving size is 1 slice

Prep Time: 20-30 minutes
Baking Time: 70 minutes

½ cup cut-up, pitted
  prunes
2 Tbsp. water
1 cup fresh *or* frozen
  cranberries, chopped
1 cup grated apple
½ cup apple juice
1 Tbsp. grated lemon peel
2 egg whites, lightly beaten
2 cups flour
¼ cup sugar blend for
  baking (Splenda)
¼ cup brown sugar blend
  (Splenda), firmly packed
1 tsp. baking powder
½ tsp. baking soda
½ tsp. cinnamon
½ tsp. nutmeg
½ cup chopped walnuts,
  optional

1. Place prunes and water
in blender and puree.
2. Mix together prune
puree, cranberries, apple,
apple juice, lemon peel, and
egg whites in a bowl.
3. In a separate large bowl,
combine flour, sugar blend for
baking, brown sugar blend,
baking powder, baking soda,
cinnamon, nutmeg, and nuts,
if you wish.

4. Stir the wet ingredients
into the dry ingredients until
just moistened. Transfer to a
9 x 5 loaf pan.
5. Bake at 350° for 1 hour
and 10 minutes, or until
toothpick inserted in center
comes out clean. Cool in the
pan for 10 minutes. Remove
and finish cooling on a wire
rack.

*Tip: To reduce the baking time,
bake in 2 smaller loaf pans.
Bake 45-50 minutes, and then
check with toothpick to see
if the loaves are fully baked.
If they are not, bake longer,
checking every 5 minutes with
a toothpick to see if they are
finished.*

Exchange List Values:
Carb 1.5

Basic Nutritional Values:
Calories 110 (Calories from Fat 2),
Total Fat 0 gm (Saturated Fat 0.0
gm, Trans Fat 0.0 gm, Polyunsat
Fat 0.1 gm, Monounsat Fat 0.0 gm,
Cholesterol 0 mg), Sodium 70 mg,
Total Carbohydrate 24 gm, Dietary
Fiber 1 gm, Sugars 11 gm, Protein 2 gm

A Tip —

   Choose breads that
list "whole-wheat flour"
instead of "enriched white
flour" as one of the first
ingredients.

Green Chili Bread

Jeanne Allen, Rye, CO

Makes 15 servings
Serving size is 2½" x 3" rectangle

Prep Time: 20-30 minutes
Baking Time: 40-60 minutes

3 cups yellow cornmeal
1½ tsp. baking powder
1 tsp. sugar
1½ tsp. salt
½ cup vegetable oil
¾ cup egg substitute
1¾ cups fat-free milk
1 cup chopped onion
1 cup cream-style corn
4-oz. can chopped green
  chilies, drained
¾ cup grated reduced-fat
  cheddar cheese

1. In a large mixing bowl,
combine cornmeal, baking
powder, sugar, and salt.
2. In a separate bowl, mix
together oil, egg substitute,
and milk. Pour wet ingredients into dry ingredients and
blend well.
3. Stir in onion, corn, chilies, and cheese. Mix gently
until vegetables and cheese
are well distributed.
4. Spoon mixture into a
greased 9 x 13 baking pan.
5. Bake at 350° for 40-60
minutes, or until tester inserted
in bread comes out clean.

Exchange List Values:
Starch 2.0, Fat 1.5

Basic Nutritional Values:
Calories 218 (Calories from Fat
82), Total Fat 9 gm (Saturated Fat

1.3 gm, Trans Fat 0.0 gm, Polyunsat Fat 2.4 gm, Monounsat Fat 4.8 gm, Cholesterol 5 mg), Sodium 439 mg, Total Carbohydrate 28 gm, Dietary Fiber 3 gm, Sugars 4 gm, Protein 6 gm

Pineapple Nut Bread

Esther Hartzler
Carlsbad, NM

Makes two 10-slice loaves
Serving size is 1 slice

Prep Time: 15-20 minutes
Baking Time: 45-60 minutes

1½ cup dry quick oats
2½ cups flour
2 tsp. salt
2 tsp. baking soda
4 eggs
¾ cup sugar blend for
  baking (Splenda)
2½-3 cups crushed
  pineapple *or* pineapple
  chunks, drained, but
  with juice reserved
1 cup shredded, dried,
  sweetened coconut
1½ cups chopped *or* broken
  pecans

1. Grease and flour two 9 x 5 loaf pans.
2. In a large mixing bowl, stir together dry oats, flour, salt, and baking soda.
3. In a separate bowl, beat eggs. Then stir in sugar blend for baking until well blended.
4. Stir wet ingredients into dry ingredients.
5. Gently stir in drained pineapple, coconut, and

pecans. If mixture seems too dry, add several tablespoons of reserved pineapple juice.
6. Pour into loaf pans. Bake at 350° for 45-60 minutes, or until tops of loaves brown, and a toothpick inserted in the middle of the tops of the loaves comes out clean.

Exchange List Values:
Carb 1.0, Fat 1.0

Basic Nutritional Values:
Calories 133 (Calories from Fat 50), Total Fat 6 gm (Saturated Fat 1.2 gm, Trans Fat 0.0 gm, Polyunsat Fat 1.3 gm, Monounsat Fat 2.6 gm, Cholesterol 26 mg), Sodium 239 mg, Total Carbohydrate 18 gm, Dietary Fiber 1 gm, Sugars 8 gm, Protein 3 gm

Pumpkin Bread

Jan McDowell
New Holland, PA
Janet Derstine
Telford, PA

Makes 3 10-slice loaves
Serving size is 1 slice

Prep Time: 15-20 minutes
Baking Time: 1 hour

1½ cups sugar blend for
  baking (Splenda)
½ cup water
¾ cup vegetable oil
4 eggs, beaten
2 cups (15-oz. can)
  prepared pumpkin
3½ cups flour
1½ tsp. salt
1 tsp. cinnamon
½ tsp. nutmeg
2 tsp. baking soda

2 cups raisins, *optional*
2 cup chopped walnuts *or*
  pecans, *optional*

1. In a large mixing bowl, dissolve sugar blend in water and oil. Add eggs and pumpkin and mix well.
2. In a separate bowl, combine all dry ingredients. Add to pumpkin mixture. Mix until all ingredients are just moistened.
3. If you wish, stir in raisins and nuts.
4. Divide into 3 greased and floured 9 x 5 loaf pans.
5. Bake at 350° for 1 hour.
6. Allow to cool in pan for 10 minutes. Remove from pan and let cool completely on wire rack before slicing.

Exchange List Values:
Carb 1.5, Fat 1.0

Basic Nutritional Values:
Calories 155 (Calories from Fat 57), Total Fat 6 gm (Saturated Fat 0.6 gm, Trans Fat 0.0 gm, Polyunsat Fat 1.8 gm, Monounsat Fat 3.5 gm, Cholesterol 28 mg), Sodium 211 mg, Total Carbohydrate 22 gm, Dietary Fiber 1 gm, Sugars 10 gm, Protein 3 gm

Tip: This is very moist pumpkin bread. Serve it with warm apple cider on a cool autumn evening. Or slice it thin, spread each slice with whipped cream cheese, and top it with another slice. Cut "sandwiches" into quarters.

Strawberry Bread

Sally Holzem
Schofield, WI

Makes 2 12-slice loaves
Serving size is 1 slice

Prep Time: 20 minutes
Baking Time: 45-60 minutes

3 cups flour
1 cup sugar blend for
  baking (Splenda)
1 tsp. baking soda
1 tsp. salt
1 tsp. cinnamon
4 eggs beaten
1 cup vegetable oil
2 10-oz. pkgs. frozen
  strawberries, thawed
  and chopped, *or* 2 cups
  fresh strawberries,
  chopped
1 cup chopped pecans,
  optional

Frosting:
half an 8-oz. block of
  fat-free cream cheese,
  softened
1 tsp. vanilla
9–10 Tbsp. light soft tub
  margarine, softened
1½ cups confectioners
  sugar
chopped nuts, *optional*

1. In a large bowl, combine
flour, sugar blend, baking
soda, salt, and cinnamon.
When well mixed, form a
well in the center of the
mixture.
2. In a separate bowl,
combine beaten eggs, veg-
etable oil, strawberries, and

chopped pecans. Pour into
well in dry ingredients and
stir until evenly mixed.
3. Spoon mixture into 2
greased and floured 9 x 5 loaf
pans.
4. Bake at 350° for 45-60
minutes, until a tester
inserted in the center of the
tops of the loaves comes out
clean.
5. Let loaves cool in pans
for 10 minutes. Remove
to wire racks and let cool
completely.
6. To make the frosting,
beat cream cheese, vanilla,
and margarine together until
creamy in a medium-sized
bowl. Gently stir in confectioners and chopped nuts
until well distributed. Spread
frosting over cooled bread.

Exchange List Values:
Carb 1.5, Fat 1.5

Basic Nutritional Values:
Calories 182 (Calories from Fat 81),
Total Fat 9 gm (Saturated Fat 1.1
gm, Trans Fat 0.0 gm, Polyunsat
Fat 2.6 gm, Monounsat Fat 4.8 gm,
Cholesterol 27 mg), Sodium 172 mg,
Total Carbohydrate 23 gm, Dietary
Fiber 1 gm, Sugars 12 gm, Protein 3 gm

Tip: This bread freezes well.

Apple Cranberry Muffins

Wendy B. Martzall
New Holland, PA

Makes 12 muffins
Serving size is 1 muffin

Prep Time: 10-20 minutes
Baking Time: 20 minutes

1¾ cups flour
¼ cup sugar
2½ tsp. baking powder
¾ tsp. salt
½ tsp. cinnamon
1 egg, well-beaten
¾ cup fat-free milk
⅓ cup vegetable oil
1 cup peeled and finely
  chopped apple
½ cup chopped frozen
  cranberries

1. In a large mixing bowl,
stir together flour, sugar,
baking powder, salt, and
cinnamon. When well mixed,
make a well in the center of
the dry ingredients.
2. In a separate bowl, blend
together egg, milk, oil, apple,
and cranberries.
3. Add all at once to dry
ingredients. Stir just until
moistened.
4. Fill paper-lined or greased
muffin cups about ⅔ full.
5. Bake at 400° for
15-20 minutes, or until tops
are lightly browned, and
toothpick inserted in center
of muffins comes out clean.
Cool in tins for 10 minutes.
Then remove and continue
cooling on wire rack.

Basic Nutritional Values:
Calories 155 (Calories from Fat 60), Total Fat 7 gm (Saturated Fat 0.6 gm, Trans Fat 0.0 gm, Polyunsat Fat 1.9 gm, Monounsat Fat 3.7 gm, Cholesterol 18 mg), Sodium 234 mg, Total Carbohydrate 21 gm, Dietary Fiber 1 gm, Sugars 7 gm, Protein 3 gm

Tip: I've used dried cranberries as well with good results. Granny Smith apples are my choice, but other baking apples work, too.

Blueberry Muffins

Lois Stoltzfus, Honey Brook, PA

Makes 16 muffins
Serving size is 1 muffin

Prep Time: 20 minutes
Baking Time: 20 minutes

2 cups flour
½ cup sugar
2 tsp. baking powder
½ tsp. baking soda
½ tsp. salt
2 eggs
1 cup vanilla *or* lemon fat-free yogurt
¼ cup oil
1 cup blueberries, fresh *or* frozen*

Crumbs:
4 Tbsp. sugar
2 Tbsp. flour
1 Tbsp. butter, at room temperature

1. In a large mixing bowl, mix dry ingredients together.

2. In another bowl, beat eggs. Add yogurt, oil, and blueberries. Gently add to dry ingredients until just moistened.

3. Place batter in greased, or paper-lined muffin tins, filling each ⅔ full.

4. Using one of the mixing bowls you've just emptied, blend crumb ingredients with a pastry blender or fork and sprinkle on top of muffins.

5. Bake at 400° for 20 minutes, or until tester inserted in tops of muffins comes out clean.

Basic Nutritional Values:
Calories 153 (Calories from Fat 44), Total Fat 5 gm (Saturated Fat 0.9 gm, Trans Fat 0.0 gm, Polyunsat Fat 1.2 gm, Monounsat Fat 2.4 gm, Cholesterol 29 mg), Sodium 179 mg, Total Carbohydrate 24 gm, Dietary Fiber 1 gm, Sugars 11 gm, Protein 3 gm

* If using frozen berries, first toss them in a separate bowl with 1 Tbsp. flour before stirring them into the batter.

Bran Flax Muffins

Ruth Fisher, Leicester, NY

Makes 15 muffins
Serving size is 1 muffin

Prep Time: 20 minutes
Baking Time: 15-20 minutes

1½ cups flour
¾ cup flaxseed meal
¾ cup oat bran

½ cup brown sugar blend (Splenda)
2 tsp. baking soda
1 tsp. baking powder
½ tsp. salt
2 tsp. cinnamon
1½ cups carrots, shredded
2 apples, peeled and shredded, *or* chopped fine
½ cup raisins, *optional*
1 cup chopped nuts
¾ cup fat-free milk
2 eggs, beaten
1 tsp. vanilla

1. In a large bowl, mix together flour, flaxseed meal, oat bran, brown sugar blend, baking soda, baking powder, salt, and cinnamon.

2. Stir in carrots, apples, raisins, and nuts.

3. In a separate bowl, combine milk, eggs, and vanilla. Pour liquid ingredients into dry ingredients and stir just until moistened. Do not over-mix.

4. Fill lightly greased muffin tins ¾ full. Bake at 350° for 15-20 minutes.

Basic Nutritional Values:
Calories 197 (Calories from Fat 74), Total Fat 8 gm (Saturated Fat 1.0 gm, Trans Fat 0.0 gm, Polyunsat Fat 5.2 gm, Monounsat Fat 1.5 gm, Cholesterol 28 mg), Sodium 297 mg, Total Carbohydrate 27 gm, Dietary Fiber 4 gm, Sugars 10 gm, Protein 6 gm

Tips:
1. You can buy flaxseed meal at bulk food or health-food stores.
2. Flaxseed is a major source of fiber.

Banana Wheat Germ Muffins

Terry Stutzman Mast
Lodi, California

Makes 12 muffins
Serving size is 1 muffin

Prep Time: 15-20 minutes
Baking Time: 18-20 minutes

1½ cups flour
1 cup toasted wheat germ
¼ cup brown sugar blend (Splenda)
1 Tbsp. baking powder
1 tsp. salt
¾ tsp. ground nutmeg
2 eggs, beaten
½ cup fat-free milk
¼ cup canola oil
1 cup (2 large) mashed ripe bananas
½ cup chopped walnuts

1. Preheat oven to 425°.
2. Lightly grease the muffin tins or line them with baking papers.
3. In a large mixing bowl, combine flour, wheat germ, sugar blend, baking powder, salt, and nutmeg. Blend well.
4. In a separate bowl, beat eggs into milk. Add canola oil and banana, continuing to beat until smooth.
5. Add banana mixture to dry ingredients, just until blended. Be careful not to over-mix.
6. Gently stir in nuts.
7. Spoon batter into muffin cups, filling ⅔ full. Bake 18-20 minutes, until muffins become a rich brown.
8. Allow to cool for 10 minutes in muffin cups, then remove and serve, or place on wire rack until completely cool and ready to be stored.
9. Serve warm or cold.

Exchange List Values:
Carb 2.0, Fat 1.5

Basic Nutritional Values:
Calories 219 (Calories from Fat 89), Total Fat 10 gm (Saturated Fat 1.2 gm, Trans Fat 0.0 gm, Polyunsat Fat 4.5 gm, Monounsat Fat 3.6 gm, Cholesterol 35 mg), Sodium 302 mg, Total Carbohydrate 26 gm, Dietary Fiber 2 gm, Sugars 8 gm, Protein 7 gm

Tip: This is a perfect, healthy use for those ripe uneaten bananas that can be found every now and then in the kitchen.
All kids love these. It's fun to see my kids, and the neighbor kids, gobble them up for snacks!

Double Chocolate Muffins

Janet Groff, Stevens, PA

Makes 18 muffins
Serving size is 1 muffin

Prep Time: 15 minutes
Baking Time: 30 minutes

½ cup dry quick oats
⅓ cup fat-free milk
1 cup flour
½ cup whole wheat flour
2 Tbsp. wheat bran
¼ cup sugar blend for baking (Splenda)
2 Tbsp. brown sugar blend (Splenda)
⅓ cup cocoa powder
¼ tsp. salt
1 rounded tsp. baking powder
1 egg
¼ cup vegetable oil
1 cup fat-free milk
1 Tbsp. vanilla
7 Tbsp. semi-sweet chocolate chips

Glaze:
1-2 Tbsp. peanut butter
1½ cups confectioners sugar
water

1. In a microwavable container, combine quick oats and ⅓ cup milk. Microwave on high 1½ minutes. Set aside.
2. In a large bowl, combine flours, wheat bran, both sugar blends, cocoa powder, salt, and baking powder.
3. In a separate bowl, stir together oats mixture, egg, oil, milk, vanilla, and chocolate chips.
4. Gently fold wet ingredients into dry ingredients, mixing just until moistened.
5. Spoon batter into 18 greased muffin cups, making each ½ full.
6. Bake at 350° for 30 minutes, or until toothpick inserted in muffin tops comes out clean. Allow muffins to cool for 10 minutes before removing from tins.
7. To make glaze: Combine peanut butter and powdered sugar in a small bowl. Add water to desired consistency and stir until smooth. Drizzle over warm muffins.

Basic Nutritional Values:
Calories 172 (Calories from Fat 51), Total Fat 6 gm (Saturated Fat 1.4 gm, Trans Fat 0.0 gm, Polyunsat Fat 1.2 gm, Monounsat Fat 2.7 gm, Cholesterol 12 mg), Sodium 70 mg, Total Carbohydrate 28 gm, Dietary Fiber 2 gm, Sugars 17 gm, Protein 3 gm

Morning Glory Muffins

Mary Jane Hoober
Shipshewana, IN

Makes 36 muffins
Serving size is 1 muffin

Prep Time: 25-30 minutes
Baking Time: 20 minutes

3 eggs
¾ cup vegetable oil
2 tsp. vanilla
½ cup sugar
2 Tbsp. sugar blend for baking (Splenda)
2 cups, plus 2 Tbsp., flour
2 tsp. baking soda
2 tsp. cinnamon
½ tsp. salt
2 cups grated carrots
1 cup raisins
½ cup nuts, chopped
½ cup grated coconut
1 apple, peeled, cored, and grated, *or* chopped finely

1. In a large mixing bowl beat eggs. Then add oil, vanilla, sugar, and sugar blend and combine well.
2. In a separate mixing bowl, stir together flour, baking soda, cinnamon, and salt. When well mixed, add remaining ingredients.
3. Pour dry-fruit ingredients into creamed ingredients. Blend just until everything is moistened.
4. Fill greased muffin tins ⅔ full. Bake at 350° for 20 minutes, or until tester inserted in center comes out clean.

Basic Nutritional Values:
Calories 120 (Calories from Fat 58), Total Fat 6 gm (Saturated Fat 0.9 gm, Trans Fat 0.0 gm, Polyunsat Fat 2.2 gm, Monounsat Fat 3.0 gm, Cholesterol 18 mg), Sodium 116 mg, Total Carbohydrate 14 gm, Dietary Fiber 1 gm, Sugars 7 gm, Protein 2 gm

Pumpkin Chip Muffins

Julia Horst
Gordonville, PA
Sherri Grindle
Goshen, IN

Makes 36 muffins
Serving size is 1 muffin

Prep Time: 10 minutes
Baking Time: 17 minutes

4 eggs
1 cup sugar blend for baking (Splenda)
15- or 16-oz. can pumpkin
¾ cup vegetable oil
¾ cup plain fat-free yogurt
3 cups flour
2 tsp. baking soda
2 tsp. baking powder
1 tsp. cinnamon
1 tsp. salt
1 cup semi-sweet chocolate chips

1. In a large bowl, beat eggs, sugar blend, pumpkin, oil, and yogurt until smooth.
2. In a separate bowl, combine flour, baking soda, baking powder, cinnamon, and salt.
3. Add dry ingredients to pumpkin mixture and mix just until moistened.
4. Fold in chocolate chips.
5. Fill paper-lined muffin cups ¾ full.
6. Bake at 400° for 17 minutes, or until tester inserted in center of muffin tops comes out clean.

Basic Nutritional Values:
Calories 139 (Calories from Fat 61), Total Fat 7 gm (Saturated Fat 1.4 gm, Trans Fat 0.0 gm, Polyunsat Fat 1.5 gm, Monounsat Fat 3.4 gm, Cholesterol 24 mg), Sodium 168 mg, Total Carbohydrate 18 gm, Dietary Fiber 1 gm, Sugars 9 gm, Protein 2 gm

Soups, Stews, and Chilis

Creamy Asparagus Soup

Mary E. Riha
Antigo, WI

Makes 4 servings
Serving size is ¾ cup

Prep Time: 30 minutes
Cooking Time: 15-20 minutes

¼ cup sesame seeds
2 Tbsp. olive oil
1 medium onion, chopped
2 medium potatoes, cubed
4 cups fat-free, reduced-sodium chicken stock, *divided*
1 lb. raw asparagus, broken in 1" pieces
dash of pepper
dash of nutmeg
sour cream, *optional*
salted sunflower seeds, *optional*

1. In stockpot, sauté sesame seeds in olive oil until brown. Add onions and potatoes. Cook and stir until potatoes begin to stick.

2. Add 2 cups stock, asparagus, and pepper. Bring to boil. Reduce heat and simmer until potatoes are done.

3. Carefully pour one-fourth of hot mixture into blender. Cover and blend until smooth. (Hold the lid on with a potholder to keep the heat from pushing it off.)

4. Put pureed soup back in stockpot. Continue blending cooked soup, one-fourth at a time. Continue to add pureed soup back into stockpot.

5. When all soup has been pureed, add 2 more cups chicken stock to soup in stockpot. Heat thoroughly.

6. Add a dash of nutmeg.

7. Top each serving with a dollop of sour cream (optional) and a sprinkling of sunflower seeds.

Exchange List Values:
Starch 1.0, Vegetable 1.0, Fat 2.0

Basic Nutritional Values: Calories 217 (Calories from Fat 104), Total Fat 12 gm (Saturated Fat 1.6 gm, Trans Fat 0.0 gm, Polyunsat Fat 2.7 gm, Monounsat Fat 6.7 gm, Cholesterol 0 mg), Sodium 511 mg, Total Carbohydrate 24 gm, Dietary Fiber 4 gm, Sugars 4 gm, Protein 7 gm

A Tip —

At the grocery store, shop primarily from the outside aisles. These sections are filled with foods that are fresh, natural, and healthy.

Southwest Bean Soup

Kathy Keener Shantz
Lancaster, PA

Makes 6-7 servings
Serving size is ¾ cup

Prep Time: 15-20 minutes
Cooking Time: 20-30 minutes

2 Tbsp. oil
1 onion, diced
4 garlic cloves, minced
2 tsp. cumin
1 tsp. chili powder
¼ tsp. ground red pepper
2 10-oz. pkg frozen corn, thawed
15-oz. can diced tomatoes
15-oz. can no-added-salt diced tomatoes
15-oz. can black beans, drained
15-oz. can kidney beans, drained
4 cups fat-free, reduced-sodium chicken broth
chopped fresh cilantro, *optional*
blue or white corn chips, *optional*
plain yogurt *or* sour cream, *optional*

1. In large saucepan, sauté onion, garlic, and seasonings in oil.
2. Stir in corn, tomatoes, beans, and chicken broth. Bring to boil. Reduce heat. Cover and simmer for 20-30 minutes.
3. Serve with optional toppings: fresh cilantro, crushed corn chips, and/or yogurt.

Exchange List Values:
Starch 2.0, Vegetable 2.0, Fat 1.0

Basic Nutritional Values:
Calories 245 (Calories from Fat 46), Total Fat 5 gm (Saturated Fat 0.4 gm, Trans Fat 0.0 gm, Polyunsat Fat 1.7 gm, Monounsat Fat 2.6 gm, Cholesterol 0 mg), Sodium 552 mg, Total Carbohydrate 43 gm, Dietary Fiber 10 gm, Sugars 8 gm, Protein 12 gm

Black Bean Sweet Potato Soup

Carisa Funk
Hillsboro, KS

Makes 4 servings
Serving size is ¾ cup

Prep Time: 10-15 minutes
Cooking Time: 20 minutes

1 Tbsp. oil
1 medium onion, chopped
2 garlic cloves, minced
2 medium-sized raw sweet potatoes, peeled and diced
1 Tbsp. chili powder
16-oz. jar salsa
1 cup water
2 15-oz. cans black beans, drained
sour cream, *optional*
fresh cilantro

1. In large saucepan, sauté onion and garlic in oil for 4 minutes.
2. Stir in sweet potatoes, chili powder, salsa, and water. Heat to boiling. Reduce heat and cook 12-15 minutes, or until potatoes are fork tender.
3. Add beans. Cook 3 more minutes.
4. Garnish individual servings with sour cream (optional) and fresh cilantro.

Exchange List Values:
Starch 3.0, Vegetable 2.0, Fat 0.5

Basic Nutritional Values:
Calories 312 (Calories from Fat 44), Total Fat 5 gm (Saturated Fat 0.5 gm, Trans Fat 0.0 gm, Polyunsat Fat 1.7 gm, Monounsat Fat 2.2 gm, Cholesterol 0 mg), **Sodium 848 mg (high sodium)**, Total Carbohydrate 57 gm, Dietary Fiber 15 gm, Sugars 12 gm, Protein 14 gm

Bean Soup with Turkey Sausage

Dorothy Reise, Severna Park, MD
D. Fern Ruth, Chalfont, PA

Makes 6 servings
Serving size is ¾ cup

Prep Time: 15-20 minutes
Cooking Time: 15-20 minutes

4 ozs. turkey kielbasa
4 cups low-sodium chicken broth
2 15-oz. cans cannelloni beans, drained and rinsed
½-1 cup onion, chopped
1 tsp. dried basil, crushed
¼ tsp. coarsely ground pepper
1 clove garlic, minced
1 carrot, peeled and sliced, *or* 1 cup baby carrots
half a red, yellow, *or* orange bell pepper, sliced
3 cups fresh spinach, cleaned, *or* 10-oz. pkg. frozen spinach
fresh parsley, chopped

1. Cut turkey kielbasa lengthwise, and then into ½" slices. Sauté in Dutch oven or large saucepan until browned, stirring occasionally so it doesn't stick.
2. Combine all ingredients in pan except spinach and parsley.
3. Bring to boil, and then reduce heat. Cover and simmer 10-15 minutes, or until onion and carrots are tender.
4. If you're using frozen spinach, add it to the soup and let it thaw in the soup pot. Stir occasionally to break up spinach and to have it heat through.
5. If you're using fresh spinach, remove stems from fresh spinach, stack, and cut into 1" strips. Remove soup from heat and stir in spinach and parsley until spinach wilts.
6. Serve immediately.

Exchange List Values:
Starch 2.0, Vegetable 2.0, Lean Meat 1.0, Fat 0.5

Basic Nutritional Values:
Calories 287 (Calories from Fat 45), Total Fat 5 gm (Saturated Fat 1.5 gm, Trans Fat 0.0 gm, Polyunsat Fat 1.4 gm, Monounsat Fat 1.1 gm, Cholesterol 20 mg), Sodium 588 mg, Total Carbohydrate 42 gm, Dietary Fiber 11 gm, Sugars 4 gm, Protein 21 gm

Variation: For a thicker soup, remove 1 cup of hot soup after Step 3 and carefully process in firmly covered blender or food processor until smooth. Stir back into soup and continue with Step 4.

Cheesy Broccoli Cauliflower Soup

Marcia S. Myer, Manheim, PA

Makes 6 servings
Serving size is ¾ cup

Prep Time: 20 minutes
Cooking Time: 40-45 minutes

4 Tbsp. canola oil
¼ cup chopped onion
½ cup flour
2 cups fat-free milk
1 cup (4 ozs.) light Velveeta cheese, cubed
2 14-oz. cans low-sodium chicken broth
2 cups chopped broccoli, fresh *or* frozen
2 cups chopped cauliflower, fresh *or* frozen
¼ cup finely chopped *or* grated carrots
¼ cup chopped celery
salt to taste
¼ tsp. pepper

1. Heat canola oil in large saucepan. Stir in onion and sauté until just tender.
2. Stir in flour until well blended. Slowly add milk over medium heat, stirring constantly until thickened and smooth.
3. Stir in cheese, continuing to stir until cheese melts. Set aside.
4. In a separate saucepan, simmer broccoli, cauliflower, carrots, and celery in chicken broth until almost tender.
5. Season with salt, if you wish, and pepper.
6. Pour cheesy sauce into vegetables and heat through.

Exchange List Values:
Carbohydrate 1.5, Lean Meat 1.0, Fat 1.5

Basic Nutritional Values:
Calories 228 (Calories from Fat 111), Total Fat 12 gm (Saturated Fat 2.3 gm, Trans Fat 0.0 gm, Polyunsat Fat 3.1 gm, Monounsat Fat 6.2 gm, Cholesterol 11 mg), Sodium 405 mg, Total Carbohydrate 20 gm, Dietary Fiber 2 gm, Sugars 9 gm, Protein 11 gm

Variations:
1. Instead of chicken broth, use 2 chicken bouillon cubes and 1¾ cups water in Step 4.

2. Instead of cauliflower, use 2 additional cups broccoli, fresh or frozen.
—**Mary Jane Musser**
Manheim, PA

Broccoli Chowder

Ruth E. Martin
Loysville, PA

Makes 6 servings
Serving size is ¾ cup

Prep Time: 15-20 minutes
Cooking Time: 20 minutes

2 cups diced potatoes, peeled *or* unpeeled
½ cup water
2 cups chopped broccoli, fresh, *or* 10-oz. pkg. chopped broccoli, frozen
2 Tbsp. onion
1 cup corn, fresh *or* frozen, thawed
¼-½ cup cooked, diced ham, *optional*
3 cups fat-free milk
½ tsp. salt, *optional*
⅛ tsp. pepper
1 tsp. powdered chicken bouillon, *or* 1 chicken bouillon cube
½ cup light Velveeta cheese, cubed

1. In medium-sized saucepan, cook potatoes in water. When potatoes are almost soft, add broccoli and onion. Cook until tender.
2. Add corn, ham, if you wish, milk, seasonings, and bouillon. Heat, but do not boil.

3. Turn off and add cubed cheese. Let cheese melt for about 3-4 minutes. Stir and serve.

Exchange List Values:
Starch 1.0, Fat-Free Milk 0.5, Vegetable 1.0

Basic Nutritional Values:
Calories 140 (Calories from Fat 12), Total Fat 1 gm (Saturated Fat 0.9 gm, Trans Fat 0.0 gm, Polyunsat Fat 0.1 gm, Monounsat Fat 0.4 gm, Cholesterol 6 mg), Sodium 358 mg, Total Carbohydrate 25 gm, Dietary Fiber 2 gm, Sugars 9 gm, Protein 9 gm

Tomato Mushroom Soup

D. Fern Ruth
Chalfont, PA

Makes 6 servings
Serving size is ¾ cup

Prep Time: 15 minutes
Cooking Time: 30 minutes

2 cups sliced fresh mushrooms
⅓ cup chopped onion
2 garlic cloves, minced
4 Tbsp. butter
6 Tbsp. flour
2 14.5-oz. cans fat-free, low-sodium chicken broth
14.5-oz. can diced tomatoes, undrained
14.5-oz. can no-salt-added diced tomatoes, undrained
4 Tbsp. chopped, fresh basil leaves, *or* 1½ Tbsp. dried basil
1 Tbsp. sugar
¼ tsp. pepper

1. In a large saucepan, sauté mushrooms, onion, and garlic in butter until tender. Remove vegetables from pan and set aside. Leave as much of the drippings as you can in the pan.
2. In the same pan, combine flour and chicken broth with drippings until smooth. Bring to boil and stir 2-4 minutes, or until thickened.
3. Return mushroom mixture to saucepan and stir into thickened chicken broth.
4. Add tomatoes, basil, sugar, and pepper. Cook over medium heat 10-15 minutes, stirring occasionally.
5. Remove from heat. Cool slightly. Then puree in tightly covered blender (¼ of the mixture at a time) until smooth.
6. Garnish with basil leaves and serve hot.

Exchange List Values:
Starch 0.5, Vegetable 2.0, Fat 1.5

Basic Nutritional Values:
Calories 148 (Calories from Fat 67), Total Fat 7 gm (Saturated Fat 0.5 gm, Trans Fat 0.0 gm, Polyunsat Fat 2.3 gm, Monounsat Fat 4.2 gm, Cholesterol 0 mg), Sodium 498 mg, Total Carbohydrate 18 gm, Dietary Fiber 3 gm, Sugars 8 gm, Protein 4 gm

Tips:
1. Flavors blend nicely when you make the soup a day ahead and allow it to stand overnight.
2. Use fresh tomatoes in season.

Fresh Vegetable Soup

Sandra Chang, Derwood, MD

Makes 6 servings
Serving size is ¾ cup

Prep Time: 25-30 minutes
Cooking Time: 60-70 minutes
Standing Time: 1 hour

3 Tbsp. canola oil
½ cup of each:
   diced celery
   diced onions
   small chunks of peeled
     carrots
   chopped cabbage
   diced zucchini
   fresh *or* frozen whole-
     kernel corn
   fresh *or* frozen cut-up
     green beans
2 cups canned whole
   tomatoes
4 cups fat-free, low-sodium
   beef stock
2 Tbsp. sugar
salt to taste
pepper to taste
½ cup fresh *or* frozen
   petite peas

1. In 4-quart saucepan, heat oil. Sauté celery, onions, carrots, cabbage, and zucchini in butter until vegetables are soft but not brown.
2. Add rest of ingredients, except ½ cup peas.
3. Simmer gently for 30-45 minutes, or until vegetables are cooked but not mushy.
4. Take pan off heat and stir in peas. Allow soup to stand for one hour before serving.

5. Reheat just until heated through and serve.

Exchange List Values:
Starch 0.5, Vegetable 2.0, Fat 1.0

Basic Nutritional Values:
Calories 140 (Calories from Fat 66), Total Fat 7 gm (Saturated Fat 0.5 gm, Trans Fat 0.0 gm, Polyunsat Fat 2.3 gm, Monounsat Fat 4.2 gm, Cholesterol 0 mg), Sodium 490 mg, Total Carbohydrate 17 gm, Dietary Fiber 3 gm, Sugars 10 gm, Protein 4 gm

Cheeseburger Soup

Marcella Heatwole,
North Lawrence, OH
Jean Hindal, Grandin, IA
Beverly High, Ephrata, PA
Sherlyn Hess, Millersville, PA

Makes 8 servings
Serving size is ¾ cup

Prep Time: 30 minutes
Cooking Time: 20-30 minutes

½ lb. 90%-lean ground beef
¾ cup chopped onions
¾ cup shredded carrots
¾ cup diced celery
¼ tsp. dried basil
1 tsp. dried parsley flakes
3 Tbsp. canola oil, *divided*
3 cups fat-free, reduced-
   sodium chicken broth
2 cups diced potatoes,
   peeled *or* unpeeled
¼ cup flour
1½ cups fat-free milk
¼-½ tsp. pepper
1 cup fat-free cheddar
   cheese, grated

½ cup reduced-fat cheddar
   cheese, grated
¼ cup sour cream

1. In saucepan, brown beef. Drain. Set aside.
2. In same saucepan, sauté onions, carrots, celery, basil, and parsley in 1 Tbsp. canola oil until vegetables are tender.
3. Add broth, potatoes, and beef. Bring to boil. Reduce heat, cover, and simmer for 10-12 minutes, or until potatoes are tender.
4. While meat and potatoes cook, in small skillet heat 2 Tbsp. canola oil. Stir in flour until smooth. Cook and stir 3-5 minutes.
5. Reduce heat to low. Add milk and pepper. Stir until mixture thickens and becomes smooth.
6. Slowly stir in grated cheese, about ½-cupful at a time. Continue to stir until cheese is fully melted and blended into white sauce.
7. Blend in sour cream. Heat, but do not boil.
8. When vegetables are tender and cheesy white sauce is finished, pour the white sauce into the vegetable mixture and gently stir together.
9. When well mixed and heated through, serve.

Exchange List Values:
Starch 1.0, Vegetable 1.0, Lean Meat 1.0, Fat 1.0

Basic Nutritional Values:
Calories 219 (Calories from Fat 83), Total Fat 9 gm (Saturated Fat 2.2 gm, Trans Fat 0.2 gm, Polyunsat Fat 1.7 gm, Monounsat Fat 4.5 gm, Cholesterol 25 mg), Sodium 445 mg, Total Carbohydrate 18 gm, Dietary Fiber 2 gm, Sugars 5 gm, Protein 16 gm

Pasta Fagioli Soup

Stacie Skelly, Millersville, PA

Makes 10 servings
Serving size is ¾ cup

Prep Time: 20 minutes
Cooking Time: 90 minutes

1 lb. 90%-lean ground beef
1 cup diced onions
1 cup julienned carrots
1 cup chopped celery
2 cloves garlic, minced
2 14.5-oz. cans no-salt-
  added diced tomatoes,
  undrained
15-oz. can red kidney
  beans, undrained
15-oz. can Great Northern
  beans, undrained
15-oz. can no-salt-added
  tomato sauce
12-oz. can low-sodium V-8
  juice
1 Tbsp. vinegar
¾ tsp. salt
1 tsp. dried oregano
1 tsp. dried basil
½ tsp. pepper
½ tsp. dried thyme
½ lb. ditali pasta*

1. Brown ground beef in a large stockpot. Drain off drippings.
2. To browned beef, add onions, carrots, celery, and garlic. Sauté for 10 minutes.
3. Add remaining ingredients, except pasta, and stir well. Simmer, covered, for 1 hour.
4. About 50 minutes into cooking time, cook pasta in a separate saucepan, according to the directions on the package.
5. Add drained pasta to the large pot of soup. Simmer for 5-10 minutes and serve.

Exchange List Values:
Starch 2.0, Vegetable 2.0,
Lean Meat 1.0

Basic Nutritional Values:
Calories 272 (Calories from Fat 43),
Total Fat 5 gm (Saturated Fat 1.6
gm, Trans Fat 0.2 gm, Polyunsat
Fat 0.6 gm, Monounsat Fat 1.7 gm,
Cholesterol 27 mg), Sodium 552 mg,
Total Carbohydrate 39 gm, Dietary
Fiber 6 gm, Sugars 9 gm, Protein 17 gm

** If you can't find these short
tubes, you can substitute elbow
macaroni.*

Hearty Beef Barley Soup

Karen Gingrich
New Holland, PA

Makes 5 servings
Serving size is ¾ cup

Preparation Time: 5-10 minutes
Cooking Time: 35 minutes

1 lb. beef tips
2 cups sliced fresh
  mushrooms
¼ tsp. garlic powder
32-oz. can (3½ cups) fat-free,
  low-sodium beef broth
2 medium-sized carrots,
  sliced
¼ tsp. dried thyme
dash of pepper
½ cup quick-cooking
  barley

1. Trim visible fat from beef.
2. Cook beef in nonstick saucepan until browned and juices evaporate, about 10 minutes, stirring often.
3. Add mushrooms and garlic powder and cook until mushrooms begin to wilt, about 5 minutes.
4. Add broth, carrots, thyme, and pepper.
5. Heat to boiling. Stir in barley. Cover and cook over low heat for 20 minutes, or until barley is tender.

Exchange List Values:
Starch 1.5, Lean Meat 2.0

Basic Nutritional Values:
Calories 227 (Calories from Fat 40),
Total Fat 4 gm (Saturated Fat 1.5
gm, Trans Fat 0.0 gm, Polyunsat
Fat 0.4 gm, Monounsat Fat 1.7 gm,
Cholesterol 56 mg), Sodium 377 mg,
Total Carbohydrate 25 gm, Dietary
Fiber 4 gm, Sugars 2 gm, Protein 22 gm

A Tip —

After you've browned ground meat, bacon, or sausage, drain and pat it dry to remove as much fat as you can.

Beef Barley Soup

Jan Rankin
Millersville, PA

Makes 6 servings
Serving size is ¾ cup

Prep Time: 15 minutes
Cooking Time: 90 minutes

2-2½-lb. chuck roast
2 cups tomato, *or* V8, juice
1 rib celery, finely chopped
2 carrots, diced
water
1 cup quick-cooking barley

1. Trim visible fat from chuck roast.
2. In large saucepan, place meat, tomato juice, celery, and carrots. Add water to cover.
3. Cook until meat is soft and tender, approximately an hour.
4. Remove meat. Cut into small pieces and return to pot.
5. Add barley. Cook 15-30 minutes more, or until barley is tender.

Exchange List Values:
Starch 2.5, Lean Meat 2.0

Basic Nutritional Values:
Calories 326 (Calories from Fat 57), Total Fat 6 gm (Saturated Fat 1.9 gm, Trans Fat 0.0 gm, Polyunsat Fat 0.6 gm, Monounsat Fat 2.8 gm, Cholesterol 75 mg), Sodium 366 mg, Total Carbohydrate 40 gm, Dietary Fiber 6 gm, Sugars 4 gm, Protein 27 gm

Chicken or Turkey Vegetable Barley Soup

Esther J. Mast
Lancaster, PA

Makes 10-12 servings
Serving size is 1½ cups

Prep Time: 45 minutes
Simmering Time: 70 minutes
(if using pre-cooked chicken or turkey)

5 qts. fresh, low-sodium chicken *or* turkey broth, fat skimmed off
2 cups diced celery
2 cups sliced carrots
2 cups green beans
1 onion, chopped
¾ cup pearl barley
2-3 cups cooked chicken *or* turkey, diced
salt and pepper to taste
fresh parsley, *if desired*

1. In soup pot, combine broth, celery, carrots, green beans, onion, and barley. Simmer approximately 1 hour, or until vegetables and barley are tender but not mushy.
2. Add cooked diced chicken, salt and pepper to taste, and heat thoroughly.
3. Serve piping hot, garnished with fresh parsley.

Exchange List Values:
Starch 1.0, Vegetable 1.0, Lean Meat 1.0, Fat 0.5

Basic Nutritional Values:
Calories 178 (Calories from Fat 43), Total Fat 5 gm (Saturated Fat 1.2 gm, Trans Fat 0.0 gm, Polyunsat Fat 1.2 gm, Monounsat Fat 1.3 gm, Cholesterol 27 mg), Sodium 240 mg, Total Carbohydrate 21 gm, Dietary Fiber 3 gm, Sugars 4 gm, Protein 14 gm

Tips:
1. Use 2 cups diced potatoes instead of barley.
2. For a tasty variation on the traditional chicken-broth flavoring, tie into a cheesecloth bag 1 bay leaf, 10 kernels whole black peppercorns, and 1 whole star anise. Place bag of spices in water while cooking a whole chicken. Simmer slowly for about 2 hours, until chicken is tender and broth is well flavored. Debone chicken and reserve for Step 2 above.

A Tip —

Make meat a side dish, rather than the whole meal. Try a few meatless meals throughout the week.

Chicken Tortellini Soup

Mary Seielstad
Sparks, NV

Makes 4-6 servings
Serving size is ¾ cup

Prep Time: 10-15 minutes
Cooking Time: 25 minutes

1 Tbsp. olive oil
4 cloves garlic, minced
5 cups low-sodium chicken broth
9-oz. pkg. frozen cheese tortellini
1½ cups diced cooked chicken
14-oz. can no-salt-added stewed tomatoes
10-oz. pkg. frozen spinach
½ tsp. pepper
1 tsp. dried basil
¼ cup grated Parmesan cheese

1. In large saucepan, heat olive oil and sauté garlic for 2 minutes over medium heat.

2. Sir in broth and tortellini and bring to a boil. Cover, reduce heat, and simmer 5 minutes.

3. Add cooked chicken, tomatoes, frozen spinach, pepper, and basil and simmer 10-15 minutes. Stir every 3 minutes or so, breaking up frozen spinach and blending it into the soup.

4. Serve when soup is heated through, along with Parmesan cheese to spoon over individual servings.

Exchange List Values:
Starch 1.5, Vegetable 1.0, Lean Meat 2.0, Fat 1.0

Basic Nutritional Values:
Calories 291 (Calories from Fat 94), Total Fat 10 gm (Saturated Fat 3.5 gm, Trans Fat 0.0 gm, Polyunsat Fat 2.0 gm, Monounsat Fat 3.9 gm, Cholesterol 54 mg), Sodium 396 mg, Total Carbohydrate 29 gm, Dietary Fiber 3 gm, Sugars 4 gm, Protein 23 gm

Chicken Noodle Soup

Josephine A. Earle
Citronelle, AL

Makes 12 servings
Serving size is ¾ cup

Prep Time: 30-40 minutes
Cooking Time: 55-60 minutes

1 cup chopped celery
1 cup chopped onion
2 Tbsp. canola oil
12 cups water
1 cup diced carrots
3 Tbsp. low-sodium chicken-flavored instant bouillon, *or* 3 low-sodium chicken bouillon cubes
½ tsp. dried marjoram leaves, *optional*
¼-½ tsp. pepper
1 bay leaf
4 cups cut-up cooked chicken
half a 12-oz. pkg. medium-sized egg noodles
1 Tbsp. chopped parsley

1. In a large Dutch oven, cook celery and onion in butter until tender.

2. Add water, carrots, bouillon, marjoram, pepper, and bay leaf. Cover. Bring to a boil. Reduce heat and simmer, covered for 30 minutes. Remove bay leaf.

3. Stir in chicken. Add noodles and parsley.

4. Cook 10 minutes longer until noodles are tender, stirring occasionally.

Exchange List Values:
Starch 0.5, Vegetable 1.0, Lean Meat 2.0

Basic Nutritional Values:
Calories 186 (Calories from Fat 59), Total Fat 7 gm (Saturated Fat 1.3 gm, Trans Fat 0.0 gm, Polyunsat Fat 1.7 gm, Monounsat Fat 2.8 gm, Cholesterol 56 mg), Sodium 450 mg, Total Carbohydrate 15 gm, Dietary Fiber 1 gm, Sugars 2 gm, Protein 16 gm

Variations:
1. Instead of cooked chicken called for above, cut up 2 lbs. uncooked skinless chicken breast, and add it to the soup in Step 2.
—Helen A. Roselle
Ellisville, IL

2. Instead of cooked chicken in the recipe above, put a whole chicken (weighing 3-4 lbs.) in Dutch oven in Step 2 above. (Eliminate bouillon.) Cook for 45-60 minutes, or until chicken is falling off the bones. Remove chicken from pot. Debone.
Return chicken meat to pot and continue with Step 3. Add 8 ozs. sliced, fresh mushrooms to Step 3, along with noodles and parsley.
—Kara Maddox,
Independence, MO

Surprise Gumbo

Brenda J Marshall
St. Marys, ON

Makes 8 servings
Serving size is ¾ cup

Prep Time: 20-30 minutes
Cooking Time: 30-40 minutes

1¼ lbs. cooked chicken, cubed*
2 medium-sized onions, cut in wedges
1 medium-sized green bell pepper, cut in narrow strips
28-oz. can whole tomatoes, undrained
¼ cup Worcestershire sauce
2 Tbsp. prepared mustard
2 Tbsp. garlic cloves, minced
1 tsp. dried thyme
1 tsp. dried rosemary
¼ tsp. pepper
½ lb. precooked shrimp
4 cups hot cooked rice

1. In large saucepan, combine chicken, onions, green pepper, tomatoes, Worcestershire sauce, mustard, garlic, thyme, rosemary, and pepper. Simmer for 25 minutes.
2. Add shrimp and cook 5 minutes more.
3. Serve over scoops of cooked rice in individual serving bowls.

Exchange List Values:
Starch 1.5, Vegetable 2.0, Very Lean Meat 3.0, Fat 1.0

Basic Nutritional Values:
Calories 316 (Calories from Fat 55), Total Fat 6 gm (Saturated Fat 1.6 gm, Trans Fat 0.0 gm, Polyunsat Fat 1.5 gm, Monounsat Fat 2.1 gm, Cholesterol 118 mg), Sodium 463 mg, Total Carbohydrate 33 gm, Dietary Fiber 2 gm, Sugars 7 gm, Protein 30 gm

---

* *If you don't have cooked chicken, cut up 1 whole skinless chicken breast (1¼-lbs.) and cook lightly in microwave. Or place raw chunks in saucepan along with just the tomatoes and simmer gently over medium heat for about 10 minutes, or until meat is losing its pinkness. Then continue with Step 1 above, adding the other ingredients listed there, and continuing to simmer them and the chicken.*

Chicken Taco Soup

Mary Puskar
Forest Hill, MD

Makes 8 servings
Serving size is ¾ cup

Prep Time: 25 minutes
Cooking Time: 40 minutes

2 chicken breast halves
3 cups water
2 stalks celery
1 medium-sized onion
2 carrots
2 Tbsp. vegetable *or* canola oil
1 Tbsp. chili powder
1 Tbsp. cumin
4.5-oz. can green chilies
14-oz. can fat-free, reduced-sodium chicken broth
14-oz. can fat-free, reduced-sodium beef broth
14.5-oz. can diced tomatoes, undrained
1 Tbsp. Worcestershire sauce
32 bite-sized, baked, low-fat tortilla chips
Monterey Jack cheese, grated, *optional*

1. In a large stockpot, cook chicken breasts in water until tender. Remove meat, reserving cooking water. When chicken is cool enough to handle, chop into bite-sized pieces. Set aside.
2. Chop celery and onion. Grate carrots.
3. In stockpot used for cooking chicken, sauté vegetables in oil.
4. Combine all ingredients in stockpot, except the cooked chicken. Cover and simmer 15 minutes.
5. Add diced chicken. Heat through.
6. Top each serving with 4 tortilla chips and, optionally, grated cheese

Exchange List Values:
Starch 0.5, Vegetable 1.0, Very Lean Meat 1.0, Fat 0.5

Basic Nutritional Values:
Calories 131 (Calories from Fat 45), Total Fat 5 gm (Saturated Fat 0.5 gm, Trans Fat 0.0 gm, Polyunsat Fat 1.5 gm, Monounsat Fat 2.5 gm, Cholesterol 18 mg), Sodium 440 mg, Total Carbohydrate 13 gm, Dietary Fiber 3 gm, Sugars 4 gm, Protein 9 gm

Scrumptious White Chili

Gloria L. Lehman
Singers Glen, VA
Lauren Bailey
Mechanicsburg, PA

Makes 6 servings
Serving size is ¾ cup

Prep Time: 20-25 minutes
Cooking Time: 25 minutes

1½ Tbsp. oil
1 large onion, chopped
2 cloves garlic, minced
2 cups chopped cooked
   chicken*
4-oz. can chopped mild
   green chilies
½-1 Tbsp. diced jalapeno
   pepper, *optional*
1½ tsp. ground cumin
1 tsp. dried oregano
10.5-oz. can low-sodium,
   condensed chicken broth
1 soup can water
15-oz. can Great Northern
   beans
½ tsp. cayenne, *or* to taste
salt to taste
2 ozs. (½ cup) reduced-fat
   Monterey Jack cheese,
   shredded
½ cup low-fat sour cream
chopped green onions,
   optional
fresh cilantro, *optional*

1. In large stockpot, sauté
onion and garlic in oil over
medium heat.
2. Add chicken, chilies,
jalapeno pepper, if you want,
cumin, oregano, chicken
broth, water, and beans

to stockpot and stir well.
Bring to a boil, reduce heat,
and simmer, covered, 10-15
minutes.
3. Just before serving, add
cayenne, salt, cheese, and
sour cream. Heat just until
cheese is melted, being careful not to let the soup boil.
4. Serve at once, garnished
with chopped green onions
and fresh cilantro, if desired.

Exchange List Values:
Starch 0.5, Vegetable 1.0,
Lean Meat 3.0, Fat 0.5

Basic Nutritional Values:
Calories 256 (Calories from Fat 91),
Total Fat 10 gm (Saturated Fat 2.6
gm, Trans Fat 0.0 gm, Polyunsat
Fat 2.1 gm, Monounsat Fat 4.0 gm,
Cholesterol 51 mg), Sodium 487 mg,
Total Carbohydrate 16 gm, Dietary
Fiber 4 gm, Sugars 4 gm, Protein 22 gm

* *If you don't have cooked
chicken, cut up 1½ lbs. skinless chicken breasts (about
1½ breasts) into 1" chunks.
Follow Step 2 and proceed with
the directions as given, being
sure to simmer until the chicken
is no longer pink.*

Black Bean Chili
Rita Steffen, Wellsboro, PA

Makes 12 servings
Serving size is ¾ cup

Prep Time: 20-25 minutes
Cooking Time: 40-70 minutes

1 lb. 90%-lean ground beef
1 large onion, chopped
2 medium green peppers,
   chopped
3 cloves garlic, minced
1-lb. can baked beans (I
   like Bush's)
1 *or* 2 1-lb. cans cooked,
   vegetarian (no pork)
   black beans, undrained
28-oz. can diced tomatoes,
   undrained
½ tsp. cumin
2 tsp. chili powder
¼ tsp. salt

1. In a large saucepan,
brown beef together with
onions, peppers, and garlic.
2. Add both kinds of
beans, tomatoes, cumin, chili
powder, and salt.
3. Simmer for 30-60 min-
utes, until flavors mingle and
the chili is heated thoroughly.
4. Serve hot.

Exchange List Values:
Starch 1.0, Vegetable 1.0,
Lean Meat 1.0

Basic Nutritional Values:
Calories 152 (Calories from Fat 33),
Total Fat 4 gm (Saturated Fat 1.3
gm, Trans Fat 0.2 gm, Polyunsat
Fat 0.3 gm, Monounsat Fat 1.4 gm,
Cholesterol 23 mg), Sodium 462 mg,
Total Carbohydrate 19 gm, Dietary
Fiber 5 gm, Sugars 6 gm, Protein 12 gm

Plum Good Chili

Susan Guarneri, Three Lakes, WI

Makes 12 servings
Serving size is ¾ cup

Prep Time: 30 minutes
Cooking Time: 2¼-2½ hours

1½ garlic cloves, minced
1 Tbsp. oil
2 lbs. 90%-lean ground
    round beef
3 large onions, sliced
2 large green peppers, sliced
1½ (16-oz. size) cans stewed
    tomatoes, undrained
2 16-oz. cans red kidney
    beans, drained
6-oz. can tomato paste
2 Tbsp. chili powder
½ tsp. white vinegar
2 dashes cayenne pepper
2 whole cloves
½ bay leaf
¼ cup low-sugar plum
    preserves *or* grape jelly
2 Tbsp. sugar blend for
    baking (Splenda)
salt and pepper to taste

1. In a large skillet, cook garlic in oil until golden. Add crumbled pieces of beef and cook 10 minutes until evenly browned. With a slotted spoon, remove beef and garlic from skillet and place in a large stockpot or saucepan. Reserve drippings in skillet.

2. Cook onions and green peppers in beef drippings in skillet until tender.

3. Add to cooked meat, along with tomatoes, beans, tomato paste, chili powder, vinegar, cayenne pepper, cloves, bay leaf, jelly, sugar blend for baking, salt, and pepper.

4. Cover and cook over low heat for 2 hours. If too dry, add additional tomatoes. If too much liquid, uncover and simmer longer.

5. Stir every 15 minutes to prevent chili from sticking or scorching. (It smells so good that you'll probably stir it more often.)

Exchange List Values:
Carbohydrate 2.0,
Lean Meat 2.0

Basic Nutritional Values:
Calories 271 (Calories from Fat 73),
Total Fat 8 gm (Saturated Fat 2.6
gm, Trans Fat 0.4 gm, Polyunsat
Fat 1.0 gm, Monounsat Fat 3.4 gm,
Cholesterol 46 mg), Sodium 299 mg,
Total Carbohydrate 30 gm, Dietary
Fiber 6 gm, Sugars 10 gm, Protein 21 gm

Baked Potato Soup

Flo Quint, Quinter, KS
Susan Nafziger, Canton, KS

Makes 8 servings
Serving size is ¾ cup

Prep Time: 30 minutes
Cooking Time: 15-20 minutes

⅓ cup canola oil
⅔ cup flour
7 cups fat-free milk
4 cups baked potatoes
    (about 5 large potatoes),
    peeled and cubed
4 green onions, sliced thin
4 strips bacon, cooked and
    crumbled

1¼ cups reduced-fat cheese,
    shredded
8 ozs. sour cream, *optional*
¾ tsp. salt, *optional*
¼ tsp. pepper, *optional*

1. Heat canola oil in large stockpot. Add flour and stir until smooth over medium heat.

2. Add milk, stirring often until thickened. Be careful not to scorch.

3. Add potatoes and onions and bring to a boil. Reduce heat and simmer 5 minutes, stirring often.

4. Remove from heat and add bacon, cheese, and optional sour cream. Stir until melted.

5. Add seasonings and blend thoroughly.

Exchange List Values:
Starch 1.5, Fat-Free Milk 1.0,
Fat 2.5

Basic Nutritional Values:
Calories 316 (Calories from Fat 122),
Total Fat 14 gm (Saturated Fat 3.0
gm, Trans Fat 0.0 gm, Polyunsat
Fat 3.0 gm, Monounsat Fat 6.8 gm,
Cholesterol 17 mg), Sodium 282 mg,
Total Carbohydrate 35 gm, Dietary
Fiber 2 gm, Sugars 13 gm, Protein 14 gm

*Variation: Instead of 7 cups
milk, you can use 4 cups milk
and 3 cups chicken broth.*

Easy Creamy Potato and Ham Soup

Lori Klassen, Mountain Lake, MN

Makes 12 servings
Serving size is ¾ cup

Prep Time: 15 minutes
Cooking Time: 30 minutes

6 cups water
7 tsp. sodium-free chicken bouillon granules
2 8-oz. pkgs. fat-free cream cheese, cubed
1½ cups extra-lean, low-sodium cubed ham, fully cooked
32-oz. pkg. frozen cubed hash brown potatoes
½ cup chopped onions
1 tsp. garlic powder
1 tsp. dill weed

1. Combine water and chicken bouillon granules in a large soup pot over heat. Stir until granules are dissolved.
2. Add cream cheese and stir until melted.
3. Add all other ingredients and simmer 20 minutes, or until vegetables are tender.

Exchange List Values:
Very Lean Meat 1.0,
Starch 1.5

Basic Nutritional Values:
Calories 136 (Calories from Fat 7),
Total Fat 1 gm (Saturated Fat 0.2
gm, Trans Fat 0.0 gm, Polyunsat
Fat 0.3 gm, Monounsat Fat 0.1 gm,
Cholesterol 13 mg], Sodium 461 mg,
Total Carbohydrate 21 gm, Dietary
Fiber 2 gm, Sugars 3 gm, Protein 10 gm

Italian Sausage Soup

Esther Porter
Minneapolis, MN

Makes 8 servings
Serving size is ¾ cup

Prep Time: 15-25 minutes
Cooking Time: 65-70 minutes

½ lb. lean turkey Italian sausage, casings removed
1 cup chopped onions
2 large garlic cloves, sliced
5 cups fat-free, no-salt-added beef stock, *or* 3 14.5-oz. cans fat-free, no-salt added beef broth
2 cups chopped *or* canned tomatoes
8-oz. can no-salt-added tomato sauce
1½ cups zucchini, sliced
1 carrot, thinly sliced
1 medium-sized green bell pepper, diced
1 cup green beans, frozen or fresh
2 Tbsp. dried basil
2 Tbsp. dried oregano
8-10-oz. pkg. cheese tortellini
salt to taste
pepper to taste
freshly grated Parmesan cheese for topping, *optional*

1. Sauté sausage in heavy Dutch oven over medium heat until cooked through, about 10 minutes, breaking it up as it browns with a wooden spoon.
2. Using a slotted spoon, transfer sausage to a large bowl. Pour off all drippings from Dutch oven. Add onions and garlic to the Dutch oven and sauté until clear, about 5 minutes.
3. Return sausage to pan. Add beef stock, tomatoes, tomato sauce, zucchini, carrot, pepper, green beans, basil, and oregano. Simmer 30-40 minutes, or until vegetables are tender.
4. Add tortellini and cook 8-10 minutes. Season to taste with salt and pepper.
5. Ladle hot soup into bowls and sprinkle with Parmesan cheese.

Exchange List Values:
Starch 1.0, Vegetable 2.0,
Lean Meat 1.0, Fat 0.5

Basic Nutritional Values:
Calories 203 (Calories from Fat 52),
Total Fat 6 gm (Saturated Fat 2.1
gm, Trans Fat 0.0 gm, Polyunsat
Fat 1.0 gm, Monounsat Fat 1.1 gm,
Cholesterol 34 mg), Sodium 422 mg,
Total Carbohydrate 26 gm, Dietary
Fiber 4 gm, Sugars 6 gm, Protein 13 gm

Variations:
1. Use leftover meat and vegetables from your refrigerator, instead of the sausage and the vegetables listed above.
2. Substitute V-8 juice for half of the beef stock or tomatoes.
3. When you're in a hurry, use Italian-style frozen vegetables instead of fresh beans, carrot, and zucchini.
4. Instead of tortellini, use ½-lb. package small pasta shells, uncooked.
   —Michelle Scribano
   Harrisonburg, VA

Sausage-Lentil Soup

Esther J. Mast
Lancaster, PA

Makes 8-10 servings
Serving size is ¾ cup

Prep Time: 10-15 minutes
Cooking Time: 45 minutes

1 lb. fresh pork sausage
2 medium onions, chopped
1 garlic clove, minced
2 cups dry lentils
½ tsp. dried basil
½ tsp. cumin
½ tsp. dried marjoram
16-oz. can stewed tomatoes
1 qt. no-salt-added tomato
  juice
1 qt. water
4 beef sodium-free bouillon
  cubes

1. In large kettle, brown sausage. Remove from kettle and drain.
2. When sausage is cool enough to handle, cut into ½"-thick slices. Set aside.
3. Add onions and garlic to kettle. Cook 5 minutes, or until onions and garlic are tender.
4. Stir in lentils, basil, cumin, marjoram, tomatoes, tomato juice, water, bouillon cubes, and browned sausage. Simmer 30 minutes, or until lentils are tender.

Exchange List Values:
Starch 1.5, Vegetable 2.0, Lean Meat 1.0, Fat 0.5

Basic Nutritional Values:
Calories 250 (Calories from Fat 65), Total Fat 7 gm (Saturated Fat 2.4 gm, Trans Fat 0.0 gm, Polyunsat Fat 1.1 gm, Monounsat Fat 3.1 gm, Cholesterol 17 mg), Sodium 409 mg, Total Carbohydrate 33 gm, Dietary Fiber 10 gm, Sugars 8 gm, Protein 15 gm

This has become a favorite soup of our family. Even the grandchildren love it!

French Onion Soup Made Light

Tanya Miseo
Bridgewater, NJ

Makes 6 servings
Serving size is ¾ cup

Prep Time: 15 minutes
Cooking Time: 2 hours and 20 minutes

8 cups Vidalia onions,
  sliced
2 Tbsp. oil
10 cups no-salt-added beef
  stock
1 tsp. pepper
½ tsp. garlic powder
1 cup white wine
6 thick slices Italian, *or*
  sourdough, bread
½ cup reduced-fat
  mozzarella cheese,
  shredded

1. In large stockpot, slice onions and sauté in oil until they caramelize, about 40 minutes.
2. Add beef stock, salt, pepper, and garlic powder to onions. Cover, bring to boil, and simmer for 1 hour.
3. Add white wine and simmer for another 30 minutes.
4. Ladle into oven-safe serving bowls. Float a piece of bread on top of soup. Sprinkle with cheese.
5. Broil for about 2 minutes until cheese melts. Serve immediately.

Exchange List Values:
Carbohydrate 2.5, Fat 1.5

Basic Nutritional Values:
Calories 263 (Calories from Fat 65), Total Fat 7 gm (Saturated Fat 1.5 gm, Trans Fat 0.0 gm, Polyunsat Fat 2.1 gm, Monounsat Fat 3.3 gm, Cholesterol 5 mg), Sodium 449 mg, Total Carbohydrate 37 gm, Dietary Fiber 4 gm, Sugars 11 gm, Protein 9 gm

---

A Tip —

Moderation is the key to healthy eating! The easiest way to cut calories is simply to eat less.

Mushroom Stew

Lauren Bailey
Mechanicsburg, PA

Makes 10 servings
Serving size is ¾ cup

Prep Time: 20 minutes
Cooking Time: 30-35 minutes

2 Tbsp. canola oil
2 bay leaves
1 large onion, chopped
2 cloves minced garlic (use
   more if you wish)
2 Tbsp. flour
1 cup chicken broth
1 cup tomato juice, *or* fresh
   puree
2 cups cut-up tomatoes,
   fresh *or* canned
1 tsp. dried thyme
1¾ Tbsp. butter
1½ lbs. fresh mushrooms,
   chopped
salt and pepper to taste
1½ cups red wine

1. In medium-sized sauce-
pan heat canola oil. Add bay
leaves and onion. Sauté until
onions are golden. Stir in garlic
and sauté one more minute.
2. Stir in flour and lower
the heat. Cook several minutes
on low, stirring constantly.
3. Add broth and to-
mato juice. Stir with whisk to
remove all lumps. Add cut-up
tomatoes.
4. In larger pot, sauté
mushrooms in 1¾ Tbsp. butter. Add thyme over high
heat. Add tomato mixture,
salt and pepper. Lower heat
and simmer for 20 minutes.

5. Add wine and stir for
one minute.

Exchange List Values:
Vegetable 2.0, Fat 1.0

Basic Nutritional Values:
Calories 97 (Calories from Fat 35),
Total Fat 4 gm (Saturated Fat 1.4
gm, Trans Fat 0.0 gm, Polyunsat
Fat 0.7 gm, Monounsat Fat 1.4 gm,
Cholesterol 6 mg), Sodium 208 mg,
Total Carbohydrate 10 gm, Dietary
Fiber 2 gm, Sugars 4 gm, Protein 3 gm

Wild Rice and Ham Chowder

Doloris Krause
Mountain Lake, MN

Makes 8 servings
Serving size is ¾ cup

Prep Time: 30 minutes
Cooking Time: 60-90 minutes

3 cups water, *or* more
¾ cup uncooked wild rice,
   rinsed
½ cup chopped onions
3 garlic cloves, minced
4 Tbsp. canola oil
½ cup flour
4 cups water
4 tsp. sodium-free bouillon
   granules
1½ cups chopped, peeled
   potatoes
½ cup chopped carrots
½ tsp. dried thyme
½ tsp. nutmeg
⅛ tsp. pepper
1 bay leaf
1½ pkgs. (10 oz.) frozen
   corn, thawed
2 cups fat-free half-and-half

3 cups (1 lb.) cubed, extra-
   lean, low-sodium ham,
   fully cooked
2 Tbsp. parsley

1. In a medium-sized
saucepan, combine 3 cups
water and wild rice. Bring
to a boil. Reduce heat, cover,
and simmer 35-40 minutes, or
until tender. (Check after 20
minutes, and then again after
30 minutes, to make sure the
rice isn't cooking dry and
scorching. Add more water if
needed.)
2. Meanwhile, in a large
saucepan, cook onions and
garlic in canola oil until crisp-
tender. Stir in flour. Cook 1
minute, stirring constantly.
3. Gradually stir 4 cups
water and bouillon into onion
and garlic. Add potatoes, carrots, thyme, nutmeg, pepper,
and bay leaf.
4. Bring vegetable mixture
to a boil. Reduce heat, cover,
and simmer 15-30 minutes.
5. Add corn to vegetables.
Cover and simmer for an
additional 15-20 minutes.
6. Stir in half-and-half,
ham, cooked wild rice, and
parsley. Cook over low heat
until heated through.
7. Remove bay leaf and
serve.

Exchange List Values:
Carbohydrate 3.0,
Lean Meat 1.0, Fat 0.5

Basic Nutritional Values:
Calories 306 (Calories from Fat 82),
Total Fat 9 gm (Saturated Fat 1.4
gm, Trans Fat 0.0 gm, Polyunsat
Fat 2.5 gm, Monounsat Fat 4.5 gm,
Cholesterol 28 mg), Sodium 504 mg,
Total Carbohydrate 41 gm, Dietary
Fiber 3 gm, Sugars 9 gm, Protein 15 gm

Aunt Marie's Tortellini Soup

Samantha Sorrentino
Tinton Falls, NJ

Makes 6 servings
Serving size is ¾ cup

Prep Time: 10 minutes
Cooking Time: 35 minutes

¼ cup chopped onions
2 cloves garlic, chopped
1 Tbsp. olive oil
14-oz. can diced tomatoes, undrained
2 14-oz. cans fat-free, low-sodium chicken broth
2-3 soup cans water
2 tsp. no-salt-added Italian seasoning (see page 254)
salt and pepper to taste
8-oz. pkg. refrigerated cheese tortellini
8-9 ozs. fresh spinach, *or* 10-oz. pkg. chopped frozen spinach, thawed

1. In large stockpot, sauté onions and garlic in olive oil for 3 minutes.
2. Add diced tomatoes, chicken broth, water, and seasonings. Simmer 20 minutes.
3. Add tortellini and simmer 8 minutes.
4. Stir in spinach and simmer 2 more minutes.

Exchange List Values:
Starch 1.0, Vegetable 1.0, Fat 1.0

Basic Nutritional Values:
Calories 162 (Calories from Fat 46), Total Fat 5 gm (Saturated Fat 1.6 gm, Trans Fat 0.0 gm, Polyunsat Fat 0.9 gm, Monounsat Fat 2.2 gm, Cholesterol 14 mg), Sodium 344 mg, Total Carbohydrate 24 gm, Dietary Fiber 3 gm, Sugars 4 gm, Protein 7 gm

Butternut Squash Soup

Stephanie O'Conner
Cheshire, CT

Makes 8 servings
Serving size is ¾ cup

Prep Time: 15-20 minutes
Cooking Time: 35 minutes

1 shallot, finely chopped
1 Tbsp. canola oil
3-lb. butternut squash, peeled and cubed
11 whole leaves of fresh sage, washed, *divided*
4 cups fat-free, low-sodium chicken stock
½ tsp. salt
¼ tsp. pepper
⅓ cup fat-free half-and-half
4 Tbsp. brown sugar blend (Splenda)
1 tsp. ground cinnamon
pinch of nutmeg

1. In stockpot, sauté the shallot in canola oil over medium heat.
2. Add squash, 3 sage leaves, chicken stock, salt, and pepper. Cover and bring to a boil. Simmer, covered, for 20-30 minutes, until squash falls apart when stuck with a fork.

3. Puree soup by portions in a firmly covered blender, 2 cups at a time. When you've finished, return pureed mixture to stockpot.
4. Stir in half-and-half, brown sugar blend, cinnamon, and nutmeg over low heat. Taste the soup to determine whether or not to add more cinnamon, sugar, salt, and pepper.
5. Serve garnished with whole leaves of fresh sage.

Exchange List Values:
Carbohydrate 1.5

Basic Nutritional Values:
Calories 111 (Calories from Fat 18), Total Fat 2 gm (Saturated Fat 0.2 gm, Trans Fat 0.0 gm, Polyunsat Fat 0.6 gm, Monounsat Fat 1.0 gm, Cholesterol 1 mg), Sodium 412 mg, Total Carbohydrate 21 gm, Dietary Fiber 1 gm, Sugars 9 gm, Protein 3 gm

A Tip —

To save time and avoid the temptation to eat out, plan your meals for the week and buy your groceries all at once.

Pumpkin Soup

Sara Harter Fredette
Goshen, IN

Makes 9 servings
Serving size is ¾ cup

Prep Time: 10-15 minutes
Cooking Time: 20 minutes

1 large onion, chopped
¾ tsp. cumin
½ tsp. cinnamon
½ tsp. ground ginger
2 Tbsp. reduced-sodium
    chicken bouillon granules
1¾ cups water
29-oz. can pumpkin
2 cups fat-free milk
1 Tbsp. honey
1 tsp. salt
2 Tbsp. soft-tub margarine
shake of Tabasco
shake of liquid smoke

1. In large saucepan, sauté onion in oil until soft. Stir in cumin, cinnamon, and ginger, and continue heating until spices are fragrant.
2. In a small saucepan, heat the water to boiling. Add bouillon and stir until dissolved. Add to saucepan.
3. Add pumpkin and simmer mixture for 10-15 minutes. Remove from heat.
4. Stir in milk, honey, salt, margarine, Tabasco, and liquid smoke.
5. When mixture has cooled to room temperature, puree in blender, 2 cups at a time.
6. Reheat before serving.

Exchange List Values:
Carbohydrate 1.0

Basic Nutritional Values:
Calories 86 (Calories from Fat 19), Total Fat 2 gm (Saturated Fat 0.5 gm, Trans Fat 0.0 gm, Polyunsat Fat 0.9 gm, Monounsat Fat 0.5 gm, Cholesterol 1 mg), Sodium 420 mg, Total Carbohydrate 15 gm, Dietary Fiber 3 gm, Sugars 9 gm, Protein 3 gm

Matt's Spicy Peanut Soup

Dawn Ranck, Lansdale, PA
Esther Nafziger, Bluffton, OH

Makes 6 servings
Serving size is ¾ cup

Prep Time: 25 minutes
Cooking Time: 30 minutes

2 Tbsp. oil
1 large onion, minced
2 garlic cloves, crushed
1 tsp. mild cayenne pepper
2 red bell peppers, seeded
    and chopped
1½ cups finely chopped
    carrots
1½ cups finely chopped
    potatoes
3 celery ribs, sliced
3¾ cups fat-free, reduced-
    sodium vegetable stock
6 Tbsp. crunchy peanut
    butter
⅔ cup frozen whole-kernel
    corn, thawed
salt to taste
freshly ground pepper to
    taste
roughly chopped peanuts,
    optional

1. In large stockpot, sauté onion and garlic in oil for 3 minutes. Add cayenne pepper. Cook 1 minute.
2. Add red peppers, carrots, potatoes, and celery. Stir well. Cook 4 minutes, stirring occasionally.
3. Add stock, peanut butter, and corn. Mix well.
4. Season with salt and pepper. Cover and bring to boil.
5. Simmer about 20 minutes, or until vegetables are tender.
6. Garnish with optional peanuts when serving.

Exchange List Values:
Starch 1.0, Vegetable 2.0, Fat 2.5

Basic Nutritional Values:
Calories 243 (Calories from Fat 122), Total Fat 14 gm (Saturated Fat 2.0 gm, Trans Fat 0.0 gm, Polyunsat Fat 4.0 gm, Monounsat Fat 6.8 gm, Cholesterol 0 mg), Sodium 354 mg, Total Carbohydrate 27 gm, Dietary Fiber 5 gm, Sugars 8 gm, Protein 7 gm

A Tip —

"Fat free" doesn't always mean healthy. Many times, fat-free foods are filled with calorie-rich "fat replacers," such as sugar.

Egg Drop Soup

Susan Guarneri
Three Lakes, WI

Makes 7 servings
Serving size is ¾ cup

Prep Time: 10 minutes
Cooking Time: 25 minutes

2 Tbsp. cornstarch
6 cups fat-free, reduced-
 sodium chicken stock
1 Tbsp. light soy sauce
3 Tbsp. white vinegar
1 small onion, minced
3 eggs, beaten
salt and pepper
sweet pepper flakes,
 optional

1. In stockpot, mix cornstarch with ½ cup cold chicken stock. When smooth, gradually add remaining chicken stock over medium heat, stirring continuously to keep cornstarch suspended and mixture smooth. Turn heat to low.

2. Add soy sauce, vinegar, and onion. Bring to low simmer (barely boiling).

3. Quickly stir in beaten eggs, swirling the broth and eggs in a circular motion to create "egg threads" in the soup. When all eggs are in the broth, allow to cook without stirring for 1 minute.

4. Remove pan from heat. Add salt and pepper to taste. Add sweet pepper flakes, if desired, before serving.

Exchange List Values:
Carbohydrate 0.5, Fat 0.5

Basic Nutritional Values:
Calories 61 (Calories from Fat 19), Total Fat 2 gm (Saturated Fat 0.7 gm, Trans Fat 0.0 gm, Polyunsat Fat 0.3 gm, Monounsat Fat 0.8 gm, Cholesterol 91 mg), Sodium 541 mg, Total Carbohydrate 5 gm, Dietary Fiber 0 gm, Sugars 2 gm, Protein 5 gm

Creamed Crab and Corn Soup

Shari Jensen, Fountain, CO

Makes 10 servings
Serving size is ¾ cup

Prep Time: 15 minutes
Cooking Time: 25-30 minutes

1 lb. lump crabmeat
2 Tbsp. canola oil
1½ cups finely chopped
 onions
2 Tbsp. flour
8 cups corn (freshly cut
 from cob is best*)
4 cups fat-free half-and-half
2 cups fat-free, reduced-
 sodium chicken broth
¼ tsp. thyme
salt and white pepper, to
 taste
2 Tbsp. chopped parsley
grated cheddar cheese,
 optional

1. Pick over crabmeat to remove any shell or cartilage. Set aside.

2. In large stockpot, heat canola oil. Add onions and sauté until clear and tender.

3. Blend in flour. Add corn kernels. Cook for 5 minutes, stirring frequently.

4. Add cream, broth, thyme, salt, and pepper. Cook over medium heat for 10 minutes, or until corn is tender. Stir often to prevent broth from scorching.

5. Add crabmeat and parsley and cook until meat is thoroughly heated.

6. Serve hot. Garnish with optional cheddar cheese if desired.

Exchange List Values:
Very Lean Meat 1.0,
Carbohydrate 2.5, Fat 0.5

Basic Nutritional Values:
Calories 252 (Calories from Fat 46), Total Fat 5 gm (Saturated Fat 1.0 gm, Trans Fat 0.0 gm, Polyunsat Fat 1.3 gm, Monounsat Fat 1.9 gm, Cholesterol 33 mg), Sodium 338 mg, Total Carbohydrate 39 gm, Dietary Fiber 4 gm, Sugars 9 gm, Protein 15 gm

* *One good-sized ear of sweet corn will yield 1-1½ cups corn kernels.*

Tip: Don't use high heat or cream will scald.

Seafood Soup

Wafi Brandt, Manheim, PA

Makes 10 servings
Serving size is ¾ cup

Prep Time: 15 minutes
Cooking Time: 45 minutes

2 cups water
1 cup (½ lb.) small veined
    shrimp (salad shrimp)
1 cup (½ lb.) small bay
    scallops
1 cup (½ lb.) crabmeat (can
    be imitation)
1 small onion, chopped
    (about 1 cup)
1 carrot, peeled and
    chopped
4-6 cups chopped potatoes
    (about 6 medium)
1 tsp. garlic salt
1½ tsp. garlic powder
1 Tbsp. Old Bay seasoning
1 Tbsp. chives
1 Tbsp. dill weed
1 Tbsp. rosemary
3 cups fat-free milk, *divided*
¼ cup flour

1. Place the water and the
3 kinds of seafood in a large
stockpot. Begin cooking over
medium heat.

2. Add chopped onion,
carrot, and potatoes. Simmer
until desired tenderness.

3. Add garlic salt, garlic
powder, Old Bay seasoning,
chives, dill weed, and
rosemary.

4. Shake together the
flour and 1 cup milk in a jar.
Add to soup, stirring until
thickened.

5. Add remaining 2 cups
milk. (More milk may be
added for a thinner soup or to
stretch it for more servings.)

Exchange List Values:
Carbohydrate 1.5,
Very Lean Meat 1.0

Basic Nutritional Values:
Calories 155 (Calories from Fat 9),
Total Fat 1 gm (Saturated Fat 0.3
gm, Trans Fat 0.0 gm, Polyunsat
Fat 0.4 gm, Monounsat Fat 0.2 gm,
Cholesterol 61 mg), Sodium 504 mg,
Total Carbohydrate 21 gm, Dietary
Fiber 2 gm, Sugars 6 gm, Protein 15 gm

Great Fish Soup

Willard E. Roth, Elkhart, IN

Makes 10 servings
Serving size is ¾ cup

Prep Time: 15 minutes
Cooking Time: 1 hour

3 Tbsp. oil
1 onion, chopped
2 cloves garlic, minced
¼ tsp. pepper
1½ tsp. salt
1 bay leaf
¼ tsp. dried thyme
1 lb. pollock, cut into
    chunks
1 lb. red snapper, cut into
    chunks
½ lb. tilapia, cut into chunks
5 cups water
1 cup white wine
1 lb. scallops
1 cup small pasta shells
12-oz. can fat-free
    evaporated milk

1. Combine oil, onion, and
garlic in large stockpot. Sauté
until onion and garlic begin
to soften. Stir in pepper, salt,
bay leaf, and thyme. Combine
well.

2. Stir in pollock, red
snapper, and tilapia. Simmer
gently for about 10 minutes.

3. Add water and wine.
Bring to a boil. Simmer for
10 more minutes.

4. Add scallops and
pasta shells. Cook about
15 minutes, or until shells are
just-tender.

5. Stir in evaporated milk.

Exchange List Values:
Very Lean Meat 4.0,
Carbohydrate 0.5, Fat 1.0

Basic Nutritional Values:
Calories 246 (Calories from Fat 57),
Total Fat 6 gm (Saturated Fat 0.8
gm, Trans Fat 0.0 gm, Polyunsat
Fat 1.9 gm, Monounsat Fat 2.8 gm,
Cholesterol 77 mg), Sodium 546 mg,
Total Carbohydrate 10 gm, Dietary
Fiber 0 gm, Sugars 5 gm, Protein 34 gm

*Tip: Use your imagination to
determine which seafood to use,
depending on what's available
and what you and your diners
like best.*

*You can also use fresh herbs
if they're available.*

*Variation: If you'd like a
thicker soup, melt 3 Tbsp.
butter in a small saucepan.
Stir in 3 Tbsp. flour. Continue
cooking over low heat, stirring
constantly for 2 minutes. Stir
this paste into hot soup in
Step 5, continuing to stir until
paste is well distributed and
broth thickens slightly. Adjust
seasonings.*

Oyster Stew

Dorothy Reise
Severna Park, MD

Makes 4 servings
Serving size is ¾ cup

Prep Time: 10-15 minutes
Cooking Time: 15 minutes

2-3 doz. fresh oysters in
    liquid
2 Tbsp. canola oil
1 Tbsp. onion, chopped
3 Tbsp. flour
3 cups milk
½ tsp. salt
½ tsp. pepper
½ tsp. parsley, chopped
pinch of celery seed,
    optional
dash of paprika, *optional*

1. In a small skillet over
medium heat, pre-cook
oysters in their own liquid
until edges curl and oysters
become plump. Set aside.

2. In large stockpot, heat
canola oil, add onion, and
sauté until soft.

3. Over medium heat, add
flour and stir until smooth.

4. Slowly add milk, stirring
constantly until thickened.

5. Add the pre-cooked
oysters and liquid, salt,
pepper, parsley, and celery
seed and paprika if you wish.
Mix well.

6. Heat thoroughly and
serve.

Exchange List Values:
Very Lean Meat 1.0,
Carbohydrate 1.0, Fat 1.5

Basic Nutritional Values:
Calories 194 (Calories from Fat 76),
Total Fat 8 gm (Saturated Fat 1.1
gm, Trans Fat 0.0 gm, Polyunsat
Fat 2.5 gm, Monounsat Fat 4.4 gm,
Cholesterol 26 mg), Sodium 468 mg,
Total Carbohydrate 18 gm, Dietary
Fiber 0 gm, Sugars 14 gm, Protein 11 gm

Crab Bisque

Jere Zimmerman
Reinholds, PA

Makes 6 servings
Serving size is ¾ cup

Prep Time: 15 minutes
Cooking Time: 20 minutes

4 Tbsp. canola oil, *divided*
½ cup finely chopped
    onions
½ cup finely chopped
    green pepper
2 green onions, finely
    chopped
¼ cup fresh parsley,
    chopped
8 ozs. fresh mushrooms,
    chopped
¼ cup flour
2 cups fat-free milk
¼ tsp. salt
¼ tsp. pepper
3 cups fat-free half-and-half
16-oz. can (2½ cups) claw
    crabmeat
grated carrot for color,
    optional

1. Heat 2 Tbsp. canola oil
in stockpot. Add onion, green
pepper, green onions, parsley,
and mushrooms. Cook until
tender. Remove vegetables
from heat and set aside.

2. In the same stockpot,
add remaining 2 Tbsp. canola
oil over low heat. Add flour
and stir until smooth. Add
milk, stirring until thickened.

3. Add reserved vegetable
mixture, salt, pepper, half-
and-half, crabmeat, and
grated carrot, if desired.

4. Heat through over low
heat, but do not boil.

Exchange List Values:
Very Lean Meat 2.0,
Carbohydrate 1.5, Fat 2.0

Basic Nutritional Values:
Calories 281 (Calories from Fat 106),
Total Fat 12 gm (Saturated Fat 1.8
gm, Trans Fat 0.0 gm, Polyunsat
Fat 3.0 gm, Monounsat Fat 5.7 gm,
Cholesterol 55 mg), Sodium 433 mg,
Total Carbohydrate 24 gm, Dietary
Fiber 1 gm, Sugars 13 gm, Protein 18 gm

Italian Clam Chowder

Susan Guarneri
Three Lakes, WI

Makes 8 servings
Serving size is ¾ cup

Prep Time: 30 minutes
Cooking Time: 4-5 hours

1 lbs. lean turkey Italian
   sausage
1 onion, chopped
4 medium potatoes,
   unpeeled and cubed
2 12-oz. cans beer
2 cups water or chicken broth
2 cups fat-free half-and-half
½ cup non-fat dry milk
1 dozen large fresh clams,
   chopped, *or* 6½-oz. can
   clams
8-oz. can minced clams
¼ tsp. salt
¼ tsp. pepper
1 tsp. dried basil

1. Cut sausage into
½" slices. Place in large
Dutch oven and brown until
no longer pink. Set sausage
aside and remove drippings.
2. Add onion, potatoes,
beer, broth, half-and-half, dry
milk, clams, salt, pepper, and
basil. Stir until well mixed.
3. Place Dutch oven in the
oven. Bake at 275° for 4-5
hours. (Do not increase the
temperature or the chowder
may boil and then the cream
will curdle.)
4. One hour before the end
of the baking time, stir in the
reserved sausage.

Exchange List Values:
Carbohydrate 2.0,
Lean Meat 3.0

Basic Nutritional Values:
Calories 335 (Calories from Fat 79),
Total Fat 9 gm (Saturated Fat 2.4
gm, Trans Fat 0.0 gm, Polyunsat
Fat 1.2 gm, Monounsat Fat 1.2 gm,
Cholesterol 87 mg), Sodium 596 mg,
Total Carbohydrate 31 gm, Dietary
Fiber 2 gm, Sugars 14 gm, Protein 31 gm

*I got this recipe from my
Italian neighbor when I lived
in Baltimore, Maryland. Fresh
clams were easy to get and this
filled up the entire family with
leftovers for lunch. The chowder
is even better the next day.*

Salmon Chowder

Ruth C. Hancock
Earlsboro, OK

Makes 8 servings
Serving size is ¾ cup

Prep Time: 25 minutes
Cooking Time: 70 minutes

½ cup chopped celery
½ cup chopped onions
½ cup chopped green
   pepper
1 clove garlic, minced
2 Tbsp. canola oil
14.5-oz. can low-sodium
   chicken broth
1 cup uncooked diced
   potatoes
1 cup shredded carrots
½ tsp. pepper
¼ tsp. dill weed
15-oz. can creamed corn
2 cups fat-free half-and-half

15-oz. can salmon,
   deboned and broken into
   small chunks, *or* 2 cups
   frozen salmon, cooked*

1. In large saucepan, sauté
celery, onions, green pepper,
and garlic in canola oil until
tender.
2. Add broth, potatoes, carrots, pepper, and dill weed.
3. Bring to a boil, reduce
heat, cover, and simmer 40
minutes, or until vegetables
are nearly tender.
4. Stir in creamed corn,
half-and-half, and salmon.
Simmer 15 minutes.

Exchange List Values:
Carbohydrate 1.5,
Lean Meat 1.0, Fat 1.0

Basic Nutritional Values:
Calories 215 (Calories from Fat 75),
Total Fat 8 gm (Saturated Fat 1.5
gm, Trans Fat 0.0 gm, Polyunsat
Fat 2.1 gm, Monounsat Fat 3.6 gm,
Cholesterol 24 mg), Sodium 508 mg,
Total Carbohydrate 22 gm, Dietary
Fiber 2 gm, Sugars 9 gm, Protein 13 gm

** You can use salmon frozen in
vacuum-sealed packages. Microwave according to directions
on the package. When done,
cut corner off package, drain
liquid, break up the salmon,
and add it to the chowder.*

*I found this recipe while waiting
for my husband who was having
an MRI. I was pleasantly
surprised the first time I made
it. My husband, who doesn't
like chowders, loves this one. It
is one of my favorites!*

Main Dishes

Beef Main Dishes

Pot Roast and Wine
Christina Ricker
Gordonville, PA

Makes 15 servings
Serving size is 4 ozs. meat

Prep Time: 15-20 minutes
Roasting Time: 1½-2 hours
Standing Time: 20 minutes

6-lb. eye round roast, no
  bone, visible fat trimmed
1-2 Tbsp. olive oil
1 cup finely chopped
  celery
1 cup finely chopped
  onions
1 bottle white cooking
  wine
salt and pepper to taste

1. In a large skillet, brown roast on all sides in 1-2 Tbsp. olive oil. Then place in a large roasting pan or Dutch oven.

2. Sprinkle chopped celery and onion over and around roast.

3. Pour white wine over all. Sprinkle salt and pepper over meat and vegetables to taste.

4. Cover and roast at 325° for 1½-2 hours, until tender.

5. While meat roasts, check liquid level to be sure the pan juices haven't all cooked off. Add ½ cup water if you can't see any liquid in the pan. Baste meat occasionally with juices.

6. Allow to stand for 20 minutes before slicing and serving with pan juices.

Exchange List Values:
Lean Meat 4.0

Basic Nutritional Values:
Calories 250 (Calories from Fat 61), Total Fat 7 gm (Saturated Fat 2.2 gm, Trans Fat 0.0 gm, Polyunsat Fat 0.3 gm, Monounsat Fat 3.1 gm, Cholesterol 79 mg), Sodium 61 mg, Total Carbohydrate 1 gm, Dietary Fiber 0 gm, Sugars 1 gm, Protein 42 gm

Savory Sweet Roast
Marie Hostetler
Nappanee, IN

Makes 8 servings
Serving size is 3 ozs. meat
and ⅛ of recipe sauce/gravy

Prep Time: 20 minutes
Roasting Time: 2 hours
Standing Time: 20 minutes

3-4 lb. lean beef roast,
  visible fat removed
1-2 Tbsp. olive oil
1 medium-sized onion,
  chopped
10.75-oz. can low-sodium,
  98% fat-free cream of
  mushroom soup
½ cup water
1 tsp. prepared mustard
½ tsp. salt
¼ cup vinegar
¼ cup sugar
1 tsp. Worcestershire sauce

1. In a large skillet, brown roast on all sides in olive oil.

2. Meanwhile, in a mixing bowl, blend together all other ingredients.

3. When roast is browned, place in roasting pan. Pour sauce ingredients over meat.

4. Cover and bake at 350° for 2 hours, or until tender.

5. Let meat stand for 20 minutes. Slice and serve with sauce.

Exchange List Values:
Carbohydrate 1.0,
Lean Meat 3.0

Basic Nutritional Values:
Calories 228 (Calories from Fat 77), Total Fat 9 gm (Saturated Fat 2.7 gm, Trans Fat 0.0 gm, Polyunsat Fat 0.7 gm, Monounsat Fat 3.9 gm, Cholesterol 75 mg), Sodium 358 mg, Total Carbohydrate 12 gm, Dietary Fiber 1 gm, Sugars 8 gm, Protein 25 gm

Tips:

1. The sauce that the roast is cooked in makes a succulent gravy. Serve over the meat, and over potatoes, rice, or pasta, if you've made one of them as a go-along.

2. I like to cut potato wedges and place them on top of the meat before roasting it. I like to do the same with julienned carrot sticks. Either of those combinations gives you a good meal all in one pan.

Pounded Swiss Steak in a Yummy Sauce
Robbin Poetzl
Springfield, OR

Makes 12 servings
Serving size is 4 ozs. meat

Prep Time: 20-30 minutes
Browning/Baking Time:
50 minutes

4-5 lbs. skirt *or* flank beef steak, about ½" thick, trimmed of visible fat
1½-2 cups flour
1 Tbsp. Italian seasoning
1 tsp. garlic powder
1 tsp. pepper
1 tsp. onion powder
1 tsp. pepper herb seasoning
2 Tbsp. canola oil

Sauce:
2 tsp. oil
½ tsp. crushed garlic
½-1 cup red wine
⅓ cup light teriyaki sauce
1 tsp. Italian seasoning
1½ cups fresh mushrooms, sliced
1 cup celery, chopped
2 14.5-oz. cans diced tomatoes, undrained

1. Cut the steak into serving-size pieces. Pound each piece to about ¼" thick. In a small bowl, mix flour with seasonings. Flour all sides of pounded steak pieces.

2. Brown floured meat, a few pieces at a time, in hot oil in a large skillet. Brown 2-3 minutes on one side and then the other side for 2-3 minutes. Place browned steak in a shallow baking dish.

3. To make the sauce, heat 2 tsp. oil in a large, heavy skillet over medium-high heat. Stir in garlic. When garlic begins to "pop" add the wine.

4. Simmer for 2-3 minutes. Then add the teriyaki sauce, Italian seasoning, mushrooms, celery, and canned tomatoes. Bring to a light boil.

5. Turn down heat and continue to cook the sauce, uncovered, until it thickens. Pour the sauce over prepared steaks.

6. Cover and bake at 350° for 15 minutes. Remove lid and bake an additional 15 minutes.

Exchange List Values:
Starch 0.5, Vegetable 1.0,
Lean Meat 4.0

Basic Nutritional Values:
Calories 291 (Calories from Fat 101), Total Fat 11 gm (Saturated Fat 3.5 gm, Trans Fat 0.0 gm, Polyunsat Fat 1.3 gm, Monounsat Fat 4.9 gm, Cholesterol 52 mg), Sodium 346 mg, Total Carbohydrate 13 gm, Dietary Fiber 1 gm, Sugars 4 gm, Protein 32 gm

Tip: For the sauce, use canned tomatoes with chopped jalapenos for a spicier flavor.

Simply Elegant Steak

Judy DeLong
Burnt Hills, NY

Makes 6 servings
Serving size is ½ cup rice
and ¾ cup meat

Prep Time: 20 minutes
Cooking Time: 30 minutes

1½ lbs. tender sirloin steak, trimmed of visible fat
1½ Tbsp. olive oil
2 large onions, sliced into rings
10.75-oz. can low-sodium, 98% fat-free cream of mushroom soup
½ cup dry sherry
4-oz. can sliced mushrooms (reserve liquid)
½ tsp. garlic salt
3 cups cooked rice

1. Cut steak into thin strips. Place in large skillet and brown in oil over high heat. Add onions and sauté until tender-crisp.
2. In mixing bowl, blend soup, sherry, mushroom liquid, and salt. Pour over steak. Top with mushrooms.
3. Reduce heat, cover, and simmer for 15-30 minutes until steak is tender, but not overdone.
4. Serve over rice.

Exchange List Values:
Starch 1.5, Vegetable 2.0, Lean Meat 3.0

Basic Nutritional Values:
Calories 347 (Calories from Fat 81), Total Fat 9 gm (Saturated Fat 2.6 gm, Trans Fat 0.1 gm, Polyunsat Fat 1.1 gm, Monounsat Fat 4.5 gm, Cholesterol 45 mg), Sodium 463 mg, Total Carbohydrate 36 gm, Dietary Fiber 2 gm, Sugars 5 gm, Protein 26 gm

Tip: For ease in slicing the steak into strips, place the meat in the freezer for 30 minutes; then slice.

Sirloin or Chuck Steak Marinade

Susan Nafziger
Canton, KS

Makes marinade for 4 steaks

Prep Time: 15 minutes

6 Tbsp. olive oil
6 Tbsp. light soy sauce
½ cup wine vinegar
½ cup white wine
½ cup water
½ cup chopped onions
⅛ tsp. garlic powder
¼ tsp. ground ginger
½ tsp. pepper
½ tsp. dry mustard

1. Mix all ingredients together, either by whisking together in a bowl, or whirring the mixture in a blender.
2. Place sirloin or chuck steak in marinade mixture and marinate for at least 1 hour per 1-inch thickness of meat.

3. When ready to grill or broil meat, drain off half the marinade and discard. Cook steak.

Exchange List Values:
Fat 2.0

Basic Nutritional Values:
Calories 116 (Calories from Fat 92), Total Fat 10 gm (Saturated Fat 1.4 gm, Trans Fat 0.0 gm, Polyunsat Fat 1.0 gm, Monounsat Fat 7.5 gm, Cholesterol 0 mg), Sodium 432 mg, Total Carbohydrate 3 gm, Dietary Fiber 0 gm, Sugars 2 gm, Protein 1 gm

Barbeque Beef Strips

Doris Ranck
Gap, PA

Makes 10 servings
Serving size is ¾ cup

Prep Time: 30 minutes
Cooking Time: 40-45 minutes

2 lbs. steak *or* London broil, trimmed of visible fat
2 Tbsp. vegetable oil
1 medium-sized onion, chopped
1 cup ketchup
1 cup no-salt-added tomato sauce
⅓ cup water
3-4 Tbsp. brown sugar, according to your taste preference
1 Tbsp. prepared mustard
1 Tbsp. Worcestershire sauce

1. Slice steak into strips about 3″ long and ⅛″ wide.

2. Place oil in large skillet. Add strips of meat and chopped onions. Brown quickly over high heat, stirring so that all sides of beef brown well. Pour off all but 2 Tbsp. drippings.

3. Combine remaining ingredients in a mixing bowl. When well mixed, pour over beef strips and onions in skillet.

4. Cover and cook slowly for 35-40 minutes, or until beef is tender. Stir occasionally.

5. Serve over cooked rice or pasta.

Exchange List Values:
Carbohydrate 1.0,
Lean Meat 2.0, Fat 0.5

Basic Nutritional Values:
Calories 201 (Calories from Fat 70),
Total Fat 8 gm (Saturated Fat 2.2 gm, Trans Fat 0.0 gm, Polyunsat Fat 1.0 gm, Monounsat Fat 3.6 gm, Cholesterol 31 mg), Sodium 367 mg, Total Carbohydrate 14 gm, Dietary Fiber 1 gm, Sugars 9 gm, Protein 18 gm

Glazed Meat Loaf
Doris Beachy
Stevens, PA

Makes 10 servings
Serving size is 1 slice
or ¹⁄₁₀ of recipe

Prep Time: 10 minutes
Baking Time: 1 hour
Standing Time: 5 minutes

1½ **lbs. 90%-lean ground beef**
¾ **cup dry quick oats**
½ **cup egg substitute**
¼ **cup chopped onions**
1 **tsp. salt**
¼ **tsp. pepper**
1 **cup tomato juice**

Sauce:
¼ **cup ketchup**
1 **Tbsp. prepared mustard**
2 **Tbsp. brown sugar**

1. In a large mixing bowl, combine ground beef with next 6 ingredients. Mix thoroughly and pack firmly into a greased 9 x 5 loaf pan.

2. In a small mixing bowl, combine sauce ingredients and pour over meat mixture.

3. Bake at 350° for 1 hour.

4. Let stand 5 minutes before slicing.

Exchange List Values:
Carbohydrate 0.5,
Lean Meat 2.0

Basic Nutritional Values:
Calories 157 (Calories from Fat 53),
Total Fat 6 gm (Saturated Fat 2.2 gm, Trans Fat 0.3 gm, Polyunsat Fat 0.4 gm, Monounsat Fat 2.4 gm, Cholesterol 42 mg), Sodium 463 mg, Total Carbohydrate 10 gm, Dietary Fiber 1 gm, Sugars 5 gm, Protein 15 gm

Variations:

1. In meat loaf, replace 1 cup tomato juice with ⅓ cup ketchup and ¾ tsp. prepared mustard.

2. Add 2 tsp. Worcestershire sauce to sauce.
—Monica Yoder
Millersburg, OH

3. After the meat loaf is mixed and shaped (Step 1 above), place loaf in the center of a greased 9 x 13 baking pan. Surround the meat with a layer of peeled and sliced potatoes (from 3 medium-sized potatoes), followed by a layer of carrot slices (from 3 medium-sized carrots), and a layer of onion quarters or slices (from 3 medium-sized onions). Top the vegetables with 2 tsp. dried parsley flakes, 1 tsp. salt, and a dash of pepper. Cover pan tightly with foil. Bake at 375° for 1 hour covered, then for 10 minutes uncovered.
—Jane Frownfelter
Grand Blanc, MI

A Tip —

There are many methods for losing weight, but what counts is simply burning more calories than you eat.

Cheesy Meat Loaf
Jean Turner
Williams Lake, BC

Makes 8 servings
Serving size is 1 slice
or ⅛ of recipe

Prep Time: 20-30 minutes
Baking Time: 1½ hours

½ cup chopped onions
½ cup chopped green
  pepper
1 tsp. corn oil
8-oz. can no-salt-added
  tomato sauce
½ cup egg substitute
1 cup fat-free white
  cheddar cheese, shredded
1 cup soft bread crumbs
½ tsp. salt
dash of pepper
¼ tsp. dried thyme
1½ lbs. 90%-lean ground
  beef
½ lb. ground pork
  tenderloin

1. In a small saucepan,
sauté onions and green pepper
in corn oil just until tender.
2. In large mixing bowl,
combine all ingredients and
mix well.
3. Shape into a loaf. Place
in greased 9 x 5 loaf pan.
4. Bake at 350° for 1½
hours.

Exchange List Values:
Carbohydrate 0.5,
Lean Meat 3.0

Basic Nutritional Values:
Calories 222 (Calories from Fat 74),
Total Fat 8 gm (Saturated Fat 3.0
gm, Trans Fat 0.4 gm, Polyunsat
Fat 0.5 gm, Monounsat Fat 3.5 gm,
Cholesterol 69 mg), Sodium 399 mg,
Total Carbohydrate 7 gm, Dietary
Fiber 1 gm, Sugars 3 gm, Protein 28 gm

10-Minute
Meat Loaf
Esther J. Yoder
Hartville, OH

Makes 6 servings
Serving size is 1 slice
or ⅙ of recipe

Prep Time: 10 minutes
Cooking Time:
  10 minutes in the microwave;
  45 minutes in the oven
Standing Time: 10 minutes,
  if cooked in the microwave

1 lb. 90%-lean ground beef
¼ cup egg substitute
½ cup dry bread crumbs
¼ cup fat-free milk
1 Tbsp. no-salt-added dry
  onion soup mix (see
  page 254)
2 Tbsp. ketchup
2 Tbsp. light soy sauce
½ cup shredded fat-free
  cheddar cheese *or* fat-
  free Swiss cheese, *or a*
  combination of the two

1. In a mixing bowl
thoroughly combine all
ingredients and shape into a
round flat loaf, like a giant
hamburger.
2. Place round loaf in a
lightly greased 8″ glass pie
plate.
3. Cover with waxed paper
and microwave for 10 min-
utes on high. Drain. Cover
with foil and let stand for 10
minutes. (This standing time
is very important!)

Exchange List Values:
Carbohydrate 0.5,
Lean Meat 3.0

Basic Nutritional Values:
Calories 186 (Calories from Fat 58),
Total Fat 6 gm (Saturated Fat 2.5
gm, Trans Fat 0.4 gm, Polyunsat
Fat 0.4 gm, Monounsat Fat 2.6 gm,
Cholesterol 47 mg), Sodium 465 mg,
Total Carbohydrate 10 gm, Dietary
Fiber 1 gm, Sugars 3 gm, Protein 20 gm

*Variation: If you prefer oven-
baked meat loaf, bake at 350°
for 45-60 minutes, uncovered.*

A Tip —

  Eat small but often.
Mini-meals spread
throughout the day can
improve glucose control
and weight loss.

Beef Roll

Susan Nafziger
Canton, KS
Ruth Ann Penner
Hillsboro, KS

Makes 12 servings
Serving size is 1 roll

Prep Time: *30 minutes*
Baking Time: *45-60 minutes*

1 cup fat-free cheddar
  cheese, shredded
1 cup coarse saltine
  cracker crumbs
½ cup chopped onions
1 cup fat-free milk
2 Tbsp. ketchup, *or*
  barbecue sauce
1 tsp. salt
¼ tsp. pepper
¼ tsp. celery salt
¼ cup brown sugar
2 lbs. 90%-lean ground
  beef

1. Mix cheese, cracker
crumbs, onions, milk, ketchup,
salt, pepper, celery salt, and
brown sugar in a large bowl.
2. Add ground beef and
mix well.
3. Form into 12 "logs," each
approximately 1" x 4". Place
side-by-side in a greased 9 x
13 baking dish.
4. Bake at 350° for 45 minutes.

Exchange List Values:
Carbohydrate 1.0,
Lean Meat 2.0

Basic Nutritional Values:
Calories 184 (Calories from Fat 60),
Total Fat 7 gm (Saturated Fat 2.5

gm, Trans Fat 0.6 gm, Polyunsat
Fat 0.3 gm, Monounsat Fat 2.9 gm,
Cholesterol 48 mg), Sodium 433 mg,
Total Carbohydrate 12 gm, Dietary
Fiber 0 gm, Sugars 6 gm, Protein 18 gm

Tips:
*1. This recipe can be made
a day ahead of time and then
served to company. I have
found a very easy way to make
uniform rolls. On a cutting
board, spread the meat mixture
into a rectangular shape
approximately the size of a
9 x 13 baking pan, and 1 inch
thick. Divide it into 12 equal-
size pieces by cutting down the
center, and then lengthwise
across 6 times. Shape each
piece into a "log."*
*2. You can make this mixture
into meatballs.*

Chuck Roast Beef Barbecue

Helen Heurich
Lititz, PA

Makes 20 servings
Serving size is ¾ cup

Prep Time: *30-40 minutes*
Baking Time: *3 hours*

3-lb. boneless chuck roast,
  visible fat removed
⅔ cup hot ketchup, *or*
  barbecue sauce
1¼ cups ketchup
3 Tbsp. lemon juice
2 Tbsp. Worcestershire
  sauce
2 Tbsp. brown sugar
1½ tsp. prepared mustard

3 Tbsp. vinegar, *optional*
1-2 medium-sized onions,
  chopped
3-4 ribs celery, chopped

1. Place beef in roast pan.
Add ½" water and cover. Roast
at 350° for about 2 hours,
until the beef is tender.
2. Cool. Pull apart with
two forks until beef is
shredded.
3. While the beef is
roasting, combine the remaining ingredients in a medium
saucepan. Cover and cook
until heated through.
4. Pour sauce over shred-
ded meat.
5. Return to oven and roast
for 1 hour at 350°.
6. Serve on hamburger
rolls.

Exchange List Values:
Carbohydrate 0.5,
Lean Meat 1.0

Basic Nutritional Values:
Calories 123 (Calories from Fat 30),
Total Fat 3 gm (Saturated Fat 1.2
gm, Trans Fat 0.0 gm, Polyunsat
Fat 0.2 gm, Monounsat Fat 1.3 gm,
Cholesterol 38 mg), Sodium 328 mg,
Total Carbohydrate 10 gm, Dietary
Fiber 0 gm, Sugars 6 gm, Protein 13 gm

A Tip —

Many "value" meals
give you more food for
less money, but the extra
calories actually make
this a bad value for your
health.

Teriyaki Burgers

Susan Kasting
Jenks, OK

Makes 4 servings
Serving size is 1 burger

Prep Time: 10 minutes
Cooking Time: 10 minutes

1 lb. 90%-lean ground beef
2 Tbsp. light soy sauce
1 Tbsp. peeled fresh
   ginger, grated
1 garlic clove, minced
¼ cup chopped green
   onions
pinch of pepper

1. Combine all ingredients in bowl.
2. Form into 4 patties.
3. Grill or broil for 10 minutes, flipping to brown both sides.

Exchange List Values:
Lean Meat 3.0

Basic Nutritional Values:
Calories 187 (Calories from Fat 84), Total Fat 9 gm (Saturated Fat 3.7 gm, Trans Fat 0.6 gm, Polyunsat Fat 0.3 gm, Monounsat Fat 3.9 gm, Cholesterol 69 mg), Sodium 355 mg, Total Carbohydrate 2 gm, Dietary Fiber 0 gm, Sugars 1 gm, Protein 23 gm

Stuffed Hamburgers

Penny Feveryear, Narvon, PA

Makes 4 servings
Serving size is 1 burger

Prep Time: 10-15 minutes
Baking Time: 30 minutes

1 lb. 90%-lean ground beef
⅓ cup dry bread crumbs
3 Tbsp. minced onions
¼ cup tomato sauce
1 tsp. Worcestershire sauce
¼ tsp. salt
¼ tsp. pepper

Stuffing:
½ cup sliced mushrooms
½ cup celery, chopped
1 Tbsp. minced onions
1 Tbsp. canola oil
2 Tbsp. fat-free milk
¼ cup dry bread crumbs

1. In a mixing bowl, blend together beef, bread crumbs, onions, tomato sauce, Worcestershire sauce, salt, and pepper. Form into 4 large cup-shaped portions and place in greased shallow baking pan.
2. To prepare stuffing, sauté mushrooms, celery, and onions in canola oil in skillet for 5 minutes. Remove from heat and stir in milk and bread crumbs.
3. Fill centers of beef cups with equal parts of stuffing, pushing sides up to form finished cups.
4. Bake at 350° for 30 minutes.

Exchange List Values:
Carbohydrate 1.0,
Lean Meat 3.0, Fat 1.0

Basic Nutritional Values:
Calories 282 (Calories from Fat 120), Total Fat 13 gm (Saturated Fat 4.0 gm, Trans Fat 0.6 gm, Polyunsat Fat 1.7 gm, Monounsat Fat 6.0 gm, Cholesterol 70 mg), Sodium 431 mg, Total Carbohydrate 15 gm, Dietary Fiber 1 gm, Sugars 3 gm, Protein 24 gm

Pizza Cups

Barbara Smith
Bedford, PA

Makes 10 servings
Serving size is 1 biscuit

Prep Time: 20 minutes
Baking Time: 12-15 minutes

¾ lb. 90%-lean ground
   beef
6-oz. can tomato paste
1 Tbsp. minced onions
½ tsp. salt
1 tsp. Italian seasoning
7.5-oz. tube low-fat
   refrigerated biscuits
½ cup fat-free mozzarella
   cheese, shredded

1. In skillet, brown beef. Drain.
2. Stir in tomato paste, onions, and seasonings.
3. Cook over low heat for 5 minutes, stirring frequently. Mixture will thicken.
4. Meanwhile, place biscuits in greased muffin tins. Press them in so they cover the bottom and sides of each cup.

5. Spoon about 2 Tbsp. meat mixture into each biscuit-lined cup. Sprinkle with cheese.

6. Bake at 400° for 12-15 minutes, or until brown.

Exchange List Values:
Starch 1.0, Lean Meat 1.0

Basic Nutritional Values:
Calories 127 (Calories from Fat 32), Total Fat 4 gm (Saturated Fat 1.2 gm, Trans Fat 0.2 gm, Polyunsat Fat 0.3 gm, Monounsat Fat 1.5 gm, Cholesterol 21 mg), Sodium 404 mg, Total Carbohydrate 13 gm, Dietary Fiber 1 gm, Sugars 2 gm, Protein 10 gm

This has often been our Friday-night, once-a-month-supper-with-a-movie.

Mexican Lasagna
Marcia S. Myer
Manheim, PA

Makes 12 servings
Serving size is 3" x 3¼" rectangle or ¹⁄₁₂ of recipe

Prep Time: 25 minutes
Cooking/Baking Time: 55 minutes

1 lb. 90%-lean ground beef
15-oz. can corn, drained
15-oz. can no-salt-added tomato sauce
1 cup picante sauce, *or* hot salsa, if you want more kick
1 Tbsp. chili powder
1½ tsp. cumin
16-oz. carton fat-free cottage cheese
½ cup egg substitute
¼ cup Parmesan cheese
1 tsp. dried oregano
½ tsp. garlic salt
12 corn tortillas
½ cup reduced-fat cheddar cheese, shredded
2 chopped green onions
chopped cilantro, *optional*
chopped lettuce, *optional*
chopped tomatoes, *optional*

1. In a large skillet, brown ground beef. Drain off drippings.

2. Add corn, tomato sauce, picante sauce or hot salsa, chili powder, and cumin. Simmer for 5 minutes.

3. In a medium-sized mixing bowl, combine cottage cheese, egg substitute, Parmesan cheese, oregano, and garlic salt. Mix well.

4. Arrange 6 tortillas on the bottom and up the sides of a greased 9 x 13 baking pan, overlapping as necessary. Top with half the meat/vegetable mixture.

5. Spoon cheese mixture over meat. Arrange remaining tortillas over cheese mixture. Top with remaining meat mixture.

6. Bake at 375° for 30 minutes or until bubbly. Remove from oven.

7. Top with cheddar cheese. Return to oven to melt cheese. Let stand 10 minutes before serving.

8. Just before serving top with green onions, and with cilantro, lettuce, and tomatoes, if you wish.

Exchange List Values:
Starch 1.0, Vegetable 1.0, Lean Meat 2.0

Basic Nutritional Values:
Calories 204 (Calories from Fat 53), Total Fat 6 gm (Saturated Fat 2.3 gm, Trans Fat 0.2 gm, Polyunsat Fat 0.7 gm, Monounsat Fat 2.1 gm, Cholesterol 30 mg), Sodium 530 mg, Total Carbohydrate 21 gm, Dietary Fiber 3 gm, Sugars 5 gm, Protein 17 gm

Variations:
1. Use 16-oz. can of diced tomatoes instead of 15-oz. can of corn in Step 2.
2. Add 1 tsp. black pepper and ¼ tsp. red pepper to Step 2.
3. Add ¼ cup sliced black olives to the toppings in Step 8.
—Mable Hershey
Marietta, PA

Zucchini Lasagna

Ruth Ann Hoover
New Holland, PA

Makes 8 servings
Serving size is 2¾" x 3½" rectangle
or ⅛ of recipe

Prep Time: 20 minutes
Cooking/Baking Time:
55 minutes

6 cups sliced raw zucchini,
  unpeeled
1 lb. 90%-lean ground beef
6-oz. can tomato paste
½ tsp. dried basil
½ tsp. dried oregano
½ tsp. salt
¼ tsp. garlic powder
1 cup fat-free cottage cheese
¼ cup egg substitute
¼ cup dry bread crumbs,
  plain *or* herb-flavored
¼ cup reduced-fat cheddar
  cheese, shredded
1 cup fat-free mozzarella
  cheese, shredded

1. Spread slices of zucchini
into a long microwave-safe
dish. Sprinkle with 2 Tbsp.
water. Cover, and cook
on high for 3½ minutes.
Stir. Cover and return to
microwave and cook on high
an additional 3½ minutes.
Stir. Cover and return to
microwave and cook on high
1½ minutes more. Drain
zucchini and set aside.
2. Meanwhile, in large
stockpot, brown ground beef.
Drain off drippings.

3. Add tomato paste, basil,
oregano, salt, garlic powder,
cottage cheese, egg substitute,
bread crumbs, cheddar
cheese, and cooked zucchini
to browned beef in stockpot.
Stir gently together until well
mixed.
4. Spoon mixture into
greased 7 x 11 baking dish.
5. Bake uncovered at 350°
for 25 minutes.
6. Sprinkle mozzarella
cheese over lasagna. Return
to oven and continue baking
20 more minutes.

Exchange List Values:
Carbohydrate 1.0,
Lean Meat 2.0

Basic Nutritional Values:
Calories 190 (Calories from Fat 53),
Total Fat 6 gm (Saturated Fat 2.3
gm, Trans Fat 0.3 gm, Polyunsat
Fat 0.4 gm, Monounsat Fat 2.2 gm,
Cholesterol 40 mg), Sodium 539
mg,Total Carbohydrate 11 gm, Dietary
Fiber 2 gm, Sugars 4 gm, Protein 22 gm

Variations:
  *1. Instead of ground beef, use
ground venison.*
  *2. Instead of ground beef, use
½ lb. ground turkey and ½ lb.
ground venison.*

A Tip —
  If you're making a
meat sauce, try reducing
the amount of meat called
for and replace it with
vegetables.

Mild Indian Curry

Vic and Christina Buckwalter
Keezletown, VA

Makes 6 servings
Serving size is ¾ cup

Prep Time: 10 minutes
Cooking Time: 15-20 minutes

1 lb. 90%-lean ground beef
1 onion, chopped
3 garlic cloves, finely
  chopped
½ tsp. ground ginger
2 tsp. coriander
2 tsp. cumin
1 tsp. turmeric
¼ tsp. ground cloves
¼ tsp. cayenne pepper
¾ cup tomato sauce
½ tsp. salt
2 Tbsp. sugar
¼ cup fat-free plain yogurt
cooked basmati rice*
topping options*: grated
  cheeses; chopped fresh
  onions; orange sections;
  sliced bananas; chopped
  papaya, mango, and/
  or tomatoes; peanuts;
  raisins

1. In a large skillet,
brown beef, onions, and
garlic together. Drain off any
drippings.
2. Add ginger, coriander,
cumin, turmeric, ground
cloves, and cayenne pepper to
beef mixture. Cook 1 minute.
3. Stir in tomato sauce, salt,
and sugar. Cook 10 minutes.

4. Just before serving, blend in yogurt.

5. Serve over basmati rice.

6. Send small bowls of each topping that you choose around the table after the rice and curry have been passed.

Exchange List Values:
Carbohydrate 1.0,
Lean Meat 2.0

Basic Nutritional Values:
Calories 167 (Calories from Fat 59), Total Fat 7 gm (Saturated Fat 2.5 gm, Trans Fat 0.4 gm, Polyunsat Fat 0.3 gm, Monounsat Fat 2.7 gm, Cholesterol 46 mg), Sodium 434 mg, Total Carbohydrate 11 gm, Dietary Fiber 1 gm, Sugars 7 gm, Protein 16 gm

*Please note that the rice and topping optional are **not** included in the nutritional analysis*

We picked up this recipe while living in East Africa. It brings back memories of the Swahili Coast.

Beef Lombardi

Lucille Amos
Greensboro, NC

*Makes 8 servings
Serving size is 3¼" x 4½" rectangle
or ⅛ of recipe*

**Prep Time: 15 minutes
Cooking/Baking Time:
75 minutes**

1 lb. 90%-lean ground beef
10-oz. can tomatoes with chilies
14-oz. can chopped tomatoes
2 tsp. sugar
½ tsp. salt
¼ tsp. pepper
6-oz. can tomato paste
1 bay leaf
½-lb. pkg. no-egg-yolk egg noodles
6 green onions, sliced
1 cup fat-free sour cream
¼ cup reduced-fat sharp cheese, grated
2 Tbsp. freshly grated Parmesan cheese
½ cup fat-free mozzarella cheese, grated

1. Brown beef in large skillet. Drain off drippings.

2. Stir into beef, both cans of tomatoes, sugar, salt, and pepper. Cover and cook for 5 minutes.

3. Add tomato paste and bay leaf. Cover and simmer 30 minutes.

4. Meanwhile, cook noodles in a saucepan according to package directions. Drain.

5. Return noodles to their saucepan and mix in sliced green onions and sour cream. Place creamy noodles in a lightly greased 9 x 13 baking pan.

6. Top with beef mixture. Sprinkle with cheeses.

7. Cover and bake at 350° for 30 minutes.

8. Uncover and bake an additional 5 minutes.

Exchange List Values:
Starch 1.5, Vegetable 2.0,
Lean Meat 2.0

Basic Nutritional Values:
Calories 285 (Calories from Fat 58), Total Fat 6 gm (Saturated Fat 2.5 gm, Trans Fat 0.3 gm, Polyunsat Fat 0.4 gm, Monounsat Fat 2.4 gm, Cholesterol 42 mg), Sodium 596 mg, Total Carbohydrate 31 gm, Dietary Fiber 4 gm, Sugars 7 gm, Protein 22 gm

Tip: Prepare the recipe in two smaller baking dishes. Freeze one for later or give it to a friend.

A Tip —

Heart disease is the number one killer of people with diabetes, which is why it's so important to manage your cholesterol, blood pressure, and glucose.

Hamburger-Potato-Carrot Bake

Eleya Raim
Oxford, IA

Makes 8 servings
Serving size is 2¼" x 4½" rectangle
or ⅛ of recipe

Prep Time: 15-20 minutes
Baking Time: 60-90 minutes
Standing Time: 5-10 minutes

1 lb. 90%-lean ground beef
½ tsp. onion powder, *or*
   1 Tbsp. dried onion soup
   mix
¼ tsp. salt, *divided*
⅛ tsp. pepper
½ cup ketchup
4 medium-sized potatoes,
   peeled and sliced
4 carrots, peeled and sliced
2 Tbsp. water
2½ oz. reduced-fat Velveeta
   cheese slices

1. Press uncooked ground beef into the bottom of a lightly greased 9" square pan. Sprinkle with onion powder, ⅛ teaspoon salt, and ⅛ teaspoon pepper.
2. Spread ketchup over top.
3. Arrange sliced potatoes on top of ground-beef layer. Sprinkle with remaining salt.
4. Arrange carrots on top of potato layer. Sprinkle with water.
5. Cover tightly with foil and bake at 350° for 1-1½ hours, or until vegetables jag tender.
6. Remove from oven. Top with cheese slices. Cover and let stand 5-10 minutes until cheese has melted.

Exchange List Values:
Starch 1.0, Vegetable 1.0,
Lean Meat 1.0, Fat 0.5

Basic Nutritional Values:
Calories 193 (Calories from Fat 51), Total Fat 6 gm (Saturated Fat 2.4 gm, Trans Fat 0.3 gm, Polyunsat Fat 0.3 gm, Monounsat Fat 2.2 gm, Cholesterol 38 mg), Sodium 431 mg, Total Carbohydrate 22 gm, Dietary Fiber 2 gm, Sugars 5 gm, Protein 14 gm

Beef & Salsa Burritos

Joyce Shackelford
Green Bay, WI

Makes 8 servings
Serving size is 1 burrito

Prep Time: 10 minutes
Cooking Time: 15 minutes

1¼ lbs. 90%-lean ground
   beef
1½ Tbsp. chili powder
1½ Tbsp. cumin, *optional*
¼ tsp. pepper
10-oz. pkg. frozen chopped
   spinach, thawed and
   squeezed dry
1¼ cups chunky salsa
1 cup fat-free cheddar
   cheese, shredded
8 medium-sized flour
   tortillas, warmed

1. In a large skillet, brown ground beef. Pour off drippings. Season meat with chili powder, cumin, if you wish, and pepper.
2. Stir in spinach and salsa. Heat through.
3. Remove from heat, stir in cheese.
4. Spoon about ½ cup beef mixture into center of each tortilla. Fold bottom edge up over filling. Fold sides to center. Serve.

Exchange List Values:
Starch 1.0, Vegetable 1.0,
Lean Meat 2.0, Fat 0.5

Basic Nutritional Values:
Calories 250 (Calories from Fat 77), Total Fat 9 gm (Saturated Fat 2.9 gm, Trans Fat 0.4 gm, Polyunsat Fat 0.9 gm, Monounsat Fat 3.7 gm, Cholesterol 44 mg), Sodium 656 mg, Total Carbohydrate 21 gm, Dietary Fiber 3 gm, Sugars 3 gm, Protein 22 gm

A Tip —

   Encourage your entire family to eat healthier with you. Meals that are good for people with diabetes are good for everybody!

Taco Tortilla Tower

Christine Lucke, Aumsville, OR

Makes 8 servings
Serving size is 1 wedge or ⅛ of recipe

Prep Time: 30 minutes
Cooking/Baking Time:
25-35 minutes

1 lb. 90%-lean ground beef
half an envelope no-salt-
 added dry taco seasoning
 mix (see page 254)
½ cup chopped onions
16-oz. can fat-free refried
 beans
½ cup fat-free sour cream
5 10" flour tortillas
1 cup fat-free cheddar
 cheese, shredded
6-oz. can black olives,
 sliced, drained
¼ cup sliced green onions
2 cups shredded lettuce
1 medium-sized tomato,
 chopped
fat-free sour cream, *optional*
salsa, *optional*

1. In a large skillet, brown
ground beef. Drain off
drippings.
2. Stir in taco seasoning
and chopped onions. Cook
until onions are transparent.
Remove from heat.
3. Add refried beans and
sour cream. Mix well.
4. Place one tortilla on a
pizza pan or stone. Spread
one-quarter of meat mixture
over the tortilla. Sprinkle with
¼ cup cheese and one-quarter
of olives and green onions.
5. Place another tortilla on
top. Repeat layering 3 more

times. Top with remaining
tortilla.
6. Bake at 375° for 20-30
minutes, or until bubbly and
browned.
7. Slice into 8 wedges.
8. Pass shredded lettuce,
chopped tomato, and, if you
wish, sour cream and salsa as
toppings.

Exchange List Values:
Starch 2.5, Lean Meat 2.0,
Fat 0.5

Basic Nutritional Values:
Calories 342 (Calories from Fat 97),
Total Fat 11 gm (Saturated Fat 3.0
gm, Trans Fat 0.3 gm, Polyunsat
Fat 1.2 gm, Monounsat Fat 5.2 gm,
Cholesterol 37 mg), Sodium 799 mg,
Total Carbohydrate 36 gm, Dietary
Fiber 5 gm, Sugars 4 gm, Protein 23 gm

*Tip: I like this recipe because
you can make it ahead, bake
it, and serve it without the fuss
and flurry of making tacos for
each person.*

Enchilada Pie

Arlene Leaman Kliewer
Lakewood, CO

Makes 12 servings
Serving size is 3¼" x 3" rectangle
or ½₂ of recipe

Prep Time: 30 minutes
Cooking/Baking Time:
55 minutes
Standing Time: 10 minutes

2 lbs. 90%-lean ground beef
1 small onion, chopped
6-oz. can of chopped black

olives, drained
2 cups no-salt-added
 tomato sauce
1-lb. can chili beans
 without meat, *or*
 Mexican-style beans,
 undrained
18 corn tortillas
2 cups fat-free chedder
 cheese, shredded
1 cup 99%-fat-free,
 low-sodium, beef broth

1. Brown beef and onion
together in large skillet.
Drain off drippings.
2. Stir in olives, tomato
sauce, and beans. Cover and
simmer until hot.
3. In a greased 9 x 13
baking pan, layer half the tortillas, followed by a layer of
half the ground beef mixture,
and a layer of one-third of
the cheese. Repeat the layers,
ending with cheese.
4. Pour broth over all.
5. Bake at 350°, uncovered,
for 45 minutes.
6. Allow to stand for 10
minutes before serving.

Exchange List Values:
Starch 1.5, Lean Meat 3.0,
Fat 0.5

Basic Nutritional Values:
Calories 308 (Calories from Fat 113),
Total Fat 13 gm (Saturated Fat 3.3
gm, Trans Fat 0.4 gm, Polyunsat
Fat 2.1 gm, Monounsat Fat 5.4 gm,
Cholesterol 48 mg), Sodium 540 mg,
Total Carbohydrate 24 gm, Dietary
Fiber 5 gm, Sugars 4 gm, Protein 24 gm

Meatball Sub Casserole

Rhoda Atzeff
Harrisburg, PA

Makes 9 servings
Serving size is 3" x 4⅓" rectangle
or ⅑ of recipe

Prep Time: 30-35 minutes
Baking Time: 50 minutes

⅓ cup chopped green
  onions
¼ cup seasoned dry bread
  crumbs
3 Tbsp. grated Parmesan
  cheese
1 lb. 90%-lean ground beef
1 lb. loaf Italian bread, cut
  into 1"-thick slices
8-oz. pkg. fat-free cream
  cheese, softened
½ cup fat-free mayonnaise
1 tsp. no-salt-added Italian
  seasoning
¼ tsp. pepper
1 cup fat-free, shredded
  mozzarella cheese,
  divided
28-oz. jar meatless, low-fat
  spaghetti sauce
1 cup water
2 garlic cloves, minced

1. In a large mixing bowl,
combine onions, crumbs, and
Parmesan cheese. Add beef
and mix well.
2. Shape into 1" balls. Place
on a rack in a shallow baking
pan.
3. Bake at 400° for 15-20
minutes, or until meat is no
longer pink.
4. Meanwhile, arrange

bread in a single layer in an
ungreased 9 x 13 baking dish.
5. Combine cream cheese,
mayonnaise, Italian seasoning, and pepper. Spread over
the bread and sprinkle with
½ cup mozzarella cheese.
6. Combine spaghetti
sauce, water, and garlic. Add
meatballs. Pour over bread-
cheese mixture. Sprinkle
with remaining mozzarella
cheese.
7. Bake, uncovered, at
350° for 30 minutes, or until
heated through.

Exchange List Values:
Carbohydrate 2.5,
Lean Meat 2.0, Fat 0.5

Basic Nutritional Values:
Calories 328 (Calories from Fat 66),
Total Fat 7 gm (Saturated Fat 2.5
gm, Trans Fat 0.3 gm, Polyunsat
Fat 1.2 gm, Monounsat Fat 2.7
gm, Cholesterol 37 mg), **Sodium
1271 mg (high sodium)**, Total
Carbohydrate 39 gm, Dietary Fiber
3 gm, Sugars 9 gm, Protein 24 gm

*Note: This dish is high in
sodium.*

Variations:
*1. If you prefer a less cheesy
dish, reduce cream cheese by
half.*
*2. To save time, use already-
prepared meatballs.*

A Tip —
Limit the amount
of sodium you eat,
especially if you have
heart disease or high
blood pressure.

Creamy Mexican Casserole

Sharon Eshleman, Ephrata, PA

Makes 10 servings
Serving size is 2⅔" x 4½" rectangle
or ¹⁄₁₀ of recipe

Prep Time: 30 minutes
Cooking/Baking Time:
35-40 minutes

¾ lb. 90%-lean ground beef
10.75-oz. can 30%-less-
  sodium tomato soup
10.75-oz. can 98%-fat-free,
  low-sodium cream of
  chicken soup
10.75-oz. can 98%-fat-free,
  low-sodium cream of
  mushroom soup
1 Tbsp. chili powder
15-oz. can no-salt-added
  kidney beans, drained
  and rinsed
10-oz. pkg. frozen corn
1 cup fat-free cheddar
  cheese, shredded
9-oz. pkg. flour tortillas,
  cut into quarters

1. Brown beef in a large
skillet or saucepan. Drain off
drippings.
2. Mix in all other ingredients except cheddar cheese
and tortillas.
3. Line the bottom of a
greased 9 x 13 baking pan with
half the quartered tortillas.
4. Spoon half the meat
mixture over the tortillas.
Cover with half the grated
cheese.
5. Repeat the layers.
6. Bake uncovered at 350°

for 25-30 minutes, or until well browned.

Basic Nutritional Values:
Calories 272 (Calories from Fat 62),
Total Fat 7 gm (Saturated Fat 2.3
gm, Trans Fat 0.2 gm, Polyunsat
Fat 1.2 gm, Monounsat Fat 2.5 gm,
Cholesterol 26 mg), Sodium 668 mg,
Total Carbohydrate 36 gm, Dietary
Fiber 5 gm, Sugars 6 gm, Protein 16 gm

Variations:
1. Use 2 cups cooked, cut-up chicken instead of the ground beef.
2. Add a 15-oz. can refried beans, in addition to, or instead of, the kidney beans, in Step 2.
3. For added zip, stir in a couple of cut-up jalapeño peppers in Step 2.

Zucchini-Hamburger Bake
Linda Overholt, Abbeville, SC

Makes 6 servings
Serving size is ¾ cup

Prep Time: 20 minutes
Cooking Time: 45-55 minutes

1 lb. 90%-lean hamburger
1 small onion, chopped
¼ tsp. pepper
2 cups pizza sauce
½ cup raw long-grain rice
4 cups zucchini, peeled and cubed
1½ cups water
¾ cup fat-free mozzarella cheese, grated

1. In a large skillet or stockpot, brown hamburger and onion together. Drain off drippings. Season meat and onion with pepper.
2. Add remaining ingredients, except cheese, and stir together. Cover and simmer over low heat until rice is soft, approximately 35-45 minutes.
3. Top with cheese and allow to melt before serving.

Basic Nutritional Values:
Calories 256 (Calories from Fat 70),
Total Fat 8 gm (Saturated Fat 2.8
gm, Trans Fat 0.4 gm, Polyunsat
Fat 0.9 gm, Monounsat Fat 2.9 gm,
Cholesterol 48 mg), Sodium 543 mg,
Total Carbohydrate 24 gm, Dietary
Fiber 3 gm, Sugars 7 gm, Protein 22 gm

Tips:
1. An electric skillet works well for making this casserole.
2. You can double the amount of zucchini if you want.

Main Dish Popover
Renee D. Groff, Manheim, PA

Makes 8 servings
Serving size is 1 slice or ⅛ of pie

Prep Time: 20 minutes
Baking Time: 30-35 minutes

1 lb. 90%-lean ground beef
½ cup chopped onions
8-oz. pkg. fat-free cream cheese, softened
¼ cup water
¼ tsp. salt
½ tsp. dried oregano

Batter for crust:
½ cup egg substitute
¾ cup flour
¼ tsp. salt
¾ cup fat-free milk
1 Tbsp. cornmeal
1 chopped tomato, *optional*

1. In a large skillet or saucepan, brown ground beef and onions together. Drain off drippings.
2. To meat and onions in pan, stir in cream cheese and water. Stir over low heat until cream cheese is melted.
3. Stir in salt and oregano and set aside.
4. Combine egg substitute, flour, salt, and milk in a small plastic container with a lid. Shake until smooth. (You may need to beat it with a fork to remove lumps.) Or mix in a mixing bowl with a whisk.
5. Pour batter into a greased 9" pie plate. Sprinkle with cornmeal.
6. Spoon meat mixture over batter, leaving ½ inch space around edges.
7. Bake at 400° for 35 minutes.
8. Top with chopped tomato, if you wish, and serve.

Basic Nutritional Values:
Calories 185 (Calories from Fat 43),
Total Fat 5 gm (Saturated Fat 1.9
gm, Trans Fat 0.3 gm, Polyunsat
Fat 0.2 gm, Monounsat Fat 2.0 gm,
Cholesterol 38 mg), Sodium 418 mg,
Total Carbohydrate 14 gm, Dietary
Fiber 1 gm, Sugars 3 gm, Protein 19 gm

Peppy Peppers

Susie Nisley, Millersburg, OH

Makes 6 servings
Serving size is ¾ cup

Prep Time: 30-40 minutes
Cooking/Baking Time:
75 minutes

1 large green pepper, diced
1 lb. 90%-lean ground beef
1 tsp. salt
¼ tsp. pepper
1 cup dry long-grain rice
1 qt. no-salt-added tomato
  juice
7 tsp. dry taco seasoning
  (see page 254)
Velveeta cheese, cubed,
  optional

1. Place pepper in greased 2-qt. casserole.
2. In skillet, brown ground beef. Drain off drippings. Season meat with salt and pepper. Spread seasoned beef over green pepper.
3. Sprinkle rice over ground beef.
4. In a saucepan, or the skillet in which you browned the beef, combine tomato juice and taco seasoning. Bring to a boil. Pour over rice and beef.
5. Cover. Bake at 350° for 60 minutes.
6. Top with Velveeta cheese if you wish. Return to oven until cheese melts.

Exchange List Values:
Starch 2.0, Vegetable 1.0,
Lean Meat 2.0

Basic Nutritional Values:
Calories 285 (Calories from Fat 63),
Total Fat 7 gm (Saturated Fat 2.5
gm, Trans Fat 0.4 gm, Polyunsat
Fat 0.5 gm, Monounsat Fat 2.8 gm,
Cholesterol 46 mg), Sodium 462 mg,
Total Carbohydrate 37 gm, Dietary
Fiber 2 gm, Sugars 7 gm, Protein 19 gm

Seven Layer Dinner with Rice

Jere Zimmerman
Reinholds, PA

Makes 6 servings
Serving size is ¾ cup

Prep Time: 20-30 minutes
Baking Time: 1½ hours

1 cup uncooked minute rice
1 cup canned whole-kernel
  corn, drained
salt and pepper to taste
2 8-oz. cans tomato sauce,
  divided
¾ cup water, *divided*
½ cup chopped onions
½ cup chopped green pepper
¾ lb. uncooked, 90%-lean
  ground beef

1. Place rice in the bottom of a greased 2-qt. casserole dish.
2. Cover with drained corn. Sprinkle with salt and pepper.
3. In a small mixing bowl, blend 1 can tomato sauce and ½ cup water. Pour over corn.
4. Top with onions and green peppers.
5. Crumble uncooked ground beef over top. Sprinkle with salt and pepper.
6. Mix second can of tomato sauce with ¼ cup water and pour over meat.
7. Cover and bake at 350° for 1 hour. Uncover and bake ½ hour longer.

Exchange List Values:
Starch 1.5, Vegetable 1.0,
Lean Meat 1.0

Basic Nutritional Values:
Calories 200 (Calories from Fat 44),
Total Fat 5 gm (Saturated Fat 1.8
gm, Trans Fat 0.3 gm, Polyunsat
Fat 0.4 gm, Monounsat Fat 2.0 gm,
Cholesterol 35 mg), Sodium 542 mg,
Total Carbohydrate 26 gm, Dietary
Fiber 2 gm, Sugars 5 gm, Protein 14 gm

A Tip —

Blood glucose levels will naturally rise after a meal. However, it is important to treat these spikes so that they do not go too high or last too long.

Reuben Casserole

Joleen Albrecht
Gladstone, MI

Makes 10 servings
Serving size is 4½" x 2⅔" rectangle
or ⅒ of recipe

Prep Time: 25 minutes
Baking Time: 25 minutes

1½ cups fat-free Thousand
  Island salad dressing
1 cup fat-free sour cream
1 Tbsp. minced onions
12 slices dark rye bread,
  cubed, *divided*
1 lb. sauerkraut, drained
  and rinsed
¾ lb. corned beef, visible
  fat trimmed, sliced and
  cut into bite-sized pieces
1 cup fat-free Swiss cheese,
  shredded

1. In a mixing bowl, stir
together dressing, sour cream,
and onions. Set aside.

2. Arrange bread cubes in
a greased 9 x 13 baking dish,
setting aside approximately
1 cup cubes for the top.

3. Top the bread with a
layer of sauerkraut, followed
by a layer of corned beef.

4. Spread dressing mixture
over corned beef. Sprinkle
with Swiss cheese.

5. Top with remaining
bread cubes.

6. Cover and bake at 350°
for 15 minutes. Uncover and
continue baking for about
10 minutes or until bubbly.

Exchange List Values:
Carbohydrate 2.0,
Lean Meat 2.0

Basic Nutritional Values:
Calories 265 (Calories from Fat 55),
Total Fat 6 gm (Saturated Fat 2.3
gm, Trans Fat 0.1 gm, Polyunsat
Fat 0.5 gm, Monounsat Fat 2.4
gm, Cholesterol 34 mg), **Sodium
1192 mg (high sodium)**, Total
Carbohydrate 31 gm, Dietary Fiber
3 gm, Sugars 8 gm, Protein 17 gm

Note: This dish is high in sodium.

Reuben Stromboli

Andrea Cunningham
Arlington, KS

Makes 8 servings
Serving size is 1 slice or ⅛ of recipe

Prep Time: 15-20 minutes
Rising Time: 15 minutes
Baking Time: 25 minutes
Standing Time: 10 minutes

3¼-3¾ cups flour, *divided*
1 pkg., or 1 Tbsp., quick-
  rise yeast
1 Tbsp. sugar
1 Tbsp. 65%-vegetable-oil
  margarine
½ tsp. salt
1 cup warm (120-130°)
  water
¼ cup fat-free Thousand
  Island salad dressing
6 ozs. thinly sliced corned
  beef, visible fat trimmed
3 ozs. reduced-fat Swiss
  cheese, sliced
8-oz. can sauerkraut,
  drained and rinsed
1 egg white, beaten

caraway seeds

1. In a large mixing bowl,
combine 2¼ cups flour, yeast,
sugar, margarine, and salt.
Stir in warm water. Mix
until a soft dough forms. Add
remaining flour if necessary.

2. Turn onto a lightly
floured surface. Knead until
smooth, about 4 minutes.

3. On a greased baking
sheet, roll dough to a 14 x 10
rectangle.

4. Spread dressing down
center third of dough. Top
with layers of beef, cheese,
and sauerkraut.

5. Make cuts from filling
to edges of dough, 1" apart
on both sides of the filling.
Alternating sides, fold the
strips at an angle across filling.

6. Cover filled dough and
let rise in a warm place for 15
minutes.

7. Brush with egg white and
sprinkle with caraway seeds.

8. Bake at 400°, uncovered,
for 25 minutes, or until
lightly browned.

9. Let stand for 10 minutes.
Cut into ¾" slices with a
sharp knife.

Exchange List Values:
Medium-Fat Meat 1.0,
Starch 3.0

Basic Nutritional Values:
Calories 336 (Calories from Fat 60),
Total Fat 7 gm (Saturated Fat 2.5
gm, Trans Fat 0.2 gm, Polyunsat
Fat 0.8 gm, Monounsat Fat 2.3 gm,
Cholesterol 22 mg), Sodium 614 mg,
Total Carbohydrate 49 gm, Dietary
Fiber 5 gm, Sugars 4 gm, Protein 20 gm

Pork Main Dishes

Pork Chops with Apples and Stuffing

Louise Bodziony
Sunrise Beach, MO

Makes 6 servings
Serving size is 1 pork chop with
small amount of apples and stuffing

Prep Time: 15 minutes
Cooking/Baking Time:
75-85 minutes

6 4-oz. boneless pork loin
   chops, 1"-thick and
   trimmed of fat
1 Tbsp. oil
24-oz. jar no-sugar-added
   apple-pie filling
ground cinnamon
6-oz. pkg. crushed stuffing
   mix, prepared*

1. In skillet, brown chops
in oil over medium-high heat.
(Do this in several batches
so as not to crowd the skillet.
The chops will brown better
if the pan isn't too full.)
   2. Spread pie filling in a
greased 9 x 13 baking pan.
Sprinkle cinnamon over pie
filling as desired.
   3. Place pork chops on top.
   4. Spoon stuffing over
chops. Cover.

5. Bake at 350° for 55-65
minutes. Uncover and bake
10 minutes longer, or until
meat thermometer reads 160°.

Exchange List Values:
Starch 1.5, Fruit 0.5,
Lean Meat 3.0

Basic Nutritional Values:
Calories 316 (Calories from Fat 97),
Total Fat 11 gm (Saturated Fat 3.0
gm, Trans Fat 0.0 gm, Polyunsat
Fat 1.4 gm, Monounsat Fat 5.3 gm,
Cholesterol 51 mg), Sodium 299 mg,
Total Carbohydrate 30 gm, Dietary
Fiber 2 gm, Sugars 10 gm, Protein 24 gm

** No fat or salt should be added
when preparing the stuffing mix.*

Sweet Pork Chops

Angie Clemens
Dayton, VA

Makes 6 servings
Serving size is 1 pork chop

Prep Time: 15 minutes
Cooking/Baking Time:
75 minutes

2 Tbsp. oil
6 4-oz. boneless pork chops,
   visible fat trimmed
1 onion, sliced
1 green pepper, sliced into
   rings
6 Tbsp. brown sugar blend
   (Splenda)
6 Tbsp. ketchup
6 Tbsp. lemon juice

1. Brown pork chops in oil
in large skillet. (Do not crowd
the skillet. The chops will
brown more fully if they're
not squeezed in the pan.)
Place browned chops in a
greased 9 x 13 baking dish.
   2. On top of each chop,
place 1 onion slice and
1 green pepper slice.
   3. In a small mixing bowl,
combine brown sugar blend,
ketchup, and lemon juice. Top
each chop with about 3 Tbsp.
of the mixture.
   4. Cover and bake at 350°
for 30 minutes. Uncover and
bake 30 minutes more.
   5. Baste occasionally
during the final 30 minutes.

Exchange List Values:
Carbohydrate 1.0,
Lean Meat 3.0, Fat 0.5

Basic Nutritional Values:
Calories 258 (Calories from Fat 110),
Total Fat 12 gm (Saturated Fat 3.2
gm, Trans Fat 0.0 gm, Polyunsat
Fat 2.0 gm, Monounsat Fat 6.3 gm,
Cholesterol 51 mg), Sodium 213 mg,
Total Carbohydrate 15 gm, Dietary
Fiber 1 gm, Sugars 10 gm, Protein 21 gm

*Tips: I like to put any extra
onions and green pepper pieces
around the edges of the baking
dish before putting the meat in
the oven.*

A Tip —

   Skipping meals is not a
good way to lose weight.
Your metabolism slows
down when you do not eat.

Spiced Pork Chops
Mary Jane Hoober
Shipshewana, IN

Makes 4 servings
Serving size is 1 pork chop

Prep Time: 15 minutes
Cooking/Baking Time:
75 minutes

½ cup flour
1½ tsp. garlic powder
1½ tsp. dry mustard
1½ tsp. paprika
½ tsp. celery salt
¼ tsp. ground ginger
⅛ tsp. dried oregano
⅛ tsp. dried basil
⅛ tsp. salt
pinch of pepper
4 6-oz. pork loin chops,
   approximately ¾"-thick,
   bone in, visible fat
   removed
1 to 2 Tbsp. oil
1 cup ketchup
1 cup water
¼ cup brown sugar blend
   (Splenda)

1. In a medium-sized mixing bowl, combine the first 10 ingredients (through pepper).
2. Dredge pork chops on both sides in dry mixture.
3. Heat oil in a skillet. Brown chops on both sides. (Do not crowd the skillet. The chops will brown better if they're not tight against each other.) Place in a greased 9 x 13 baking dish.
4. In a small bowl, combine ketchup, water, and brown sugar blend. Pour over chops.

5. Bake uncovered, at 350° for 1 hour, or until tender.

Exchange List Values:
Carbohydrate 1.0,
Lean Meat 3.0, Fat 0.5

Basic Nutritional Values:
Calories 275 (Calories from Fat 97), Total Fat 11 gm (Saturated Fat 2.8 gm, Trans Fat 0.0 gm, Polyunsat Fat 1.7 gm, Monounsat Fat 5.2 gm, Cholesterol 71 mg), Sodium 148 mg, Total Carbohydrate 15 gm, Dietary Fiber 1 gm, Sugars 7 gm, Protein 26 gm

Baked Pork Chops with Gravy
Margaret Jarrett
Anderson, IN

Makes 4 servings
Serving size is 1 pork chop

Prep Time: 15 minutes
Cooking/Baking Time:
75 minutes

1 Tbsp. oil
4 pork chops, bone in,
   visible fat removed
10.75-oz. can 90%-fat-free,
   low-sodium cream of
   mushroom soup
¾ cup water
½ tsp. ground ginger
¼ tsp. rosemary
¼ cup fat-free sour cream

1. Brown pork chops in oil in skillet. (Reserve the drippings.) Lay the browned chops in a lightly greased baking dish.
2. In a small mixing bowl, mix the mushroom soup, water, ginger, and rosemary together. Pour over the chops.
3. Cover and bake at 350° for 50 minutes.
4. Uncover. Bake 10 more minutes.
5. While the chops are baking, make a gravy by heating the drippings. Stir in the sour cream and heat without boiling. Serve with the baked chops.

Exchange List Values:
Carbohydrate 0.5,
Lean Meat 4.0

Basic Nutritional Values:
Calories 256 (Calories from Fat 108), Total Fat 12 gm (Saturated Fat 3.4 gm, Trans Fat 0.0 gm, Polyunsat Fat 2.2 gm, Monounsat Fat 5.5 gm, Cholesterol 75 mg), Sodium 360 mg, Total Carbohydrate 7 gm, Dietary Fiber 1 gm, Sugars 2 gm, Protein 27 gm

A Tip —
   Reducing the amount of saturated fats in your diet has a great effect on your cholesterol levels.

Pork Chops and Cabbage

Shirley Hedman
Schenectady, NY

Makes 4 servings
Serving size is 1 pork chop

Prep Time: 10 minutes
Cooking Time: 1-2 hours

4 6-oz. pork chops, bone
  in, visible fat removed
2 Tbsp. oil
dash of salt
dash of pepper
dash of garlic powder
1 medium-sized head of
  cabbage, shredded
8-oz. can tomato sauce
¼ cup water

1. In a large skillet or saucepan, brown pork chops on one side in oil. Turn.
2. Season with salt, pepper, and garlic powder.
3. Top chops with cabbage.
4. In a small bowl, mix together tomato sauce and water until smooth. Pour over cabbage. Cover pan.
5. Cook slowly over low heat for 1½ hours, stirring occasionally, until chops and cabbage are tender, but not overdone.

Exchange List Values:
Lean Meat 4.0, Fat 0.5,
Vegetable 3.0

Basic Nutritional Values:
Calories 302 (Calories from Fat 129),
Total Fat 14 gm (Saturated Fat 3.1
gm, Trans Fat 0.0 gm, Polyunsat
Fat 2.8 gm, Monounsat Fat 7.2 gm,
Cholesterol 71 mg), Sodium 435 mg,
Total Carbohydrate 17 gm, Dietary
Fiber 6 gm, Sugars 11 gm, Protein 29 gm

Cranberry-Glazed Pork Roast

Cova Rexroad
Kingsville, MD

Makes 6 servings
Serving size is 4 ozs. meat

Prep Time: 15 minutes
Baking Time: 2 hours
Standing Time: 25-30 minutes

2½-3-lb. pork roast,
  boneless, visible fat
  trimmed
1 tsp. salt
½-¼ tsp. pepper
16-oz. can whole-berry
  cranberry sauce
½ cup orange juice
¼ cup brown sugar blend
  (Splenda)

1. Rub the pork roast with salt and pepper. Bake uncovered at 350° for 1½ hours.
2. Meanwhile, combine cranberry sauce, orange juice, and brown sugar blend in a small saucepan. Cook over low heat until mixture comes to a boil, making a thin sauce.
3. After the meat has baked, brush ¼ of the sauce over the roast and bake uncovered another 30 minutes.

4. Remove the roast from the pan and place it on a serving platter. Cover with foil and allow to stand for 25-30 minutes. Slice thinly and serve with the remaining sauce.

Exchange List Values:
Carbohydrate 2.0,
Lean Meat 3.0

Basic Nutritional Values:
Calories 295 (Calories from Fat 73),
Total Fat 8 gm (Saturated Fat 2.9
gm, Trans Fat 0.0 gm, Polyunsat
Fat 0.8 gm, Monounsat Fat 3.5 gm,
Cholesterol 83 mg), Sodium 361 mg,
Total Carbohydrate 27 gm, Dietary
Fiber 1 gm, Sugars 26 gm, Protein 28 gm

Variation: For the glaze, use ¼ cup honey, 1 tsp. grated orange peel, ⅛ tsp. cloves, and ⅛ tsp. nutmeg, instead of orange juice and brown sugar.
  —Chris Peterson
  Green Bay, WI

A Tip —

Studies have shown that people over 65 can pack on muscle at the same rate as people decades younger.

Pear Pork Stir-Fry

Polly Anna Glaser
New Ulm, MN

Makes 8 servings
Serving size is ¾ cup

Prep Time: 5 minutes
Cooking Time: 20-25 minutes

16-oz. can pear slices,
    drained (reserve liquid)
12 ozs. lean pork tenderloin,
    cut into julienned strips
2 Tbsp. vegetable oil
3 carrots, cut in ½"-thick
    slices
1 medium-sized onion,
    diced
1 red pepper, diced
3 Tbsp. brown sugar
3 Tbsp. red wine vinegar
1 Tbsp. cornstarch
2 Tbsp. light soy sauce
dash of pepper

1. Cut pears slices in half.
Set aside.
2. In a skillet, sauté pork
over high heat in oil until
lightly browned, stirring
constantly.
3. Add the vegetables and
cook just until tender-crisp,
about 5 minutes, stirring
frequently.
4. In a small bowl, com-
bine pear liquid with brown
sugar, vinegar, cornstarch,
soy sauce, and pepper. When
smooth, stir into pork and
vegetables.
5. Add pears. Cook,
stirring gently 1-2 minutes,
until sauce thickens.
6. Serve over rice.

Exchange List Values:
Carbohydrate 2.5,
Lean Meat 2.0, Fat 0.5

Basic Nutritional Values:
Calories 305 (Calories from Fat 86),
Total Fat 10 gm (Saturated Fat 1.3
gm, Trans Fat 0.0 gm, Polyunsat
Fat 2.4 gm, Monounsat Fat 5.0 gm,
Cholesterol 46 mg), Sodium 359 mg,
Total Carbohydrate 38 gm, Dietary
Fiber 5 gm, Sugars 27 gm, Protein 19 gm

Pork Thai Stew

Marilyn Mowry
Irving, TX

Makes 8 servings
Serving size is ½ cup rice
with ¾ cup stew

Prep Time: 15 minutes
Cooking Time: 3 hours and
15 minutes

2 lbs. pork tenderloin,
    visible fat trimmed,
    cubed
2 Tbsp. oil
2 garlic cloves, minced
2 cups sliced red bell
    pepper
2 Tbsp. white wine or rice
    wine vinegar
¼ cup light teriyaki sauce
1 tsp. crushed red pepper
    flakes
½ cup water
¼ cup creamy peanut
    butter
4 cups cooked rice
sliced green onions, *optional*
chopped peanuts, *optional*

1. In large skillet, brown
meat in oil.
2. Add garlic, bell pepper,
wine, teriyaki sauce, and red
pepper flakes.
3. Simmer, covered,
1½ hours on stove. Stir in
½ cup water. Cover and
continue simmering over low
heat for another 1½ hours, or
until meat is very tender.
4. Remove skillet from
heat. While meat is still in
skillet, shred the meat using
2 forks to pull it apart. Stir in
peanut butter.
5. Serve over cooked rice.
Garnish with chopped green
onions and chopped peanuts,
if you wish.

Exchange List Values:
Starch 2.0, Lean Meat 3.0

Basic Nutritional Values:
Calories 314 (Calories from Fat 98),
Total Fat 11 gm (Saturated Fat 2.1
gm, Trans Fat 0.0 gm, Polyunsat
Fat 2.6 gm, Monounsat Fat 5.3 gm,
Cholesterol 61 mg), Sodium 243 mg,
Total Carbohydrate 27 gm, Dietary
Fiber 1 gm, Sugars 3 gm, Protein 27 gm

Mother's Baked Ham

Dawn Ranck, Lansdale, PA

Makes 8 servings
Serving size is ⅛ of recipe

Prep Time: 10 minutes
Baking Time: 60-75 minutes

2 1-lb. slices boneless, extra-lean, low-sodium ham steaks, each 1¼" thick
1 tsp. dried mustard
4 Tbsp. brown sugar blend (Splenda)
fat-free milk to cover ham

1. Place ham in large baking pan.
2. Rub with mustard.
3. Sprinkle with brown sugar blend.
4. Add enough milk to barely cover ham. (Pour milk in along the side of the meat slices so as not to wash off the mustard and sugar.)
5. Cover with foil.
6. Bake at 325° for 60-75 minutes, or until milk is absorbed.

Exchange List Values:
Carbohydrate 0.5,
Lean Meat 2.0

Basic Nutritional Values:
Calories 130 (Calories from Fat 16), Total Fat 2 gm (Saturated Fat 0.7 gm, Trans Fat 0.0 gm, Polyunsat Fat 0.3 gm, Monounsat Fat 0.7 gm, Cholesterol 45 mg), **Sodium 804 mg (high sodium)**, Total Carbohydrate 8 gm, Dietary Fiber 0 gm, Sugars 8 gm, Protein 18 gm

Note: This dish is high in sodium.

Pineapple Glaze for Ham

Starla Kreider
Mohrsville, PA

Makes 4 cups, or 16 servings
Serving size is ¼ cup

Prep Time: 5 minutes
Cooking Time: 10 minutes

¼ cup water
¾ cup brown sugar blend (Splenda)
1½ Tbsp. ketchup
1½ Tbsp. light soy sauce
1½ tsp. dry mustard
1½ cups crushed pineapple, drained
2¼ Tbsp. cornstarch
½ cup water

1. Combine first 6 ingredients in a saucepan. Bring to a boil.
2. In a small mixing bowl, combine cornstarch and ½ cup water until smooth. Add to boiling mixture. Stir continuously and cook until clear.
3. Spoon over ham slices before baking. Or serve as a topping for cooked sweet potatoes or for cooked rice.

Exchange List Values:
Carbohydrate 1.0

Basic Nutritional Values:
Calories 62 (Calories from Fat 1), Total Fat 0 gm (Saturated Fat 0.0 gm, Trans Fat 0.0 gm, Polyunsat Fat 0.0 gm, Monounsat Fat 0.0 gm, Cholesterol 0 mg), Sodium 73 mg, Total Carbohydrate 13 gm, Dietary Fiber 0 gm, Sugars 11 gm, Protein 0 gm

Ham Loaf

Inez Rutt, Bangor, PA

Makes 8 servings
Serving size is 1 slice
or ⅛ of recipe

Prep Time: 20-30 minutes
Baking Time: 1-1¼ hours

¾ lb. extra-lean, low-sodium ground ham
¾ lb. ground pork tenderloin
1 egg
¼ cup minced onions
½ cup cracker crumbs
½ cup fat-free milk
pepper to taste

Glaze:
¼ cup brown sugar blend (Splenda)
1 Tbsp. dry mustard
¼ cup vinegar

1. In a large mixing bowl, mix ham, pork, egg, onions, cracker crumbs, milk, and pepper together until well blended. Form into a loaf, and then place in greased loaf pan.
2. Make glaze by mixing brown sugar blend, dry mustard, and vinegar together until smooth.
3. Pour glaze over top of ham loaf.
4. Bake at 350° for 1-1¼ hours, or until well browned. Baste occasionally with glaze during baking.

Exchange List Values:
Carbohydrate 1.0,
Lean Meat 2.0

Basic Nutritional Values:
Calories 152 (Calories from Fat 28),
Total Fat 3 gm (Saturated Fat 0.9
gm, Trans Fat 0.2 gm, Polyunsat
Fat 0.4 gm, Monounsat Fat 1.2 gm,
Cholesterol 66 mg), Sodium 375 mg,
Total Carbohydrate 12 gm, Dietary
Fiber 0 gm, Sugars 8 gm, Protein 17 gm

*Variation: Add 8-oz. can
crushed pineapple and juice to
the glaze.*
—**Mary E. Wheatley**
Mashpee, MA
—**Janice Yoskovich**
Carmichaels, PA

Potato, Ham, and Cheese Casserole
Vera Martin, East Earl, PA

Makes 6 servings
Serving size is 3" x 4½" rectangle
or ⅙ of recipe

Prep Time: 10-15 minutes
Baking Time: 40-45 minutes
Standing Time: 10 minutes

1 cup egg substitute
½ cup reduced-fat cheddar
    cheese, shredded
½ cup fat-free milk
pinch of onion salt
2 medium-sized raw
    potatoes, peeled and
    shredded, about 2 cups-
    worth
½ cup chipped ham

1. In a bowl, combine egg
substitute, cheese, milk and
onion salt. Then add the
shredded potatoes and the
chipped ham.

2. Stir everything together
well, and put into a greased
9 x 9 baking dish, or a
10" glass pie plate.
3. Bake at 350° for about
40-45 minutes, or until set,
and knife inserted in center
comes out clean.
4. Allow to stand 10 min-
utes before cutting to serve.

Exchange List Values:
Starch 0.5, Lean Meat 1.0

Basic Nutritional Values:
Calories 103 (Calories from Fat 22),
Total Fat 2 gm (Saturated Fat 1.4
gm, Trans Fat 0.0 gm, Polyunsat
Fat 0.2 gm, Monounsat Fat 0.6 gm,
Cholesterol 13 mg), Sodium 301 mg,
Total Carbohydrate 11 gm, Dietary
Fiber 1 gm, Sugars 2 gm, Protein 10 gm

We like this dish for breakfast
or for a light lunch.

Scalloped Potatoes and Ham
Sandra Chang, Derwood, MD

Makes 4 servings
Serving size is ¾ cup

Prep Time: 15 minutes
Cooking Time: 30 minutes
Standing Time: 5 minutes

4 medium-sized potatoes,
    peeled and sliced
¼ cup onions, chopped
1 Tbsp. flour, *divided*
⅛ tsp. salt
⅛ tsp. pepper
1 cup extra-lean, low-
    sodium cooked ham,
    diced

1⅔ cups milk
1 Tbsp. 65%-vegetable-oil
    stick margarine
½ cup (2 ozs.) reduced-fat
    cheddar cheese, shredded
sprinkle of paprika

1. Arrange half of potatoes
in greased 2-qt. microwavable
casserole dish.
2. Sprinkle with onions,
1½ tsp. flour, ⅛ tsp. salt, and
pinch of pepper.
3. Layer remaining
potatoes into dish. Add a
layer of ham. Sprinkle with
remaining flour, and pepper.
4. Pour milk over top. Dot
with margarine.
5. Cover and microwave at
50% power for 30 minutes,
or until potatoes are tender.
Rotate dish one-quarter turn
every 8 minutes.
6. Sprinkle with cheese
and paprika.
7. Microwave, uncovered,
at 50% power for 2 minutes,
or until cheese is melted.
8. Cover and let stand for
5 minutes before serving.

Exchange List Values:
Starch 2.0, Lean Meat 1.0,
Fat-Free Milk 0.5

Basic Nutritional Values:
Calories 278 (Calories from Fat 55),
Total Fat 6 gm (Saturated Fat 2.7
gm, Trans Fat 0.4 gm, Polyunsat
Fat 1.0 gm, Monounsat Fat 1.8 gm,
Cholesterol 28 mg), Sodium 557 mg,
Total Carbohydrate 40 gm, Dietary
Fiber 3 gm, Sugars 10 gm, Protein 16 gm

Ham and Pea Casserole

Marcia S. Myer
Manheim, PA

Makes 8 servings
Serving size is 2¾" x 3½" rectangle or ⅛ of recipe

Prep Time: 35-40 minutes
Baking Time: 30 minutes

10.75-oz. can 98%-fat-free, low-sodium cream of mushroom soup
1 soup can of milk
½ tsp. garlic powder
2 cups extra-lean, low-sodium cooked ham, cubed
1 cup frozen peas, thawed
2 cups cooked macaronis
2 ozs. light Velveeta cheese, cubed
2 slices torn bread
1 Tbsp. 65%-vegetable-oil stick margarine

1. In a large mixing bowl, whisk together soup, milk, and garlic powder until smooth.
2. Gently stir in ham, peas, macaronis, and cheese cubes.
3. Spoon into a greased 2-qt., 7 x 11 baking dish.
4. In the mixing bowl, combine the bread and margarine. Spoon over casserole.
5. Bake at 350°, uncovered, for 30 minutes, or until heated through and bread topping is browned.

Exchange List Values:
Carbohydrate 1.5,
Lean Meat 1.0

Basic Nutritional Values:
Calories 180 (Calories from Fat 34), Total Fat 4 gm (Saturated Fat 1.4 gm, Trans Fat 0.2 gm, Polyunsat Fat 1.1 gm, Monounsat Fat 1.0 gm, Cholesterol 21 mg), Sodium 622 mg, Total Carbohydrate 23 gm, Dietary Fiber 2 gm, Sugars 7 gm, Protein 13 gm

Smoked Sausage Oriental

Ruth Feister
Narvon, PA

Makes 6 servings
Serving size is ¾ cup

Prep Time: 10-15 minutes
Cooking Time: 10-15 minutes

1 lb. low-fat smoked sausage, cut into ¾" thick chunks
1 Tbsp. canola oil
1 medium-sized onion, chopped
3 small tomatoes, chopped
1 Tbsp. cornstarch
½ tsp. ginger
1 Tbsp. vinegar
1 Tbsp. light soy sauce
½ cup low-sugar apricot preserves

1. Brown sausage chunks in oil.
2. Stir in onion and brown it in the meat drippings.
3. Add tomatoes, and cook over low heat for 5 minutes.

4. Meanwhile, in a small bowl, combine cornstarch and ginger. Mix in vinegar and soy sauce, stirring until smooth. Add preserves and combine well.
5. Stir into sausage-vegetable mixture.
6. Cook covered over low heat, stirring occasionally, until sauce thickens.
7. When heated through, serve over rice.

Exchange List Values:
Carbohydrate 2.0,
Lean Meat 1.0, Fat 0.5

Basic Nutritional Values:
Calories 215 (Calories from Fat 53), Total Fat 6 gm (Saturated Fat 1.5 gm, Trans Fat 0.0 gm, Polyunsat Fat 2.1 gm, Monounsat Fat 2.2 gm, Cholesterol 32 mg), **Sodium 749 mg (high sodium)**, Total Carbohydrate 31 gm, Dietary Fiber 1 gm, Sugars 18 gm, Protein 10 gm

Note: This dish is high in sodium.

Variations: If you want, add 1 green pepper, chunked, to Step 3, and 2 cups drained pineapple chunks to Step 6.

A Tip —

Serving sizes are important! Use measuring cups at home to serve your food. This can help you get a feel for serving sizes.

Sausage Tortellini

Christie Detamore-Hunsberger
Harrisonburg, VA

Makes 8 servings
Serving size is ¾ cup

Prep Time: 25-30 minutes
Cooking Time: 65-80 minutes

1 lb. low-fat smoked
   sausage, cut into ½" slices
1 cup chopped onions
2 cloves garlic, minced
5 cups fat-free, no-salt-added
   beef broth
½ cup water
½ cup red cooking wine
14-oz. can diced tomatoes,
   undrained
14-oz. can no-salt-added
   diced tomatoes,
   undrained
1 cup thinly sliced carrots
½ tsp. dried basil
½ tsp. dried oregano
16-oz. can no-salt-added
   tomato sauce
½ cup sliced zucchini,
   optional
16-oz. pkg. tortellini
3 Tbsp. parsley

1. In large stockpot, brown
sausage in its own drippings.
When well browned, stir in
onions, and garlic. Cook until
browned.
2. Add next 9 ingredients
(through the tomato sauce),
cover, and simmer 35-40
minutes.
3. Add zucchini if you wish,
and tortellini. Simmer another
20-25 minutes over low heat,
or until tortellini is cooked.
4. Stir in parsley and serve.

Exchange List Values:
Starch 2.5, Vegetable 2.0,
Fat 0.5

Basic Nutritional Values:
Calories 269 (Calories from Fat 26),
Total Fat 3 gm (Saturated Fat 0.9
gm, Trans Fat 0.0 gm, Polyunsat
Fat 1.2 gm, Monounsat Fat 0.6 gm,
Cholesterol 18 mg), Sodium 587 mg,
Total Carbohydrate 47 gm, Dietary
Fiber 4 gm, Sugars 10 gm, Protein 12 gm

Favorite Casserole

Laverne Nafziger
Goshen, IN

Makes 6 servings
Serving size is 4" x 2" rectangle
or ⅙ of recipe

Prep Time: 30 minutes
Cooking/Baking Time:
55-70 minutes

½ lb. bulk sausage
2 Tbsp. chopped onions
1 clove garlic, minced
2 cups no-egg-yolk
   dry noodles, cooked
   according to package
   directions
1 cup fat-free cottage cheese
1 cup fat-free milk
10.75-oz. can 98%-fat-free,
   low-sodium cream of
   mushroom soup
1 cup fat-free cheddar
   cheese, shredded
¾ cup egg substitute

1. Brown sausage, onions,
and garlic in skillet. Drain off
drippings.
2. In large bowl, mix all
ingredients except cheddar
cheese and egg substitute.
Pour into a greased 8 x 12, or
2-qt., baking dish.
3. Beat egg substitute with
fork. Add cheddar cheese.
Pour over top of casserole.
4. Bake uncovered at 350°
for 45-60 minutes, or until
bubbly and browned.

Exchange List Values:
Carbohydrate 1.5,
Lean Meat 2.0

Basic Nutritional Values:
Calories 227 (Calories from Fat 61),
Total Fat 7 gm (Saturated Fat 2.4
gm, Trans Fat 0.0 gm, Polyunsat
Fat 1.1 gm, Monounsat Fat 2.7 gm,
Cholesterol 21 mg), **Sodium 834 mg
(high sodium)**, Total Carbohydrate
19 gm, Dietary Fiber 1 gm, Sugars
6 gm, Protein 20 gm

Note: This dish is high in sodium.

A Tip —

To lose a pound of body
weight, a person needs to
burn 3,500 more calories
than they take in.

Sausage and Corn Casserole

Julia Horst, Gordonville, PA

Makes 6 servings
Serving size is ¾ cup

Prep Time: 20 minutes
Cooking/Baking Time:
50 minutes

½ lb. bulk sausage
2 cups cooked corn
2 cups cooked, diced
 potatoes
4 hard-boiled egg whites
 (yolks discarded), diced
1 Tbsp. canola oil
1 tsp. minced onions
¼ cup flour
¼ tsp. salt
2 cups fat-free milk
½ cup dry bread crumbs

1. Brown sausage in skillet, stirring to break up chunks. Drain off drippings.
2. Layer meat, corn, potatoes, and egg whites in a 3-qt. greased casserole dish.
3. In a saucepan, heat canola oil. Sauté onions until just softened.
4. Stir in flour and salt. Stir over low heat for about 2 minutes until slightly browned.
5. Gradually pour in milk, stirring constantly until mixture begins to bubble. Continue stirring until sauce begins to thicken. Continue cooking another minute or 2, until sauce becomes smooth and thickened, stirring constantly.

6. Pour white sauce over casserole ingredients. Mix lightly.
7. Spoon bread crumbs evenly over casserole.
8. Bake uncovered at 350° for 30 minutes, or until heated through.

Exchange List Values:
Starch 2.5, Lean Meat 1.0, Fat 0.5

Basic Nutritional Values:
Calories 267 (Calories from Fat 79), Total Fat 9 gm (Saturated Fat 2.4 gm, Trans Fat 0.0 gm, Polyunsat Fat 1.7 gm, Monounsat Fat 4.0 gm, Cholesterol 16 mg), Sodium 470 mg, Total Carbohydrate 36 gm, Dietary Fiber 3 gm, Sugars 7 gm, Protein 13 gm

Italian Barbecue

Pat Bishop, Bedminster, PA

Makes 10 servings
Serving size is 1 sandwich

Prep Time: 10 minutes
Cooking Time: 80 minutes

1 lb. bulk sausage,
 uncooked
1 lb. chipped steak, visible
 fat trimmed, uncooked
4 large onions, cut in rings
2 medium-sized green
 peppers, sliced
4-oz. can sliced
 mushrooms, drained
28-oz. jar low-fat spaghetti
 sauce
1 Tbsp. dried oregano
salt to taste
10 hot dog rolls

1. In a large skillet, brown the sausage. Remove from pan and set aside.
2. Brown chipped steak in the sausage drippings in the same skillet. Pull steak apart with 2 forks. Remove from pan and set aside.
3. Brown onions and peppers in skillet drippings. Stir meats back in and add remaining ingredients. Cover and simmer 1 hour.
4. Serve on hot dog rolls.

Exchange List Values:
Starch 3.0, Vegetable 3.0, Lean Meat 1.0, Fat 0.5

Basic Nutritional Values:
Calories 396 (Calories from Fat 78), Total Fat 9 gm (Saturated Fat 3.1 gm, Trans Fat 0.0 gm, Polyunsat Fat 1.6 gm, Monounsat Fat 3.3 gm, Cholesterol 32 mg), **Sodium 1013 mg (high sodium)**, Total Carbohydrate 60 gm, Dietary Fiber 5 gm, Sugars 14 gm, Protein 21 gm

Note: This dish is high in sodium.

Pork Tenderloin Sandwiches

Karen Kirstein
Schenectady, NY

Makes 4 servings
Serving size is 1 sandwich

Prep Time: 15 minutes
Cooking Time: 15 minutes

1 lb. pork tenderloin,
    trimmed of all visible fat
¼ tsp. salt
⅛ tsp. pepper
⅓ cup flour
1 egg, beaten
1 Tbsp. vegetable oil
½ cup fat-free sour cream
1 tsp. horseradish
romaine lettuce
red onion, thinly sliced
4 sandwich rolls

1. Slice tenderloin into 4 ¼"-thick slices and pound flat.

2. In a small bowl, mix flour with salt and pepper. Dip meat slices into flour and then into beaten egg. Fry in oil until brown. Turn and brown other side. (Be careful not to crowd the pan so the meat can brown well and cook through.) Set finished slices aside and keep warm while you brown the rest.

3. Meanwhile, in a small bowl, mix sour cream with horseradish.

4. To serve, place meat, lettuce, and onion on rolls and top with sour cream mixture.

Exchange List Values:
Starch 2.0, Lean Meat 3.0

Basic Nutritional Values:
Calories 349 (Calories from Fat 87), Total Fat 10 gm (Saturated Fat 2.1 gm, Trans Fat 0.0 gm, Polyunsat Fat 2.4 gm, Monounsat Fat 4.2 gm, Cholesterol 117 mg), Sodium 430 mg, Total Carbohydrate 30 gm, Dietary Fiber 1 gm, Sugars 4 gm, Protein 31 gm

Ham & Cheese Ring

Desi Rineer
Millersville, PA

Makes 8 servings
Serving size is 1 crescent roll

Prep Time: 20 minutes
Baking Time: 25 minutes

1 Tbsp. canola oil
2 Tbsp. prepared mustard
1 tsp. lemon juice
2 Tbsp. chopped onions
¼ cup parsley
1 cup chopped broccoli,
    fresh or frozen (thawed)
1 cup extra-lean, low-
    sodium chopped or
    shredded ham
1 cup fat-free cheddar
    cheese, shredded
1 8-oz. refrigerated tube,
    containing 8 reduced-fat
    crescent rolls

1. In a medium-sized mixing bowl, mix together canola oil, mustard, and lemon juice.

2. Add onions, parsley, broccoli, ham, and cheese. Blend well.

3. In a lightly greased baking dish, arrange crescent rolls in a circle with points out like a star and centers overlapping.

4. Place meat/vegetable mixture in center and fold ends of rolls into the middle.

5. Bake at 350° for 25 minutes.

Exchange List Values:
Starch 1.0, Lean Meat 1.0, Fat 0.5

Basic Nutritional Values:
Calories 154 (Calories from Fat 61), Total Fat 7 gm (Saturated Fat 2.3 gm, Trans Fat 0.0 gm, Polyunsat Fat 1.1 gm, Monounsat Fat 2.8 gm, Cholesterol 9 mg), Sodium 550 mg, Total Carbohydrate 15 gm, Dietary Fiber 1 gm, Sugars 4 gm, Protein 10 gm

A Tip —

Be prepared for eating out. Many chain restaurants make their nutrition information available online or in stores. Take advantage!

Stromboli
Monica Kehr
Portland, MI

Makes 6 servings
Serving size is 1 slice

Prep Time: *20 minutes*
Rising Time: *30-40 minutes*
Baking Time: *20 minutes*
Standing Time: *10 minutes*

1-lb. loaf frozen bread
  dough, thawed, *or*
¾ cup water
2 Tbsp. oil
2 cups bread flour
½ tsp. sugar
½ tsp. salt
2 tsp. dry yeast
Italian seasoning
1 cup fat-free mozzarella
  cheese, grated
2 ozs. turkey pepperoni,
  sliced
4 ozs. extra-lean, low-sodium
  cooked ham, chipped
½ cup sliced black olives
⅓ cup sliced mushrooms,
  optional
2 Tbsp. chopped onions,
  optional
2 Tbsp. chopped green or
  red bell pepper, *optional*

1. Make dough in bread machine, or use 1 loaf frozen bread dough, thawed. Roll dough to 10 x 15 rectangle on lightly floured surface.

2. Sprinkle dough with Italian seasoning. Cover entire rectangle with cheese, pepperoni, ham, black olives, and any of the other ingredients you want. Press toppings down gently into dough.

3. Starting with the long side of the rectangle, roll dough up into a log shape. Seal ends by pinching dough together.

4. Carefully lift onto a lightly greased baking sheet. Cover and allow to rise 30-40 minutes.

5. Bake on sheet for 20 minutes at 400°, or until lightly browned.

6. Allow to stand for 10 minutes before slicing.

Exchange List Values:
Starch 2.5, Lean Meat 1.0,
Fat 0.5

Basic Nutritional Values:
Calories 290 (Calories from Fat 48),
Total Fat 5 gm (Saturated Fat 1.4
gm, Trans Fat 0.0 gm, Polyunsat
Fat 1.5 gm, Monounsat Fat 1.9 gm,
Cholesterol 24 mg), **Sodium 1101 mg
(high sodium)**, Total Carbohydrate
40 gm, Dietary Fiber 2 gm, Sugars
4 gm, Protein 18 gm

Note: This dish is high in sodium.

Tip: Microwave pepperoni slices between paper towels before putting in stromboli to eliminate some calories.

Lamb
Main Dishes

Hoosier
Lamb Chops
Willard E. Roth, Elkhart, IN

Makes 6 servings
Serving size is 1 chop

Prep Time: *10 minutes*
Cooking Time: *20 minutes*

1 Tbsp. oil
6 4-oz. lean lamb chops
1 onion, finely chopped
1 Tbsp. balsamic vinegar
1 tsp. coarsely ground
  black pepper
¼ cup reduced-sugar
  black currant *or* black
  raspberry jam
¼ cup red wine
1 Tbsp. fresh mint,
  chopped

1. Heat oil in skillet over medium heat. Cook chops, 2 or 3 at a time, for 2 minutes per side until browned. Set aside. Reserve drippings.

2. Sauté onion for 1 minute in same skillet. Add vinegar, pepper, jam, and wine to skillet. Cook until thickened. Stir in fresh mint.

3. Return chops to skillet. Cook 2-3 minutes per side, or until just done. Adjust seasoning. Serve.

Basic Nutritional Values:
Calories 160 (Calories from Fat 64),
Total Fat 7 gm (Saturated Fat 1.9
gm, Trans Fat 0.0 gm, Polyunsat
Fat 1.0 gm, Monounsat Fat 3.4 gm,
Cholesterol 46 mg), Sodium 42 mg,
Total Carbohydrate 7 gm, Dietary
Fiber 0 gm, Sugars 5 gm, Protein 15 gm

*Tip: This sauce makes a good
gravy for couscous. If you want
to do that, double the amounts
of the sauce ingredients and
proceed according to the recipe.*

A Tip —

Take advantage of
the time you have on
weekends. Cook and bake
in large quantities and
freeze portions for meals
later in the week.

Chicken Main Dishes

Almond Lemon Chicken

Judi Janzen
Salem, OR

*Makes 6 servings
Serving size is 1 chicken breast half
with ⅙ of almond/lemon sauce*

**Prep Time: 35-40 minutes
Marinating Time: 1 hour
Cooking Time: 25-30 minutes**

5 Tbsp. lemon juice
3 Tbsp. prepared mustard
2 cloves garlic, finely
    chopped
3 Tbsp. olive oil
6 4-oz. boneless, skinless
    chicken breast halves
⅔ cup (2-oz. pkg) sliced
    almonds
2 cups chicken broth
1 tsp. cornstarch dissolved
    in 1 Tbsp. water
2 Tbsp. low-sugar orange
    or lemon marmalade
2 Tbsp. chopped fresh
    parsley
¼ tsp. red pepper flakes

1. In a large bowl, combine
first 3 ingredients. Stir in
olive oil. Add chicken and
marinate one hour at room
temperature.
2. Meanwhile, in large dry
skillet, toast almonds until

golden. Remove almonds
from pan and set aside.
3. Drain chicken, reserving
marinade. Spray skillet with
small amount of vegetable
spray. Cook chicken over
medium-high heat in skillet
until brown on each side,
about 6-10 minutes total, or
until tender. Remove and
keep warm.
4. Pour marinade into pan.
Add chicken broth and cornstarch mixture. Cook over
high heat, until it boils and
is reduced by slightly more
than half, about 5 minutes.
Stir occasionally to loosen
browned bits from skillet and
to keep sauce smooth.
5. Add marmalade and
stir over medium heat until
melted. Stir in parsley and
red pepper flakes.
6. Return chicken to pan
and heat through.
7. Place chicken on
serving platter. Spoon sauce
over. Sprinkle with toasted
almonds.

Basic Nutritional Values:
Calories 269 (Calories from Fat 133),
Total Fat 15 gm (Saturated Fat 2.1
gm, Trans Fat 0.0 gm, Polyunsat
Fat 2.5 gm, Monounsat Fat 9.3 gm,
Cholesterol 66 mg), Sodium 312 mg,
Total Carbohydrate 6 gm, Dietary
Fiber 1 gm, Sugars 3 gm, Protein 27 gm

Lemon Chicken

Ruth Shank
Gridley, IL

Makes 10 servings
Serving size is 4 ozs. or ⅒ of recipe

Prep Time: 10-15 minutes
Baking Time: 40-50 minutes

3 lbs. boneless, skinless
 chicken breasts
¼ cup lemon juice
¼ tsp. garlic powder
¼ tsp. pepper
½ tsp. salt
2 tsp. dried oregano leaves
olive oil

1. Trim excess fat from
chicken breasts and cut into
10 serving-sized pieces.
2. Arrange chicken pieces in
a greased 9 x 13 baking dish.
3. In a small mixing bowl,
combine lemon juice, garlic
powder, pepper, salt, and
oregano. Pour over chicken.
4. Bake, uncovered, at 375°
for 40-50 minutes. Brush
with olive oil every 10 to 15
minutes, turning chicken
pieces over occasionally.

Exchange List Values:
Very Lean Meat 4.0, Fat 0.5

Basic Nutritional Values:
Calories 156 (Calories from Fat 30),
Total Fat 3 gm (Saturated Fat 0.9
gm, Trans Fat 0.0 gm, Polyunsat
Fat 0.7 gm, Monounsat Fat 1.2 gm,
Cholesterol 79 mg), Sodium 186 mg,
Total Carbohydrate 1 gm, Dietary
Fiber 0 gm, Sugars 0 gm, Protein 29 gm

Crusty Baked Chicken Breast

Eileen Eash
Carlsbad, NM

Makes 10 servings
Serving size is ¾ cup
or ⅒ of recipe

Prep Time: 20-25 minutes
Baking Time: 20 minutes

2 cups dry bread crumbs
⅓ cup freshly grated
 Parmesan cheese
1 tsp. paprika
1 tsp. garlic salt
1 tsp. pepper
4 Tbsp. chopped parsley
½ cup low-fat buttermilk
1 tsp. Worcestershire sauce
1 tsp. dry mustard
4 8-oz. whole boneless,
 skinless chicken breasts,
 cut in strips

1. In a shallow bowl,
combine bread crumbs,
cheese, paprika, garlic salt,
pepper, and parsley.
2. In another shallow bowl,
combine buttermilk, Worcestershire sauce, and mustard.
3. Dip chicken pieces in
buttermilk mixture and then
roll in crumbs. Place coated
chicken in a greased 9 x 13
baking dish in a single layer.
4. Pour remaining but-
termilk over chicken.
5. Bake at 400° for 20
minutes.

Exchange List Values:
Very Lean Meat 3.0,
Starch 1.0, Fat 0.5

Basic Nutritional Values:
Calories 195 (Calories from Fat 38),
Total Fat 4 gm (Saturated Fat 1.4
gm, Trans Fat 0.0 gm, Polyunsat
Fat 0.9 gm, Monounsat Fat 1.3 gm,
Cholesterol 55 mg), Sodium 336 mg,
Total Carbohydrate 14 gm, Dietary
Fiber 1 gm, Sugars 2 gm, Protein 23 gm

*Variation: In Step 2, use 1
stick (½ cup) melted butter,
instead of buttermilk. Use 2
tsp. prepared mustard instead
of dry mustard.*
  —Erma Martin
  East Earl, PA

Savory Stir-Fried Chicken Breasts

Carolyn Baer
Conrath, WI

Makes 8 servings
Serving size is 1 chicken breast half

Prep Time: 10 minutes
Cooking Time: 6-8 minutes

1 cup flour
2½ tsp. seasoning salt
1 tsp. paprika
1 tsp. poultry seasoning
1 tsp. ground mustard
½ tsp. pepper
4 8-oz. whole boneless,
 skinless chicken breasts,
 cubed into 1½" pieces
¼ cup canola oil

1. In a plastic bag, combine flour, seasoning salt, paprika, poultry seasoning, ground mustard, and pepper.

2. Add chicken breast cubes and shake bag until chicken is well coated.

3. In a large skillet, sauté coated chicken in canola oil for 6-8 minutes. Stir constantly while sautéing.

Exchange List Values:
Starch 0.5, Fat 2.0, Very Lean Meat 3.0

Basic Nutritional Values:
Calories 232 (Calories from Fat 88), Total Fat 10 gm (Saturated Fat 1.3 gm, Trans Fat 0.0 gm, Polyunsat Fat 2.7 gm, Monounsat Fat 5.0 gm, Cholesterol 66 mg), Sodium 420 mg, Total Carbohydrate 9 gm, Dietary Fiber 0 gm, Sugars 0 gm, Protein 25 gm

Tip: This way of making chicken breasts keeps them moist, and it is so easy to prepare quickly. Be sure to make the breasts as you finish preparing your meal so you don't have to keep them warm. They are best when eaten immediately.

Chicken-Veggies-Peanut Stir-Fry
Becky Gehman
Bergton, VA

Makes 8 servings
Serving size is ¾ cup

Prep Time: 25 minutes
Cooking Time: 10-12 minutes

Chicken and Vegetables:
2 Tbsp. olive oil
1 medium-sized carrot, sliced thin
1 medium-sized green pepper, sliced thin
1 cup mushrooms, sliced thin
2 cups broccoli, cut into small pieces
1-1½ lbs. boneless, skinless, uncooked chicken breast, cut into 1" pieces
5-oz. can water chestnuts, sliced and drained
¾ cup unsalted ground peanuts

Sauce:
¼ cup cornstarch
2 Tbsp. brown sugar
½ tsp. minced gingerroot *or* ground ginger
1 clove garlic, minced
¼ cup light soy sauce
2 Tbsp. cider vinegar
1 cup fat-free, low-sodium chicken *or* beef broth
2 Tbsp. cooking wine
2 Tbsp. water

1. Make the stir-fry sauce by mixing the first 4 ingredients in a jar with a tight lid. Add the remaining ingredients and shake until well mixed. Set aside.

2. In a large skillet or wok, heat oil. Stir-fry carrot, pepper, mushrooms, and broccoli for 3-5 minutes.

3. Add chicken and water chestnuts and continue stir-frying until the chicken is no longer pink.

4. Add stir-fry sauce to chicken and vegetables. Stir while heating over medium heat, just until the sauce has thickened.

5. Spoon onto platter and sprinkle with peanuts. Serve with rice.

Exchange List Values:
Carbohydrate 1.0, Fat 1.5, Very Lean Meat 2.0

Basic Nutritional Values:
Calories 209 (Calories from Fat 84), Total Fat 9 gm (Saturated Fat 1.5 gm, Trans Fat 0.0 gm, Polyunsat Fat 2.1 gm, Monounsat Fat 5.2 gm, Cholesterol 33 mg), Sodium 396 mg, Total Carbohydrate 15 gm, Dietary Fiber 3 gm, Sugars 6 gm, Protein 16 gm

A Tip —

Heart disease is the number one killer of people with diabetes, which is why it's so important to manage your cholesterol, blood pressure, and glucose.

Chicken Marengo

Bernadette Veenstra
Rockford, MI

Makes 4 servings
Serving size is 1 breast half

Prep Time: 15-20 minutes
Cooking Time: 25-35 minutes

1 Tbsp. oil
4 4-oz. bone-in chicken
   breast halves, skin
   removed
1 Tbsp. flour
½ tsp. dried basil
¼ tsp. garlic powder
⅛ tsp. pepper
½ cup white wine, *or*
   chicken broth
2 Tbsp. tomato paste
14.5-oz. can stewed
   tomatoes
14.5-oz. can no-salt-added
   stewed tomatoes
half a coarsely chopped
   green pepper
1 onion, cut into 8 wedges
½ cup halved *or* sliced
   olives
1 lb. cooked wide no-egg-
   yolk noodles

1. Brown all sides of chicken in oil in a large skillet.
2. In a medium-sized bowl, mix together flour, basil, garlic powder, pepper, wine or broth, tomato paste and tomatoes. Pour over chicken.
3. Bring to a boil. Reduce heat, cover, and simmer 20-25 minutes. About halfway through, add green pepper, onion, and olives. Stir occasionally.

4. When finished cooking, debone chicken. Stir back into sauce.
5. Serve over noodles.

Exchange List Values:
Starch 2.5, Vegetable 3.0,
Very Lean Meat 3.0, Fat 1.5

Basic Nutritional Values:
Calories 446 (Calories from Fat 94),
Total Fat 10 gm (Saturated Fat 1.7
gm, Trans Fat 0.0 gm, Polyunsat
Fat 2.6 gm, Monounsat Fat 4.9 gm,
Cholesterol 113 mg), Sodium 531 mg,
Total Carbohydrate 52 gm, Dietary
Fiber 5 gm, Sugars 9 gm, Protein 36 gm

Chicken Monterey

Sally Holzem
Schofield, WI

Makes 4 servings
Serving size is 1 chicken breast half

Prep Time: 15 minutes
Baking Time: 30 minutes

4 4-oz. boneless, skinless
   chicken breast halves
⅛ tsp. pepper
⅓ cup bottled barbecue
   sauce
2 slices bacon, cooked as
   crisp as you like
1 cup fat-free cheddar
   cheese, shredded
4 scallions, trimmed and
   sliced
1 small tomato, chopped

1. Heat oven to 350°.
2. Place chicken in a single layer in a greased baking dish.
3. Sprinkle with pepper. Spoon on the barbecue sauce.
4. Bake in 350° oven for 25 minutes, or until all pink is gone.
5. Top each breast half with ½ slice of cooked bacon. Sprinkle with cheddar cheese.
6. Bake in oven 5 more minutes.
7. Top each breast half with fresh scallions and tomatoes just before serving.

Exchange List Values:
Carbohydrate 0.5,
Very Lean Meat 5.0

Basic Nutritional Values:
Calories 228 (Calories from Fat 38),
Total Fat 4 gm (Saturated Fat 1.2
gm, Trans Fat 0.0 gm, Polyunsat
Fat 0.8 gm, Monounsat Fat 1.6 gm,
Cholesterol 72 mg), Sodium 643 mg,
Total Carbohydrate 12 gm, Dietary
Fiber 1 gm, Sugars 7 gm, Protein 34 gm

Mexican Stuffed Chicken

Karen Waggoner, Joplin, MO

Makes 6 servings
Serving size is 1 chicken breast half

Prep Time: 20 minutes
Baking Time: 25-35 minutes

6 4-oz. boneless skinless chicken breast halves
4 ozs. fat-free mozzarella cheese, cut into 6 strips
2 4-oz. cans chopped green chilies, drained
½ cup dry bread crumbs
¼ cup grated Parmesan cheese
1 Tbsp. chili powder
¼ tsp. ground cumin
2 egg whites
2 Tbsp. water
¾ cup flour

1. Cover each chicken breast with plastic wrap and, on a cutting board, flatten each with a mallet to ⅛" thickness.
2. Place a cheese strip in the middle of each and top with a mound of chilies. Roll up and tuck in ends. Secure with toothpick. Set aside each breast half on a platter.
3. In a shallow dish, mix together bread crumbs, Parmesan cheese, chili powder, and cumin.
4. In another dish, whip egg whites with water.
5. In a third shallow dish, coat chicken with flour. Dip into whipped egg whites. Roll in crumb mixture.

6. Place, seam-side down, in a greased 9 x 13 baking dish.
7. Bake, uncovered, at 400° for 25-35 minutes, or until chicken juices run clear.
8. Be sure to remove toothpicks before serving.

Exchange List Values:
Carbohydrate 1.0,
Very Lean Meat 5.0

Basic Nutritional Values:
Calories 256 (Calories from Fat 43), Total Fat 5 gm (Saturated Fat 1.6 gm, Trans Fat 0.0 gm, Polyunsat Fat 1.0 gm, Monounsat Fat 1.5 gm, Cholesterol 72 mg), Sodium 577 mg, Total Carbohydrate 15 gm, Dietary Fiber 2 gm, Sugars 2 gm, Protein 34 gm

Chicken Angelo

Elaine Rineer
Lancaster, PA

Makes 4 servings
Serving size is 1 chicken breast half

Prep Time: 20 minutes
Baking Time: 30-35 minutes

½ lb. fresh mushrooms, sliced, *divided*
2 eggs, beaten
1 cup dried bread crumbs
4 4-oz. boneless, skinless chicken breast halves
2 Tbsp. canola oil
4 ozs. fat-free mozzarella cheese, shredded
¾ cup fat-free, reduced-sodium chicken broth

1. Place half of mushrooms in greased 9 x 13 baking pan.
2. Beat eggs in a shallow bowl. Place bread crumbs in another shallow bowl. Dip chicken in egg. Then dip in bread crumbs, spooning bread crumbs over all sides of the chicken.
3. Heat canola oil in skillet. Brown chicken on both sides in batches; do not crowd the skillet. As you finish browning pieces, place them on top of the mushrooms.
4. Arrange remaining mushrooms over chicken. Top with cheese. Pour broth over top, being careful not to disturb the cheese.
5. Bake uncovered at 350° for 30-35 minutes.
6. Serve with angel-hair pasta. Garnish with parsley.

Exchange List Values:
Starch 1.0, Fat 2.0,
Very Lean Meat 5.0

Basic Nutritional Values:
Calories 350 (Calories from Fat 115), Total Fat 13 gm (Saturated Fat 2.1 gm, Trans Fat 0.0 gm, Polyunsat Fat 3.4 gm, Monounsat Fat 6.0 gm, Cholesterol 149 mg), Sodium 648 mg, Total Carbohydrate 17 gm, Dietary Fiber 1 gm, Sugars 3 gm, Protein 38 gm

A Tip —

Use a pedometer to count the steps you take, and aim for 10,000 steps a day minimum. Anything less than that is considered sedentary!

Polynesian Chicken

Sheila Plock
Boalsburg, PA

Makes 6 servings
*Serving size is 1 chicken breast half
with fruit and sauce*

Prep Time: 15 minutes
Baking Time: 75 minutes

**6 4-oz. boneless, skinless
chicken breast halves
1 onion, sliced in rings
16-oz. can juice-packed
sliced peaches, drained
16-oz. can juice-packed dark
sweet cherries, drained
1 cup sweet-and-sour sauce
¾ cup barbecue sauce**

1. Place chicken in bottom
of a greased 9 x 13 baking
pan.
2. Place onions over
chicken. Arrange peaches
over onions. Top with cherries.
3. In a small mixing bowl,
mix together sweet-and-sour
sauce and barbecue sauce.
Spoon evenly over all other
ingredients.
4. Cover. Bake at 350° for
30 minutes. Uncover and
bake another 45 minutes.

Exchange List Values:
Carbohydrate 2.0,
Very Lean Meat 3.0

Basic Nutritional Values:
Calories 279 (Calories from Fat 26),
Total Fat 3 gm (Saturated Fat 0.8
gm, Trans Fat 0.0 gm, Polyunsat
Fat 0.7 gm, Monounsat Fat 1.0 gm,

Cholesterol 66 mg), Sodium 664 mg,
Total Carbohydrate 38 gm, Dietary
Fiber 2 gm, Sugars 30 gm, Protein 25 gm

Brandied Peach Chicken

Shari Jensen
Fountain, CO

Makes 6 servings
Serving size is 1 chicken breast half

Prep Time: 20 minutes
Baking Time: 45 minutes

**6 4-oz. boneless, skinless
chicken breast halves
1 tsp. salt
½ cup finely chopped
white onions
½ cup chopped unsalted
cashews
½ tsp. ground ginger
5 fresh medium-sized
peaches, peeled, *divided*
2 Tbsp. 65%-vegetable-oil
stick margarine, melted
¼ cup brown sugar blend
(Splenda)
2 tsp. prepared mustard
1 cup fat-free sour cream
1 Tbsp. brandy**

1. Cut a pocket in the side
of each chicken breast, or
pound chicken breasts to ¼"
thickness between sheets of
waxed paper. Sprinkle with
salt.
2. Prepare filling in a
mixing bowl by combining
onions, chopped nuts, ginger,
and 3 of the peaches cut into
small pieces.

3. Divide peach mixture
between the six chicken
breasts by stuffing it into the
created pockets or by placing
it on top of each flat cutlet,
rolling and securing the
stuffed meat with a toothpick.
4. Pour melted margarine
into a foil-lined 9 x 13 baking
dish. Place chicken on top of
margarine.
5. Bake uncovered at 350°
for 25 minutes. Turn chicken
over and bake 20 minutes
longer.
6. While chicken bakes the
last 20 minutes, combine the
remaining 2 peaches (sliced),
brown sugar blend, mustard,
sour cream, and brandy in a
saucepan.
7. Heat for 5 minutes over
medium heat, making sure
it doesn't boil. Serve over
chicken breasts.

Exchange List Values:
Carbohydrate 2.0, Fat 1.5,
Very Lean Meat 4.0

Basic Nutritional Values:
Calories 349 (Calories from Fat 103),
Total Fat 11 gm (Saturated Fat 2.5
gm, Trans Fat 0.5 gm, Polyunsat
Fat 2.6 gm, Monounsat Fat 5.0 gm,
Cholesterol 70 mg), Sodium 525 mg,
Total Carbohydrate 26 gm, Dietary
Fiber 2 gm, Sugars 21 gm, Protein 30 gm

A Tip —

Pick a meal plan you
can stick with! Starvation
diets and bizarre food
plans can't be followed for
a lifetime and are often
followed by weight gain.

Cranberry Chili Chicken

Kelly Bailey
Mechanicsburg, PA

Makes 6 servings
Serving size is 1 chicken breast half with sauce

Prep Time: 5-10 minutes
Cooking Time: 20 minutes

½ cup chili sauce
2 Tbsp. low-sugar orange marmalade
½ cup whole-berry cranberry sauce
¼ tsp. ground allspice
6 4-oz. boneless, skinless chicken breast halves
2 tsp. vegetable oil

1. In a small mixing bowl, combine chili sauce, orange marmalade, cranberry sauce, and allspice. Set aside.
2. In a large skillet, brown several breast halves at a time in oil for about 5 minutes on each side. (Be careful not to crowd the skillet or the breasts won't brown as well.) Place browned breasts on a platter until all are finished browning.
3. Return all breasts to skillet. Pour chili-cranberry mixture over chicken. Cover and simmer 8 minutes. Uncover and continue cooking 2 more minutes, or until chicken is cooked and sauce is of desired consistency.

Exchange List Values:
Carbohydrate 1.0, Fat 0.5,
Very Lean Meat 3.0

Basic Nutritional Values:
Calories 206 (Calories from Fat 39),
Total Fat 4 gm (Saturated Fat 0.9
gm, Trans Fat 0.0 gm, Polyunsat
Fat 1.1 gm, Monounsat Fat 1.8 gm,
Cholesterol 66 mg), Sodium 332 mg,
Total Carbohydrate 16 gm, Dietary
Fiber 0 gm, Sugars 13 gm, Protein 25 gm

Chicken Breasts with Fresh Fruit

Robin Schrock
Millersburg, OH

Makes 4 servings
Serving size is 1 chicken breast half with ⅓ cup fruit sauce

Prep Time: 15-20 minutes
Cooking Time: 15 minutes

1½ Tbsp. olive oil
½ tsp. salt
½ tsp. pepper
¼ tsp. garlic powder
4 4-oz. boneless, skinless chicken breast halves
2 Tbsp. canola oil
8-oz. can pineapple tidbits, drained, *or* fresh pineapple chunks
1 cup fresh, quartered strawberries
1 kiwi, peeled, quartered, and sliced
¼ cup chopped red onions
half a 4-oz. can chopped green chilies
1 tsp. cornstarch
⅓ cup orange juice

1. In a small bowl, combine olive oil, salt, pepper, and garlic powder. Spread over one side of each chicken breast.
2. In skillet, sauté chicken in canola oil, seasoned side down, 4-6 minutes. Turn and cook another 4-6 minutes, or until chicken juices run clear.
3. While chicken is sauting, cut up fruit and onions into mixing bowl. Stir in chilies.
4. In a small bowl, combine cornstarch and juice until smooth.
5. Remove cooked chicken from skillet to serving platter. Keep warm. Stir juice mixture into skillet and bring to a boil. Cook and stir for 1-2 minutes, or until thickened. Remove from heat and pour over fruit/onion/chilies mixture. Gently toss to coat.
6. Serve about ⅓ cup fruit sauce over each chicken breast.

Exchange List Values:
Very Lean Meat 4.0,
Fruit 1.0, Fat 2.5

Basic Nutritional Values:
Calories 302 (Calories from Fat 137),
Total Fat 15 gm (Saturated Fat 2.0
gm, Trans Fat 0.0 gm, Polyunsat
Fat 3.4 gm, Monounsat Fat 8.9 gm,
Cholesterol 66 mg), Sodium 421 mg,
Total Carbohydrate 16 gm, Dietary
Fiber 3 gm, Sugars 11 gm, Protein 25 gm

A Tip —

Cook once and serve often! When you're preparing meals, cook extra for leftovers.

Bruschetta Chicken Bake

Jennifer Yoder Sommers
Harrisonburg, VA

Makes 6 servings
Serving size is ¾ cup

Prep Time: 20 minutes
Cooking/Baking Time:
40-45 minutes

1½ lbs. boneless, skinless
   chicken breasts, cut into
   bite-sized pieces
14.5-oz. can no-salt-added
   diced tomatoes,
   undrained
2 cloves garlic, minced
6-oz. pkg. stuffing mix,
   chicken-flavored
½ cup water
1 tsp. dried basil leaves
½ cup low-fat mozzarella
   cheese, shredded

1. Place chicken pieces in
a microwave-safe shallow
baking dish. Sprinkle with
2 Tbsp. water. Cover with
waxed paper. Microwave on
high for 3 minutes. Stir. Cover
and microwave on high for
another 3 minutes. Allow
chicken to stand for 5 minutes.
   2. Meanwhile, place
tomatoes with liquid in medium-sized mixing bowl. Add
garlic, stuffing mix, and ½ cup
water. Stir just until stuffing is
moistened. Set aside.
   3. Place cooked chicken
in a greased 9 x 13 baking
dish. Sprinkle with basil and
cheese. Top with stuffing
mixture.

4. Bake at 400°, uncovered,
for 30 minutes, or until
heated through.

Exchange List Values:
Very Lean Meat 4.0,
Starch 1.5, Fat 0.5

Basic Nutritional Values:
Calories 274 (Calories from Fat 48),
Total Fat 5 gm (Saturated Fat 1.8
gm, Trans Fat 0.0 gm, Polyunsat
Fat 0.8 gm, Monounsat Fat 1.2 gm,
Cholesterol 72 mg), Sodium 586 mg,
Total Carbohydrate 25 gm, Dietary
Fiber 2 gm, Sugars 5 gm, Protein 31 gm

Chicken Scallopine

Betsy Chutchian
Grand Prairie, TX

Makes 8 servings
Serving size is 1 chicken breast half
with sauce

Prep Time: 5-10 minutes
Cooking Time: 25-30 minutes

8 4-oz. boneless, skinless
   chicken breast halves
½ tsp. salt
¼ tsp. pepper
¼ cup flour
1 Tbsp. canola oil
¼ lb. fresh mushrooms,
   sliced
2 tsp. lemon juice
2 Tbsp. olive oil
¼ lb. extra-lean, low-sodium
   ham, cut into thin strips
½ cup dry sherry
½ cup fat-free, low-sodium
   chicken broth

1. Place chicken breasts
between 2 sheets of plastic

wrap and pound with a mallet or rolling pin to flatten.
   2. Place salt, pepper, and
flour in shallow bowl. Dip
each breast half into mixture,
coating both sides well.
   3. Heat canola oil in skillet.
Add mushrooms and sauté
about 5 minutes.
   4. Remove mushrooms and
sprinkle with lemon juice. Set
aside.
   5. Heat olive oil with
remaining canola oil in
skillet. Add several chicken
breasts to the skillet (do not
crowd them), and sauté until
lightly browned on both sides.
Remove chicken pieces as they
brown and keep them warm
on a platter covered with foil.
   6. Add ham to skillet and
brown. Remove and keep
warm in a separate bowl.
   7. Add sherry and broth to
skillet, bringing to a boil and
cooking for 2 minutes.
   8. Stir up any brown
particles in the skillet so that
they flavor the sauce. Return
chicken and mushrooms to
skillet. Bring sauce to a boil
again, then simmer uncovered
for 3-5 minutes, until reduced
by one-third.
   9. Place chicken on a
serving platter.
   10. Spoon ham and mushrooms on top of chicken.
   11. Pour sauce over chicken
and serve.

Exchange List Values:
Carbohydrate 0.5, Fat 1.0,
Very Lean Meat 4.0

Basic Nutritional Values:
Calories 219 (Calories from Fat 74),
Total Fat 8 gm (Saturated Fat 1.5
gm, Trans Fat 0.0 gm, Polyunsat
Fat 1.5 gm, Monounsat Fat 4.6 gm,

Cholesterol 72 mg), Sodium 351 mg, Total Carbohydrate 5 gm, Dietary Fiber 0 gm, Sugars 1 gm, Protein 27 gm

Chicken Stuffin' Casserole

Janice Muller, Derwood, MD

Makes 8 servings
Serving size is 4½" x 3¼" rectangle

Prep Time: 20 minutes
Baking Time: 80 minutes

8-oz. pkg. bread stuffing
1⅔ cups sugar-free
    applesauce
1 Tbsp. celery flakes
1 tsp. poultry seasoning
½ tsp. sage
1 Tbsp. onion flakes
4 cups de-boned chicken
10.75-oz. can cream of
    chicken soup
½ soup-can of fat-free milk
pepper, black *or* lemon

1. In a large bowl, mix stuffing and applesauce together. Add celery flakes, poultry seasoning, sage, onion flakes, and enough water to make a moist stuffing mix.
2. Spread the stuffing into a greased 9 x 13 pan. Distribute chicken over the stuffing.
3. In a separate bowl, mix the soup and milk together. Pour over the casserole.
4. Finally, sprinkle the seasoned pepper heavily over the entire surface of the casserole.

5. Bake covered at 350° for 1 hour. Remove cover and continue to bake until the surface has browned and has a "crunchy" appearance, approximately 20 minutes more.

Exchange List Values:
Carbohydrate 2.0,
Lean Meat 3.0

Basic Nutritional Values:
Calories 304 (Calories from Fat 66), Total Fat 7 gm (Saturated Fat 1.8 gm, Trans Fat 0.0 gm, Polyunsat Fat 1.6 gm, Monounsat Fat 2.5 gm, Cholesterol 66 mg), Sodium 543 mg, Total Carbohydrate 33 gm, Dietary Fiber 3 gm, Sugars 8 gm, Protein 26 gm

✓ Amish Roast

Vonda Ebersole
Mt. Pleasant Mills, PA
Miriam Witmer, Lititz, PA

Makes 12 servings
Serving size is ¾ cup

Prep Time: 30 minutes
Baking Time: 1-1½ hours

½ stick (¼ cup) 65%-vege-
    table-oil stick margarine
25 slices of bread, cubed
1 cup celery, chopped
1 small onion, chopped
2-3 cups fat-free milk
1¼ cups egg substitute
½ tsp. pepper
1¼ tsp. garlic salt
5 cups cooked, cubed
    chicken

1. Melt margarine.
2. In a very large bowl, pour melted margarine over bread cubes. Stir thoroughly to distribute margarine through the bread cubes.
3. In another mixing bowl, combine chopped celery and onion, milk, egg substitute, and seasonings.
4. Pour mixture over bread cubes. Add diced chicken. Mix well.
5. Place in greased roasting pans or casseroles. Cover each one.
6. Bake for 1 hour at 250°, stirring every 15 minutes. Continue baking until heated through.

Exchange List Values:
Starch 2.0, Lean Meat 3.0

Basic Nutritional Values:
Calories 308 (Calories from Fat 84), Total Fat 9 gm (Saturated Fat 2.2 gm, Trans Fat 0.5 gm, Polyunsat Fat 3.0 gm, Monounsat Fat 2.8 gm, Cholesterol 53 mg), Sodium 574 mg, Total Carbohydrate 29 gm, Dietary Fiber 1 gm, Sugars 5 gm, Protein 25 gm

My grandmother made this for Thanksgiving and Christmas get-togethers.
—Vonda Ebersole

A Tip —

When eating fast food, choose grilled, broiled, baked, or rotisserie sandwiches. Stay away from breaded meats, mayonnaise, and cheese.

Cordon Bleu Casserole

Denise Martin, Lancaster, PA

Makes 12 servings
Serving size is 3¼″ x 3″ rectangle
or ¹⁄₁₂ of recipe

Prep Time: 20 minutes
Baking Time: 30 minutes

5 cups cubed, fully cooked
  chicken breast
2½ cups cubed, fully
  cooked, extra-lean, low-fat
  ham
½ cup fat-free cheddar
  cheese, shredded
1 cup chopped onions
2 Tbsp. canola oil
⅓ cup flour
2 cups fat-free half-and-half
1 tsp.-1 Tbsp. dill weed,
  according to your taste
  preference
⅛-1 tsp. dry mustard,
  according to your taste
  preference
⅛-½ tsp. ground nutmeg,
  according to your taste
  preference

Topping:
1 cup dry bread crumbs
¼-1 tsp. dill weed,
  according to your taste
  preference
¼ cup fat-free cheddar
  cheese, shredded
¼-½ cup chopped walnuts,
  according to your taste
  preference

1. In a large bowl, combine
chicken, ham, and cheese. Set
aside.

2. In saucepan, sauté
onions in canola oil until
tender. Add flour. Stir to form
a paste.
3. Over low heat, gradually
add half-and-half, stirring
constantly. Bring to a boil,
and boil 1 minute or until
thickened.
4. Add dill, mustard,
and nutmeg and mix well.
Remove from heat and pour
over meat/cheese mixture.
Spoon into a greased 9 x 13
baking pan.
5. In the large mixing
bowl, toss together bread
crumbs and dill. Stir in
cheese and walnuts. Sprinkle
over casserole.
6. Bake uncovered at
350° for 30 minutes, or until
heated through.

Exchange List Values:
Carbohydrate 1.0, Fat 1.0,
Very Lean Meat 4.0

Basic Nutritional Values:
Calories 255 (Calories from Fat 69),
Total Fat 8 gm (Saturated Fat 1.5
gm, Trans Fat 0.0 gm, Polyunsat
Fat 2.6 gm, Monounsat Fat 2.6 gm,
Cholesterol 66 mg), Sodium 456 mg,
Total Carbohydrate 16 gm, Dietary
Fiber 1 gm, Sugars 5 gm, Protein 28 gm

Tip: This recipe can be
prepared the day before through
Step 4. When ready to heat,
remove from the refrigerator
and sprinkle on topping. Add
5-10 minutes to the baking time.

Garden Chicken Casserole

Virginia Bender, Dover, DE

Makes 12 servings
Serving size is 3″ x 3¼″ rectangle

Prep Time: 10 minutes
Baking Time: 60 minutes

3 10.75-oz. cans fat-free,
  reduced-sodium cream
  of chicken soup
1½ cups fat-free mayonnaise
¼ cup chopped onions
2 cups chopped celery
8-oz. can sliced water
  chestnuts, drained
4 cups diced, cooked
  chicken
2 cups cooked rice
½ cup sliced almonds
1 sleeve butter snack
  crackers, crushed

1. In a large mixing bowl,
combine soup, mayonnaise,
onions, celery, water
chestnuts, chicken, rice, and
almonds. Pour into a greased
9 x 13 baking pan.
2. Sprinkle with crackers.
3. Bake at 350° for 60
minutes.

Exchange List Values:
Carbohydrate 2.0,
Lean Meat 2.0, Fat 0.5

Basic Nutritional Values:
Calories 289 (Calories from Fat 94),
Total Fat 10 gm (Saturated Fat 2.3
gm, Trans Fat 0.0 gm, Polyunsat
Fat 2.7 gm, Monounsat Fat 4.4 gm,
Cholesterol 49 mg), Sodium 685 mg,
Total Carbohydrate 29 gm, Dietary
Fiber 2 gm, Sugars 5 gm, Protein 18 gm

Variations:

1. In place of water chestnuts, stir in 4 hard-cooked chopped eggs.

2. Replace cracker/butter topping with a layer of 3 cups crushed potato chips, followed by a layer of 2 cups shredded cheddar cheese.

—**Violette Harris Denney**
Carrollton, GA

Cheesy Chicken Tetrazzini

Andrea Yoder, Drexel, MO

Makes 16 servings
Serving size is 2¼" x 3¼" rectangle or ¹⁄₁₆ of recipe

Prep Time: 20 minutes
Cooking/Baking Time:
60 minutes
Standing Time: 20-30 minutes

4 lbs. boneless, skinless chicken breasts
3 reduced-sodium chicken bouillon cubes
8 ozs. uncooked spaghetti
10.75-oz. can cream of chicken soup
10.75-oz. can cream of mushroom soup
4-oz. can chopped green chilies, drained
2-oz. jar diced pimentos, drained
6 Tbsp. freshly grated Parmesan cheese
1 cup (4 ozs.) reduced-fat cheddar cheese, shredded
1 cup fat-free milk
⅛ tsp. garlic powder

4-oz. can sliced mushrooms
½ cup sliced almonds, *optional*

1. Place chicken and bouillon cubes in large stockpot. Cover with water. Cover pot and bring to a boil. Continue simmering until chicken is tender.

2. Lift chicken out of broth. Reserve broth.

3. Allow chicken to cool, and then cut into cubes. Set chicken aside.

4. While chicken is cooling, cook spaghetti in chicken broth according to package directions (adding enough water to equal one quart). Drain.

5. In a large mixing bowl, mix together soups, chilies, pimentos, cheeses, milk, garlic powder, mushrooms, and almonds.

6. Add spaghetti and chicken and mix well.

7. Bake in a greased 9 x 13 baking casserole for 30 minutes. Allow to stand for 20 or 30 minutes before serving.

Exchange List Values:
Starch 1.0, Fat 0.5,
Very Lean Meat 4.0

Basic Nutritional Values:
Calories 248 (Calories from Fat 55), Total Fat 6 gm (Saturated Fat 2.4 gm, Trans Fat 0.0 gm, Polyunsat Fat 1.1 gm, Monounsat Fat 1.8 gm, Cholesterol 76 mg), Sodium 387 mg, Total Carbohydrate 16 gm, Dietary Fiber 1 gm, Sugars 2 gm, Protein 30 gm

Tip: Sprinkle with bread crumbs and paprika before baking, if you wish.

Honey Chicken

Lisa Cutler
Willow Street, PA
Christie Detamore-Hunsberger
Harrisonburg, VA

Makes 8 servings
Serving size is 1 chicken breast half

Prep Time: 15-20 minutes
Baking Time: 50-60 minutes

8 4-oz. boneless, skinless chicken breast halves
¼ cup soft, low-fat tub margarine
½ cup honey
¼ cup prepared mustard
½ tsp. salt
1 tsp. curry
1 Tbsp. dry *or* **minced onion,** *optional*

1. Wash and pat chicken dry. Arrange in a greased 9 x 13 baking pan.

2. Melt margarine in a medium-sized saucepan and then add remaining ingredients. Mix well and pour over chicken.

3. Bake uncovered, basting every 15 minutes, at 350° for 50-60 minutes, or until chicken is cooked through but not burned.

Exchange List Values:
Carbohydrate 1.0, Fat 1.0,
Very Lean Meat 3.0

Basic Nutritional Values:
Calories 218 (Calories from Fat 48), Total Fat 5 gm (Saturated Fat 1.0 gm, Trans Fat 0.0 gm, Polyunsat Fat 1.2 gm, Monounsat Fat 2.4 gm, Cholesterol 66 mg), Sodium 333 mg, Total Carbohydrate 18 gm, Dietary Fiber 0 gm, Sugars 18 gm, Protein 24 gm

Turkey or Chicken Curry

Angie Clemens
Dayton, VA

Makes 10 servings
Serving size is ¾ cup

Prep Time: 30 minutes
Cooking Time: 75 minutes

⅔ cup minced onions
1 cup chopped apples
2 Tbsp. vegetable oil
¼ cup flour
1 Tbsp. curry powder
hot sauce to taste
1 qt. fat-free, reduced-
    sodium chicken broth
2 cloves garlic, crushed
2 pieces dried gingerroot,
    or ½ tsp. powdered
    ginger
1 sliced large tomato, *or*
    1 qt. stewed tomatoes,
    drained, *optional*
2 cups diced cooked turkey
    or chicken

1. In a large skillet, heat onions and apples in oil. Cook, covered, until clear, stirring several times.
2. Add flour and curry.
3. Slowly stir in hot sauce, if you wish, and the broth until well blended. Add garlic, ginger, and tomato, if you wish.
4. Bring to a boil. Cover and simmer 1 hour, stirring occasionally.
5. Add meat and cook long enough to heat through.
6. Serve over rice along with serving dishes of chutney,

sliced green onions, shredded coconut, peanuts, pineapple chunks, and raisins or craisins, if you wish.

Exchange List Values:
Carbohydrate 0.5,
Lean Meat 1.0

Basic Nutritional Values:
Calories 105 (Calories from Fat 39), Total Fat 4 gm (Saturated Fat 0.7 gm, Trans Fat 0.0 gm, Polyunsat Fat 1.3 gm, Monounsat Fat 2.0 gm, Cholesterol 21 mg), Sodium 221 mg, Total Carbohydrate 6 gm, Dietary Fiber 1 gm, Sugars 2 gm, Protein 10 gm

Tip: Bake the rice while preparing the curry. We prefer the texture of baked rice, and I don't have to worry about it cooking over or burning on the stove.

Easy Chicken Fajitas

Jessica Hontz
Coatesville, PA

Makes 6 servings
Serving size is 1 fajita

Prep Time: 20 minutes
Marinating Time: 4-8 hours,
    or overnight
Cooking Time: 10 minutes

1 lb. boneless, skinless
    chicken breasts
2 Tbsp. dry no-salt-added
    Italian seasoning mix
    (see recipe on page 254)
8-oz. bottle fat-free Italian
    salad dressing
1 cup salsa

1 green pepper, sliced
half a medium-sized
    onion, sliced
6 7-8″-flour tortillas

Optional Toppings:
shredded Monterey Jack
    cheese
shredded lettuce
sour cream
chopped tomatoes
salsa
hot pepper sauce

1. Cut chicken into thin strips. Place in large mixing bowl.
2. Add dry salad dressing mix and salad dressing. Mix well. Cover and marinate 4-8 hours in the fridge.
3. In a large skillet, combine drained chicken strips, salsa, and pepper and onion slices. Stir-fry until chicken is cooked and peppers and onions are soft.
4. Place chicken mix in tortillas with your choice of optional toppings.

Exchange List Values:
Starch 1.5, Vegetable 1.0,
Very Lean Meat 2.0, Fat 1.0

Basic Nutritional Values:
Calories 257 (Calories from Fat 50), Total Fat 6 gm (Saturated Fat 1.4 gm, Trans Fat 0.0 gm, Polyunsat Fat 1.2 gm, Monounsat Fat 2.5 gm, Cholesterol 44 mg), **Sodium 710 mg (high sodium)**, Total Carbohydrate 30 gm, Dietary Fiber 3 gm, Sugars 4 gm, Protein 21 gm

Note: This recipe is high in sodium.

Variation: The cooked chicken can also be used on salads.

Mexican Chicken Bake

Gretchen H. Maust
Keezletown, VA

Makes 8 servings
Serving size is ¾ cup or ⅛ of recipe

Prep Time: 20 minutes
Baking Time: 1 hour

2 cups cooked brown rice
1 lb. cooked skinless
   chicken breast, cubed
2 14.5-oz. cans diced
   tomatoes, undrained
15-oz. can black beans,
   drained
1 cup corn
1 cup red bell pepper, diced
1 cup green pepper, diced
1 Tbsp. cumin
1 Tbsp. chili powder
½ tsp. salt
¼ tsp. pepper
4 garlic cloves, minced
1 cup reduced-fat cheddar
   cheese, shredded

1. Spread rice on bottom of greased 3-4-qt. casserole dish.
2. In a large mixing bowl, combine remaining ingredients, except cheese. Pour over rice. Cover.
3. Bake at 375° for 45 minutes. Remove from oven. Top with cheese. Reduce heat to 300°. Bake, uncovered, for an additional 15 minutes, or until bubbly.

Exchange List Values:
Starch 2.0, Fat 0.5,
Very Lean Meat 3.0

Basic Nutritional Values:
Calories 280 (Calories from Fat 57), Total Fat 6 gm (Saturated Fat 2.5 gm, Trans Fat 0.0 gm, Polyunsat Fat 1.0 gm, Monounsat Fat 1.9 gm, Cholesterol 58 mg), Sodium 561 mg, Total Carbohydrate 30 gm, Dietary Fiber 6 gm, Sugars 6 gm, Protein 27 gm

Variation: For a vegetarian version of this dish, leave out the chicken.

Stuffed Quesadillas

Stacy Schmucker Stoltzfus
Enola, PA

Makes 4 servings
Serving size is 1 full quesadilla

Prep Time: 20-25 minutes
Cooking Time: 6-10 minutes

8 6" corn tortillas
1 cup fat-free mozzarella
   cheese, shredded
1 cup canned black beans,
   drained
¼ cup diced onions
½ cup chopped cilantro
2 plum tomatoes, chopped
1 red or green bell pepper,
   chopped
2 cups shredded, cooked
   chicken
1 lime, cut into wedges
sour cream and salsa,
   optional

1. Place 4 tortillas onto workspace. Sprinkle ⅛ cup cheese over each tortilla.
2. Dividing each ingredient into 4 parts, continue layering on each tortilla in this order: black beans, onions, cilantro, tomatoes, pepper, and chicken. Top each with ⅛ cup cheese.
3. Squeeze lime juice over all. Cover with remaining tortillas.
4. Heat large skillet on medium-high heat. Place 2 tortilla stacks in hot skillet and cook 3-5 minutes, or until tortilla is browned.
5. Carefully flip onto other side and cook until cheese is melted.
6. Remove from pan and cut with a pizza cutter into fourths. Keep warm.
7. Continue with the remaining 2 tortilla stacks, browning and flipping until done. Cut into fourths, also.
8. Serve with sour cream and salsa on the side, if desired.

Exchange List Values:
Starch 2.5, Fat 0.5,
Very Lean Meat 4.0

Basic Nutritional Values:
Calories 360 (Calories from Fat 63), Total Fat 7 gm (Saturated Fat 1.7 gm, Trans Fat 0.0 gm, Polyunsat Fat 2.1 gm, Monounsat Fat 2.2 gm, Cholesterol 66 mg), Sodium 479 mg, Total Carbohydrate 37 gm, Dietary Fiber 8 gm, Sugars 5 gm, Protein 35 gm

A Tip —

Fiber is power food. Eat as many fiber-rich foods as possible.

Curried Chicken Pitas

Sharon Eshleman
Ephrata, PA

Makes 8 servings
Serving size is ½ filled pita pocket

Prep Time: 15 minutes

½ cup fat-free mayonnaise
1 Tbsp. honey
1 Tbsp. pickle relish
¾-1 tsp. curry powder, according to your taste preference
2 cups cubed cooked chicken
1 cup halved grapes *or* chopped apples
½ cup chopped pecans
4 pita breads, halved
8 lettuce leaves

1. In a bowl, combine mayonnaise, honey, pickle relish, and curry powder.
2. Stir in chicken, grapes, and pecans.
3. Line pita halves with lettuce. Spoon ½ cup chicken mixture into each pita and slice in half before serving.

Exchange List Values:
Starch 1.0, Lean Meat 1.0, Carbohydrate 1.0, Fat 0.5

Basic Nutritional Values:
Calories 235 (Calories from Fat 74), Total Fat 8 gm (Saturated Fat 1.2 gm, Trans Fat 0.0 gm, Polyunsat Fat 2.2 gm, Monounsat Fat 4.0 gm, Cholesterol 31 mg), Sodium 330 mg, Total Carbohydrate 27 gm, Dietary Fiber 2 gm, Sugars 8 gm, Protein 14 gm

Chicken and Broccoli Pita Sandwiches

Vonnie Oyer
Hubbard, OR

Makes 8 servings
Serving size is ½ filled pita pocket

Prep Time: 15 minutes

---

2 cups chopped cooked chicken
2 tomatoes, chopped
1½ cups chopped raw broccoli
1 hard-cooked egg, chopped
⅓ cup cooked rice
½ cup fat-free cheddar cheese, shredded
1 avocado, chopped, *optional*
4 pita breads

Dressing:
2 Tbsp. honey
2 Tbsp. prepared mustard
¾ cup fat-free mayonnaise

1. Mix chicken, tomatoes, broccoli, egg, rice, cheese, and avocado together in a large bowl.
2. Mix dressing ingredients in a small bowl.
3. Pour dressing over chicken mixture and stir gently.
4. Cut pita breads in half. Fill with chicken mixture. Cut in half again before serving.

Exchange List Values:
Carbohydrate 1.0, Starch 1.0, Lean Meat 1.0

Basic Nutritional Values:
Calories 221 (Calories from Fat 34), Total Fat 4 gm (Saturated Fat 1.0 gm, Trans Fat 0.0 gm, Polyunsat Fat 0.9 gm, Monounsat Fat 1.3 gm, Cholesterol 58 mg), Sodium 476 mg, Total Carbohydrate 29 gm, Dietary Fiber 2 gm, Sugars 8 gm, Protein 17 gm

---

I first had this at the home of an older woman in our church. I had hung wallpaper for her, and then enjoyed her company and these pocket sandwiches for lunch.

Variations: If you'd like a zestier flavor, add salt, pepper, and curry powder, to taste, to the dressing.

A Tip —

When visiting your doctor, plan ahead. Write down all of the questions you want to ask beforehand.

Chicken Salad Sandwiches

Rosalie Duerksen
Canton, KS

Makes 6 servings
Serviung size is 1 sandwich

Prep Time: 15 minutes

12.5-oz can cooked
  chicken, drained
¼ cup diced celery
¼ cup golden raisins
¼ cup dried cranberries
¼ cup sliced almonds
¼ tsp. salt
⅛ tsp. pepper
¾ cup fat-free mayonnaise
6 slices whole-wheat bread

1. Place drained chicken in
a bowl. Add celery, raisins,
cranberries, almonds, salt,
and pepper.
2 Stir in mayonnaise until
well blended.
3. Spread onto bread.

Exchange List Values:
Starch 1.0, Fruit 0.5, Fat 0.5,
Very Lean Meat 2.0

Basic Nutritional Values:
Calories 207 (Calories from Fat 38),
Total Fat 4 gm (Saturated Fat 0.4
gm, Trans Fat 0.0 gm, Polyunsat
Fat 1.0 gm, Monounsat Fat 2.1 gm,
Cholesterol 31 mg), Sodium 602 mg,
Total Carbohydrate 26 gm, Dietary
Fiber 3 gm, Sugars 11 gm, Protein 17 gm

Turkey Main Dishes

Turkey Stir-Fry

Arianne Hochstetler
Goshen, IN

Makes 6 servings
Serving size is ¾ cup

Prep Time: 15-20 minutes
Cooking Time: 20 minutes

1½ lbs. boneless turkey,
  cut into strips
1 Tbsp. cooking oil
1 large onion, chopped
1 carrot, julienned
half a green pepper, sliced
2 cups fresh, sliced
  mushrooms
1 cup fat-free, no-salt-added
  chicken broth
3 Tbsp. cornstarch
3 Tbsp. light soy sauce
½ tsp. ginger
1 tsp. curry powder
2 cups pea pods, trimmed,
  or 2 cups frozen stir-fry
  vegetables
⅓ cup cashews, *optional*

A Tip —

  Cook at home as much
as possible. Eating at
restaurants gives you less
control over your food
and often means more fat
and calories.

---

1. In a large skillet or
wok, stir-fry turkey in oil
over medium-high heat until
no longer pink, about 5-6
minutes. Remove turkey from
pan and keep warm.
2. Stir-fry the onion,
carrot, green pepper, and
mushrooms until crisp-tender,
about 5 minutes.
3. In a small bowl, combine
chicken broth, cornstarch,
soy sauce, ginger, and curry
powder until smooth.
4. Add to the skillet. Cook
and stir until thickened and
bubbly.
5. Return turkey to skillet
with pea pods. Cook and stir
until heated through.
6. Serve over cooked rice.
Top with cashews, if desired.

Exchange List Values:
Vegetable 2.0, Lean Meat 2.0

Basic Nutritional Values:
Calories 172 (Calories from Fat 47),
Total Fat 5 gm (Saturated Fat 1.1
gm, Trans Fat 0.0 gm, Polyunsat
Fat 1.5 gm, Monounsat Fat 1.9 gm,
Cholesterol 40 mg), Sodium 417 mg,
Total Carbohydrate 13 gm, Dietary
Fiber 2 gm, Sugars 4 gm, Protein 18 gm

---

*Variation: You can use sliced
beef, pork, or chicken instead of
turkey.*

Tips:
  *1. Chop all the vegetables
before you cut the turkey into
strips. Then all ingredients are
ready to go as you need them.*
  *2. Cook the rice at the same
time as you are preparing and
cooking the stir-fry.*

109

Orange-Glazed Turkey Cutlets

Rosemarie Fitzgerald
Gibsonia, PA

Makes 4 servings
Serving size is 3 ozs. turkey breast
with 4 tsp. marmalade sauce
or ¼ of recipe

Prep Time: 10 minutes
Cooking Time: 10 minutes

1 lb. turkey breast cutlets
   or slices
salt and pepper to taste
ground cinnamon to taste
2 tsp. oil
⅓ cup reduced-sugar
   orange marmalade
⅛ tsp. ground cinnamon
⅛ tsp. ground nutmeg
⅛ tsp. ground ginger

1. Lightly sprinkle one side of cutlets with salt, pepper, and cinnamon.

2. In large non-stick skillet, over medium-high heat, sauté turkey cutlets in oil for 1-2 minutes per side, or until turkey is no longer pink in the center. Do in batches if your skillet isn't large enough to hold the cutlets all at once with space around each one.

3. Remove turkey as it finishes browning to platter and keep warm.

4. In small saucepan, over medium heat, combine marmalade, cinnamon, nutmeg, and ginger. Cook 1-2 minutes or until marmalade melts and mixture is heated through.

5. To serve, spoon marmalade sauce over cutlets.

Exchange List Values:
Carbohydrate 0.5,
Very Lean Meat 4.0

Basic Nutritional Values:
Calories 175 (Calories from Fat 26),
Total Fat 3 gm (Saturated Fat 0.4 gm, Trans Fat 0.0 gm, Polyunsat Fat 0.8 gm, Monounsat Fat 1.4 gm, Cholesterol 74 mg), Sodium 47 mg, Total Carbohydrate 8 gm, Dietary Fiber 0 gm, Sugars 7 gm, Protein 27 gm

Savory Turkey

Clara Newswanger
Gordonville, PA

Makes 12 servings
Serving size is 3 ozs. turkey
with sauce

Prep Time: 15 minutes
Baking Time: 35-45 minutes

½ cup onions, chopped
2 Tbsp. canola oil
2 9-oz. cans mushrooms,
   drained
4 Tbsp. flour
2 cubes reduced-sodium
   beef bouillon
1 cup water
2 Tbsp. light soy sauce
2 lbs. boneless skinless
   turkey thighs, cut in 2"
   chunks

A Tip —
   There is no such thing as a single "diabetic diet" that works for everyone.

1. In medium-sized saucepan, sauté onions in canola oil.

2. Add mushrooms and flour. Stir until well mixed.

3. Add bouillon cubes, water, and soy sauce, Mix well and bring to a boil.

4. Meanwhile, place turkey thighs in a greased baking dish. Pour sauce over thighs.

5. Bake uncovered at 350° for 35-45 minutes, or until tender.

Exchange List Values:
Carbohydrate 0.5,
Lean Meat 3.0

Basic Nutritional Values:
Calories 207 (Calories from Fat 70), Total Fat 8 gm (Saturated Fat 1.9 gm, Trans Fat 0.0 gm, Polyunsat Fat 2.3 gm, Monounsat Fat 2.5 gm, Cholesterol 67 mg), Sodium 379 mg, . Total Carbohydrate 6 gm, Dietary Fiber 2 gm, Sugars 1 gm, Protein 27 gm

Seafood Main Dishes

Shrimp with Ginger and Lime

Joy Uhler
Richardson, TX

Makes 4 servings
Serving size is ¼ recipe

Prep Time: 15-20 minutes
Cooking Time: 10 minutes

3 Tbsp. lime juice
4 Tbsp. olive oil, *divided*
1 Tbsp. minced gingerroot
1 Tbsp. brown sugar
1 tsp. grated lime zest
1 tsp. sesame seed oil
1 large garlic clove, minced
1 lb. cooked shrimp,
   peeled and deveined
cooked rice*
2 Tbsp. cilantro, chopped

1. In a large mixing bowl, stir together lime juice, 3 Tbsp. olive oil, gingerroot, brown sugar, lime zest, sesame seed oil, and garlic clove.

2. Stir in shrimp and mix well so that they're covered with the marinade. Allow shrimp to marinate for 15 minutes.

3. Pour 1 Tbsp. olive oil into large skillet or wok. Spoon in shrimp mixture and stir-fry until heated through.

4. Serve over prepared rice. Sprinkle with chopped cilantro.

Exchange List Values:
Very Lean Meat 2.0, Fat 2.0

Basic Nutritional Values:
Calories 155 (Calories from Fat 88), Total Fat 10 gm (Saturated Fat 1.4 gm, Trans Fat 0.0 gm, Polyunsat Fat 1.4 gm, Monounsat Fat 6.6 gm, Cholesterol 131 mg), Sodium 152 mg, Total Carbohydrate 2 gm, Dietary Fiber 0 gm, Sugars 2 gm, Protein 14 gm

** Rice is **not** included in the nutritional analysis.*

Sesame Shrimp and Asparagus

Karen Kay Tucker
Manteca, CA

Makes 6 servings
Serving size is ¾ cup

Prep Time: 30 minutes
Cooking Time: 10 minutes

1½ lbs. fresh asparagus
1 Tbsp. sesame seeds
3 Tbsp. canola oil
2 small red onions, sliced
   in rings
1½ lbs. large shrimp,
   peeled and deveined
4 tsp. light soy sauce
¼ tsp. salt

1. About 30 minutes before serving, prepare asparagus. Hold base of each stalk firmly and bend. The end will break off at the spot where it becomes too tough to eat. Discard ends or freeze and use when making stock.

2. Wash and trim asparagus. Then cut into 2″ pieces and steam in ½″ water in saucepan until crisp-tender. Plunge asparagus into cold water to stop cooking. Set aside.

3. In a large skillet or wok, over medium heat, toast sesame seeds until golden brown, stirring seeds and shaking skillet often. Remove seeds to small bowl.

4. In same skillet or wok, over medium-high heat, heat oil until hot. Add onions and shrimp. Cook until shrimp are pink, about 5 minutes.

5. Drain asparagus. Add to skillet with shrimp. Stir in sesame seeds, soy sauce, and salt. Heat until asparagus is warm.

Exchange List Values:
Vegetable 1.0, Fat 1.5,
Very Lean Meat 2.0

Basic Nutritional Values:
Calories 174 (Calories from Fat 79), Total Fat 9 gm (Saturated Fat 0.8 gm, Trans Fat 0.0 gm, Polyunsat Fat 2.8 gm, Monounsat Fat 4.6 gm, Cholesterol 131 mg), Sodium 384 mg, Total Carbohydrate 8 gm, Dietary Fiber 2 gm, Sugars 3 gm, Protein 17 gm

Cajun Shrimp

Mary Ann Potenta
Bridgewater, NJ

Makes 5 servings
Serving size is 4 ozs. shrimp

Prep Time: just minutes!
Cooking Time: 10-12 minutes

3 Tbsp. canola oil, *divided*
½ cup chopped green
  onions
1 tsp. minced garlic
1 tsp. cayenne pepper
½ tsp. white pepper
½ tsp. black pepper
¼ tsp. dry mustard
¼ tsp. salt
1 tsp. Tabasco sauce
2 lbs. shrimp, peeled and
  cleaned
cooked rice*

1. Heat 2 Tbsp. canola oil in large skillet. Add onions and garlic and sauté till clear, but not brown, about 1 minute.
2. Add peppers, mustard, and salt. Cook and stir for 3 minutes.
3. Mix in 1 Tbsp. canola oil and Tabasco sauce until blended.
4. Add shrimp. Cook just until pink. Do not overcook.
5. Serve over cooked rice.

Exchange List Values:
Very Lean Meat 3.0,
Fat 2.0

Basic Nutritional Values:
Calories 187 (Calories from Fat 87), Total Fat 10 gm (Saturated Fat 0.9 gm, Trans Fat 0.0 gm, Polyunsat Fat 3.0 gm, Monounsat Fat 5.2 gm, Cholesterol 209 mg), Sodium 364 mg, Total Carbohydrate 1 gm, Dietary Fiber 1 gm, Sugars 0 gm, Protein 23 gm

* *Rice is **not** included in the nutritional analysis.*

Note: *This is hot! You can tone things down by reducing the amounts of the 3 peppers and the Tabasco sauce.*

Shrimp Primavera

Elaine Rineer
Lancaster, PA

Makes 4 servings
Serving size is ¾ cup

Prep Time: 20 minutes
Cooking Time: 10 minutes

1 Tbsp., plus 1 tsp.,
  vegetable *or* olive oil
1½ cups chopped broccoli
½ cup thinly sliced carrots
1 cup sliced mushrooms
2 garlic cloves, minced
1 cup fat-free, reduced-
  sodium chicken broth
1 Tbsp. cornstarch
1 lb. shrimp, peeled and
  deveined
2 Tbsp. grated Parmesan
  cheese
2 Tbsp. parsley

1. In large skillet or wok, sauté broccoli and carrots in oil. Stir-fry until carrots are crisp-tender.
2. Stir in mushrooms and garlic. Stir-fry 1 minute.
3. In a small bowl, whisk together broth and cornstarch. Pour over vegetables.
4. Add shrimp. Cook until shrimp turns pink and sauce thickens.
5. Stir in remaining ingredients.

Exchange List Values:
Vegetable 1.0, Fat 1.0,
Very Lean Meat 2.0

Basic Nutritional Values:
Calories 155 (Calories from Fat 57), Total Fat 6 gm (Saturated Fat 1.0 gm, Trans Fat 0.0 gm, Polyunsat Fat 1.7 gm, Monounsat Fat 3.1 gm, Cholesterol 133 mg), Sodium 321 mg, Total Carbohydrate 7 gm, Dietary Fiber 2 gm, Sugars 2 gm, Protein 17 gm

Baked Scallops

Rosemarie Fitzgerald
Gibsonia, PA

Makes 4 servings
Serving size is ¾ cup

Prep Time: 10 minutes
Baking Time: 15 minutes

1 lb. scallops
½ cup dry bread crumbs
2 tsp. 65%-vegetable-oil
  stick margarine
½ cup white wine
3 Tbsp. freshly grated
  Parmesan cheese
salt and pepper to taste
¼ cup chopped fresh
  parsley

1. Rinse scallops and pat dry. Place in large mixing bowl and sprinkle with bread crumbs. Toss to coat.

2. Place in a greased baking dish, large enough to hold the scallops in one layer.

3. Cut margarine into bits and divide over the scallops. Pour wine into bottom of baking dish, being careful not to disturb the bread-crumb coating on the scallops.

4. Bake, uncovered, at 350° for 15 minutes. Remove from oven and turn on broiler.

5. Sprinkle scallops with Parmesan cheese. Place under broiler for 5-10 seconds, until cheese has browned slightly. Watch carefully to keep from burning.

6. Season with salt and freshly ground pepper. Sprinkle with chopped parsley.

Exchange List Values:
Starch 0.5, Fat 1.0,
Very Lean Meat 3.0

Basic Nutritional Values:
Calories 189 (Calories from Fat 43), Total Fat 5 gm (Saturated Fat 1.4 gm, Trans Fat 0.3 gm, Polyunsat Fat 1.3 gm, Monounsat Fat 1.1 gm, Cholesterol 49 mg), Sodium 377 mg, Total Carbohydrate 10 gm, Dietary Fiber 1 gm, Sugars 1 gm, Protein 23 gm

---

A Tip —

Everyday activities burn calories and can help with weight loss. Just mowing the lawn can burn 200 calories!

Scallops Au Gratin
Anne Jones
Ballston Lake, NY

Makes 4 servings
Serving size is ¾ cup

Prep Time: 15 minutes
Baking Time: 20-30 minutes

16 butter-flavored crackers
½ tsp. paprika
½ tsp. garlic powder
1 lb. bay scallops
2 Tbsp. canola oil
2 Tbsp. sherry
½ cup fat-free Swiss cheese, shredded

1. Crush crackers in plastic bag. Add paprika and garlic powder and mix.

2. Add scallops to bag and shake to coat.

3. Place scallops in a greased 8 x 8 baking pan, or 4 greased individual baking dishes.

4. In a small saucepan, warm canola oil and add sherry. Stir to mix. Pour over scallops, dividing if using small baking dishes.

5. Bake at 375° for 15 minutes. Cover with Swiss cheese and continue baking until bubbly.

Exchange List Values:
Starch 0.5, Fat 2.0,
Very Lean Meat 3.0

Basic Nutritional Values:
Calories 244 (Calories from Fat 101), Total Fat 11 gm (Saturated Fat 1.1 gm, Trans Fat 0.0 gm, Polyunsat Fat 3.7 gm, Monounsat Fat 5.5 gm, Cholesterol 48 mg), Sodium 503 mg, Total Carbohydrate 9 gm, Dietary Fiber 0 gm, Sugars 2 gm, Protein 24 gm

---

Crab-Topped Catfish
Vicki Hill
Memphis, TN

Makes 6 serving
Serving size is 1 fillet with topping

Prep Time: 5-10 minutes
Baking Time: 27 minutes

6 4-oz. catfish fillets
6-oz. can white crabmeat, drained and flaked
½ cup fat-free mayonnaise
1 tsp. lemon juice
paprika
⅓ cup sliced almonds

1. Place catfish on greased cookie sheet.

2. Bake, uncovered, at 350° for 22 minutes, or until fish flakes easily with a fork. Drain.

3. Meanwhile, combine crab, mayonnaise, and lemon juice in a bowl.

4. After fish has baked for 22 minutes, spoon crab mix evenly over fish. Sprinkle with paprika and sliced almonds.

5. Return to oven and bake uncovered at 350° for 5 minutes more.

Exchange List Values:
Lean Meat 4.0

Basic Nutritional Values:
Calories 215 (Calories from Fat 98), Total Fat 11 gm (Saturated Fat 2.1 gm, Trans Fat 0.0 gm, Polyunsat Fat 2.1 gm, Monounsat Fat 5.9 gm, Cholesterol 82 mg), Sodium 286 mg, Total Carbohydrate 4 gm, Dietary Fiber 1 gm, Sugars 1 gm, Protein 24 gm

Oven-Fried Catfish

Karen Waggoner
Joplin, MO

Makes 4 servings
Serving size is 1 fillet

Prep Time: 15 minutes
Baking Time: 25-30 minutes

4 6-oz. catfish fillets
1 cup cornflake crumbs
¼ tsp. celery salt
½ tsp. onion powder
¼ tsp. paprika
⅛ tsp. pepper
1 egg white
2 Tbsp. fat-free milk

1. Pat fish dry with paper towels. Set aside.
2. In glass pie plate, combine crumbs, celery salt, onion powder, paprika, and pepper.
3. In a shallow bowl, beat egg white. Add milk.
4. Dip fillets in egg white mixture, then dip into crumb mixture, coating well.
5. Place in greased 9 x 13 baking dish.
6. Bake, uncovered, at 350° for 25-30 minutes, or until fish flakes easily with a fork.

Exchange List Values:
Starch 1.5, Lean Meat 4.0

Basic Nutritional Values:
Calories 340 (Calories from Fat 110), Total Fat 12 gm (Saturated Fat 2.7 gm, Trans Fat 0.0 gm, Polyunsat Fat 2.3 gm, Monounsat Fat 6.3 gm, Cholesterol 98 mg), Sodium 448 mg, Total Carbohydrate 24 gm, Dietary Fiber 1 gm, Sugars 3 gm, Protein 32 gm

Seafood Enchiladas

Joleen Albrecht
Gladstone, MI

Makes 6 servings
Serving size is 1 filled enchilada

Prep Time: 15 minutes
Baking Time: 30 minutes

1 onion, chopped
1 Tbsp. canola oil
¾-1 lb. crabmeat, flaked
⅓ cup low-fat Colby cheese, shredded, *divided*
6 7-8" flour tortillas
1 cup fat-free milk
½ cup fat-free sour cream
1½ tsp. parsley
¼ tsp. garlic powder

1. In a medium-sized saucepan, sauté onions in canola oil. Remove from heat and stir in crabmeat and 2 Tbsp. cheese.
2. Place equal amount of mixture into each tortilla. Roll up tortillas and place seam-side down in a greased 8 x 8 or 9 x 13 baking pan.
3. Combine milk, sour cream, parsley, and garlic powder in the saucepan. Heat until blended and warmed through.
4. Pour sauce over enchiladas and sprinkle with remaining cheese.
5. Bake uncovered at 350° for 30 minutes.

Exchange List Values:
Starch 2.0, Lean Meat 2.0

Basic Nutritional Values:
Calories 272 (Calories from Fat 71), Total Fat 8 gm (Saturated Fat 2.0 gm, Trans Fat 0.0 gm, Polyunsat Fat 1.8 gm, Monounsat Fat 3.6 gm, Cholesterol 53 mg), Sodium 507 mg, Total Carbohydrate 29 gm, Dietary Fiber 2 gm, Sugars 5 gm, Protein 18 gm

Home-Baked Fish Fingers

Andrea Cunningham
Arlington, KS

Makes 4 servings
Serving size is ¾ cup or ¼ recipe

Prep Time: 15 minutes
Baking Time: 20 minutes

1 lb. codfish, whiting, *or* orange roughy fillets
¾ cup dry bread crumbs
½ cup egg substitute
2 Tbsp. 65%-vegetable-oil stick margarine, melted

Tartar Sauce:
1 pickle, chopped
½ cup fat-free mayonnaise
1 lemon

1. Wash the fillets, then pat them dry with paper towels. Cut into long pieces.
2. Place bread crumbs in a shallow bowl. Put egg substitute in another shallow bowl.
3. Dip each strip of fish into the eggs; then roll in bread crumbs until coated.
4. Lay fish in a greased 9 x 13 baking pan. Drizzle melted margarine over fish fingers.

5. Bake at 400° for 20 minutes, or until golden brown, turning once.

6. Meanwhile, combine ingredients for tartar sauce. Serve with fish fingers.

Exchange List Values:
Carbohydrate 1.5, Fat 0.5,
Very Lean Meat 3.0

Basic Nutritional Values:
Calories 229 (Calories from Fat 55),
Total Fat 6 gm (Saturated Fat 1.3
gm, Trans Fat 0.8 gm, Polyunsat
Fat 2.1 gm, Monounsat Fat 1.5 gm,
Cholesterol 49 mg), Sodium 529 mg,
Total Carbohydrate 20 gm, Dietary
Fiber 2 gm, Sugars 4 gm, Protein 25 gm

A Tip —

To save time and avoid the temptation to eat out, plan your meals for the week and buy your groceries all at once.

Salmon Croquettes
Margaret Moffitt
Bartlett, TN

Makes 6 servings
Serving size is 1 croquette

Prep Time: 25 minutes
Cooking Time: 6-8 minutes

**14.75-oz. can of salmon,
   drained and deboned**
½ cup egg substitute
**½ cup dry bread crumbs *or*
   finely crushed crackers**
1 Tbsp. flour
⅛ tsp. salt
¼ tsp. black pepper
¼ cup grated onions
¼ cup chopped celery
2 Tbsp. vegetable oil, *divided*

1. Mix all ingredients together except vegetable oil. Form into 6 croquettes.

2. Pour 1 Tbsp. oil into skillet and heat. Sauté croquettes in hot skillet without crowding them. (Do in batches if necessary.)

3. When croquettes brown on one side, turn them over and continue cooking until both sides are brown. Add second Tbsp. of oil if needed.

Exchange List Values:
Starch 0.5, Lean Meat 2.0,
Fat 0.5

Basic Nutritional Values:
Calories 182 (Calories from Fat 84),
Total Fat 9 gm (Saturated Fat 1.4
gm, Trans Fat 0.0 gm, Polyunsat
Fat 2.7 gm, Monounsat Fat 4.6 gm,
Cholesterol 25 mg), Sodium 459 mg,
Total Carbohydrate 9 gm, Dietary
Fiber 1 gm, Sugars 1 gm, Protein 15 gm

Variations:
Use only ¼ cup egg substitute. Instead of salt, pepper, onions, and celery, mix in 2 Tbsp. ketchup and 1 tsp. paprika.
—**Barbara W. Glueck**
Jenks, OK

Add the following to the full recipe above: ¼ cup finely chopped red bell pepper, ¼ cup finely chopped green pepper, 1 Tbsp. Worcestershire sauce. Shape into patties. Beat 1 egg in a shallow bowl; place 1 cup bread crumbs in another shallow bowl. Dip each patty into the beaten egg, and then into the bread crumbs. Proceed with Steps 2 and 3. Serve finished patties with ½ Tbsp. medium or hot salsa on top.
—**Kathy Novy**
Pueblo, CO

Instead of the celery, use ¼ cup shredded carrots. Add 1 Tbsp. Worcestershire sauce and ¼ tsp. dried basil or dried oregano to the full recipe above.
—**Esther J. Yoder**
Hartville, OH

Replace the onion and celery with 2 Tbsp. Dijon mustard and 1 Tbsp. dried onion flakes in the full recipe above.
—**Shirley Hinh**
Wayland, IA

A Tip —

Omega-3 fatty acids are great for your health. They're found in fish, soybeans, nuts, and a variety of other foods.

Baked Salmon

Erma Brubaker
Harrisonburg, VA

Makes 4 servings
Serving size is 3½ ozs. salmon
or ¼ of recipe

Prep Time: 5 minutes
Baking Time: 30-45 minutes

1 lb. fresh salmon, cut into
    4 pieces
nonfat cooking spray
seasoning salt
¼ cup fat-free mayonnaise
parsley

1. Spray baking dish with
cooking spray. Spray salmon
with cooking spray and
arrange in baking dish.
2. Sprinkle with seasoning
salt, spread with mayonnaise,
and top with parsley.
3. Bake, uncovered, at 350°
for 30-45 minutes.

Exchange List Values:
Lean Meat 4.0

Basic Nutritional Values:
Calories 201 (Calories from Fat 87),
Total Fat 10 gm (Saturated Fat 1.7
gm, Trans Fat 0.0 gm, Polyunsat
Fat 2.1 gm, Monounsat Fat 4.7 gm,
Cholesterol 77 mg), Sodium 163 mg,
Total Carbohydrate 2 gm, Dietary
Fiber 0 gm, Sugars 1 gm, Protein 24 gm

*Tip: Mayonnaise keeps the
salmon moist. For quick clean-
up, bake on an open piece of
tin foil.*

Oyster Sage Dressing

J.B. Miller
Indianapolis, IN

Makes 8 servings
Serving size is 3¼" x 4½" rectangle
or ⅛ of recipe

Prep Time: 40 minutes
Baking Time: 40 minutes

1-lb. loaf whole wheat
    bread, cut into 1" cubes
2 Tbsp. canola oil
1 large onion, chopped
4 ribs celery, chopped
1 Tbsp. dried sage
2 Tbsp. fresh parsley,
    chopped
1-1½ cups chicken stock
1 pint freshly shucked
    oysters with liquor,
    chopped if they're large
½ tsp. black pepper

1. If the bread you plan to
use is very fresh, cube it and
place it in a large uncovered
bowl overnight.
2. Heat oil in a very large
skillet or stockpot. Sauté
onions and celery in butter
until just tender.
3. Stir into bread in large
bowl. Add sage and parsley.
Toss gently to combine.
4. Fold in chicken stock,
just enough to moisten bread.
5. Fold in oysters and
oyster liquor. Season with
pepper.
6. Transfer to a greased
9 x 13 baking dish. Cover
with foil.

7. Bake at 375° for 30
minutes.
8. Remove foil and
continue baking until top
is lightly browned, about
10 more minutes.

Exchange List Values:
Starch 2.0, Fat 1.0,
Very Lean Meat 1.0

Basic Nutritional Values:
Calories 227 (Calories from Fat 66),
Total Fat 7 gm (Saturated Fat 0.8
gm, Trans Fat 0.0 gm, Polyunsat
Fat 2.0 gm, Monounsat Fat 3.2 gm,
Cholesterol 31 mg), Sodium 444 mg,
Total Carbohydrate 32 gm, Dietary
Fiber 5 gm, Sugars 6 gm, Protein 10 gm

Scalloped Corn and Oysters

Evelyn Page
Lance Creek, WY

Makes 6 servings
Serving size is 3⅓" x 4" rectangle
or ⅙ of recipe

Prep Time: 5-7 minutes
Baking Time: 60 minutes

2 15.25-oz. cans whole-
    kernel corn, drained
1 15.25-oz. can creamed
    corn
1 cup oysters, drained
⅛-¼ tsp. pepper
2-oz. jar pimentos, drained
8 soda crackers with
    unsalted tops, crumbled
2½ Tbsp. 65%-vegetable-oil
    stick margarine
¼ cup fat-free half-and-half

1. Place a layer of half the corns, followed by a layer of half the oysters in a greased 8 x 10 baking dish. Sprinkle with half the pepper.

2. Spoon half the pimentos over top, and half the cracker crumbs.

3. Melt the margarine in a small pan. Spoon half of it over the cracker crumbs.

4. Repeat the layers.

5. Pour half-and-half over top. Drizzle with remaining margarine.

6. Bake uncovered at 350° for 1 hour.

Exchange List Values:
Starch 2.0, Fat 1.0

Basic Nutritional Values:
Calories 214 (Calories from Fat 59), Total Fat 7 gm (Saturated Fat 1.3 gm, Trans Fat 0.6 gm, Polyunsat Fat 2.2 gm, Monounsat Fat 1.8 gm, Cholesterol 13 mg), Sodium 559 mg, Total Carbohydrate 35 gm, Dietary Fiber 3 gm, Sugars 11 gm, Protein 6 gm

Meatless Main Dishes

Vegetarian Black Bean Burritos

Maricarol Magill
Freehold, NJ

Makes 8 burritos
Serving size is 1 filled burrito

Prep Time: 10 minutes
Cooking/Baking time:
40 minutes

1¼ cup water
½ cup long-grain rice
8 7-8″ flour tortillas
10-oz. pkg. frozen corn
15-oz. can spicy black-bean chili
8-oz. can no-salt-added tomato sauce
shredded reduced-fat cheddar, Monterey Jack, or pepper Jack cheese, *optional**

1. In a medium-sized saucepan, bring water to a boil.

2. Stir in rice. Cover. Simmer over low heat until rice is cooked, about 20 minutes.

3. Meanwhile, wrap tortillas in foil. Heat oven to 350° and then heat tortillas until warm, about 15 minutes.

4. When rice is done, stir in corn, black-bean chili, and tomato sauce. Heat to boiling over medium-high heat. Boil one minute.

5. Assemble burritos by spooning rice mixture onto tortillas. Top with cheese of your choice, if desired. Fold in tops of tortillas and roll up.

Exchange List Values:
Starch 3.0, Fat 0.5

Basic Nutritional Values:
Calories 255 (Calories from Fat 35), Total Fat 4 gm (Saturated Fat 0.9 gm, Trans Fat 0.0 gm, Polyunsat Fat 0.9 gm, Monounsat Fat 1.9 gm, Cholesterol 0 mg), Sodium 613 mg, Total Carbohydrate 49 gm, Dietary Fiber 5 gm, Sugars 4 gm, Protein 8 gm

* The optional cheese is not included in the nutritional analysis.

A Tip —

Make meat a side dish, rather than the whole meal. Try a few meatless meals throughout the week.

Black Bean and Butternut Burritos

Janelle Myers-Benner
Harrisonburg, VA

Makes 8 burritos
Serving size is 1 filled burrito

Prep Time: 45 minutes
Baking Time: 15-20 minutes

1 Tbsp. oil
1 small or medium-sized
  onion, chopped
3-4 cups butternut squash,
  cut into ½" cubes
½ tsp. cumin
¼ tsp. cinnamon
½ tsp. salt
2 cups cooked, *or* a 15-oz.
  can, black beans, drained
8 7-8" tortillas
½ cup reduced-fat grated
  cheese
sour cream
cilantro, *if you wish*
salsa

1. In a large skillet or
saucepan, heat oil. Sauté
onions until tender.
2. Add squash. Cover and
cook over medium heat until
tender.
3. Add cumin, cinnamon,
and salt. Add beans. Cover,
and heat through.
4. Put ⅛ of mixture in
each tortilla, top with 1 Tbsp.
cheese, and roll up. Place
seam-side down in a greased
9 x 13 baking pan.
5. Bake uncovered in 350°
oven for about 15-20 minutes,
until heated through.
6. Serve with sour cream

and salsa, and cilantro if you
wish.

Exchange List Values:
Starch 2.5, Fat 1.0

Basic Nutritional Values:
Calories 260 (Calories from Fat 64),
Total Fat 7 gm (Saturated Fat 1.9
gm, Trans Fat 0.0 gm, Polyunsat
Fat 1.4 gm, Monounsat Fat 3.2 gm,
Cholesterol 5 mg), Sodium 501 mg,
Total Carbohydrate 40 gm, Dietary
Fiber 6 gm, Sugars 3 gm, Protein 10 gm

*Tips: Tortillas freeze well with
the mixture inside so I often make
a double or triple batch. You can
also freeze just the filling.*

Taco-Ritto

Marlene Fonken
Upland, CA

Makes 4 servings
Serving size is 1 filled soft taco

Prep Time: 20-25 minutes
Cooking Time: 5 minutes

1 Tbsp., plus 1 tsp.,
  vegetable oil
1½ cups broccoli florets
1 cup sliced fresh
  mushrooms
½ cup chopped green
  peppers
½ cup sliced onions
½ cup diced tomatoes
½ cup fat-free cheddar
  cheese, shredded
4 1-oz. flour tortillas,
  warmed

1. In a skillet, heat oil
over medium-high heat. Add
broccoli, mushrooms, green
peppers, and onions. Stir-fry
until tender-crisp, about
2-5 minutes.
2. Remove from heat and
stir in tomatoes and cheese.
Stir until cheese is partially
melted.
3. Divide among the
4 tortillas. Roll up to eat!

Exchange List Values:
Starch 1.0, Vegetable 2.0,
Fat 1.0

Basic Nutritional Values:
Calories 183 (Calories from Fat 64),
Total Fat 7 gm (Saturated Fat 0.9
gm, Trans Fat 0.0 gm, Polyunsat
Fat 1.9 gm, Monounsat Fat 3.8 gm,
Cholesterol 1 mg), Sodium 340 mg,
Total Carbohydrate 22 gm, Dietary
Fiber 3 gm, Sugars 4 gm, Protein 8 gm

*Tip: Add some taco sauce to
Step 2 if you wish.*

A Tip —

Eat slowly. You'll find
that you enjoy food more
and eat less when you take
time to savor each bite.

Black Bean and Kale or Spinach Tostada

Peg Zannotti, Tulsa, OK

Makes 6 servings
Serving size is 1 filled tostada

Prep Time: 15 minutes
Baking Time: 25 minutes

1 bunch green onions, chopped
3 garlic cloves, minced
1½ tsp. cumin
1½ tsp. coriander
1 Tbsp. poblano pepper, minced
1 Tbsp. olive oil
15-oz. can black beans, drained and rinsed
½ cup orange juice
1 bunch (1 lb.) kale, *or* 3 cups fresh spinach, chopped
salt to taste
6 6″ corn tortillas
⅓ cup grated reduced-fat cheese of your choice
⅓-½ cup sour cream, *optional*

1. In a large skillet, sauté onions, garlic, cumin, coriander, and poblano in olive oil for 8 minutes. (Wear gloves when you deseed the pepper, and do not allow the pepper to touch your eyes or skin.)
2. Add black beans and cook for 3 minutes, stirring and mashing the beans with the back of a spoon.
3. Add orange juice and kale or spinach. Cover and simmer for about 10 minutes, stirring frequently.
4. Add salt to taste.
5. Heat tortillas by lightly frying them, microwaving them, or heating them in the oven for several minutes.
6. For each serving, start with a heated tortilla, cover it generously with the black bean mixture, 1 Tbsp. cheese, and 1-2 Tbsp. sour cream if you wish.

Exchange List Values:
Starch 1.5, Vegetable 1.0, Fat 1.0

Basic Nutritional Values:
Calories 179 (Calories from Fat 44), Total Fat 5 gm (Saturated Fat 1.3 gm, Trans Fat 0.0 gm, Polyunsat Fat 0.8 gm, Monounsat Fat 2.3 gm, Cholesterol 5 mg), Sodium 133 mg, Total Carbohydrate 28 gm, Dietary Fiber 7 gm, Sugars 5 gm, Protein 8 gm

Tip: The filling in this recipe also works well as a dip for chips.

A Tip —

Be prepared for eating out. Many chain restaurants make their nutrition information available online or in stores. Take advantage!

Double Corn Tortilla Casserole

Kathy Keener Shantz
Lancaster, PA

Makes 6 servings
Serving size is ¾ cup

Prep Time: 15-20 minutes
Baking Time: 30 minutes

8 corn tortillas
1¼ cups fat-free mozzarella cheese, shredded
1 cup frozen corn
4 green onions sliced, about ½ cup
2 eggs, beaten
1 cup low-fat buttermilk
4-oz. can diced green chilies

1. Tear 4 tortillas into bite-sized pieces. Arrange in greased 2-qt. baking dish.
2. Top with half the cheese, half the corn, and half the green onions. Repeat layers.
3. In a mixing bowl, stir together eggs, buttermilk, and chilies. Gently pour over tortilla mixture.
4. Bake at 325° for 30 minutes, or until knife inserted in center comes out clean.

Exchange List Values:
Starch 1.5, Lean Meat 1.0

Basic Nutritional Values:
Calories 177 (Calories from Fat 28), Total Fat 3 gm (Saturated Fat 0.8 gm, Trans Fat 0.0 gm, Polyunsat Fat 0.8 gm, Monounsat Fat 1.0 gm, Cholesterol 75 mg), Sodium 449 mg, Total Carbohydrate 24 gm, Dietary Fiber 3 gm, Sugars 4 gm, Protein 13 gm

Exceptional Eggplant Casserole

Lisa Good, Harrisonburg, VA

Makes 8 servings
Serving size is ¾ cup

Prep Time: 15-20 minutes
Baking Time: 45-50 minutes

½ cup chopped onions
½ cup chopped green
  peppers
½ cup chopped celery
1 tsp. oil
2 8-oz. cans tomato sauce
2½ Tbsp. brown sugar blend
  (Splenda)
1½ tsp. dried oregano
½ tsp. minced garlic
1 medium-sized eggplant,
  peeled or unpeeled,
  sliced in ⅛"-thick slices
1 cup reduced-fat
  mozzarella cheese

1. In a large skillet or
saucepan, sauté the onions,
green peppers, and celery in
the oil.
2. Add the tomato sauce,
brown sugar blend, oregano,
and garlic to the sautéed
vegetables. Mix well.
3. Layer one-third of the
sauce mixture, one-third of
the eggplant, and one-third of
the cheese into a greased 2-qt.
baking dish. Repeat the layers
twice.
4. Bake uncovered at 350°
for 45-50 minutes.

Exchange List Values:
Vegetable 3.0, Fat 0.5

Basic Nutritional Values:
Calories 107 (Calories from Fat 26),
Total Fat 3 gm (Saturated Fat 1.3
gm, Trans Fat 0.0 gm, Polyunsat
Fat 0.5 gm, Monounsat Fat 0.7 gm,
Cholesterol 8 mg), Sodium 449 mg,
Total Carbohydrate 16 gm, Dietary
Fiber 3 gm, Sugars 10 gm, Protein 6 gm

Eggplant Pita

Donna Conto
Saylorsburg, PA

Makes filling for 4 pita sandwiches,
or 8 servings
Serving size is ½ filled pita pocket

Prep Time: 10 minutes
Standing Time: 2 hours
Cooking Time: 5 minutes

1 large eggplant, peeled
  and diced
¼ cup canola oil
½ tsp. garlic salt
½ tsp. pepper
½ tsp. salt
15-oz. can diced tomatoes,
  drained
1 small onion, chopped
2 Tbsp. parsley
4 pita breads

1. Heat oil in skillet. Add
eggplant, garlic salt, pepper,
and ½ tsp. salt. Sauté for 5
minutes until soft. Drain off
excess oil.
2. Put seasoned eggplant in
mixing bowl. Add tomatoes,
onion, and parsley.
3. Mix well, stuff in pita
bread halves, and serve
immediately.

Exchange List Values:
Starch 1.0, Vegetable 2.0,
Fat 1.0

Basic Nutritional Values:
Calories 182 (Calories from Fat 67),
Total Fat 7 gm (Saturated Fat 0.6
gm, Trans Fat 0.0 gm, Polyunsat
Fat 2.3 gm, Monounsat Fat 4.1 gm,
Cholesterol 0 mg), Sodium 447 mg,
Total Carbohydrate 26 gm, Dietary
Fiber 3 gm, Sugars 5 gm, Protein 4 gm

Baked Southwest Grits

Jane Steele, Moore, OK

Makes 10 servings
Serving size is ¾ cup

Prep Time: 25 minutes
Baking Time: 45 minutes

4 cups water
¼ tsp. salt
1 cup uncooked grits
½ cup egg substitute
1 Tbsp. canola oil
minced garlic to taste
4-oz. can chopped green
  chilies
1 cup grated reduced-fat
  Mexican cheese, *divided*

1. Place water in large
saucepan, add salt, and cover.
Bring to boil.
2. Add grits and stir for
1 minute.
3. Cover and cook until
thick and creamy, about 5-7
minutes. Stir occasionally.
4. Beat egg substitute
in a small bowl. Stir in ¼
cup cooked grits and blend

together. Add mixture to saucepan of grits.

5. Heat oil in a medium-sized pan. Stir in garlic, chilies, and ¾ cup cheese. Add to the grits mixture and stir well.

6. Spoon into a greased 2-qt. casserole. Top with remaining ¼ cup cheese.

7. Bake uncovered at 350° for 45 minutes.

Exchange List Values:
Starch 1.0, Fat 1.0

Basic Nutritional Values:
Calories 110 (Calories from Fat 36), Total Fat 4 gm (Saturated Fat 1.3 gm, Trans Fat 0.0 gm, Polyunsat Fat 0.5 gm, Monounsat Fat 1.5 gm, Cholesterol 8 mg), Sodium 214 mg, Total Carbohydrate 13 gm, Dietary Fiber 1 gm, Sugars 0 gm, Protein 6 gm

Jamaican Rice and Beans
Lorraine Pflederer, Goshen, IN

Makes 5 servings
Serving size is 1 cup

Prep Time: 10 minutes
Cooking Time: 30 minutes
Standing Time: 5 minutes

¾ cup light coconut milk
1½ cups water
scant ½ tsp. allspice
½ tsp. salt
3 fresh thyme sprigs, *or*
   1 tsp. dried thyme
1 garlic clove, crushed
1 cup long-grain white rice
15-oz. can dark red kidney
   beans, drained and
   rinsed

1. Combine first 6 ingredients (through garlic) in a medium-sized saucepan over medium-high heat. Cover and bring to a boil.

2. Stir in rice. Reduce the heat to low. Cover and cook 20 minutes, or until all the liquid is absorbed. Check periodically to make sure the rice isn't sticking.

3. Remove pan from heat. Remove the thyme sprigs and discard.

4. Gently stir in the beans. Cover and let stand 5 minutes before serving.

Exchange List Values:
Starch 3.0

Basic Nutritional Values:
Calories 245 (Calories from Fat 22), Total Fat 2 gm (Saturated Fat 1.3 gm, Trans Fat 0.0 gm, Polyunsat Fat 0.3 gm, Monounsat Fat 0.4 gm, Cholesterol 0 mg), Sodium 347 mg, Total Carbohydrate 47 gm, Dietary Fiber 4 gm, Sugars 2 gm, Protein 8 gm

Spinach Souffle
Kaye Taylor, Florissant, MO

Makes 8 servings
Serving size is ½ cup

Prep Time: 5-10 minutes
Baking Time: 60-75 minutes

4 Tbsp. flour
2 ozs. reduced-fat Colby
   cheese, grated
2 ozs. fat-free cheddar
   cheese, grated
2 Tbsp. 65%-vegetable-oil
   stick margarine, melted
1-lb. carton fat-free, small-
   curd cottage cheese
¾ cup egg substitute
⅛ tsp. pepper
10-oz. pkg. chopped
   spinach, thawed and
   squeezed dry

1. Blend together flour, cheeses, and margarine in a large mixing bowl.

2. Stir in remaining ingredients.

3. Pour into a greased 2-qt. baking casserole.

4. Bake uncovered at 325° for 60-75 minutes, or until knife inserted in center comes out clean.

Exchange List Values:
Carbohydrate 0.5, Fat 0.5,
Very Lean Meat 2.0

Basic Nutritional Values:
Calories 126 (Calories from Fat 33), Total Fat 4 gm (Saturated Fat 1.4 gm, Trans Fat 0.4 gm, Polyunsat Fat 0.9 gm, Monounsat Fat 1.0 gm, Cholesterol 8 mg), Sodium 436 mg, Total Carbohydrate 8 gm, Dietary Fiber 1 gm, Sugars 2 gm, Protein 15 gm

Apple-Stuffed Acorn Squash

Susan Guarneri, Three Lakes, WI

Makes 4 servings
Serving size is ½ stuffed squash

Prep Time: 20 minutes
Baking Time: 50 minutes

2 1¼-lb. acorn squashes
3 tart apples, *divided*
1 Tbsp. fresh lemon juice,
   taken from half a lemon
   (reserve the other half)
1½ tsp. grated lemon rind,
   taken from half a lemon
   (reserve the other half)
2 Tbsp. 65%-vegetable-oil
   stick margarine, melted,
   divided
2½ Tbsp. brown sugar
   blend, (Splenda)
½ tsp. salt
1 tsp. cinnamon

1. Cut each squash in half. Scoop out seeds. Place in baking dish, cut-side down, and add ½" boiling water. Bake, covered with aluminum foil, at 400° for 20 minutes.
2. Pare, core, and dice 2 apples. In small bowl, mix with lemon juice, rind, 1 Tbsp. margarine, and brown sugar blend.
3. Remove squash halves from oven. Brush cut halves with remaining 1 Tbsp. margarine. Sprinkle with salt and cinnamon.
4. Fill squash halves with apple mixture.
5. Place squash halves cut-side up in baking dish.

Add ½" boiling water. Cover with foil and bake 30 minutes longer.
6. Before serving, pour pan juices over squash. Garnish each half with slices from the reserved apple and the reserved lemon half.

Exchange List Values:
Starch 1.5, Fruit 1.5, Fat 0.5

Basic Nutritional Values:
Calories 218 (Calories from Fat 45), Total Fat 5 gm (Saturated Fat 1.1 gm, Trans Fat 0.8 gm, Polyunsat Fat 1.7 gm, Monounsat Fat 1.3 gm, Cholesterol 0 mg), Sodium 354 mg, Total Carbohydrate 44 gm, Dietary Fiber 9 gm, Sugars 26 gm, Protein 2 gm

Tomato-Artichoke Scallop

Clara Earle Baskin, Quinton, NJ

Makes 8 servings
Serving size is ¾ cup

Prep Time: 20 minutes
Baking Time: 10-15 minutes

2 Tbsp. olive oil
½ cup finely chopped onions
2 Tbsp. finely chopped
   scallions
14-oz. can artichoke
   hearts, drained
35-oz. can whole plum
   tomatoes, drained
½ tsp. fresh, *or* pinch of
   dried, basil
1-2 tsp. sugar, your
   preference
salt and pepper to taste
¼ cup grated Parmesan
   cheese

1. In a large skillet or saucepan, heat oil. Sauté onions and scallions until tender.
2. Rinse artichokes and cut into quarters. Add to skillet.
3. Stir in tomatoes and basil. Heat 2 to 3 minutes, stirring occasionally.
4. Season with sugar, salt, and pepper. Turn into greased shallow baking dish. Sprinkle with Parmesan cheese.
5. Bake at 325° for 10-15 minutes, or until vegetables are tender.

Exchange List Values:
Vegetable 1.0, Fat 1.0

Basic Nutritional Values:
Calories 71 (Calories from Fat 41), Total Fat 5 gm (Saturated Fat 1.0 gm, Trans Fat 0.0 gm, Polyunsat Fat 0.5 gm, Monounsat Fat 2.8 gm, Cholesterol 3 mg), Sodium 193 mg, Total Carbohydrate 6 gm, Dietary Fiber 1 gm, Sugars 3 gm, Protein 2 gm

A Tip —

Remember that healthy changes are for a lifetime. Quick fixes, fad diets, and magic pills will eventually put you right back where you started.

Sun-Dried Tomato Casserole

Barbara Jean Fabel, Wausau, WI

Makes 12 servings
Serving size is ¾ cup

Prep Time: 15-20 minutes
Standing Time: 8 hours or
overnight, plus 10 minutes
Baking Time: 40 minutes

1¾ 9-oz. pkgs. reduced-fat
cheese ravioli (look for
them in the dairy case)
half an 8-oz. jar sun-dried
tomatoes in oil, drained
and chopped
1 cup fat-free cheddar
cheese, shredded
1 cup fat-free mozzarella
cheese, shredded
2 cups egg substitute
2½ cups fat-free milk
1-2 Tbsp. fresh basil,
snipped, *or* 1-2 tsp. dried
basil

1. Grease a 3-qt. baking
dish. Place uncooked ravioli
evenly in bottom.
2. Sprinkle ravioli with
tomatoes. Top evenly with
cheeses. Set aside.
3. In a mixing bowl, whisk
egg substitute and milk until
well combined. Pour over
layers in casserole dish.
4. Cover and chill for 8
hours or overnight.
5. Bake, uncovered, at 350°
for 40 minutes, until center
is set and knife inserted in
center comes out clean.
6. Let stand 10 minutes
before serving. Just before
serving, sprinkle with basil.

Exchange List Values:
Very Lean Meat 2.0,
Starch 1.5

Basic Nutritional Values:
Calories 181 (Calories from Fat 26),
Total Fat 3 gm (Saturated Fat 1.4
gm, Trans Fat 0.0 gm, Polyunsat
Fat 0.3 gm, Monounsat Fat 1.2 gm,
Cholesterol 16 mg), Sodium 467 mg,
Total Carbohydrate 21 gm, Dietary
Fiber 1 gm, Sugars 6 gm, Protein 17 gm

*Tip: If you don't like sun-dried
tomatoes, replace them with
something you do like, such as
sliced black olives or artichokes.*

Double Cheese Zucchini Bake

Janet Schaeffer, Lansing, IL

Makes 15 servings
Serving size is 2½" x 3" rectangle
or ¹⁄₁₅ of recipe

Prep Time: 15-20 minutes
Baking Time: 35-40 minutes

2 Tbsp. olive oil
1 clove garlic, chopped
8 medium-sized, peeled
or unpeeled, zucchini,
sliced
1 cup Italian-seasoned
bread crumbs, *divided*
¾ cup reduced-fat Monterey
Jack cheese, shredded
½ cup freshly grated
Parmesan cheese
1 Tbsp. no-salt-added
Italian seasoning (see
recipe on page 254)
¾ cup egg substitute
2 cups fat-free half-and-half

1. In large saucepan, heat
olive oil. Add garlic and cook
about 3 minutes.
2. Add zucchini to garlic
and oil. Sauté until soft, about
10 minutes.
3. Stir in ½ cup bread
crumbs, Monterey Jack
cheese, Parmesan cheese, and
Italian seasoning. Blend well.
4. Spoon mixture into a
greased 9 x 13, or larger,
baking dish.
5. Pour egg substitute into
a mixing bowl. Mix in half-
and-half. Pour over baking
dish contents and let it settle
into the zucchini mixture.
6. Top with remaining
bread crumbs.
7. Bake at 350°, uncovered,
for 35-40 minutes, or until
knife inserted in center comes
out clean.

Exchange List Values:
Carbohydrate 1.0, Fat 0.5

Basic Nutritional Values:
Calories 108 (Calories from Fat 37),
Total Fat 4 gm (Saturated Fat 1.3
gm, Trans Fat 0.0 gm, Polyunsat
Fat 0.4 gm, Monounsat Fat 1.9 gm,
Cholesterol 6 mg), Sodium 217 mg,
Total Carbohydrate 12 gm, Dietary
Fiber 2 gm, Sugars 4 gm, Protein 6 gm

*Tip: You can make the dish
the day before serving it and
refrigerate it unbaked. If you
put it in the oven cold, increase
the baking time to 50-60
minutes.*

Zucchini Babka

Esther J. Mast
Lancaster, PA

Makes 8 servings
Serving size is ¾ cup

Prep Time: 20 minutes
Baking Time: 30-45 minutes

¾ cup egg substitute
¼ cup vegetable oil
4 cups diced zucchini,
    peeled or unpeeled
1 medium-sized onion,
    chopped
1 cup all-purpose, reduced-
    fat baking mix
½ cup reduced-fat cheddar
    cheese, grated
½ tsp. salt
1 tsp. dried oregano
dash of pepper
Parmesan cheese

1. Pour egg substitute into
a large mixing bowl. Blend
in oil.
2. Add zucchini, onions,
baking mix, cheese, salt,
oregano, and pepper. Mix
well.
3. Pour into greased 1½-2-qt.
baking dish. Sprinkle with
Parmesan cheese.
4. Bake at 350° for 30-45
minutes, or until nicely
browned.

Exchange List Values:
Starch 0.5, Vegetable 1.0,
Fat 2.0

Basic Nutritional Values:
Calories 156 (Calories from Fat 81),
Total Fat 9 gm (Saturated Fat 1.3
gm, Trans Fat 0.0 gm, Polyunsat
Fat 2.3 gm, Monounsat Fat 4.9 gm,

Cholesterol 4 mg), Sodium 400 mg,
Total Carbohydrate 14 gm, Dietary
Fiber 1 gm, Sugars 3 gm, Protein 6 gm

Variations:
   1. Use 3 cups zucchini and
1 cup cheese in the batter.
   2. Use 1 clove minced garlic
instead of onions.
   —Evie Hershey
     Atglen, PA

   3. Use 3 cups zucchini and 1
cup egg substitute.
   4. Use 2 Tbsp. parsley,
½ tsp. salt, and ½ tsp. dried
oregano.
   —Joyce Kreiser
     Manheim, PA
   —Virginia Martin
     Harrisonburg, VA
   —Joanne Kennedy
     Plattsburgh, NY

   5. Use 1 cup egg substitute.
   6. Add ½ cup shredded
Swiss cheese to the batter, and
sprinkle the Parmesan cheese
on top.
   —Becky Frey
     Lebanon, PA

A Tip —

   Try to eat at least 20–35
grams of fiber everyday.

Veggie Burgers

Esther Becker
Gordonville, PA

Makes 14 servings
Serving size is 1 burger

Prep Time: 20 minutes
(after soaking and cooking)
Cooking Time: 8-10 minutes

1 cup dry oat bran
1 cup dry oats
1 cup cooked brown rice
½ cup dry lentils, soaked
    and cooked
½ cup dry black beans,
    soaked and cooked
½ cup dry black-eyed peas,
    soaked and cooked
½ cup salsa
½ cup chopped onions
half a green pepper, chopped
half-square of tofu, at
    room temperature
half an 8-oz. pkg. fat-free
    cream cheese, softened
cooking oil

1. Mix all ingredients
together and shape into
14 patties.
2. Brown on both sides in a
skillet in enough oil to cover
the bottom of the pan.

Exchange List Values:
Carbohydrate 1.5,
Lean Meat 1.0

Basic Nutritional Values:
Calories 143 (Calories from Fat 17),
Total Fat 2 gm (Saturated Fat 0.4
gm, Trans Fat 0.0 gm, Polyunsat
Fat 0.8 gm, Monounsat Fat 0.5 gm,
Cholesterol 1 mg), Sodium 117 mg,
Total Carbohydrate 25 gm, Dietary
Fiber 6 gm, Sugars 2 gm, Protein 10 gm

Pastas and Pizzas

Macaronis and Cheese

Elaine Rineer
Lancaster, PA

Makes 9 servings
Serving size is ½ cup

Prep Time: 20 minutes
Baking Time: 20-25 minutes

8 ozs. shell macaronis
2 Tbsp. canola oil
2 Tbsp. flour
1 tsp. salt
1 tsp. dry mustard
2½ cups fat-free milk
⅔ cup reduced-fat sharp
  cheddar cheese,
  shredded, *divided*
¼ cup dry bread crumbs
paprika

1. Cook shells according to package directions. Drain and set aside.
2. While shells are cooking, heat 2 Tbsp. canola oil in a large saucepan.
3. Blend in flour, salt, and dry mustard.
4. Add milk. Heat, stirring constantly until sauce thickens and is smooth.
5. Add ½ cup cheese. Heat until melted, continuing to stir.
6. Combine sauce and cooked macaronis. Pour into a greased 2-qt. casserole.
7. Top macaronis and cheese with remaining cheese, bread crumbs, and paprika.
8. Bake uncovered at 375° for 20-25 minutes.

Exchange List Values:
Starch 1.5, Fat 0.5,
Fat-Free Milk 0.5

Basic Nutritional Values:
Calories 168 (Calories from Fat 37), Total Fat 4 gm (Saturated Fat 1.3 gm, Trans Fat 0.0 gm, Polyunsat Fat 0.8 gm, Monounsat Fat 1.5 gm, Cholesterol 7 mg), Sodium 380 mg, Total Carbohydrate 25 gm, Dietary Fiber 1 gm, Sugars 5 gm, Protein 8 gm

Variation: Use evaporated milk instead of regular milk. Use 2 Tbsp. Parmesan cheese instead of buttered bread crumbs as topping.
  —Andrea Cunningham
  Arlington, KS

A Tip —

   In Okinawa they had a principle called *hara hachi bu*—stop eating when you're "80% full." Not coincidentally, Okinawans were renowned for long life spans.

Tomato-y Penne Pasta

Joy Sutter
Perkasie, PA

Makes 8 servings
Serving size is 1¼ cups

Prep Time: 15 minutes
Cooking Time: 25 minutes

1 Tbsp. butter
1 Tbsp. olive oil
1 small onion, chopped
28-oz. can Italian plum
    tomatoes, drained,
    seeded, and chopped
1 cup fat-free half-and-half
¼ cup vodka
¼ tsp. dried crushed red
    pepper flakes
salt and pepper to taste
1 lb. penne pasta
¼ cup, or more, freshly
    grated Parmesan cheese
2 Tbsp., or more, minced
    fresh chives

1. In a large heavy sauce-pan, melt butter with oil over medium heat.
2. Add onions and sauté until translucent. Add tomatoes and cook uncovered until almost no liquid remains.
3. Stir in half-and-half, vodka, and red pepper flakes, and boil until the mixture reaches a sauce consistency, about 2 minutes. Add salt and pepper to taste.
4. Meanwhile, cook pasta according to package directions. Drain.
5. Pour hot sauce over cooked pasta.
6. Toss and sprinkle with Parmesan cheese and chives.

Exchange List Values:
Starch 3.0, Fat 1.0

Basic Nutritional Values:
Calories 299 (Calories from Fat 50), Total Fat 6 gm (Saturated Fat 2.0 gm, Trans Fat 0.0 gm, Polyunsat Fat 0.7 gm, Monounsat Fat 2.0 gm, Cholesterol 8 mg), Sodium 137 mg, Total Carbohydrate 49 gm, Dietary Fiber 3 gm, Sugars 6 gm, Protein 10 gm

Tip: You can prepare this sauce a day ahead of when you want to use it. Just cover and refrigerate until you need it.

A Tip —

Avoid restaurants that offer only buffet-style eating. You will almost always eat more at a buffet.

Easy Fettucine Alfredo

Trish Propst
Tinton Falls, NJ

Makes 6 servings
Serving size is ¾ cup

Preparation time: 5-10 minutes
Cooking time: 15 minutes

8 ozs. fettucine noodles
½ cup fat-free half-and-half
6½ Tbsp. freshly grated
    Parmesan cheese
½ tsp. salt
dash of pepper
2 tsp. parsley

1. Cook noodles according to package. Drain and keep warm.
2. In a medium-sized saucepan, heat half-and-half over low heat.
3. Stir in cheese, salt, and pepper.
4. Pour sauce over hot noodles. Sprinkle with parsley. Serve.

Exchange List Values:
Starch 2.0, Fat 0.5

Basic Nutritional Values:
Calories 197 (Calories from Fat 28), Total Fat 3 gm (Saturated Fat 1.4 gm, Trans Fat 0.0 gm, Polyunsat Fat 0.4 gm, Monounsat Fat 0.8 gm, Cholesterol 7 mg), Sodium 264 mg, Total Carbohydrate 33 gm, Dietary Fiber 2 gm, Sugars 2 gm, Protein 9 gm

Spinach Pesto

Vic and Christina Buckwalter
Keezletown, VA

Makes 12 servings, or 1½ cups
Serving size is 2 Tbsp.

Prep Time: 15 minutes
Cooking Time: 12 minutes

Pesto:
4 packed cups fresh
   spinach leaves
3 garlic cloves
2 Tbsp. pine nuts
¼ packed cup fresh basil,
   or 1½ Tbsp. dried basil
7 Tbsp. extra-virgin olive oil
⅛ tsp. salt

Process Pesto ingredients in blender until smooth. Store in refrigerator or freeze for later use.

Exchange List Values:
Fat 2.0

Basic Nutritional Values:
Calories 100 (Calories from Fat 96), Total Fat 11 gm (Saturated Fat 1.4 gm, Trans Fat 0.0 gm, Polyunsat Fat 1.6 gm, Monounsat Fat 7.3 gm, Cholesterol 0 mg), Sodium 40 mg, Total Carbohydrate 1 gm, Dietary Fiber 0 gm, Sugars 0 gm, Protein 1 gm

Tip: This pesto makes an excellent pizza topping, along with your favorite cheeses.

A Tip —

Herbs and spices are a great way to add flavor to meals without adding fat or calories.

Linguine Spinach Pesto

Vic and Christina Buckwalter
Keezletown, VA

Makes 6 servings
Serving size is 1 cup

Prep Time: 15 minutes
Cooking Time: 12 minutes

1 lb. linguine, *or* pasta of
   your choice
½ cup spinach pesto from
   previous recipe
2 Tbsp. Parmesan cheese,
   freshly grated
2 Tbsp. pasta water

1. Cook 1 lb. linguine according to package directions. Drain, saving 2 Tbsp. of pasta water.
2. Mix together ½ cup of pesto, Parmesan cheese, and reserved pasta water. Stir mixture into pasta.

Exchange List Values:
Starch 3.0, Fat 1.0

Basic Nutritional Values:
Calories 266 (Calories from Fat 61), Total Fat 7 gm (Saturated Fat 1.1 gm, Trans Fat 0.0 gm, Polyunsat Fat 1.2 gm, Monounsat Fat 3.9 gm, Cholesterol 1 mg), Sodium 33 mg, Total Carbohydrate 43 gm, Dietary Fiber 2 gm, Sugars 2 gm, Protein 8 gm

Variations:
1. Sometimes we toss chopped fresh tomatoes from the garden into Step 2.

Southwestern Pesto Pasta

Carrie Wood
Paxton, MA

Makes 6 servings
Serving size is 1 cup

Prep Time: 10 minutes
Cooking Time: 10-12 minutes

¾ cup loosely packed
   cilantro leaves
¾ cup loosely packed flat
   parsley
2 Tbsp. toasted pepitas
   (pumpkin seeds)
1 clove garlic, peeled
½ cup fat-free feta cheese,
   crumbled
5 Tbsp. extra-virgin olive oil
salt to taste
1 lb. spaghetti *or* linguine

1. Process all ingredients except pasta in a food processor until a rough paste is formed, adding additional water if the paste seems too dry.
2. Cook spaghetti or linguine according to package directions. Drain.
3. Toss pesto thoroughly with hot pasta and then serve.

Exchange List Values:
Starch 3.0, Fat 2.0

Basic Nutritional Values:
Calories 323 (Calories from Fat 99), Total Fat 11 gm (Saturated Fat 1.5 gm, Trans Fat 0.0 gm, Polyunsat Fat 1.9 gm, Monounsat Fat 6.8 gm, Cholesterol 0 mg), Sodium 155 mg, Total Carbohydrate 45 gm, Dietary Fiber 3 gm, Sugars 2 gm, Protein 11 gm

Spaghetti! Quick!

Helen E. Shenk
Quarryville, PA

Makes 10 servings
Serving size is ¾ cup

Prep Time: 10-15 minutes
Baking Time: 10-45 minutes

9-10 ozs. dry spaghetti
1½ cups reduced-fat sharp
  cheddar cheese, shredded
2 10-oz. pkgs. frozen
  spinach, thawed and
  squeezed dry
½ lb. sliced fresh
  mushrooms
1½ cups fat-free sour cream
dash of oregano
½ cup chopped onions
salt to taste
pepper to taste

1. Cook spaghetti in large
stockpot according to package
directions. Drain and return
to stockpot.
2. Add cheese. Stir until
well mixed and partially
melted.
3. Add remaining ingredi-
ents. Mix well.
4. Pour into greased 3-qt.
baking dish.
5. Bake at 350° for 10-15
minutes if spaghetti is still
warm; 30-45 minutes if not.

Exchange List Values:
Starch 1.5, Vegetable 1.0,
Lean Meat 1.0

Basic Nutritional Values:
Calories 197 (Calories from Fat 40),
Total Fat 4 gm (Saturated Fat 2.2
gm, Trans Fat 0.0 gm, Polyunsat
Fat 0.4 gm, Monounsat Fat 1.1 gm,

Cholesterol 15 mg), Sodium 203 mg,
Total Carbohydrate 25 gm, Dietary
Fiber 3 gm, Sugars 3 gm, Protein 12 gm

*Variation: Use fresh spinach
instead of frozen. Use spaghetti
squash instead of the pasta.*
  —Tina Hartman
    Lancaster, PA

Sausage Ziti Bake

Margaret Morris
Middle Village, NY

Makes 8 servings
Serving size is 3¼" x 4½" rectangle
or ⅛ of recipe

Prep Time: 15 minutes
Baking Time: 45 minutes

1 lb. lean turkey Italian
  sausage
1 lb. uncooked ziti
2 cups sliced fresh
  mushrooms
1 large onion, chopped
26-oz. jar fat-free,
  low-sodium tomato and
  basil pasta sauce
salt to taste
pepper to taste
4 ozs. reduced-fat mozzarella
  cheese, shredded

1. Brown sausage in large
stockpot.
2. Meanwhile, cook the
ziti according to the package
directions. Drain.
3. After sausage is browned
remove it to a bowl and drain
off all drippings. Add mushrooms and onions to stockpot.
Cook gently until tender.
4. Stir in sauce, sausage,
cooked and drained ziti, salt,
and pepper. Spoon into a
greased 9 x 13 baking dish.
Cover.
5. Bake at 350° for 30-40
minutes, or until heated the
whole way through.
6. Sprinkle with cheese.
Bake uncovered an additional
5 minutes.

Exchange List Values:
Starch 3.0, Vegetable 2.0,
Lean Meat 2.0, Fat 0.5

Basic Nutritional Values:
Calories 411 (Calories from Fat 88),
Total Fat 10 gm (Saturated Fat 3.3
gm, Trans Fat 0.0 gm, Polyunsat
Fat 1.4 gm, Monounsat Fat 1.6 gm,
Cholesterol 52 mg), Sodium 487 mg,
Total Carbohydrate 55 gm, Dietary
Fiber 3 gm, Sugars 11 gm, Protein 26 mg

A Tip —

Heart disease is the number one killer of people with
diabetes, which is why it's so important to manage your
cholesterol, blood pressure, and glucose.

Cheesy Chicken Casserole

Miriam Christophel
Goshen, IN

Makes 6 servings
Serving size is ¾ cup or ⅙ of recipe

Prep Time: 20-30 minutes
Baking Time: 30 minutes for oven or 8-10 minutes for microwave

½ cup fat-free mayonnaise,
¾ cup reduced-fat sharp
   cheddar cheese, shredded,
   divided
1½ cups chopped, cooked
   chicken breast
1½ cups dry (4 ozs.) rotini,
   cooked and drained
2 cups mixed frozen
   vegetables
¼ cup fat-free milk
½ tsp. dried basil leaves

1. In a large mixing bowl, combine all ingredients except ¼ cup cheese.
2. Spoon into a greased 1½-qt. casserole. Sprinkle with reserved ¼ cup cheese.
3. Bake uncovered at 350° for 40 minutes, or until heated through.

Exchange List Values:
Starch 1.5, Fat 0.5,
Very Lean Meat 2.0

Basic Nutritional Values:
Calories 209 (Calories from Fat 42),
Total Fat 5 gm (Saturated Fat 2.2
gm, Trans Fat 0.0 gm, Polyunsat
Fat 0.5 gm, Monounsat Fat 1.3 gm,
Cholesterol 40 mg), Sodium 314 mg,
Total Carbohydrate 23 gm, Dietary
Fiber 2 gm, Sugars 4 gm, Protein 18 gm

Variation: To make this in the microwave, be sure to use a microwave-safe casserole. Heat on high 8-10 minutes, or until thoroughly heated.

Chicken Manicotti

Lori Showalter
New Hope, VA

Makes 4 servings
Serving size is 2 stuffed shells or ¼ of recipe

Prep Time: 30 minutes
Baking Time: 65-70 minutes

¾ lb. boneless, skinless
   chicken breasts
1½ tsp. garlic powder
8 uncooked manicotti
   shells
26-oz. jar fat-free, low-
   sodium tomato and basil
   pasta sauce, *divided*
⅓ lb. meatless, soy-based
   sausage, cooked and
   drained
¼ lb. fresh mushrooms,
   sliced, *or* canned
   mushrooms, drained
1 cup (4 ozs.) reduced-
   fat mozzarella cheese,
   shredded
⅓ cup water

1. Cut chicken into small chunks. In large bowl, toss chicken with garlic powder.
2. Stuff chicken into manicotti shells.
3. Spread 1 cup pasta sauce in the bottom of a greased 7 x 11 baking dish. Arrange stuffed shells on top of sauce.

4. Sprinkle with sausage and mushrooms. Pour remaining pasta sauce over top.
5. Sprinkle with cheese.
6. Spoon water around the edge of the dish. Cover and bake at 375° for 65-70 minutes, or until chicken juices run clear and pasta is tender.

Exchange List Values:
Carbohydrate 2.5,
Lean Meat 4.0

Basic Nutritional Values:
Calories 394 (Calories from Fat 83),
Total Fat 9 gm (Saturated Fat 3.2
gm, Trans Fat 0.0 gm, Polyunsat
Fat 1.8 gm, Monounsat Fat 2.3 gm,
Cholesterol 64 mg), Sodium 552 mg,
Total Carbohydrate 41 gm, Dietary
Fiber 4 gm, Sugars 14 gm, Protein 39 gm

Tip: I like to double the recipe and freeze the second dish for another meal. The dish can be frozen for up to one month. When ready to use, thaw it in the refrigerator; then let it stand at room temperature for 30 minutes before baking as directed.

129

Creamy Chicken Lasagna

Joanne E. Martin
Stevens, PA

Makes 10 servings
Serving size is 2⅔″ x 4¼″ rectangle
or ⅒ of recipe

Prep Time: 30 minutes
Baking Time: 40-45 minutes
Standing Time: 15 minutes

8 ozs. lasagna noodles
10.75-oz. can 98%-fat-free, reduced-sodium cream of mushroom soup
10.75-oz. can 98%-fat-free, reduced-sodium cream of chicken soup
¼ cup grated Parmesan cheese
1 cup fat-free sour cream
3 cups diced cooked chicken breast
1 cup reduced-fat mozzarella cheese, grated, *divided*

1. Cook noodles as directed on package. Drain.
2. In a large mixing bowl, blend soups, Parmesan cheese, and sour cream. Stir in diced chicken.
3. Put one-fourth of creamy chicken mixture in the bottom of a greased 9 x 13 baking pan.
4. Alternate layers of ⅓ noodles, ⅓ chicken mixture, and ⅓ mozzarella cheese, repeating the layers 2 more times.
5. Bake uncovered at 350° for 40-45 minutes.
6. Allow to stand for 15 minutes before serving.

Exchange List Values:
Carbohydrate 1.5, Fat 0.5, Very Lean Meat 3.0

Basic Nutritional Values:
Calories 252 (Calories from Fat 50), Total Fat 6 gm (Saturated Fat 2.4 gm, Trans Fat 0.0 gm, Polyunsat Fat 1.1 gm, Monounsat Fat 1.4 gm, Cholesterol 50 mg), Sodium 399 mg, Total Carbohydrate 24 gm, Dietary Fiber 1 gm, Sugars 3 gm, Protein 23 gm

Southwestern Shells

Elaine Rineer, Lancaster, PA

Makes 6 servings
Serving size is 4 stuffed shells

Prep Time: 30-35 minutes
Baking Time: 25-35 minutes

1 lb. 90%-lean ground beef
1 medium-sized onion, chopped
16-oz. jar salsa
8-oz. can no-salt-added tomato sauce
½ cup water
1 tsp. chili powder
4-oz. can chopped green chilies, drained
24 jumbo shells, cooked

1. In large nonstick skillet, brown ground beef and onion together.
2. Meanwhile, mix together in a mixing bowl the salsa, tomato sauce, and water.
3. When meat and onions are brown, stir chili powder, chilies, and ½ cup salsa sauce mix into the meat. Mix well.
4. Pour half of remaining salsa sauce mixture into a greased 9 x 13 baking pan.
5. Fill each shell with 1-2 Tbsp. meat mixture. Place in baking dish.
6. Pour remaining sauce over shells. Cover with foil.
7. Bake at 350° for 20-30 minutes. Uncover. Bake 5 more minutes.

Exchange List Values:
Starch 2.0, Vegetable 1.0, Lean Meat 2.0

Basic Nutritional Values:
Calories 293 (Calories from Fat 63), Total Fat 7 gm (Saturated Fat 2.6 gm, Trans Fat 0.4 gm, Polyunsat Fat 0.6 gm, Monounsat Fat 2.7 gm, Cholesterol 46 mg), Sodium 545 mg, Total Carbohydrate 36 gm, Dietary Fiber 4 gm, Sugars 7 gm, Protein 21 gm

Mexican Lasagna

Diane Eby, Holtwood, PA

Makes 12 servings
Serving size is 3″ x 3¼″ rectangle
or ⅟₁₂ of recipe

Prep Time: 20-30 minutes
Baking Time: 1 hour, plus 5 minutes
Standing Time: 15 minutes

1 lb. 90%-lean ground beef
16-oz. can fat-free refried beans
4-oz. can chopped green chilies
1¼ oz. no-salt-added taco seasoning (see recipe on page 254)
2 Tbsp. hot salsa
12 ozs. uncooked lasagna noodles

¾ cup (6 ozs.) reduced-fat
Monterey Jack cheese,
shredded, *divided*
16-oz. jar mild salsa
2 cups water
2 cups (16 ozs.) fat-free
sour cream
2¼-oz. can sliced ripe
olives, drained
3 green onions, chopped

1. In a large nonstick skillet, cook beef over medium heat until no longer pink. Drain off drippings.
2. Add the beans, chilies, taco seasoning, and hot salsa to the beef. Mix well.
3. In a deep greased 9 x 13 baking dish or lasagna pan, layer one-third of the uncooked noodles topped by one-third of the meat mixture. Sprinkle with ¼ cup cheese. Repeat layers twice.
4. Combine mild salsa and water; pour over top.
5. Cover and bake at 350° for 1 hour or until heated through.
6. Uncover. Top with sour cream, olives, and onions. Bake 5 minutes longer uncovered. Let stand 10-15 minutes before serving.

Exchange List Values:
Starch 2.0, Lean Meat 2.0

Basic Nutritional Values:
Calories 274 (Calories from Fat 56),
Total Fat 6 gm (Saturated Fat 2.3
gm, Trans Fat 0.2 gm, Polyunsat
Fat 0.5 gm, Monounsat Fat 2.3 gm,
Cholesterol 32 mg), Sodium 578 mg,
Total Carbohydrate 33 gm, Dietary
Fiber 4 gm, Sugars 5 gm, Protein 18 gm

Tip: You can prepare this up to 24 hours in advance. Cover it and keep it chilled. Remove

from the refrigerator 30 minutes before baking. You may need to bake it 15 minutes longer (covered, and before adding toppings in Step 6) if it's still quite cold when you put it in the oven.

Pastitsio
Sheila Soldner, Lititz, PA

*Makes 12 servings
Serving size is 3" x 3¼" rectangle
or ¹⁄₁₂ of recipe*

Prep Time: 30-45 minutes
Baking Time: 35 minutes

1 large onion, grated
1 lb. 90%-lean ground beef
½ cup tomato sauce
½ tsp. sugar
½ tsp. nutmeg
¼ tsp. pepper
1 tsp. salt
1 lb. ziti
4 Tbsp. canola oil, *divided*
3 Tbsp. Romano cheese,
grated
1 cup egg substitute, *divided*
5½ Tbsp. flour, *divided*
3 cups fat-free milk, *divided*
¼ cup reduced-fat cheddar
cheese, grated
dash of nutmeg
dash of salt
dash of pepper

1. Brown onion and ground beef in large nonstick skillet until moisture is absorbed.
2. Add tomato sauce, sugar, nutmeg, pepper, and salt and simmer for 15 minutes.
3. Meanwhile, boil ziti in water in a large stockpot for 10

minutes. Drain and rinse with cold water. Place in large bowl.
4. Heat 1 Tbsp. canola oil. Then pour the heated oil, Romano cheese and ½ cup egg substitute over ziti. Mix gently.
5. Grease a 9 x 13 baking pan, or a deep lasagna pan. Place half the ziti in the bottom of the pan. Pour meat/tomato mixture on top of ziti. Cover with remaining ziti.
6. In a small mixing bowl, whisk together ½ Tbsp. flour and 1 cup milk. Pour over the baking dish contents.
7. Make the cream sauce by heating 3 Tbsp. canola oil in a medium-sized saucepan. Add 5 Tbsp. flour and blend well. Add 2 cups milk slowly. Cook over medium heat, stirring constantly until thickened and smooth.
8. Remove pan from heat. Add ½ cup egg substitute to mixture and stir until smooth.
9. Spoon sauce over ziti. Top with grated cheddar cheese. Sprinkle with nutmeg, salt, and pepper.
10. Bake uncovered at 350° for 35 minutes.

Exchange List Values:
Starch 2.5, Lean Meat 1.0,
Fat 1.0

Basic Nutritional Values:
Calories 311 (Calories from Fat 86),
Total Fat 10 gm (Saturated Fat 2.3
gm, Trans Fat 0.2 gm, Polyunsat
Fat 1.8 gm, Monounsat Fat 4.5 gm,
Cholesterol 28 mg), Sodium 385 mg,
Total Carbohydrate 38 gm, Dietary
Fiber 2 gm, Sugars 7 gm, Protein 18 gm

Tip: I have found this to be a great dish to serve at Christmas or other get-togethers when I have a large crowd to feed.

Quick Shrimp Pasta

Sandra Chang
Derwood, MD

Makes 9 servings
Serving size is 1 cup or ⅑ of recipe

Prep Time: 30 minutes
Cooking Time: 20 minutes

1 lb. spaghetti
1 Tbsp. vegetable oil
1 lb. raw shrimp, peeled
   and deveined
kosher salt
ground black pepper
1 medium-sized zucchini,
   unpeeled and cut into
   ½" pieces
3 cloves garlic, minced
3 Tbsp. extra-virgin olive oil
⅓ cup fresh flat-leaf
   parsley
½ tsp. cracked black
   pepper
½ cup grated Parmesan
   cheese, *divided*

1. Cook spaghetti according to package directions. When finished cooking, drain, return to cooking pot, and keep warm.
2. Meanwhile, in a large skillet, heat 1 Tbsp. vegetable oil over high heat until smoking hot.
3. Place shrimp in pan and sear for 1 to 2 minutes per side, or until just cooked through. Stir in a dash of kosher salt and a dash of pepper. Remove seasoned shrimp to a large serving bowl and keep warm.
4. Sauté zucchini pieces and minced garlic briefly in skillet until crisp-tender.
5. Add zucchini and garlic to shrimp.
6. Mix in olive oil, parsley, pepper, and ¼ cup Parmesan cheese.
7. Add cooked pasta and remaining cheese. Toss well and serve.

Exchange List Values:
Starch 2.5, Lean Meat 1.0, Fat 1.0

Basic Nutritional Values:
Calories 304 (Calories from Fat 81), Total Fat 9 gm (Saturated Fat 1.8 gm, Trans Fat 0.0 gm, Polyunsat Fat 1.5 gm, Monounsat Fat 5.0 gm, Cholesterol 63 mg), Sodium 112 mg, Total Carbohydrate 40 gm, Dietary Fiber 3 gm, Sugars 2 gm, Protein 15 gm

Variation: Substitute 1½ lbs. scallops for the shrimp for a different quick meal.

A Tip —

If you're traveling and an airline meal doesn't fit your meal plan, bring your own food. Having food is essential, especially if you take insulin.

Low-Fat Fettucine Alfredo with Veggies and Shrimp

Norma Grieser
Clarksville, MI

Makes 4-6 servings
Serving size is 1 cup or ⅙ of recipe

Prep Time: 15 minutes
Cooking Time: 30 minutes

2 Tbsp. onions, chopped
2 Tbsp. oil, *divided*
2 cups sliced asparagus *or*
   broccoli
½ cup nonfat dry milk
1½ cups skim milk
1½ Tbsp. flour
2 Tbsp. fat-free cream
   cheese, at room
   temperature
⅔ cup grated Parmesan, *or*
   mozzarella, cheese
9 ozs. fettucine
1 tsp. minced garlic
½ lb. raw shrimp, peeled
   and deveined, *or* ½ lb.
   fresh scallops

1. In a large skillet, sauté onions in 1 Tbsp. oil. Add asparagus or broccoli and stir-fry until just crisp-tender.
2. Combine milks and flour in a saucepan and whisk together until smooth. Cook until thickened.
3. In a small bowl, mix cream cheese with a small amount of white sauce until the cheese softens. Stir into rest of white sauce.
4. In a large stockpot, cook pasta according to directions

on box. Drain and keep warm. Pour stir-fried vegetables into cooked pasta.

5. Pour remaining oil into large skillet and sauté seafood and garlic. Add to pasta.

6. Pour sauce over pasta and toss.

Exchange List Values:
Carbohydrate 3.0,
Lean Meat 2.0, Fat 0.5

Basic Nutritional Values:
Calories 354 (Calories from Fat 85), Total Fat 9 gm (Saturated Fat 2.5 gm, Trans Fat 0.0 gm, Polyunsat Fat 2.1 gm, Monounsat Fat 4.1 gm, Cholesterol 55 mg), Sodium 235 mg, Total Carbohydrate 46 gm, Dietary Fiber 3 gm, Sugars 8 gm, Protein 22 gm

Shrimp and Mushroom Linguine

Cyndie Marrara
Port Matilda, PA

Makes 5 servings
Serving size is 1¼ cups or ⅕ recipe

Preparation Time: 10 minutes
Cooking Time: 30 minutes

2 cups fresh mushroom
  slices
3 Tbsp. canola oil
¼ cup flour
⅛ tsp. pepper
3 cups fat-free milk
2 cups peeled and cooked
  shrimp
¼ cup Parmesan cheese
8 ozs. linguine
Parmesan cheese, *optional*

1. In a large skillet, sauté mushrooms in canola oil. Blend in flour and pepper.

2. Add milk, and stir constantly until thickened.

3. Add shrimp and ¼ cup Parmesan cheese. Heat thoroughly.

4. Meanwhile, cook linguine according to package directions. Drain.

5. Combine shrimp sauce with linguine. Toss lightly and sprinkle with additional Parmesan cheese, if desired.

Exchange List Values:
Carbohydrate 3.0, Fat 1.5,
Very Lean Meat 3.0

Basic Nutritional Values:
Calories 398 (Calories from Fat 104), Total Fat 12 gm (Saturated Fat 1.9 gm, Trans Fat 0.0 gm, Polyunsat Fat 3.2 gm, Monounsat Fat 5.7 gm, Cholesterol 117 mg), Sodium 230 mg, Total Carbohydrate 47 gm, Dietary Fiber 2 gm, Sugars 10 gm, Protein 26 gm

Tip: I've doubled and tripled this recipe with no problem. The sauce is not really thick, so don't think you did something wrong. The pasta thickens the dish when you mix the sauce and cooked pasta together.

Simple Shrimp Scampi

Anne Jones, Ballston Lake, NY

Makes 4 servings
Serving size is 1¼ cups or ¼ recipe

Prep Time: 5 minutes
Cooking Time:
  5 minutes for the Scampi
  30 minutes for the pasta

2 Tbsp. olive oil
2 cloves garlic, crushed
1 Tbsp. lemon juice
1 Tbsp. dried parsley
1 lb. shrimp, shelled and
  deveined
2 Tbsp. freshly grated
  Parmesan cheese, *divided*
½ lb. cooked rotini *or*
  pasta of your choice

1. In a large skillet or wok, heat olive oil over low heat.

2. Add garlic, lemon juice, and parsley. Cook until garlic is tender.

3. Add shrimp and 1 Tbsp. Parmesan cheese. Cook over low heat until shrimp becomes opaque, stirring frequently, about 3 minutes.

4. Serve over pasta. Sprinkle with 1 Tbsp. Parmesan cheese.

Exchange List Values:
Starch 3.0, Fat 1.0,
Very Lean Meat 2.0

Basic Nutritional Values:
Calories 346 (Calories from Fat 84), Total Fat 9 gm (Saturated Fat 1.7 gm, Trans Fat 0.0 gm, Polyunsat Fat 1.4 gm, Monounsat Fat 5.5 gm, Cholesterol 133 mg), Sodium 177 mg, Total Carbohydrate 42 gm, Dietary Fiber 2 gm, Sugars 2 gm, Protein 22 gm

Spaghetti with Red Clam Sauce

Kate Good
Lancaster, PA
Rebecca Fennimore
Harrisonburg, VA

Makes 9 servings
Serving size is 1¼ cups or ⅑ recipe

Prep Time: 10-15 minutes
Cooking Time: 15-25 minutes

1 lb. spaghetti
1 Tbsp. olive oil
1 large onion, chopped
2 6.5-oz cans chopped
  clams, with their juice
¼ cup dry white wine
1 cup crushed tomatoes
pinch of red pepper flakes
¼ tsp. salt
pinch of ground pepper
¼ cup fresh parsley
Parmesan cheese, *optional*

1. Cook pasta according to package directions in large stockpot. Drain pasta, reserving ½ cup of cooking liquid. Keep pasta warm.
2. While pasta is cooking, heat oil in a skillet. Add onion and brown.
3. Stir in clams with juice, wine, tomatoes, red pepper flakes, salt, and pepper.
4. Reduce heat and simmer uncovered until sauce is thickened slightly, about 5 minutes.
5. Stir sauce, parsley, and reserved pasta cooking liquid into cooked pasta in stockpot. Cover and cook 1 minute.

6. Serve immediately, with Parmesan cheese for individual servings if you wish.

Exchange List Values:
Carbohydrate 3.0,
Very Lean Meat 1.0

Basic Nutritional Values:
Calories 260 (Calories from Fat 26), Total Fat 3 gm (Saturated Fat 0.4 gm, Trans Fat 0.0 gm, Polyunsat Fat 0.7 gm, Monounsat Fat 1.2 gm, Cholesterol 13 mg), Sodium 213 mg, Total Carbohydrate 45 gm, Dietary Fiber 3 gm, Sugars 5 gm, Protein 12 gm

Lazy Linguine with White Clam Sauce

Anne Jones
Ballston Lake, NY

Makes 8 servings
Serving size is 1 cup or ⅛ recipe

Prep Time: 20 minutes
Cooking Time: 20 minutes

2 Tbsp. canola oil
4 cloves garlic, crushed
½ cup diced onions
2 Tbsp. flour
2 6-oz. cans chopped clams
1 cup fat-free milk
¾ tsp. salt
¼-½ tsp. pepper
1 Tbsp. parsley
1 lb. linguine
shredded Parmesan
  cheese, *optional*

1. In a medium-sized saucepan, heat oil. Sauté garlic and onions until tender.
2. Add flour and stir until smooth.
3. Drain clams, reserving liquid.
4. Stir milk and reserved clam juice into flour mixture. Continue heating over medium heat, stirring constantly until thickened.
5. Add salt, pepper, parsley, and clams. Warm through.
6. Meanwhile, prepare linguine according to package directions.
7. Drain linguine. Place in large serving bowl. Stir clam sauce into it. Sprinkle with shredded Parmesan cheese, if you wish.

Exchange List Values:
Starch 3.0, Fat 0.5,
Very Lean Meat 1.0

Basic Nutritional Values:
Calories 294 (Calories from Fat 45), Total Fat 5 gm (Saturated Fat 0.5 gm, Trans Fat 0.0 gm, Polyunsat Fat 1.6 gm, Monounsat Fat 2.2 gm, Cholesterol 14 mg), Sodium 306 mg, Total Carbohydrate 48 gm, Dietary Fiber 2 gm, Sugars 5 gm, Protein 14 gm

A Tip —

If you plan on having a big meal, try to get in a little extra physical activity beforehand to compensate for the extra calories.

Creamy Salmon Casserole

Mary Jane Ebersole
Millmont, PA

Makes 6 servings
Serving size is ⅙ recipe

Prep Time: 25 minutes
Baking Time: 35 minutes

2 cups dry macaronis
2 Tbsp. canola oil
¼ cup chopped onions
2 Tbsp. parsley
⅓ cup flour
⅛ tsp. salt
¼ tsp. pepper
¼ tsp. Old Bay Seasoning, *optional*
3 cups fat-free milk
½ cup reduced-fat cheddar cheese, shredded
14.75-oz. can salmon, drained and de-boned
½ cup dry bread crumbs

1. Cook macaronis according to package directions. Drain and set aside.
2. Meanwhile, heat canola oil in a large saucepan. Add onions and parsley. Cook 5 minutes, stirring occasionally.
3. Stir in flour, salt, pepper, and Old Bay Seasoning if you wish.
4. Gradually add milk, stirring constantly.
5. Blend in cheese and salmon.
6. Add cooked macaronis. Mix well.
7. Pour into a greased 2-qt. casserole.
8. Sprinkle crumbs over casserole contents.
9. Bake uncovered at 350° for 35 minutes.

Exchange List Values:
Fat 1.0, Fat-Free Milk 0.5, Starch 2.5, Lean Meat 2.0

Basic Nutritional Values:
Calories 392 (Calories from Fat 109), Total Fat 12 gm (Saturated Fat 2.8 gm, Trans Fat 0.0 gm, Polyunsat Fat 3.0 gm, Monounsat Fat 5.4 gm, Cholesterol 34 mg), Sodium 555 mg, Total Carbohydrate 45 gm, Dietary Fiber 2 gm, Sugars 8 gm, Protein 25 gm

Creamy Crab-Stuffed Shells

James R. Johnston
Pahrump, NV

Makes 8 servings
Serving size is 3 shells

Prep Time: 45 minutes
Baking Time: 30 minutes

24 jumbo pasta shells
1 Tbsp. chopped green pepper
1 Tbsp. chopped red onions
3 Tbsp. canola oil, *divided*
12 ozs. crabmeat
½ tsp. pepper
1 tsp. Old Bay Seasoning
1 egg, beaten
2 Tbsp., plus 1½ cups fat-free milk, *divided*
½ cup fat-free mayonnaise
2 Tbsp. flour
½ cup grated Parmesan cheese
Old Bay Seasoning

1. Cook pasta according to package directions. Drain and set aside.
2. Sauté green pepper and onions in 1 Tbsp. canola oil in skillet until tender. Remove from heat.
3. Combine crabmeat, pepper, Old Bay, egg, 2 Tbsp. milk, and mayonnaise with sautéed vegetables.
4. Spoon mixture into shells.
5. Place a single layer of shells in a greased 9 x 13 baking pan.
6. Heat 2 Tbsp. canola oil in the skillet. Gradually whisk in flour. Then slowly add 1½ cups milk, stirring continuously until mixture thickens.
7. When white sauce is thickened and smooth, stir in Parmesan cheese.
8. Drizzle sauce over shells. Sprinkle with additional Old Bay Seasoning.
9. Bake uncovered for 30 minutes.

Exchange List Values:
Carbohydrate 2.0, Lean Meat 1.0, Fat 1.0

Basic Nutritional Values:
Calories 249 (Calories from Fat 78), Total Fat 9 gm (Saturated Fat 1.8 gm, Trans Fat 0.0 gm, Polyunsat Fat 2.1 gm, Monounsat Fat 4.1 gm, Cholesterol 57 mg), Sodium 389 mg, Total Carbohydrate 26 gm, Dietary Fiber 1 gm, Sugars 5 gm, Protein 16 gm

Crazy Crust Pizza

Pamela Metzler
Gilman, WI

Makes 8 serving
Serving size is 1 slice

Prep Time: 20 minutes
Baking Time: 20 minutes
Standing Time: 5 minutes

2 cups flour
1 cup egg substitute
1 tsp. salt
1½ cups milk
¾ lb. 90%-lean ground beef
½-1 cup chopped onions,
    according to your taste
    preference
2 tsp. dried oregano
¼ tsp. salt
pepper to taste
26-oz. can no-salt-added
    tomato sauce
¼ cup reduced-fat
    mozzarella cheese,
    shredded
¼ cup reduced-fat cheddar
    cheese, shredded

1. In a mixing bowl, mix
together flour, egg substitute,
1 tsp. salt, and milk until
smooth. Pour onto a greased
and floured jelly-roll pan.
    2. In a large skillet, brown
ground beef and onions.
Season with oregano, ¼ tsp.
salt, and pepper. Stir in
tomato sauce. Pour over
crust.
    3. Sprinkle cheeses evenly
over top.
    4. Bake at 475° for 20 min-
utes. Let stand 5 minutes
before cutting.

Exchange List Values:
Starch 2.0, Vegetable 1.0,
Lean Meat 1.0, Fat 0.5

Basic Nutritional Values:
Calories 261 (Calories from Fat 46),
Total Fat 5 gm (Saturated Fat 2.2
gm, Trans Fat 0.2 gm, Polyunsat
Fat 0.3 gm, Monounsat Fat 1.8 gm,
Cholesterol 31 mg), Sodium 547 mg,
Total Carbohydrate 34 gm, Dietary
Fiber 2 gm, Sugars 9 gm, Protein 18 gm

Personal Pizza

Ruth Shank
Gridley, IL

Makes 8 servings
Serving size is 1 individual pizza

Prep Time: 10-20 minutes
Resting Time: 10 minutes
Baking Time: 9-12 minutes,
    per baking sheet

3 cups flour
1½ cups whole wheat flour
2 Tbsp., *or* 2 envelopes,
    rapid-rise yeast
¾ tsp. salt
1½ tsp. sugar
1½ cups hot (120-130°)
    water
cornmeal
2 cups pizza *or* spaghetti
    sauce
1 cup reduced-fat mozzarella
    cheese, shredded
various pizza toppings,
    optional*

1. Stir flours, yeast, salt, and
sugar together in a large bowl.
    2. Stir in hot water until
dough pulls away from sides
of the bowl.

3. Turn out onto floured
surface and knead 5 minutes,
until smooth.
    4. Place dough on a floured
surface, cover with plastic
wrap, and let rest 10 minutes.
(Dough will just start to rise.)
    5. Divide dough into
8 pieces. Shape each piece
into a disk.
    6. Put oven rack in lowest
position. Preheat oven to 500°.
    7. Sprinkle a cookie sheet
with cornmeal and place
individual dough crusts on
the sheet. (You'll be able to fit
more than one dough crust on
a sheet.)
    8. Top each dough crust
with ¼ cup pizza sauce,
2 Tbsp. mozzarella cheese,
and, optionally, your favorite
toppings.
    9. Bake on the oven's
lowest rack position at 500°
for 9-12 minutes.

Exchange List Values:
Starch 3.5, Vegetable 1.0,
Fat 0.5

Basic Nutritional Values:
Calories 322 (Calories from Fat 36),
Total Fat 4 gm (Saturated Fat 1.7
gm, Trans Fat 0.0 gm, Polyunsat
Fat 0.9 gm, Monounsat Fat 0.7 gm,
Cholesterol 8 mg), Sodium 563 mg,
Total Carbohydrate 59 gm, Dietary
Fiber 5 gm, Sugars 5 gm, Protein 14 gm

** Please check food lists (e.g.:
Exchanges) or food labels for
nutritional information about
your favorite toppings.*

*With individual-sized pizzas,
each person may choose the
toppings s/he likes best.*

Pillow Pizza

Sharon Miller, Holmesville, OH

Makes 12 servings
Serving size is 3" x 3¼" rectangle

Prep Time: 20 minutes
Baking Time: 20 minutes

2 tubes refrigerated low-fat biscuits (10 biscuits per tube)
1 lb. 90%-lean ground beef
16-oz. can pizza sauce
optional ingredients:
  chopped onions
  chopped peppers
  canned mushrooms
  pepperoni
1 cup reduced-fat mozzarella cheese, shredded

1. Cut each biscuit into quarters and place in the bottom of a greased 9 x 13 baking dish.
2. In a skillet, brown beef. Drain off drippings. Add sauce to beef in skillet and stir together.
3. Pour over biscuit quarters.
4. Top with any optional ingredients as you would a pizza. Sprinkle cheese over top.
5. Bake at 400° for 20 minutes.

Exchange List Values:
Starch 1.0, Vegetable 1.0, Lean Meat 1.0, Fat 0.5

Basic Nutritional Values:
Calories 183 (Calories from Fat 55), Total Fat 6 gm (Saturated Fat 2.4 gm, Trans Fat 0.2 gm, Polyunsat Fat 0.7 gm, Monounsat Fat 2.2 gm, Cholesterol 28 mg), Sodium 548 mg, Total Carbohydrate 19 gm, Dietary Fiber 1 gm, Sugars 4 gm, Protein 13 gm

Pizza Roll-Ups

Vonnie Oyer, Hubbard, OR

Makes 12 servings
Serving size is 1 roll-up

Prep Time: 30 minutes
Standing and Rising Times: 1½ hours
Baking Time: 20-25 minutes

1½ Tbsp. yeast
½ tsp. sugar
⅜ cup warm (110-115°) water
1½ Tbsp. sugar
1½ Tbsp. no-trans-fat shortening
1⅓ tsp. salt
1½ cups hot (120-130°) water
5-6 cups flour
1¼ cups reduced-fat mozzarella cheese, shredded
½ tsp. salt
½ tsp. parsley
1 tsp. no-salt-added Italian seasoning (see recipe on page 254)
¼ tsp. pepper
2 cups no-salt-added tomato sauce
1½ tsp. sugar
1½ tsp. no-salt-added Italian seasoning (see recipe on page 254)
1½ tsp. parsley
1½ tsp. dried basil
½ tsp. garlic powder
¼ tsp. pepper

1. In a small bowl dissolve yeast and ½ tsp. sugar in ⅜ cup water.
2. In a large bowl, combine 1½ Tbsp. sugar, shortening, salt and hot water. Add yeast mixture.
3. Stir in flour. Knead for 10 minutes, or until smooth and elastic. Place in greased bowl, turning once.
4. Let rise to double. Punch down and let rest 10 minutes.
5. Roll dough into a 14"-wide strip, ¼" thick.
6. In a small bowl, mix cheese with salt, parsley, 1 tsp. Italian seasoning, and ¼ tsp. pepper. Sprinkle over dough. Press slightly into dough.
7. Roll up dough beginning with a narrow end, like a jelly roll. Cut roll into 12 slices, each about ¾" thick.
8. Grease 2 baking sheets, or line with bakers paper. Place roll-ups on baking sheets, cut-side up, and let stand 10-20 minutes.
9. Bake at 400° for 20-25 minutes.
10. Mix tomato sauce and the seasonings and herbs in a saucepan. Heat. Serve roll-ups with small bowls of sauce for dunking.

Exchange List Values:
Starch 3.0, Fat 0.5

Basic Nutritional Values:
Calories 258 (Calories from Fat 34), Total Fat 4 gm (Saturated Fat 1.5 gm, Trans Fat 0.0 gm, Polyunsat Fat 0.8 gm, Monounsat Fat 1.0 gm, Cholesterol 6 mg), Sodium 453 mg, Total Carbohydrate 46 gm, Dietary Fiber 2 gm, Sugars 6 gm, Protein 9 gm

Tips: You can add chopped pepperoni with the cheese and seasonings (Step 6) if you wish.

Chicken Fajita Pizza

Ann Henderson, Cincinnati, OH

Makes 12 servings
Serving size is 1 slice

Prep Time: 20-30 minutes
Baking Time: 15-20 minutes

1 Tbsp. oil
1 small boneless skinless
　chicken breast, about ¾
　lb., cut into 2" x ½" strips
1 clove garlic, pressed, *or*
　½ tsp. garlic powder
1-2 tsp. chili powder,
　according to your taste
　preference
½ tsp. salt
1 cup onions, thinly sliced
1 cup combination of
　green, red, and orange
　pepper slices
13½-oz. pkg. refrigerated
　pizza crust
cornmeal
½ cup salsa *or* picante sauce
⅔ cup reduced-fat Monterey
　Jack cheese, shredded

1. Heat oil in skillet. Add chicken strips and stir-fry just until lightly browned.

2. Stir in garlic, chili powder, and salt. Add onions and peppers and cook for 1 minute until tender-crisp.

3. Unroll dough and roll onto cornmeal-covered pizza stone. Par-bake dough at 425° for 8-10 minutes.

4. Spoon chicken and vegetable mixture onto crust. Cover with salsa and cheese.

5. Bake at 425° for about more 5 minutes, or until crust is browning.

Exchange List Values:
Starch 1.0, Vegetable 1.0,
Fat 1.0

Basic Nutritional Values:
Calories 153 (Calories from Fat 39),
Total Fat 4 gm (Saturated Fat 1.3
gm, Trans Fat 0.0 gm, Polyunsat
Fat 1.1 gm, Monounsat Fat 1.3 gm,
Cholesterol 21 mg), Sodium 468 mg,
Total Carbohydrate 19 gm, Dietary
Fiber 1 gm, Sugars 3 gm, Protein 11 gm

Pasta Pizza Pronto

Shari Jensen, Fountain, CO

Makes 9 servings
Serving size is 1 slice

Prep Time: 20 minutes
Baking Time: 37-40 minutes

Crust:
2 cups uncooked macaronis
¾ cup egg substitute
⅓ cup finely chopped onions
¼ cup reduced-fat cheddar
　cheese, shredded

Topping:
1½ cups prepared pizza *or*
　pasta sauce
3-oz. pkg. sliced turkey
　pepperoni
2.25-oz. can sliced olives,
　drained
1 cup toppings: mix *or* select
　sliced mushrooms, diced
　cooked ham *or* chicken,
　diced bell peppers
⅓ cup reduced-fat
　mozzarella cheese,
　shredded

1. In a saucepan, cook macaronis according to package directions. Drain well.

2. In a large bowl, stir together egg substitute, onions, cheddar cheese, and cooked macaronis.

3. Spread pasta mixture evenly on generously greased 14-16" pizza pan.

4. Bake at 375° for 25 minutes on lower oven rack. Remove from oven.

5. Top with your favorite pizza or pasta sauce. Spread to within ½" of edge, using the back of a spoon.

6. Top evenly with pepperoni, olives, and 1 cup of the other toppings.

7. Finish by sprinkling with mozzarella cheese.

8. Return to oven and bake 12-15 minutes longer, until cheese is bubbly.

9. Remove from oven and slice with pizza cutter into 9 slices. Serve warm.

Exchange List Values:
Starch 1.0, Vegetable 1.0,
Lean Meat 1.0, Fat 0.5

Basic Nutritional Values:
Calories 177 (Calories from Fat 40),
Total Fat 4 gm (Saturated Fat 1.5
gm, Trans Fat 0.0 gm, Polyunsat
Fat 0.8 gm, Monounsat Fat 1.5 gm,
Cholesterol 16 mg), Sodium 425 mg,
Total Carbohydrate 23 gm, Dietary
Fiber 2 gm, Sugars 3 gm, Protein 11 gm

Tips:
1. Don't overload with toppings. Stay within the 1-cup suggestion.
2. Using the lower shelf of oven will crisp the crust. If not available in your oven, the middle shelf is okay.
3. Keep pasta pieces touching each other. No gaps.

Vegetables

Oven Roasted Vegetables & Herbs

Bonnie Goering
Bridgewater, VA

Makes 5 servings
Serving size is ¾ cup or ⅕ recipe

Prep Time: 10 minutes
Baking Time: 45-60 minutes

3 potatoes, cut in 1" pieces
3 carrots, cut in 1" pieces
2 onions, cut in wedges
¼ cup olive oil
2 Tbsp. minced fresh, *or*
  ¾ tsp. dried, rosemary
2 Tbsp. minced fresh, *or*
  ¾ tsp. dried, thyme
1 Tbsp. fresh, *or* 1 tsp.
  dried parsley
¾ tsp. salt
¼ tsp. freshly ground
  black pepper
½ lb. freshly mushrooms,
  cut into halves or
  quarters

1. Combine potatoes, carrots, and onions in a large mixing bowl.
2. Drizzle olive oil over vegetables.
3. In a small bowl, combine rosemary, thyme, parsley, salt, and pepper. Sprinkle over vegetables.
4. Arrange vegetables in a single layer on a large greased baking sheet.
5. Bake at 400° for 30 minutes.
6. Remove from oven and stir in mushrooms. Return to oven and continue baking for another 15-30 minutes, or until potatoes and carrots are tender.

A Tip —

To cut fat, saturated fat, and calories, use a butter spray instead of real butter on vegetables, baked potatoes, and popcorn.

Exchange List Values:
Starch 1.0, Vegetable 3.0, Fat 2.0

Basic Nutritional Values:
Calories 228 (Calories from Fat 102), Total Fat 11 gm (Saturated Fat 1.5 gm, Trans Fat 0.0 gm, Polyunsat Fat 1.3 gm, Monounsat Fat 8.0 gm, Cholesterol 0 mg), Sodium 389 mg, Total Carbohydrate 30 gm, Dietary Fiber 5 gm, Sugars 7 gm, Protein 4 gm

Garden Vegetable Medley

Ruth Fisher, Leicester, NY

Makes 4 servings
Serving size is ¾ cup or ¼ recipe

Prep Time: 10 minutes
Cooking Time: 20 minutes

1 Tbsp. olive oil
4 cups zucchini, chopped
  into ½" pieces
1 cup chopped onions
1 red *or* green pepper,
  chopped
2 medium-sized tomatoes,
  chopped
¼ tsp. garlic powder
½ tsp. salt
4 slices of your favorite
  reduced-fat cheese

1. Heat oil in stir-fry pan over medium heat. Add zucchini and onions. Heat until tender, about 10 minutes.

2. Add peppers and tomatoes and stir-fry until just tender.

3. Stir in garlic powder and salt.

4. Lay cheese over top. Turn off heat and let stand until cheese is melted.

Exchange List Values:
Vegetable 3.0, Fat 1.5

Basic Nutritional Values:
Calories 138 (Calories from Fat 61), Total Fat 7 gm (Saturated Fat 2.4 gm, Trans Fat 0.0 gm, Polyunsat Fat 0.7 gm, Monounsat Fat 3.4 gm, Cholesterol 10 mg), Sodium 298 mg, Total Carbohydrate 14 gm, Dietary Fiber 3 gm, Sugars 8 gm, Protein 7 gm

Variations:
1. Use only 3 cups zucchini and add 1 baby eggplant, cut up into ½" pieces.
2. Substitute 1-2 tsp. dried Italian seasoning for garlic powder and salt.
3. Instead of slices of cheese, sprinkle liberally with Parmesan cheese.
—Stephanie O'Conner
  Cheshire, CN

Peas with Bacon & Crispy Leeks

J.B.Miller, Indianapolis, IN

Makes 12 servings
Serving size is ¾ cup or 1/12 recipe

Prep Time: 15 minutes
Cooking Time: 45 minutes

3 large leeks
2 Tbsp. olive oil
4 fresh thyme springs, *or*
  ½ tsp. ground thyme
salt and pepper to taste
6 thick slices of bacon
1 cup reduced-sodium,
  98%-fat-free chicken
  broth, *divided*
¾ cup fat-free half-and-half
30 ozs. frozen baby peas,
  thawed
salt and pepper
1 tsp. cornstarch
1 Tbsp. water

1. Using only the white and tender green part of the leeks, slice the leeks crosswise into ¼" thick pieces. Separate into rings. Wash and pat dry.

2. Arrange leeks in a single layer on a large baking sheet. Drizzle with 2 Tbsp. olive oil. Sprinkle with thyme. Bake at 400° for 15 minutes, or until crisp.

3. Transfer leeks and thyme to a plate and season lightly with salt and pepper.

4. Cook bacon in a skillet until brown and crispy. Remove bacon and discard drippings. Place bacon on paper towels. When drained, crumble.

5. Add ½ cup chicken broth to skillet and cook uncovered until broth is reduced by half.

6. Add half-and-half. Cook until the creamy broth is reduced by half.

7. Stir in peas, crumbled bacon, and the remaining ½ cup broth. Bring to a boil.

8. If using fresh thyme sprigs, discard. Season cooked mixture lightly with salt and pepper.

9. In a small bowl, stir cornstarch into water until smooth. Stir into hot sauce. Continue stirring until it thickens slightly.

10. Spoon the peas into a serving dish and top with the reserved crispy leeks just before serving.

Exchange List Values:
Starch 0.5, Vegetable 1.0, Fat 1.0

Basic Nutritional Values:
Calories 114 (Calories from Fat 36), Total Fat 4 gm (Saturated Fat 0.9 gm, Trans Fat 0.0 gm, Polyunsat Fat 0.5 gm, Monounsat Fat 2.3 gm, Cholesterol 4 mg), Sodium 190 mg, Total Carbohydrate 14 gm, Dietary Fiber 4 gm, Sugars 5 gm, Protein 5 gm

Spinach Quiche

Mary Jane Hoober
Shipshewana, IN

Makes 8 servings
Serving size is ¾ cup or ⅛ recipe

Prep Time: 20 minutes
Baking Time: 30-35 minutes

2 slices bacon
1 cup fat-free sour cream
3 eggs, separated
2 Tbsp. flour
⅛ tsp. pepper
10-oz. pkg. frozen chopped
  spinach, thawed and
  squeezed dry
⅓ cup reduced-fat sharp
  cheddar cheese, shredded
½ cup dry bread crumbs

1. Fry bacon. When crisp, drain. Then crumble and set aside.
2. In a large mixing bowl, combine sour cream, egg yolks, flour, and pepper.
3. In a separate bowl, beat egg whites until stiff peaks form. Gently stir one-fourth of egg whites into sour cream mixture. When well blended, fold in remaining egg whites.
4. In a greased round 2-qt. baking dish, layer spinach, sour-cream mixture, cheese, and bacon in casserole dish.
6. Sprinkle bread crumbs over bacon.
7. Bake, uncovered, at 350° for 30-35 minutes, or until a knife inserted in the center comes out clean.

Exchange List Values:
Carbohydrate 0.5,
Lean Meat 1.0

Basic Nutritional Values:
Calories 109 (Calories from Fat 31), Total Fat 3 gm (Saturated Fat 1.4 gm, Trans Fat 0.0 gm, Polyunsat Fat 0.5 gm, Monounsat Fat 1.1 gm, Cholesterol 61 mg), Sodium 188 mg, Total Carbohydrate 9 gm, Dietary Fiber 1 gm, Sugars 2 gm, Protein 8 gm

Cheesy Spinach or Broccoli Casserole

Christie Detamore-Hunsberger
Harrisonburg, VA

Makes 6 servings
Serving size is 3" x 4¼" rectangle
or ⅙ of recipe

Prep Time: 20 minutes
Baking Time: 30 minutes
Standing Time: 10 minutes

¾ cup egg substitute
2 Tbsp. flour
10-oz. pkg. chopped spinach
  or broccoli, thawed
4 ozs. fat-free cottage
  cheese
¾ cup (3 ozs.) reduced-fat
  cheddar cheese, grated
1-1½ tsp. dried oregano,
  according to your taste
  preference
¾ tsp. dried basil
⅛ tsp. pepper
¼ cup dry bread crumbs
1 Tbsp. Parmesan cheese

1. In a large mixing bowl, beat egg substitute and flour until smooth.
2. If you're using spinach, squeeze it dry. Then add it (or the broccoli) and the cottage and cheddar cheeses, oregano, basil, and pepper to the egg mixture. Stir.
3. Spray 9 x 9 glass baking dish with no-stick pan spray. Pour mixture into dish. Sprinkle with bread crumbs and Parmesan cheese.
4. Bake uncovered at 375° for 30 minutes. Let stand 10 minutes before serving.

Exchange List Values:
Carbohydrate 0.5,
Lean Meat 1.0

Basic Nutritional Values:
Calories 99 (Calories from Fat 25), Total Fat 3 gm (Saturated Fat 1.4 gm, Trans Fat 0.0 gm, Polyunsat Fat 0.3 gm, Monounsat Fat 0.7 gm, Cholesterol 9 mg), Sodium 280 mg, Total Carbohydrate 9 gm, Dietary Fiber 2 gm, Sugars 1 gm, Protein 10 gm

Stir-Fried Broccoli

Vicki Dinkel, Sharon Springs, KS

Makes 4 servings
Serving size is ¾ cup or ¼ recipe

Prep Time: 15 minutes
Cooking Time: 5 minutes

1 onion, diced
1 Tbsp. oil
1 lb. broccoli florets, cut in
   pieces, fresh *or* frozen
½ cup reduced-sodium,
   98%-fat-free chicken
   broth
1 tsp. cornstarch
2 Tbsp. light soy sauce
1 tsp. sugar

1. Brown onion in oil in
a large skillet. Add broccoli.
Stir-fry 3 minutes.
2. In a small bowl,
combine chicken broth,
cornstarch, soy sauce, and
sugar. Add to broccoli. Cook
1-2 minutes until sauce clears.
3. Serve over cooked rice.

Exchange List Values:
Vegetable 2.0, Fat 1.0

Basic Nutritional Values:
Calories 93 (Calories from Fat 35),
Total Fat 4 gm (Saturated Fat 0.3
gm, Trans Fat 0.0 gm, Polyunsat
Fat 1.3 gm, Monounsat Fat 2.1 gm,
Cholesterol 0 mg), Sodium 381 mg,
Total Carbohydrate 12 gm, Dietary
Fiber 4 gm, Sugars 5 gm, Protein 5 gm

Variations:
1. Replace half of broccoli
with cauliflower or any other
vegetable of your choice.
2. Add strips of boneless skin-
less chicken breasts to Step 1.

Surfside Summer Squash

Ginny Cutler, Westminster, MD

Makes 8 servings
Serving size is 4½" x 3¼" rectangle
or ⅛ of recipe

Prep Time: 25-30 minutes
Baking Time: 30 minutes

5 medium-sized summer
   squash
½ cup egg substitute
½ cup fat-free milk
1 medium onion, chopped
¾ cup reduced-fat cheddar
   cheese, grated
1 tomato, chopped
2 Tbsp. Parmesan cheese
1 cup Italian bread crumbs

1. Cut up or slice squash.
Steam or microwave until just
tender. Drain and set aside.
2. In a mixing bowl, beat
together egg substitute and
milk. Add onion, cheddar
cheese, and tomato.
3. Add squash to egg/cheese
mixture.
4. Pour into a greased 9 x 13
baking dish.
5. Sprinkle with Parmesan
cheese and bread crumbs.
6. Bake uncovered at 400°
for 30 minutes.

Exchange List Values:
Carbohydrate 1.0,
Lean Meat 1.0

Basic Nutritional Values:
Calories 136 (Calories from Fat 35),
Total Fat 4 gm (Saturated Fat 2.0
gm, Trans Fat 0.0 gm, Polyunsat
Fat 0.4 gm, Monounsat Fat 1.1 gm,

Cholesterol 10 mg), Sodium 373 mg,
Total Carbohydrate 18 gm, Dietary
Fiber 2 gm, Sugars 6 gm, Protein 9 gm

Baked Cabbage

Karen Gingrich, New Holland, PA

Makes 6 servings
Serving size is ¾ cup or ⅙ recipe

Prep Time: 20 minutes
Cooking/Baking Time: 45 minutes

1 medium-sized head of
   cabbage
water
½ tsp. salt
1½ cups fat-free milk
1 Tbsp. flour
½ tsp. salt
½ tsp. pepper
1 Tbsp. stick corn-oil
   margarine
½ cup reduced-fat sharp
   cheddar cheese, grated

1. Cut cabbage in wedges
¾" thick. Cook, covered,
in a saucepan in ½" water,
sprinkled with ½ tsp. salt, for
10 minutes. Drain and place
cabbage in a greased 2-qt.
baking casserole.
2. While cabbage is cook-
ing (Step 1), warm milk in a
small saucepan until it forms
a skin but does not boil.
3. Sprinkle cabbage with
flour, ½ tsp. salt, and pepper.
4. Pour hot milk over,
being careful not to wash off
the flour and seasonings. Dot
with margarine. Top with
grated cheese.
5. Bake, uncovered, at 350°
for 35 minutes.

Basic Nutritional Values:
Calories 110 (Calories from Fat 37), Total Fat 4 gm (Saturated Fat 1.6 gm, Trans Fat 0.3 gm, Polyunsat Fat 0.8 gm, Monounsat Fat 1.1 gm, Cholesterol 8 mg), Sodium 445 mg, Total Carbohydrate 14 gm, Dietary Fiber 4 gm, Sugars 9 gm, Protein 7 gm

Carrots with Sausage and Rosemary

J.B. Miller, Indianapolis, IN

Makes 12 servings
Serving size is ¾ cup or 1/12 recipe

Preparation Time: 15 minutes
Cooking Time: 20 minutes

3 lbs. carrots, sliced crosswise, about ¼″ thick
2 Tbsp. extra-virgin olive oil
¾ lb. lean turkey sweet Italian sausage, removed from casing
1 medium-sized onion, finely chopped
1 Tbsp., plus 1 tsp., chopped fresh rosemary, or 2 tsp. dried rosemary
1 Tbsp. tomato paste
½ cup water
salt and pepper
¼ cup chopped parsley

1. In a large pot, boil carrots in salt water over moderately high heat until tender, about 7 minutes. Do not overcook. Drain carrots.

2. In a large, deep skillet, heat olive oil. Add sausage and cook over moderate heat, breaking up the meat with a wooden spoon until no pink remains.

3. Add onions and rosemary to sausage. Cook over moderately low heat, stirring occasionally until onions are softened, about 6 minutes.

4. Stir in carrots and cook until heated through.

5. In a small bowl, blend tomato paste with water. Add to carrots. Season with salt and pepper.

6. Remove from heat and stir in parsley just before serving.

Basic Nutritional Values:
Calories 124 (Calories from Fat 53), Total Fat 6 gm (Saturated Fat 1.3 gm, Trans Fat 0.0 gm, Polyunsat Fat 0.7 gm, Monounsat Fat 2.3 gm, Cholesterol 22 mg), Sodium 255 mg, Total Carbohydrate 12 gm, Dietary Fiber 3 gm, Sugars 5 gm, Protein 7 gm

We often serve this at Thanksgiving. It's a great alternative to more traditional vegetables at holiday-times.

A Tip —

Be wary of any diet that claims you can eat all you want of one food and lose weight. Unfortunately, there is no "magic" diet.

Cheesy Cauliflower

Joan Erwin, Sparks, NV

Makes 6 servings
Serving size is ¾ cup or 1/6 recipe

Prep Time: 5-10 minutes
Baking Time: 11 minutes

1 head of cauliflower
1 Tbsp. water
1 cup mayonnaise
1 Tbsp. prepared mustard
½ cup chopped green *or* red onions
¼ cup reduced-fat Monterey Jack cheese, shredded
¼ cup reduced-fat sharp cheddar cheese, shredded

1. Place whole cauliflower head in microwavable glass baking dish. Add water. Cover. Microwave on high for 9 minutes, until crisp-cooked.

2. Meanwhile, combine mayonnaise, mustard, and onions in a small bowl. Spread over cooked cauliflower. Sprinkle with cheeses.

3. Cover and microwave on high for 1 minute, or until cheese is melted.

Basic Nutritional Values:
Calories 81 (Calories from Fat 21), Total Fat 2 gm (Saturated Fat 1.2 gm, Trans Fat 0.0 gm, Polyunsat Fat 0.2 gm, Monounsat Fat 0.6 gm, Cholesterol 7 mg), Sodium 417 mg, Total Carbohydrate 11 gm, Dietary Fiber 3 gm, Sugars 5 gm, Protein 5 gm

---

Variation: You may break the cauliflower into florets and proceed with Step 1.

Stuffed Peppers

Stacy Schmucker Stoltzfus
Enola, PA

Makes 4 servings
Serving size is 2 stuffed pepper halves

Prep Time: 15-20 minutes
Baking Time: 25 minutes

**4 large bell peppers of any
color**
½ lb. 90%-lean ground beef
half or a whole onion, diced
1 cup cooked rice
¼ cup crushed soda crackers
¾ cup chopped tomatoes
salt and pepper to taste
**¼ cup reduced-fat cheddar
cheese, grated**

1. Cut peppers in half
through their stem ends. Seed
and de-vein. In covered pan,
par-boil for 5 minutes in 1 inch
of water. Drain and cool.
2. In a skillet, brown meat
and onion. Drain.
3. In a mixing bowl, stir
together meat and onion, rice,
crackers, tomatoes, salt, and
pepper.
4. Place peppers in a greased
9 x 13 pan and divide the meat
mixture among the halves.
5. Bake, uncovered, at 350°
for 20 minutes. Remove from
oven and top with cheese.
6. Turn oven to 400°.
Return pan to oven and heat
stuffed peppers for 5 more
minutes.

Exchange List Values:
Starch 1.0, Vegetable 2.0,
Lean Meat 1.0, Fat 1.0

Basic Nutritional Values:
Calories 230 (Calories from Fat 64),
Total Fat 7 gm (Saturated Fat 2.9
gm, Trans Fat 0.4 gm, Polyunsat
Fat 0.5 gm, Monounsat Fat 2.8 gm,
Cholesterol 39 mg), Sodium 147 mg,
Total Carbohydrate 26 gm, Dietary
Fiber 4 gm, Sugars 6 gm, Protein 16 gm

Stewed Tomatoes

Esther J. Mast, Lancaster, PA

Makes 5 servings
Serving size is ¾ cup or ⅕ recipe

Prep Time: 5 minutes
Cooking Time: 10 minutes

2 Tbsp. chopped onions
**2 Tbsp. freshly chopped
celery leaves**
2 tsp. butter
**2 cups canned diced
tomatoes, undrained**
2 Tbsp. cornstarch
**2 Tbsp. sugar blend for
baking (Splenda)**
¼ tsp. salt
⅛ tsp. cinnamon

1. In a large skillet or
saucepan, sauté onions and
celery leaves in butter until
soft but not brown.
2. Add tomatoes and stir in
well.
3. In a small bowl, com-
bine cornstarch, sugar blend
for baking, salt, and cinnamon. Pour just enough tomato
mixture into dry mixture
to moisten. Immediately
stir into remaining tomato
mixture. Continue cooking
and stirring until thickened.

Exchange List Values:
Carbohydrate 1.0

Basic Nutritional Values:
Calories 66 (Calories from Fat 15),
Total Fat 2 gm (Saturated Fat 1.0
gm, Trans Fat 0.0 gm, Polyunsat
Fat 0.1 gm, Monounsat Fat 0.4 gm,
Cholesterol 4 mg), Sodium 330 mg,
Total Carbohydrate 13 gm, Dietary
Fiber 1 gm, Sugars 8 gm, Protein 1 gm

*Tip: If the mixture gets too
thick, add water until the
tomatoes reach the consistency
you want.*

Variations:
*1. Stir 1½ tsp. prepared
mustard into Step 2.*
*2. Butter and toast 3 slices of
bread. Then cut them into cubes
and place them on top of the
casserole at the end of Step 3.
Slide under broiler to brown.*
—**Dorothy Hartley**
Carmichaels, PA

*3. Stir 1 Tbsp. fresh basil,
chopped, or ¾ tsp. dried basil,
into Step 2.*
*4. If you add #2 Variation
(just above), sprinkle the
buttered toast with a dusting of
dried oregano before cutting the
toast into cubes.*
—**Colleen Heatwole**
Burton, MI

*I got this recipe from the school
cafeteria where I worked when
our sons were in junior high
school. It became a family
favorite—served as a side dish
to macaroni and cheese.*
—**Esther J. Mast**
Lancaster, PA

Squash Apple Bake

Lavina Hochstedler
Grand Blanc, MI

Makes 8 servings
Serving size is ¾ cup or ⅛ recipe

Prep Time: 20 minutes
Baking Time: 45-50 minutes

3 Tbsp. brown sugar
⅓ cup orange juice, *or* apple juice, *or* apple cider
4 cups cubed butternut *or* buttercup squash, *divided*
¼ tsp. salt, *divided*
2 apples, cored and thinly sliced, *divided*
¼ cup raisins, *divided*
cinnamon
1 Tbsp. butter

1. Combine brown sugar and juice in a small mixing bowl. Set aside.
2. Place half the cubed squash in a greased 2-qt. baking dish. Sprinkle with half the salt.
3. Follow with a layer of half the apples and raisins. Sprinkle generously with cinnamon.
4. Repeat the layers.
5. Pour juice mixture over all. Dot with butter.
6. Cover and bake at 350° for 45-50 minutes, or until tender.

Exchange List Values:
Carbohydrate 1.5

Basic Nutritional Values:
Calories 92 (Calories from Fat 14), Total Fat 2 gm (Saturated Fat 0.9 gm, Trans Fat 0.0 gm, Polyunsat Fat 0.1 gm, Monounsat Fat 0.4 gm, Cholesterol 4 mg), Sodium 88 mg, Total Carbohydrate 21 gm, Dietary Fiber 2 gm, Sugars 14 gm, Protein 1 gm

Variation: Stir 1 Tbsp. orange rind into Step 1.
—Christie Detamore-Hunsberger
Harrisonburg, VA

Aunt Mary's Baked Corn

Becky Frey, Lebanon, PA
Doris Beachy, Stevens, PA
Cynthia Morris
Grottoes, VA
Susie Nisley
Millersburg, OH

Makes 6 servings
Makes 1½-2-quart casserole
Serving size is ¾ cup or ⅙ recipe

Prep Time: 15 minutes
Standing Time: 1 hour
Baking Time: 1 hour

1½ cups fat-free milk
1 Tbsp. soft-tub corn-oil margarine
3 cups creamed corn, fresh, frozen, *or* canned
3 Tbsp. cornstarch
3 eggs, beaten
1 Tbsp. sugar blend for baking (Splenda)
⅛ tsp. pepper

1. In a small saucepan, heat milk until it forms a skin but does not boil. Stir in margarine.
2. While margarine melts, mix corn and cornstarch in a good-sized mixing bowl until cornstarch is dissolved. Add beaten eggs, sugar blend, and pepper. Mix in milk and margarine.
3. Put in a greased 1½-2-qt. baking dish.
4. Let stand for 1 hour.
5. Bake, uncovered, at 350° for 1 hour, or until set in the middle.

Exchange List Values:
Carbohydrate 2.0, Fat 1.0

Basic Nutritional Values:
Calories 192 (Calories from Fat 44), Total Fat 5 gm (Saturated Fat 1.1 gm, Trans Fat 0.0 gm, Polyunsat Fat 1.2 gm, Monounsat Fat 1.5 gm, Cholesterol 107 mg), Sodium 475 mg, Total Carbohydrate 30 gm, Dietary Fiber 1 gm, Sugars 14 gm, Protein 7 gm

When my mom's cousins had their annual Christmas dinner at a local firehall, we always had ham, candied sweet potatoes, and baked corn, among other things. (The second cousins brought cookies, and we had many varieties to choose from after the main course!)
—Becky Frey
Lebanon, PA

A Tip —

Go to www.diabetes.org for more information on diabetes, meal planning, and ways to volunteer.

Spiced Sweet Potatoes

J.B. Miller, Indianapolis, IN

Makes 4 servings
Serving size is ½ cup or ¼ recipe

Prep Time: 10-15 minutes
Baking Time: 30-40 minutes

1 tsp. coriander seeds
½ tsp. fennel seeds
½ tsp. dried oregano
½ tsp. dried hot red pepper flakes
½ tsp. salt
1 lb. medium-sized sweet potatoes with skins left on
3 Tbsp. vegetable oil

1. Coarsely grind all spices in coffee/spice grinder. (This yields a potent flavor, releasing the oils just before they're added to the other ingredients.) Add salt.
2. Cut potatoes lengthwise into 1"-wide wedges. Place them in a large mixing bowl. Toss them with the vegetable oil and spice mixture.
3. When well coated, place them in a single layer on a greased baking sheet.
4. Bake at 425° for 15 minutes. Turn them over and bake another 15 minutes, or until soft. Check the potatoes ever 5 minutes after you've turned them over to be sure they don't burn.

Exchange List Values:
Starch 1.5, Fat 1.5

Basic Nutritional Values:
Calories 179 (Calories from Fat 97),

Total Fat 11 gm (Saturated Fat 0.8 gm, Trans Fat 0.0 gm, Polyunsat Fat 3.2 gm, Monounsat Fat 6.3 gm, Cholesterol 0 mg), Sodium 324 mg, Total Carbohydrate 20 gm, Dietary Fiber 3 gm, Sugars 6 gm, Protein 2 gm

Yam Fries

Kathy Keener Shantz
Lancaster, PA

Makes 6 servings
Serving size is ¾ cup or ⅙ recipe

Prep Time: 10 minutes
Baking Time: 20 minutes

2 Tbsp. olive oil
1 tsp. salt
1 tsp. pepper
1 tsp. curry
½ tsp. hot sauce
4 5¼-oz. (medium-sized) yams, sliced like French fries, with skins left on

1. In a large mixing bowl, combine oil, salt, pepper, curry, and hot sauce.
2. Stir in sliced yams.
3. When thoroughly coated, spread on lightly greased baking sheet.
4. Bake at 375° for 20 minutes, or until tender.

Exchange List Values:
Starch 1.0, Fat 1.0

Basic Nutritional Values:
Calories 114 (Calories from Fat 42), Total Fat 5 gm (Saturated Fat 0.6 gm, Trans Fat 0.0 gm, Polyunsat Fat 0.5 gm, Monounsat Fat 3.3 gm, Cholesterol 0 mg), Sodium 419 mg, Total Carbohydrate 17 gm, Dietary Fiber 3 gm, Sugars 5 gm, Protein 2 gm

Baked Sweet Potatoes

Mable Hershey, Marietta, PA

Makes 20 servings
Serving size is ¾ cup or ¹⁄₂₀ recipe

Prep Time: 30 minutes
Baking Time: 1-1½ hours

20 5¼-oz. (medium-sized) sweet potatoes
3 Tbsp. butter
1½ Tbsp. flour
1 tsp. salt
½ cup brown sugar blend (Splenda)
¼ cup dark corn syrup
½ cup water

1. In a large stockpot, boil sweet potatoes for 10 minutes, or until they slightly soften.
2. Peel and arrange in a greased 9 x 13 baking dish.
3. In a saucepan, melt butter. Add flour, salt, brown sugar blend, syrup, and water. Stir until well blended.
4. Cook until slightly thickened.
5. Pour over sweet potatoes. Bake, uncovered, at 350° for 1-1½ hours, or until sauce carmelizes over potatoes. Baste potatoes every 10-15 minutes with the sauce during the baking time.

Exchange List Values:
Carbohydrate 1.0, Fat 0.5

Basic Nutritional Values:
Calories 92 (Calories from Fat 16), Total Fat 2 gm (Saturated Fat 1.1 gm, Trans Fat 0.0 gm, Polyunsat Fat 0.1 gm, Monounsat Fat 0.4 gm,

Cholesterol 5 mg), Sodium 150 mg, Total Carbohydrate 17 gm, Dietary Fiber 1 gm, Sugars 11 gm, Protein 1 gm

Variations:
1. Substitute 1 cup apricot nectar for the water and 3 Tbsp. cornstarch for 1½ Tbsp. flour.
2. Use raw orange yams instead of sweet potatoes.
—Mable Hershey
Marietta, PA

3. After pouring sauce over potatoes, top them with 8 marshmallows cut into pieces and ½ cup chopped nuts. Pour 1 cup light cream over all.
—Emma Oberholtzer
Bamberg, SC

Baked Lima Beans
Jean Butzer, Batavia, NY

Makes 10 servings
Serving size is ¾ cup or ¹⁄₁₀ recipe

Prep Time: 5-10 minutes
Soaking Time: 8 hours, or overnight
Cooking Time: 1 hour, plus 2 hours

1 lb. dried lima beans
⅓ cup brown sugar blend for baking (Splenda)
¼ cup canola oil
1¾ tsp. salt
1 Tbsp. dried mustard
2 Tbsp. light corn syrup
1 cup fat-free sour cream

1. Place beans in a large soup pot and cover with water. Allow to soak for 8 hours, or overnight.

2. Cook in soaking water, covered, until almost tender. Drain and rinse.

3. In a large mixing bowl, combine cooked beans, brown sugar blend, canola oil, salt, mustard, corn syrup, and sour cream. Pour into a greased 2½-qt. casserole and cover.

4. Bake at 300° for 2 hours, stirring several times.

5. Mixture will be thin when taken from the oven, but it thickens as it cools.

Exchange List Values:
Carbohydrate 2.0, Fat 1.0, Very Lean Meat 1.0

Basic Nutritional Values:
Calories 240 (Calories from Fat 56), Total Fat 6 gm (Saturated Fat 0.5 gm, Trans Fat 0.0 gm, Polyunsat Fat 1.9 gm, Monounsat Fat 3.3 gm, Cholesterol 2 mg), Sodium 425 mg, Total Carbohydrate 33 gm, Dietary Fiber 8 gm, Sugars 11 gm, Protein 11 gm

Spicy Green Beans
Miriam Kauffman
Harrisonburg, VA

Makes 8 servings
Serving size is ¾ cup or ⅛ recipe

Prep Time: 25 minutes
Cooking and Baking Time: 75 minutes

3 cups canned tomatoes
2 Tbsp. minced onions
2 Tbsp. diced celery
½-1 tsp. dried oregano, according to your taste preference
½-1 tsp. chili powder, according to your taste preference
1 Tbsp. sugar
1 bay leaf
dash of red pepper
¼ tsp. garlic salt
⅛ tsp. ground cloves
⅛ tsp. pepper
2 Tbsp. flour
1 qt. canned green beans
½ cup dry bread crumbs

1. In a large saucepan, combine all ingredients except flour, beans, and bread crumbs. Simmer, covered, for 15 minutes.

2. Meanwhile, drain the beans, reserving 2 Tbsp. liquid. Place the beans in a large mixing bowl.

3. Pour the reserved bean liquid into a small bowl. Mix in flour to form a paste.

4. Add the paste to the tomato mixture. Cook until thickened. Pour thickened sauce over beans. Stir well.

5. Place mixture in a greased 3-qt. baking dish. Bake, covered, at 350° for 45 minutes.

6. Top with dry bread crumbs. Bake, uncovered, an additional 15 minutes.

Exchange List Values:
Carbohydrate 1.0

Basic Nutritional Values:
Calories 74 (Calories from Fat 6), Total Fat 1 gm (Saturated Fat 0.1 gm, Trans Fat 0.0 gm, Polyunsat Fat 0.3 gm, Monounsat Fat 0.1 gm, Cholesterol 0 mg), Sodium 458 mg, Total Carbohydrate 16 gm, Dietary Fiber 3 gm, Sugars 6 gm, Protein 3 gm

Many Beans Casserole

Donna Neiter
Wausau, WI

Makes 10 servings
Serving size is ¾ cup or ¹⁄₁₀ recipe

Prep Time: 20 minutes
Baking Time: 45 minutes

½ lb. bacon, diced
½ lb. 90%-lean ground beef
1 cup chopped onions
2 15-oz. cans fat-free, low-sodium baked beans
15-oz. can lima beans, drained and rinsed
15-oz. can kidney beans, drained and rinsed
15-oz. can butter beans, drained and rinsed
½ cup barbecue sauce
½ cup salt-free ketchup
¼ cup sugar blend for baking (Splenda)
¼ cup brown sugar blend (Splenda)
2 Tbsp. prepared mustard
2 Tbsp. molasses
½ tsp. chili powder

1. In a large skillet, brown bacon and beef. Drain, discarding all drippings. Cook onions in skillet until just tender.
2. Transfer to a greased 2½-quart baking dish. Add beans and mix well.
3. In a small bowl, combine barbecue sauce, ketchup, sugar blends, mustard, molasses, salt, and chili powder. Stir combination into beef and bean mixture.
4. Cover and bake at 350° for 30 minutes. Uncover and bake for 15 minutes.

Exchange List Values:
Carbohydrate 3.5,
Lean Meat 1.0, Fat 0.5

Basic Nutritional Values:
Calories 360 (Calories from Fat 45), Total Fat 5 gm (Saturated Fat 1.7 gm, Trans Fat 0.1 gm, Polyunsat Fat 0.6 gm, Monounsat Fat 2.1 gm, Cholesterol 21 mg), Sodium 636 mg, Total Carbohydrate 58 gm, Dietary Fiber 11 gm, Sugars 25 gm, Protein 19 gm

Variations:
1. Use 1 lb. bulk sausage of your preference instead of the bacon and ground beef.
—**Karen Denney**
Roswell, GA

2. Stir 1 or 2 6.5-oz. cans mushroom stems and pieces, drained, into Step 2.
—**Ruth Shank**
Gridley, IL

A Tip —

If you have gastroparesis (slow emptying of the stomach), eat small meals, avoid fatty foods, and limit foods like lentils and legumes.

Sweet and Sour Beets

Shirley Taylor
Yuba City, CA

Makes 6 servings
Serving size is ¾ cup or ⅙ recipe

Prep Time: 10 minutes
Cooking Time: 30 minutes

¼ cup sugar blend for baking (Splenda)
1 Tbsp. cornstarch
¼ tsp. salt
2 whole cloves
½ cup vinegar
3 15-oz. cans sliced beets, drained
3 Tbsp. reduced-sugar orange marmalade
2 Tbsp. soft-tub corn-oil margarine

1. Combine sugar blend, cornstarch, salt, and cloves in a large heavy saucepan. Stir in vinegar. Cook over medium heat, stirring constantly, until thickened and bubbly.
2. Add beets to sauce. Cover and cook 15 minutes.
3. Stir in marmalade and margarine until both melt.

Exchange List Values:
Carbohydrate 1.5, Fat 0.5

Basic Nutritional Values:
Calories 117 (Calories from Fat 25), Total Fat 3 gm (Saturated Fat 0.5 gm, Trans Fat 0.0 gm, Polyunsat Fat 1.4 gm, Monounsat Fat 0.7 gm, Cholesterol 0 mg), Sodium 394 mg, Total Carbohydrate 23 gm, Dietary Fiber 2 gm, Sugars 18 gm, Protein 1 gm

Amish Onion Pie

Kathi Rogge
Alexandria, IN

Makes 8 servings
Serving size is 1 slice

Prep Time: 30 minutes
Cooking/Baking Time:
75 minutes

4 regular-sized slices of
bacon, diced
2 cups chopped onions
1 cup fat-free sour cream
½ cup egg substitute
1 Tbsp. flour
½ tsp. salt
¼ tsp. pepper
9″ low-fat pie shell,
unbaked (see page 245)
caraway seeds, optional

1. Sauté bacon in a large skillet until evenly browned. Drain and discard drippings. Crumble bacon and set aside.
2. Sauté onions in skillet until softened. Return crumbled bacon to skillet.
3. Stir in sour cream, egg substitute, flour, salt, and pepper. Mix well.
4. Pour filling into pie crust.
5. Sprinkle with caraway seeds, if you wish.
6. Bake at 425° for 1 hour, or until onions are golden brown.

Exchange List Values:
Carbohydrate 1.0,
Lean Meat 1.0, Fat 0.5

Basic Nutritional Values:
Calories 151 (Calories from Fat 49),
Total Fat 5 gm (Saturated Fat 1.2 gm, Trans Fat 0.4 gm, Polyunsat Fat 1.1 gm, Monounsat Fat 2.5 gm, Cholesterol 6 mg), Sodium 311 mg, Total Carbohydrate 17 gm, Dietary Fiber 1 gm, Sugars 3 gm, Protein 6 gm

Up-Town Rice

Judy Buller
Bluffton, OH

Makes 8 servings
Serving size is ¾ cup or ⅛ recipe

Prep Time: 15-20 minutes
Cooking/Baking Time:
55 minutes

1½ cups uncooked white
rice
½ lb. sliced fresh, or 4-oz.
can sliced, mushrooms
½ cup slivered almonds
2 Tbsp. chopped onions
¼ cup canola oil
3 cups reduced-sodium,
98%-fat-free chicken
broth
1 Tbsp. parsley

1. Sauté rice, mushrooms, almonds, and onions in canola oil for 10-15 minutes on medium heat, stirring constantly. When almonds look slightly toasted and rice has a yellow cast, remove from heat.
2. Add broth and parsley and mix well. Pour into a greased 3-qt. casserole dish.
3. Cover and bake at 325° for 40 minutes.
4. Stir before serving.

Exchange List Values:
Starch 2.0, Fat 2.0

Basic Nutritional Values:
Calories 257 (Calories from Fat 101), Total Fat 11 gm (Saturated Fat 0.9 gm, Trans Fat 0.0 gm, Polyunsat Fat 3.1 gm, Monounsat Fat 6.6 gm, Cholesterol 0 mg), Sodium 190 mg, Total Carbohydrate 33 gm, Dietary Fiber 2 gm, Sugars 1 gm, Protein 6 gm

Variations:
1. Add ½ cup chopped celery to Step 1.
2. Instead of 3 cups chicken broth, use 14-oz. can chicken broth, ⅓ cup water, and 1-2 Tbsp. soy sauce.
—Amber Swarey
Honea Path, SC

A Tip —

When a recipes calls for oil, use canola oil or olive oil. These are brimming with good monounsaturated fats.

Green Chili Rice
John D. Allen, Rye, CO

Makes 6 servings
Serving size is ¾ cup or ⅙ recipe

Prep Time: 20 minutes
Baking Time: 35 minutes

2 ozs. reduced-fat Monterey
Jack cheese
3 cups fat-free sour cream
2 4-oz. cans chopped green
chilies, drained
3 cups cooked white rice
salt to taste
pepper to taste

1. Cut Monterey Jack
cheese into strips.
2. In a small bowl, com-
bine sour cream and chilies.
3. Season rice with salt and
pepper.
4. Layer one-third of the
rice, half the sour cream
mixture, and half the cheese
strips into a greased casserole
dish. Repeat the layers, ending
with a layer of rice on top.
5. Bake, covered, at 350°
for 35 minutes.

Exchange List Values:
Carbohydrate 2.0,
Very Lean Meat 2.0

Basic Nutritional Values:
Calories 230 (Calories from Fat 20),
Total Fat 2 gm (Saturated Fat 1.2
gm, Trans Fat 0.0 gm, Polyunsat
Fat 0.1 gm, Monounsat Fat 0.5 gm,
Cholesterol 18 mg), Sodium 228 mg,
Total Carbohydrate 28 gm, Dietary
Fiber 1 gm, Sugars 4 gm, Protein 13 gm

*Variation: Replace rice with
cooked macaronis or hominy.*

Potatoes and Onions
Christie Anne Detamore-Hunsberger, Harrisonburg, VA

Makes 10 servings
*Serving size is 2⅔" x 4½" rectangle
or ⅒ of recipe*

Prep Time: 15-20 minutes
Baking Time: 1 hour

6 large potatoes, thickly
sliced
4 to 6 medium-sized
onions, thinly sliced
2 Tbsp. butter
1 large garlic clove, minced
¼ tsp. pepper
¼ tsp. celery seed
paprika

1. Cover bottom of a
greased 9 x 13 glass baking
dish with half the potato
slices. Top with half the
onion slices. Create a second
layer of potatoes followed by
a second layer of onion slices.
2. Melt butter in a small
saucepan. Stir in garlic,
pepper, and celery seed. Pour
over potatoes and onions.
3. Bake at 400° for 40 minutes, covered with foil.
4. Remove from oven and
sprinkle with paprika.
5. Bake for an additional
20 minutes, uncovered.

Exchange List Values:
Starch 1.5, Vegetable 1.0,
Fat 0.5

Basic Nutritional Values:
Calories 158 (Calories from Fat 22),
Total Fat 2 gm (Saturated Fat 1.5
gm, Trans Fat 0.0 gm, Polyunsat

Fat 0.2 gm, Monounsat Fat 0.6 gm,
Cholesterol 6 mg), Sodium 23 mg,
Total Carbohydrate 32 gm, Dietary
Fiber 3 gm, Sugars 4 gm, Protein 3 gm

Spinach Potatoes
Janet Derstine, Telford, PA

Makes 8 servings
Serving size is ¾ cup or ⅛ recipe

Prep Time: 25 minutes
Baking Time: 25 minutes

6 medium-sized potatoes,
cooked soft and peeled
2 tsp. chives
1 cup fat-free sour cream
¾ cup reduced-fat sharp
cheddar cheese, grated
¼ tsp. dill weed
1-2 tsp. salt, according to
your taste preference
¼ tsp. pepper
10-oz. box frozen chopped
spinach, thawed and
squeezed dry

1. Mash all ingredients
together except spinach.
2. When thoroughly
blended, stir in spinach until
well distributed.
3. Place in greased cas-
serole dish and bake for 25
minutes, uncovered, at 350°.

Exchange List Values:
Starch 1.5, Fat 0.5

Basic Nutritional Values:
Calories 141 (Calories from Fat 22),
Total Fat 2 gm (Saturated Fat 1.4
gm, Trans Fat 0.0 gm, Polyunsat
Fat 0.2 gm, Monounsat Fat 0.6 gm,
Cholesterol 10 mg), Sodium 425 mg,
Total Carbohydrate 21 gm, Dietary
Fiber 3 gm, Sugars 3 gm, Protein 7 gm

Variation: Instead of 1 cup grated cheese, use 8-oz. pkg. cream cheese at room temperature.

—**Doyle Rounds**
Bridgewater, VA

Potato Casserole

Marilyn Wanner
New Holland, PA

*Makes 8 servings
Serving size is 3¼" x 4⅓" rectangle or ⅛ of recipe*

*Prep Time: 30-40 minutes
Baking Time: 40-45 minutes*

6-8 medium red potatoes,
  cooked and diced
½ cup fat-free sour cream
½ cup fat-free Ranch
  dressing
3 Tbsp. fried bacon,
  crumbled
2 Tbsp. chopped parsley
½ cup reduced-fat cheddar
  cheese, shredded
1 cup cornflakes, crushed
¼ cup butter, melted

1. Layer potatoes in a greased 9 x 13 baking pan.
2. In a small bowl, mix together sour cream and Ranch dressing. Spread over potatoes.
3. Sprinkle with bacon, parsley, and cheese.
4. In the small bowl, mix together cornflakes and butter. Top casserole with mixture.
5. Bake, uncovered, at 350° for 40-45 minutes.

Exchange List Values:
Starch 2.0, Fat 0.5

Basic Nutritional Values:
Calories 175 (Calories from Fat 27), Total Fat 3 gm (Saturated Fat 1.3 gm, Trans Fat 0.0 gm, Polyunsat Fat 0.4 gm, Monounsat Fat 1.0 gm, Cholesterol 11 mg), Sodium 379 mg, Total Carbohydrate 31 gm, Dietary Fiber 2 gm, Sugars 4 gm, Protein 6 gm

---

Tips:
  Crush the cornflakes in a plastic bag for less mess.
  Don't peel the potatoes if you want to retain their beautiful color.

Crusty Twice-Baked Potatoes

Amy Jensen, Fountain, CO

*Makes 4 servings
Serving size is 1 potato*

*Prep Time: 10 minutes
Baking Time: 60-65 minutes*

4 large baking potatoes
3 Tbsp. soft-tub corn-oil
  margarine, melted
½ cup cornflake crumbs
2 Tbsp. sesame seeds
½ tsp. salt
¼ tsp. pepper
½ tsp. garlic powder

1. Scrub potatoes. Prick with a fork and bake at 425° for 45 minutes, or until tender but not mushy.
2. Remove from oven and cool. Peel, keeping the potatoes whole.

---

3. Cut deep gashes, ¼" apart, crosswise across the top and almost through to the bottom of each potato. Brush surface and inside each gash with melted margarine.
4. Combine crumbs, seeds, salt, pepper, and garlic powder in a mixing bowl.
5. Spoon crumb mixture over potatoes, spreading each one slightly so the crumbs fall between the gashes.
6. Place potatoes cut-side up in a 9 x 13, or other shallow, baking dish. Bake at 375° for 15-20 minutes, or until heated through and browned.

Exchange List Values:
Starch 2.5, Fat 1.0

Basic Nutritional Values:
Calories 240 (Calories from Fat 74), Total Fat 8 gm (Saturated Fat 1.4 gm, Trans Fat 0.0 gm, Polyunsat Fat 4.0 gm, Monounsat Fat 2.3 gm, Cholesterol 0 mg), Sodium 471 mg, Total Carbohydrate 39 gm, Dietary Fiber 3 gm, Sugars 4 gm, Protein 4 gm

---

Variation: Crumble bleu cheese over the crumb-topped potatoes, just before Step 6.

A Tip —

If you take insulin, know your carbohydrate-to-insulin ratio. This will tell you how much insulin to take to cover the carbs you eat.

Golden Potato Casserole

Andrea Igoe
Poughkeepsie, NY

Makes 12 servings
Serving size is 3¼" x 3" rectangle
or ¹⁄₁₂ of recipe

Prep Time: 20 minutes
Cooking/Baking Time: 1½-2 hours
Chilling Time: 3-4 hours,
or overnight

8 large potatoes
1 cup reduced-fat cheddar
cheese, grated
1 bunch of scallions,
chopped fine
1 tsp. salt
⅛ tsp. pepper
2 cups fat-free sour cream
3-4 Tbsp. fat-free milk
¾ cup bread crumbs
2 Tbsp. soft-tub corn-oil
margarine, melted

1. Boil potatoes until tender but firm. Chill thoroughly 3-4 hours or overnight. Peel and grate.
2. In a large mixing bowl, stir cheese and grated potatoes together.
3. Fold in scallions, salt, pepper, sour cream, and milk. Mix well.
4. Spread in a greased 9 x 13 baking dish.
5. Combine bread crumbs and margarine. Sprinkle over potatoes.
6. Bake at 350° for 60 minutes.

Exchange List Values:
Starch 2.0, Fat 0.5

Basic Nutritional Values:
Calories 201 (Calories from Fat 35), Total Fat 4 gm (Saturated Fat 1.5 gm, Trans Fat 0.0 gm, Polyunsat Fat 0.9 gm, Monounsat Fat 1.0 gm, Cholesterol 11 mg), Sodium 362 mg, Total Carbohydrate 31 gm, Dietary Fiber 3 gm, Sugars 4 gm, Protein 8 gm

Potluck Potatoes

Mattie Yoder,
Millersburg, OH

Makes 15 servings
Serving size is ¾ cup or ¹⁄₁₅ recipe

Prep Time: 45-50 minutes
Chilling Time: 3 hours
Cooking/Baking Time: 1¾ hours

2 lbs. potatoes
1 pint fat-free sour cream
1½ cups light Velveeta
cheese, cubed
¼ tsp. salt
1 tsp. pepper
10.75-oz. can reduced-
sodium 98%-fat-free
cream of chicken soup
4 Tbsp. soft-tub corn-oil
margarine
2 cups crushed cornflakes

1. Peel potatoes. Cook in large stockpot until soft. Cool in refrigerator.
2. When potatoes are fully chilled, shred or put through ricer into a large mixing bowl.

3. In a large saucepan, stir sour cream, Velveeta, salt, pepper, and soup together. Heat over low heat until cheese is melted.
4. Pour over shredded potatoes and mix gently but well. Spoon into a 5-quart greased casserole.
5. In a saucepan, melt margarine. Stir in crushed cornflakes. Top casserole with mixture.
6. Bake, uncovered, at 350° for 45 minutes.

Exchange List Values:
Starch 1.5, Fat 1.0

Basic Nutritional Values:
Calories 167 (Calories from Fat 35), Total Fat 4 gm (Saturated Fat 1.4 gm, Trans Fat 0.0 gm, Polyunsat Fat 1.3 gm, Monounsat Fat 1.0 gm, Cholesterol 9 mg), Sodium 463 mg, Total Carbohydrate 24 gm, Dietary Fiber 1 gm, Sugars 5 gm, Protein 7 gm

Variation: Use cream of celery soup instead of cream of chicken soup.
—Jere Zimmerman
Reinholds, PA

A Tip —

Baked potatoes and salads are healthy foods that often get topped with unhealthy additions, so be careful with the dressings, cheeses, and bacon bits. They can add up!

Crusty Baked Potatoes

Anna Stoltzfus
Honey Brook, PA

Makes 6 servings
Serving size is ¾ cup or ⅙ recipe

Prep Time: 15 minutes
Baking Time: 60 minutes

1 cup saltine cracker
  crumbs
⅛ tsp. salt
1 tsp. dried oregano
1 tsp. seasoning salt
1 tsp. parsley flakes
4 Tbsp. canola oil
4 medium-sized potatoes,
  sliced

1. In a shallow bowl, add seasonings to cracker crumbs.
2. Place canola oil in another shallow bowl.
3. Dip potato slices in the oil. Then dredge in cracker crumbs.
4. When coated, place slices in a greased baking dish.
5. Bake, uncovered, at 375° for 60 minutes.

Exchange List Values:
Starch 2.0, Fat 2.0

Basic Nutritional Values:
Calories 240 (Calories from Fat 97),
Total Fat 11 gm (Saturated Fat 0.9
gm, Trans Fat 0.4 gm, Polyunsat
Fat 3.0 gm, Monounsat Fat 6.3 gm,
Cholesterol 0 mg), Sodium 441 mg,
Total Carbohydrate 33 gm, Dietary
Fiber 3 gm, Sugars 1 gm, Protein 4 gm

Oven-Fried Potatoes

Robin Schrock
Millersburg, OH

Makes 8 servings
Serving size is 3 wedges

Prep Time: 10 minutes
Baking Time: 1 hour

4 large baking potatoes,
  unpeeled
⅓ cup vegetable oil
2 Tbsp. Parmesan cheese
½ tsp. salt
¼ tsp. garlic powder
¼ tsp. paprika
⅛ tsp. pepper

1. Cut each potato lengthwise into 6 wedges.
2. Place wedges skin-side down in a greased 9 x 13 baking dish.
3. In a mixing bowl, combine oil, cheese, salt, garlic powder, paprika, and pepper. Brush over potatoes. Or, mix all ingredients except the potatoes in a large mixing bowl. When thoroughly blended, stir in potato wedges. Stir until they're well covered. Then place in a single layer in the baking dish.
4. Bake at 375° for 1 hour.

Exchange List Values:
Starch 2.0, Fat 1.5

Basic Nutritional Values:
Calories 225 (Calories from Fat 87),
Total Fat 10 gm (Saturated Fat 0.9
gm, Trans Fat 0.0 gm, Polyunsat
Fat 2.8 gm, Monounsat Fat 5.5 gm,
Cholesterol 1 mg), Sodium 172 mg,
Total Carbohydrate 32 gm, Dietary
Fiber 3 gm, Sugars 2 gm, Protein 4 gm

Variation: To create a crustier finish on the potatoes, add 3 Tbsp. flour to Step 3. And increase the Parmesan cheese to ⅓ cup.
  —**Jere Zimmerman**
    Reinholds, PA
  —**Jena Hammond**
    Traverse City, MI
  —**Sara Wilson**
    Blairstown, MO

A Tip —

  You don't need "special" vitamins for diabetes, but everyone needs proper vitamins and minerals for health, whether they have diabetes or not.

Corn Bread Stuffing

Janice Muller
Derwood, MD

Makes 6 servings
Serving size is ¾ cup or ⅙ recipe

Prep Time: 15 minutes
Baking Time: 30 minutes

1 cup chopped onions
1 cup chopped celery
2 Tbsp. canola oil
8-oz. pkg. corn bread
    stuffing
16-oz. jar unsweetened
    applesauce
½ tsp. dried thyme
½ tsp. dried marjoram
½ tsp. poultry seasoning
¼ tsp. lemon-pepper
⅓ cup boiling water

1. In a large skillet, sauté onions and celery in canola oil until soft.

2. Add stuffing mix, applesauce, herbs, seasonings, and boiling water. Toss until evenly moist.

3. Stuff turkey, or if baking separately, spoon into a buttered 1-qt. baking dish.

4. Cover with foil. Put in a 325° oven during the last 30 minutes that your turkey is baking. Or bake at 325° for 30 minutes on its own.

Exchange List Values:
Starch 2.0, Fruit 0.5,
Vegetable 1.0, Fat 1.0

Basic Nutritional Values:
Calories 237 (Calories from Fat 57),
Total Fat 6 gm (Saturated Fat 0.4
gm, Trans Fat 0.0 gm, Polyunsat
Fat 1.9 gm, Monounsat Fat 3.4 gm,
Cholesterol 0 mg), Sodium 452 mg,
Total Carbohydrate 41 gm, Dietary
Fiber 3 gm, Sugars 10 gm, Protein 4 gm

Grilled Veggies

Tim Smith
Rutledge, PA

Makes 6 servings
Serving size is ¾ cup

Prep Time: 10-20 minutes
Grilling Time: 20-40 minutes

2 large potatoes
1 medium zucchini
1 medium yellow squash
1 small red onion
1 small white onion
2 Tbsp. crushed garlic
1 tsp. pepper
½ tsp. white pepper
1 Tbsp. fresh basil leaves
3 Tbsp. oil

1. Slice potatoes paper-thin.

2. Slice zucchini and squash ¼" thick.

3. Slice onions.

4. Combine all ingredients in a large mixing bowl.

5. Cut a piece of heavy-duty foil large enough to hold all ingredients. Spoon vegetables into center of foil. Close tightly.

6. Place on preheated grill. Grill over medium heat for 20-40 minutes, turning every 5 minutes. Open and jag potatoes after 20 minutes to see if the vegetables are done to your liking. Close up and continue grilling if you want them more tender, checking again after 10 minutes. Continue until they are as tender as you want them.

Exchange List Values:
Starch 1.0, Vegetable 1.0,
Fat 1.0

Basic Nutritional Values:
Calories 155 (Calories from Fat 65),
Total Fat 7 gm (Saturated Fat 0.6
gm, Trans Fat 0.0 gm, Polyunsat
Fat 2.2 gm, Monounsat Fat 4.1 gm,
Cholesterol 0 mg), Sodium 8 mg,
Total Carbohydrate 21 gm, Dietary
Fiber 3 gm, Sugars 4 gm, Protein 3 gm

Salads

Festive Tossed Salad

Cheryl A. Lapp
Parkesburg, PA
Yvonne Kauffman Boettger
Harrisonburg, VA
Sally Holzem
Schofield, WI

Makes 10 servings
Serving size is ¾ cup

Prep Time: 30 minutes

4 Tbsp. granular Splenda
2½ Tbsp. cider, *or* red
    wine, vinegar
1 Tbsp. lemon juice
1 Tbsp. finely chopped
    onions
¼ tsp. salt
¼ cup olive oil
1 tsp. poppy seeds
10 cups torn romaine
    lettuce
1 cup fat-free Swiss cheese,
    shredded
1 medium-sized apple,
    cored and cubed

1 medium-sized pear,
    cored and cubed
¼ cup dried cranberries
⅓ cup chopped cashews

1. In a blender, combine first 5 ingredients until well blended.
2. With blender running, gradually add oil. Add poppy seeds and blend.
3. In salad bowl, combine lettuce, cheese, apple, pear, and cranberries.
4. Just before serving, drizzle salad with desired amount of dressing. Add cashews and toss to coat.

Variation: Add 1 tsp. Dijon mustard to the dressing in Step 1.
—Jennifer Eberly
Harrisonburg, VA

A Tip —

Dark green leafy vegetables (such as fresh spinach and romaine) supply more vitamins than iceberg lettuce.

Dried Cherry Salad

Stacy Schmucker Stoltzfus
Enola, PA

Makes 12 servings
Serving size is ¾ cup

Prep Time: 20 minutes
Cooking Time: 10 minutes

half a head of romaine
lettuce, chopped
half a head of red leaf
lettuce, chopped
half a large red onion,
sliced
1 cup dried cherries
½ cup reduced-fat feta
cheese
⅓ cup sugar
1 cup pecan halves

Raspberry Dressing:
4 Tbsp. raspberry vinegar
½ tsp. Tabasco sauce
½ tsp. salt
4 Tbsp. granular Splenda
pepper to taste
1 Tbsp. chopped parsley
⅓ cup vegetable oil

1. Place lettuces in a large
salad bowl. Sprinkle with
onion slices, dried cherries,
and feta cheese.
2. In skillet, over medium
heat, combine ⅓ cup sugar
and pecans. Stir constantly
until sugar melts and pecans
are coated. Immediately pour
pecans onto waxed paper to
cool.
3. Sprinkle cooled nuts
over salad.
4. To make dressing,
combine vinegar, Tabasco

sauce, salt, 4 Tbsp. granular
Splenda, pepper, and parsley
in a small mixing bowl. While
whisking, slowly pour in oil
until emulsified. Just before
serving, pour over salad.

Exchange List Values:
Carbohydrate 1.0, Fat 2.5

Basic Nutritional Values:
Calories 195 (Calories from Fat 121),
Total Fat 13 gm (Saturated Fat 1.4
gm, Trans Fat 0.0 gm, Polyunsat
Fat 3.7 gm, Monounsat Fat 7.7 gm,
Cholesterol 1 mg), Sodium 122 mg,
Total Carbohydrate 18 gm, Dietary
Fiber 2 gm, Sugars 13 gm, Protein 3 gm

Caesar Salad

Colleen Heatwole
Burton, MI

Makes 8 servings
Serving size is ¾ cup

Prep Time: 15-20 minutes

8-12 cups romaine lettuce,
or spring mix, torn into
bite-sized pieces
¼ cup vegetable oil
3 Tbsp. red wine vinegar
1 tsp. Worcestershire sauce
½ tsp. salt
¾ tsp. dry mustard powder
1 large garlic clove, minced
1½–2 Tbsp. fresh lemon
juice
dash of pepper
¼-½ cup grated Parmesan
cheese
1½ cups Caesar-flavored,
or garlic, croutons

1. Place lettuce in a large
bowl.
2. Combine next 6 ingre-
dients in a blender or food
processor.
3. Add fresh lemon juice
and process until smooth.
4. Just before serving, toss
with lettuce.
5. Sprinkle with pepper.
Add Parmesan cheese and
toss well. Serve croutons
separately.

Exchange List Values:
Carbohydrate 0.5, Fat 2.0

Basic Nutritional Values:
Calories 119 (Calories from Fat 84),
Total Fat 9 gm (Saturated Fat 1.4
gm, Trans Fat 0.0 gm, Polyunsat
Fat 2.3 gm, Monounsat Fat 5.0 gm,
Cholesterol 3 mg), Sodium 273 mg,
Total Carbohydrate 7 gm, Dietary
Fiber 1 gm, Sugars 1 gm, Protein 3 gm

Tips:
1. I have made this on more
Sundays than I can count. I
prepare the lettuce, blend the
6 ingredients, and get the hard
cheese ready for my son to
grate. I always use fresh lemon
or fresh lime.
2. My family prefers a tart
dressing. My friend adds
1 Tbsp. sugar.

Greek Salad

Ruth Feister
Narvon, PA

Makes 8 servings
Serving size is ¾ cup

Prep Time: 20 minutes

head of torn romaine
 lettuce
1 medium-sized cucumber
 sliced thin
2 medium-sized tomatoes,
 cut in pieces
half a red onion, finely
 chopped
parsley
4-oz. can sliced black
 olives, drained
2 ozs. crumbled feta cheese
several artichoke hearts,
 quartered, *optional*

Dressing:
¼ cup fat-free, reduced-
 sodium chicken stock
2 Tbsp. red wine vinegar
2 tsp. lemon juice
1 tsp. sugar
½ tsp. dried basil
½ tsp. dried oregano

1. Combine dressing
ingredients in a jar with a
tightly fitting lid. Shake until
mixed well.
 2. Place lettuce, cucumber,
tomatoes, onions, and parsley
in a large serving bowl.
 3. Just before serving,
drizzle with dressing and
toss.
 4. Top with olives, cheese,
and artichoke hearts, if you
wish.

Exchange List Values:
Vegetable 1.0, Fat 1.0

Basic Nutritional Values:
Calories 63 (Calories from Fat 31),
Total Fat 3 gm (Saturated Fat 1.3
gm, Trans Fat 0.1 gm, Polyunsat
Fat 0.3 gm, Monounsat Fat 1.4 gm,
Cholesterol 6 mg), Sodium 179 mg,
Total Carbohydrate 7 gm, Dietary
Fiber 2 gm, Sugars 4 gm, Protein 2 gm

Grand Tossed Salad

Kathy Hertzler
Lancaster, PA
Carol Stroh
Akron, NY

Makes 8 servings
Serving size is ¾ cup

Prep Time: 45-60 minutes
Cooking Time: 10 minutes

½ cup sliced almonds
8 tsp. sugar
medium-sized head of
 romaine lettuce
medium-sized head of red
 or green leaf lettuce
2 green onions, sliced
2 ribs of celery, sliced
11-oz. can mandarin
 oranges, drained
¼ cup oil
1 Tbsp. granular Splenda
2 Tbsp. white wine vinegar
1 Tbsp. snipped parsley
¼ tsp. salt
Tabasco sauce to taste

1. Cook almonds and sugar
over low heat, stirring constantly until sugar is melted
and almonds are coated. Cool
and break apart.
 2. Toss together lettuces,
onions, celery, oranges, and
sugared almonds.
 3. Blend together oil,
granular Splenda, vinegar,
parsley, salt, and Tabasco
sauce. Just before serving,
pour over salad. Toss to mix.

Exchange List Values:
Carbohydrate 1.0, Fat 2.0

Basic Nutritional Values:
Calories 145 (Calories from Fat 97),
Total Fat 11 gm (Saturated Fat 0.8
gm, Trans Fat 0.0 gm, Polyunsat
Fat 3.0 gm, Monounsat Fat 6.4 gm,
Cholesterol 0 mg), Sodium 100 mg,
Total Carbohydrate 11 gm, Dietary
Fiber 3 gm, Sugars 8 gm, Protein 3 gm

A Tip —

 Folic acid, which is
found in green, leafy
vegetables, plays an
important role in a
number of chemical
processes in your body.
Try to get 180–200 mcg
per day.

Bibb Lettuce with Pecans and Oranges

Betty K. Drescher
Quakertown, PA

Makes 8 servings
Serving size is ¾ cup

Prep Time: 10-15 minutes

4 heads Bibb lettuce
½ cup pecan halves,
  toasted
2 oranges, peeled and
  sliced

Dressing:
¼ cup vinegar
2 Tbsp. granular Splenda
¼ cup vegetable oil
½ tsp. salt
half a small onion,
  chopped
1 tsp. dry mustard
2 Tbsp. water

1. Place lettuce, pecans, and oranges in a salad bowl.
2. Combine dressing ingredients in blender. (You can make this ahead of time and refrigerate it.)
3. Toss dressing with salad ingredients just before serving.

Exchange List Values:
Carbohydrate 0.5, Fat 2.0

Basic Nutritional Values:
Calories 138 (Calories from Fat 105), Total Fat 12 gm (Saturated Fat 0.9 gm, Trans Fat 0.0 gm, Polyunsat Fat 3.4 gm, Monounsat Fat 6.7 gm, Cholesterol 0 mg), Sodium 150 mg, Total Carbohydrate 9 gm, Dietary Fiber 3 gm, Sugars 5 gm, Protein 2 gm

Blueberry Spinach Salad

Judi Robb
Manhattan, KS

Makes 8 servings
Serving size is ¾ cup

Prep Time: 15-20 minutes

¼ cup vegetable oil
¼ cup raspberry vinegar
2 tsp. Dijon mustard
1 tsp.-1 Tbsp. sugar,
  according to your taste
  preference
½ tsp. salt
10-oz. pkg. fresh torn
  spinach
1 oz. bleu cheese, crumbled
1 cup fresh blueberries
⅓ cup chopped pecans,
  toasted

1. In a jar with a tight-fitting lid, combine oil, vinegar, mustard, sugar, and salt. Shake well.
2. In a large salad bowl, toss spinach, bleu cheese, blueberries, and pecans.
3. Just before serving, add dressing and toss gently.

Exchange List Values:
Carbohydrate 0.5, Fat 2.0

Basic Nutritional Values:
Calories 128 (Calories from Fat 103), Total Fat 11 gm (Saturated Fat 1.4 gm, Trans Fat 0.0 gm, Polyunsat Fat 3.1 gm, Monounsat Fat 6.3 gm, Cholesterol 3 mg), Sodium 253 mg, Total Carbohydrate 6 gm, Dietary Fiber 2 gm, Sugars 3 gm, Protein 2 gm

Spinach Salad with Walnut Dressing

Dolores Metzler
Lewistown, PA

Makes 8 servings
Serving size is ¾ cup

Prep Time: 15 minutes
Standing Time: 30 minutes

Dressing:
3 Tbsp. vegetable oil
1 Tbsp. honey
¼ tsp. salt
2 Tbsp. lemon juice
2 tsp. Dijon mustard
dash of pepper
½ cup walnuts, chopped
2 Tbsp. sliced green onions

Salad:
4-6 cups spinach *and/or*
  other greens
½ cup reduced-fat Swiss
  cheese, diced
1 cup diced fresh fruit
  (apples, peaches, and
  pears are all good,
  dipped in lemon juice to
  keep from discoloring)

1. Mix oil, honey, salt, lemon juice, mustard, pepper, walnuts, and onions in a jar with a tight-fitting lid.
2. Cover and shake until well mixed. Then let stand for 30 minutes to enhance flavor.
3. Mix spinach, Swiss cheese, and diced fruit in a large mixing bowl.
4. Just before serving, add dressing to salad and toss together.

Basic Nutritional Values:
Calories 136 (Calories from Fat 100),
Total Fat 11 gm (Saturated Fat 1.3
gm, Trans Fat 0.0 gm, Polyunsat
Fat 5.2 gm, Monounsat Fat 4.0 gm,
Cholesterol 3 mg), Sodium 148 mg,
Total Carbohydrate 7 gm, Dietary
Fiber 1 gm, Sugars 4 gm, Protein 4 gm

Spinach-Strawberry Salad

Pat Bechtel
Dillsburg, PA
Sarah M. Balmer
Manheim, PA

Makes 8 servings
Serving size is ¾ cup

Prep Time: 20 minutes

12 ozs. fresh spinach
1 qt. fresh strawberries,
 sliced
2 Tbsp. sesame seeds
1 Tbsp. poppy seeds

Dressing:
¼ cup vegetable oil
¼ cup granular Splenda
1½ tsp. grated onion
¼ tsp. Worcestershire
 sauce
¼ tsp. paprika
¼ cup cider vinegar

1. Layer spinach, strawberries, sesame seeds, and poppy
seeds in a large salad bowl.
2. Combine the dressing
ingredients in a blender.
Blend for 2 minutes.

3. Just before serving pour
the dressing over the spinach
and toss lightly to coat the
spinach and berries.

Basic Nutritional Values:
Calories 132 (Calories from Fat 100),
Total Fat 11 gm (Saturated Fat 1.0
gm, Trans Fat 0.0 gm, Polyunsat
Fat 4.0 gm, Monounsat Fat 5.5 gm,
Cholesterol 0 mg), Sodium 37 mg,
Total Carbohydrate 8 gm, Dietary
Fiber 3 gm, Sugars 4 gm, Protein 2 gm

*This is one of our favorite salads.
I make the dressing and store it in
the refrigerator. Then I make the
amount of salad I want and just
add as much dressing as it needs.*

Variations:
*1. For the dressing, use ¼
cup honey, heated until thin,
instead of the ½ cup sugar.*
 —Ellie Oberholtzer
 Smoketown, PA
*2. To the salad itself, add 1
cup shredded Monterey Jack
cheese and ½ cup chopped
walnuts.*
 —Tina Snyder
 Manheim, PA

A Tip —

Antioxidants protect
the body from harmful
free radicals, which can
destroy cell membranes
and DNA.

Salad with Hot Bacon Dressing

Joanne E. Martin, Stevens, PA

*Makes 16 servings (2 cups dressing)
Serving size is 2 cups salad greens
and 2 Tbsp. dressing*

Prep Time: 15 minutes
Cooking Time: 7 minutes

6-8 strips of bacon
¾ cup sugar blend for
 baking (Splenda)
2 eggs, beaten
⅓ cup vinegar
⅔ cup water

32 cups salad greens
1 cup grated carrots
hard-cooked eggs, *optional*

1. In a skillet, brown
bacon. Drain off drippings.
Crumble and set aside.
2. In the same skillet, mix
sugar blend, beaten eggs,
vinegar, and water. Bring
to boil, stirring up browned
bacon drippings. Stir dressing
until slightly thickened.
3. Stir in bacon.
4. Just before serving, toss
warm salad dressing with
mixture of salad greens, grated
carrots, and hard-cooked eggs.

Basic Nutritional Values:
Calories 76 (Calories from Fat 16),
Total Fat 2 gm (Saturated Fat 0.5
gm, Trans Fat 0.0 gm, Polyunsat
Fat 0.3 gm, Monounsat Fat 0.7 gm,
Cholesterol 29 mg), Sodium 84 mg,
Total Carbohydrate 13 gm, Dietary
Fiber 1 gm, Sugars 11 gm, Protein 3 gm

Black Bean Taco Salad with Lime Vinaigrette

Joy Sutter
Perkasie, PA

Makes 6 servings
Serving size is ¾ cup

Prep Time: 15-20 minutes (if the chicken is already cooked)

Vinaigrette:
¼ cup chopped, seeded tomatoes
¼ cup chopped fresh cilantro
2 Tbsp. olive oil
1 Tbsp. cider vinegar
1 tsp. grated lime rind
1 Tbsp. fresh lime juice
¼ tsp. salt
¼ tsp. ground cumin
¼ tsp. chili powder
¼ tsp. black pepper
1 garlic clove, peeled

Salad:
8 cups thinly sliced lettuce
1½ cups roasted, boneless chicken breast pieces
1 cup chopped tomatoes
1 cup diced onions
½ cup reduced-fat sharp cheddar cheese, grated
15-oz. can black beans, drained and rinsed
2 cups (3 ozs.) baked, low-fat tortilla chips

1. Combine vinaigrette ingredients in a blender or food processor until smooth.
2. Combine lettuce, chicken, tomatoes, onions, cheese, and black beans in a large bowl.
3. Add vinaigrette and toss well to coat. Serve with chips.

Exchange List Values:
Starch 1.5, Vegetable 1.0, Lean Meat 2.0

Basic Nutritional Values:
Calories 251 (Calories from Fat 74), Total Fat 8 gm (Saturated Fat 2.0 gm, Trans Fat 0.0 gm, Polyunsat Fat 1.2 gm, Monounsat Fat 4.4 gm, Cholesterol 35 mg), Sodium 346 mg, Total Carbohydrate 27 gm, Dietary Fiber 6 gm, Sugars 4 gm, Protein 19 gm

Broccoli Slaw

Bonnie Heatwole
Springs, PA

Makes 8 servings
Serving size is ¾ cup

Prep Time: 15 minutes

16-oz. pkg. broccoli slaw
¼ cup sunflower seeds
¼ cup slivered almonds
2 3-oz. pkgs. chicken-flavored Ramen noodles
1 cup diced green onions

Dressing:
¼ cup vegetable oil
¼ cup white vinegar
3 Tbsp. granular Splenda
2 seasoning packets from Ramen noodles

1. Combine salad ingredients in a large bowl.
2. Shake the dressing ingredients together in a jar with a tight-fitting lid. (The dressing is probably more than needed for the amount of salad, so begin by adding only half of what you've made. Add more if you need it.) Add the dressing right before serving. Toss to mix.

Exchange List Values:
Carbohydrate 1.5, Fat 2.0

Basic Nutritional Values:
Calories 198 (Calories from Fat 107), Total Fat 12 gm (Saturated Fat 0.9 gm, Trans Fat 0.0 gm, Polyunsat Fat 3.9 gm, Monounsat Fat 5.7 gm, Cholesterol 0 mg), Sodium 254 mg, Total Carbohydrate 23 gm, Dietary Fiber 4 gm, Sugars 4 gm, Protein 5 gm

Variations:
1. Instead of broccoli slaw, use 10-oz. pkg. cole slaw mix, 6-oz. pkg. fresh spinach, and 2 cups shredded lettuce. Add 3 Tbsp. sesame seeds, lightly toasted to the salad.
—**Sharon Eshleman**
Ephrata, PA

2. Instead of broccoli slaw, use 6-oz. pkg. fresh spinach and half a head of torn romaine lettuce. Substitute walnuts or pecans for the almonds, if you wish.
—**Elena Yoder**
Carlsbad, NM
—**Colleen Heatwole**
Burton, MI
—**Betty Moore**
Plano, IL
—**Clara Newswanger**
Gordonville, PA
—**LuAnna Hochstedler**
East Earl, PA

Broccoli Salad

Sherlyn Hess
Millersville, PA
Ruth Zendt
Mifflintown, PA

Makes 8 servings
Serving size is ¾ cup

Prep Time: 20 minutes
Chilling Time: 2 hours

1 cup raisins
2 cups boiling water
6 cups chopped broccoli tops
⅔ cup chopped red onions
10 strips of bacon, cooked
    and crumbled
¼ cup shredded carrots
½ cup fat-free Ranch dressing
½ cup fat-free mayonnaise
2 Tbsp. vinegar
¼ cup granular Splenda

1. Soak raisins for a few minutes in boiling water. Drain.
2. Combine plumped raisins, broccoli, onions, bacon, and carrots.
3. Whisk together remaining ingredients in a separate bowl. Pour over broccoli mixture. Toss to mix.
4. Refrigerate at least 2 hours before serving.

Exchange List Values:
Fruit 1.0, Carbohydrate 0.5, Vegetable 1.0, Fat 0.5

Basic Nutritional Values:
Calories 152 (Calories from Fat 35), Total Fat 4 gm (Saturated Fat 1.2 gm, Trans Fat 0.0 gm, Polyunsat Fat 0.6 gm, Monounsat Fat 1.5 gm, Cholesterol 10 mg), Sodium 438 mg, Total Carbohydrate 26 gm, Dietary Fiber 3 gm, Sugars 16 gm, Protein 5 gm

Variations:
1. Add 1 cup grated cheese and/or ½ cup chopped peanuts to Step 2.
—**Ruth Zendt,** Mifflintown, PA

2. Add 1 cup chopped celery and ½ cup hulled sunflower seeds to Step 2.
—**Jean Butzer,** Batavia, NY

Trees & Seeds Salad

Nanci Keatley
Salem, OR

Makes 10 servings
Serving size is ¾ cup

Prep Time: 10-20 minutes
Chilling Time: 30 minutes

4 cups cauliflower florets
3 cups cut-up broccoli
1 cup diced red onions
2 pts. cherry tomatoes,
    halved
8 slices bacon, cooked and
    diced
3 Tbsp. sesame seeds
¼ cup sunflower seeds
¼ cup slivered almonds

Dressing:
1 cup mayonnaise
4 Tbsp. granular Splenda
3 Tbsp. cider vinegar
½ tsp. salt
½ tsp. pepper

1. In a large serving bowl, combine cauliflower, broccoli, onions, tomatoes, bacon, seeds, and nuts.

2. In a separate bowl, mix together mayonnaise, granular Splenda, vinegar, salt, and pepper. Pour over vegetables.
3. Refrigerate at least 30 minutes to blend flavors.

Exchange List Values:
Carbohydrate 1.0, Fat 1.5

Basic Nutritional Values:
Calories 136 (Calories from Fat 63), Total Fat 7 gm (Saturated Fat 1.2 gm, Trans Fat 0.0 gm, Polyunsat Fat 2.4 gm, Monounsat Fat 2.9 gm, Cholesterol 6 mg), Sodium 426 mg, Total Carbohydrate 14 gm, Dietary Fiber 4 gm, Sugars 6 gm, Protein 6 gm

Tip: This is great to make ahead. Mix all ingredients together except the dressing. Chill, then add the dressing half an hour before serving. Refrigerate until serving time.

Variations:
1. Change the "green" base of this salad to: 3 cups shredded cabbage or coleslaw mix; 2 cups broken cauliflower; 2 cups chopped broccoli.
—**Teresa Martin**
    Gordonville, PA

2. Add ⅓ cup grated Parmesan cheese to the Dressing in Step 2.
—**Phyllis Smith**
    Goshen, IN

3. Add 8 sliced radishes to Step 1.
—**Sara Wilson**
    Blairstown, MO

Spring Pea Salad

Dottie Schmidt, Kansas City, MO

Makes 4 servings
Serving size is ¾ cup

Prep Time: 20 minutes
Chilling Time: 30 minutes

10-oz. pkg. frozen peas
1 cup diced celery
1 cup chopped fresh
  cauliflower florets
¼ cup diced green onions
3 Tbsp. chopped cashews
2 Tbsp. crisp-cooked and
  crumbled bacon
¼ cup fat-free sour cream
⅓ cup fat-free Ranch salad
  dressing
¼ tsp. Dijon mustard
1 small clove garlic, minced

1. Thaw peas. Drain.
2. In a large mixing bowl, combine peas, celery, cauliflower, onion, cashews, and bacon with sour cream.
3. In a small bowl, mix together Ranch dressing, mustard, and minced garlic. Begin by pouring only half the dressing over salad mixture. Toss gently. Add more if needed. (The dressing amount is generous.) Chill before serving.

Exchange List Values:
Carbohydrate 1.5, Fat 1.0

Basic Nutritional Values:
Calories 160 (Calories from Fat 48), Total Fat 5 gm (Saturated Fat 1.4 gm, Trans Fat 0.0 gm, Polyunsat Fat 1.0 gm, Monounsat Fat 2.6 gm, Cholesterol 7 mg), Sodium 400 mg, Total Carbohydrate 21 gm, Dietary Fiber 5 gm, Sugars 7 gm, Protein 8 gm

Cabbage Slaw with Vinegar Dressing

Betty Hostetler
Allensville, PA

Makes 12 servings
Serving size is ¾ cup

Prep Time: 30-45 minutes
Chilling Time: 3-4 hours

8 cups grated cabbage
¼ cup grated carrots
¼ cup diced celery
¼ cup chopped red pepper
¼ cup chopped yellow
  pepper
⅛ cup chopped green
  pepper
1 Tbsp. celery seed
¾-1 cup sugar
1 tsp. salt
½ cup white vinegar
¼ cup, plus 2 Tbsp., oil

1. Combine vegetables, celery seed, sugar, and salt in a large mixing bowl. Mix well.
2. In a small saucepan, bring vinegar to a boil. Add oil. Pour over vegetables. Mix well.
3. Refrigerate for 3-4 hours before serving.

Exchange List Values:
Vegetable 1.0, Fat 1.5

Basic Nutritional Values:
Calories 79 (Calories from Fat 65), Total Fat 7 gm (Saturated Fat 0.5 gm, Trans Fat 0.0 gm, Polyunsat Fat 2.1 gm, Monounsat Fat 4.2 gm, Cholesterol 0 mg), Sodium 159 mg, Total Carbohydrate 4 gm, Dietary Fiber 1 gm, Sugars 2 gm, Protein 1 gm

Variations:
1. Add 1 medium-sized onion, chopped to the vegetables in Step 1.
2. Reduce celery seed to 1 tsp. and add 1½ tsp. mustard seed and ½ tsp. turmeric.
—**Emilie Kimpel**
Arcadia, MI

Creamy Coleslaw

Tammy Yoder
Belleville, PA

Makes 6 servings
Serving size is ¾ cup

Prep Time: 10 minutes
Chilling Time: 30 minutes

half a head of cabbage
½ cup reduced-fat
  mayonnaise
2 Tbsp. vinegar
2½ Tbsp. granular Splenda
pinch of salt
pinch of pepper
1 Tbsp. celery seed, *or* to
  taste
¼ cup grated carrots

1. Shred cabbage. Place in a large mixing bowl.
2. Mix all remaining ingredients together in another bowl.
3. Stir dressing into shredded cabbage, mixing well.
4. Chill for 30 minutes before serving.

Exchange List Values:
Carbohydrate 0.5, Fat 1.5

Basic Nutritional Values:
Calories 94 (Calories from Fat 63), Total Fat 7 gm (Saturated Fat 1.1 gm, Trans Fat 0.0 gm, Polyunsat Fat 3.7 gm, Monounsat Fat 1.8 gm, Cholesterol 6 mg), Sodium 192 mg, Total Carbohydrate 8 gm, Dietary Fiber 2 gm, Sugars 5 gm, Protein 2 gm

---

Variations:
1. If you're short on time, use a bag of prepared shredded cabbage with carrots.
2. For added zest, stir ½ tsp. dry mustard into the dressing in Step 2.
—**Maricarol Magill**
Freehold, NJ

Cranberry Coleslaw

Carolyn Baer, Conrath, WI

Makes 7 servings
Serving size is ¾ cup

Prep Time: 15 minutes
Chilling Time: 45 minutes

½ cup reduced-fat
   mayonnaise
2 Tbsp. honey
2 Tbsp. vinegar
¼ cup fresh cranberries,
   chopped, *or* snipped
   dried cranberries
5 cups shredded cabbage
   (1 small head)

1. Combine mayonnaise, honey, and vinegar. Stir in cranberries.
2. Place shredded cabbage in a large bowl.
3. Pour dressing over cabbage. Toss to coat.

4. Cover and chill for 45 minutes.

Exchange List Values:
Carbohydrate 0.5, Fat 1.0

Basic Nutritional Values:
Calories 88 (Calories from Fat 52), Total Fat 6 gm (Saturated Fat 0.9 gm, Trans Fat 0.0 gm, Polyunsat Fat 3.1 gm, Monounsat Fat 1.4 gm, Cholesterol 5 mg), Sodium 156 mg, Total Carbohydrate 10 gm, Dietary Fiber 1 gm, Sugars 8 gm, Protein 1 gm

---

This salad is very pretty for holiday parties, but it is delicious anytime.

Crispy, Crunchy Cabbage Salad

Jolyn Nolt, Leola, PA
Karen Stoltzfus
Alto, MI
Andrea O'Neil
Fairfield, CT

Makes 5 servings
Serving size is ¾ cup

Prep Time: 10-15 minutes

---

1 whole chicken breast,
   cooked and diced, *or*
   2 5-oz. cans cooked
   chicken
2 Tbsp. toasted sesame
   seeds
2 ozs. slivered toasted
   almonds
half a head of cabbage,
   shredded fine
2 green onions, sliced
3-oz. pkg. chicken-flavored
   dry Ramen noodles

Dressing:
1 pkg. Ramen noodle
   seasoning mix
1½ Tbsp. granular Splenda
3 Tbsp. vegetable oil
3 Tbsp. red wine vinegar
¼ tsp. salt
½ tsp. pepper

1. In a large bowl, combine chicken with sesame seeds, almonds, cabbage, onions, and uncooked noodles, broken apart.
2. In a separate bowl, mix dressing ingredients together, stirring until dry ingredients are dissolved. Add to salad ingredients. Toss together gently.
3. Cover and refrigerate until serving time.

Exchange List Values:
Starch 1.0, Vegetable 1.0, Very Lean Meat 2.0, Fat 3.0

Basic Nutritional Values:
Calories 303 (Calories from Fat 162), Total Fat 18 gm (Saturated Fat 1.7 gm, Trans Fat 0.0 gm, Polyunsat Fat 5.2 gm, Monounsat Fat 10.0 gm, Cholesterol 29 mg), Sodium 448 mg, Total Carbohydrate 22 gm, Dietary Fiber 4 gm, Sugars 6 gm, Protein 17 gm

---

Tip: This salad is also tasty without the chicken.

Variation: Add 1-2 grated carrots and ½ cup sunflower seeds to Step 1.
—**Tabitha Schmidt**
Baltic, OH

Greek Cabbage Salad

Colleen Heatwole, Burton, MI

Makes 10 servings
Serving size is ¾ cup

Prep Time: 30 minutes
Chilling Time: 1 hour

6-8 cups thinly sliced
    cabbage
½ cup sliced black olives
½ cup thinly sliced red
    onions
½ cup reduced-fat feta
    cheese, diced *or* crumbled

Dressing:
1 cup apple cider vinegar
6 Tbsp. oil
1 tsp. dry mustard
½ tsp. celery seed

1. Combine first 4 salad
ingredients in a large bowl.
2. Combine dressing
ingredients in a blender or
food processor, or beat well
with a whisk.

3. Add salad dressing to
cabbage mixture. Chill in
refrigerator at least 1 hour
before serving to combine
flavors.

Exchange List Values:
Vegetable 1.0, Fat 2.0

Basic Nutritional Values:
Calories 115 (Calories from Fat 91),
Total Fat 10 gm (Saturated Fat 1.3
gm, Trans Fat 0.0 gm, Polyunsat
Fat 2.6 gm, Monounsat Fat 5.7 gm,
Cholesterol 2 mg), Sodium 162 mg,
Total Carbohydrate 4 gm, Dietary
Fiber 1 gm, Sugars 2 gm, Protein 2 gm

Potato Salad

Gladys Shank, Harrisonburg, VA
Sheila Soldner, Lititz, PA
Sue Suter, Millersville, PA

Makes 10 servings
Serving size is ¾ cup

Prep Time: 20-30 minutes
Cooking Time: 45 minutes
Cooling Time: 3-4 hours

8 medium-sized potatoes,
    diced, peeled or
    unpeeled
1½ tsp. salt
water
4 hard-boiled eggs, diced
½-1 cup celery, chopped
¼-1 cup onions, chopped

Dressing:
2 eggs, beaten
⅓ cup granular Splenda
1 tsp. cornstarch
⅓ cup vinegar
⅓ cup fat-free milk
3 Tbsp. soft-spread tub
    margarine

1 tsp. prepared mustard
1 cup fat-free mayonnaise

1. Cooked diced potatoes in
salt water to a firm softness
(don't let them get mushy).
Cool.
2. Cook eggs. Cool, peel,
and dice.
3. Mix cooled potatoes and
eggs with celery and onions.
4. Mix eggs, granular
Splenda, cornstarch, vinegar,
and milk in a saucepan and
cook until thickened. Add
margarine, mustard, and
mayonnaise. Cool.
5. Pour cooled dressing
over potatoes, eggs, celery,
and onions.
6. Refrigerate and chill for
several hours before serving.

Exchange List Values:
Starch 1.5, Fat 1.0

Basic Nutritional Values:
Calories 173 (Calories from Fat 50),
Total Fat 6 gm (Saturated Fat 1.4
gm, Trans Fat 0.0 gm, Polyunsat
Fat 1.6 gm, Monounsat Fat 1.8 gm,
Cholesterol 127 mg), Sodium 251 mg,
Total Carbohydrate 25 gm, Dietary
Fiber 2 gm, Sugars 5 gm, Protein 6 gm

Variations:
*1. Stir 1 tsp. celery seed
into the dressing (Step 4), or
substitute celery seed for the
celery if you wish.*
    —Ruth Schrock
      Shipshewana, IN

*2. Shred the potatoes after
they're cooked, instead of cubing
them before they're cooked. And
substitute ⅓ cup sour cream for
the milk in the dressing.*
    —Martha Belle Burkholder
      Waynesboro, VA

Easy Red Potato Salad

Becky Harder, Monument, CO

Makes 6 servings
Serving size is ¾ cup

Prep Time: 20 minutes
Cooking Time: 20 minutes
Standing Time: 30 minutes

2 lbs. red potatoes
⅓ cup cider vinegar
2 medium-sized ribs of
   celery, chopped
⅓ cup sliced green onions,
   including some green
   tops
½ cup reduced-fat
   mayonnaise
½ cup fat-free sour cream
½ tsp. salt
½ tsp. pepper
sprinkle of paprika

1. Place potatoes in pot
and cover with water. Cover
and bring to a boil over high
heat. Reduce heat to medium-
low. Cover and simmer 10
minutes, or until potatoes are
tender in the center. Drain
and cool.
2. Cut potatoes into
quarters, or eighths if they're
large. Place in large mixing
bowl. Pour vinegar over them
and stir.
3. Let the potatoes stand
for 30 minutes while you
prepare the celery and
onions. Stir the potatoes
occasionally.
4. Mix mayonnaise, sour
cream, salt, and pepper
together in a small bowl.

5. Add the celery and
onions to the potatoes. Toss
gently.
6. Stir in dressing and mix
together gently. Sprinkle with
a dash of paprika. Chill until
ready to serve.

Exchange List Values:
Starch 2.0, Fat 1.0

Basic Nutritional Values:
Calories 216 (Calories from Fat 62),
Total Fat 7 gm (Saturated Fat 1.1
gm, Trans Fat 0.0 gm, Polyunsat
Fat 3.7 gm, Monounsat Fat 1.6 gm,
Cholesterol 8 mg), Sodium 413 mg,
Total Carbohydrate 33 gm, Dietary
Fiber 3 gm, Sugars 4 gm, Protein 5 gm

Variations:
   1. Add 3 hard-cooked eggs,
chopped, to Step 5.
   2. Use ¾ tsp. celery seed
instead of the chopped celery.
   —Lori Newswanger
   Lancaster, PA

Creamy Dill Pasta Salad

Jan Mast, Lancaster, PA

Makes 10 servings
Serving size is ¾ cup

Prep Time: 15 minutes
Cooking Time: 12-15 minutes

3 cups uncooked tri-color
   spiral pasta
6-oz. can black olives,
   halved and drained
½ cup red pepper, chopped
½ cup green pepper,
   chopped

½ cup onions, chopped
2 tomatoes, chopped
1 Tbsp. dill weed

Dressing:
¾ cup reduced-fat
   mayonnaise
2 Tbsp. prepared mustard
¼ cup vinegar
2½ Tbsp. granular Splenda

1. Cook pasta according
to package directions, being
careful not to overcook. Rinse
in cool water. Drain well.
Place in large mixing bowl.
2. Add vegetables and dill
weed and toss.
3. In a mixing bowl,
combine mayonnaise, mus-
tard, vinegar, and granular
Splenda.
4. Pour over pasta and
vegetables and stir to coat.
5. Chill and serve.

Exchange List Values:
Starch 1.0, Vegetable 1.0,
Fat 1.5

Basic Nutritional Values:
Calories 174 (Calories from Fat 77),
Total Fat 9 gm (Saturated Fat 1.3
gm, Trans Fat 0.0 gm, Polyunsat
Fat 3.6 gm, Monounsat Fat 2.8 gm,
Cholesterol 5 mg), Sodium 282 mg,
Total Carbohydrate 22 gm, Dietary
Fiber 2 gm, Sugars 4 gm, Protein 4 gm

A Tip —

   Add vegetables
wherever you can—
soups, sandwiches,
omelets, frozen pizzas,
and sauces are all
enhanced by extra
vegetables.

Greek Orzo Salad

Lavina Hochstedler
Grand Blanc, MI

Makes 8 servings
Serving size is ¾ cup

Prep Time: 20 minutes
Cooking Time: 12 minutes
Chilling Time: 2-24 hours

1 cup uncooked orzo pasta
6 tsp. olive oil, *divided*
1 medium-sized red onion,
   finely chopped
½ cup minced fresh parsley
⅓ cup cider vinegar
1½ tsp. dried oregano
1 tsp. salt
1 tsp. sugar
⅛ tsp. pepper
1 large tomato, chopped
1 large red pepper, chopped
1 medium-sized cucumber,
   peeled, seeded, and
   chopped
½ cup black olives, sliced
   and drained, *optional*
½ cup reduced-fat feta
   cheese, crumbled

1. Cook pasta according to directions. Drain.

2. In a large mixing bowl, toss cooked orzo with 2 tsp. olive oil.

3. In a separate bowl, combine the onion, parsley, vinegar, oregano, salt, sugar, pepper, and remaining oil. Pour over orzo and toss to coat.

4. Cover and refrigerate 2-24 hours.

5. Just before serving, gently stir in tomato, red pepper, cucumber, olives, if you wish, and cheese.

Exchange List Values:
Starch 1.0, Vegetable 2.0,
Fat 1.0

Basic Nutritional Values:
Calories 160 (Calories from Fat 46),
Total Fat 5 gm (Saturated Fat 1.3
gm, Trans Fat 0.0 gm, Polyunsat
Fat 0.6 gm, Monounsat Fat 2.9 gm,
Cholesterol 2 mg), Sodium 414 mg,
Total Carbohydrate 23 gm, Dietary
Fiber 2 gm, Sugars 5 gm, Protein 6 gm

Summer Pasta Salad

Judy Govotsos
Frederick, MD

Makes 18 servings
Serving size is ¾ cup

Prep Time: 8-10 minutes
Cooking Time: 15 minutes

1 lb. uncooked penne *or*
   corkscrew pasta
1 yellow pepper, sliced
1 green pepper, sliced
1 red pepper, sliced
1 red onion, sliced
8 ozs. crumbled feta
   cheese, *optional*
½ lb. pitted Kalamata
   olives, *optional*
cherry tomatoes, *optional*
16-oz. bottle reduced-fat
   Caesar salad dressing
10-oz. pkg. chicken strips,
   cooked, *optional*

1. Cook pasta according to package directions. Drain.

2. In a large mixing bowl, combine all ingredients except salad dressing and chicken.

3. Pour dressing over pasta mixture. Toss.

4. Add chicken, if you wish, immediately before serving.

Exchange List Values:
Starch 1.0, Vegetable 1.0,
Fat 1.0

Basic Nutritional Values:
Calories 163 (Calories from Fat 50),
Total Fat 6 gm (Saturated Fat 0.9
gm, Trans Fat 0.0 gm, Polyunsat
Fat 3.1 gm, Monounsat Fat 1.2 gm,
Cholesterol 1 mg), Sodium 282 mg,
Total Carbohydrate 24 gm, Dietary
Fiber 1 gm, Sugars 2 gm, Protein 4 gm

Variations:

1. Instead of yellow and red peppers, substitute 2 cups cut-up broccoli florets in Step 2.

2. Instead of feta cheese, use 1 cup shredded cheddar cheese.

3. Instead of Caesar salad dressing, use Three-Cheese Ranch dressing.

—**Lois Smith**
   Millersville, PA

A Tip —

   Buying grated, chopped, precooked, and presliced foods will save preparation time when you're cooking foods at home.

Pasta Salad with Tuna

Sheila Soldner
Lititz, PA

Makes 8 servings
Serving size is ¾ cup

Prep Time: 15 minutes
Cooking Time: 15 minutes

½ lb. uncooked rotini pasta
12.5-oz. can solid white tuna, drained and flaked
2 cups thinly sliced cucumber
1 large tomato, seeded and sliced, *or* ½ pint cherry *or* grape tomatoes
½ cup sliced celery
¼ cup chopped green pepper
¼ cup sliced green onions
¾ cup bottled Italian dressing
¼ cup fat-free mayonnaise
1 Tbsp. prepared mustard
1 tsp. dill weed
¼ tsp. salt
⅛ tsp. pepper

1. Prepare rotini according to package directions. Drain.
2. In a large bowl, combine rotini, tuna, cucumbers, tomato, celery, green pepper, and onions.
3. In a small bowl, blend together Italian dressing, mayonnaise, mustard, and seasonings. Add to salad mixture. Toss to coat.
4. Cover and chill. Toss gently before serving.

Exchange List Values:
Starch 1.5, Vegetable 1.0, Very Lean Meat 1.0, Fat 2.0

Basic Nutritional Values:
Calories 268 (Calories from Fat 105), Total Fat 12 gm (Saturated Fat 1.7 gm, Trans Fat 0.0 gm, Polyunsat Fat 6.5 gm, Monounsat Fat 2.6 gm, Cholesterol 12 mg), Sodium 463 mg, Total Carbohydrate 26 gm, Dietary Fiber 2 gm, Sugars 5 gm, Protein 14 gm

A Tip —
While a daily vitamin never hurts, it's better to get your vitamins and minerals directly from healthy foods.

Crab Pasta Salad

April Swartz
Lake Cadessa, MI

Makes 16 servings
Serving size is ¾ cup

Prep Time: 20 minutes
Cooking Time: 8-10 minutes

16-oz. box uncooked pasta of your choice
½-1 lb. imitation crab, your choice of amount
4-oz. jar sliced pimentos, drained
4-oz. can sliced black olives, drained
1 small onion, diced
16-oz. bottle light Ranch dressing

1. Cook pasta according to package directions, until firm-soft. Drain and cool in a large mixing bowl.
2. Cut up crab into bite-sized pieces. Add to pasta.
3. Stir in pimentos, olives, and onions.
4. Pour dressing over top. Toss until well coated.

Exchange List Values:
Carbohydrate 2.0, Fat 1.5

Basic Nutritional Values:
Calories 207 (Calories from Fat 75), Total Fat 8 gm (Saturated Fat 1.2 gm, Trans Fat 0.0 gm, Polyunsat Fat 0.3 gm, Monounsat Fat 0.6 gm, Cholesterol 3 mg), Sodium 435 mg, Total Carbohydrate 27 gm, Dietary Fiber 2 gm, Sugars 3 gm, Protein 6 gm

Orzo and Corn Off the Cob

Karen Kay Tucker
Manteca, CA

Makes 8 servings
Serving size is ¾ cup

Prep Time: 30 minutes
Cooking Time: 8-9 minutes

4 fresh ears of corn, *or*
    2 cups canned *or* frozen
    (thawed)
1¼ cups uncooked orzo
1 cup black olives, pitted
    and halved
1 medium-sized red sweet
    pepper, chopped
¼ cup thinly sliced green
    onions
¼ cup finely snipped fresh,
    or 1 Tbsp. and 1 tsp.
    dried basil
¼ cup finely snipped fresh
    parsley, *or* 1 Tbsp. and
    1 tsp. dried parsley
¼ cup olive oil
2 Tbsp. white wine vinegar
¼ tsp. salt
¼ tsp. pepper

1. Cut corn off the cob,
about 2 cups-worth. Set aside.
2. Bring a large pot of
lightly salted water to a
boil. Add orzo and cook,
stirring occasionally for 8 to
9 minutes, or until tender,
adding corn during the last
3 minutes of cooking time.
Drain and place in a large
serving bowl.
3. Stir in the olives, sweet
pepper, green onion, basil,
and parsley.

4. In a small bowl, combine
the olive oil, vinegar, salt, and
pepper. Whisk together.
5. Pour dressing over
orzo mixture. Toss gently to
combine.

Exchange List Values:
Starch 2.0, Fat 1.5

Basic Nutritional Values:
Calories 228 (Calories from Fat 83),
Total Fat 9 gm (Saturated Fat 1.3
gm, Trans Fat 0.0 gm, Polyunsat
Fat 1.2 gm, Monounsat Fat 6.3 gm,
Cholesterol 0 mg), Sodium 226 mg,
Total Carbohydrate 33 gm, Dietary
Fiber 3 gm, Sugars 4 gm, Protein 5 gm

Linguine Salad with Peanut Sauce

Gretchen H. Maust
Keezletown, VA

Makes 6 servings
Serving size is ¾ cup

Prep Time: 15 minutes
Cooking Time: 15 minutes

8-oz. box dry linguine
½-1 cup chopped scallions
1 diced cucumber
3 Tbsp. peanut butter
⅓ cup cider, *or* rice, vinegar
¼ cup soy sauce
¼ cup warm water
5 tsp. sesame oil
2 cloves minced garlic
½ tsp. 5-spice powder
hot sauce to taste
dark green lettuce leaves,
    optional
toasted sesame seeds
    and tomato wedges for
    garnish, *optional*

1. Cook linguine as directed
on box, but undercook slightly.
Drain. Rinse with cool water.
2. In a large bowl, combine
linguini, scallions, and
cucumber.
3. In a separate bowl,
whisk together peanut butter,
vinegar, soy sauce, water, oil,
garlic, 5-spice powder, and
hot sauce.
4. If you choose to include
lettuce, arrange it on a platter.
Spoon linguine mixture into
the middle of the platter.
Drizzle dressing over top.
Garnish with sesame seeds
and tomato wedges if desired.

Exchange List Values:
Starch 2.0, Fat 1.5

Basic Nutritional Values:
Calories 243 (Calories from Fat 78),
Total Fat 9 gm (Saturated Fat 1.4
gm, Trans Fat 0.0 gm, Polyunsat
Fat 3.0 gm, Monounsat Fat 3.6 gm,
Cholesterol 0 mg), Sodium 425 mg,
Total Carbohydrate 34 gm, Dietary
Fiber 2 gm, Sugars 5 gm, Protein 8 gm

Variations:
    1. For a heartier dish, add
cubed cooked chicken or turkey.
    2. Serve hot, replacing the
cucumbers with cooked zucchini.

Tip: I like to triple the
peanut sauce and keep it in the
refrigerator to use as a salad
dressing or dipping sauce for
grilled chicken.

Tuna Salad

Frances Schrag, Newton, KS

Makes 4 servings
Serving size is ¾ cup

Prep Time: 15 minutes

6-oz. packed-in-water can
   tuna, drained
2 Tbsp. onion, chopped
3 Tbsp. pickle, chopped
½ cup chopped celery
3 hard-cooked eggs, diced
⅛ tsp. salt
⅛ tsp. pepper
2 Tbsp. light Ranch
   dressing *or* mayonnaise

Combine all ingredients in
a good-sized mixing bowl.

Exchange List Values:
Carbohydrate 0.5,
Lean Meat 2.0

Basic Nutritional Values:
Calories 130 (Calories from Fat 46),
Total Fat 5 gm (Saturated Fat 1.4
gm, Trans Fat 0.0 gm, Polyunsat
Fat 0.9 gm, Monounsat Fat 1.8 gm,
Cholesterol 173 mg), Sodium 426 mg,
Total Carbohydrate 5 gm, Dietary
Fiber 0 gm, Sugars 1 gm, Protein 15 gm

*Tip: Serve as a salad on
lettuce leaves, or use to fill
sandwiches. Or spread the
salad on split English muffins,
top with cheese, and broil
until the cheese melts. (Please
note that the lettuce, bread,
English muffins, and cheese are
optional and are not included in
the recipe analysis.)*

Variations:
   *1. Mix 1½ tsp. prepared
mustard into the salad in Step 1.*
   *2. Instead of the salt and pepper,
use ½ tsp. Mrs. Dash seasoning.*
   —**Lauren Eberhard**
   Seneca, IL

Albacore Tuna Stuffed Tomato

Joe Barker
Carlsbad, NM

Makes 8 servings
Serving size is 2 tomato halves

Prep Time: 1 hour

8 4-oz. Roma tomatoes
2 6-oz. packed-in-water cans
   albacore tuna, drained
1 Tbsp. fat-free mayonnaise
½ tsp. prepared mustard
1½ tsp. bleu cheese
   dressing
2 tsp. green onion, thinly
   sliced
1½ tsp. chives, chopped
1½ tsp. black olives,
   chopped
1½ tsp. cucumber, chopped
1½ tsp. red bell pepper,
   chopped
1½ tsp. yellow bell pepper,
   chopped
celery leaves
paprika
6-8 mint leaves

1. Cut tomatoes in half and
remove seeds and veins. Keep
for another use. Keep the
tomato shells cool.
   2. Mix remaining ingredients together in a bowl.
   3. Stuff tomato halves with
tuna mixture.
   4. Sprinkle paprika lightly
over top.
   5. Garnish each tomato
with a mint leaf.
   6. Keep cold until ready to
serve.

Exchange List Values:
Carbohydrate 0.5,
Very Lean Meat 1.0

Basic Nutritional Values:
Calories 69 (Calories from Fat 10),
Total Fat 1 gm (Saturated Fat 0.3
gm, Trans Fat 0.0 gm, Polyunsat
Fat 0.5 gm, Monounsat Fat 0.3 gm,
Cholesterol 12 mg), Sodium 166 mg,
Total Carbohydrate 4 gm, Dietary
Fiber 1 gm, Sugars 3 gm, Protein 11 gm

A Tip —
   Make sure the food
you eat has plenty of
color. If you have yellow,
green, and red on your
plate, you're probably
looking at a healthy meal.

Asparagus, Apple, and Chicken Salad

Betty Salch
Bloomington, IL
Wilma Stoltzfus
Honey Brook, PA

Makes 4 servings
Serving size is ¾ cup

Prep Time: 20 minutes
Cooking Time: 3-4 minutes,
if using pre-cooked chicken

1 cup fresh asparagus, cut
　into 1"-long pieces
2 Tbsp. cider vinegar
2 Tbsp. vegetable oil
2 tsp. honey
2 tsp. minced fresh parsley
½ tsp. salt
¼ tsp. pepper
1 cup cubed cooked
　chicken, *or* 5-oz. can
　cooked chicken
½ cup diced red apples,
　unpeeled
2 cups torn mixed greens
alfalfa sprouts, *optional*

1. In a small saucepan,
cook asparagus in a small
amount of water until crisp-
tender, about 3-4 minutes.
Drain and cool.

2. In a good-sized mixing
bowl, combine the next 6
ingredients.

3. Stir in the chicken,
apples, and asparagus. Toss.

4. Serve over greens.
Garnish with alfalfa sprouts
if you wish.

Exchange List Values:
Carbohydrate 0.5,
Lean Meat 1.0, Fat 1.5

Basic Nutritional Values:
Calories 164 (Calories from Fat 88),
Total Fat 10 gm (Saturated Fat 1.2
gm, Trans Fat 0.0 gm, Polyunsat
Fat 2.7 gm, Monounsat Fat 5.1 gm,
Cholesterol 31 mg), Sodium 331 mg,
Total Carbohydrate 8 gm, Dietary
Fiber 1 gm, Sugars 6 gm, Protein 12 gm

Asparagus Bean Salad

Carol Coggin
Jacksonville, FL

Makes 6 servings
Serving size is ¾ cup

Prep Time: 20 minutes
Cooking Time: 10 minutes
Chilling Time: 1 hour

1 lb. fresh asparagus, cut
　in 1" pieces
6 dried tomatoes
2 cloves garlic, minced
1½ Tbsp. brown sugar
3 Tbsp. olive oil
4 Tbsp. rice vinegar
2 Tbsp. water
1½ tsp. Dijon mustard
¼ tsp. sage
¼ tsp. salt
¼ tsp. pepper
15-oz. can white navy
　beans, rinsed and
　drained
¼ cup chopped onions
3 tsp. capers, drained
3 Tbsp. grated Parmesan
　cheese

1. Place cut-up asparagus
in a saucepan. Add 1" water.
Cover and cook just until
crisp-tender. Drain and chill.

2. Place dried tomatoes
in a saucepan with 1" water.
Cover and place over medium
heat for about 4 minutes, or
until they plump up. Drain.
Then chop into small chunks
and chill.

3. In a small bowl, whisk
together garlic, brown sugar,
oil, vinegar, water, mustard,
sage, salt, and pepper.

4. In a large mixing bowl,
toss together the asparagus,
tomatoes, beans, onions, and
capers.

5. Pour the dressing over
all. Mix well and chill for an
hour before serving.

6. Sprinkle with Parmesan
cheese to serve.

Exchange List Values:
Starch 1.0, Vegetable 1.0,
Lean Meat 1.0, Fat 0.5

Basic Nutritional Values:
Calories 187 (Calories from Fat 75),
Total Fat 8 gm (Saturated Fat 1.4
gm, Trans Fat 0.0 gm, Polyunsat
Fat 1.0 gm, Monounsat Fat 5.4 gm,
Cholesterol 3 mg), Sodium 305 mg,
Total Carbohydrate 23 gm, Dietary
Fiber 5 gm, Sugars 8 gm, Protein 8 gm

A Tip —

Raid your local farmer's
market whenever possible.
These places are a treasure
trove of fresh, nutritious,
and delicious foods.

Black Bean Fiesta Salad

Lorraine Pflederer
Goshen, IN

Makes 6 servings
Serving size is ¾ cup

Prep Time: 30 minutes
Chilling Time: 2-8 hours,
  or overnight

15-oz. can black beans,
  rinsed and drained
1 cup frozen corn, thawed
1 green pepper, diced
1 sweet red pepper, diced
1 cup diced red onions
2 celery ribs, chopped
½ cup reduced-fat Monterey
  Jack cheese, cubed
3 Tbsp. lemon juice
3 Tbsp. red wine, *or* cider,
  vinegar
2 Tbsp. olive oil
2 garlic cloves, minced
1 Tbsp. no-salt-added
  Italian seasoning (see
  page 254)
1 tsp. pepper
½ tsp. ground cumin

1. In a large bowl, combine
beans, corn, peppers, onions,
celery, and cheese.
2. In a jar with a tight-fitting lid, combine the remaining ingredients. Shake well.
3. Pour over vegetable
mixture and toss gently.
4. Cover and chill for
2 hours or overnight.

Exchange List Values:
Starch 1.0, Vegetable 1.0,
Lean Meat 1.0, Fat 0.5

Basic Nutritional Values:
Calories 180 (Calories from Fat 64),
Total Fat 7 gm (Saturated Fat 1.9
gm, Trans Fat 0.0 gm, Polyunsat
Fat 0.8 gm, Monounsat Fat 3.9 gm,
Cholesterol 7 mg), Sodium 167 mg,
Total Carbohydrate 23 gm, Dietary
Fiber 6 gm, Sugars 5 gm, Protein 8 gm

Boston Bean Salad

Joyce Shackelford
Green Bay, WI

Makes 10 servings
Serving size is ¾ cup

Prep Time: 30 minutes
Chilling Time: 4-8 hours,
  or overnight

14-oz. can navy beans,
  rinsed and drained
15-oz. can red kidney
  beans, rinsed and
  drained
15-oz. can black beans,
  rinsed and drained
1 cup (2 ribs) celery, sliced
½ cup green onions, sliced
½ cup vinegar
¼ cup molasses
¼ cup oil
1 Tbsp. Dijon mustard
¼ tsp. pepper
lettuce leaves to line the
  salad bowl
2 cups curly endive lettuce
  leaves, torn
2 slices bacon, crisp-
  cooked and crumbled

1. In a large bowl, combine
all the beans, celery, and
green onions.
2. In a jar with a tight-fitting lid, combine vinegar,
molasses, oil, mustard, and
pepper. Shake well.
3. Pour dressing over bean
mixture. Chill 4-24 hours.
4. Line a large bowl with
lettuce leaves.
5. Stir endive and bacon
into bean mixture. Spoon
bean mixture into salad bowl.

Exchange List Values:
Starch 1.5, Fat 1.0,
Carbohydrate 0.5

Basic Nutritional Values:
Calories 190 (Calories from Fat 58),
Total Fat 6 gm (Saturated Fat 0.6
gm, Trans Fat 0.0 gm, Polyunsat
Fat 1.9 gm, Monounsat Fat 3.5 gm,
Cholesterol 1 mg), Sodium 218 mg,
Total Carbohydrate 27 gm, Dietary
Fiber 6 gm, Sugars 7 gm, Protein 8 gm

Green Bean Salad

Jean H. Robinson
Cinnaminson, NJ

Makes 8 servings
Serving size is ¾ cup

Prep Time: 20 minutes
Cooking Time: 10 minutes
Chilling Time: 2 hours

4 cups water
1 Tbsp. salt
2 lbs. fresh green beans,
  cut into 2″ pieces
1 rib celery, chopped fine
½ cup chopped green onions
2 cups cherry tomatoes,
  halved
½ cup reduced-fat feta
  cheese

Dressing:
6 Tbsp. oil
2 Tbsp. rice vinegar
1 tsp. Dijon mustard
salt to taste
pepper to taste

1. Bring water and salt to a
boil in a large stockpot. Place
beans into boiling water and
cook for 6 minutes. Remove
from stove and drain. Plunge
beans immediately into ice
water. Drain.

2. In a large mixing bowl,
combine beans, celery,
onions, tomatoes, and cheese.

3. In a jar with a tight-fitting lid, combine oil, vinegar,
mustard, salt, and pepper.
Shake well.

4. Pour dressing over bean
mixture. Toss.

5. Chill for at least 2 hours
before serving.

Exchange List Values:
Vegetable 2.0, Fat 1.5

Basic Nutritional Values:
Calories 125 (Calories from Fat 77),
Total Fat 9 gm (Saturated Fat 1.3
gm, Trans Fat 0.0 gm, Polyunsat
Fat 2.3 gm, Monounsat Fat 4.5 gm,
Cholesterol 2 mg), Sodium 142 mg,
Total Carbohydrate 10 gm, Dietary
Fiber 4 gm, Sugars 3 gm, Protein 4 gm

Colorful Bean Salad

Patricia Eckard
Singers Glen, VA
Betty B. Dennison
Grove City, PA

Makes 6 servings
Serving size is ¾ cup

Prep Time: 30 minutes
Cooking Time: 5 minutes
Chilling Time: 2-8 hours,
  or overnight

15-oz. can green beans,
  drained
15-oz. can peas, drained
15-oz. can shoepeg corn,
  drained
15-oz. can baby lima
  beans, drained
1 medium-sized red onion,
  chopped
4-oz. jar pimentos, drained
½ cup chopped celery
½ cup chopped red bell
  pepper

Dressing:
¾ cup apple cider vinegar
½ cup granular Splenda

1. Mix all vegetables
together in a large bowl.

2. Combine vinegar and
granular Splenda in a small
saucepan. Bring to a boil.
Boil for 3 minutes, stirring
occasionally.

3. Pour over vegetables.
Cover and refrigerate 2-8
hours, or overnight.

Exchange List Values:
Starch 1.5, Vegetable 2.0

Basic Nutritional Values:
Calories 159 (Calories from Fat 9),
Total Fat 1 gm (Saturated Fat 0.2
gm, Trans Fat 0.0 gm, Polyunsat
Fat 0.5 gm, Monounsat Fat 0.2 gm,
Cholesterol 0 mg), Sodium 507 mg,
Total Carbohydrate 32 gm, Dietary
Fiber 7 gm, Sugars 10 gm, Protein 7 gm

Variations:
1. Add a 4-oz. can sliced
mushrooms, drained; a 15-oz.
can of kidney beans, rinsed and
drained; and a 15-oz. can of
yellow wax beans, rinsed and
drained, to Step 1.

2. Add ½ cup oil, 1 tsp.
celery salt, and ¼ tsp. pepper
to the dressing, and whisk
together—without cooking the
mixture. Proceed with Step 3.
—Mary Lynn Miller
  Reinholds, PA

A Tip —

Restaurant portions are
generally big enough for
two or three! Split one
course with your dinner
mates or immediately
save half for later.

Marinated Mushrooms

Lisa Harnish
Christiana, PA

Makes 12 servings
Serving size is 4-5 mushrooms

***Prep Time:** 10 minutes*
***Cooking Time:** 20 minutes*

2 lbs. (50-60) medium-
   sized fresh mushrooms
2 cloves garlic
1 cup red wine vinegar
1 cup water
½ cup olive oil
½ cup vegetable oil
1 bay leaf
1 tsp. salt
½ tsp. dried thyme leaves
12 whole black
   peppercorns
fresh parsley

1. Clean mushrooms and set aside.
2. Flatten garlic or use garlic press.
3. In Dutch oven, combine all ingredients except mushrooms and parsley.
4. Bring to a boil. Reduce heat and simmer 5 minutes.
5. Add mushrooms and simmer uncovered 10 minutes.
6. Remove from heat and let stand until cooled slightly.
7. Transfer mushrooms and marinade to a storage container. Cover and refrigerate until ready to serve.

8. To serve, remove mushrooms from marinade and place in serving dish. Garnish with fresh parsley.

Exchange List Values:
Vegetable 1.0, Fat 1.0

Basic Nutritional Values:
Calories 75 (Calories from Fat 59), Total Fat 7 gm (Saturated Fat 0.6 gm, Trans Fat 0.0 gm, Polyunsat Fat 1.3 gm, Monounsat Fat 4.1 gm, Cholesterol 0 mg), Sodium 68 mg, Total Carbohydrate 4 gm, Dietary Fiber 1 gm, Sugars 1 gm, Protein 2 gm

A Tip —

Fats can be good for you. Monounsaturated fats, like those found in nuts, olive oil, and canola oil, are essential to good health.

Refreshing Cucumber Salad

Kathy Alderfer, Broadway, VA

Makes 4 servings
Serving size is ¾ cup

***Prep Time:** 15 minutes*
***Chilling Time:** 1 hour*

¼ cup reduced-fat
   mayonnaise
¼ cup fat-free sour cream
1 Tbsp. sugar
1 Tbsp. vinegar
1 tsp. dill weed
salt and pepper to taste
2 6-oz. cucumbers, thinly
   sliced (to make 3 cups)
1 cup grape tomatoes, halved
2-4 small green onions,
   sliced into rings, amount
   according to your
   preference

1. In a medium-sized mixing bowl, mix mayonnaise, sour cream, sugar, vinegar, dill, salt, and pepper. Blend thoroughly.
2. Add cucumbers, tomatoes, and green onions to creamy mixture and stir together.
3. Allow to marinate in refrigerator for at least 1 hour before serving.

Exchange List Values:
Carbohydrate 0.5, Fat 1.0, Vegetable 1.0

Basic Nutritional Values:
Calories 96 (Calories from Fat 46), Total Fat 5 gm (Saturated Fat 0.8 gm, Trans Fat 0.0 gm, Polyunsat Fat 2.8 gm, Monounsat Fat 1.2 gm, Cholesterol 6 mg), Sodium 142 mg, Total Carbohydrate 10 gm, Dietary Fiber 1 gm, Sugars 7 gm, Protein 2 gm

Marinated Garden Tomatoes

Bonnie Goering, Bridgewater, VA

Makes 10 servings
Serving size is ¾ cup

Prep Time: 10 minutes
Chilling Time: 1 hour or more

6 large firm tomatoes, cut
   in wedges
½ cup sliced onions
½ cup sliced green bell
   pepper
¼ cup olive oil
2 Tbsp. red wine vinegar
¼ tsp. garlic powder
½ tsp. salt
¼ tsp. pepper
1 Tbsp. granular Splenda
2 Tbsp. minced fresh, *or*
   2 tsp., parsley flakes
1 Tbsp. snipped fresh, *or*
   1 tsp. dried, thyme

1. Arrange tomatoes, onions, and peppers in a flat dish.
2. In a jar with a tight-fitting lid, mix together oil, vinegar, garlic powder, salt, pepper, and granular Splenda. Pour over vegetables.
3. In a small bowl, combine parsley and thyme and sprinkle on top.
4. Refrigerate for one hour or more before serving.

Exchange List Values:
Vegetable 1.0, Fat 1.0

Basic Nutritional Values:
Calories 74 (Calories from Fat 51), Total Fat 6 gm (Saturated Fat 0.8 gm, Trans Fat 0.0 gm, Polyunsat Fat 0.7 gm, Monounsat Fat 4.1 gm,

Cholesterol 0 mg), Sodium 123 mg, Total Carbohydrate 6 gm, Dietary Fiber 2 gm, Sugars 4 gm, Protein 1 gm

Summer Vegetable Cheese Salad

Jan Mast, Lancaster, PA

Makes 8 servings
Serving size is ¾ cup

Prep Time: 15 minutes
Chilling Time: 1 hour

1¼ cups fat-free cheddar
   cheese, shredded
1¼ cups fat-free mozzarella
   cheese, shredded
½ cup reduced-fat Monterey
   Jack cheese, shredded
1 medium-sized cucumber,
   chopped
1 medium-sized tomato,
   seeded and chopped
1 onion, thinly sliced
1 cup green and red
   pepper, chopped
8 lettuce leaves

Dressing:
½ cup fat-free sour cream
¼ cup fat-free mayonnaise
1 Tbsp. lemon juice
1 garlic clove, minced
½ tsp. Dijon mustard
½ tsp. dried basil
½ tsp. paprika
1 tsp. sugar

1. In a large mixing bowl, combine cheeses, cucumber, tomato, onion, and green and red peppers.
2. In a separate bowl, combine sour cream, mayonnaise, lemon juice, garlic, mustard,

basil, paprika, and sugar.
3. Pour dressing over cheese and vegetables. Toss to coat.
4. Chill for 1 hour.
5. Serve in a lettuce-lined bowl.

Exchange List Values:
Carbohydrate 0.5,
Very Lean Meat 2.0

Basic Nutritional Values:
Calories 118 (Calories from Fat 15), Total Fat 2 gm (Saturated Fat 0.9 gm, Trans Fat 0.0 gm, Polyunsat Fat 0.1 gm, Monounsat Fat 0.4 gm, Cholesterol 11 mg), Sodium 519 mg, Total Carbohydrate 10 gm, Dietary Fiber 1 gm, Sugars 5 gm, Protein 14 gm

Beet Salad

Dorothy Lingerfelt, Stonyford, CA

Makes 6 servings
Serving size is ¾ cup

Prep Time: 10 minutes
Cooking Time: 5 minutes
Chilling Time: 4 hours

16-oz. can diced beets,
   drained, juice reserved
0.3-oz. pkg. sugar-free
   lemon gelatin
⅔ cup orange juice
1 tsp. grated onion
2-3 tsp. grated horseradish,
   depending upon how
   much zip you like
1 tsp. vinegar
½ tsp. salt
⅔ cup chopped celery

1. Drain beets, reserving juice.
2. Pour beet juice into a 1-cup measure. Fill to the top

with water. Pour into a small saucepan. Bring to a boil.

3. Dissolve gelatin in boiling beet juice. Stir in orange juice, onion, horseradish, vinegar, and salt. Mix well.

4. Chill beet-gelatin mixture until slightly thickened.

5. Stir in beets and celery. Pour into mold.

6. Chill until firm. Unmold on a serving plate.

Exchange List Values:
Carbohydrate 0.5

Basic Nutritional Values:
Calories 38 (Calories from Fat 1), Total Fat 0 gm (Saturated Fat 0.0 gm, Trans Fat 0.0 gm, Polyunsat Fat 0.1 gm, Monounsat Fat 0.0 gm, Cholesterol 0 mg), Sodium 415 mg, Total Carbohydrate 9 gm, Dietary Fiber 1 gm, Sugars 6 gm, Protein 1 gm

Pickled Beets and Eggs
Beverly Flatt-Getz
Warriors Mark, PA

Makes 12 servings
Serving size is 1 egg and
2 whole small beets

Prep Time: 15 minutes
Cooking Time: 15 minutes
Chilling Time: 1-2 days

12 eggs
¾ cup vinegar
1 cup sugar
2 16-oz. cans whole red beets

1. Hard-cook eggs. Peel and prick whites slightly with fork.

2. In saucepan, heat vinegar.

3. Add sugar and stir over heat until dissolved.

4. Stir in beet juice and heat through.

5. Put eggs in a large jar with a lid. Pour juice over eggs. Add beets on top. Refrigerate for 1-2 days.

6. To serve, cut eggs in half lengthwise. Place on a serving dish, along with the red beets.

Exchange List Values:
Vegetable 1.0,
Medium-Fat Meat 1.0

Basic Nutritional Values:
Calories 97 (Calories from Fat 45), Total Fat 5 gm (Saturated Fat 1.5 gm, Trans Fat 0.0 gm, Polyunsat Fat 0.7 gm, Monounsat Fat 1.9 gm, Cholesterol 212 mg), Sodium 167 mg, Total Carbohydrate 6 gm, Dietary Fiber 1 gm, Sugars 5 gm, Protein 7 gm

Tip: In order to have the eggs be uniformly colored, stir them every few hours. And the longer the eggs are in the beet juice, the more they absorb its flavor.

Deviled Eggs
Leona Yoder, Hartville, OH

Makes 4 servings
Serving size is 2 egg halves

Cooking Time: 15-20 minutes
Prep Time: 10 minutes

4 eggs
⅛ tsp. salt
2 tsp. vinegar
1 Tbsp. fat-free mayonnaise
⅛ tsp. pepper
¼ tsp. prepared mustard

1 Tbsp. fat-free half-and-half
¼ cup finely chopped red onions
paprika *or* fresh parsley leaves

1. Place eggs in a saucepan. Cover with water. Cover pan and bring water to boil.

2. Remove pan with eggs from heat. Keep covered and allow eggs to sit in hot water for 15 minutes. Remove eggs from pan and allow to cool. Peel carefully.

3. Cut eggs in half lengthwise. Remove yolks and place in a small bowl. Mash until smooth.

4. Add other ingredients to mashed yolks and mix well.

5. Refill the whites and garnish with paprika or parsley just before serving.

Exchange List Values:
Medium-Fat Meat 1.0

Basic Nutritional Values:
Calories 84 (Calories from Fat 45), Total Fat 5 gm (Saturated Fat 1.6 gm, Trans Fat 0.0 gm, Polyunsat Fat 0.7 gm, Monounsat Fat 1.9 gm, Cholesterol 212 mg), Sodium 183 mg, Total Carbohydrate 2 gm, Dietary Fiber 0 gm, Sugars 1 gm, Protein 7 gm

Tip: You can use this recipe as the filling for egg salad sandwiches. Simply cut up the hard-cooked eggs (whites and yolks) and mix gently with the other ingredients.

Zippy Fruit Salad

Violette Harris Denney
Carrollton, GA

Makes 8 servings
Serving size is ¾ cup

Prep Time: 20 minutes
Cooking Time: 10 minutes
Chilling Time: 4 hours

½ cup water
21-oz. can light cherry pie
  filling
0.6-oz. pkg. sugar-free
  cherry gelatin
15-oz. can crushed
  pineapple
half a 12-oz. can of
  sugar-free Coke
1 cup chopped nuts
2 apples, chopped

1. In a saucepan, combine
water and pie filling. Bring to
a boil, stirring frequently.
2. Reduce heat and cook for
5 minutes, stirring frequently.
Remove from heat.
3. Add gelatin. Mix
until dissolved. Cool until the
mixture starts to congeal.
4. Fold in pineapple, Coke,
nuts, and apples. Pour into
serving bowl. Chill until
firm.

Exchange List Values:
Fruit 2.0, Fat 2.0

Basic Nutritional Values:
Calories 197 (Calories from Fat 91),
Total Fat 10 gm (Saturated Fat 0.9
gm, Trans Fat 0.0 gm, Polyunsat
Fat 7.2 gm, Monounsat Fat 1.5 gm,
Cholesterol 0 mg), Sodium 29 mg,
Total Carbohydrate 27 gm, Dietary
Fiber 3 gm, Sugars 22 gm, Protein 3 gm

Strawberry Gelatin Salad

Vonda Ebersole
Mt. Pleasant Mills, PA

Makes 12 servings
Serving size is ¾ cup

Prep Time: 15 minutes
Chilling Time: 3-4 hours

2 cups water
0.6-oz. pkg. sugar-free
  strawberry gelatin
4 cups fresh *or* frozen
  strawberries
15-oz. can crushed
  pineapples, undrained
3 large bananas, sliced

1. Bring water to a boil in
a saucepan. Stir gelatin into
boiling water until dissolved.
2. Stir in additional
ingredients.
3. Refrigerate until gelatin
is firm.

Exchange List Values:
Fruit 1.0

Basic Nutritional Values:
Calories 63 (Calories from Fat 3),
Total Fat 0 gm (Saturated Fat 0.0
gm, Trans Fat 0.0 gm, Polyunsat
Fat 0.1 gm, Monounsat Fat 0.1 gm,
Cholesterol 0 mg), Sodium 9 mg, Total
Carbohydrate 16 gm, Dietary Fiber
2 gm, Sugars 10 gm, Protein 1 gm

*Tip: If you're in a hurry, use
frozen strawberries. They'll
speed up the gelling process.*

Frozen Waldorf Salad

Bonita Ensenberger
Albuquerque, NM

Makes 9 servings
*Serving size is 2⅔″ x 2⅔″ rectangle
or ⅑ of recipe*

Prep Time: 20 minutes
**Freezing Time: 8 hours,
  or overnight**

8 ozs. fat-free cream cheese,
  softened
½ cup fat-free mayonnaise
2 cups fat-free frozen
  whipped topping,
  slightly thawed
1 cup apples, unpeeled and
  chopped
½ cup celery, sliced
1 cup seedless grapes,
  halved
¾ cup crushed pineapple,
  drained
¾ cup English walnuts,
  toasted and chopped

1. In a large mixing bowl,
whip together cream cheese
and mayonnaise, either by
hand or with a mixer or food
processor. Fold in whipped
topping.
2. Fold in apples, celery,
grapes, and pineapple.
3. Pour into a greased 8 x 8
baking dish. Cover and freeze
for 8 hours or overnight.
4. Remove from freezer
10-15 minute before serving.
Cut into squares. Top each
serving with toasted walnuts.

Exchange List Values:
Carbohydrate 1.0, Fat 1.5

Basic Nutritional Values:
Calories 155 (Calories from Fat 59),
Total Fat 7 gm (Saturated Fat 0.6
gm, Trans Fat 0.0 gm, Polyunsat
Fat 4.7 gm, Monounsat Fat 0.9 gm,
Cholesterol 3 mg), Sodium 286 mg,
Total Carbohydrate 17 gm, Dietary
Fiber 1 gm, Sugars 10 gm, Protein 5 gm

Favorite Blueberry Salad
Vicki Hill
Memphis, TN

Makes 12 servings
Serving size is 3¼" x 3" rectangle

Prep Time: 10-20 minutes
Chilling Time: 4 hours

**0.6-oz. pkg. sugar-free
  raspberry gelatin**
1½ cups boiling water
**2½ cups fresh *or* frozen (no
  sugar added) blueberries**
½ cup water
**20-oz. can crushed
  pineapple, undrained**
**8-oz. pkg. fat-free cream
  cheese, softened**
1 cup fat-free sour cream
2 Tbsp. granular Splenda
½ cup chopped nuts

1. In a large saucepan or
mixing bowl, dissolve gelatin
in 1½ cups boiling water.
2. Stir in blueberries,
pineapple, and ½ cup water.
Pour into a 9 x 13 pan. Chill
until set, about 4 hours.

3. Meanwhile, cream
together cream cheese,
sour cream, and granulated
Splenda, either by hand, or
with an electric mixer or food
processor. Spread on top of
congealed salad.
4. Sprinkle with nuts.

Exchange List Values:
Fruit 1.0, Fat 1.0

Basic Nutritional Values:
Calories 110 (Calories from Fat 32),
Total Fat 4 gm (Saturated Fat 0.3
gm, Trans Fat 0.0 gm, Polyunsat
Fat 2.4 gm, Monounsat Fat 0.5 gm,
Cholesterol 4 mg), Sodium 153 mg,
Total Carbohydrate 13 gm, Dietary
Fiber 2 gm, Sugars 10 gm, Protein 5 gm

Holiday Cranberry Mousse
Rhoda Atzeff
Harrisburg, PA

Makes 10 servings
Serving size is 2⅔" x 4½" rectangle
or ¹⁄₁₀ of recipe

Prep Time: 30 minutes
Chilling Time: 4-5 hours

**20-oz. can crushed
  pineapple, juice reserved**
**0.6-oz. pkg. sugar-free
  strawberry gelatin**
1 cup water
**1-lb. can whole-berry
  cranberry sauce**
3 Tbsp. fresh lemon juice
1 tsp. grated lemon peel
¼ tsp. ground nutmeg
2 cups fat-free sour cream
½ cup chopped pecans

1. Drain pineapple well,
reserving all juice.
2. Add juice to gelatin in a
2-qt. saucepan. Stir in water.
Bring to a boil, stirring to
dissolve gelatin. Remove from
heat.
3. Blend in cranberry
sauce, lemon juice, lemon
peel, and nutmeg.
4. Chill until mixture
thickens slightly, about 1-2
hours.
5. Blend sour cream
into gelatin mixture. Fold
in drained pineapple and
pecans.
6. Pour into a 1-qt. mold, or
into a 9 x 13 pan.
7. Chill until firm, about
2-3 hours. Unmold onto a
plate or cut into squares and
serve.

Exchange List Values:
Fruit 2.0, Fat 1.0

Basic Nutritional Values:
Calories 176 (Calories from Fat 38),
Total Fat 4 gm (Saturated Fat 0.4
gm, Trans Fat 0.0 gm, Polyunsat
Fat 1.2 gm, Monounsat Fat 2.5 gm,
Cholesterol 5 mg), Sodium 50 mg,
Total Carbohydrate 27 gm, Dietary
Fiber 1 gm, Sugars 26 gm, Protein 5 gm

Lemon Cream Salad

Helen J. Myers, Silver Spring, MD

Makes 10 servings
Serving size is ¾ cup

Prep Time: 20 minutes
Chilling Time: 4 hours

10 ozs. sugar-free lemon-
   lime soda
1 cup miniature
   marshmallows
2 3-oz. pkgs. fat-free
   cream cheese, cubed
0.6-oz. pkg. sugar-free
   lemon-flavored gelatin
20-oz. can crushed
   pineapple with juice
¾ cup chopped pecans,
   optional
8-oz. carton fat-free
   whipped topping

1. In a heavy saucepan,
combine soda, marshmal-
lows, and cream cheese.
Bring to boil over low heat.
Remove from heat.
2. Add gelatin, stirring
until dissolved.
3. Stir in pineapple and
pecans. Chill until the
consistency of unbeaten egg
whites, about an hour.
4. Fold in whipped topping.
Pour into lightly oiled mold.
Chill until firm, about 3 hours.

Exchange List Values:
Carbohydrate 1.5

Basic Nutritional Values:
Calories 101 (Calories from Fat 1),
Total Fat 0 gm (Saturated Fat 0.0
gm, Trans Fat 0.0 gm, Polyunsat

Fat 0.0 gm, Monounsat Fat 0.0 gm,
Cholesterol 2 mg), Sodium 144 mg,
Total Carbohydrate 20 gm, Dietary
Fiber 0 gm, Sugars 14 gm, Protein 3 gm

Cranberry Salad

Mary Lynn Miller
Reinholds, PA

Makes 8 servings
Serving size is ¾ cup

Prep Time: 30-40 minutes
Chilling Time: 6-8 hours,
**   or overnight**

4 cups fresh cranberries,
   rinsed and drained
4 oranges (2 peeled,
   2 unpeeled)
4 apples, peeled and cut
   into quarters
1 cup granulated Splenda

1. Grind cranberries,
oranges, and apples. Mix well.
2. Pour granulated Splenda
over fruit and mix well.
3. Refrigerate for 6-8 hours
before serving.

Exchange List Values:
Fruit 2.0

Basic Nutritional Values:
Calories 111 (Calories from Fat
4), Total Fat 0 gm (Saturated Fat
0.0 gm, Trans Fat 0.0 gm, Polyunsat
Fat 0.1 gm, Monounsat Fat 0.0 gm,
Cholesterol 0 mg), Sodium 1 mg, Total
Carbohydrate 28 gm, Dietary Fiber
6 gm, Sugars 21 gm, Protein 1 gm

Orange Sherbet Salad

Marlys Martins, Waukon, IA

Makes 6 servings
Serving size is ¾ cup

Prep Time: 15-20 minutes
Chilling Time: 3-4 hours

1 cup water
0.6-oz. pkg. sugar-free
   orange gelatin
1 cup orange juice
1 pint orange sherbet
11-oz. can mandarin
   oranges, drained

1. Bring water to a boil in
a saucepan. Stir in gelatin
until dissolved. Pour into an
electric mixer bowl.
2. Add orange juice and
sherbet. Beat with mixer at
low speed until smooth.
3. Fold in oranges.
4. Pour into serving bowl.
Refrigerate until firm, about
3-4 hours.

Exchange List Values:
Carbohydrate 1.5

Basic Nutritional Values:
Calories 103 (Calories from Fat 10),
Total Fat 1 gm (Saturated Fat 0.6
gm, Trans Fat 0.0 gm, Polyunsat
Fat 0.1 gm, Monounsat Fat 0.3 gm,
Cholesterol 0 mg), Sodium 41 mg,
Total Carbohydrate 22 gm, Dietary
Fiber 2 gm, Sugars 19 gm, Protein 1 gm

Sea Foam
Pear Salad

Esther J. Mast
Lancaster, PA

Makes 12 servings
Serving size is ¾ cup

Prep Time: 15 minutes
Chilling Time: 4 hours

29-oz. can pears, drained,
 with juice reserved
1 cup reserved pear juice
0.3-oz. pkg. sugar-free
 lime gelatin
8-oz. pkg. fat-free cream
 cheese, softened
2 cups frozen fat-free
 whipped topping, thawed

1. Mash drained pears and set aside.
2. In a saucepan, heat pear juice to the boiling point and add lime gelatin. Stir until dissolved.
3. With an electric mixer, beat softened cream cheese until smooth and creamy. Gradually add gelatin mixture. Continue beating with electric mixer until blended.
4. Chill until thickened but not until stiff, about 1 hour.
5. Fold in mashed pears and whipped topping.
6. Pour into mold or glass serving dish to set fully, about 3 hours.

Exchange List Values:
Carbohydrate 1.0

Basic Nutritional Values:
Calories 76 (Calories from Fat 1),
Total Fat 0 gm (Saturated Fat 0.0

gm, Trans Fat 0.0 gm, Polyunsat Fat 0.0 gm, Monounsat Fat 0.0 gm, Cholesterol 2 mg), Sodium 149 mg, Total Carbohydrate 14 gm, Dietary Fiber 1 gm, Sugars 9 gm, Protein 3 gm

Easy Fruit Salad

Shirley Sears
Tiskilwa, IL

Makes 12 servings
Serving size is ¾ cup

Prep Time: 20-25 minutes
Chilling Time: 3-4 hours

20-oz. can juice-packed
 pineapple chunks,
 drained and halved
11-oz. can juice-packed
 mandarin oranges,
 drained
15-oz. can juice-packed
 apricot halves, drained
 and quartered
15-oz. can juice-packed
 peach slices, drained
 and quartered
2 cups fresh green grapes,
 halved
3 bananas, sliced
24-oz. jar no-sugar-added
 peach pie filling
½ cup pecan halves,
 optional

1. In a large mixing bowl, stir all drained, canned fruit together.
2. Add grapes and sliced bananas.
3. Mix in peach pie filling.
4. Refrigerate several hours before serving.
5. Garnish with pecan

halves just before serving, if you wish.

Exchange List Values:
Fruit 1.5

Basic Nutritional Values:
Calories 102 (Calories from Fat 2), Total Fat 0 gm (Saturated Fat 0.1 gm, Trans Fat 0.0 gm, Polyunsat Fat 0.1 gm, Monounsat Fat 0.0 gm, Cholesterol 0 mg), Sodium 4 mg, Total Carbohydrate 26 gm, Dietary Fiber 3 gm, Sugars 20 gm, Protein 1 gm

Tips:
 1. Drain the fruit well.
 2. If you need a larger salad just use larger cans or more cans of fruit. You could add marshmallows or apples, too, if you want.

This is quick to make. I keep these canned ingredients on hand all the time for last-minute preparation. I only need to purchase fresh grapes and bananas. My mom introduced me to this recipe in 1968, and I've given it to others many times.

A Tip —

 Fruit is perhaps the best between-meal snack. It's portable, delicious, and healthy.

Grandma's Special Fruit Salad

Jan Moore, Wellsville, KS

Makes 6 servings
Serving size is ¾ cup

Prep Time: 15 minutes
Cooking Time: 5 minutes
Chilling Time: 1-2 hours

1 apple
1 orange, peeled
½ cup strawberries
1 kiwi
1 peach
2 apricots
1 banana
15-oz. can sliced pineapple, drained, with juice reserved
½ cup orange juice
¼ cup reserved pineapple juice
2 tsp. cornstarch
1 egg, beaten
2½ Tbsp. grated coconut
½ cup pecans, chopped

1. Cut all fruit into bite-sized pieces and place in a large bowl.
2. In a small saucepan, heat orange juice over medium heat.
3. Mix cornstarch and pineapple juice together in a small bowl. Add to heated orange juice.
4. Add egg, stirring until sauce thickens.
5. Pour over fruit. Add coconut and pecans and mix well.
6. Chill 1-2 hours and then serve.

Exchange List Values:
Fruit 2.0, Fat 2.0

Basic Nutritional Values:
Calories 205 (Calories from Fat 78), Total Fat 9 gm (Saturated Fat 1.4 gm, Trans Fat 0.0 gm, Polyunsat Fat 2.1 gm, Monounsat Fat 4.4 gm, Cholesterol 35 mg), Sodium 19 mg, Total Carbohydrate 32 gm, Dietary Fiber 4 gm, Sugars 24 gm, Protein 4 gm

Apple Salad

Vera Campbell, Dayton, VA

Makes 8 servings
Serving size is ¾ cup

Prep Time: 15 minutes

4 large apples of your favorite kind, diced
1 large banana, diced
¼ cup raisins
⅓ cup peanuts

Dressing:
⅓ cup fat-free mayonnaise or salad dressing
¼ cup peanut butter
¼ tsp. vanilla
1 tsp. lemon juice
¼ cup fat-free half-and-half
½ cup brown sugar blend (Splenda)

1. Combine apples, banana, raisins, and peanuts in a large bowl.
2. In a small bowl, mix together mayonnaise, peanut butter, vanilla, lemon juice, half-and-half, and brown sugar blend until smooth.
3. Just before serving, toss the dressing with the fruit.

Exchange List Values:
Fruit 2.0, Fat 2.0

Basic Nutritional Values:
Calories 209 (Calories from Fat 69), Total Fat 8 gm (Saturated Fat 1.3 gm, Trans Fat 0.0 gm, Polyunsat Fat 2.2 gm, Monounsat Fat 3.5 gm, Cholesterol 1 mg), Sodium 170 mg, Total Carbohydrate 33 gm, Dietary Fiber 4 gm, Sugars 24 gm, Protein 4 gm

Tip: *You can use this either as a salad or as a light dessert.*

Variation: *For a more caramel-like dressing, eliminate the mayonnaise or salad dressing.*

Double Apple Salad

Anne Nolt, Thompsontown, PA

Makes 12 servings
Serving size is ¾ cup

Prep Time: 20 minutes
Chilling Time: 1 hour

1 large golden delicious apple, unpeeled and diced
1 large red delicious apple, unpeeled and diced
1 tsp. lemon juice
20-oz. can pineapple chunks, drained
1 cup miniature marshmallows
½ cup, plus 2 Tbsp., shredded coconut
½ cup chopped walnuts
¼ cup raisins
¼ cup fat-free mayonnaise
2 Tbsp. thinly sliced celery

1. In a large mixing bowl, toss apples with lemon juice until coated.

2. Gently stir in pineapple, marshmallows, coconut, walnuts, raisins, mayonnaise, and celery.

3. Mix well and transfer to a serving bowl. Cover and chill for 1 hour before serving.

Exchange List Values:
Fruit 1.0, Fat 0.5, Carbohydrate 0.5

Basic Nutritional Values:
Calories 114 (Calories from Fat 42), Total Fat 5 gm (Saturated Fat 1.4 gm, Trans Fat 0.0 gm, Polyunsat Fat 2.4 gm, Monounsat Fat 0.5 gm, Cholesterol 0 mg), Sodium 49 mg, Total Carbohydrate 19 gm, Dietary Fiber 2 gm, Sugars 15 gm, Protein 1 gm

Wheat Berry Salad

Sara Harter Fredette
Goshen, MA

Makes 6 servings
Serving size is ¾ cup

Prep Time: 5 minutes
Cooking Time: 1 hour
Chilling Time: 2-4 hours

1⅓ cups dry wheat berries
1 qt. water
⅓ cup raspberry vinegar
2½ Tbsp. olive oil
¼ cup fresh parsley, chopped
3 scallions, sliced
½ cup dried cranberries
Tabasco to taste
1 Tbsp. lemon juice
¼ tsp. salt
1 Tbsp. sesame oil

1. In a medium-sized saucepan, simmer wheat berries in 1 qt. water for 1 hour, or until tender. (You can also soak the berries overnight and then simmer them for 40 minutes.) Rinse and cool to room temperature.

2. In a large mixing bowl, mix wheat berries with the remaining ingredients.

3. Chill for 2-3 hours.

4. Taste and add more of any of the last 4 ingredients for additional flavor.

Exchange List Values:
Starch 2.0, Fruit 0.5, Fat 1.5

Basic Nutritional Values:
Calories 242 (Calories from Fat 81), Total Fat 9 gm (Saturated Fat 1.3 gm, Trans Fat 0.0 gm, Polyunsat Fat 1.9 gm, Monounsat Fat 5.2 gm, Cholesterol 0 mg), Sodium 107 mg, Total Carbohydrate 36 gm, Dietary Fiber 5 gm, Sugars 7 gm, Protein 6 gm

Mandarin Couscous Salad

Lourene G. Bender
Harrisonburg, VA

Makes 7 servings
Serving size is ¾ cup

Prep Time: 25 minutes

1⅓ cups water
1 cup uncooked couscous
1 cup frozen peas
11-oz. can mandarin oranges, drained
½ cup slivered almonds, toasted
⅓ cup red onions, chopped

¼ cup red wine vinegar
2 Tbsp. olive oil
4 tsp. sugar
¼ tsp. salt
¼ tsp. hot pepper sauce, *or* slightly more, if you wish

1. Bring water to a boil in a saucepan. Stir in couscous, cover, and remove from heat. Let stand 5 minutes.

2. Fluff with fork and add frozen peas.

3. In a mixing bowl, combine oranges, almonds, and onions. Stir into couscous/peas mixture.

4. Combine vinegar, oil, sugar, salt, and hot pepper sauce in a jar with a lid. Shake well.

5. Pour dressing over couscous mixture and toss to coat.

6. Serve at room temperature or chilled.

Exchange List Values:
Starch 2.0, Fat 1.5

Basic Nutritional Values:
Calories 208 (Calories from Fat 75), Total Fat 8 gm (Saturated Fat 0.9 gm, Trans Fat 0.0 gm, Polyunsat Fat 1.5 gm, Monounsat Fat 5.6 gm, Cholesterol 0 mg), Sodium 110 mg, Total Carbohydrate 28 gm, Dietary Fiber 4 gm, Sugars 7 gm, Protein 6 gm

Variations:
1. Use fresh oranges instead of mandarin oranges.
2. Instead of peas use diced cucumbers or cut-up blanched green beans.

Tofu Salad

Sara Harter Fredette
Goshen, MA

Makes 6 servings
Serving size is ¾ cup

Prep Time: 10 minutes
Cooking Time: 10 minutes
Chilling Time: 2-3 hours

1 pkg. extra-firm tofu, cubed
1 carrot, grated
1 scallion, sliced
1 clove garlic, minced
⅓-½ cup sunflower seeds
1 Tbsp. light soy sauce
2 Tbsp. lemon juice and rind
2 Tbsp. olive oil
¼ tsp. salt
⅛ tsp. pepper

1. In a saucepan, steam tofu in 1″ of water for 10 minutes.
2. Drain, and cool. Crumble with fork.
3. Place crumbled tofu, carrot, scallion, garlic, and seeds in a large mixing bowl. Combine gently.
4. In a jar with a tight-fitting lid, combine all remaining ingredients.
5. Pour dressing over the tofu/veggies mixture. Combine well.
6. Cover and chill for 1-2 hours.

Exchange List Values:
Carbohydrate 0.5, Fat 0.5, Medium-Fat Meat 1.0

Basic Nutritional Values:
Calories 120 (Calories from Fat 82), Total Fat 9 gm (Saturated Fat 1.2 gm, Trans Fat 0.0 gm, Polyunsat Fat 3.4 gm, Monounsat Fat 4.2 gm, Cholesterol 0 mg), Sodium 231 mg, Total Carbohydrate 4 gm, Dietary Fiber 1 gm, Sugars 2 gm, Protein 6 gm

Raspberry Vinaigrette

Colleen Heatwole
Burton, MI

Makes 8 servings
Serving size is 2 Tbsp.

Prep Time: 5-10 minutes

1 cup raspberries, fresh *or* frozen and thawed
¼ cup raspberry vinegar
2 Tbsp. olive oil
1 Tbsp. honey
¼ tsp. dry mustard

1. Blend all ingredients in food processor or blender.
2. Refrigerate.

Exchange List Values:
Fat 1.0

Basic Nutritional Values:
Calories 47 (Calories from Fat 31), Total Fat 3 gm (Saturated Fat 0.5 gm, Trans Fat 0.0 gm, Polyunsat Fat 0.4 gm, Monounsat Fat 2.5 gm, Cholesterol 0 mg), Sodium 1 mg, Total Carbohydrate 4 gm, Dietary Fiber 1 gm, Sugars 3 gm, Protein 0 gm

Zesty French Dressing

Erma Rutt
Newmanstown, PA

Makes 16 servings
Serving size is 2 Tbsp.

Prep Time: 5-10 minutes

1 small onion, chopped
⅔ cup vegetable oil
¼ cup granular Splenda
⅓ cup vinegar
2 Tbsp. ketchup
1½ tsp. Worcestershire sauce
1 tsp. salt
1 tsp. prepared mustard
1 tsp. paprika
½ tsp. garlic powder
½ tsp. celery seed

1. Combine all ingredients in blender.
2. Blend until smooth.
3. Store in refrigerator.

Exchange List Values:
Fat 2.0

Basic Nutritional Values:
Calories 89 (Calories from Fat 83), Total Fat 9 gm (Saturated Fat 0.7 gm, Trans Fat 0.0 gm, Polyunsat Fat 2.7 gm, Monounsat Fat 5.4 gm, Cholesterol 0 mg), Sodium 178 mg, Total Carbohydrate 2 gm, Dietary Fiber 0 gm, Sugars 1 gm, Protein 0 gm

A Tip —

Instead of calorie-rich condiments or rich sauces, use dried herbs to flavor your dishes.

Favorite Balsamic Dressing

Ann Bender
Fort Defiance, VA

Makes 8 servings
Serving size is 1 Tbsp.

Prep Time: 5 minutes

¼ cup olive oil
2 Tbsp. balsamic vinegar
1 tsp. prepared mustard
1 clove garlic
1 Tbsp. granular Splenda
⅛ tsp. salt
⅛ tsp. pepper

1. Combine olive oil, vinegar, mustard, garlic, granular Splenda, salt, and pepper in blender.
2. Blend until smooth.
3. Store in refrigerator.

Exchange List Values:
Fat 1.5

Basic Nutritional Values:
Calories 64 (Calories from Fat 61), Total Fat 7 gm (Saturated Fat 0.9 gm, Trans Fat 0.0 gm, Polyunsat Fat 0.7 gm, Monounsat Fat 5.0 gm, Cholesterol 0 mg), Sodium 45 mg, Total Carbohydrate 1 gm, Dietary Fiber 0 gm, Sugars 1 gm, Protein 0 gm

Country Sweet-and-Sour Dressing

Annabelle Unternahrer
Shipshewana, IN

Makes 26 servings
Serving size is 2 Tbsp.

Prep Time: 5 minutes
Chilling Time: 1 hour

¾ cup granular Splenda
½ cup fat-free mayonnaise
1¼ cups olive oil
½ tsp. pepper
1½ tsp. celery seed
¾ cup cider vinegar
2 Tbsp. dry mustard
2 Tbsp. chopped onions

1. In a blender, combine all ingredients.
2. Blend on high for 2 minutes.
3. Refrigerate 1 hour before serving. Refrigerate any leftover dressing.

Exchange List Values:
Fat 2.0

Basic Nutritional Values:
Calories 102 (Calories from Fat 95), Total Fat 11 gm (Saturated Fat 1.4 gm, Trans Fat 0.0 gm, Polyunsat Fat 1.0 gm, Monounsat Fat 7.7 gm, Cholesterol 0 mg), Sodium 33 mg, Total Carbohydrate 2 gm, Dietary Fiber 0 gm, Sugars 1 gm, Protein 0 gm

Ranch Dressing

Pat Unternahrer
Wayland, IA

Makes 6 servings
Serving size is 2 Tbsp.

Prep Time: 5 minutes

⅔ cup fat-free cottage cheese
2 Tbsp. fat-free milk
1 Tbsp. tarragon vinegar
1 garlic clove, minced
1 Tbsp. sliced green onions

1. Blend cottage cheese, milk, vinegar, and garlic in blender or food processor.
2. Add green onions and blend just to combine.
3. Store in refrigerator.

Exchange List Values:
Free food

Basic Nutritional Values:
Calories 22 (Calories from Fat 0), Total Fat 0 gm (Saturated Fat 0.0 gm, Trans Fat 0.0 gm, Polyunsat Fat 0.0 gm, Monounsat Fat 0.0 gm, Cholesterol 1 mg), Sodium 94 mg, Total Carbohydrate 2 gm, Dietary Fiber 0 gm, Sugars 1 gm, Protein 3 gm

A Tip —

When having a salad, don't pour on the dressing. Instead, use the fork-and-dip method of lightly dipping a bite of salad into the dressing.

Desserts

Crisps, Cobblers, & Puddings

Cherry Berry Cobbler

Carol DiNuzzo, Latham, NY

Makes 6 servings
Serving size is ¾ cup

Prep Time: 10 minutes
Baking Time: 30 minutes

21-oz. can reduced-sugar cherry pie filling
10-oz. pkg. frozen, no-sugar-added red raspberries, thawed, juice reserved
1 tsp. lemon juice
½ cup flour
2 Tbsp. sugar blend for baking (Splenda)
⅛ tsp. salt
1 Tbsp. butter
2 tsp. canola oil
1 tsp. reserved raspberry juice

1. In a saucepan, combine pie filling, raspberries, and lemon juice. Bring to a boil over medium heat.
2. Turn into a greased 1-qt. casserole.
3. In a bowl, mix together flour, sugar blend, and salt. With a pastry cutter, blend in butter and oil until crumbly. Pour in raspberry juice and stir with a fork until the mixture is evenly moistened. Sprinkle over fruit.
4. Bake at 375° for 30 minutes, or until cobbler is fully baked (when a toothpick inserted into the center comes out clean) and gently browned.
5. Serve warm (not hot) alone, or over ice cream.

Exchange List Values:
Carbohydrate 2.0, Fat 0.5

Basic Nutritional Values:
Calories 172 (Calories from Fat 34), Total Fat 4 gm (Saturated Fat 1.3 gm, Trans Fat 0.0 gm, Polyunsat Fat 0.7 gm, Monounsat Fat 1.5 gm, Cholesterol 5 mg), Sodium 82 mg, Total Carbohydrate 34 gm, Dietary Fiber 2 gm, Sugars 25 gm, Protein 2 gm

A Tip —

People with diabetes can enjoy sugar like everyone else, as long as it's accounted for in a meal plan and medication regimen.

Apple Pear Crisp

Christie Detamore-Hunsberger
Harrisonburg, VA

Makes 12 servings
Serving size is 3" x 3¼" rectangle

Prep Time: 20 minutes
Baking Time: 45 minutes

3 to 4 large apples, peeled and sliced (use baking apples if you can find them)
3 to 4 large pears, peeled and sliced
¼ cup sugar blend for baking (Splenda)
1 Tbsp. lemon juice
1 Tbsp. flour

Topping:
1 cup flour
½ cup brown sugar blend (Splenda)
⅔ cup dry oats, quick *or* rolled (rolled have more texture)
½ tsp. cinnamon
1 Tbsp. cold butter
1½ Tbsp. canola oil
2 Tbsp. apple juice

1. In a large bowl, mix together apples, pears, sugar, lemon juice, and flour. Place in a greased 9 x 13 baking dish.
2. In the same bowl, mix dry topping ingredients.
3. Cut butter into chunks. With a pastry cutter, blend oil and butter into the dry topping until crumbly. Pour in apple juice and stir with a fork until the mixture is evenly moistened. Sprinkle over fruit mixture.
4. Bake uncovered at 375° for 45 minutes.

Exchange List Values:
Carbohydrate 2.5, Fat 0.5

Basic Nutritional Values:
Calories 195 (Calories from Fat 30), Total Fat 3 gm (Saturated Fat 0.8 gm, Trans Fat 0.0 gm, Polyunsat Fat 0.8 gm, Monounsat Fat 1.4 gm, Cholesterol 3 mg), Sodium 10 mg, Total Carbohydrate 39 gm, Dietary Fiber 3 gm, Sugars 23 gm, Protein 2 gm

Cranberry Pudding

Barbara Jean Fabel
Wausau, WI

Makes 12 servings
Serving size is 3" x 2¼" rectangle

Prep Time: 10 minutes
Baking Time: 30 minutes

Pudding:
2 cups flour
½ cup sugar blend for baking (Splenda)
¼ tsp. salt
4 tsp. baking powder
1 cup fat-free milk, or more
4 tsp. butter, melted
2 cups raw cranberries, cut in half

Sauce:
2 cups fat-free half-and-half
⅓ cup sugar blend for baking (Splenda)
2 Tbsp. cornstarch
⅛ tsp. salt
1½ tsp. butter

1. To make pudding, mix ingredients together in order named.
2. Bake in a greased 9 x 9 baking pan at 400° for 30 minutes.
3. While the pudding is baking, make the sauce by scalding the half-and-half.
4. In a small bowl, combine the sugar blend, cornstarch, and salt. When thoroughly mixed add to the hot half-and-half in the saucepan.
5. Bring to a boil, stirring constantly until mixture thickens. Stir in butter.
6. Serve hot over hot pudding.

Exchange List Values:
Carbohydrate 2.5

Basic Nutritional Values:
Calories 192 (Calories from Fat 23), Total Fat 3 gm (Saturated Fat 1.4 gm, Trans Fat 0.0 gm, Polyunsat Fat 0.2 gm, Monounsat Fat 0.5 gm, Cholesterol 8 mg), Sodium 257 mg, Total Carbohydrate 38 gm, Dietary Fiber 1 gm, Sugars 18 gm, Protein 4 gm

This has been our family's Christmas dessert for 3 generations!

Fruit Cobbler

Abbie Christie
Berkeley Heights, NJ

Makes 8 servings
Serving size is 4½" x 2¼" rectangle

Prep Time: 10 minutes
Baking Time: 30-45 minutes

1 Tbsp. butter
3 Tbsp. canola oil
1 cup flour
1 cup fat-free milk
½ cup sugar blend for
  baking (Splenda)
2 tsp. baking powder
dash of salt
3-4 cups fresh fruit

1. Preheat oven to 350°.
2. Melt butter in a greased 9 x 9 baking dish.
3. Add all other ingredients except fruit. Stir well.
4. Arrange fruit on top of dough.
5. Bake 40-55 minutes, or until lightly browned and fruit is tender.
6. Serve warm with ice cream or milk.

Exchange List Values:
Carbohydrate 2.0, Fat 1.0

Basic Nutritional Values:
Calories 200 (Calories from Fat 63), Total Fat 7 gm (Saturated Fat 1.4 gm, Trans Fat 0.0 gm, Polyunsat Fat 1.7 gm, Monounsat Fat 3.5 gm, Cholesterol 4 mg), Sodium 115 mg, Total Carbohydrate 32 gm, Dietary Fiber 2 gm, Sugars 19 gm, Protein 3 gm

Tip: Use fruit that is in season. The more fruit the better!

In the summer, we would pick blackberries at my sister-in-law's farm, and she would make this for dessert. I always think of her when I make it.

Rhubarb Crisp

Carolyn Lehman Henry
Clinton, NY

Makes 12 servings
Serving size is 3" x 3¼" rectangle

Prep Time: 30 minutes
Baking Time: 35 minutes

2 qts. rhubarb cut in 1" pieces
½ cup sugar blend for
  baking (Splenda)
⅓ cup flour

Topping:
1 cup flour
¼ cup sugar blend for
  baking (Splenda)
¼ cup brown sugar blend
  (Splenda)
½ cup dry rolled oats
2¼ tsp. butter, melted
1½ Tbsp. canola oil
2 Tbsp. apple juice

1. Combine first 3 ingredients and pour into a greased 9 x 13 baking pan.
2. In a large bowl, combine the flour, sugar blends, and oats. With a pastry cutter, blend in the butter and oil until crumbly. Pour in apple juice and stir with a fork until the mixture is evenly moistened. Sprinkle topping over rhubarb mixture.

3. Bake uncovered at 375° for 35 minutes.

Exchange List Values:
Carbohydrate 2.0, Fat 0.5

Basic Nutritional Values:
Calories 172 (Calories from Fat 27), Total Fat 3 gm (Saturated Fat 0.6 gm, Trans Fat 0.0 gm, Polyunsat Fat 0.7 gm, Monounsat Fat 1.3 gm, Cholesterol 2 mg), Sodium 10 mg, Total Carbohydrate 33 gm, Dietary Fiber 2 gm, Sugars 17 gm, Protein 3 gm

Variation: Speed things up by preparing this in a microwave. Place the first 3 ingredients in a greased glass 9 x 13 baking pan. Cover with plastic and microwave on high for 3 minutes.
After placing the topping ingredients over the rhubarb, microwave the dish uncovered on high for 8-10 minutes, or until the rhubarb is tender.
—Wendy Nice
  Goshen, IN

A Tip —

Contrary to a popular myth, eating sugar does not cause diabetes. Genetics, age, obesity, and lifestyle contribute to diabetes—not eating sugar.

Frozen Fruit Slush
Ida Stoltzfus
Free Union, VA

Makes 20 servings
Serving size is ½ cup

Prep Time: 20 minutes
Freezing Time: 4-8 hours,
or overnight

1 cup granular Splenda
pinch of salt
2 cups warm water
6-oz. can orange juice
 concentrate
20-oz. can pineapple
 tidbits, undrained
8 bananas, sliced
1 pt. frozen peaches,
 partially thawed
1-2 cups red or green
 grapes

1. In a large mixing bowl,
dissolve granular sweetener
and salt in water.
2. Add orange juice concentrate and pineapple. Mix well.
3. Fold in bananas,
peaches, and grapes. Mix
well.
4. Pour into a 9 x 13 pan.
Freeze.
5. Before serving, put slush
in refrigerator for 1-2 hours.

A Tip —
 Sugar substitutes are
a great way to add flavor
to dishes without adding
calories.

Exchange List Values:
Fruit 1.5

Basic Nutritional Values:
Calories 96 (Calories from Fat 2),
Total Fat 0 gm (Saturated Fat 0.1
gm, Trans Fat 0.0 gm, Polyunsat
Fat 0.1 gm, Monounsat Fat 0.0 gm,
Cholesterol 0 mg), Sodium 2 mg, Total
Carbohydrate 24 gm, Dietary Fiber
2 gm, Sugars 18 gm, Protein 1 gm

Tips:
 *1. You can substitute manda-
rin oranges or canned peaches
for frozen peaches.*
 *2. I sometimes put the slush
into 4- or 6-oz. containers to
freeze. Individual cups make
excellent lunch-box ingredients
or appetizers for a brunch.*

Variation:
 *1. Reduce the number of
bananas to 2. Substitute 2 cups
sliced fresh or frozen strawberries for the grapes.*
 —Janet Oberholtzer
 Ephrata, PA

Ice Cream-in-a-Bag
Annabelle Unternahrer
Shipshewana, IN

Makes 5 servings
Serving size is ½ cup

Prep Time: 10 minutes
Shaking Time: 10-15 minutes

2 cups fat-free milk
⅓ cup granular Splenda
1 tsp. vanilla
5 cups ice
¾ cup rock salt
¼ cup water

1. In a 1-qt. resealable
bag, combine milk, granular
sweetener, and vanilla.
2. In a 1-gallon resealable
bag, combine ice, salt, and
water. Then add bag with ice
cream mix in it.
3. Close gallon bag very
securely. Wrap with a heavy
towel.
4. Shake 10-15 minutes, or
until ice cream is frozen.

Exchange List Values:
Fat-Free Milk 0.5

Basic Nutritional Values:
Calories 52 (Calories from Fat 1),
Total Fat 0 gm (Saturated Fat 0.1
gm, Trans Fat 0.0 gm, Polyunsat
Fat 0.0 gm, Monounsat Fat 0.1 gm,
Cholesterol 2 mg), Sodium 54 mg,
Total Carbohydrate 8 gm, Dietary
Fiber 0 gm, Sugars 8 gm, Protein 4 gm

---

*Kids ages 3-90 love to make
this recipe.*

Chocolate Mocha Sauce

Lorraine Arnold
Rhinebeck, NY
Jane S. Lippincott
Wynnewood, PA

Makes 16 servings
Serving size is 2 Tbsp.

Prep Time: 5 minutes
Cooking Time: 15 minutes

¾ cup unsweetened cocoa
powder
½ cup fat-free half-and-half
½ cup fat-free milk
1 Tbsp. butter
1 Tbsp. dry instant coffee
⅛ tsp. salt
½ cup brown sugar blend
(Splenda)
½ cup granular Splenda
1 tsp. vanilla

1. Mix all ingredients
except vanilla in a heavy
saucepan. Bring to a boil over
medium-high heat.
2. Turn heat down and
simmer 5 minutes. When
cool, stir in vanilla.
3. Serve with brownies or
vanilla ice cream.

Exchange List Values:
Carbohydrate 1.0

Basic Nutritional Values:
Calories 57 (Calories from Fat 12),
Total Fat 1 gm (Saturated Fat 0.8
gm, Trans Fat 0.0 gm, Polyunsat
Fat 0.0 gm, Monounsat Fat 0.4 gm,
Cholesterol 3 mg), Sodium 37 mg,
Total Carbohydrate 10 gm, Dietary
Fiber 1 gm, Sugars 8 gm, Protein 1 gm

*My grandmother made this sauce
when I was a child. She will soon
be 100 years old, and she no
longer cooks. But my sister and I
still make her recipes.*

Hot Fudge Sauce

Doris Bachman
Putnam, IL

Makes 16 servings
Serving size is 2 Tbsp.

Prep Time: 12 minutes
Cooking Time: 12 minutes

1 cup granular Splenda
⅓ cup unsweetened cocoa
powder
2 Tbsp., + 1 tsp., flour
pinch of salt
1 cup water
1 Tbsp. butter

1. In a saucepan, mix all
dry ingredients together well.
2. Pour in water, stirring
until well mixed. Add butter
and bring to a boil.
3. Cook slowly for 8
minutes, stirring often.

Exchange List Values:
Free food

Basic Nutritional Values:
Calories 20 (Calories from Fat 9),
Total Fat 1 gm (Saturated Fat 0.6
gm, Trans Fat 0.0 gm, Polyunsat
Fat 0.0 gm, Monounsat Fat 0.3 gm,
Cholesterol 2 mg), Sodium 6 mg, Total
Carbohydrate 3 gm, Dietary Fiber
1 gm, Sugars 2 gm, Protein 0 gm

Chocolate Ice Cream Syrup

Christine Weaver
Reinholds, PA

Makes 24 servings
Serving size is 2 Tbsp.

Prep Time: 5 minutes
Cooking Time: 30 minutes

½ cup semi-sweet
chocolate chips
1⅔ Tbsp. butter
2 cups granular Splenda
12-oz. can fat-free
evaporated milk

1. Microwave the chocolate
and butter in a microwave-safe
dish, stirring a few times, for
approximately 3-4 minutes.
2. Transfer chocolate
to a heavy saucepan. Add
granular sweetener and milk
alternately, stirring until
blended.
3. Cook 15 minutes over
low heat, stirring frequently.
4. Serve warm over ice
cream. Refrigerate leftovers.

Exchange List Values:
Carbohydrate 0.5, Fat 0.5

Basic Nutritional Values:
Calories 47 (Calories from Fat 18),
Total Fat 2 gm (Saturated Fat 1.2
gm, Trans Fat 0.0 gm, Polyunsat
Fat 0.1 gm, Monounsat Fat 0.6 gm,
Cholesterol 3 mg), Sodium 26 mg,
Total Carbohydrate 6 gm, Dietary
Fiber 0 gm, Sugars 6 gm, Protein 1 gm

Blueberry Sauce

Jeannine Dougherty
Tyler, TX

Makes 20 servings
Serving size is 2 Tbsp.

Prep Time: 5 minutes
Cooking Time:15-20 minutes

2 Tbsp. sugar blend for
  baking (Splenda)
2 tsp. cornstarch
pinch of salt
½ cup water
2 cups fresh or frozen
  blueberries
2 tsp. lemon juice

1. In a medium-sized
saucepan, combine sugar
blend, cornstarch, and salt.
Mix well.
2. Add water and blueber-
ries. Mix well.
3. Bring mixture to a boil,
stirring constantly. Cook until
thick and translucent.
4. Remove from heat and
stir in lemon juice.

Exchange List Values:
Free food

Basic Nutritional Values:
Calories 14 (Calories from Fat 0),
Total Fat 0 gm (Saturated Fat 0.0
gm, Trans Fat 0.0 gm, Polyunsat
Fat 0.0 gm, Monounsat Fat 0.0 gm,
Cholesterol 0 mg), Sodium 1 mg, Total
Carbohydrate 4 gm, Dietary Fiber
0 gm, Sugars 3 gm, Protein 0 gm

*Here's a great dessert—or quick
meal: place a waffle or a couple
of thin pancakes on a plate. Add
a scoop of good ice cream and
cover with warm blueberry sauce.*

*When cold, this sauce is also
very good over plain ice cream,
yogurt, or cottage cheese. Or
serve it as a topping for pound
cake or angel food cake.*

Raspberry Sauce

Jennifer Kuh
Bay Village, OH

Makes 16 servings
Serving size is 2 Tbsp.

Prep Time: 5 minutes

12-oz. bag frozen
  raspberries
½ cup confectioners sugar
¼ tsp. lemon juice
¼ cup amaretto

1. Blend all ingredients in a
blender until smooth.
2. Pour/drain through a
strainer to separate seeds.
3. Serve over pound cake,
ice cream, frozen yogurt,
yogurt, chocolate mousse,
pancakes, or waffles.
4. Refrigerate unused
portion.

Exchange List Values:
Carbohydrate 0.5

Basic Nutritional Values:
Calories 36 (Calories from Fat 0),
Total Fat 0 gm (Saturated Fat 0.0
gm, Trans Fat 0.0 gm, Polyunsat
Fat 0.0 gm, Monounsat Fat 0.0 gm,
Cholesterol 0 mg), Sodium 1 mg, Total
Carbohydrate 7 gm, Dietary Fiber
0 gm, Sugars 7 gm, Protein 0 gm

Lemon Butter

Lois Niebauer
Pedricktown, NJ

Makes 28 servings
Serving size is 2 Tbsp.

Prep Time: 20 minutes
Baking Time: 15-20 minutes

3 large lemons
4 large eggs
1 cup granular Splenda
2 cups water
2-3 Tbsp. butter
3½ Tbsp. cornstarch

1. Wash lemons. Finely
grate the yellow part of the
skins. Set aside.
2. Squeeze juice of lemons.
Get rid of seeds.
3. In a small bowl, beat
eggs to break up the egg
whites.
4. In a saucepan, combine
all ingredients. Bring to a low
boil, stirring constantly.
5. When mixture thickens,
remove from heat. Pour into a
bowl and chill.
6. Serve as a side dish like
applesauce, or over cake or
gingerbread.

Exchange List Values:
Fat 0.5

Basic Nutritional Values:
Calories 27 (Calories from Fat 14),
Total Fat 2 gm (Saturated Fat 0.7
gm, Trans Fat 0.0 gm, Polyunsat
Fat 0.1 gm, Monounsat Fat 0.5 gm,
Cholesterol 32 mg), Sodium 18 mg,
Total Carbohydrate 2 gm, Dietary
Fiber 0 gm, Sugars 1 gm, Protein 1 gm

Oreo Ice Cream Dessert

Wanda Marshall, Massillon, OH

Makes 24 servings
Serving size is 2¼" x 2" rectangle

Prep Time: 20 minutes
Freezing Time: 8 hours,
or overnight

25 reduced-fat Oreo cookies
2 Tbsp canola oil
2 Tbsp. instant coffee
powder
6 cups (1½-qts.) light
vanilla ice cream,
partially softened
⅔ cup fat-free chocolate
syrup
salted pecans, *optional*

1. Crush Oreo cookies and mix with canola oil. Cover bottom of 9 x 13 pan with the mixture.
2. Blend coffee into softened ice cream using mixer. Drop spoonfuls of ice cream over the crust. Carefully spread the mixture over the cookie crust, being careful not to disturb the crust.
3. Pour chocolate syrup over ice cream. Swirl chocolate syrup through ice cream using a table knife.
4. Sprinkle salted pecans over top, if you wish, and place in freezer.
5. Freeze for 8 hours, or overnight, before cutting into pieces to serve.

Exchange List Values:
Carbohydrate 1.5, Fat 0.5

Basic Nutritional Values:
Calories 135 (Calories from Fat 40), Total Fat 4 gm (Saturated Fat 1.4 gm, Trans Fat 0.0 gm, Polyunsat Fat 0.7 gm, Monounsat Fat 1.9 gm, Cholesterol 10 mg), Sodium 94 mg, Total Carbohydrate 22 gm, Dietary Fiber 0 gm, Sugars 15 gm, Protein 2 gm

---

Variations:
1. Use hot fudge sauce instead of chocolate sauce.
2. Use peanuts instead of pecans.
3. After freezing (Step 5), spread an 8-oz. container of thawed whipped topping over the nuts. Then top with a cup of cookie crumbs. Freeze again for 4 hours before cutting to serve.
—Pam Hochstedler
Kalona, IA

Frozen Heath Bar Mocha Mousse

Ida Stoltzfus, Free Union, VA

Makes 24 servings
Serving size is 2¼" x 2" rectangle

Prep Time: 20-30 minutes
Chilling Time: 30-60 minutes
Freezing Time: 6 hours,
or overnight
Thawing Time: 1 hour

1½ cups crushed reduced-
fat Oreo cookies
2 tsp. butter, melted
2 Tbsp. canola oil
2 tsp. apple juice
2¾ cups fat-free cold milk
2 1-oz. pkgs. fat-free, sugar-
free instant chocolate
pudding
3 tsp. instant coffee powder

2 Tbsp. hot water
1 ice cube
8 ozs. frozen fat-free
whipped topping, thawed
½ cup, plus 1 Tbsp., crushed
Heath Bars, *divided*

1. Mix crushed Oreos, butter, canola oil, and apple juice. Press into a 9 x 13 pan. Put into freezer until pudding is made.
2. In a mixing bowl, stir together pudding and milk. Chill until of soft-set consistency.
3. Mix coffee powder with hot water in a mug until dissolved. Add ice cube until mixture cools. Remove any remaining cube.
4. Fold cooled coffee and whipped topping into soft-set pudding until blended.
5. Add ½ cup crushed Heath Bars.
6. Spoon into cookie crust in pan, being careful not to disturb the crust crumbs.
7. Garnish with 1 Tbsp. crushed Heath Bars.
8. Freeze for 6 hours, or overnight.
9. Thaw in refrigerator for 1 hour prior to serving.

Exchange List Values:
Carbohydrate 1.0, Fat 1.0

Basic Nutritional Values:
Calories 105 (Calories from Fat 38), Total Fat 4 gm (Saturated Fat 1.4 gm, Trans Fat 0.0 gm, Polyunsat Fat 0.7 gm, Monounsat Fat 1.7 gm, Cholesterol 3 mg), Sodium 187 mg, Total Carbohydrate 15 gm, Dietary Fiber 0 gm, Sugars 8 gm, Protein 2 gm

Caramel Pudding

Esther S. Martin
Ephrata, PA

Makes 16 servings
Serving size is ¾ cup

Prep Time: 10 minutes
Cooking Time: 15-20 minutes
Chilling Time: 2-3 hours

2½ Tbsp. butter
1½ Tbsp. canola oil
1 cups brown sugar blend
   (Splenda)
½ cup water
2 qts. fat-free milk
pinch of salt
1½ cups egg substitute
6 Tbsp. cornstarch
6 Tbsp. flour
1 Tbsp. vanilla
whipped topping *or*
   whipped cream, *optional*

1. In heavy saucepan, heat butter with oil until butter is melted. Add brown sugar blend. Bring to a boil and continue simmering until mixture browns. Stir occasionally so it doesn't stick and burn.

2. Remove from heat and add water. Stir in milk and salt. Return pan to stove over low heat.

3. In a blender, mix egg substitute, cornstarch, and flour.

4. Add to caramel-milk mixture and heat until boiling, stirring constantly or whisking as mixture thickens.

5. Remove from stove and add vanilla.

6. Pour into two serving dishes.

7. Chill. Top with whipped topping or whipped cream just before serving, if you wish.

Exchange List Values:
Carbohydrate 1.5, Fat 1.0

Basic Nutritional Values:
Calories 165 (Calories from Fat 29), Total Fat 3 gm (Saturated Fat 1.4 gm, Trans Fat 0.0 gm, Polyunsat Fat 0.5 gm, Monounsat Fat 1.3 gm, Cholesterol 7 mg), Sodium 113 mg, Total Carbohydrate 24 gm, Dietary Fiber 0 gm, Sugars 18 gm, Protein 7 gm

Rice Pudding

Judy Koczo
Plano, IL

Makes 12 servings
Serving size is ⅓ cup or 1/12 of recipe

Prep Time: 30 minutes
Cooking Time: 25-30 minutes
Chilling Time: 2-3 hours

1⅓ cups uncooked,
   converted rice
¼ cup sugar blend for
   baking (Splenda)
pinch of salt
½ tsp. nutmeg
4 tsp. butter
1 tsp. vanilla
5 cups fat-free milk
5-oz. can fat-free
   evaporated milk
2 egg yolks
3 Tbsp. fat-free milk
whipped topping, *optional*
cinnamon, *optional*

1. Combine all ingredients—except egg yolks and 3 Tbsp. milk—in a pan. Cover and cook over low heat. After it comes to a slow boil, cook for 20 minutes.

2. While rice is cooking, beat 2 egg yolks with 3 Tbsp. milk in a small bowl.

3. When rice is cooked, remove rice from heat. Add egg-yolk mixture immediately.

4. Refrigerate until chilled and then serve. Garnish with whipped topping and sprinkles of cinnamon, if you wish.

Exchange List Values:
Carbohydrate 2.0, Fat 0.5

Basic Nutritional Values:
Calories 167 (Calories from Fat 22), Total Fat 2 gm (Saturated Fat 1.4 gm, Trans Fat 0.0 gm, Polyunsat Fat 0.2 gm, Monounsat Fat 0.8 gm, Cholesterol 42 mg), Sodium 73 mg, Total Carbohydrate 29 gm, Dietary Fiber 0 gm, Sugars 11 gm, Protein 7 gm

A Tip —

Every person can make a difference in the fight against diabetes. Call 1-800-DIABETES to see how you can volunteer.

Tapioca Pudding

Miriam Christophel, Goshen, IN

Makes 5 servings
Serving size is ¾ cup

Prep Time: 10 minutes
Cooking Time: 15 minutes
Cooling Time: 20 minutes-2 hours

3 Tbsp. dry instant tapioca
2½ Tbsp. sugar blend for
   baking (Splenda)
⅛ tsp. salt
1 egg, beaten
3 cups fat-free milk
¾ tsp. vanilla

1. In a 2-quart saucepan, combine all ingredients except vanilla. Let stand 5 minutes.
2. Bring ingredients to a boil, stirring constantly. Boil for 1 minute.
3. Remove from heat. Stir in vanilla.
4. Stir once after cooling for 20 minutes.
5. Serve warm or cold.

Exchange List Values:
Carbohydrate 1.5

Basic Nutritional Values:
Calories 111 (Calories from Fat 10), Total Fat 1 gm (Saturated Fat 0.5 gm, Trans Fat 0.0 gm, Polyunsat Fat 0.1 gm, Monounsat Fat 0.5 gm, Cholesterol 45 mg), Sodium 139 mg, Total Carbohydrate 19 gm, Dietary Fiber 0 gm, Sugars 14 gm, Protein 6 gm

This is good just as it is, or with a sliced banana and some whipped cream stirred in. It is our kids' favorite dessert. I like it because it isn't as sweet as some puddings are.

Strawberr-i-oca

Pauline Hindal
Grandin, MI

Makes 12 servings
Serving size is ¾ cup

Prep Time: 15 minutes
Cooking Time: 20 minutes
Chilling Time: 4 hours

4 cups water
½ cup sugar blend for
   baking (Splenda)
¾ cup dry minute tapioca
¼ tsp. salt
0.6-oz. pkg. sugar-free
   strawberry gelatin
1 qt. partially frozen no-
   sugar-added strawberries
2 bananas, *optional*
1-2 cups fat-free whipped
   topping *or* fat-free
   whipped cream

1. In a 4-quart saucepan mix together water, sugar blend, tapioca, and salt. Cook on high, stirring until sugar is dissolved and mixture comes to a boil. Turn to medium-low and continue cooking for 10 minutes, stirring frequently.
2. Remove from heat. Add gelatin and stir until dissolved.
3. Add partially frozen strawberries and sliced bananas, if you wish.
4. Pour into a serving bowl and refrigerate until soft-set.
5. Fold in whipped topping and refrigerate until fully set.

Exchange List Values:
Carbohydrate 1.5

Basic Nutritional Values:
Calories 95 (Calories from Fat 0), Total Fat 0 gm (Saturated Fat 0.0 gm, Trans Fat 0.0 gm, Polyunsat Fat 0.0 gm, Monounsat Fat 0.0 gm, Cholesterol 0 mg), Sodium 64 mg, Total Carbohydrate 23 gm, Dietary Fiber 1 gm, Sugars 11 gm, Protein 0 gm

Pumpkin Ginger Squares

Margaret Culbert
Lebanon, PA
Gina Hargitt
Quinter, KS

Makes 20 servings
Serving size is 2⅔" x 2¼" rectangle

Prep Time: 20 minutes
Baking Time: 50-55 minutes
Chilling Time: 2 hours

1 cup flour
½ cup dry quick oats
¼ cup brown sugar blend
   (Splenda)
1 Tbsp. butter, softened
1 Tbsp., plus 1 tsp., canola
   oil
1½ Tbsp. apple juice
2 cups pumpkin
12-oz. can fat-free
   evaporated milk
2 eggs
⅓ cup sugar blend for
   baking (Splenda)
½ tsp. salt
1 tsp. cinnamon
½ tsp ginger
½ cup chopped pecans *or*
   walnuts
¼ cup brown sugar blend
   (Splenda)
1 Tbsp. butter, melted

1. In a large mixing bowl, mix together flour, quick oats, and ¼ cup brown sugar blend. When well mixed, blend in butter and oil with a pastry cutter until crumbly. Pour in apple juice and stir with a fork until the mixture is evenly moistened.

2. Press into the bottom of a lightly greased 9 x 13 baking pan. Bake at 350° for 15 minutes.

3. In the same mixing bowl, combine pumpkin, evaporated milk, eggs, sugar blend for baking, salt, cinnamon, and ginger. Mix well.

4. Spoon pumpkin mixture over baked crust, being careful not to disturb the crumbs. Return to oven and bake another 20 minutes at 350°.

5. Meanwhile, combine pecans or walnuts, ¼ cup brown sugar blend and 1 Tbsp. melted butter. Sprinkle over baked pumpkin.

6. Return to oven and bake 15-20 minutes more at 350°.

7. Allow to cool completely before cutting into 20 equal pieces to serve.

Exchange List Values:
Starch 1.0, Fat 1.0

Basic Nutritional Values:
Calories 133 (Calories from Fat 42), Total Fat 5 gm (Saturated Fat 1.1 gm, Trans Fat 0.0 gm, Polyunsat Fat 1.0 gm, Monounsat Fat 2.2 gm, Cholesterol 14 mg), Sodium 94 mg, Total Carbohydrate 19 gm, Dietary Fiber 1 gm, Sugars 11 gm, Protein 3 gm

Pumpkin Cream
Esther J. Mast
Lancaster, PA

Makes 10 servings
Serving size is ¾ cup

Prep Time: 5 minutes
Cooking Time: 15-20 minutes
Chilling Time: 1-2 hours

2 cups pumpkin, canned or freshly sieved
2 cups fat-free milk
4 Tbsp. cornstarch
½ cup sugar blend for baking (Splenda)
1 tsp. salt
1 tsp. cinnamon
½ tsp. nutmeg
2 eggs, beaten
1 tsp. cold water
8-oz. container fat-free whipped topping, *divided*

1. Combine pumpkin and milk in a microwavable dish. Microwave on high for 10-15 minutes, or until liquid reaches boiling point.

2. In a mixing bowl, mix together cornstarch, sugar blend, salt, cinnamon, and nutmeg. Beat in the eggs and water.

A Tip —
Choose nonfat milk whenever possible. If you simply don't like the taste of nonfat, try 1% milk.

3. Stir into the pumpkin/milk mixture and microwave on high an additional 5 minutes, or until thickened.

4. Chill in refrigerator.

5. Reserve some of the whipped topping as a garnish and mix the remainder into the cooled, thickened pumpkin.

Exchange List Values:
Carbohydrate 2.0

Basic Nutritional Values:
Calories 137 (Calories from Fat 11), Total Fat 1 gm (Saturated Fat 0.5 gm, Trans Fat 0.0 gm, Polyunsat Fat 0.1 gm, Monounsat Fat 0.4 gm, Cholesterol 43 mg), Sodium 284 mg, Total Carbohydrate 27 gm, Dietary Fiber 2 gm, Sugars 16 gm, Protein 3 gm

This is a creamy alternative to pumpkin pie, with much less work.

Mother's Pumpkin Pudding

Dawn Ranck
Lansdale, PA

Makes 6 servings
Serving size is ¾ cup

Prep Time: 15 minutes
Baking Time: 1 hour

½ cup egg substitute
2 cups mashed pumpkin
¼ cup sugar blend for
  baking (Splenda)
1 Tbsp. flour
¼ tsp. salt
5 Tbsp. shredded, dried,
  sweetened coconut
dash of cinnamon
dash of nutmeg
1 cup fat-free milk
8 full-sized marshmallows

1. Combine all ingredients except marshmallows in a large mixing bowl.
2. Pour into a greased 9 x 9 baking dish.
3. Bake at 350° for 30 minutes.
4. Top with marshmallows. Bake an additional 30 minutes.
5. Serve warm or chilled.

Exchange List Values:
Carbohydrate 2.0

Basic Nutritional Values:
Calories 137 (Calories from Fat 14), Total Fat 2 gm (Saturated Fat 1.3 gm, Trans Fat 0.0 gm, Polyunsat Fat 0.0 gm, Monounsat Fat 0.1 gm, Cholesterol 1 mg), Sodium 172 mg, Total Carbohydrate 28 gm, Dietary Fiber 3 gm, Sugars 22 gm, Protein 5 gm

Lemon Almond Torte

Kathy Hertzler, Lancaster, PA

Makes 12 servings
Serving size is ¹⁄₁₂ of recipe

Prep Time: 15-20 minutes
Baking Time: 50 minutes
Cooling Time: 15 minutes

1 Tbsp. butter, softened
1 Tbsp. canola oil
1½ Tbsp. apple juice
½ cup sugar blend for
  baking (Splenda)
1½ cups finely ground
  almonds, *divided*
1 cup egg substitute
1 tsp. vanilla
1 tsp. lemon extract
1 tsp. almond extract
1 Tbsp. grated lemon rind
1 cup flour
1 tsp. baking powder
¼ tsp. salt
¼ cup fresh lemon juice

Glaze:
¼ cup fresh lemon juice
1½-2 cups confectioners
  sugar
10 whole almonds, *optional*

1. In a large electric mixing bowl, cream together butter, canola oil, apple juice, sugar blend for baking, and 1 cup finely ground almonds until fluffy. Add a little water during this process if it becomes crumbly
2. Add egg substitute and beat well.
3. Add 3 extracts and lemon rind. Beat again to incorporate.
4. In a separate mixing bowl,

stir together flour, baking powder, and salt. Add to creamed mixture alternately with lemon juice.
5. Spoon batter into a greased and floured 8" springform pan.
6. Bake at 350° for 50 minutes. Cool for 15 minutes. Release springform pan.
7. While cake is still warm, and with the pan sides removed, whisk together lemon juice and confectioners sugar to make the glaze.
8. Spread glaze generously over top and sides of cake. Sprinkle remaining ground almonds over glaze while it is still wet. Garnish with whole almonds if you wish.

Exchange List Values:
Carbohydrate 2.5, Fat 1.5

Basic Nutritional Values:
Calories 259 (Calories from Fat 96), Total Fat 11 gm (Saturated Fat 1.4 gm, Trans Fat 0.0 gm, Polyunsat Fat 2.4 gm, Monounsat Fat 6.3 gm, Cholesterol 3 mg), Sodium 127 mg, Total Carbohydrate 36 gm, Dietary Fiber 2 gm, Sugars 24 gm, Protein 7 gm

Gooey Apple Dumplings

Kathy Deal, Noblesville, IN

Makes 12 servings
Serving size is 1 dumpling

Prep Time: 15-25 minutes
Cooking/Baking Time:
50-70 minutes

2 8" pie crusts, unbaked
(see recipe on page 245)

4 firm baking apples
(Granny Smith are good)
6 tsp. brown sugar blend
(Splenda)
12 dashes of cinnamon

Syrup:
½ cup sugar blend for
baking (Splenda)
1 cup water
2 tsp. butter
¼ tsp. cinnamon

1. In a medium-sized saucepan, mix the syrup ingredients together. Boil 3 minutes, watching carefully that the mixture doesn't boil over.

2. Meanwhile, cut the pie crusts into 6 even sections.

3. Divide sliced, pared apples over the divided crust. Top each with ½ teaspoon brown sugar blend and a dash of cinnamon.

4. Wrap up each dumpling. Seal the seam with a dab of water.

5. Place in a greased 9 x 13 baking pan. Pour syrup over top.

6. Bake at 350° for 40-60 minutes, or until nicely browned.

Exchange List Values:
Carbohydrate 2.0, Fat 1.0

Basic Nutritional Values:
Calories 180 (Calories from Fat 55), Total Fat 6 gm (Saturated Fat 1.4 gm, Trans Fat 0.5 gm, Polyunsat Fat 1.3 gm, Monounsat Fat 2.7 gm, Cholesterol 2 mg), Sodium 67 mg, Total Carbohydrate 30 gm, Dietary Fiber 1 gm, Sugars 16 gm, Protein 1 gm

Apple Bake
Barbara Sparks
Glen Burnie, MD

Makes 8 servings
Serving size is 1 slice

Prep Time: 10-15 minutes
Baking Time: 20-30 minutes

⅓ cup sugar blend for
baking (Splenda)
¾ cup flour
pinch of salt
1½ tsp. baking powder
½ tsp. cinnamon, *or* to taste
2 eggs
¾ tsp. vanilla
¾ cup chopped nuts
1½ cups Gala apples,
chopped, *or* other baking
apple, peeled or unpeeled
a little water to thin

1. Lightly grease an 8" or 9" pie plate.

2. Thoroughly mix all ingredients and spread in pie plate.

3. Bake at 350° for 20-30 minutes, until top is browned. (The mix will puff up to fit the pie plate.)

4. Serve with or without sauce listed in the following recipe.

Exchange List Values:
Carbohydrate 1.5, Fat 1.5

Basic Nutritional Values:
Calories 181 (Calories from Fat 79), Total Fat 9 gm (Saturated Fat 1.1 gm, Trans Fat 0.0 gm, Polyunsat Fat 5.5 gm, Monounsat Fat 1.5 gm, Cholesterol 53 mg), Sodium 86 mg, Total Carbohydrate 22 gm, Dietary Fiber 2 gm, Sugars 12 gm, Protein 5 gm

Sauce for Apple Bake
Christine Heuser
Farmingdale, NJ

Makes 6-8 servings
Serving size is 2 Tbsp.

Prep Time: 10-15 minutes
Baking Time: 20-30 minutes

½ cup sugar blend for
baking (Splenda)
1 Tbsp. butter, cut in pieces
½ cup fat-free half-and-half
1 tsp. vanilla

1. Place all ingredients in a saucepan. Stir.

2. Bring to a boil over medium-high heat. Cook 3 minutes, stirring frequently.

3. Spoon 2 Tbsp. sauce on top of each slice of apple bake.

Exchange List Values:
Carbohydrate 1.0

Basic Nutritional Values:
Calories 72 (Calories from Fat 15), Total Fat 2 gm (Saturated Fat 1.0 gm, Trans Fat 0.0 gm, Polyunsat Fat 0.1 gm, Monounsat Fat 0.4 gm, Cholesterol 5 mg), Sodium 25 mg, Total Carbohydrate 14 gm, Dietary Fiber 0 gm, Sugars 13 gm, Protein 0 gm

A Tip —

Never skip insulin in an attempt to lose weight! The high blood glucose is too dangerous to justify any weight loss.

Apple Custard Dessert

Barbara Smith
Bedford, PA

Makes 24 servings
Serving size is 2¼" x 2" rectangle

Prep Time: 15 minutes
Baking Time: 35-45 minutes

1 18½-oz. pkg. butter-recipe
  golden cake mix
½ cup sweetened, shredded
  or flaked coconut
2 Tbsp. canola oil
2 Tbsp. apple juice
6 cups sliced firm baking
  apples, approximately
  6 peeled, sliced apples
1 cup water
¼ cup lemon juice
whipped topping *or* ice
  cream, *optional*

1. Combine dry cake mix
and coconut in a large bowl.
Add canola oil and apple juice.

2. Place sliced apples in a
greased 9 x 13 baking dish.
Sprinkle crumb mixture over
apples.

3. In a small bowl, com-
bine water and lemon juice.
Pour over apples and crumbs.

4. Bake at 350° for 35-45
minutes, or until lightly
browned and set.

5. Cool slightly and serve
with whipped topping or ice
cream, if you wish.

Exchange List Values:
Carbohydrate 1.5, Fat 0.5

Basic Nutritional Values:
Calories 132 (Calories from Fat 35),
Total Fat 4 gm (Saturated Fat 1.4
gm, Trans Fat 0.2 gm, Polyunsat
Fat 1.0 gm, Monounsat Fat 1.3 gm,
Cholesterol 0 mg), Sodium 101 mg,
Total Carbohydrate 23 gm, Dietary
Fiber 1 gm, Sugars 16 gm, Protein 1 gm

Chocolate Raspberry Torte

Pam McAllister
Wooster, OH

Makes 12 servings
Serving size is 1 slice

Prep Time: 35 minutes
Baking Time: 25-30 minutes
Cooling Time: 1 hour

18.25-oz. pkg. chocolate
  cake mix
3-oz. pkg. fat-free cream
  cheese, softened
¾ cup fat-free cold milk
1-oz. pkg. fat-free, sugar-
  free instant vanilla
  pudding
8-oz. container frozen fat-
  free whipped topping,
  thawed
2 cups fresh raspberries
confectioners sugar
fresh mint and additional
  raspberries, *optional*

1. Prepare the cake according to package directions,
using 3 greased and floured
9" round cake pans.

2. Bake at 350° for 25-30
minutes, or until toothpick
inserted in center comes out
clean.

3. Cool for 10 minutes in
pan. Remove from pans to
wire racks to cool completely.

4. While the cake is
baking, beat the cream cheese
in a mixing bowl until fluffy.

5. In a separate bowl,
combine milk and pudding.
Add to cream cheese mixture
and mix well.

6. Fold whipped topping
and raspberries into creamy
mixture.

7. Place one cake layer on
a serving plate. Spread with
half the creamy fruit filling.
Repeat layers, ending with a
cake layer.

8. Just before serving, dust
with confectioners sugar.
Garnish with mint leaves and
raspberries if you wish. Store
in the refrigerator until the
moment you're ready to serve.

Exchange List Values:
Carbohydrate 3.0, Fat 1.0

Basic Nutritional Values:
Calories 247 (Calories from Fat 62),
Total Fat 7 gm (Saturated Fat 1.4
gm, Trans Fat 0.0 gm, Polyunsat
Fat 2.2 gm, Monounsat Fat 2.7 gm,
Cholesterol 1 mg), Sodium 525 mg,
Total Carbohydrate 43 gm, Dietary
Fiber 2 gm, Sugars 21 gm, Protein 4 gm

*Tip: You can substitute sliced
fresh strawberries for raspberries.*

Graham Cracker Pudding Cake

Sandi Degan
Kintnersville, PA

Makes 24 servings
Serving size is 2¼" x 2⅛" rectangle

Prep Time: 20-30 minutes
Chilling Time: 12-24 hours

Cake:
4 1-oz. pkgs. fat-free, sugar-
 free instant vanilla
 pudding
3 cups fat-free milk
8 ozs. frozen fat-free
 whipped topping, thawed
14-oz. box graham crackers

Frosting:
2 ozs. semi-sweet chocolate
1½ cups confectioners
 sugar
3 Tbsp. fat-free milk
1 tsp. vanilla
1 tsp. light corn syrup
2 Tbsp. melted butter

1. In a large mixing bowl,
mix pudding and milk until
thickened. Fold in whipped
topping.
2. Layer bottom of 9 x
13 dish with whole graham
crackers. Top with one-third
of the pudding.
3. Repeat layers, ending
with a layer of crackers.
4. Melt the chocolate either
in the microwave or in a
double boiler.
5. Mix melted chocolate,
confectioners sugar, milk,
vanilla, corn syrup, and
melted butter together.

6. Cover top cracker layer
with frosting.
7. Refrigerate 12-24 hours.

Exchange List Values:
Carbohydrate 2.0, Fat 0.5

Basic Nutritional Values:
Calories 164 (Calories from Fat 30),
Total Fat 3 gm (Saturated Fat 1.3
gm, Trans Fat 0.0 gm, Polyunsat
Fat 0.7 gm, Monounsat Fat 1.2 gm,
Cholesterol 3 mg), Sodium 331 mg,
Total Carbohydrate 31 gm, Dietary
Fiber 1 gm, Sugars 14 gm, Protein 2 gm

Chocolate Chip Date Cake with Topping

Shari Jensen, Fountain, CO
Rebecca Meyerkorth
Wamego, KS

Makes 9 servings
Serving size is 3" x 3" square

Prep Time: 20 minutes
Baking Time: 30-35 minutes

1 cup chopped dates
1½ cups boiling water
1¾ tsp. baking soda,
 divided
3 Tbsp. canola oil, at room
 temperature
½ cup sugar blend for
 baking (Splenda)
1½ cups flour
½ cup egg substitute
1 tsp. vanilla

Topping:
2 Tbsp. sugar blend for
 baking (Splenda)
2 Tbsp. chopped walnuts

¼ cup (1½ ozs.) chocolate
 chips

1. Combine dates, boiling
water, and 1 tsp. baking soda
in a small bowl. Let cool.
2. In a large mixing bowl,
mix together canola oil and
sugar blend.
3. In a separate bowl,
combine flour and ¾ tsp.
baking soda. Stir into
creamed mixture.
4. Add egg substitute and
vanilla. Stir well.
5. Stir in cooled dates.
6. Pour into a lightly greased
9" square baking dish.
7. Make topping by com-
bining sugar, walnuts, and
chocolate chips. Sprinkle over
cake batter.
8. Bake at 375° for 30-35
minutes. (Warning: The cake
will likely sink in the middle.
Despite that, it's ready to
serve when a toothpick
inserted in the center comes
out clean.) Serve warm or
cold.

Exchange List Values:
Carbohydrate 2.5, Fat 1.5

Basic Nutritional Values:
Calories 245 (Calories from Fat 67),
Total Fat 7 gm (Saturated Fat 1.3
gm, Trans Fat 0.0 gm, Polyunsat
Fat 2.3 gm, Monounsat Fat 3.4 gm,
Cholesterol 0 mg), Sodium 273 mg,
Total Carbohydrate 42 gm, Dietary
Fiber 2 gm, Sugars 24 gm, Protein 4 gm

Almond Bake

Jeanne Allen, Rye, CO

Makes 12 servings
Serving size is 3" x 3¼" rectangle

Prep Time: 25 minutes
Baking Time: 30 minutes

2½ cups white *or* yellow
   cake mix
1 egg, beaten
¼ cup canola oil
1 tsp. almond extract
2 3-oz. pkgs. fat-free cream
   cheese, softened
2 eggs
1½ cups confectioners sugar
½ cup sliced almonds

1. In a large mixing bowl,
combine cake mix, egg, canola
oil, and extract. Spread in a
greased 9 x 13 baking pan.

2. In the same mixing
bowl, blend cream cheese and
eggs. Add confectioners sugar.
Mix well.

3. Spoon over bottom layer,
spreading carefully. Sprinkle
almonds over top.

4. Bake at 350° for 30
minutes, or until golden
brown. Serve warm with
optional whipped cream or
ice cream, if desired.

Exchange List Values:
Carbohydrate 2.5, Fat 1.5

Basic Nutritional Values:
Calories 261 (Calories from Fat 90),
Total Fat 10 gm (Saturated Fat 1.2
gm, Trans Fat 0.0 gm, Polyunsat
Fat 2.7 gm, Monounsat Fat 5.2 gm,
Cholesterol 55 mg), Sodium 299 mg,
Total Carbohydrate 38 gm, Dietary
Fiber 1 gm, Sugars 27 gm, Protein 6 gm

Blueberry Crinkle

Makes 8 servings
Serving size is 2" x 4" rectangle

Prep Time: 15-20 minutes
Baking Time: 20 minutes

¼ cup brown sugar blend
   (Splenda)
¾ cup dry quick oats
½ cup flour, white *or*
   whole wheat
½ tsp. cinnamon
dash of salt
1 Tbsp. butter, at room
   temperature
1 Tbsp. canola oil
4 tsp. apple juice
4 cups blueberries, fresh or
   frozen
2 Tbsp. sugar
2 Tbsp. instant tapioca
2 Tbsp. lemon juice
½ tsp. grated lemon peel

1. In a large bowl, combine
brown sugar blend, oats,
flour, cinnamon, and salt.
With a pastry cutter, blend
butter and oil with dry
ingredients until crumbly.
Pour in apple juice and stir
with fork until mixture is
evenly moistened. Set aside.

2. In a separate bowl, stir
together blueberries, sugar,
tapioca, lemon juice, and
lemon peel.

3. Spoon into a greased
8" square baking pan. Sprinkle crumbs over blueberries.

4. Bake at 375° for 20
minutes.

Exchange List Values:
Carbohydrate 2.0, Fat 0.5

Basic Nutritional Values:
Calories 180 (Calories from Fat 36),
Total Fat 4 gm (Saturated Fat 1.2
gm, Trans Fat 0.0 gm, Polyunsat
Fat 0.9 gm, Monounsat Fat 1.6 gm,
Cholesterol 4 mg), Sodium 14 mg,
Total Carbohydrate 34 gm, Dietary
Fiber 3 gm, Sugars 17 gm, Protein 3 gm

A Tip —

All foods can fit
into your meal plan,
as long as the amounts
are reasonable—even a
couple of bites of your
favorite dessert.

Mom's Cherry Pudding Cake

Willard E. Roth, Elkhart, IN

Makes 8 servings
Serving size is ⅛ of recipe

Prep Time: 10-15 minutes
Baking Time: 25 minutes

½ cup sugar blend for baking (Splenda)
2 tsp. butter, at room temperature
1 egg, beaten
1 tsp. baking soda
1 cup flour
15-oz. can pitted red sour cherries, *divided*, juice reserved
1 Tbsp. cornstarch

1. In a large mixing bowl, cream butter and sugar blend. Stir in egg.
2. In a separate bowl, mix together baking soda and flour. Stir into the creamed mixture until well blended.
3. Fold in 1 cup cherries (reserve the juice and any remaining cherries).
4. Spread into an 8" round cake pan.
5. Bake at 350° for 25 minutes.
6. While the cake is baking make the glaze. Pour the reserved juice from the cherries into a saucepan. Stir in cornstarch. Cook over medium heat until thickened, stirring constantly. Stir in remaining cherries. Serve warm over warm pudding cake.

Exchange List Values:
Carbohydrate 2.5

Basic Nutritional Values:
Calories 166 (Calories from Fat 16), Total Fat 2 gm (Saturated Fat 0.8 gm, Trans Fat 0.0 gm, Polyunsat Fat 0.2 gm, Monounsat Fat 0.5 gm, Cholesterol 29 mg), Sodium 177 mg, Total Carbohydrate 35 gm, Dietary Fiber 1 gm, Sugars 12 gm, Protein 3 gm

This is a family favorite, prepared for generations without a formal recipe.

Lemon Fluff

Helen J. Myers, Silver Spring, MD
Arleta Petersheim, Haven, KS

Makes 20 servings
Serving size is 2⅔" x 2¼" rectangle

Prep Time: 20 minutes
Baking Time: 15 minutes
Cooling Time: 30-45 minutes

2 Tbsp. butter, softened
¼ cup canola oil
1½ cups flour
1 cup chopped nuts, *divided*
8-oz. pkg. fat-free cream cheese, softened
1 cup confectioners sugar
2 1-oz. pkgs. fat-free, sugar-free instant lemon pudding
3½ cups cold fat-free milk
8-oz. container frozen, fat-free whipped topping, thawed

1. Beat soft butter, canola oil, and flour together. Spread in a greased 9 x 13 baking pan.
2. Sprinkle ½ cup nuts over top, pushing slightly into dough.
3. Bake at 350° for 12-15 minutes. Remove from oven. Cool.
4. Beat cream cheese until fluffy. Stir in sugar until well mixed. Spread mixture carefully over crust, being sure not to pull up the crust as you go.
5. In a mixing bowl, mix pudding with milk. When thickened, spread over cream cheese layer.
6. Top with whipped topping. Garnish with remaining nuts.

Exchange List Values:
Starch 2.0, Fat 0.5

Basic Nutritional Values:
Calories 201 (Calories from Fat 35), Total Fat 4 gm (Saturated Fat 1.5 gm, Trans Fat 0.0 gm, Polyunsat Fat 0.9 gm, Monounsat Fat 1.0 gm, Cholesterol 11 mg), Sodium 362 mg, Total Carbohydrate 31 gm, Dietary Fiber 3 gm, Sugars 4 gm, Protein 8 gm

Variation: Replace lemon pudding and nuts with vanilla pudding and coconut, or with chocolate pudding and nuts.

A Tip —

Go to www.mypyramid.gov for more information on healthy eating and exercise.

Peanut Butter and Hot Fudge Pudding Cake

Bernadette Veenstra
Rockford, MI

Makes 12 servings
Serving size is 3" x 3¼" rectangle

Prep Time: 15 minutes
Baking Time: 30 minutes

1 cup flour
¾ cup sugar blend for baking (Splenda), *divided*
1½ tsp. baking powder
⅔ cup fat-free milk
2 Tbsp. oil
1 tsp. vanilla
7 Tbsp. peanut butter
6 Tbsp. cocoa powder
2 cups hot water

1. In a large mixing bowl, mix together flour, ¼ cup sugar blend, and baking powder.
2. Add milk, oil, and vanilla. Stir until smooth.
3. Stir in peanut butter.
4. Place mixture in a greased 9 x 13 baking pan.
5. In a small bowl, combine ½ cup sugar blend and cocoa powder. Sprinkle on top.
6. Pour water over everything.
7. Bake at 400° for 30 minutes.

Exchange List Values:
Carbohydrate 1.5, Fat 1.5

Basic Nutritional Values:
Calories 175 (Calories from Fat 69), Total Fat 8 gm (Saturated Fat 1.4 gm, Trans Fat 0.0 gm, Polyunsat Fat 2.1 gm, Monounsat Fat 3.8 gm, Cholesterol 0 mg), Sodium 100 mg, Total Carbohydrate 24 gm, Dietary Fiber 2 gm, Sugars 14 gm, Protein 4 gm

Butterscotch Pie Dessert

Karen Stoltzfus, Alto, MI

Makes 16 servings
Serving size is 3¾" x 2½" rectangle

Prep Time: 15-20 minutes
Baking Time: 20-25 minutes
Cooling Time: 30-45 minutes

1½ cups flour
½ cup chopped walnuts
2 tsp. butter, melted
5 tsp. canola oil
2 Tbsp. apple juice
8-oz. pkg. fat-free cream cheese
1 cup confectioners sugar
2 1-oz. pkgs. fat-free, sugar-free instant butterscotch pudding
3 cups fat-free milk
1 tsp. vanilla
8-oz. container frozen, fat-free whipped topping, thawed
3½ Tbsp. butterscotch chips

A Tip —

Fat-free and sugar-free foods can still contain calories! Be sure to read the nutrient information on all foods you eat.

---

1. Combine flour and nuts in a mixing bowl. With a pastry cutter, blend butter and oil into flour-walnut mixture until crumbly. Pour in apple juice and stir with a fork until the mixture is moistened. Press into a greased 9 x 13 baking pan. Bake at 350° for 20 minutes. Cool.
2. In a mixing bowl, beat cream cheese until fluffy. Beat in powdered sugar until creamy. Spread over crust, being careful not to pull the crust up.
3. In the same mixing bowl, beat pudding, milk, and vanilla until thickened. Spread over top of cream cheese layer.
4. Spread whipped topping over pudding. Sprinkle with butterscotch chips.

Exchange List Values:
Carbohydrate 2.0, Fat 1.0

Basic Nutritional Values:
Calories 199 (Calories from Fat 49), Total Fat 5 gm (Saturated Fat 1.4 gm, Trans Fat 0.0 gm, Polyunsat Fat 2.3 gm, Monounsat Fat 1.5 gm, Cholesterol 4 mg), Sodium 288 mg, Total Carbohydrate 30 gm, Dietary Fiber 1 gm, Sugars 14 gm, Protein 5 gm

---

Variations:
1. Replace butterscotch pudding and butterscotch chips with chocolate pudding and chocolate chips.
2. Replace butterscotch pudding and butterscotch chips with pistachio pudding and chopped walnuts.

Fresh Plum Kuchen

Scarlett von Bernuth
Canon City, CO

Makes 9 servings
Serving size is 3" x 3" square

Prep Time: 10-15 minutes
Baking Time: 50-60 minutes

1 Tbsp. butter, softened
1 Tbsp. canola oil
6 Tbsp. sugar blend for
   baking (Splenda)
2 eggs
1 tsp. grated lemon peel
1 cup flour
1 tsp. baking powder
¼ cup fat-free milk
2 cups fresh plums (about
   4 medium-sized ones)
1 Tbsp. cinnamon
¼ cup brown sugar blend
   (Splenda)

1. In a mixing bowl, cream butter, canola oil and sugar blend together.
2. Beat in the eggs and lemon peel.
3. In a separate bowl, combine the flour and baking powder.
4. Stir the flour mixture into the creamed ingredients. Add the milk, mixing well.
5. Grease a 9 x 9 baking pan. Sprinkle greased bottom and sides lightly with sugar. Spoon in batter.
6. Slice the plums and arrange on top of dough.
7. In a small bowl, stir together the cinnamon and brown sugar. Sprinkle over the plums.

8. Bake at 350° for 50-60 minutes. Let cool and serve with whipped topping or ice cream, if you wish.

Exchange List Values:
Carbohydrate 2.0, Fat 0.5

Basic Nutritional Values:
Calories 172 (Calories from Fat 38), Total Fat 4 gm (Saturated Fat 1.3 gm, Trans Fat 0.0 gm, Polyunsat Fat 0.7 gm, Monounsat Fat 1.7 gm, Cholesterol 51 mg), Sodium 70 mg, Total Carbohydrate 29 gm, Dietary Fiber 1 gm, Sugars 18 gm, Protein 3 gm

Pineapple Cheese Torte

Diane Eby, Holtwood, PA

Makes 16 servings
Serving size is 2" x 3" rectangle

Prep Time: 15-20 minutes
Cooking/Baking Time:
   45 minutes
Chilling Time: 8 hours,
   or overnight

Pat-in-the-Pan Crust:
1 cup flour
1¼ cups confectioners sugar
¼ cup finely chopped
   almonds
2 Tbsp. butter, softened
2 Tbsp. canola oil
1 Tbsp. pineapple juice

Filling:
2 8-oz. pkgs. fat-free cream
   cheese, softened
¼ cup sugar blend for
   baking (Splenda)
2 eggs
⅔ cup unsweetened
   pineapple juice

Pineapple Topping:
¼ cup flour
2 Tbsp. sugar blend for
   baking (Splenda)
20-oz. can crushed
   pineapple, juice drained
   and reserved
1 cup fat-free whipped
   topping
fresh strawberries, *optional*

1. Combine crust ingredients in a mixing bowl. Pat into the bottom of an 8 x 12 baking dish.
2. Bake at 350° for 20 minutes.
3. Meanwhile, beat cream cheese in a mixing bowl until fluffy. Beat in sugar blend and eggs until fluffy. Stir in juice. Pour filling over hot crust.
4. Return pan to oven and bake at 350° for 20 minutes, or until center is set. Cool.
5. To make topping, combine flour and sugar in a saucepan. Stir in 1 cup reserved pineapple juice. Bring to a boil, stirring constantly. Boil and stir 1 minute. Remove from heat.
6. Fold in drained pineapple. Cool.
7. Fold whipped topping into cooled pineapple topping. Spread carefully over dessert.
8. Refrigerate 6 hours or overnight. Garnish with strawberries, if you wish, just before serving.

Exchange List Values:
Carbohydrate 2.0, Fat 1.0

Basic Nutritional Values:
Calories 201 (Calories from Fat 45), Total Fat 5 gm (Saturated Fat 1.3 gm, Trans Fat 0.0 gm, Polyunsat Fat 1.0 gm, Monounsat Fat 2.4 gm, Cholesterol 34 mg), Sodium 222 mg, Total Carbohydrate 31 gm, Dietary Fiber 1 gm, Sugars 21 gm, Protein 6 gm

Fresh Raspberry Soup

Esther Nafziger
Bluffton, OH

Makes 6 servings
Serving size is ¾ cup

Prep Time: 10 minutes
Cooking Time: 10 minutes
Cooling Time: 6 hours,
   or overnight

7 cups (2 lbs.) fresh
   raspberries
3 Tbsp., sugar blend for
   baking (Splenda)
2 Tbsp. cornstarch
2 cups fresh orange juice
½ tsp. grated orange rind
⅔ cup water
⅔ cup, plus 2 Tbsp., fat-free,
   sucralose-sweetened
   vanilla yogurt, *divided*
6 fresh mint leaves *or*
   sprigs

1. Place raspberries in an electric blender or food processor. Cover and process until smooth. Strain and discard seeds.

2. In a medium-sized, non-aluminum saucepan, combine raspberry puree, sugar blend, cornstarch, orange juice, orange rind, and water. Stir well.

3. Cook over medium heat, stirring constantly, until mixture comes to a boil. Reduce heat and simmer 1 minute, stirring constantly. Remove from heat. Cool to room temperature.

4. Pour into a large bowl, cover, and chill thoroughly. Allow 4 hours, or overnight.

5. Add ⅔ cup yogurt to cooled raspberry mixture, stirring well.

6. Ladle into individual bowls and garnish each serving with 1 tsp. yogurt and a mint leaf or sprig.

Exchange List Values:
Carbohydrate 2.5

Basic Nutritional Values:
Calories 153 (Calories from Fat 9), Total Fat 1 gm (Saturated Fat 0.0 gm, Trans Fat 0.0 gm, Polyunsat Fat 0.5 gm, Monounsat Fat 0.1 gm, Cholesterol 1 mg), Sodium 18 mg, Total Carbohydrate 36 gm, Dietary Fiber 10 gm, Sugars 23 gm, Protein 3 gm

Cookies & Bars

Chocolate-Almond Biscotti

Beth Maurer
Columbus Grove, OH

Makes 48 biscotti slices
Serving size is 1 biscotti

Prep Time: 30-40 minutes
Baking Time: 40-47 minutes
   per sheet
Cooling Time: 2 hours

1½ cups sliced almonds,
   toasted, *divided*
2 Tbsp. butter, softened
6 Tbsp. canola oil
1 cup sugar blend for
   baking (Splenda)
⅔ cup unsweetened cocoa
   powder
1 tsp. baking powder
1 tsp. baking soda
½ tsp. salt
¾ cup egg substitute
1 tsp. almond extract
3½ cups flour
2 blocks (4 ozs.) white
   almond bark, melted

1. Preheat the oven to 350°. Lightly grease a cookie sheet and set it aside.

2. Place ¾ cup almonds in a food processor and pulse until ground.

3. In a large electric mixer bowl, beat butter and canola oil with mixer. Add sugar blend and beat until well mixed.

4. Add cocoa powder, baking powder, baking soda, and salt to mixer bowl. Beat until combined.

5. Beat in egg substitute and almond extract. Stir in ground almonds.

6. Add flour by cupfuls, mixing well after each addition. Batter will be quite stiff, and you may need to add the last cup of flour by hand.

7. Remove from mixer, and by hand stir in remaining ¾ cup sliced almonds.

8. Divide dough in half. On waxed paper, and with floured hands, shape dough into two 14"-long rolls.

9. Place rolls on greased and floured cookie sheet, at least 5" apart. Flatten slightly.

10. Bake 25-30 minutes, or until wooden pick inserted near center comes out clean.

11. Cool on cookie sheet for 1 hour. On a cutting board, cut each roll diagonally into ½" thick slices, about 24 slices from each roll.

12. Place slices cut-side down on the same cookie sheets you used for the first baking. Bake at 350° for 8 minutes.

13. Turn cookies over and bake 7-9 more minutes, or until cookies are dry and beginning to get crisp.

14. Remove from cookie sheets to wire racks. Cool completely.

15. With a spoon, drizzle melted almond bark over tops of biscotti.

16. Store in an airtight container.

Exchange List Values:
Carbohydrate 1.0, Fat 1.0

Basic Nutritional Values:
Calories 108 (Calories from Fat 46), Total Fat 5 gm (Saturated Fat 1.4 gm, Trans Fat 0.0 gm, Polyunsat Fat 1.0 gm, Monounsat Fat 2.4 gm, Cholesterol 1 mg), Sodium 71 mg, Total Carbohydrate 14 gm, Dietary Fiber 1 gm, Sugars 6 gm, Protein 2 gm

---

These are great in the morning with coffee or in the evening as dessert. They are perfect for dipping in your favorite hot beverage.

I made these for my mother as part of her Christmas gift. They disappeared very quickly, and she keeps asking me to make more!

Chocolate Chip Toffee Cookies

Luanne Berkey
Canby, OR

Makes about 6½ dozen cookies
Serving size is 1 cookie

Prep Time: 15 minutes
Baking Time: 10 minutes per sheet

¼ **cup butter, at room temperature**
¼ **cup canola oil**
½ **cup brown sugar blend (Splenda)**
½ **cup sugar blend for baking (Splenda)**
2 **eggs**
1 **tsp. vanilla**
2 **cups flour**
1 **tsp. baking soda**
1 **tsp. baking powder**
¼ **tsp. salt**
2 **cups dry quick oats**
1 **cup grated coconut**
1 **cup chocolate chips**
½ **cup toffee bits**

1. In a large electric mixing bowl, or by hand, cream butter, canola oil and sugar blends thoroughly.

2. Add eggs and vanilla and mix until fluffy.

3. In a separate bowl, sift together flour, baking soda, baking powder, and salt. Add to creamed mixture alternately with the dry oatmeal.

4. Mix in coconut, chocolate chips, and toffee bits by hand.

5. Drop onto greased cookie sheet. Bake at 375° for approximately 10 minutes.

Exchange List Values:
Carbohydrate 0.5, Fat 0.5

Basic Nutritional Values:
Calories 67 (Calories from Fat 28), Total Fat 3 gm (Saturated Fat 1.4 gm, Trans Fat 0.0 gm, Polyunsat Fat 0.4 gm, Monounsat Fat 1.0 gm, Cholesterol 8 mg), Sodium 45 mg, Total Carbohydrate 9 gm, Dietary Fiber 0 gm, Sugars 5 gm, Protein 1 gm

---

Variations: Substitute raisins, cut-up gumdrops, or white chocolate chips for the chocolate chips and toffee bits.

Chocolate Chip Cookies

Mary Martins, Fairbank, IA

Makes 5 dozen small cookies
Serving size is 1 small cookie

Prep Time: 15 minutes
Baking Time: 9 minutes per sheet
Chilling Time: 1 hour

¼ cup butter, at room
    temperature
¾ cup canola oil
1 cup brown sugar
1 cup sugar
3 eggs, beaten
3½ cups flour
2 tsp. cream of tartar
2 tsp. baking soda
½ tsp. salt
1 tsp. vanilla
6 ozs. chocolate chips
1 cup chopped nuts,
    optional

1. In a large mixing bowl, combine butter, canola oil, sugars, and eggs.
2. In a separate mixing bowl, sift together flour, cream of tartar, baking soda, and salt.
3. Add about one-third of the dry ingredients to the creamed mixture. Mix well. Add half of the remaining dry ingredients and mix well. Add the remaining dry ingredients and mix until thoroughly blended.
4. Stir in vanilla, chocolate chips, and nuts, if you wish. Chill in the fridge for 60 minutes.
5. Drop by small spoonfuls onto a greased cookie sheet.
6. Bake at 400° for about 9 minutes, or until lightly browned

Exchange List Values:
Carbohydrate 1.0, Fat 0.5

Basic Nutritional Values:
Calories 102 (Calories from Fat 42), Total Fat 5 gm (Saturated Fat 1.3 gm, Trans Fat 0.0 gm, Polyunsat Fat 0.9 gm, Monounsat Fat 2.2 gm, Cholesterol 13 mg), Sodium 72 mg, Total Carbohydrate 14 gm, Dietary Fiber 0 gm, Sugars 9 gm, Protein 1 gm

---

Tips:
1. If you like smaller cookies, make the spoonfuls in Step 5 about the size of a level teaspoon.
2. I usually bake a cookie-sheet full and then cover the rest of the dough and keep it in the refrigerator for a day or so so that I can have freshly baked cookies.
3. Use macadamia nuts in Step 4 for a real treat.
    —**Barb Yoder**, Angola, IN

Quick Chocolate Sandwich Cookies

Connie Miller, Shipshewana, IN

Makes 6 dozen cookies
Serving size is 1 cookie

Prep Time: 30 minutes
Baking Time: 10 minutes per sheet

2 18¼-oz. pkgs. chocolate
    cake mix
1 cup vegetable oil
1 cup egg substitute

Filling:
8-oz. pkg. fat-free cream
    cheese, softened
¼ cup butter, at room
    temperature
2½ cups confectioners
    sugar
1 tsp. vanilla

1. In a mixing bowl, combine the cake mixes, oil, and egg subtitute. Mix well.
2. Dust your hands with cocoa powder, if you have some nearby, and then roll the dough into 1″ balls.
3. Place balls 2 inches apart on ungreased baking sheets. Do not flatten.
4. Bake at 350° for 8-10 minutes. Take out after 10 minutes, even if they don't look like they're done.
5. Cool 5 minutes before removing to wire racks. (Cookies will flatten as they cool.)
6. In a mixing bowl, beat cream cheese and butter together.
7. Add confectioners sugar and vanilla. Beat until smooth.
8. Spread on half the cookies and top with remaining cookies.
9. Store in the refrigerator.

Exchange List Values:
Carbohydrate 1.0, Fat 1.0

Basic Nutritional Values:
Calories 112 (Calories from Fat 48), Total Fat 5 gm (Saturated Fat 1.4 gm, Trans Fat 0.0 gm, Polyunsat Fat 1.2 gm, Monounsat Fat 2.5 gm, Cholesterol 2 mg), Sodium 180 mg, Total Carbohydrate 15 gm, Dietary Fiber 1 gm, Sugars 10 gm, Protein 1 gm

Ginger Snaps

Joan Brown, Warriors Mark, PA

Makes 3 dozen cookies
Serving size is 1 ginger snap

Prep Time: 30 minutes
Baking Time: 15 minutes per sheet

¾ cup zero-trans-fat solid
  shortening
1 cup sugar
1 egg
¼ cup molasses
2 cups flour
1½ tsp. baking soda
¾ tsp. allspice
1 tsp. cinnamon
1 tsp. ginger
¼ cup sugar

1. In an electric mixing bowl, cream shortening and 1 cup sugar together. Add unbeaten egg and molasses. Beat until smooth.

2. In a separate bowl, sift together flour, baking soda, allspice, cinnamon, and ginger. Gradually add to creamed mixture. Mix well.

3. Roll into 1" balls. Roll in ¼ cup sugar. Place on ungreased cookie sheets.

4. Bake at 350° for 15 minutes.

Exchange List Values:
Carbohydrate 1.0, Fat 0.5

Basic Nutritional Values:
Calories 100 (Calories from Fat 40), Total Fat 4 gm (Saturated Fat 1.1 gm, Trans Fat 0.0 gm, Polyunsat Fat 1.5 gm, Monounsat Fat 1.8 gm, Cholesterol 6 mg), Sodium 55 mg, Total Carbohydrate 14 gm, Dietary Fiber 0 gm, Sugars 8 gm, Protein 1 gm

Variation: Instead of allspice, use ¾-1 tsp. ground cloves.
—Cova Rexroad
  Kingsville, MD

Soft, Chewy Molasses Cookies

Martha Ann Auker
Landisburg, PA

Makes 3 dozen cookies
Serving size is 1 cookie

Prep Time: 10 minutes
Baking Time: 8-10 minutes per cookie sheet

6 Tbsp. butter, at room
  temperature
2 Tbsp. canola oil
1 cup brown sugar
1 egg
2 cups flour
2 tsp. baking soda
2 tsp. ginger
2 tsp. cinnamon
4 Tbsp. black strap molasses
¼ cup sugar

1. In an electric mixing bowl, cream together butter, canola oil and brown sugar. Add egg. Mix well.

2. In a separate bowl, mix together flour, baking soda, ginger, and cinnamon. Add to creamed mixture, alternately with the molasses, until well blended.

3. Shape batter into 1" balls. Roll each in sugar. Place 2" apart on a greased cookie sheet.

4. Bake at 350° for 8-10 minutes.

5. Let stand on cookie sheet about 2 minutes before removing to wire rack to cool.

Exchange List Values:
Carbohydrate 1.0, Fat 0.5

Basic Nutritional Values:
Calories 86 (Calories from Fat 26), Total Fat 3 gm (Saturated Fat 1.3 gm, Trans Fat 0.0 gm, Polyunsat Fat 0.4 gm, Monounsat Fat 1.0 gm, Cholesterol 11 mg), Sodium 89 mg, Total Carbohydrate 14 gm, Dietary Fiber 0 gm, Sugars 9 gm, Protein 1 gm

Variation: Add ½ tsp. ground cloves to Step 2, if you wish.
—**Marjora Miller**
  Archbold, OH

A Tip —

Find healthy ways to replace nervous eating. A walk around the block, talking with a friend, or simply keeping food out of reach can help.

Peanut Butter Chocolate Chip Cookies

Wendy B. Martzall
New Holland, PA

Makes 7 dozen small cookies
Serving size is 1 small cookie

Prep Time: 10 minutes
Baking Time: 8-10 minutes
 per sheet

1 cup peanut butter
3 Tbsp. butter, at room
 temperature
3 Tbsp. canola oil
6 Tbsp. sugar blend for
 baking (Splenda)
6 Tbsp. brown sugar blend
 (Splenda)
1 tsp. vanilla
2 large eggs
2 cups flour
1 tsp. baking soda
2 cups semi-sweet
 chocolate chips

1. Preheat oven to 375°.
2. Beat together peanut
butter, butter, canola oil,
sugar blends, and vanilla
with an electric mixer.
3. Beat in eggs. Gradually
beat in flour and baking soda.
4. Stir in chocolate chips by
hand.
5. Drop by rounded
teaspoons, 2 inches apart, on
ungreased cookie sheets.
6. Bake 8-10 minutes, or
until lightly browned.
7. Cool on cookie sheets for
1 minute before removing.
Cool completely on wire racks.

Exchange List Values:
Carbohydrate 0.5, Fat 0.5

Basic Nutritional Values:
Calories 65 (Calories from Fat 34),
Total Fat 4 gm (Saturated Fat 1.3
gm, Trans Fat 0.0 gm, Polyunsat
Fat 0.7 gm, Monounsat Fat 1.6 gm,
Cholesterol 6 mg), Sodium 35 mg,
Total Carbohydrate 7 gm, Dietary
Fiber 0 gm, Sugars 4 gm, Protein 1 gm

Variations:
 *1. Use the same dough, but
get a different result! After Step
3, refrigerate the dough for half
an hour or so, so that it's easy
to handle.*
 *Using a 7-oz. pkg. of minia-
ture peanut butter cups, wrap
a ball of cookie dough around
each little peanut butter cup.
Place the wrapped balls in the
fridge for 1 hour.*
 *When ready to bake,
place balls 2 inches apart on
ungreased cookie sheets. Bake
at 350° for 12-14 minutes, or
until the bottom edges of the
balls are golden.*
 *After the baked balls have
cooled, drizzle them with melted
chocolate chips.*
 —**Stacy Schmucker**
 Stoltzfus, Enola, PA

 *2. After Step 3, chill the
dough for half an hour in the
fridge. Then roll into small
walnut-sized balls and place
each ball in a cup in a mini-
muffin tin.*
 *Bake at 375° for 8-9 minutes.
Remove from oven. Gently press
1 miniature peanut butter cup
into each cookie.*
 *Cool in pan 10 minutes.
Remove from pan and finish
cooling on a wire rack.*
 —**Carol Sherwood**
 Batavia, NY

Mom's Sugar Cookies

Marie Skelly
Babylon, NY

Makes 3 dozen cookies
Serving size is 1 cookie

Prep Time: 15-20 minutes
Baking Time: 8-12 minutes
 per sheet

1 cup sugar
½ cup zero-trans-fat solid
 shortening
1 egg
2 Tbsp. milk
½ tsp. vanilla
2 cups flour
2 tsp. baking powder
½ tsp. salt
¼ cup sugar

1. In an electric mixing
bowl, cream 1 cup sugar and
shortening together. Add egg,
milk, and vanilla. Beat well.
2. In a separate bowl, mix
dry ingredients together. Add
to creamed mixture.
3. Stir well. Then work
with hands until a stiff dough
forms.
4. Lightly flour a work
surface. Roll dough to
¼" thickness. Cut with
cookie cutters and place
on ungreased cookie sheet.
Sprinkle lightly with granulated sugar.
5. Bake at 375° for 8-12
minutes until lightly browned
on edges. Cool on cooling
racks.

Exchange List Values:
Carbohydrate 1.0, Fat 0.5

Basic Nutritional Values:
Calories 81 (Calories from Fat 27),
Total Fat 3 gm (Saturated Fat 0.8
gm, Trans Fat 0.0 gm, Polyunsat
Fat 1.0 gm, Monounsat Fat 1.2 gm,
Cholesterol 6 mg), Sodium 55 mg,
Total Carbohydrate 12 gm, Dietary
Fiber 0 gm, Sugars 7 gm, Protein 1 gm

*Variation: Instead of vanilla,
use ¾-1½ tsp. almond extract,
according to your taste preference.*
—Barb Yoder
Angola, IN

Crinkle-Top Cookies
Esther J. Mast
Lancaster, PA

Makes 4 dozen cookies
Serving size is 1 cookie

Prep Time: 10-20 minutes
Chilling Time: 2 hours
Baking Time: 9-10 minutes
per cookie sheet

2 cups chocolate chips,
divided
1½ cups flour
1½ tsp. baking powder
¼ tsp. salt
1 Tbsp. butter, at room
temperature
½ cup sugar blend for
baking (Splenda)
2 egg whites
1½ tsp. vanilla extract
¼ cup water
¼ cup confectioners sugar

1. Melt 1 cup chocolate
chips (3 min. at 60% power
in microwave). Stir until
smooth. Set aside.
2. In a mixing bowl,
combine flour, baking
powder, and salt. Set aside.
3. In a large mixing bowl
cream together butter and
sugar blend. Add egg whites
and vanilla.
4. Stir in melted chocolate.
Then add flour mixture
alternately with water.
5. Stir in remaining 1 cup
chocolate chips.
6. Refrigerate at least 2
hours until dough is firm.
Roll into 1" balls and roll in

A Tip —

If you're headed to
a party with lots of
unhealthy options, have a
small snack before you go
to lessen the temptation.

confectioners sugar. Place on
greased cookie sheet.
7. Bake at 350° approxi-
mately 10 minutes. Don't
over-bake.

Exchange List Values:
Carbohydrate 0.5, Fat 0.5

Basic Nutritional Values:
Calories 61 (Calories from Fat 21),
Total Fat 2 gm (Saturated Fat 1.4
gm, Trans Fat 0.0 gm, Polyunsat
Fat 0.1 gm, Monounsat Fat 0.8 gm,
Cholesterol 1 mg), Sodium 28 mg,
Total Carbohydrate 10 gm, Dietary
Fiber 1 gm, Sugars 7 gm, Protein 1 gm

*I got this recipe from a friend
in my weight-loss group. Using
egg whites and sugar substitute,
plus eating only 1 cookie at
a meal, allows you to enjoy
dessert occasionally!*

Mexican Wedding Cakes

Leona Yoder
Hartville, OH

Makes 3 dozen dollar-size cookies
Serving size is 1 dollar-size cookie

Prep Time: 15 minutes
Chilling Time: 2 hours
Baking Time: 15-20 minutes
*   per sheet*

¼ cup butter, at room
    temperature
¾ cup canola oil
½ cup sugar
½ tsp. salt
2 tsp. vanilla
2 cups flour
1 cup chopped nuts
¼ cup confectioners sugar

1. Cream butter, canola oil, and sugar together in a large bowl with an electric mixer.
2. Add salt, vanilla, flour, and nuts. Mix well.
3. Chill dough for 2 hours.
4. Shape dough into balls. Place on lightly greased baking sheets. Flatten with the bottom of a drinking glass which has a design, dipped in flour.
5. Bake at 325° until lightly brown, about 15-20 minutes.
6. When cookies are cool, rub their tops lightly in confectioners sugar.

Exchange List Values:
Carbohydrate 0.5, Fat 1.5

Basic Nutritional Values:
Calories 114 (Calories from Fat 74),
Total Fat 8 gm (Saturated Fat 1.4
gm, Trans Fat 0.0 gm, Polyunsat
Fat 3.0 gm, Monounsat Fat 3.4 gm,
Cholesterol 3 mg), Sodium 42 mg,
Total Carbohydrate 9 gm, Dietary
Fiber 0 gm, Sugars 4 gm, Protein 1 gm

Cloud Cookies

Esther J. Mast
Lancaster, PA

Makes 6 dozen cookies
Serving size is 1 cookie

Prep Time: 15 minutes
Baking Time: 9-10 minutes
*   per sheet*

4 cups flour, slightly
    heaping
1 tsp. baking soda
3 tsp. baking powder
1 tsp. salt
¾ cup butter, softened
¼ cup canola oil
2 cups sugar
3 eggs
1½ tsp. vanilla
1 cup low-fat buttermilk

1. Sift together flour, baking soda, baking powder, and salt. Set aside.
2. In an electric mixing bowl, cream together butter, canola oil, and sugar.
3. Add eggs, one at a time, beating well each time. Add vanilla and mix well.
4. Add flour mixture alternately with buttermilk.
5. Drop by spoonsfuls onto greased cookie sheets. Make the cookies as large or small as you wish.
6. Bake at 350° for 9-10 minutes, until tops are slightly firm.

Exchange List Values:
Carbohydrate 1.0, Fat 0.5

Basic Nutritional Values:
Calories 75 (Calories from Fat 27),
Total Fat 3 gm (Saturated Fat 1.4
gm, Trans Fat 0.0 gm, Polyunsat
Fat 0.4 gm, Monounsat Fat 1.0 gm,
Cholesterol 14 mg), Sodium 85 mg,
Total Carbohydrate 11 gm, Dietary
Fiber 0 gm, Sugars 6 gm, Protein 1 gm

Tips:
*   1. The amount of flour is the key in this recipe. Too little makes them flat; too much gives them a biscuit texture.*
*   2. Don't over-bake. When the tops are just firm enough not to indent, the cookies are perfect!*

I received this recipe from Harvella Stutzman, my son's mother-in-law, now my friend. These have become my 10 grandchildren's favorite cookie!

A Tip —

    Most recipes will taste fine if you cut out one-third to one-half of the butter or oil.

Forgotten Cookies
Penny Blosser
Beavercreek, OH

Makes 2 dozen cookies
Serving size is 1 cookie

Prep Time: 10-20 minutes
Baking Time: overnight

2 egg whites
⅔ cup sugar
1 tsp. vanilla
pinch of salt
½ cup chocolate chips
½ cup chopped nuts

1. Preheat oven to 350°.
2. Beat egg whites until foamy in a large mixing bowl.
3. Gradually add sugar and beat until stiff.
4. Fold in remaining ingredients.
5. Line a cookie sheet with foil. Spray the foil with nonstick cooking spray.
6. Drop cookies by rounded teaspoonfuls onto foil-lined cookie sheet.
7. Place in oven. Turn oven OFF immediately!
8. Leave cookies in oven until oven is completely cool, or overnight.

Exchange List Values:
Carbohydrate 0.5, Fat 0.5

Basic Nutritional Values:
Calories 57 (Calories from Fat 24), Total Fat 3 gm (Saturated Fat 0.8 gm, Trans Fat 0.0 gm, Polyunsat Fat 1.2 gm, Monounsat Fat 0.6 gm, Cholesterol 0 mg), Sodium 5 mg, Total Carbohydrate 8 gm, Dietary Fiber 0 gm, Sugars 8 gm, Protein 1 gm

I usually make these just as I finish baking. It's a sweet way to cool the oven.

Harvest Cookies
Sherlyn Hess
Millersville, PA

Makes 4 dozen small cookies
Serving size is 1 small cookie

Prep Time: 30 minutes
Baking Time: 15 minutes
**   per sheet**

1½ cups raisins
boiling water
1 cup zero-trans-fat solid
**   shortening**
1 cup sugar
1 cup mashed pumpkin
1 egg
2 cups flour
1 tsp. baking soda
1 tsp. cinnamon
½ tsp. salt

Frosting:
2 Tbsp. butter
½ cup brown sugar
2 Tbsp. fat-free evaporated
**   milk**
1 cup confectioners sugar
1 tsp. vanilla

1. Place raisins in a small bowl and cover with boiling water.
2. In an electric mixing bowl, cream together shortening, sugar, pumpkin, and egg.
3. In a separate bowl, mix together dry ingredients. Stir into creamed mixture.
4. Drain raisins and fold into batter.
5. Drop by teaspoonfuls onto greased cookie sheets.
6. Bake at 350° for 8 minutes.
7. In a double boiler, heat butter, brown sugar, and evaporated milk until sugar is melted. Stir frequently.
8. Add confectioners sugar and vanilla, mixing until well blended.
9. Drizzle or spread on hot cookies.

Exchange List Values:
Carbohydrate 1.0, Fat 1.0

Basic Nutritional Values:
Calories 115 (Calories from Fat 45), Total Fat 5 gm (Saturated Fat 1.4 gm, Trans Fat 0.0 gm, Polyunsat Fat 1.5 gm, Monounsat Fat 2.0 gm, Cholesterol 6 mg), Sodium 58 mg, Total Carbohydrate 17 gm, Dietary Fiber 0 gm, Sugars 12 gm, Protein 1 gm

A Tip —

Limit the amount of sodium you eat, especially if you have heart disease or high blood pressure.

Apricot Bars

Jean Butzer
Batavia, NY

Makes 20 2" x 2" bars
Serving size is 1 bar

Prep Time: 15 minutes
Cooking/Baking Time:
60-65 minutes

⅔ cup dried apricots
2 Tbsp., plus ¼ cup, sugar,
divided
3 Tbsp. butter, softened
1⅓ cups flour, *divided*
½ cup brown sugar blend
(Splenda)
2 eggs, well beaten
½ tsp. baking powder
¼ tsp. salt
½ tsp. vanilla
½ cup chopped nuts
¼ cup confectioners sugar

1. In a small saucepan, cover apricots with water. Stir in 2 Tbsp. sugar. Boil for 10 minutes.
2. Drain fruit, cool, and cut into bite-sized pieces. Set aside.
3. In a mixing bowl, combine butter and ¼ cup sugar. Stir in 1 cup flour until crumbly.
4. Spread creamed mixture into greased 8 x 10 baking pan, packing it down. Bake at 350° for 25 minutes.
5. Meanwhile, gradually beat brown sugar blend into eggs in a mixing bowl.
6. In a separate bowl, combine ⅓ cup flour, baking powder, and salt. Add to brown sugar/egg mixture.

7. Stir in vanilla, nuts, and apricots.
8. Spread over baked layer and bake an additional 25-30 minutes, or until lightly browned.
9. Cool in pan. Cut into bars and roll in confectioners sugar.

Exchange List Values:
Carbohydrate 1.5, Fat 0.5

Basic Nutritional Values:
Calories 127 (Calories from Fat 39), Total Fat 4 gm (Saturated Fat 1.4 gm, Trans Fat 0.0 gm, Polyunsat Fat 1.6 gm, Monounsat Fat 0.9 gm, Cholesterol 26 mg), Sodium 59 mg, Total Carbohydrate 19 gm, Dietary Fiber 1 gm, Sugars 12 gm, Protein 2 gm

Polynesian Cookies

Wilma Haberkamp
Fairbank, IA

Makes about 4½ dozen cookies
Serving size is 1 cookie

Prep Time: 30 minutes
Baking Time: 8-10 minutes
per sheet

1½ cups sugar
½ cup butter, at room
temperature
½ cup canola oil
1 large egg
1 tsp. vanilla
3½ cups flour
1 tsp. baking soda
½ tsp. salt
8.5-oz. can crushed
pineapple with juice
1 cup chopped nuts

1. In an electric mixer bowl, cream sugar, butter, and canola oil together. Add egg and vanilla.
2. In a separate bowl, sift together flour, baking soda, and salt.
3. Add dry ingredients to creamed mixture alternately with pineapple until mixed well. Add nuts.
4. Drop by teaspoonfuls onto ungreased baking sheet.
5. Bake at 375° for 8-10 minutes, or just until lightly browned. The finished cookies will be soft and cake-like.

Exchange List Values:
Carbohydrate 1.0, Fat 1.0

Basic Nutritional Values:
Calories 103 (Calories from Fat 49), Total Fat 5 gm (Saturated Fat 1.4 gm, Trans Fat 0.0 gm, Polyunsat Fat 1.8 gm, Monounsat Fat 1.9 gm, Cholesterol 8 mg), Sodium 58 mg, Total Carbohydrate 13 gm, Dietary Fiber 0 gm, Sugars 6 gm, Protein 1 gm

Tips:
1. When storing cookies, use a sheet of waxed paper between layers to keep them from sticking together.
2. I often bake a sheet or two at a time and refrigerate the rest of the dough until I need it.
3. This dough will keep a week or more in the refrigerator.

Raspberry Almond Shortbread Thumbprints

Sherlyn Hess, Millersville, PA

Makes about 3½ dozen cookies
Serving size is 1 cookie

Prep Time: 35 minutes
Baking Time: 8-10 minutes
per sheet

⅔ cup sugar
7 Tbsp. butter, softened
½ cup canola oil
½ tsp. almond extract
2 cups flour
½ cup raspberry jelly

Glaze:
1 cup confectioners sugar
1½ tsp. almond extract
2-3 tsp. water

1. In an electric mixer bowl, combine sugar, butter, canola oil, and ½ tsp. almond extract until creamy.

2. Add flour. Mix well.

3. Shape into 1" balls. Place 2" apart on ungreased cookie sheets.

4. With your thumb, make an indentation in the center of each cookie. Fill each indentation with ¼ tsp. jam.

5. Bake at 350° for 8-10 minutes. Do not brown.

6. Remove from cookie sheets onto wire racks. Cool 10 minutes.

7. Combine confectioners sugar, 1½ tsp. almond extract, and water. Drizzle over cookies. Cool completely.

Exchange List Values:
Carbohydrate 1.0, Fat 1.0

Basic Nutritional Values:
Calories 97 (Calories from Fat 19), Total Fat 2 gm (Saturated Fat 0.4 gm, Trans Fat 0.0 gm, Polyunsat Fat 0.5 gm, Monounsat Fat 0.9 gm, Cholesterol 18 mg), Sodium 286 mg, Total Carbohydrate 16 gm, Dietary Fiber 2 gm, Sugars 3 gm, Protein 5 gm

Tip: I cool these cookies on racks. Then when I drizzle them with the glaze, the excess falls through the rack and the cookies have a nicer look than when the glaze puddles around them.

Almond Bars

Darla Sathre
Baxter, MN

Makes 20 2¼" x 2⅖" bars
Serving size is 1 bar

Prep Time: 30 minutes
Cooling Time: 1-2 hours
Baking Time: 35 minutes

Crust:
2 cups flour
½ cup confectioners sugar
1 Tbsp butter, at room temperature
2 Tbsp. canola oil
2¼ Tbsp. apple juice

Filling:
8-oz. pkg. fat-free cream cheese, at room temperature
2 eggs
¼ cup sugar blend for baking (Splenda)
1 tsp. almond extract

Frosting:
¾ cup confectioners sugar
2 Tbsp. butter, at room temperature
½ tsp. almond extract
1 Tbsp. fat-free milk

1. To make the crust, mix the flour and ½ cup confectioners sugar together. With a pastry cutter, blend oil and butter into the dry topping. Pour in apple juice and stir with a fork until the mixture is evenly moistened.

2. Pat into a lightly greased 9 x 13 baking pan. Bake at 350° for 20 minutes.

3. Meanwhile, prepare the filling by beating all 4 ingredients together with an electric mixer until fluffy.

4. Pour filling over baked hot crust.

5. Bake another 15 minutes. Cool for 1-2 hours.

6. Prepare frosting by creaming sugar and butter together until smooth. Stir in extract and milk until well blended.

7. Spread over cooled bars.

Exchange List Values:
Carbohydrate 1.5, Fat 0.5

Basic Nutritional Values:
Calories 133 (Calories from Fat 34), Total Fat 4 gm (Saturated Fat 1.4 gm, Trans Fat 0.0 gm, Polyunsat Fat 0.6 gm, Monounsat Fat 1.5 gm, Cholesterol 27 mg), Sodium 100 mg, Total Carbohydrate 21 gm, Dietary Fiber 0 gm, Sugars 10 gm, Protein 4 gm

A Tip —

To cut fat when baking, substitute two egg whites for one whole egg.

Date Krumble

Marie Mahorney
Las Vegas, NV

Makes 20 2¼" x 2⅔" bars
Serving size is 1 bar

Prep Time: 25-30 minutes
Cooking/Baking Time:
50-55 minutes

Filling:
½ lb. pitted dates
1½ cups water

Batter:
7 Tbsp. solid zero-trans-fat
shortening
½ cup brown sugar blend
(Splenda)
1 egg
2 cups flour
2 cups dry quick oats
1 tsp. baking soda
1 tsp. vanilla

1. Mix dates and water
in a saucepan. Boil until
thickened. Set aside.
2. In an electric mixer
bowl, cream shortening,
brown sugar blend, and egg
together.
3. Mix in flour, dry oats,
baking soda, and vanilla.
Mixture will be crumbly.
4. Pat half of crumb
mixture firmly into the
bottom of a greased 9 x 13
baking pan.
5. Top with the date
mixture.
6. Sprinkle remaining
crumb mixture on top and
press down gently.
7. Bake at 350° for 30-35
minutes.

Exchange List Values:
Carbohydrate 2.0, Fat 0.5

Basic Nutritional Values:
Calories 175 (Calories from Fat 46),
Total Fat 5 gm (Saturated Fat 1.3
gm, Trans Fat 0.0 gm, Polyunsat
Fat 1.7 gm, Monounsat Fat 2.0 gm,
Cholesterol 11 mg), Sodium 69 mg,
Total Carbohydrate 28 gm, Dietary
Fiber 2 gm, Sugars 13 gm, Protein 3 gm

Pumpkin Pie Squares

Gina Hargitt, Quinter, KS

Makes 20 2¼" x 2⅔" bars
Serving size is 1 bar

Prep Time: 30 minutes
Baking Time: 45-50 minutes

1 cup flour
½ cup dry quick *or* rolled
oats
¼ cup brown sugar blend
(Splenda)
1½ Tbsp. butter, at room
temperature
1 Tbsp. canola oil
1 Tbsp. apple juice
2 cups pumpkin
12-oz. can fat-free
evaporated milk
2 eggs
6 Tbsp. sugar blend for
baking (Splenda)
½ tsp. salt
½ tsp. ginger
1 tsp. cinnamon
¼ tsp. cloves
1 Tbsp. butter, at room
temperature
2 Tbsp. brown sugar blend
(Splenda)
¼ cup pecans

1. In a mixing bowl,
combine flour, dry oatmeal,
and ¼ cup brown sugar
blend. With a pastry cutter,
blend oil and butter into the
dry topping until crumbly.
Pour in apple juice and stir
with a fork until the mixture
is evenly moistened.
2. Spread in a greased
9 x 13 baking pan. Bake at
350° for 15 minutes.
3. Meanwhile, combine
pumpkin, evaporated milk,
eggs, sugar blend for baking,
salt, ginger, cinnamon, and
cloves in the same mixing
bowl.
4. Pour over baked crust.
Return to oven and bake for
20 minutes.
5. Combine 1 Tbsp. butter,
2 Tbsp. brown sugar blend,
and pecans. Sprinkle over
pumpkin filling. Bake an
additional 15-20 minutes.

Exchange List Values:
Carbohydrate 1.0, Fat 1.0

Basic Nutritional Values:
Calories 123 (Calories from Fat 36),
Total Fat 4 gm (Saturated Fat 1.3
gm, Trans Fat 0.0 gm, Polyunsat
Fat 0.7 gm, Monounsat Fat 1.6 gm,
Cholesterol 26 mg), Sodium 100 mg,
Total Carbohydrate 18 gm, Dietary
Fiber 1 gm, Sugars 11 gm, Protein 3 gm

Butterscotch Bars

Dottie Geraci, Burtonsville, MD

Makes 25 2¼" x 1¾" bars
Serving size is 1 bar

Prep Time: 20 minutes
Baking Time: 40 minutes

---

1 Tbsp. butter, at room
   temperature
1 Tbsp. canola oil
2 tsp. apple juice
¾ cup brown sugar blend
   (Splenda), *divided*
1¼ cups all-purpose flour,
   divided
½ cup egg substitute
1½ tsp. vanilla extract
1 tsp. baking powder
½ tsp. salt
½ cup chopped walnuts
7 Tbsp. butterscotch
   morsels

1. In a small mixing bowl, cream butter, canola oil, apple juice, and ¼ cup brown sugar blend together until light and fluffy. Blend in 1 cup flour and mix until crumbly.

2. Pat mixture into an ungreased 7 x 11 x 1½ baking pan. Bake at 350° for 10 minutes. Remove from oven.

3. In the mixing bowl, beat egg substitute with ½ cup brown sugar blend and vanilla.

4. In a separate bowl, combine ¼ cup flour, baking powder, and salt. Add to egg mixture. Stir in nuts.

5. Spread over baked crust. Sprinkle with butterscotch morsels.

6. Bake 30 minutes more. Cool and cut into 25 equal bars.

Exchange List Values:
Starch 2.0, Fat 0.5

Basic Nutritional Values:
Calories 201 (Calories from Fat 35), Total Fat 4 gm (Saturated Fat 1.5 gm, Trans Fat 0.0 gm, Polyunsat Fat 0.9 gm, Monounsat Fat 1.0 gm, Cholesterol 11 mg), Sodium 362 mg, Total Carbohydrate 31 gm, Dietary Fiber 3 gm, Sugars 4 gm, Protein 8 gm

Banana Cream Bars

Marsha Sabus, Fallbrook, CA

Makes 50 1½" x 2" bars
Serving size is 1 bar

Prep Time: 15-20 minutes
Baking Time: 25-30 minutes
Cooling Time: 45-60 minutes

---

4 Tbsp. butter, at room
   temperature
4 Tbsp. canola oil
1½ cups sugar
2 large eggs
2 tsp. vanilla
¾ cup fat-free sour cream
2 cups flour
¼ tsp. salt
1 tsp. baking soda
2 large, *or* 3 medium-sized,
   ripe bananas, mashed

Frosting:
3-oz. pkg. fat-free cream
   cheese, at room
   temperature
4 Tbsp. butter, softened
3 Tbsp. fat-free milk
1 tsp. vanilla
2 cups confectioners sugar
½ cup chopped nuts,
   optional

1. In a large electric mixer bowl, cream 4 Tbsp. butter, 4 Tbsp. canola oil and 1½ cups sugar together.

2. Add the unbeaten eggs and beat thoroughly. Add 2 tsp. vanilla and sour cream. Mix well.

3. In a separate mixing bowl, blend together flour, salt, and baking soda. Add alternately with the mashed bananas to the creamed ingredients. Mix well after each addition.

4. Spoon into a greased 15 x 10 x 1 baking pan. Bake at 350° for 25-30 minutes, or until toothpick inserted in center comes out clean. Cool on wire racks.

5. Meanwhile, make frosting by beating together cream cheese, 4 Tbsp. butter, milk, 1 tsp. vanilla, and confectioners sugar. Spread over cooled bars and sprinkle with nuts if you wish.

Exchange List Values:
Carbohydrate 1.0, Fat 0.5

Basic Nutritional Values:
Calories 100 (Calories from Fat 29), Total Fat 3 gm (Saturated Fat 1.3 gm, Trans Fat 0.0 gm, Polyunsat Fat 0.5 gm, Monounsat Fat 1.2 gm, Cholesterol 14 mg), Sodium 67 mg, Total Carbohydrate 16 gm, Dietary Fiber 0 gm, Sugars 11 gm, Protein 1 gm

Cheesecake Bars
Leona Yoder
Hartville, OH

Makes 12 2" x 2⅔" bars
Serving size is 1 bar

Prep Time: 10-15 minutes
Baking Time: 40 minutes

1 cup flour
2½ Tbsp. brown sugar
  blend (Splenda)
2 Tbsp. butter, melted
1 Tbsp. canola oil
8-oz. pkg. fat-free cream
  cheese, at room
  temperature
2 Tbsp. sugar blend for
  baking (Splenda)
1 large egg
1 Tbsp. lemon juice
2 Tbsp. fat-free milk
1 tsp. vanilla

1. Mix flour, brown sugar
blend, butter, and canola
oil together in an electric
mixing bowl. Reserve 1 cup
mixture. Press remainder into
a greased 8 x 8 baking pan.
2. Bake at 350° for 15
minutes.
3. Meanwhile, in the
mixing bowl, beat together
the remaining ingredients.
Spread on baked crust.
4. Top with reserved
crumbs and bake for 25
minutes, or until set.

Exchange List Values:
Carbohydrate 1.0, Fat 1.0

Basic Nutritional Values:
Calories 114 (Calories from Fat 32),
Total Fat 4 gm (Saturated Fat 1.4

gm, Trans Fat 0.0 gm, Polyunsat
Fat 0.5 gm, Monounsat Fat 1.4 gm,
Cholesterol 25 mg), Sodium 155 mg,
Total Carbohydrate 14 gm, Dietary
Fiber 0 gm, Sugars 6 gm, Protein 4 gm

Philly Chippers
Erma Hoover, Lititz, PA

Makes 24 3¾" x 1½" bars
Serving size is 1 bar

Prep Time: 12-15 minutes
Baking Time: 15-30 minutes

1 Tbsp. butter, at room
  temperature
6 Tbsp. canola oil
8-oz. pkg. cream cheese, at
  room temperature
6 Tbsp. sugar blend for
  baking (Splenda)
6 Tbsp. brown sugar blend
  (Splenda)
¼ cup egg substitute
1 tsp. vanilla
¼ cup fat-free milk
2½ cups flour
1 tsp. baking powder
1 tsp. salt
⅔ cup chocolate chips

1. In a large mixing bowl,
cream together butter, canola
oil, cream cheese, and sugar
blends.
2. Add egg substitute,
vanilla, and milk. Mix well.
3. In a separate bowl,
combine flour, baking
powder, and salt. Blend into
creamed mixture.
4. Fold in chocolate chips.
5. Pour into a greased
9 x 13 baking pan.

6. Bake at 350° for 15-30
minutes, or until done in the
center, but not dry around the
edges.

Exchange List Values:
Carbohydrate 1.5, Fat 1.0

Basic Nutritional Values:
Calories 145 (Calories from Fat 50),
Total Fat 6 gm (Saturated Fat 1.4
gm, Trans Fat 0.0 gm, Polyunsat
Fat 1.2 gm, Monounsat Fat 2.7 gm,
Cholesterol 2 mg), Sodium 189 mg,
Total Carbohydrate 20 gm, Dietary
Fiber 1 gm, Sugars 9 gm, Protein 3 gm

Chocolate Peanut Bars
Andrea Zuercher
Lawrence, KS

Makes 24 2¼" x 1½" bars
Serving size is 1 bar

Prep Time: 10 minutes
Cooking Time: 3-5 minutes
Chilling Time: 1 hour

½ cup light corn syrup
2 Tbsp. brown sugar blend
  (Splenda)
dash of salt
¾ cup chunky peanut butter
1 tsp. vanilla
2 cups crispy rice cereal
1 cup cornflakes, slightly
  crushed
½ cup chocolate chips

1. Combine corn syrup,
brown sugar blend, and salt
in a heavy saucepan. Bring to
a full boil.
2. Stir in peanut butter.
Remove from heat.

3. Stir in remaining ingredients.

4. Press into a buttered 9 x 9 baking pan.

5. Chill about 1 hour before cutting and removing from pan.

Basic Nutritional Values:
Calories 105 (Calories from Fat 48), Total Fat 5 gm (Saturated Fat 1.4 gm, Trans Fat 0.0 gm, Polyunsat Fat 1.3 gm, Monounsat Fat 2.4 gm, Cholesterol 0 mg), Sodium 83 mg, Total Carbohydrate 13 gm, Dietary Fiber 1 gm, Sugars 7 gm, Protein 2 gm

Tips:

1. This recipe can be easily doubled for a larger quantity.

2. It's a nice no-bake treat during the hot summertime.

A Tip —

A little weight gain is normal when you begin to get your blood glucose under control.

Chocolate Oatmeal Chews
Bertha Burkholder
Hillsville, VA

Makes 20 2⅔" x 2¼" bars
Serving size is 1 bar

Prep Time: 10 minutes
Baking Time: 15-18 minutes

1 Tbsp. butter, at room temperature
1 Tbsp. canola oil
1⅔ Tbsp. apple juice
½ cup brown sugar blend (Splenda)
1¼ cups flour
1½ cups dry quick oats
½ tsp. baking soda
½ tsp. salt
4 cups mini marshmallows
½ cup, plus 2 Tbsp., chocolate chips

1. In an electric mixing bowl, cream butter, canola oil, apple juice, and brown sugar blend together.

2. In a separate bowl, combine flour, dry oats, baking soda, and salt.

3. Blend dry ingredients into creamy mixture thoroughly.

4. Set aside 1½ cups batter. Press remainder into a greased 9 x 13 baking pan.

5. Sprinkle "crust" with mini marshmallows and chocolate chips.

6. Top with reserved batter.

7. Bake at 375° for 15-18 minutes, or until set in the middle and not dry around the edges. Cool and cut into bars.

Basic Nutritional Values:
Calories 145 (Calories from Fat 30), Total Fat 3 gm (Saturated Fat 1.4 gm, Trans Fat 0.0 gm, Polyunsat Fat 0.5 gm, Monounsat Fat 1.2 gm, Cholesterol 2 mg), Sodium 100 mg, Total Carbohydrate 26 gm, Dietary Fiber 1 gm, Sugars 16 gm, Protein 2 gm

Variatons:

1. After Step 4, sprinkle "crust" with 2 cups chocolate chips and 1 cup sliced almonds. In a mixing bowl, whisk 12-oz. jar caramel ice cream topping and ¼ cup flour together. Drizzle over chocolate chips and nuts. Proceed with Step 6 above.

—Stacy Schmucker
Stoltzfus, Enola, PA

2. After Step 4, spread "crust" with a mixture of a 14-oz. can sweetened condensed milk and ⅓ cup peanut butter. Combine reserved batter and 1 cup M&Ms. Sprinkle over top, pressing down lightly. Bake at 350° for 20 minutes.

—Lawina Good
Harrisonburg, VA

3. Follow Variation 2 immediately above, except add 1 cup chocolate chips to the reserved batter/M&M mixture.

—Erma Rutt
Newmanstown, PA

Raspberry Walnut Shortbread

Joyce Nolt
Richland, PA

Makes 20 2⅗" x 2½" bars
Serving size is 1 bar

Prep Time: 10-15 minutes
Baking Time: 40-45 minutes

2½ cups flour
½ cup sugar blend for
  baking (Splenda)
1½ Tbsp. butter, at room
  temperature
2½ Tbsp. canola oil
2⅓ Tbsp. apple juice
⅔ cup low-sugar raspberry
  jam, beaten until
  softened
1 cup egg substitute
½ cup brown sugar blend
  (Splenda)
2 tsp. vanilla
4 Tbsp. flour
¼ tsp. salt
¼ tsp. baking soda
2 cups chopped walnuts

1. Combine 2½ cups flour,
sugar blend for baking,
butter, canola oil, and apple
juice in a mixing bowl. Press
into the bottom of a greased 9
x 13 baking pan.
2. Bake at 350° for 20 minutes. Remove from oven.
3. Spread raspberry jam
over shortbread, being careful
not to disturb the crust.
4. In the mixing bowl, beat
together egg substitute, brown
sugar blend, and vanilla.
5. In a separate bowl,
combine 4 Tbsp. flour, salt,

and baking soda.
6. Add dry ingredients to
egg mixture. Mix well.
7. Spoon over jam and
spread lightly to corners.
8. Sprinkle walnuts over
top.
9. Return to oven. Bake
20-25 minutes longer. Cool
before cutting into bars.

Exchange List Values:
Carbohydrate 2.0, Fat 2.0

Basic Nutritional Values:
Calories 248 (Calories from Fat 95),
Total Fat 11 gm (Saturated Fat 1.4
gm, Trans Fat 0.0 gm, Polyunsat
Fat 6.3 gm, Monounsat Fat 2.3 gm,
Cholesterol 2 mg), Sodium 76 mg,
Total Carbohydrate 33 gm, Dietary
Fiber 1 gm, Sugars 18 gm, Protein 5 gm

Deliciously Chocolate Brownies

Alice Whitman
Lancaster, PA
Michelle Martin
Ephrata, PA

Makes 24 servings
Serving size is 2¼" x 2⅛" rectangle

Prep Time: 10-15 minutes
Baking Time: 28-30 minutes

1 Tbsp. butter, melted
7 Tbsp. canola oil
½ cup, plus 2 Tbsp.,
  unsweetened cocoa
  powder
1 cup sugar blend for
  baking (Splenda)
1 cup egg substitute
1½ cups flour
pinch of salt

½ cup chopped nuts
6 Tbsp. miniature
  chocolate chips

1. In a mixing bowl,
combine butter, canola oil,
and cocoa powder until well
blended.
2. Add sugar blend, egg
substitute, flour, and salt. Stir
with a fork. (Stirring with a
fork keeps the brownies from
becoming too cakey.)
3. Stir in chopped nuts.
Spread in a greased 9 x 13
baking pan.
4. Bake at 350° for 25 minutes. Do not over-bake.
5. Sprinkle with chocolate
chips. Return to oven for
3-4 minutes, or just until
chocolate melts.
6. Cool completely before
cutting with a plastic knife—
which will cut clean.

Exchange List Values:
Carbohydrate 1.0, Fat 1.5

Basic Nutritional Values:
Calories 140 (Calories from Fat 67),
Total Fat 7 gm (Saturated Fat 1.4
gm, Trans Fat 0.0 gm, Polyunsat
Fat 2.5 gm, Monounsat Fat 3.1 gm,
Cholesterol 1 mg), Sodium 24 mg,
Total Carbohydrate 17 gm, Dietary
Fiber 1 gm, Sugars 10 gm, Protein 3 gm

A Tip —

Eating too much fat
does not make you fat—
eating too many calories
leads to weight gain.

Microwave Brownies

Sandra Chang
Derwood, MD

Makes 16 brownies
Serving size is 1 square

Prep Time: 10 minutes
Cooking Time: 9-12 minutes

1 cup sifted flour
½ tsp. baking powder
½ tsp. salt
1 Tbsp. butter
1 Tbsp. canola oil
1 oz. unsweetened chocolate
½ cup sugar blend for
   baking (Splenda)
½ cup egg substitute
1 tsp. vanilla extract
½ cup chopped nuts

1. Sift together flour, baking powder, and salt. Set aside.
2. Place butter, canola oil, and chocolate in an 8"-square glass baking dish. Microwave at 50 percent power for 3 minutes, or until melted.
3. Stir sugar blend into melted mixture. Add egg substitute and vanilla, beating well.
4. Gradually stir in dry ingredients, blending well. Add nuts.
5. Microwave on high for 5-6 minutes, or until the top is no longer wet, or a toothpick inserted in the center comes out clean. Rotate dish ¼ turn every 2 minutes while microwaving.
6. Cool in baking dish, then cut into 2" squares.

Exchange List Values:
Carbohydrate 1.0, Fat 1.0

Basic Nutritional Values:
Calories 104 (Calories from Fat 45), Total Fat 5 gm (Saturated Fat 1.3 gm, Trans Fat 0.0 gm, Polyunsat Fat 2.1 gm, Monounsat Fat 1.3 gm, Cholesterol 2 mg), Sodium 132 mg, Total Carbohydrate 13 gm, Dietary Fiber 1 gm, Sugars 6 gm, Protein 2 gm

Chocolate Chip Blonde Brownies

Vera Martin
East Earl, PA

Makes 20 brownies
Serving size is 2⅔" x 2¼" rectangle

Prep Time: 15 minutes
Baking Time: 25 minutes
Cooling Time: 20 minutes

1 Tbsp. butter
3 Tbsp. canola oil
1 Tbsp. hot water
1 cup brown sugar blend
   (Splenda)
2 eggs
2 tsp. vanilla
2 cups flour
1 tsp. baking powder
¼ tsp. baking soda
1 tsp. salt
½ cup chopped nuts,
   optional
½ cup chocolate chips

1. In a good-sized saucepan, melt butter with canola oil. Add water and brown sugar blend. Cool for 20 minutes.
2. Add eggs and vanilla. Beat well.
3. In a mixing bowl, combine flour, baking powder, baking soda, and salt.
4. Add dry ingredients to egg/sugar mixture. Mix well and add nuts if desired.
5. Spread into a greased 9 x 13 baking pan. Sprinkle chocolate chips over the top.
6. Bake at 350° for 25 minutes. Cool slightly. Cut into squares with a plastic knife—which will make clean cuts.

Exchange List Values:
Carbohydrate 1.5, Fat 1.0

Basic Nutritional Values:
Calories 146 (Calories from Fat 41), Total Fat 5 gm (Saturated Fat 1.4 gm, Trans Fat 0.0 gm, Polyunsat Fat 0.8 gm, Monounsat Fat 2.0 gm, Cholesterol 23 mg), Sodium 164 mg, Total Carbohydrate 22 gm, Dietary Fiber 1 gm, Sugars 12 gm, Protein 2 gm

Tip: These will be chewy in the center. Don't over-bake.

A Tip —

Make a shopping list before you go to the grocery store and stick to it. Buying only items on the list will help you avoid unhealthy impulse purchases.

Apple Brownies
Wendy B. Martzall
New Holland, PA

Makes 20 brownies
Serving size is 2⅔" x 2¼" rectangle

Prep Time: 20-25 minutes
Baking Time: 40-50 minutes

3 Tbsp. butter, at room
  temperature
3 Tbsp. canola oil
1 cup sugar blend for
  baking (Splenda)
2 eggs, beaten
2 cups flour
1 tsp. baking powder
1 tsp. baking soda
2 tsp. cinnamon
3 cups apples, peeled and
  thinly sliced
1 cup chopped walnuts,
  optional

1. In an electric mixing
bowl, cream butter, canola oil,
and sugar blend for baking
together.
2. Add eggs and mix well.
3. In a separate bowl,
combine flour, baking
powder, baking soda, and
cinnamon.
4. Stir into creamed
mixture, mixing well.
5. Fold in apples, and walnuts if you wish, thoroughly.
Batter will be stiff.
6. Spread in a greased 9 x 13
baking pan.
7. Bake 40-50 minutes at
350°, or until cake pulls away
from pan.
8. Cool in pan, then cut
into squares.

Exchange List Values:
Carbohydrate 1.5, Fat 0.5

Basic Nutritional Values:
Calories 135 (Calories from Fat 41),
Total Fat 5 gm (Saturated Fat 1.4
gm, Trans Fat 0.0 gm, Polyunsat
Fat 0.8 gm, Monounsat Fat 1.9 gm,
Cholesterol 26 mg), Sodium 101 mg,
Total Carbohydrate 22 gm, Dietary
Fiber 1 gm, Sugars 12 gm, Protein 2 gm

Cherry Brownies
Jolyn Nolt
Leola, PA

Makes 20 brownies
Serving size is 2⅔" x 2¼" rectangle

Prep Time: 5-10 minutes
Baking Time: 30 minutes

1½ cups flour
1 cup sugar blend for
  baking (Splenda)
½ cup unsweetened cocoa
  powder
½ tsp. salt
½ cup canola oil
4 eggs
2 tsp. vanilla
½ cup chopped nuts,
  optional
2 cups light cherry pie
  filling
confectioners sugar,
  optional

1. In an electric mixing
bowl, combine flour, sugar
blend, cocoa powder, salt,
canola oil, eggs, vanilla, and
nuts if you wish. Beat with
mixer.

2. Stir in pie filling with a
spoon or spatula.
3. Pour into a greased
9 x 13 baking pan.
4. Bake at 350° for 30
minutes.
5. Remove from oven, cool
slightly, and sprinkle with
confectioners sugar, if you
wish. Cut when the brownies
have cooled.

Exchange List Values:
Carbohydrate 1.5, Fat 1.0

Basic Nutritional Values:
Calories 160 (Calories from Fat 62),
Total Fat 7 gm (Saturated Fat 0.9
gm, Trans Fat 0.0 gm, Polyunsat
Fat 1.8 gm, Monounsat Fat 3.7 gm,
Cholesterol 42 mg), Sodium 77 mg,
Total Carbohydrate 23 gm, Dietary
Fiber 1 gm, Sugars 14 gm, Protein 3 gm

Cakes

Moist Chocolate Cake

Rosalie Duerksen, Canton, KS

Makes 9 servings
Serving size is 2⅔" x 2⅔" square

Prep Time: 15 minutes
Baking Time: 30 minutes

1 cup flour
½ cup sugar blend for
   baking (Splenda)
1 tsp. baking powder
1 tsp. baking soda
½ cup unsweetened cocoa
   powder
1 cup hot water, or brewed
   coffee
1 egg
¼ cup canola oil
½ tsp. vanilla
1 Tbsp. confectioners sugar

1. In a mixing bowl,
combine flour, sugar blend,
baking powder, baking soda,
cocoa powder, and hot water
or coffee.
   2. Add egg and canola oil.
Mix well.
   3. Pour into a greased
8"-square baking pan.
   4. Bake at 350° for 30 minutes, or until toothpick inserted
in center comes out clean.
   5. Cool. Dust with confectioners sugar. Cut and serve.

Exchange List Values:
Carbohydrate 1.5, Fat 1.5

Basic Nutritional Values:
Calories 172 (Calories from Fat 68),
Total Fat 8 gm (Saturated Fat 1.0
gm, Trans Fat 0.0 gm, Polyunsat
Fat 2.0 gm, Monounsat Fat 4.1 gm,
Cholesterol 24 mg), Sodium 190 mg,
Total Carbohydrate 25 gm, Dietary
Fiber 2 gm, Sugars 12 gm, Protein 3 gm

*Tip: This cake is just the right
size for a small family, and very
easy to make.*

One Step Chocolate Cake

Brenda J. Marshall
ON, Canada

Makes 12 servings
Serving size is 1 slice

Prep Time: 15 minutes
Baking Time: 40-45 minutes

½ cup sugar blend for
   baking (Splenda)
1 egg
½ cup unsweetened cocoa
   powder
⅓ cup canola oil
1 tsp. vanilla
1½ cups flour
1½ tsp. baking powder
1 tsp. baking soda
pinch of salt
½ cup hot brewed coffee

Frosting:
¼ cup chopped semi-sweet
   chocolate
¼ cup fat-free half-and-half

raspberries, *optional*

1. Place sugar blend, egg,
cocoa powder, canola oil,
vanilla, flour, baking powder,
baking soda, salt, and coffee
in food processor or large
electric mixer bowl. Process
in food processor (or mixing
bowl with mixer) until smooth.
   2. Spoon batter into a
buttered 8" springform pan
with a round of parchment
paper covering the bottom.
   3. Bake at 350° for 40-45
minutes. Cool on rack.
Remove cake from pan and
place on serving plate.
   4. To make frosting, combine chocolate and half-and-
half in microwave-safe bowl.
Cover and microwave for
1 minute on high. Stir to melt.
Pour into center of cake and
allow to run down the sides.
   5. If desired, top with
raspberries right before
serving.

Exchange List Values:
Carbohydrate 1.5, Fat 1.5

Basic Nutritional Values:
Calories 174 (Calories from Fat 70),
Total Fat 8 gm (Saturated Fat 1.4
gm, Trans Fat 0.0 gm, Polyunsat
Fat 1.9 gm, Monounsat Fat 4.1 gm,
Cholesterol 0 mg), Sodium 167 mg,
Total Carbohydrate 25 gm, Dietary
Fiber 2 gm, Sugars 11 gm, Protein 3 gm

Chocolate Sheet Cake

Robin Schrock
Millersburg, OH

Makes 18 servings
Serving size is 2⅗" x 3⅕" rectangle

Prep Time: 30 minutes
Baking Time: 20 minutes
Cooling Time: 1½ hours

Cake:
⅔ cup canola oil
5 Tbsp. unsweetened cocoa
   powder
1 cup water
2 eggs, beaten
1 Tbsp vinegar
1 tsp. baking soda
1 tsp. baking powder
½ cup low-fat buttermilk
1 Tbsp. vanilla extract
1 cup sugar blend for
   baking (Splenda)
2 cups flour
½ tsp. salt

Frosting:
2 Tbsp. butter
2 Tbsp. canola oil
2½ Tbsp. unsweetened
   cocoa powder
¼ cup fat-free milk
½ tsp. vanilla extract
1 cup confectioners sugar

1. To make cake, combine canola oil, cocoa powder, and water in a small saucepan. Bring to a rolling boil, stirring occasionally. Remove from heat and cool.

2. When cooled, pour slowly into mixing bowl. Add eggs, vinegar, baking soda, baking powder, buttermilk, and vanilla. Mix well.

3. In a separate bowl, mix together sugar blend, flour, and salt. Add to liquid mixture and blend thoroughly.

4. Pour into a 13 x 16 x 1½ cake pan. Bake at 350° for 20 minutes.

5. Allow cake to cool to room temperature.

6. When ready to ice, make frosting by combining butter, canola oil, cocoa powder, and milk in the saucepan. Bring to a rolling boil.

7. When slightly cool, add vanilla. Gradually add confectioners sugar, beating to make a spreadable consistency.

8. Ice cooled cake with frosting.

Exchange List Values:
Carbohydrate 1.5, Fat 1.5

Basic Nutritional Values:
Calories 160 (Calories from Fat 78), Total Fat 9 gm (Saturated Fat 1.4 gm, Trans Fat 0.0 gm, Polyunsat Fat 2.2 gm, Monounsat Fat 4.6 gm, Cholesterol 20 mg), Sodium 131 mg, Total Carbohydrate 19 gm, Dietary Fiber 1 gm, Sugars 11 gm, Protein 2 gm

A Tip —

A healthy diet and regular exercise are absolutely the best ways to prevent type 2 diabetes.

Chocolate Raspberry Cheesecake

LaRee Eby
Portland, OR

Makes 20 servings
Serving size is 2⅔" x 2¼" rectangle

Prep Time: 35 minutes
Baking Time: 50 minutes

Crust:
2 cups crushed reduced-fat
   Oreo cookies
¼ cup canola oil

Filling:
2 8-oz. pkgs. fat-free
   cream cheese, at room
   temperature
½ cup sugar blend for
   baking (Splenda)
2 eggs
1 tsp. vanilla
1½ Tbsp. lemon juice
2 cups fat-free sour cream
½ cup powdered baking
   cocoa
3 cups fresh raspberries

Glaze:
1 cup low-sugar raspberry,
   or blackberry, jelly
1 Tbsp. lemon juice
1½ Tbsp. cornstarch
1 Tbsp. cold water

1. Mix crushed Oreos and canola oil together in a mixing bowl. Press into a lightly greased 9 x 13 baking pan.

2. Beat cream cheese with sugar blend in a mixing bowl until smooth.

3. Add eggs, vanilla, and lemon juice. Mix until well blended.

4. Add sour cream and cocoa powder. Beat 1 minute.

5. Spoon cream cheese mixture over the crumb layer, being careful not to disturb the crumbs.

6. Bake at 275° for 50 minutes on the middle shelf of the oven. Allow to cool slowly in the oven with the door ajar for up to an hour.

7. Place raspberries on top of cooled cheesecake.

8. While the cake is cooling, melt jelly in a small saucepan. Add lemon juice and bring to a boil, stirring constantly.

9. In a small bowl, dissolve cornstarch in cold water. Stir mixture into jelly mixture and cook until thickened. Remove from heat.

10. Pour glaze over raspberries. Refrigerate the cake for 4-8 hours, or overnight.

Exchange List Values:
Carbohydrate 1.5, Fat 1.0

Basic Nutritional Values:
Calories 174 (Calories from Fat 44), Total Fat 5 gm (Saturated Fat 1.1 gm, Trans Fat 0.0 gm, Polyunsat Fat 1.1 gm, Monounsat Fat 2.4 gm, Cholesterol 28 mg), Sodium 241 mg, Total Carbohydrate 24 gm, Dietary Fiber 2 gm, Sugars 16 gm, Protein 7 gm

Black Bottom Cake or Cupcakes
Joleen Albrecht
Gladstone, MI

Makes 18 servings of cake, or about 18 cupcakes
Serving size is 3″ x 2⅙″ rectangle, or 1 cupcake

Prep Time: 20 minutes
Baking Time: 20-25 minutes

8 ozs. fat-free cream cheese, at room temperature
1 egg
2½ Tbsp. sugar blend for baking (Splenda)
⅜ tsp. salt, *divided*
½ cup, plus 1 Tbsp., semi-sweet chocolate chips
1½ cups flour
¼ cup unsweetened cocoa powder
½ cup sugar blend for baking (Splenda)
¼ tsp. salt
½ tsp. baking soda
1 cup cold water
⅓ cup vegetable oil
1 Tbsp. vinegar
1 Tbsp. vanilla

1. Mix cream cheese, egg, 2½ Tbsp. sugar blend, and ⅛ tsp. salt together with an electric mixer.

2. Stir in the chocolate chips by hand. Set aside.

3. Combine and mix the remaining ingredients in a separate bowl.

4. Pour cake batter into a greased 9 x 13 baking pan.

5. Spoon cream cheese mixture on top. Swirl with a fork.

6. Bake at 350° for 25 minutes, or until a toothpick inserted in the center comes out clean.

Exchange List Values:
Carbohydrate 1.5, Fat 1.0

Basic Nutritional Values:
Calories 148 (Calories from Fat 55), Total Fat 6 gm (Saturated Fat 1.4 gm, Trans Fat 0.0 gm, Polyunsat Fat 1.3 gm, Monounsat Fat 3.0 gm, Cholesterol 13 mg), Sodium 211 mg, Total Carbohydrate 20 gm, Dietary Fiber 1 gm, Sugars 11 gm, Protein 4 gm

To make cupcakes, line cupcake pans with cupcake papers.

Spoon batter into the cups, making each about half-full. Put about 1 tablespoon cream cheese mixture on top of each. Bake at 350° for 20-25 minutes, or until toothpick inserted in centers comes out clean.

Chocolate Chip Zucchini Cake

Vonda Ebersole
Mt. Pleasant Mills, PA
Bernice Esau
North Newton, KS

Makes 20 servings
Serving size is 2⅔" x 2½" rectangle

Prep Time: 20 minutes
Baking Time: 45 minutes

1 Tbsp. butter, softened
½ cup canola oil
¾ cup, plus 2 Tbsp., sugar
  blend for baking (Splenda)
2 eggs
½ cup buttermilk
1 tsp. vanilla
1 tsp. salt
1 tsp. baking soda
2½ cups flour
4 tbsp. unsweetened cocoa
  powder
2 cups grated zucchini,
  peeled or unpeeled
¼ cup chocolate chips

1. In a large mixing bowl,
cream butter, canola oil, and
sugar blend together.
2. Beat in eggs.
3. Add milk, vanilla, and salt.
4. In a separate bowl, sift
together baking soda, flour,
and cocoa powder. Stir into
creamed mixture.
5. Gently stir in zucchini.
6. Grease a 9 x 13 baking
pan. Sprinkle flour lightly
over its bottom and sides.
Pour in batter. Sprinkle with
chocolate chips.
7. Bake at 325° for 45
minutes.

Exchange List Values:
Carbohydrate 1.5, Fat 1.5

Basic Nutritional Values:
Calories 169 (Calories from Fat 68),
Total Fat 8 gm (Saturated Fat 1.4
gm, Trans Fat 0.0 gm, Polyunsat
Fat 1.8 gm, Monounsat Fat 3.8 gm,
Cholesterol 23 mg), Sodium 199 mg,
Total Carbohydrate 23 gm, Dietary
Fiber 1 gm, Sugars 10 gm, Protein 3 gm

Sponge Cake

Cathy Boshart, Lebanon, PA

Makes 20 servings
Serving size is 2⅔" x 2¼" rectangle

Prep Time: 15 minutes
Baking Time: 35-40 minutes

4 eggs
2 cups flour
2 cups sugar
2 tsp. baking powder
1 cup hot milk
1 tsp. vanilla extract

1. In a mixing bowl, beat
eggs well.
2. In a separate bowl, mix
together flour, sugar, and baking powder. Add alternately
with milk to the beaten eggs.
3. Stir in vanilla.
4. Pour batter into a greased
tube pan or a 9 x 13 baking pan.
5. Bake at 350° for 35-40
minutes.

Exchange List Values:
Carbohydrate 2.0

Basic Nutritional Values:
Calories 143 (Calories from Fat 10),
Total Fat 1 gm (Saturated Fat 0.3
gm, Trans Fat 0.0 gm, Polyunsat
Fat 0.2 gm, Monounsat Fat 0.4 gm,

Cholesterol 43 mg), Sodium 56 mg,
Total Carbohydrate 30 gm, Dietary
Fiber 0 gm, Sugars 21 gm, Protein 3 gm

Angel Food Cake

Pauline Hindal, Grandin, MI

Makes 16 servings
Serving size is 1 slice

Prep Time: 10-15 minutes
Baking Time: 35-40 minutes

2 cups egg whites, at room
  temperature
1⅛ cups flour
2 cups sugar, divided
½ tsp. salt
1½ tsp. cream of tarter
1 tsp. vanilla extract

1. Place egg whites in the
large bowl of an electric mixer.
2. In a separate bowl,
sift flour and 1 cup sugar
together. Set aside.
3. Add salt to egg whites
and beat on high speed until
foamy, about half a minute.
4. Add cream of tarter to egg
whites. Continue beating until
whites are stiff, but not dry,
approximately 2½-3 minutes.
5. Quickly sprinkle 1 cup
sugar into whites. Beat on a
slower speed while sprinkling
in the sugar. Then increase
mixer to the highest speed,
just until the sugar is blended
in and very stiff peaks form.
6. Sprinkle in the flour/
sugar mixture and vanilla.
Blend in quickly by hand,
using a spatula and a gentle
folding motion from the sides
toward the center of the bowl.

7. Spoon gently into an ungreased tube pan. Cut carefully through the batter—going the whole way around the pan—with a knife to release large bubbles.

8. Bake at 350° for 35-40 minutes, or until the top is springy when touched.

Exchange List Values:
Carbohydrate 2.0

Basic Nutritional Values:
Calories 146 (Calories from Fat 1), Total Fat 0 gm (Saturated Fat 0.0 gm, Trans Fat 0.0 gm, Polyunsat Fat 0.0 gm, Monounsat Fat 0.0 gm, Cholesterol 0 mg), Sodium 123 mg, Total Carbohydrate 32 gm, Dietary Fiber 0 gm, Sugars 25 gm, Protein 4 gm

Tips:
1. Do not open the oven door while the cake is baking.
2. I like to use an electric knife to cut angel food cakes.
3. Strawberr-i-oca (page 245) is a great topping for this cake.

My Favorite Blueberry Cake
Mary E. Wheatley, Mashpee, MA

Makes 16 servings
Serving size is 1 slice

Prep Time: 15 minutes
Baking Time: 1 hour, or more if using frozen berries

2 Tbsp. butter, at room temperature
2 Tbsp. canola oil
½ cup, plus 1 Tbsp., sugar blend for baking (Splenda), *divided*
1 cup, plus 1 Tbsp., flour, *divided*
1 tsp. baking powder
½ tsp. salt
2 eggs
3 cups fresh blueberries*
2 Tbsp. freshly squeezed lemon juice
1 Tbsp. confectioners sugar

1. In a large bowl, cream the butter and canola oil with ½ cup sugar blend until light and fluffy.

2. In another bowl, mix together 1 cup flour, baking powder, and salt. Beat into the butter mixture.

3. Beat in the eggs, one at a time. This will be a stiff batter.

4. Place batter into a lightly buttered 9" springform pan.

5. Toss berries with 1 tablespoon sugar blend, lemon juice, and 1 tablespoon flour. (*If using frozen berries, do not thaw them. And increase the amount of flour to 2-3 Tbsp.) Spread evenly over top of batter.

6. Bake 1 hour at 350°. (*Frozen berries may require more than an hour.) Check that the cake is done by inserting a toothpick in its center. It will come out clean if the cake is fully baked.

7. Cool cake in pan. Remove sides of pan and move onto a cake plate, berry-side up. Sprinkle lightly with confectioners sugar when serving.

Exchange List Values:
Carbohydrate 1.0, Fat 1.0

Basic Nutritional Values:
Calories 113 (Calories from Fat 36), Total Fat 4 gm (Saturated Fat 1.3 gm, Trans Fat 0.0 gm, Polyunsat Fat 0.7 gm, Monounsat Fat 1.7 gm,

Cholesterol 30 mg), Sodium 115 mg, Total Carbohydrate 18 gm, Dietary Fiber 1 gm, Sugars 10 gm, Protein 2 gm

A special lemon sauce for this cake is listed in the next recipe.

Lemon Sauce for My Favorite Blueberry Cake
Stacy Schmucker Stoltzfus
Enola, PA

Makes 16 servings
Serving size is ¹/₁₆ of recipe

Prep Time: 10 minutes
Cooking Time: 10 minutes

½ cup sugar blend for baking (Splenda)
2⅔ Tbsp. butter
¼ cup water
¾ tsp. fresh lemon zest
3 Tbsp. fresh lemon juice
1 egg, well beaten

1. Combine all sauce ingredients in a non-aluminum saucepan. Bring to a boil over medium heat, stirring occasionally.

2. Serve warm with warm squares of blueberry cake.

Exchange List Values:
Carbohydrate 0.5, Fat 0.5

Basic Nutritional Values:
Calories 158 (Calories from Fat 21), Total Fat 2 gm (Saturated Fat 1.0 gm, Trans Fat 0.0 gm, Polyunsat Fat 0.3 gm, Monounsat Fat 0.6 gm, Cholesterol 35 mg), Sodium 214 mg, Total Carbohydrate 30 gm, Dietary Fiber 2 gm, Sugars 10 gm, Protein 4 gm

Strawberry Shortcake

Joyce Kreiser, Manheim, PA

Makes 20 servings
Serving size is 2⅔" x 2¼" rectangle

Prep Time: 8-12 minutes
Baking Time: 30-35 minutes

¾ cup sugar blend for baking (Splenda)
2 Tbsp. butter, softened
3 eggs
4 cups flour
4 tsp. baking powder
1 tsp. salt
1 cup fat-free milk
5 cups (¼ cup per serving) sliced strawberries

1. Beat together sugar blend and butter.
2. Add eggs and mix well.
3. In a separate bowl, sift together flour, baking powder, and salt.
4. Add to creamed sugar mixture alternately with milk.
5. Bake at 350° in a greased and floured 9 x 13 baking pan until lightly browned on top, about 30-35 minutes.
6. Serve topped with sliced strawberries and milk in bowls.

Exchange List Values:
Carbohydrate 2.0

Basic Nutritional Values:
Calories 158 (Calories from Fat 21), Total Fat 2 gm (Saturated Fat 1.0 gm, Trans Fat 0.0 gm, Polyunsat Fat 0.3 gm, Monounsat Fat 0.6 gm, Cholesterol 35 mg), Sodium 214 mg, Total Carbohydrate 30 gm, Dietary Fiber 2 gm, Sugars 10 gm, Protein 4 gm

---

Tip: Another way to serve this cake is to slice 1½ qts. strawberries into a bowl, sprinkle the berries with 3 Tbsp. sugar, then cover and refrigerate the bowl for ½ hour or more before serving. The sugar over the sliced berries makes a great syrup.

Banana Nut Cake

Margaret Culbert
Lebanon, PA

Makes 15 servings
Serving size is 2½" x 3" rectangle

Prep Time: 15-17 minutes
Baking Time: 30-40 minutes

2 cups sifted flour
1 tsp. baking powder
1 tsp. baking soda
½ tsp. salt
¾ cup sugar blend for baking (Splenda)
¼ cup zero-trans-fat shortening
½ cup low-fat buttermilk
1½ cups sliced bananas
2 eggs
1 tsp. vanilla
½ cup walnuts

1. Sift flour, baking powder, baking soda, and salt together in a large bowl.
2. Combine sugar blend, shortening, buttermilk, bananas, eggs, and vanilla in a food processor. Cover and process on high until smooth.

3. Remove feeder cap and add walnuts. Continue to process only until nuts are chopped.
4. Pour these creamed ingredients into the dry ingredients. Mix just until combined.
5. Pour batter into a greased and floured 9 x 13 baking pan.
6. Bake at 350° for 30-40 minutes, or until toothpick inserted in center comes out clean.

Exchange List Values:
Carbohydrate 2.0, Fat 1.0

Basic Nutritional Values:
Calories 184 (Calories from Fat 63), Total Fat 7 gm (Saturated Fat 1.4 gm, Trans Fat 0.0 gm, Polyunsat Fat 3.2 gm, Monounsat Fat 2.1 gm, Cholesterol 28 mg), Sodium 204 mg, Total Carbohydrate 27 gm, Dietary Fiber 1 gm, Sugars 12 gm, Protein 4 gm

---

A Tip —

Eat plenty of green leafy vegetables; red, orange, and yellow fruits and vegetables; citrus fruits; nuts and seeds; and meat and fish. They are good for your heart and help prevent cancer.

Unbelievable Carrot Cake

Sue Hamilton
Minooka, IL

Makes 20 servings
Serving size is 2⅔" x 2¼" rectangle

Prep Time: 5-10 minutes
Baking Time: 30 minutes
Cooling Time: 1 hour

Cake:
1 2-layer spice cake mix
2 cups (½ lb.) shredded carrots
1 cup crushed pineapples with juice
3 egg whites
½ cup All-Bran cereal

Frosting:
2 3-oz. pkgs. fat-free cream cheese, softened
1 cup granular Splenda
1 tsp. vanilla
4 ozs. (⅓ of a 12-oz. container) fat-free frozen whipped topping, thawed

1. Combine all cake ingredients thoroughly.
2. Pour into a 9 x 13 baking pan sprayed with non-fat cooking spray.
3. Bake at 350° for 30 minutes. Cool completely.
4. Beat together cream cheese, Splenda, and vanilla.
5. Fold in the whipped topping. Frost cake and refrigerate.

Exchange List Values:
Carbohydrate 2.0

Basic Nutritional Values:
Calories 145 (Calories from Fat 17), Total Fat 2 gm (Saturated Fat 0.6 gm, Trans Fat 0.0 gm, Polyunsat Fat 0.0 gm, Monounsat Fat 0.6 gm, Cholesterol 1 mg), Sodium 246 mg, Total Carbohydrate 29 gm, Dietary Fiber 1 gm, Sugars 17 gm, Protein 3 gm

Tip: There is no need to shred carrots yourself anymore, because you can now buy them in a bag all ready to use.

Carrot Cake

Janelle Myers-Benner
Harrisonburg, VA

Makes 20 servings
Serving size is 2⅔" x 2¼" rectangle

Prep Time: 45 minutes
Baking Time: 40-50 minutes

½ cup canola oil
2½ Tbsp. sugar blend for baking (Splenda)
½ cup brown sugar blend (Splenda)
4 eggs
½ cup unsweetened applesauce
2 cups whole wheat pastry flour
1 tsp. baking soda
1 tsp. baking powder
1 tsp. salt
2 tsp. cinnamon
2 cups grated carrots, about 3 large carrots
¼ cup grated coconut
1 cup crushed pineapple, drained
¾ cup nuts, *optional*
2 tsp. vanilla

Cream Cheese Frosting:
3-oz. pkg. fat-free cream cheese, softened
1 Tbsp. butter, softened
2 cups confectioners sugar
1 tsp. vanilla
2 Tbsp. fat-free milk

1. In a large mixing bowl, cream together oil and both sugar blends. Stir in the eggs and the applesauce.
2. In a separate bowl, sift together the flour, baking soda, baking powder, salt, and cinnamon. Add to creamed mixture.
3. Stir in the carrots, coconut, pineapple, nuts, if desired, and vanilla.
4. Pour into a greased 9 x 13 baking pan. Bake at 325° for 40-50 minutes, or until toothpick inserted in center comes out clean.
5. To make the frosting, mix cream cheese, butter, confectioners sugar, and vanilla together. Add milk until you reach a spreadable consistency.

Exchange List Values:
Carbohydrate 2.0, Fat 1.5

Basic Nutritional Values:
Calories 212 (Calories from Fat 68), Total Fat 8 gm (Saturated Fat 1.4 gm, Trans Fat 0.0 gm, Polyunsat Fat 1.9 gm, Monounsat Fat 3.8 gm, Cholesterol 44 mg), Sodium 259 mg, Total Carbohydrate 32 gm, Dietary Fiber 2 gm, Sugars 20 gm, Protein 3 gm

This is the cake my mom made for our wedding. We couldn't wait until our 1st anniversary to eat the top of the cake!

Cajun Pineapple Cake

Jan Sams, Lancaster, PA
Kay Magruder, Seminole, OK

Makes 20 servings
Serving size is 2⅔" x 2¼" rectangle

Prep Time: 20 minutes
Baking Time: 50 minutes

3 cups flour
½ tsp. salt
¾ cup sugar blend for
   baking (Splenda)
1½ tsp. baking soda
2 eggs
15-oz. can crushed
   pineapple, undrained
¼ cup orange juice

Frosting:
6 Tbsp. sugar blend for
   baking (Splenda)
¼ cup fat-free evaporated
   milk
2 tsp. butter
2 Tbsp. canola oil
1 cup chopped pecans
½ cup shredded coconut

1. Make the cake by combining the flour, salt, sugar blend, and baking soda in a large mixing bowl.
2. In a separate bowl, mix together eggs, pineapple, and orange juice.
3. Add wet ingredients to dry ingredients. Mix well.
4. Pour into a greased 9 x 13 baking pan.
5. Bake at 325° for 50 minutes, or until a toothpick inserted in the center comes out clean.

6. While the cake is baking, place the sugar blend, milk, butter, and canola oil for the frosting in a saucepan. Bring to a boil. Continue simmering until the butter is melted. Cool.
7. Stir in pecans and coconut. Mix well.
8. Spread topping on hot cake. Place under broiler for a few minutes until lightly browned. But watch carefully so the topping doesn't burn!

Exchange List Values:
Carbohydrate 2.0, Fat 1.0

Basic Nutritional Values:
Calories 196 (Calories from Fat 64), Total Fat 7 gm (Saturated Fat 1.4 gm, Trans Fat 0.0 gm, Polyunsat Fat 1.7 gm, Monounsat Fat 3.6 gm, Cholesterol 22 mg), Sodium 171 mg, Total Carbohydrate 30 gm, Dietary Fiber 1 gm, Sugars 15 gm, Protein 3 gm

Lemony Cheese Cake

Ruth Osborne
Carmichael, PA

Makes 12 servings
Serving size is 1 slice

Prep Time: 10-20 minutes
Baking Time: 45-60 minutes

Crust:
2 cups graham cracker
   crumbs
2 Tbsp. sugar
1 Tbsp. butter
1 Tbsp. canola oil

Filling:
4 eggs

3 8-oz. pkgs. fat-free cream
   cheese, softened
4 Tbsp. flour
2 Tbsp. lemon juice
½ cup sugar blend for
   baking (Splenda)
1 tsp. vanilla

1. Prepare crust by combining graham cracker crumbs and sugar.
2. Melt butter with canola oil and stir into cracker mixture.
3. Press combined ingredients around sides and bottom of a 9" springform pan.
4. Bake 2-4 minutes at 350°. Set aside.
5. Put eggs in an electric mixer bowl and beat slightly.
6. Add all other filling ingredients and blend with mixer until smooth.
7. Spoon over top of graham cracker crust, being careful not to disturb the crumbs.
8. Bake at 350° for 40-55 minutes, or until set in the middle.

Exchange List Values:
Carbohydrate 2.0, Fat 1.0

Basic Nutritional Values:
Calories 214 (Calories from Fat 47), Total Fat 5 gm (Saturated Fat 1.4 gm, Trans Fat 0.0 gm, Polyunsat Fat 1.2 gm, Monounsat Fat 2.1 gm, Cholesterol 80 mg), Sodium 515 mg, Total Carbohydrate 27 gm, Dietary Fiber 0 gm, Sugars 15 gm, Protein 11 gm

Tip: To keep a cheesecake from cracking, either place a dish of water in the oven along with the cheesecake, or wrap the springform pan with foil and place the filled pan in a dish of water to bake.

Kiwi Pineapple Cheesecake

Mable Hershey
Marietta, PA

Makes 14 servings
Serving size is 1 wedge

Prep Time: 30 minutes
Baking Time: 8-10 minutes
Chilling Time: 7 hours,
  or overnight

1¾ cups crushed reduced-
  fat vanilla wafers (about
  50 wafers)
2 Tbsp. sugar blend for
  baking (Splenda)
1½ Tbsp. butter, melted
1½ Tbsp. canola oil
1 Tbsp. pineapple juice

Filling:
20-oz. can sliced
  pineapples, ½ cup and
  1 Tbsp. juice reserved
1 envelope unflavored
  gelatin
2 8-oz. pkgs. fat-free cream
  cheese, softened
15 ozs. fat-free ricotta
  cheese
1 cup confectioners sugar
1 Tbsp. grated fresh orange
  peel
1 tsp. vanilla

Topping:
½ cup low-fat orange
  marmalade
1 kiwi fruit peeled, halved,
  and sliced

1. Drain pineapple, separately reserving ½ cup and 1 Tbsp. juice.
2. In a bowl, combine wafer crumbs and sugar blend. Stir in melted butter, canola oil and 1 Tbsp. pineapple juice.
3. Press into the bottom and 2 inches up the sides of a 9" springform pan. Bake at 350° for 8 minutes. Cool on wire rack; then refrigerate for 30 minutes.
4. Pour ½ cup pineapple juice into a small saucepan. Sprinkle gelatin over juice. Let stand for 1 minute.
5. Cook over low heat, stirring until gelatin is completely dissolved. Cool to room temperature, about 10 minutes.
6. While the juice is cooling, beat together the cream cheese and ricotta cheese in a large electric mixer bowl until smooth. Stir in confectioners sugar until smooth.
7. Gradually add gelatin mixture, orange peel, and vanilla to the cheese mixture. Beat on low speed until well mixed. Spoon half into crust.
8. Cut four pineapple rings in half and arrange in spoke-fashion over the filling.
9. Spoon remaining filling over pineapple.
10. Refrigerate in the baking pan for 6 hours, or overnight.
11. Beat marmalade until soft and spreadable. Brush 6 Tbsp. on top of thoroughly chilled cheesecake.

12. Cut remaining pineapple rings in half and arrange over marmalade.
13. Place kiwi slices between pineapple rings and brush with remaining marmalade.
14. Just before serving, run knife around the edge of the pan to loosen. Remove sides of pan, cut cake into wedges, and serve.

Exchange List Values:
Fat-Free Milk 0.5, Fat 0.5,
Carbohydrate 2.0

Basic Nutritional Values:
Calories 224 (Calories from Fat 36),
Total Fat 4 gm (Saturated Fat 1.4
gm, Trans Fat 0.0 gm, Polyunsat
Fat 0.7 gm, Monounsat Fat 1.7 gm,
Cholesterol 17 mg), Sodium 288 mg,
Total Carbohydrate 36 gm, Dietary
Fiber 1 gm, Sugars 29 gm, Protein
10 gm

Tip: To evenly press crumbs into a springform pan, place another round cake pan down on top of the crumbs, pressing gently. This will make the corner/bend from the bottom to the sides less thick and will help to make very straight sides. When you take the springform pan sides off, the sides of the cake will look even.

Frozen Mocha Cheesecake

Stacy Schmucker Stoltzfus
Enola, PA
Ilene Bontrager
Arlington, KS

Makes 20 servings
Serving size is 2⅔" x 2¼" rectangle

Prep Time: 20-25 minutes
Freezing Time: 6 hours,
or overnight

1¼ cups crushed chocolate
    wafer cookies
¼ cup sugar
3 Tbsp. butter, melted
8-oz. pkg. fat-free cream
    cheese, softened
14-oz. can fat-free sweetened
    condensed milk
⅔ cup fat-free chocolate
    syrup
2 Tbsp. instant coffee
    granules
1 tsp. hot water
1 cup frozen fat-free
    whipped topping,
    thawed (plus extra for
    garnish, *optional*)
1 cup chocolate chips,
    optional

1. Reserve a few cookie crumbs for garnish. In a small bowl, combine remaining cookie crumbs, sugar, and butter. Pat crumbs firmly on the bottom and up the sides of a 9 x 13 baking pan, or a 9" springform pan. Refrigerate while preparing rest of cake.
2. In a large mixing bowl, beat cream cheese until fluffy.

3. Add milk and syrup and combine well.
4. In a small bowl, dissolve coffee granules in hot water. Add to creamed mixture. Mix well.
5. Fold in whipped topping.
6. Pour into prepared pan. Cover and freeze about 6 hours, or until firm.
7. If you choose to top the cheesecake with chocolate chips, melt them in microwave (about 30 seconds). Stir. Place in plastic baggie, and cut off a small part of one corner.
8. Squeeze chocolate onto waxed paper into 16 or 20 shapes (hearts, fun squiggles, etc.). Place in refrigerator until firm.
9. If desired, just before serving, place a dollop of whipped topping on each piece of cake. Gently lift chocolate shapes off waxed paper and lean each one into a dollop, so it stands up. Sprinkle with reserved crumbs.
10. Serve chilled.

Exchange List Values:
Carbohydrate 2.0, Fat 0.5

Basic Nutritional Values:
Calories 156 (Calories from Fat 25),
Total Fat 3 gm (Saturated Fat 1.4
gm, Trans Fat 0.0 gm, Polyunsat
Fat 0.4 gm, Monounsat Fat 1.3 gm,
Cholesterol 6 mg), Sodium 162 mg,
Total Carbohydrate 28 gm, Dietary
Fiber 0 gm, Sugars 23 gm, Protein 4 gm

Please note that the optional whipped topping and chocolate shapes in this recipe are not included in the nutritional analysis.

No-Bake Raspberry Cheesecake

Arlene M. Kopp
Lineboro, MD

Makes 12 servings
Serving size is 3¼" x 3" rectangle

Prep Time: 30 minutes
Chilling Time: 4-5 hours

0.35-oz. pkg. sugar-free
    raspberry gelatin
1 cup boiling water
8-oz. pkg. fat-free cream
    cheese, softened
½ cup sugar
½ cup granular Splenda
1 tsp. vanilla
1⅓ cups (19-20 crackers)
    graham cracker crumbs
1½ Tbsp. melted butter
1½ Tbsp. canola oil
3 Tbsp. lemon juice
12-oz. can fat-free
    evaporated milk, chilled

1. Place a large mixing bowl in the fridge. (You'll need it later to whip the milk.)
2. Combine gelatin and boiling water in a small bowl, stirring until gelatin is dissolved. Cool.
3. In a medium-sized mixing bowl, cream together cream cheese, sugar, sweetener, and vanilla. Mix well.
4. Add gelatin. Mix well. Chill until it begins to set.

5. Meanwhile, combine cracker crumbs, butter, and oil in a small bowl. Press two-thirds of crumbs into the bottom of a 9 x 13 pan.

6. Combine lemon juice and milk in the bowl you've been chilling. Whip until it's stiff and holds a peak.

7. Lightly fold gelatin mixture into whipped mixture.

8. Pour into crumb crust in pan, being careful not to disturb the crumbs. Sprinkle top with remaining crumbs.

9. Chill until set, about 2-3 hours.

Exchange List Values:
Carbohydrate 1.5, Fat 1.0

Basic Nutritional Values:
Calories 151 (Calories from Fat 38), Total Fat 4 gm (Saturated Fat 1.2 gm, Trans Fat 0.0 gm, Polyunsat Fat 0.9 gm, Monounsat Fat 1.8 gm, Cholesterol 7 mg), Sodium 242 mg, Total Carbohydrate 22 gm, Dietary Fiber 0 gm, Sugars 15 gm, Protein 6 gm

---

A Tip —

Exercise is like a miracle drug—it boosts your metabolism, increases muscle mass so you burn more calories, improves your body's response to insulin, and naturally lowers glucose.

Oatmeal Cake
Shari Jensen
Fountain, CO
Barb Yoder
Angola, IN

Makes 20 servings
Serving size is 2⅔" x 2¼" rectangle

Prep Time: 15 minutes
Baking Time: 50 minutes

1¼ cups boiling water
1 cup dry quick oats
½ cup sugar blend for baking (Splenda)
½ cup brown sugar blend (Splenda)
¼ cup zero-trans-fat shortening
½ cup egg substitute
1½ cups sifted flour
1 tsp. baking soda
½ tsp. salt
1 tsp. cinnamon

Topping:
¼ cup brown sugar blend (Splenda)
¼ cup sweetened coconut, shredded *or* flaked
½ cup chopped walnuts
½ tsp. vanilla
2 tsp. melted butter
2 Tbsp. fat-free evaporated milk

1. Pour boiling water over quick oats in a small bowl. Let stand a few minutes.

2. Cream together sugar blends, shortening, and egg substitute. Add oatmeal mixture.

3. In a small bowl, combine flour, baking soda, salt, and cinnamon. Add to egg/oatmeal mixture.

4. Pour into a greased and floured 9 x 13 baking pan. Bake at 350° for 40-45 minutes.

5. Meanwhile, make topping by combining ¼ cup brown sugar blend, coconut, walnuts, vanilla, butter, and evaporated milk in a mixing bowl.

6. Spread over cake as soon as it is comes out of the oven. Turn on broiler and place cake under broiler for 3-5 minutes, until golden and bubbly. Watch carefully so it doesn't burn.

7. Remove from broiler and let cool before serving.

Exchange List Values:
Carbohydrate 1.5, Fat 1.0

Basic Nutritional Values:
Calories 161 (Calories from Fat 50), Total Fat 6 gm (Saturated Fat 1.4 gm, Trans Fat 0.0 gm, Polyunsat Fat 2.4 gm, Monounsat Fat 1.5 gm, Cholesterol 1 mg), Sodium 142 mg, Total Carbohydrate 23 gm, Dietary Fiber 1 gm, Sugars 13 gm, Protein 3 gm

---

Variation: Instead of finishing the cake with the topping above, in Step 4, after the cake is in the baking pan but before putting it in the oven, scatter 5 cups (6-oz. pkg.) peanut butter cups, chopped, over the batter. Bake at 350° for 40-45 minutes. Let cool before cutting into squares and serving.
—**Joan Miller**
Wayland, IA

Moist Creamy Coconut Cake

Kathy Bless, Fayetteville, PA

Makes 20 servings
Serving size is 2⅔" x 2¼" rectangle

Prep Time: 10 minutes
Baking Time: about 30 minutes
Chilling Time: 8 hours,
  or overnight

1 pkg. yellow cake mix
¼ cup canola oil
¾ cup egg substitute
1¼ cups fat-free milk
¼ cup sugar blend for
  baking (Splenda)
⅔ cup flaked sweetened
  coconut, *divided*
8-oz. container frozen fat-
  free whipped topping,
  thawed
1 tsp. vanilla

1. Prepare cake mix as
directed on package, except
use ¼ cup canola oil in place
of butter, and ¾ cup egg
substitute in place of eggs.
Bake in a greased 9 x 13 pan.
2. Cool 15 minutes. Poke
holes in the cake with a fork.
3. Meanwhile, combine
milk, sugar blend, and ⅓ cup
coconut in a saucepan. Bring
to a boil. Reduce heat and
simmer 1 minute.
4. Spoon evenly over warm
cake. Cool completely.
5. Fold together ⅓ cup
coconut, whipped topping,
and vanilla. Spread over
cooled cake.
6. Chill overnight. Store in
refrigerator.

Exchange List Values:
Carbohydrate 2.0, Fat 1.0

Basic Nutritional Values:
Calories 188 (Calories from Fat 59),
Total Fat 7 gm (Saturated Fat 1.4
gm, Trans Fat 0.0 gm, Polyunsat
Fat 2.0 gm, Monounsat Fat 2.9 gm,
Cholesterol 1 mg), Sodium 209 mg,
Total Carbohydrate 29 gm, Dietary
Fiber 0 gm, Sugars 17 gm, Protein 3 gm

Mixed Fruit Cake

Merle E. Mast
Keezletown, VA

Makes 24 servings
Serving size is 1 slice

Prep Time: 30 minutes
Cooking/Baking Time:
  90 minutes

3 cups chopped dried fruits
  (vary these as you like):
½ cup raisins *or* currants
½ cup dates
1 cup figs
¾ cup dried apricots
¼ cup dried cranberries,
  or dried tart cherries
2 cups water
½ cup sugar blend for
  baking (Splenda)
4½ Tbsp. butter
3 cups flour
1 tsp. baking soda
2 tsp. cinnamon
½ tsp. cloves
½ tsp. salt
1 cup chopped nuts,
  optional

1. Combine chopped fruit,
water, sugar blend, and butter
in a saucepan. Bring to a boil,
cover, and simmer over low
heat for 20 minutes.
2. Meanwhile, stir together
flour, soda, cinnamon, cloves,
and salt in a mixing bowl.
3. Add fruit mixture,
and nuts, if you wish. Stir
together until well blended.
4. Spread mixture into two
greased 4½ x 8½ x 2½ loaf
pans.
5. Bake at 325° for 60
minutes, or until cakes test
done. Invert onto rack and
cool.

Exchange List Values:
Carbohydrate 2.0

Basic Nutritional Values:
Calories 147 (Calories from Fat 23),
Total Fat 3 gm (Saturated Fat 1.4
gm, Trans Fat 0.0 gm, Polyunsat
Fat 0.2 gm, Monounsat Fat 0.6 gm,
Cholesterol 6 mg), Sodium 119 mg,
Total Carbohydrate 30 gm, Dietary
Fiber 2 gm, Sugars 16 gm, Protein 2 gm

A Tip —

  Drinking less alcohol,
quitting smoking, and
getting more exercise are
not only better for your
health, they will also
save you money on health
care, since you may be
able to use less insulin.

Poppy Seed Cake

Helen Goering
Moundridge, KS

Makes 15 servings
Serving size is 1 slice

Prep Time: 20-30 minutes
Baking Time: 25-30 minutes

1 cup sugar blend for
  baking (Splenda)
¼ cup solid zero-trans-fat
  shortening
½ cup poppy seeds, finely
  ground
2 eggs
⅓ cup fat-free buttermilk
2 cups flour
1 tsp. baking soda
1 tsp. vanilla
¾ cup boiling water

1. In a large mixing bowl,
cream together sugar blend,
shortening, and ground poppy
seeds.
2. Add eggs and buttermilk.
Mix well.
3. Sift flour and baking soda
into mixture. Blend thoroughly.
4. Add vanilla and hot
water. Blend in well.
5. Place in a greased 9" or
10" tube pan or a greased
9 x 13 baking pan.
6. Bake at 350° for 25-30
minutes, or until a toothpick
inserted in center comes out
clean.

Exchange List Values:
Carbohydrate 2.0, Fat 1.0

Basic Nutritional Values:
Calories 180 (Calories from Fat 57),
Total Fat 6 gm (Saturated Fat 1.3
gm, Trans Fat 0.0 gm, Polyunsat
Fat 2.7 gm, Monounsat Fat 2.0 gm,
Cholesterol 28 mg), Sodium 101 mg,
Total Carbohydrate 27 gm, Dietary
Fiber 1 gm, Sugars 14 gm, Protein 4 gm

Vicki's Lovely Lazy Daizy Cake

Dorothy Van Deest
Memphis, TN

Makes 20 servings
Serving size is 2⅔" x 2¼" rectangle

Prep Time: 30 minutes
Baking Time: 33-43 minutes

1 cup egg substitute
1 cup sugar blend for
  baking (Splenda)
2 tsp. vanilla
2 cups flour
2 tsp. baking powder
1½ tsp. salt
1½ tsp. butter
1 Tbsp. canola oil
¾ cup scalded fat-free
  milk

Topping:
2½ Tbsp. brown sugar
  blend (Splenda)
3 Tbsp. fat-free half-and-
  half
1 Tbsp. butter
½ cup shredded sweetened
  coconut
½ cup chopped walnuts

1. In a large mixing bowl,
combine egg substitute
with sugar blend, beating
constantly. Add vanilla.
2. Sift flour, baking
powder, and salt together
in a separate bowl. Stir into
egg/sugar mixture.
3. Stir butter and canola
oil into scalded milk, stirring
until the butter melts. Add to
batter and mix well.
4. Pour into a greased
9 x 13 cake pan. Bake at 350°
for 30-40 minutes.
5. While the cake is
baking, prepare topping.
Mix all topping ingredients
in a saucepan. Heat over
medium-low heat until the
butter melts and the topping
is bubbling.
6. Test cake with toothpick.
When done, spread immedi-
ately with topping.
7. Change oven to broiler
and set cake under broiler
until bubbly. Watch carefully;
it doesn't take long!
8. Serve hot or cold.

Exchange List Values:
Carbohydrate 1.5, Fat 1.0

Basic Nutritional Values:
Calories 144 (Calories from Fat 38),
Total Fat 4 gm (Saturated Fat 1.4
gm, Trans Fat 0.0 gm, Polyunsat
Fat 1.7 gm, Monounsat Fat 0.9 gm,
Cholesterol 3 mg), Sodium 251 mg,
Total Carbohydrate 23 gm, Dietary
Fiber 1 gm, Sugars 13 gm, Protein 3 gm

Lemon Glaze Cake

Terry Stutzman Mast
Lodi, CA
Nancy Wagner Graves
Manhattan, KS

Makes 20 servings
Serving size is 2⅔" x 2¼" rectangle

Prep Time: 10 minutes
Cooking Time: 30-35 minutes

Cake:
1 yellow cake mix
4 eggs
¾ cup oil
¾ cup water
0.35-oz. pkg. sugar-free
lemon gelatin

Glaze:
juice and grated rind of
2 lemons
2 cups confectioners sugar

1. In a large mixing bowl, mix together cake mix, eggs, oil, water, and gelatin.
2. Pour into a lightly greased 9 x 13 baking pan. Bake at 350° for 30-35 minutes, or until a toothpick inserted in the center comes out clean.
3. While the cake is baking, mix lemon juice, lemon rind, and confectioners together in a mixing bowl.
4. While the baked cake is still warm, poke holes all over it with a fork. Drizzle thoroughly with the glaze.
5. Allow cake to cool before cutting into squares and serving.

Exchange List Values:
Carbohydrate 2.0, Fat 2.0

Basic Nutritional Values:
Calories 248 (Calories from Fat 110), Total Fat 12 gm (Saturated Fat 1.3 gm, Trans Fat 0.0 gm, Polyunsat Fat 3.7 gm, Monounsat Fat 6.5 gm, Cholesterol 43 mg), Sodium 190 mg, Total Carbohydrate 33 gm, Dietary Fiber 0 gm, Sugars 23 gm, Protein 2 gm

Ah, the annual summer picnic with folks from the church in Normal, Illinois, where I grew up. This was a regular contribution of Ruth Rowe, a family friend.

Variation: Substitute a 3.4-oz. box of lemon instant pudding for the box of gelatin. Stir 1 tsp. almond flavoring and 1 heaping tsp. poppy seeds into batter in Step 1.
    Pour cake into a greased bundt pan and bake at 350° for 35 minutes, or until a toothpick comes out clean when inserted in the center.
    —Beth Maurer
        Columbus Grove, OH

A Tip —
    Wear a medical alert bracelet or necklace that says "diabetes"—not to call attention to your condition, but to tell medical personnel to check your sugar level if an emergency happened.

Orange Streusel Cake

Lori Newswanger
Lancaster, PA

Makes 16 servings
Serving size is 1 slice

Prep Time: 20 minutes
Baking Time: 30-35 minutes

Streusel:
½ cup brown sugar blend
(Splenda)
1 cup chopped nuts *or*
sliced almonds
¼ cup flour
1 Tbsp. butter, melted
1 Tbsp. canola oil
1 tsp. grated fresh orange
zest

Cake:
¼ cup, plus 2 Tbsp.,
canola oil
¼ cup sugar blend for
baking (Splenda)
¾ cup egg substitute
1 tsp. grated fresh orange
zest
½ tsp. vanilla
2 cups flour
1 tsp. baking powder
1 tsp. baking soda
⅔ cup orange juice

Glaze:
2½ tsp. orange juice
½ cup confectioners sugar

1. To make the streusel, combine brown sugar blend, nuts, flour, butter, canola oil, and orange zest in a mixing bowl. Mix till crumbly and set aside.

2. To make the cake, beat together canola oil and sugar blend.

3. Mix in egg substitute. Add orange zest and vanilla and beat well.

4. In a separate bowl, combine flour, baking powder, and baking soda. Add to egg mixture alternately with orange juice.

5. Spoon half the batter into a greased 9" or 10" tube pan. Sprinkle with half the streusel. Top with remaining batter and then a layer of the remaining streusel.

6. Bake at 350° for 30-35 minutes, or until a toothpick comes out clean. Cool on a wire rack.

7. Prepare glaze by combining orange juice and confectioners sugar.

8. Turn cake right side up onto a serving plate. Drizzle with glaze.

9. Slice and serve.

Exchange List Values:
Carbohydrate 2.0, Fat 2.0

Basic Nutritional Values:
Calories 242 (Calories from Fat 107), Total Fat 12 gm (Saturated Fat 1.4 gm, Trans Fat 0.0 gm, Polyunsat Fat 5.5 gm, Monounsat Fat 4.5 gm, Cholesterol 2 mg), Sodium 130 mg, Total Carbohydrate 29 gm, Dietary Fiber 1 gm, Sugars 14 gm, Protein 4 gm

Orange Lemon Pound Cake
Judi Manos
West Islip, NY

Makes 20 servings
Serving size is 1 slice

Prep Time: 20 minutes
Baking Time: 45-60 minutes
Cooling Time: 15 minutes

2⅔ Tbsp. butter, softened
5⅓ Tbsp. canola oil
1 cup sugar blend for baking (Splenda)
1 egg, at room temperature
2 egg whites, at room temperature
3 cups flour
½ tsp. salt
½ tsp. baking soda
½ tsp. baking powder
1 cup low-fat buttermilk
1 tsp. vanilla
1 tsp. lemon extract

Glaze:
2 tsp. orange juice
2 tsp. lemon juice
1 cup confectioners sugar

1. In a large mixing bowl, cream together butter, canola oil, and sugar blend until very well mixed.

2. Add egg, and egg whites one at a time. Beat well after each addition.

3. In a separate bowl, combine flour, salt, baking soda, and baking powder.

4. Add dry ingredients to creamed mixture alternately with buttermilk. End with dry ingredients.

5. Stir in vanilla and lemon extract.

6. Spoon batter into a well greased and floured 10" tube pan. Bake at 350° for 45-60 minutes, or until cake tests done with a toothpick.

7. Combine all glaze ingredients in a mixing bowl. Blend well.

8. Cool cake on a wire rack for 15 minutes. Remove from pan. Place cake on the wire rack over a plate that is slightly larger than the cake. Punch holes in the still-warm cake with a toothpick and drizzle glaze over the cake until it is absorbed.

Exchange List Values:
Carbohydrate 2.0, Fat 1.0

Basic Nutritional Values:
Calories 188 (Calories from Fat 52), Total Fat 6 gm (Saturated Fat 1.4 gm, Trans Fat 0.0 gm, Polyunsat Fat 1.3 gm, Monounsat Fat 2.7 gm, Cholesterol 15 mg), Sodium 132 mg, Total Carbohydrate 31 gm, Dietary Fiber 1 gm, Sugars 16 gm, Protein 3 gm

Variation: In addition to the vanilla and lemon extract in the batter, add ½ tsp. coconut extract, 1 tsp. almond extract, and ½ tsp. butter flavoring.
—Ann Bender
Fort Defiance, VA

Sunny Spice Cake

Karla Baer
North Lime, OH

Makes 20 servings
Serving size is 2⅔" x 2¼" rectangle

Prep Time: 10 minutes
Baking Time: 35 minutes

1 spice cake mix
3 1-oz. pkgs. fat-free, sugar-
 free butterscotch instant
 pudding
2 cups fat-free milk
2 eggs
20 peach halves, drained
20 Tbsp. frozen fat-free
 whipped topping,
 thawed

1. In a mixing bowl, blend together cake mix, pudding mix, milk, and eggs.
2. Pour into a greased 9 x 13 baking pan. Bake at 350° for 35 minutes.
3. Cool.
4. When ready to serve, cut into serving-sized pieces. Place a peach half on each serving of cake. Top each with a Tbsp. of whipped topping.

Exchange List Values:
Carbohydrate 2.5

Basic Nutritional Values:
Calories 168 (Calories from Fat 21), Total Fat 2 gm (Saturated Fat 0.8 gm, Trans Fat 0.0 gm, Polyunsat Fat 0.1 gm, Monounsat Fat 0.8 gm, Cholesterol 22 mg), Sodium 247 mg, Total Carbohydrate 35 gm, Dietary Fiber 1 gm, Sugars 22 gm, Protein 3 gm

Pound Cake

Janna Zimmerman
Flemington, NJ

Makes 20 servings
Serving size is 1 slice

Prep Time: 10 minutes
Baking Time: 1¼-1½ hours

2⅔ Tbsp. butter, softened
5⅓ Tbsp. canola oil
1½ cups sugar blend for
 baking (Splenda)
1 cup fat-free sour cream
1 tsp. vanilla
½ tsp. baking powder
2 eggs
2 egg whites
3 cups flour

1. In a large mixing bowl, cream butter, canola oil, and sugar blend together.
2. Blend in sour cream, vanilla, and baking powder.
3. Add egg and egg whites, one at a time, beating well after each addition.
4. Add flour and mix well.
5. Pour into a greased bundt pan. Bake at 325° for 1¼-1½ hours, or until a toothpick inserted in the center comes out clean.

Exchange List Values:
Carbohydrate 2.0, Fat 1.0

Basic Nutritional Values:
Calories 192 (Calories from Fat 54), Total Fat 6 gm (Saturated Fat 1.4 gm, Trans Fat 0.0 gm, Polyunsat Fat 1.3 gm, Monounsat Fat 2.8 gm, Cholesterol 26 mg), Sodium 39 mg, Total Carbohydrate 29 gm, Dietary Fiber 1 gm, Sugars 15 gm, Protein 4 gm

Bernice's Rhubarb Sour Cream Cake

Bonnie Heatwole
Springs, PA

Makes 20 servings
Serving size is 2⅔" x 2¼" rectangle

Prep Time: 20 minutes
Baking Time: 40 minutes

2 Tbsp. butter, softened
¾ cup brown sugar blend
 (Splenda)
2 large eggs
1 tsp. vanilla
2⅓ cups flour
1 tsp. baking soda
1 tsp. salt
4 cups rhubarb, cut in ½"
 slices
1 cup fat-free sour cream

Topping:
¼ cup sugar blend for
 baking (Splenda)
1 tsp. cinnamon
1 cup chopped nuts
frozen whipped topping,
 thawed, *optional*

1. In a large mixing bowl, cream together butter and ¾ cup brown sugar blend until fluffy.
2. Add eggs and vanilla. Mix well.
3. In a separate bowl, combine flour, baking soda, and salt. Add to creamed mixture. Mix well.
4. Stir in rhubarb and sour cream. Mix well.
5. Spread batter in a greased 9 x 13 baking pan.

6. To make the topping, combine ¼ cup sugar blend, cinnamon, and nuts in a small bowl. Sprinkle on top of batter.

7. Bake at 350° for 40 minutes, or until top springs back or toothpick comes out clean.

8. Serve warm with whipped topping, if you wish, for dessert or for breakfast as a coffee cake.

Exchange List Values:
Carbohydrate 1.5, Fat 1.0

Basic Nutritional Values:
Calories 171 (Calories from Fat 52), Total Fat 6 gm (Saturated Fat 1.3 gm, Trans Fat 0.0 gm, Polyunsat Fat 3.0 gm, Monounsat Fat 1.0 gm, Cholesterol 25 mg), Sodium 204 mg, Total Carbohydrate 23 gm, Dietary Fiber 1 gm, Sugars 11 gm, Protein 4 gm

---

A Tip —

Anything that raises your pulse and makes you breathe harder— swimming, walking, jogging, dancing, or biking—is aerobic. Find something you enjoy and do it for 30 minutes, three or four times a week.

Aunt Allie's Molasses Cake with Lemon Sauce

Mary D. Smith
Moneta, VA
Virginia Bender
Dover, DE

Makes 20 servings
Serving size is 2⅔" x 2¼" rectangle

Prep Time: 20 minutes
Baking Time: 40-45 minutes
Cooling Time: 45 minutes

---

2 eggs
½ cup sugar blend for baking (Splenda)
2⅔ Tbsp. butter, softened
5⅓ Tbsp. canola oil
1 cup molasses
2 tsp. cinnamon
1 tsp. ginger
3 cups flour
1⅔ cups boiling water
2 tsp. baking soda

Lemon Sauce:
¼ cup sugar blend for baking (Splenda)
⅛ tsp. salt
1½ Tbsp. cornstarch
1⅓ cups boiling water
grated rind and juice of 2 lemons

1. By hand, combine eggs, sugar blend, butter, and canola oil. Mix well.

2. Add molasses, cinnamon, and ginger. Mix well.

3. Stir in flour. Mix well.

4. In a small bowl, combine boiling water and baking soda. Add to batter. Mix well.

5. Pour batter into a greased 9 x 13 baking pan.

6. Bake at 325° for 40-45 minutes. Cool.

7. Combine sugar blend, salt, and cornstarch in a saucepan.

8. Add boiling water. Stir until smooth. Cook over low heat until thickened and clear, stirring constantly.

9. Remove from heat. Stir in lemon rind and juice. Stir until well blended.

10. Serve molasses cake with lemon sauce.

Exchange List Values:
Carbohydrate 2.0, Fat 1.0

Basic Nutritional Values:
Calories 198 (Calories from Fat 54), Total Fat 6 gm (Saturated Fat 1.4 gm, Trans Fat 0.0 gm, Polyunsat Fat 1.3 gm, Monounsat Fat 2.8 gm, Cholesterol 25 mg), Sodium 168 mg, Total Carbohydrate 34 gm, Dietary Fiber 1 gm, Sugars 17 gm, Protein 3 gm

Pumpkin Yummy Dessert with Frosting

LuAnna Hochstedler
East Earl, PA
Marolyn Minnich
Westover, MD

Makes 20 servings
Serving size is 2⅔″ x 2¼″ rectangle

Prep Time: 15-20 minutes
Baking Time: 50 minutes

29-oz. can pumpkin
¼ tsp. salt
2 tsp. cinnamon
½ tsp. ginger
¼ tsp. cloves
½ cup brown sugar blend (Splenda)
¾ cup egg substitute
12-oz. can fat-free evaporated milk
1 pkg. yellow, *or* spice, cake mix
1½ Tbsp. butter, melted

Topping:
8-oz. pkg. fat-free cream cheese, softened
½ cup confectioners sugar
8-oz. container frozen fat-free whipped topping, thawed

1. In a large mixing bowl, combine pumpkin, salt, cinnamon, ginger, cloves, sugar blend, and egg substitute. Blend well.
2. Add milk and blend thoroughly.
3. Pour batter into a greased 9 x 13 baking pan.

4. Sprinkle batter with cake mix.
5. Pour butter over top.
6. Bake at 350° for 50-60 minutes.
7. In a mixing bowl, beat cream cheese until creamy. Fold in confectioners sugar and blend well. Fold in whipped topping.
8. Spread over cooled cake.

Exchange List Values:
Carbohydrate 2.5, Fat 1.0

Basic Nutritional Values:
Calories 221 (Calories from Fat 37), Total Fat 4 gm (Saturated Fat 1.1 gm, Trans Fat 0.0 gm, Polyunsat Fat 1.2 gm, Monounsat Fat 1.5 gm, Cholesterol 5 mg), Sodium 336 mg, Total Carbohydrate 39 gm, Dietary Fiber 2 gm, Sugars 24 gm, Protein 6 gm

Root Beer Cake

Charlotte Hill
Rapid City, SD

Makes 16 servings
Serving size is 3″ x 2″ rectangle

Prep Time: 20-25 minutes
Baking Time: 30-35 minutes
Cooling Time: 1 hour

½ cup sugar blend for baking (Splenda)
1 Tbsp. butter, softened
3 Tbsp. canola oil
½ tsp. vanilla
2 eggs
2 cups flour
1 Tbsp. baking powder
1 tsp. salt
⅔ cup root beer

Frosting:
1 Tbsp. butter, softened
1 Tbsp. canola oil
⅛ tsp. salt
2 cups confectioners sugar
2-4 Tbsp. fat-free milk
⅓ cup root beer, chilled

1. In a large electric mixer bowl, combine all cake ingredients and blend on low speed. Increase to medium speed and beat for another 3 minutes.
2. Pour into a greased and floured 8 x 12 baking pan and bake at 375° for 30-35 minutes.
3. To make frosting, beat together butter, canola oil, salt, confectioners sugar, and milk in a medium-sized bowl. Blend in enough root beer to make frosting spreadable.
4. Spread on cooled cake.

Exchange List Values:
Carbohydrate 2.0, Fat 1.0

Basic Nutritional Values:
Calories 193 (Calories from Fat 52), Total Fat 6 gm (Saturated Fat 1.4 gm, Trans Fat 0.0 gm, Polyunsat Fat 1.2 gm, Monounsat Fat 2.7 gm, Cholesterol 30 mg), Sodium 255 mg, Total Carbohydrate 33 gm, Dietary Fiber 0 gm, Sugars 20 gm, Protein 2 gm

Pies

Apple Cream Pie

Barb Stutzman, Carlock, IL

Makes 10 servings
Serving size is 1 slice

Prep Time: 30 minutes
Baking Time: 60-65 minutes

Filling:
1 cup fat-free half-and-half
½ cup, plus 2 Tbsp., sugar
   blend for baking (Splenda)
⅓ cup flour, or more
1 tsp. vanilla
dash of salt
4 cups baking apples,
   sliced thin
unbaked 9″ pie shell (see
   recipe on page 245)

Topping:
½ cup flour
2½ Tbsp. sugar blend for
   baking (Splenda)
2 tsp. butter, cut in small
   pieces
2 tsp. canola oil
2 tsp. apple juice
cinnamon

1. Combine filling ingredients, except apples, in a mixing bowl.
2. Place apples in the unbaked pie shell. Pour filling mixture over apples.
3. To make topping, blend flour, sugar blend, butter, canola oil, and apple juice together with a pastry blender until crumbs form.

4. Sprinkle crumbs over apples. Sprinkle cinnamon over apples to taste.
5. Bake at 450° for 15 minutes. Reduce heat to 350°. Bake an additional 45-50 minutes.

Exchange List Values:
Carbohydrate 2.5, Fat 1.0

Basic Nutritional Values:
Calories 225 (Calories from Fat 49), Total Fat 5 gm (Saturated Fat 1.3 gm, Trans Fat 0.3 gm, Polyunsat Fat 1.1 gm, Monounsat Fat 2.2 gm, Cholesterol 4 mg), Sodium 68 mg, Total Carbohydrate 41 gm, Dietary Fiber 2 gm, Sugars 23 gm, Protein 3 gm

Variation: Substitute 1 cup sour cream for the half-and-half in the filling.
—Jeanne Heyerly, Chenoa, IL

Greatest Apple Pie

Lynette Nisly, Lancaster, PA

Makes 10 servings
Serving size is 1 slice

Prep Time: 30 minutes
Baking Time: 45-55 minutes

Filling:
½ cup sugar blend for
   baking (Splenda)
2 Tbsp. flour
1 tsp. cinnamon
dash of nutmeg
dash of salt
6 cups peeled and sliced
   apples (Rome is my
   favorite)
unbaked 9″ pie shell (see
   recipe on page 245)

Crumb Topping:
2 Tbsp. brown sugar blend
   (Splenda)
2 Tbsp. sugar blend for
   baking (Splenda)
¾ cup flour
1½ Tbsp. solid zero-trans-
   fat shortening
2 tsp. apple juice

1. To prepare filling, combine sugar blend, flour, cinnamon, nutmeg, and salt in a large bowl.
2. Add sliced apples and mix well. Put apple mixture in unbaked pie crust.
3. To prepare topping, combine sugar blends and flour in a medium-sized bowl.
4. Cut in shortening with a pastry blender or fork until crumbly. Add apple juice and mix until the crumbles are moistened Sprinkle over apples.
5. Bake at 400° for 45-55 minutes.

Exchange List Values:
Carbohydrate 2.5, Fat 1.0

Basic Nutritional Values:
Calories 219 (Calories from Fat 48), Total Fat 5 gm (Saturated Fat 1.1 gm, Trans Fat 0.3 gm, Polyunsat Fat 1.5 gm, Monounsat Fat 2.3 gm, Cholesterol 0 mg), Sodium 39 mg, Total Carbohydrate 41 gm, Dietary Fiber 2 gm, Sugars 24 gm, Protein 2 gm

When my husband and I were dating, I made this pie for him and he loved it. After that, he decided to think more seriously about our future together. He has convinced our children that I make the best apple pie, which they are not shy about stating whenever apple pie is served.

Harvest Cranberry Apple Pie

Janelle Reitz, Lancaster, PA

Makes 10 servings
Serving size is 1 slice

Prep Time: 20 minutes
Baking Time: 55-60 minutes

½ cup sugar blend for
  baking (Splenda)
2 Tbsp. cornstarch
½ tsp. allspice
2 tsp. cinnamon
4 large tart baking apples,
  pared, cored, and sliced
1 cup fresh, whole
  cranberries*
½ cup chopped walnuts
unbaked 9" pie shell (see
  recipe on page 245)
1½ tsp. butter, cut into
  pieces

1. In a large mixing
bowl, combine sugar blend,
cornstarch, allspice, and
cinnamon.
2. Add apples, cranberries,
and nuts. (*Frozen cranberries also work in this pie.
Allow them to thaw before
stirring them into the mix.)
Toss to coat.
3. Fill unbaked pie crust
with fruit mixture and dot
with butter.
4. Bake at 400° for 55-60
minutes, or until filling is
bubbly. (You may need to
loosely cover the edges of
the crust with foil to prevent
it from burning during the
last 30 minutes of the baking
time.)

Exchange List Values:
Carbohydrate 2.0, Fat 1.5

Basic Nutritional Values:
Calories 201 (Calories from Fat 72),
Total Fat 8 gm (Saturated Fat 1.3
gm, Trans Fat 0.3 gm, Polyunsat
Fat 3.7 gm, Monounsat Fat 2.2 gm,
Cholesterol 2 mg), Sodium 42 mg,
Total Carbohydrate 32 gm, Dietary
Fiber 3 gm, Sugars 20 gm, Protein 2 gm

Crumb-Topped Blueberry Pie

Dawn Shertzer
Mechanicsburg, PA

Makes 10 servings
Serving size is 1 slice

Prep Time: 15-20 minutes
Baking Time: 25 minutes
Cooling/Chilling Time: 4 hours

1 cup water, *divided*
½ cup sugar blend for
  baking (Splenda)
3 Tbsp. cornstarch
1 pint blueberries
8" pie crust, unbaked (see
  recipe on page 245)
¾ cup flour
¼ cup dry quick *or* rolled
  oats
2 Tbsp. sugar blend for
  baking (Splenda)
2 Tbsp. brown sugar blend
  (Splenda)
2 tsp. butter, at room
  temperature
1 Tbsp. canola oil
1½ Tbsp. apple juice

1. Pour ¾ cup water into
saucepan. Add ½ cup sugar
blend for baking.

2. Heat over high heat,
stirring until sugar blend is
dissolved.
3. Pour remaining ¼ cup
water into a small bowl.
Add cornstarch. Whisk until
smooth. Add to sugar water.
4. Bring to a boil while stirring until thick and bubbly.
5. Add blueberries. Stir
until heated through.
6. Pour into crust.
7. Combine flour, oats,
and sugar blends in a mixing
bowl. With a pastry cutter,
blend oil and butter into the
dry topping until crumbly.
Pour in apple juice and stir
with a fork until the mixture
is evenly moistened.
8. Top pie with crumb
topping.
9. Bake at 425° for 25
minutes.
10. Cool to room tem-
perature, and then refrigerate
3 hours to allow filling to set.

Exchange List Values:
Starch 2.0, Fat 0.5

Basic Nutritional Values:
Calories 201 (Calories from Fat 35),
Total Fat 4 gm (Saturated Fat 1.5
gm, Trans Fat 0.0 gm, Polyunsat
Fat 0.9 gm, Monounsat Fat 1.0 gm,
Cholesterol 11 mg), Sodium 362 mg,
Total Carbohydrate 31 gm, Dietary
Fiber 3 gm, Sugars 4 gm, Protein 8 gm

Tips:
  *1. You can use this recipe for
other fruits, also.*
  *2. If the sugar syrup does not
thicken as much as you like,
add more cornstarch.*

Cranberry Pie

Sandra Chang
Derwood, MD

Makes 10 servings
Serving size is 1 slice

Prep Time: 20 minutes
Baking Time: 35-40 minutes

2 cups fresh cranberries
½ cup walnuts, chopped
¾ cup sugar blend for baking (Splenda), *divided*
2 tsp. unsalted butter, melted
1⅓ Tbsp. canola oil
1 cup flour
1 tsp. almond extract
2 eggs, slightly beaten

1. Pour cranberries and nuts into a greased 10″ pie pan.
2. Sprinkle with 6 Tbsp. sugar blend.
3. In a mixing bowl, add remaining 6 Tbsp. sugar blend to butter and canola oil and blend together thoroughly.
4. Stir in flour and almond extract and mix together.
5. Add eggs and blend well.
6. Pour over cranberries and nuts.
7. Bake at 325° for 35 to 40 minutes.

Exchange List Values:
Carbohydrate 2.0, Fat 1.0

Basic Nutritional Values:
Calories 191 (Calories from Fat 69), Total Fat 8 gm (Saturated Fat 1.4 gm, Trans Fat 0.0 gm, Polyunsat Fat 3.6 gm, Monounsat Fat 2.2 gm, Cholesterol 44 mg), Sodium 15 mg, Total Carbohydrate 27 gm, Dietary Fiber 2 gm, Sugars 17 gm, Protein 4 gm

Fruit and Cream Pie

Mary Jones
Marengo, OH

Makes 8 servings
Serving size is 1 slice

Prep Time: 15 minutes
Chilling Time: 4 hours

half an 8-oz. pkg. fat-free cream cheese, at room temperature
½ cup confectioners sugar
½ cup frozen fat-free whipped topping, thawed
9″ store-bought, reduced-fat graham cracker crust
0.35-oz. pkg. sugar-free gelatin (flavor to match fruit)
1-oz. box fat-free, sugar-free instant vanilla pudding
1¼ cups water
2 cups sliced fruit of your choice—strawberries, peaches, etc.
8 Tbsp. fat-free whipped topping

1. Mix together cream cheese and confectioners sugar until smooth.
2. Fold in whipped topping. Spread in crust. Refrigerate.
3. In saucepan, combine gelatin, pudding mix, and water until smooth. Stir constantly over medium heat until mixture comes to a boil. Remove from heat.

4. Stir in fruit. Spoon over cream-cheese layer.
5. Refrigerate 4 hours. Garnish with whipped topping just before serving.

Exchange List Values:
Carbohydrate 2.0, Fat 0.5

Basic Nutritional Values:
Calories 187 (Calories from Fat 33), Total Fat 4 gm (Saturated Fat 1.0 gm, Trans Fat 1.5 gm, Polyunsat Fat 0.6 gm, Monounsat Fat 1.0 gm, Cholesterol 2 mg), Sodium 366 mg, Total Carbohydrate 33 gm, Dietary Fiber 1 gm, Sugars 17 gm, Protein 3 gm

A Tip —

When flying, keep your medications and glucose meter with you in your carry-on luggage so there's no chance of things being lost.

Easy Peach Cream Pie

Doyle Rounds, Bridgewater, VA

Makes 8 servings
Serving size is 1 slice

Prep Time: 15 minutes if using
a bought pie crust; 30 minutes
if making your own
Baking Time: 40-50 minutes

3 cups peeled and sliced fresh peaches
9″ unbaked pie shell (see recipe on page 245)
2 eggs
½ cup sugar blend for baking (Splenda)
¼ cup flour
dash of salt
1 cup fat-free half-and-half
1 tsp. vanilla extract
cinnamon, *optional*

1. Fill pie shell with peaches.
2. In mixing bowl, beat eggs slightly. Blend in sugar blend, flour, and salt.
3. Stir half-and-half and vanilla into sugar/flour mixture. Blend well and pour over peaches.
4. Sprinkle with cinnamon if you wish.
5. Bake at 375° for 40-50 minutes, or until center shakes slightly when moved. Don't over-bake.
6. Serve warm. For a firmer pie, chill before serving. Refrigerate leftovers.

Exchange List Values:
Carbohydrate 2.5, Fat 0.5

Basic Nutritional Values:
Calories 209 (Calories from Fat 53), Total Fat 6 gm (Saturated Fat 1.3 gm, Trans Fat 0.4 gm, Polyunsat Fat 1.2 gm, Monounsat Fat 2.4 gm, Cholesterol 55 mg), Sodium 95 mg, Total Carbohydrate 34 gm, Dietary Fiber 1 gm, Sugars 20 gm, Protein 4 gm

Tips:
1. If the pie crust can't accommodate all the filling, put the extra in a small greased baking dish. Bake it along with the pie until the filling is set.
2. To prevent the crust edges from becoming too brown, cover the edges with foil after baking 30 minutes.

Fresh Peach Pie

Lavon Martins, Postville, IA
Darlene E. Miller
South Hutchinson, KS

Makes 8 servings
Serving size is 1 slice

Prep Time: 15 minutes
Cooking Time: 10 minutes
Chilling Time: 30 minutes

6 Tbsp. sugar blend for baking (Splenda)
½ tsp. salt
1 cup water
3 Tbsp. cornstarch
2 Tbsp. white corn syrup
0.35-oz. pkg. sugar-free peach gelatin
4-6 peaches
9″ baked pie crust (see recipe on page 245)

1. In a saucepan, combine sugar blend, salt, water, cornstarch, and syrup. Cook until

clear, stirring constantly.
2. Add gelatin and stir until dissolved. Cool in fridge for 30 minutes.
3. Slice peaches. Place in pie crust.
4. Pour filling over peaches. Chill until ready to serve.
5. Serve with whipped cream or ice cream.

Exchange List Values:
Carbohydrate 2.0, Fat 0.5

Basic Nutritional Values:
Calories 173 (Calories from Fat 38), Total Fat 4 gm (Saturated Fat 0.8 gm, Trans Fat 0.4 gm, Polyunsat Fat 1.0 gm, Monounsat Fat 1.9 gm, Cholesterol 0 mg), Sodium 206 mg, Total Carbohydrate 33 gm, Dietary Fiber 1 gm, Sugars 18 gm, Protein 2 gm

Variation: Replace the peach gelatin with strawberry gelatin. And use 1 qt. strawberries, fresh or frozen, instead of the peaches.
—**June S. Groff**, Denver, PA

Hawaiian Delight Pie

Freda Imler, Eldon, MO
Josephine Earle
Citronelle, AL

Makes 10 servings
Serving size is 1 slice

Prep Time: 10 minutes
Baking Time: 50 minutes

1 cup egg substitute
½ cup sugar blend for baking (Splenda)

1 cup grated *or* flaked coconut
1 cup drained crushed pineapple
pinch of salt
8″ reduced-fat graham cracker pie crust

1. Mix first 5 ingredients in a mixing bowl.
2. Pour into unbaked pie shell.
3. Bake at 350° for 10 minutes, and then at 325° for 40 minutes, or until lightly browned and knife inserted in middle comes out clean.

Exchange List Values:
Carbohydrate 1.5, Fat 1.0

Basic Nutritional Values:
Calories 157 (Calories from Fat 36), Total Fat 4 gm (Saturated Fat 1.8 gm, Trans Fat 1.2 gm, Polyunsat Fat 0.4 gm, Monounsat Fat 0.9 gm, Cholesterol 0 mg), Sodium 136 mg, Total Carbohydrate 26 gm, Dietary Fiber 1 gm, Sugars 18 gm, Protein 3 gm

Tip: If you use a foil pie pan, fill it, and then place it on a cookie sheet to bake. That will help the bottom crust to bake more fully.
—Jeanne Heyerly
Chenoa, IL

Mile-High Strawberry Pie
Violette Harris Denney
Carrolton, GA

Makes 12 servings
Serving size is 1 slice

Prep Time: 20-25 minutes
Freezing Time: 4 hours, or overnight

10-oz. pkg. frozen, unsweetened strawberries, chopped, but not thawed
2 egg whites
1 cup granular Splenda
2 Tbsp. lemon juice
8-oz. carton frozen fat-free whipped topping, thawed
9″ store-bought, reduced-fat graham cracker pie crust

1. Combine strawberries, egg whites, granular sweetener, and lemon juice in an electric mixer. Beat at high speed until very stiff, 10-15 minutes.
2. Fold in whipped topping.
3. Pile into crust. Freeze at least 3-4 hours.
4. Remove from freezer 30 minutes before serving.

Exchange List Values:
Carbohydrate 1.5

Basic Nutritional Values:
Calories 118 (Calories from Fat 22), Total Fat 2 gm (Saturated Fat 0.7 gm, Trans Fat 1.0 gm, Polyunsat Fat 0.4 gm, Monounsat Fat 0.7 gm, Cholesterol 0 mg), Sodium 88 mg, Total Carbohydrate 21 gm, Dietary Fiber 1 gm, Sugars 9 gm, Protein 1 gm

Frozen Strawberry Pie
Betty Salch, Bloomington, IL

Makes 16 servings (8 per pie)
Serving size is 1 slice

Prep Time: 20 minutes
Freezing Time: 3-4 hours

8-oz. pkg. fat-free cream cheese, at room temperature
1 cup granular Splenda
1 tsp. vanilla
4 cups chopped fresh strawberries
12-oz. carton frozen fat-free whipped topping, thawed
½ cup chopped pecans, toasted
2 9″ chocolate crumb crusts

1. In a large bowl, beat the cream cheese, sweetener, and vanilla until smooth.
2. Beat in the strawberries. Fold in whipped topping and pecans.
3. Pour mixture into crusts. Cover and freeze for 3-4 hours, or until firm.
4. Remove from the freezer 15-20 minutes before serving.

Exchange List Values:
Carbohydrate 2.0, Fat 1.5

Basic Nutritional Values:
Calories 193 (Calories from Fat 65), Total Fat 7 gm (Saturated Fat 1.2 gm, Trans Fat 2.0 gm, Polyunsat Fat 1.3 gm, Monounsat Fat 2.5 gm, Cholesterol 2 mg), Sodium 222 mg, Total Carbohydrate 27 gm, Dietary Fiber 2 gm, Sugars 12 gm, Protein 4 gm

Gingerberry Lattice Pie

Jan Sams, Lancaster, PA

Makes 10 servings
Serving size is 1 slice

Prep Time: *30 minutes*
Baking Time: *50 minutes*

15¼-oz. can crushed
  pineapple, juice reserved
3 cups fresh *or* frozen
  cranberries
½ cup, plus 2 Tbsp.,
  sugar blend for baking
  (Splenda)
¼ cup cornstarch
1-2 Tbsp. chopped
  crystallized ginger, *or*
  ½ tsp. ground ginger
dough for 2 9" pie crusts
  (see recipe on page 245)

1. Drain pineapple, reserving juice.
2. Add water to pineapple juice to make 1 cup.
3. In a medium saucepan, combine cranberries and pineapple juice. Bring to a boil. Reduce heat. Simmer, uncovered, for 5 minutes, or until cranberries pop.
4. In a small bowl, combine sugar blend and cornstarch. Stir into cranberries. Cook until bubbly, stirring constantly. Remove from heat.
5. Stir in drained pineapple and ginger.
6. Fit half the pie dough into a 9" pie plate.
7. Pour filling into pie crust. If there's more filling than will fit in the crust, grease a small baking dish and place the extra filling in it. Bake it alongside the pie.
8. Cut strips from the other half of the pie dough to make a lattice. Arrange the strips over the filling. Cover the lattice-topped pie with foil.
9. Bake at 375° for 25 minutes. Remove foil. Bake an additional 20-25 minutes until golden brown.

Exchange List Values:
Carbohydrate 3.0, Fat 0.5

Basic Nutritional Values:
Calories 237 (Calories from Fat 59), Total Fat 7 gm (Saturated Fat 1.2 gm, Trans Fat 0.6 gm, Polyunsat Fat 1.6 gm, Monounsat Fat 3.0 gm, Cholesterol 0 mg), Sodium 76 mg, Total Carbohydrate 43 gm, Dietary Fiber 2 gm, Sugars 22 gm, Protein 2 gm

Lemon Sour Cream Pie

Lilli Peters, Dodge City, KS

Makes 8 servings
Serving size is 1 slice

Prep Time: *15 minutes*
Cooking Time: *20-30 minutes*
Cooling Time: *1 hour*

⅓ cup sugar blend for
  baking (Splenda)
3½ Tbsp. cornstarch
1 Tbsp. finely grated
  lemon rind (reserve juice
  and several slices)
½ cup fresh lemon juice
2 egg yolks, slightly beaten
1 cup fat-free milk
1 cup fat-free sour cream
9" deep baked pie shell
  (see recipe on page 245)
2 cups fat-free whipped
  topping
lemon twists for garnish

1. In a heavy saucepan, combine sugar blend, cornstarch, lemon rind, lemon juice, egg yolks, and milk. Cook over medium heat until thickened. Stir frequently.
2. Cool to room temperature.
3. Stir sour cream into pie filling. Pour into pie shell.
4. Cover with whipped topping. Garnish with lemon twists.
5. Refrigerate until ready to serve.

Exchange List Values:
Carbohydrate 2.5, Fat 1.0

Basic Nutritional Values:
Calories 226 (Calories from Fat 49), Total Fat 5 gm (Saturated Fat 1.3 gm, Trans Fat 0.4 gm, Polyunsat Fat 1.2 gm, Monounsat Fat 2.4 gm, Cholesterol 57 mg), Sodium 92 mg, Total Carbohydrate 35 gm, Dietary Fiber 0 gm, Sugars 17 gm, Protein 5 gm

A Tip —

An occasional drink can actually be good for your health! Limit daily drinks to two per day for men and one for women.

Microwave Lemon Pie

Jean Butzer, Batavia, NY

Makes 10 servings
Serving size is 1 slice

Prep Time: 20 minutes
Cooking Time: 10-12 minutes
Cooling Time: 2 hours

baked 9" pie shell (see
  recipe on page 245)
½ cup sugar blend for
  baking (Splenda)
4 Tbsp. cornstarch
¼ tsp. salt
1 cup water, *divided*
3 egg yolks, slightly beaten
1 tsp. butter, at room
  temperature
⅓ cup lemon juice
10 Tbsp. fat-free whipped
  topping

1. Combine sugar blend,
cornstarch, salt, and ¼ cup
water in a 1½-qt. microwavable casserole.

2. Microwave remaining
¾ cup water on high for 2-3
minutes until boiling. Stir
into sugar mixture. Microwave on high 4-6 minutes
until very thick. Stir every
2 minutes.

3. In a separate bowl, add
a little hot mixture into egg
yolks. Then blend yolks well
into sugar mixture. Microwave on high 1 minute.

4. Stir in butter. Then add
lemon juice. Cool slightly and
turn into pie shell.

5. Serve cooled, topped
with whipped topping.

Exchange List Values:
Carbohydrate 2.0, Fat 1.0

Basic Nutritional Values:
Calories 186 (Calories from Fat 47),
Total Fat 5 gm (Saturated Fat 1.4
gm, Trans Fat 0.3 gm, Polyunsat
Fat 1.0 gm, Monounsat Fat 2.2 gm,
Cholesterol 65 mg), Sodium 106 mg,
Total Carbohydrate 33 gm, Dietary
Fiber 0 gm, Sugars 21 gm, Protein 2 gm

Tips:
*1. To make a large deep-dish
pie, you can double this recipe.*
*2. This is also good served in
custard cups as a pudding with
no crust.*
*3. The microwave is a
wonderful way to make the
lemon filling—no need to worry
about it sticking to the bottom
of the pan as it thickens.*

Key Lime Pie

Norma I. Gehman
Ephrata, PA

Makes 10 servings
Serving size is 1 slice

Prep Time: 20 minutes
Baking Time: 25-28 minutes
**Chilling Time: 8 hours,
  or overnight**

1½ cups graham cracker
  crumbs
¼ cup firmly packed
  brown sugar blend
  (Splenda)
1 Tbsp. butter, melted
3 Tbsp. canola oil
14-oz. can fat-free
  sweetened condensed
  milk

½ cup key lime juice
2 egg whites
¼ tsp. cream of tartar
2 Tbsp. sugar

1. Combine first 4 ingredients. Press into a 10" pie pan.

2. Bake at 350° for 10 minutes, or until lightly browned.
Cool.

3. In a mixing bowl, stir
milk and lime juice together
until blended. Pour into crust.

4. In a clean mixing bowl,
beat egg whites with cream
of tartar at high speed until
foamy.

5. Gradually beat sugar
into the egg whites until
the sugar dissolves and soft
peaks are formed, about 2-4
minutes.

6. Spread egg-white
meringue over filling. Bake at
325° for 25-28 minutes.

7. Chill 8 hours, or overnight.

Exchange List Values:
Carbohydrate 3.0, Fat 1.0

Basic Nutritional Values:
Calories 250 (Calories from Fat 60),
Total Fat 7 gm (Saturated Fat 1.2
gm, Trans Fat 0.0 gm, Polyunsat
Fat 1.9 gm, Monounsat Fat 4.2 gm,
Cholesterol 3 mg), Sodium 138 mg,
Total Carbohydrate 42 gm, Dietary
Fiber 0 gm, Sugars 34 gm, Protein 5 gm

Pumpkin Pie

Wafi Brandt
Manheim, PA

Makes 8 servings
Serving size is 1 slice

Prep Time: 15-20 minutes
Baking Time: 40-50 minutes

9″ unbaked pie shell (see
  recipe on page 245)
2 eggs
¼ cup brown sugar blend
  (Splenda)
2½ Tbsp. sugar blend for
  baking (Splenda)
¼ tsp. salt
1¼ tsp. cinnamon
¼ tsp. ginger
¼ tsp. nutmeg
dash of allspice
⅔ tsp. vanilla
1⅓ cups pumpkin
1⅓ cups milk
2 tsp. cornstarch

1. Beat eggs in a large mixing bowl. Add all remaining
ingredients as listed. Whisk
until very smooth.
2. Pour into unbaked pie
shell.
3. Bake at 350° for 40-50
minutes, until set and browned.

Exchange List Values:
Carbohydrate 2.0, Fat 1.0

Basic Nutritional Values:
Calories 179 (Calories from Fat 49),
Total Fat 5 gm (Saturated Fat 1.3
gm, Trans Fat 0.4 gm, Polyunsat
Fat 1.1 gm, Monounsat Fat 2.4 gm,
Cholesterol 54 mg), Sodium 158 mg,
Total Carbohydrate 27 gm, Dietary
Fiber 2 gm, Sugars 14 gm, Protein 4 gm

Sour Cream Raisin Pie

Kay Magruder
Seminole, OK

Makes 10 servings
Serving size is 1 slice

Prep Time: 20 minutes
Cooking/Baking Time:
  30 minutes
Cooling Time: 45-60 minutes

1 cup sour cream
½ cup raisins
½ cup sugar blend for
  baking (Splenda)
¼ tsp. ground cloves
½ tsp. cinnamon
dash of salt
4 eggs, separated and
  divided
2 Tbsp. sugar
9″ baked pie crust, cooled
  (see recipe on page 245)

1. In a medium-sized
saucepan, blend together
sour cream, raisins, ½ cup
sugar blend, spices, salt, 1
egg white, and 4 egg yolks.
(Reserve the 3 other whites
for the meringue.) Cook over
low heat until raisins plump
and are tender.
2. Let pie filling and crust
cool completely before pouring the filling into the crust.
3. Prepare the meringue
topping by beating the
3 reserved egg whites until
stiff.

4. Fold in 2 Tbsp. sugar,
beating gently until the sugar
is incorporated. Then increase
beating to top speed until
meringue turns glossy and
stiff peaks form.
5. Pile meringue on cooled
pie filling in crust. Bake at
350° for about 12 minutes,
until golden brown.

Exchange List Values:
Carbohydrate 2.0, Fat 1.0

Basic Nutritional Values:
Calories 184 (Calories from Fat 48),
Total Fat 5 gm (Saturated Fat 1.2
gm, Trans Fat 0.3 gm, Polyunsat
Fat 1.1 gm, Monounsat Fat 2.3 gm,
Cholesterol 87 mg), Sodium 79 mg,
Total Carbohydrate 27 gm, Dietary
Fiber 1 gm, Sugars 18 gm, Protein 5 gm

A Tip —

  Drinking a sports drink
while you're exercising is
fine, but be sure to watch
the carbohydrate content.

White Christmas Pie
Carolyn Bell
Quinter, KS

Makes 16 servings (8 per pie)
Serving size is 1 slice

Prep Time: 30 minutes
Chilling Time: 1-2 hours

14-oz. can fat-free
  sweetened condensed
  milk
⅓ cup lemon juice
⅓ cup sweetened coconut,
  grated
½ cup chopped pecans
16-oz. can crushed
  pineapples, drained
½ tsp. pineapple flavoring
12-oz. carton fat-free
  whipped topping
2 8″ baked pie shells (see
  next recipe)

1. In a large mixing bowl,
combine milk, lemon juice,
coconut, pecans, pineapple,
and pineapple flavoring.
2. Fold in whipped topping.
Pour into pie shells. Chill at
least 1 hour before serving.

Exchange List Values:
Carbohydrate 2.5, Fat 1.0

Basic Nutritional Values:
Calories 231 (Calories from Fat 64),
Total Fat 7 gm (Saturated Fat 1.4
gm, Trans Fat 0.4 gm, Polyunsat
Fat 1.8 gm, Monounsat Fat 4.0 gm,
Cholesterol 0 mg), Sodium 89 mg,
Total Carbohydrate 37 gm, Dietary
Fiber 1 gm, Sugars 21 gm, Protein 3 gm

Basic Pie Crust
Graham Kerr
from his book,
Charting a Course to Wellness

Makes 1 8″ or 9″ pie crust
Serving size is 1 slice

Prep Time: 10 minutes
Baking Time: 10-12 minutes

¾ cup cake flour
½ tsp. sugar
¹⁄₁₆ tsp. salt
1 Tbsp. non-aromatic olive
  oil
2 Tbsp. hard margarine
  (65% vegetable oil
  variety), frozen for 15
  minutes
½ tsp. vinegar
2 Tbsp. ice water

1. In a mixing bowl, stir
together cake flour, sugar,
and salt.
2. Cut in olive oil and hard
margarine with a pastry
cutter or two knives until
crumbly.
3. Sprinkle vinegar and
ice water over dough. Toss
with a fork until the dough is
moistened and forms a ball.
4. Roll out on a lightly
floured surface.
5. Fold dough gently
in half, without creasing.
Then fold in half again, also
without creasing. Lift into pie
plate and unfold, patting it
into place and crimping the
edges between your thumb
and forefinger.

6. If your recipe calls for
a baked crust, jag the crust
at several places over the
bottom and sides. Bake at
400° for 10-12 minutes, until
lightly browned.

Exchange List Values:
Starch 0.5, Fat 1.0

Basic Nutritional Values:
Calories 82 (Calories from Fat 36),
Total Fat 4 gm (Saturated Fat 0.7
gm, Trans Fat 0.4 gm, Polyunsat
Fat 1.0 gm, Monounsat Fat 1.9 gm,
Cholesterol 0 mg), Sodium 45 mg,
Total Carbohydrate 10 gm, Dietary
Fiber 0 gm, Sugars 0 gm, Protein 1 gm

Snacks, Candies and Beverages

Sugared Almonds and Pecans

Linda Hartzler, Minonk, IL

Makes 28 servings
Serving size is ¼ cup

Prep Time: 15 minutes
Baking Time: 1 hour

1 egg white
1 Tbsp. water
1-2 tsp. cinnamon, according
    to your taste preference
1 tsp. vanilla
½ cup sugar blend for
    baking (Splenda)
1 lb. almonds and/or pecans

1. In a large bowl, beat together egg white and water until fluffy.
2. Stir in cinnamon, vanilla, sugar blend, and nuts.
3. Spread in a single layer on a baking sheet with sides.
4. Bake at 200° for 1 hour, stirring every 15 minutes.
5. Cool completely before storing.

Exchange List Values:
Carbohydrate 0.5, Fat 2.0

Basic Nutritional Values:
Calories 121 (Calories from Fat 93), Total Fat 10 gm (Saturated Fat 0.8 gm, Trans Fat 0.0 gm, Polyunsat Fat 2.7 gm, Monounsat Fat 6.3 gm, Cholesterol 0 mg), Sodium 2 mg, Total Carbohydrate 6 gm, Dietary Fiber 2 gm, Sugars 4 gm, Protein 3 gm

Pretzel Treat

Shelia Heil, Lancaster, PA

Makes 50 pretzel treats
Serving size is 1 pretzel treat

Prep Time: 10 minutes per
**   8-oz. bag**
Baking Time: 4-6 minutes per
**   cookie sheet**

50 Hershey Kisses
50 waffle-shaped pretzels
50 chocolate M&Ms

1. Unwrap Hershey Kisses.
2. Preheat oven to 170°.
3. Place pretzels in a single layer on a baking sheet.
4. Top each pretzel with

1 Hershey Kiss.
5. Bake for 4-6 minutes, until chocolate feels soft when touched.
6. Remove from oven. Quickly press an M&M candy into the center of each Hershey Kiss.
7. Allow to cool before storing.
8. Refrigerate if necessary.

Exchange List Values:
Carbohydrate 0.5, Fat 0.5

Basic Nutritional Values:
Calories 46 (Calories from Fat 15), Total Fat 2 gm (Saturated Fat 0.9 gm, Trans Fat 0.0 gm, Polyunsat Fat 0.2 gm, Monounsat Fat 0.3 gm, Cholesterol 1 mg), Sodium 91 mg, Total Carbohydrate 7 gm, Dietary Fiber 0 gm, Sugars 3 gm, Protein 1 gm

Tips:
1. Use green and red M&Ms for Christmas.
2. Use multi-colored M&Ms for birthdays.
3. This is a good activity for children or senior adults who need supervision!
4. To share as gifts, place handfuls of these pretzel treats into clear or colored plastic wrap and tie with colorful ribbon.

Cheesy Pretzels

Kim Jensen
Thornton, CO

Makes 16 pretzels
Serving size is 1 pretzel

Prep Time: 10-15 minutes
Baking Time: 20 minutes

1½ cups flour
⅔ cup fat-free milk
½ cup reduced-fat cheddar
  cheese, shredded
2 Tbsp. butter
2 tsp. baking powder
1 tsp. sugar
1 tsp. salt
1 egg, beaten
2 tsp. kosher salt

1. In a large bowl, mix the first 7 ingredients with a fork until blended.
2. Divide dough into 16 equal pieces. With your hands, roll each portion into a rope about 12-14″ long. Lay them on greased cookie sheets, forming each into a pretzel shape as you do so.
3. Brush each pretzel lightly with beaten egg and sprinkle with salt.
4. Bake at 400° for 20 minutes, or until golden brown.

Exchange List Values:
Starch 0.5, Fat 0.5

Basic Nutritional Values:
Calories 72 (Calories from Fat 22), Total Fat 2 gm (Saturated Fat 1.4 gm, Trans Fat 0.0 gm, Polyunsat Fat 0.2 gm, Monounsat Fat 0.7 gm, Cholesterol 19 mg), Sodium 473 mg, Total Carbohydrate 10 gm, Dietary Fiber 0 gm, Sugars 1 gm, Protein 3 gm

Tip: You can substitute onion or garlic salt for the kosher salt.

Caramel Popcorn

Janelle Reitz
Lancaster, PA
Starla A. Diem
Denmark, SC

Makes 12 1-cup servings
Serving size is 1 cup

Prep Time: 10 minutes
Cooking/Baking Time:
75-80 minutes
Cooling Time: 1 hour

12 cups popped popcorn,
  unsalted, air-popped
½ cup brown sugar blend
  (Splenda)
¼ cup light corn syrup
2 Tbsp. butter
¼ tsp. salt
¼ tsp. baking soda
¼ tsp. vanilla

1. Place popped popcorn in two 9 x 13 greased baking pans. Preheat oven to 250°.
2. Combine brown sugar blend, corn syrup, butter, and salt in a heavy saucepan.
3. Cook 7-10 minutes, stirring constantly, bringing mixture to a boil over medium heat. Boil 4 minutes. Do not stir.
4. Remove from heat. Add baking soda and vanilla. Pour over popcorn, stirring to coat evenly.
5. Bake for 1 hour, stirring every 15 minutes.

6. Cool on waxed paper. Break apart into pieces. Store in tightly-covered container.

Exchange List Values:
Carbohydrate 1.5

Basic Nutritional Values:
Calories 107 (Calories from Fat 20), Total Fat 2 gm (Saturated Fat 1.3 gm, Trans Fat 0.0 gm, Polyunsat Fat 0.2 gm, Monounsat Fat 0.6 gm, Cholesterol 5 mg), Sodium 98 mg, Total Carbohydrate 19 gm, Dietary Fiber 1 gm, Sugars 12 gm, Protein 1 gm

Variaton: For a real treat, add 1½ cups broken cashews to the popcorn in Step 1.
—Dawn Derstine
Souderton, PA

A Tip —

Check your blood sugar as soon as you get up, before you do anything else, and then treat as needed. Starting the day with a normal blood sugar level will make it easier to keep your level under control throughout the day.

Sweet Snack Mix

Ruth Ann Penner
Hillsboro, KS

Makes 80 servings
Serving size is ¼ cup

Prep Time: 10 minutes
Cooking Time: 2-5 minutes
Cooling Time: 2-3 hours

14 cups popped popcorn, unsalted, air-popped
3 cups crisp rice cereal
2 cups salted peanuts
½ lb. white almond bark
1½ Tbsp. creamy peanut butter

1. In a large bowl, combine popped popcorn, cereal, and peanuts.
2. Place bark and peanut butter in a microwave-safe bowl. Heat on high for 1 minute. Stir. Heat on high for 15 seconds. Stir. If the mixture isn't yet melted, continue heating on high for 15-second periods, stirring between each.
3. Pour melted mixture over popcorn mixture, stirring to coat.
4. Spread on waxed paper. Allow to stand for at least 2 hours.
5. Break up and store in an airtight container.

Exchange List Values:
Carbohydrate 0.5, Fat 0.5

Basic Nutritional Values:
Calories 47 (Calories from Fat 26), Total Fat 3 gm (Saturated Fat 1.2 gm, Trans Fat 0.0 gm, Polyunsat

Fat 0.6 gm, Monounsat Fat 1.0 gm, Cholesterol 0 mg), Sodium 43 mg, Total Carbohydrate 5 gm, Dietary Fiber 1 gm, Sugars 2 gm, Protein 1 gm

Tip: Look for the almond bark in the baking section of the grocery store.

Granola Bars

Barbara Kuhns, Millersburg, OH
Kim Stoll, Abbeville, SC
Lydia Stoltzfus, East Earl, PA
Christine Weaver, Reinholds, PA

Makes 40 servings
Serving size is 1 bar

Prep Time: 5-10 minutes
Cooking Time: 5-10 minutes

2 cups (1 pkg.) graham crackers, crushed
5 cups dry quick oats
4½ cups crisp rice cereal
½ cup canola oil
½ cup peanut butter
¾ cup honey
2 10-oz. pkgs. marshmallows
½ cup chocolate M&Ms, frozen
½ cup chocolate chips, frozen

1. In a large bowl, combine crushed graham crackers, dry oats, and crisp rice cereal.
2. In a saucepan, combine canola oil, peanut butter, and honey. Stir frequently, heating until until well mixed.
3. Add marshmallows. Heat until marshmallows are melted, stirring constantly.

4. Pour over dry mixture. Mix well.
5. Add M&Ms and chocolate chips. Mix well.
6. Press onto a greased baking sheet. Cut into 40 pieces.

Exchange List Values:
Carbohydrate 2.0, Fat 1.0

Basic Nutritional Values:
Calories 197 (Calories from Fat 61), Total Fat 7 gm (Saturated Fat 1.4 gm, Trans Fat 0.0 gm, Polyunsat Fat 1.7 gm, Monounsat Fat 3.0 gm, Cholesterol 0 mg), Sodium 79 mg, Total Carbohydrate 33 gm, Dietary Fiber 2 gm, Sugars 21 gm, Protein 3 gm

Variations:
1. Add 1 cup each of any of the following to Step 1: grated coconut, almonds, raisins, other dried fruit.
—**Lori Showalter**
New Hope, VA

2. Add 2 tsp. vanilla to Step 2.
—**Julie Newman**
Sidney, BC

3. Add 1 cup all-bran cereal, ¼ cup sunflower seeds, and ¼ cup sesame seeds to Step 1.
—**Frances Schrag**
Newton, KS
—**Esther Zimmerman**
Ephrata, PA

Salted Peanut Squares

John D. Allen
Rye, CO

Makes 50 servings
Serving size is 1 piece

Prep Time: 5 minutes
Cooking Time: 5 minutes
Chilling Time: 1 hour

16-oz. jar salted peanuts
1½ Tbsp. canola oil
½ 10-oz. pkg. (5 ozs.)
  peanut butter chips
2 cups miniature
  marshmallows
14-oz. can fat-free
  sweetened condensed
  milk

1. Cover the bottom of a greased 9 x 13 baking pan with half the salted peanuts.
2. In a saucepan, melt peanut butter chips in canola oil.
3. Stir in marshmallows and milk. Heat until melted.
4. Pour over peanuts.
5. Top with remaining peanuts.
6. Chill. Cut into 50 equal squares.

Exchange List Values:
Carbohydrate 2.0, Fat 1.0

Basic Nutritional Values:
Calories 187 (Calories from Fat 38), Total Fat 4 gm (Saturated Fat 1.2 gm, Trans Fat 0.3 gm, Polyunsat Fat 0.8 gm, Monounsat Fat 1.7 gm, Cholesterol 20 mg), Sodium 158 mg, Total Carbohydrate 34 gm, Dietary Fiber 0 gm, Sugars 18 gm, Protein 2 gm

Peanut Butter Clusters

Ruth Ann Gingrich
New Holland, PA

Makes 60 pieces
Serving size is 1 piece

Prep Time: 5-10 minutes
Cooking Time: 3-5 minutes
Cooling Time: 1 hour

2 cups light corn syrup
2 cups peanut butter
1 cup sugar blend for
  baking (Splenda)
1 12-oz. box cornflakes, *or*
  12 cups cornflakes

1. Mix corn syrup, peanut butter, and sugar blend in a large saucepan.
2. While stirring constantly over medium heat, bring to a boil.
3. Immediately remove from heat and stir in cornflakes until coated evenly.
4. Drop by spoonfuls onto waxed paper.
5. When fully cooled, store in airtight container, placing a sheet of waxed paper between each layer.

Exchange List Values:
Carbohydrate 1.0, Fat 1.0

Basic Nutritional Values:
Calories 115 (Calories from Fat 41), Total Fat 5 gm (Saturated Fat 0.9 gm, Trans Fat 0.0 gm, Polyunsat Fat 1.3 gm, Monounsat Fat 2.1 gm, Cholesterol 0 mg), Sodium 97 mg, Total Carbohydrate 18 gm, Dietary Fiber 1 gm, Sugars 10 gm, Protein 3 gm

Tip: You must stir constantly in Step 2 so the mixture doesn't burn. As soon as it reaches the boiling point, remove from heat!

Honey Milk Balls

Sherry Goss Lapp
Lancaster, PA

Makes 28 balls
Serving size is 1 ball

Prep Time: 10 minutes

½ cup honey
½ cup peanut butter
1 cup powdered milk
1 cup dry quick oats

1. In a large mixing bowl, mix together honey and peanut butter.
2. Stir in milk and oats, mixing well.
3. Roll mixture into small balls.

Exchange List Values:
Carbohydrate 0.5, Fat 0.5

Basic Nutritional Values:
Calories 66 (Calories from Fat 24), Total Fat 3 gm (Saturated Fat 0.5 gm, Trans Fat 0.0 gm, Polyunsat Fat 0.8 gm, Monounsat Fat 1.2 gm, Cholesterol 0 mg), Sodium 37 mg, Total Carbohydrate 9 gm, Dietary Fiber 1 gm, Sugars 7 gm, Protein 2 gm

This is a great, healthy snack that children can help to make.

Cranberry Clusters

Edwina Stoltzfus
Narvon, PA

Makes 48 clusters
Serving size is 1 cluster

Prep Time: 5-10 minutes
Cooking Time: 2-4 minutes
Standing Time: 1 hour

2 cups (12-oz. pkg.) semi-
  sweet chocolate chips
⅔ cup craisins
⅔ cup peanuts

1. Place chocolate chips
in a microwave-safe bowl.
Microwave at 50% for 1
minute. Stir. Microwave at
50% for 15 seconds. Stir.
Continue microwaving at
50% for 15-second periods,
followed by stirring, until the
chips are melted.
2. Stir in craisins and
peanuts.
3. Drop by small teaspoonfuls onto waxed paper. Let
stand until set.

Exchange List Values:
Carbohydrate 0.5, Fat 0.5

Basic Nutritional Values:
Calories 51 (Calories from Fat 28),
Total Fat 3 gm (Saturated Fat 1.4
gm, Trans Fat 0.0 gm, Polyunsat
Fat 0.4 gm, Monounsat Fat 1.2 gm,
Cholesterol 0 mg), Sodium 17 mg,
Total Carbohydrate 6 gm, Dietary
Fiber 1 gm, Sugars 5 gm, Protein 1 gm

Variations: Use white choco-
late chips instead of chocolate
chips, cashews instead of
peanuts, and raisins or dried
cherries instead of craisins.

Easy Fudge

Barbara Tenney, Delta, PA

Makes 36 servings
Serving size is 1 piece

Prep Time: 5 minutes
Cooking Time: 12-15 minutes

⅔ cup fat-free evaporated
  milk
¾ cup sugar blend for
  baking (Splenda)
½ tsp. salt
1½ cups mini-marsh-
  mallows, *or* diced large
  marshmallows
1¼ cups semi-sweet
  chocolate chips
1 tsp. vanilla
½ cup chopped nuts

1. Place first 3 ingredients
in saucepan. Mix and heat
over medium heat. Bring to a
boil, stirring continuously.
2. Boil 5 minutes and
remove from heat.
3. Add remaining ingredi-
ents and stir until marshmallows and chocolate chips melt.
4. Pour into a buttered
9 x 9 pan. Cut into squares
while still warm and chill.

Exchange List Values:
Carbohydrate 0.5, Fat 0.5

Basic Nutritional Values:
Calories 68 (Calories from Fat 27),
Total Fat 3 gm (Saturated Fat 1.4
gm, Trans Fat 0.0 gm, Polyunsat
Fat 0.4 gm, Monounsat Fat 1.3 gm,
Cholesterol 0 mg), Sodium 49 mg,
Total Carbohydrate 10 gm, Dietary
Fiber 1 gm, Sugars 10 gm, Protein 1 gm

Variations: Replace chocolate
chips with peanut butter chips.

Fruity Yogurt
Ice Pops

Paula King
Flanagan, IL

Makes 10 servings
Serving size is 1 pop

Prep Time: 5 minutes
Freezing Time: 8 hours,
  or overnight

32 ozs. (or 5⅓ 6-oz.
  containers) fat-free,
  sugar-free strawberry
  yogurt
8-oz. can unsweetened
  crushed pineapple,
  undrained
1 Tbsp. honey

1. Combine yogurt, pine-
apple, and honey in a blender
or food processor, blending
until smooth.
2. Pour into 10 plastic
molds or 3-oz. paper cups.
Top with holders or insert
wooden sticks.
3. Freeze until firm, about
8 hours or overnight.

Exchange List Values:
Fruit 0.5, Fat-Free Milk 0.5

Basic Nutritional Values:
Calories 49 (Calories from Fat 0),
Total Fat 0 gm (Saturated Fat 0.0
gm, Trans Fat 0.0 gm, Polyunsat
Fat 0.0 gm, Monounsat Fat 0.0 gm,
Cholesterol 2 mg), Sodium 43 mg,
Total Carbohydrate 10 gm, Dietary
Fiber 0 gm, Sugars 8 gm, Protein 3 gm

Tip: You can use other flavors
of yogurt and other fruits. Just
make sure you use the correct
amounts of each.

Mochaccino

Jenelle Miller
Marion, SD

Makes 20 servings
Serving size is 1 cup

Prep Time: 15 minutes

12 Tbsp. freshly ground
  coffee granules
10 cups water
¾ cup fat-free non-dairy
  powdered creamer
½ cup fat-free chocolate
  syrup
½ cup fat-free caramel
  syrup
⅓ cup granular Splenda
10 cups coarsely crushed ice
whipped cream and
  additional syrup, *optional*

1. Brew coffee (with 10 cups
water) in coffeemaker. Pour
into a 2-qt. pitcher.
2. Add creamer, syrups,
and sugar substitute. Whisk
together. Cool in refrigerator.
3. To use, place ½ cup
coffee mix in blender with
½ cup crushed ice. Blend for
1 minute.
4. Pour into a tall glass.
Top with whipped cream and
drizzle with syrup, if you wish.

Exchange List Values:
Carbohydrate 1.0

Basic Nutritional Values:
Calories 73 (Calories from Fat 0),
Total Fat 0 gm (Saturated Fat 0.0
gm, Trans Fat 0.0 gm, Polyunsat
Fat 0.0 gm, Monounsat Fat 0.0 gm,
Cholesterol 0 mg), Sodium 36 mg,
Total Carbohydrate 17 gm, Dietary
Fiber 0 gm, Sugars 11 gm, Protein 0 gm

Mint Lemonade Concentrate

Stacy Schmucker Stoltzfus
Enola, PA
Virginia M. Eberly
Loysville, PA

Makes 32 servings
Serving size is ¼ cup concentrate
mixed with ¾ cup water

Prep Time: 10 minutes
Cooking Time: 10 minutes
Cooling Time: 1-2 hours

2 cups fresh tea leaves
  (stems are okay to use, too)
1 qt. water
¾ cup sugar blend for
  baking (Splenda)
12-oz. can frozen lemonade
  concentrate
6-oz. can frozen orange
  juice concentrate

1. Wash tea leaves and put
in a large bowl.
2. Combine water and
sugar blend in a saucepan.
Boil for 10 minutes.
3. Pour over tea leaves.
Cover and let cool. Squeeze
water out of leaves, remove
them, and compost.
4. Add juice concentrates to
tea. Stir until thawed.
5. To serve, mix 1 part
concentrate to 3 parts water.

Exchange List Values:
Carbohydrate 1.0

Basic Nutritional Values:
Calories 57 (Calories from Fat 0),
Total Fat 0 gm (Saturated Fat 0.0
gm, Trans Fat 0.0 gm, Polyunsat
Fat 0.0 gm, Monounsat Fat 0.0 gm,
Cholesterol 0 mg), Sodium 2 mg, Total
Carbohydrate 15 gm, Dietary Fiber
0 gm, Sugars 14 gm, Protein 0 gm

*Tip: At the end of the growing
season, I make quantities of the
concentrate and freeze it to use
in the winter.*

A Tip —

   Most of us drink too
many calories. Simply
cutting out sugary drinks
can eliminate hundreds
of calories a day.

3-2-1 Lemonade

Tabitha Schmidt, Baltic, OH

Makes 16 servings
Serving size is 1 cup

Prep Time: 15 minutes

3 lemons
2 cups granular Splenda
water and ice to make a
   gallon

1. Thinly slice lemons,
discarding tips.
2. Place in a one-gallon
pitcher and add sweetener.
Stir thoroughly until lemon
slices are well-covered with
sugar. Let stand for 10 minutes.
3. Add ice and water to
make one gallon.
4. Serve immediately or
within hours, putting a lemon
slice in each glass if desired.

Exchange List Values:
Free food

Basic Nutritional Values:
Calories 13 (Calories from Fat 0),
Total Fat 0 gm (Saturated Fat 0.0
gm, Trans Fat 0.0 gm, Polyunsat
Fat 0.0 gm, Monounsat Fat 0.0 gm,
Cholesterol 0 mg), Sodium 11 mg,
Total Carbohydrate 3 gm, Dietary
Fiber 0 gm, Sugars 3 gm, Protein 0 gm

Tips:
*1. If you have left-over
lemonade, remove the lemons if
you won't be using it within 24
hours. The rinds can turn bitter
if left in too long.*
*2. To get the maxium flavor
from the lemons, mash the
sugar and lemon slices together
(Step 2) until well blended.*

Mint Tea

Carol Eberly, Harrisonburg, VA

Makes 4 servings
Serving size is 1 cup

Prep Time: 15-20 minutes
Steeping Time: 10 minutes

4 cups water
3 Lipton family-size tea
   bags (only Lipton!)
8-10 stalks fresh mint tea, *or*
   2 Boston's mint tea bags,
   or 8-10 stalks dried mint
1¼ cups granular Splenda

1. Heat 4 cups water to boil
in the microwave or on the
stove.
2. Remove from heat and
add family-size tea bags and
mint tea or tea bags.
3. Let steep at least 10
minutes.
4. Remove tea bags and
mint.
5. Add granular sweetener.
Stir until dissolved.
6. Add enough water to
make a gallon.
7. Serve over ice in glasses.

Exchange List Values:
Free food

Basic Nutritional Values:
Calories 10 (Calories from Fat 0),
Total Fat 0 gm (Saturated Fat 0.0
gm, Trans Fat 0.0 gm, Polyunsat
Fat 0.0 gm, Monounsat Fat 0.0 gm,
Cholesterol 0 mg), Sodium 7 mg, Total
Carbohydrate 2 gm, Dietary Fiber
0 gm, Sugars 2 gm, Protein 0 gm

*Tip: In the summer when the
tea grows, I cut it off and dry it
for use in the winter.*

Indian Tea

Terry Stutzman Mast
Lodi, CA

Makes 4 servings
Serving size is 1 cup

Prep Time: 5 minutes
Steeping Time: 5-10 minutes

4 cups water
3 black (regular *or* decaf)
   tea bags
3 whole cloves
1" piece of gingerroot,
   chopped
3 pods cardamom, opened
   for seeds
1 stick cinnamon, chopped
6-oz. can evaporated skim
   milk
¼ cup granular Splenda

1. Bring water to a boil in
a covered saucepan. Turn off
heat.
2. Place tea bags in to steep
for 5 minutes. Keep covered.
3. In a tea ball or muslin
bag (tied shut) place cloves,
gingerroot, cardamom seeds,
and chopped cinnamon. Place
into steeping tea.
4. After 5 minutes, remove
tea bags. (If you prefer a
stronger tea, allow the tea
bags to steep a few more
minutes until tea is darker.)
5. Stir in evaporated milk.
6. Add granular sweetener,
stirring until dissolved.
7. Remove tea ball or spice
bag and serve.

Exchange List Values:
Carbohydrate 0.5

Basic Nutritional Values:
Calories 46 (Calories from Fat 1),
Total Fat 0 gm (Saturated Fat 0.1
gm, Trans Fat 0.0 gm, Polyunsat
Fat 0.0 gm, Monounsat Fat 0.0 gm,
Cholesterol 2 mg), Sodium 62 mg,
Total Carbohydrate 7 gm, Dietary
Fiber 0 gm, Sugars 7 gm, Protein 4 gm

Strawberry Banana Smoothie

Ann Bender, Fort Defiance, VA

Makes 5 servings
Serving size is 1 cup

Prep Time: 5 minutes

1 banana
1 cup frozen unsweetened
  strawberries
½ cup orange juice
¼ cup granular Splenda
½ cup pineapple, crushed
  or cubes
1 tray of ice cubes
1 cup yogurt, optional
peaches *or* blueberries,
  optional

1. Place ingredients in a blender in the order listed.
2. Blend until ice is dissolved (1-2 minutes).

Exchange List Values:
Fruit 1.0

Basic Nutritional Values:
Calories 58 (Calories from Fat 2),
Total Fat 0 gm (Saturated Fat 0.0
gm, Trans Fat 0.0 gm, Polyunsat
Fat 0.1 gm, Monounsat Fat 0.0 gm,
Cholesterol 0 mg), Sodium 1 mg, Total
Carbohydrate 15 gm, Dietary Fiber
1 gm, Sugars 10 gm, Protein 1 gm

This is exceptionally good—and welcome—on a hot day or night.

Orange Crème Smoothie

Dale Peterson, Rapid City, SD

Makes 3 servings
Serving size is 1 cup

Prep Time: 5 minutes

2 cups fat-free milk
½ cup fat-free plain yogurt
½ cup frozen orange juice
  concentrate
4 tsp. granular Splenda
1 banana, sliced

1. Blend all ingredients in blender or food processor.
2. Serve cold.

Exchange List Values:
Fruit 1.5, Fat-Free Milk 0.5

Basic Nutritional Values:
Calories 145 (Calories from Fat 3),
Total Fat 0 gm (Saturated Fat 0.2
gm, Trans Fat 0.0 gm, Polyunsat
Fat 0.0 gm, Monounsat Fat 0.1 gm,
Cholesterol 3 mg), Sodium 81 mg,
Total Carbohydrate 30 gm, Dietary
Fiber 1 gm, Sugars 25 gm, Protein 7 gm

Variations:
1. Add 4-6 ice cubes to the blender to make the smoothie slushy.
2. Make the smoothie without adding any sweetener.
—Annabelle Unternahrer
Shipshewana, IN

Red Velvet Punch

J.B. Miller
Indianapolis, IN

Makes 24 servings
Serving size is ¾ cup

Prep Time: 15 minutes

8 cups light cranberry
  juice cocktail
1 cup each, thawed frozen
  concentrate of orange
  juice, lemon juice, and
  pineapple juice
2 cups grape juice
block of ice
2 qts. diet ginger ale
lemon and lime slices

1. Mix all ingredients together in large punch bowl.
2. When well blended, add a block of ice.
3. Just before serving add 2 quarts ginger ale.
4. Garnish with slices of lemon and lime.

Exchange List Values:
Fruit 1.5

Basic Nutritional Values:
Calories 91 (Calories from Fat 1),
Total Fat 0 gm (Saturated Fat 0.0
gm, Trans Fat 0.0 gm, Polyunsat
Fat 0.0 gm, Monounsat Fat 0.0 gm,
Cholesterol 0 mg), Sodium 45 mg,
Total Carbohydrate 23 gm, Dietary
Fiber 0 gm, Sugars 21 gm, Protein 1 gm

Tip: Instead of a solid block of ice, substitute an ice ring with slices of citrus and cherries inbedded in the ice.

Low-Sodium Mixes and Sauce

Italian Seasoning Mix

Madelyn L. Wheeler, Zionsville, IN

Makes 13 servings
Serving size is 1 Tbsp.

6 tsp. marjoram, dried
6 tsp. thyme leaves, dried
6 tsp. rosemary, dried
6 tsp. savory, ground
3 tsp. dry sage, ground
6 tsp. oregano leaves, dried
6 tsp. basil leaves, dried

Combine all ingredients.

Exchange List Values:
Vegetable 2.0, Lean Meat 4.0

Basic Nutritional Values:
Calories 8 (Calories from Fat 2),
Total Fat 0 gm (Saturated Fat 0.1 gm,
Polyunsat Fat 0.1 gm, Monounsat Fat
0.0 gm, Cholesterol 0 mg), Sodium 1
mg, Total Carbohydate 2 gm, Dietary
Fiber 1 gm, Sugars 0 gm, Protein 0 gm

*This recipe should be made
with dried leaves if available,
rather than ground, except for
the savory and sage.*

Taco Seasoning Mix, Low-Sodium

Madelyn L. Wheeler, Zionsville, IN

Makes 3 servings
Serving size is 7 tsp. or ⅓ of recipe

6 tsp. chili powder
5 tsp. paprika
4½ tsp. cumin seed
3 tsp. onion powder
1 tsp. garlic powder
⅔ Tbsp. dry cornstarch

1. Combine all ingredients in bowl.
2. One-third of mix (about 7 tsp.) is equivalent to 1 pkg. (1.25 oz.) purchased taco seasoning mix.

Exchange List Values:
Carbohydrate 0.5

Basic Nutritional Values:
Calories 56 (calories from Fat 19),
Total Fat 2 gm (Saturated Fat 0.0 gm,
Polyunsat Fat 0.9 gm, Monounsat Fat
0.7 gm, Cholesterol 0 mg), Sodium 61
mg, Total Carbohydrate 10 gm, Dietary
Fiber 3 gm, Sugars 3 gm, Protein 2 gm

Onion Soup Mix, Salt-Free

Madelyn L. Wheeler, Zionsville, IN

Makes 1 serving
*(equivalent to 1 pkg. purchased
dry onion soup mix)*

2⅔ Tbsp. dried onion, minced, flaked, or chopped
4 tsp. beef instant bouillon powder, sodium-free
1 tsp. onion powder
¼ tsp. celery seed

Combine all ingredients.

Exchange List Values:
Carbohydrate 1.5

Basic Nutritional Values:
Calories 106 (calories from Fat 2),
Total Fat 0 gm (Saturated Fat 0.0 gm,
Polyunsat Fat 0.1 gm, Monounsat Fat
0.1 gm, Cholesterol 0 mg), Sodium
5 mg, Total Carbohydrate 23 gm,
Dietary Fiber 2 gm, Sugars 11 gm,
Protein 2 gm

Phyllis' Homemade Barbecue Sauce

Phyllis Barrier
Little Rock, AR

Makes 16 servings
Serving size is 2 Tbsp.

2 8-oz. cans tomato sauce, no-added-salt
¼ cup cider vinegar
brown sugar substitute to equal 2 Tbsp.
½ cup fresh onions, minced
1 tsp. garlic powder
½ tsp. dry mustard powder
6 tsp. chili powder
⅛ tsp. Tabasco sauce
½ tsp. black pepper
6 tsp. Worcestershire sauce
1 tsp. paprika
1 tsp. liquid smoke
¼ tsp. salt

Mix all ingredients together and cook in microwave until minced onion is tender and sauce has thickened.

Exchange List Values:
Carbohydrate 0.5

Basic Nutritional Values:
Calories 24 (calories from Fat 2),
Total Fat 0 gm (Saturated Fat 0.0 gm,
Polyunsat Fat 0.1 gm, Monounsat Fat
0.0 gm, Cholesterol 0 mg), Sodium 81
mg, Total Carbohydrate 5 gm, Dietary
Fiber 1 gm, Sugars 5 gm, Protein 0 gm

A Week of Menus

If you're trying to stick to a daily meal plan with a specific number of calories, here is help. Each day in this Week of Menus is designed with 3 meals and 2 snacks, for a total of about 1500 calories.

One or two recipes each day comes from this *Fix-It and Enjoy-It Diabetic Cookbook*, making it easy to eat healthfully, despite busy lives and chaotic schedules.

You'll quickly see the Exchange Value for each part of the meal, as well as the nutritional breakdown of each food. In addition, the total number of nutrients for each day's menu is given, and then compared to healthy, nutritional goals. You'll soon see how easy it is to eat well.

Sunday

Food Item	Serving Amount	Exchanges	Cal	Carb (g)	Prot (g)	Fat (g)	Sod (mg)
Breakfast							
Scrambled Egg Muffins (page 24)	1 muffin	1 Lean Meat, ½ Fat	69	2	8	3	327
Toast, whole-wheat	2 slices	2 Starch	153	26	8	2	292
Jelly or preserves, low or reduced sugar	2 tsp.	Free Food	16	4	0	0	0
Milk, fat-free	1 cup	1 Fat-Free Milk	83	12	8	0	108
			322	44	25	5	726
Morning Snack							
Orange, fresh	1 orange	1 Fruit	62	15	1	0	0
			62	15	1	0	0
Lunch							
Chicken, no skin, roasted	3 ozs.	3 Lean Meat	161	0	25	6	73
Mashed potatoes	½ cup	1 Starch	64	14	1	1	91
Green beans, fresh cooked	½ cup	1 Vegetable	22	5	1	0	1
Carrots, fresh cooked	½ cup	1 Vegetable	35	8	1	0	51
Roll, whole grain	1 small roll	1 Starch	88	16	2	1	170
Margarine, 67% oil (Smart Balance)	½ Tbsp.	1 Fat	42	0	0	5	45
Cantaloupe melon	1 cup	1 Fruit	56	13	1	0	14
			468	56	31	14	445
Dinner							
Bread, rye	2 slices	2 Starch	166	31	5	2	422
Ham, extra lean, lower sodium, roasted	1 oz.	1 Very Lean Meat	30	1	5	1	230
Swiss cheese, reduced-fat	1 oz.	1 Medium-Fat Meat	70	0	9	4	130
Mustard	2 tsps	Free Food	7	1	0	0	112
Garden Salad Mix	2 cups	1 Vegetable	30	6	2	0	25
Salad dressing, balsamic vinaigrette	1 Tbsp.	½ Fat	38	2	0	2	145
Ice cream, light, vanilla	½ cup	1 Carb, 1 Fat	100	15	3	4	45
Hot Fudge Sauce (page 188)	2 Tbsp.	Free Food	20	3	0	1	6
			461	59	25	14	1116
Evening Snack							
Popcorn, popped, no salt or fat added	3 cups	1 Starch	92	19	3	1	1
Peanuts, dry roasted, no salt	10 peanuts	1 Fat	59	2	2	5	1
Milk, fat-free	1 cup	1 Fat-Free Milk	83	12	8	0	108
			233	33	14	6	109

Sunday—Totals for the Day

Nutrient	Quantity	DRI Comparison	% of Day's Calories	Goals
Calories	1546			1450 to 1550
Fat	40 grams		23%	10 to 30 %
Saturated fat	12 grams		7%	0 to 10 %
Trans fatty acids, total	0 grams			
Polyunsaturated fat	9 grams		5%	
Monounsaturated fat	14 grams		8%	
Cholesterol	139 milligrams			0 to 300 mg
Sodium	2397 milligrams			0 to 2400 mg
Carbohydrate	208 grams		53%	40 to 55%
Dietary fiber	28 grams			25 to 45 grams
Sugars	83 grams			
Protein	96 grams		24%	10 to 35 %
Calcium	1168 milligrams			More than 1000 mg
Carb (Breakfast)	44 grams			
Carb (AM Snack)	15 grams			
Carb (Lunch)	56 grams			
Carb (PM Snack)	0 grams			
Carb (Dinner)	59 grams			
Carb (EV Snack)	33 grams			
Iron	12 milligrams	Low		18 to 45 mg
Magnesium	338 milligrams			320 to 1280 mg
Phosphorus	1449 milligrams			More than 700 mg
Potassium	3128 milligrams	Low		More than 4700 mg
Vitamin A_RAE	884 micrograms			700 to 2800 mcg
Vitamin C	188 milligrams			75 to 300 mg
Vitamin B12	5 micrograms			More than 2.4 mcg
Folate, total	381 micrograms	Low		More than 400 mcg
Thiamine	2 milligrams			More than 1.1 mg
Riboflavin	3 milligrams			More than 1 mg
Niacin	22 milligrams			More than 14 mg
Vitamin B6	2 milligrams			More than 1.3 mg

Monday

Food Item	Serving Amount	Exchanges	Cal	Carb (g)	Prot (g)	Fat (g)	Sod (mg)
Breakfast							
Milk, fat-free	1 cup	1 Fat-Free Milk	83	12	8	0	108
Toast, whole-wheat	2 slices	2 Starch	153	26	8	2	292
Peanut butter, smooth or crunchy	2 Tbsp.	High-Fat Meat	192	6	8	17	160
			428	**44**	**24**	**19**	**559**
Morning Snack							
Orange juice, fresh	½ cup	1 Fruit	56	13	1	0	1
			56	**13**	**1**	**0**	**1**
Lunch							
Sausage-Lentil Soup (page 60)	1 cup	1½ Starch, 2 Vegetable, 1 Lean Meat	250	33	15	7	409
Bread sticks, crisp	2 sticks (4″ x ½″)	½ Starch	41	7	1	1	66
Apple, with peel	1 small apple (2½″)	1 Fruit	54	14	0	0	1
			345	**54**	**17**	**8**	**476**
Dinner							
Beef pot roast, lean meat only, cooked	4 ozs.	4 Lean Meat	245	0	37	9	75
Plantain, ripe, cooked	⅓ cup, slices	1 Starch	59	16	0	0	3
Rice, brown, cooked	⅓ cup	1 Starch	71	15	2	1	3
Chayote squash, cooked	½ cup	1 Vegetable	19	4	0	0	1
Garden Salad Mix	2 cups	1 Vegetable	30	6	2	0	25
Salad dressing, balsamic vinaigrette	1 Tbsp.	½ Fat	38	2	0	2	145
Mango, fresh	½ mango, small	1 Fruit	68	18	1	0	2
Coffee, brewed	1 cup	Free Food	5	1	0	0	5
			535	**62**	**42**	**14**	**259**
Evening Snack							
Yogurt, nonfat, vanilla	1 cup	1 Fat-Free Milk	89	15	7	0	119
Vanilla wafer cookies	5 wafers	1 Carb	88	15	1	3	70
			177	**30**	**8**	**3**	**189**

Monday—Totals for the Day

Nutrient	Quantity	DRI Comparison	% of Day's Calories	Goals
Calories	1542			1450 to 1550
Fat	45 grams		26%	10 to 30 %
Saturated fat	11 grams		7%	0 to 10 %
Trans fatty acids, total	0 grams			
Polyunsaturated fat	10 grams		5%	
Monounsaturated fat	19 grams		11%	
Cholesterol	152 milligrams			0 to 300 mg
Sodium	1484 milligrams			0 to 2400 mg
Carbohydrate	202 grams		51%	40 to 55%
Dietary fiber	29 grams			25 to 45 grams
Sugars	95 grams			
Protein	93 grams		23%	10 to 35 %
Calcium	777 milligrams	Low		More than 1000 mg
Carb (Breakfast)	44 grams			
Carb (AM Snack)	13 grams			
Carb (Lunch)	54 grams			
Carb (PM Snack)	0 grams			
Carb (Dinner)	62 grams			
Carb (EV Snack)	30 grams			
Iron	16 milligrams	Low		18 to 45 mg
Magnesium	386 milligrams			320 to 1280 mg
Phosphorus	1307 milligrams			More than 700 mg
Potassium	3695 milligrams	Low		More than 4700 mg
Vitamin A_RAE	592 micrograms	Low		700 to 2800 mcg
Vitamin C	171 milligrams			75 to 300 mg
Vitamin B12	7 micrograms			More than 2.4 mcg
Folate, total	520 micrograms			More than 400 mcg
Thiamine	1 milligrams			More than 1.1 mg
Riboflavin	2 milligrams			More than 1 mg
Niacin	20 milligrams			More than 14 mg
Vitamin B6	2 milligrams			More than 1.3 mg

Tuesday

Food Item	Serving Amount	Exchanges	Cal	Carb (g)	Prot (g)	Fat (g)	Sod (mg)
Breakfast							
Milk, fat-free	1 cup	1 Fat-Free Milk	83	12	8	0	108
Wheaties Cereal	1½ cups	2 Starch	160	36	5	1	326
			243	**49**	**13**	**2**	**434**
Morning Snack							
Banana, fresh	1 extra small	1 Fruit	71	19	1	0	1
			71	**19**	**1**	**0**	**1**
Lunch							
Tuna Salad (page 169)	¼ recipe	½ Carb, 2 Lean Meat	130	5	15	5	426
Bread, whole-wheat	2 slices	2 Starch	138	26	5	2	295
Carrots, fresh, raw	1 cup, strips	1 Vegetable	50	12	1	0	84
Plum, fresh	1 plum	½ Fruit	30	8	0	0	0
			348	**50**	**22**	**8**	**805**
Dinner							
Salmon, fresh, broiled	4 ozs.	4 Lean Meat	245	0	31	12	75
Potato, boiled, with peel	½ medium potato	1 Starch	62	14	1	0	3
Margarine, 67% oil (Smart Balance)	½ Tbsp.	1 Fat	42	0	0	5	45
Kale, fresh, cooked	½ cup	1 Vegetable	18	4	1	0	15
Roll, whole grain	1 small roll	1 Starch	88	16	2	1	170
Margarine, 67% oil (Smart Balance)	½ Tbsp.	1 Fat	42	0	0	5	45
Garden Salad Mix	2 cups	1 Vegetable	30	6	2	0	25
Salad dressing, ranch, light	1 Tbsp.	½ Fat	35	3	0	0	175
Grapes, fresh seedless, small	17 grapes	1 Fruit	60	15	1	0	2
			622	**59**	**38**	**26**	**555**
Evening Snack							
Healthy Hummus (page 10)	2 Tbsp.	½ Starch, 1½ Fat	105	5	2	9	35
Pita bread, whole wheat	½ pita	1 Starch	70	15	3	1	65
Milk, fat-free	½ cup	1 Fat-Free Milk	42	6	4	0	54
			216	**26**	**9**	**10**	**153**

Tuesday—Totals for the Day

Nutrient	Quantity	DRI Comparison	% of Day's Calories	Goals
Calories	1502			1450 to 1550
Fat	46 grams		27%	10 to 30 %
Saturated fat	10 grams		6%	0 to 10 %
Trans fatty acids, total	0 grams			
Polyunsaturated fat	10 grams		6%	
Monounsaturated fat	21 grams		12%	
Cholesterol	283 milligrams			0 to 300 mg
Sodium	1949 milligrams			0 to 2400 mg
Carbohydrate	202 grams		52%	40 to 55%
Dietary fiber	25 grams			25 to 45 grams
Sugars	71 grams			
Protein	82 grams		21%	10 to 35 %
Calcium	616 milligrams	Low		More than 1000 mg
Carb (Breakfast)	49 grams			
Carb (AM Snack)	19 grams			
Carb (Lunch)	50 grams			
Carb (PM Snack)	0 grams			
Carb (Dinner)	59 grams			
Carb (EV Snack)	26 grams			
Iron	23 milligrams			18 to 45 mg
Magnesium	321 milligrams			320 to 1280 mg
Phosphorus	1355 milligrams			More than 700 mg
Potassium	3190 milligrams	Low		More than 4700 mg
Vitamin A_RAE	1929 micrograms			700 to 2800 mcg
Vitamin C	109 milligrams			75 to 300 mg
Vitamin B12	15 micrograms			More than 2.4 mcg
Folate, total	581 micrograms			More than 400 mcg
Thiamine	2 milligrams			More than 1.1 mg
Riboflavin	3 milligrams			More than 1 mg
Niacin	37 milligrams			More than 14 mg
Vitamin B6	3 milligrams			More than 1.3 mg

Wednesday

Food Item	Serving Amount	Exchanges	Cal	Carb (g)	Prot (g)	Fat (g)	Sod (mg)
Breakfast							
Milk, fat-free	1 cup	1 Fat-Free Milk	83	12	8	0	108
Bagel, plain	½ large (4" diameter)	2 Starch	155	30	6	1	302
Cream cheese, reduced-fat (neufchatel)	1½ Tbsp.	1 Fat	54	1	2	5	92
			292	**43**	**16**	**6**	**501**
Morning Snack							
Pineapple, fresh	¾ cup	1 Fruit	56	15	1	0	1
			56	**15**	**1**	**0**	**1**
Lunch							
Mild Indian Curry (page 76)	¾ cup	1 Carb, 2 Lean Meat	167	11	16	7	434
Rice, white, cooked	⅓ cup	1 Starch	68	15	1	0	1
Naan	¼ large (8" x 2")	1 Starch	75	13	2	2	90
Margarine, 67% oil (Smart Balance)	1 Tbsp.	2 Fat	85	0	0	9	90
Chutney	1 Tbsp.	1 Carb	60	14	0	0	170
Broccoli, fresh, raw	1 cup	1 Vegetable	30	6	2	0	29
			485	**59**	**22**	**18**	**814**
Dinner							
Beef tenderloin, lean, broiled	4 ozs.	4 Lean Meat	218	0	32	9	67
Garlic Bread (page 15)	½ slice	1 Starch, ½ Fat	96	12	4	3	242
Grilled Veggies (page 154)	⅙ recipe	1 Starch, 1 Vegetable, 1 Fat	155	21	3	7	8
Fresh fruit salad	¾ cup	1 Fruit	59	15	1	0	4
Roll, whole grain	1 small roll	1 Starch	88	16	2	1	170
			529	**49**	**40**	**20**	**321**
Evening Snack							
Milk, fat-free	½ cup	1 Fat-Free Milk	42	6	4	0	54
Oatmeal, cooked	½ cup	1 Starch	73	13	3	1	1
			156	**25**	**11**	**1**	**109**

Wednesday—Totals for the Day

Nutrient	Quantity	DRI Comparison	% of Day's Calories	Goals
Calories	1518			1450 to 1550
Fat	45 grams		27%	10 to 30 %
Saturated fat	15 grams		9%	0 to 10 %
Trans fatty acids, total	0 grams			
Polyunsaturated fat	8 grams		5%	
Monounsaturated fat	18 grams		11%	
Cholesterol	173 milligrams			0 to 300 mg
Sodium	1747 milligrams			0 to 2400 mg
Carbohydrate	190 grams		50%	40 to 55%
Dietary fiber	15 grams	Low		25 to 45 grams
Sugars	71 grams			
Protein	90 grams		24%	10 to 35 %
Calcium	764 milligrams	Low		More than 1000 mg
Carb (Breakfast)	43 grams			
Carb (AM Snack)	15 grams			
Carb (Lunch)	59 grams			
Carb (PM Snack)	0 grams			
Carb (Dinner)	49 grams			
Carb (EV Snack)	25 grams			
Iron	14 milligrams	Low		18 to 45 mg
Magnesium	244 milligrams	Low		320 to 1280 mg
Phosphorus	1208 milligrams			More than 700 mg
Potassium	2748 milligrams	Low		More than 4700 mg
Vitamin A_RAE	404 micrograms	Low		700 to 2800 mcg
Vitamin C	190 milligrams			75 to 300 mg
Vitamin B12	6 micrograms			More than 2.4 mcg
Folate, total	293 micrograms	Low		More than 400 mcg
Thiamine	1 milligrams			More than 1.1 mg
Riboflavin	2 milligrams			More than 1 mg
Niacin	21 milligrams			More than 14 mg
Vitamin B6	2 milligrams			More than 1.3 mg

Thursday

Food Item	Serving Amount	Exchanges	Cal	Carb (g)	Prot (g)	Fat (g)	Sod (mg)
Breakfast							
Yogurt, non-fat, vanilla	1 cup	1 Fat-Free Milk	89	15	7	0	119
English muffin, whole-wheat	1 muffin	2 Starch	126	25	5	1	220
Margarine, 67% oil (Smart Balance)	1 Tbsp.	2 Fat	85	0	0	9	90
			300	**40**	**13**	**11**	**429**
Morning Snack							
Strawberry Banana Smoothie (page 253)	1 cup	1 Fruit	58	15	1	0	1
			58	**15**	**1**	**0**	**1**
Lunch							
Personal Pizza (page 136)	1 individual pizza	3½ Starch, ½ Fat, 1 Vegetable	322	59	14	4	563
Garden Salad Mix	2 cups	1 Vegetable	30	6	2	0	25
Salad dressing, balsamic, vinaigrette	1 Tbsp.	½ Fat	38	2	0	3	145
			390	**67**	**15**	**8**	**733**
Dinner							
Meatless ground crumbles, soy based (Boca)	1 cup	3 Very Lean Meat, ½ Carb	120	12	26	1	540
Jamaican Rice and Beans (page 121)	1 cup	3 Starch	245	47	8	2	347
Cashews, unsalted	9 cashews	1½ Fat	77	4	2	6	2
Mixed vegetables (no corn, peas, or pasta)	½ cup	1 Vegetable	20	3	1	0	15
Strawberries, fresh	1¼ cups	1 Fruit	57	13	1	1	2
			519	**80**	**38**	**10**	**906**
Evening Snack							
Cottage cheese, creamed, 4.5% milkfat	½ cup	2 Lean Meat	108	3	13	5	420
Crackers, graham	3 crackers	1 Starch	89	16	1	2	127
			197	**19**	**14**	**7**	**547**

Thursday—Totals for the Day

Nutrient	Quantity	DRI Comparison	% of Day's Calories	Goals
Calories	1464			1450 to 1550
Fat	36 grams		21%	10 to 30 %
Saturated fat	10 grams		6%	0 to 10 %
Trans fatty acids, total	0 grams			
Polyunsaturated fat	9 grams		5%	
Monounsaturated fat	12 grams		7%	
Cholesterol	29 milligrams			0 to 300 mg
Sodium	2617 milligrams	High		0 to 2400 mg
Carbohydrate	221 grams	High	58%	40 to 55%
Dietary fiber	30 grams			25 to 45 grams
Sugars	51 grams			
Protein	82 grams		21%	10 to 35 %
Calcium	1010 milligrams			More than 1000 mg
Carb (Breakfast)	40 grams			
Carb (AM Snack)	15 grams			
Carb (Lunch)	67 grams			
Carb (PM Snack)	0 grams			
Carb (Dinner)	80 grams			
Carb (EV Snack)	19 grams			
Iron	18 milligrams			18 to 45 mg
Magnesium	341 milligrams			320 to 1280 mg
Phosphorus	1401 milligrams			More than 700 mg
Potassium	2560 milligrams	Low		More than 4700 mg
Vitamin A_RAE	391 micrograms	Low		700 to 2800 mcg
Vitamin C	191 milligrams			75 to 300 mg
Vitamin B12	4 micrograms			More than 2.4 mcg
Folate, total	632 micrograms			More than 400 mcg
Thiamine	3 milligrams			More than 1.1 mg
Riboflavin	2 milligrams			More than 1 mg
Niacin	25 milligrams			More than 14 mg
Vitamin B6	2 milligrams			More than 1.3 mg

Friday

Food Item	Serving Amount	Exchanges	Cal	Carb (g)	Prot (g)	Fat (g)	Sod (mg)
Breakfast							
Milk, fat-free	1 cup	1 Fat-Free Milk	83	12	8	0	108
Oatmeal, cooked	1 cup	2 Starch	145	25	6	2	2
			228	**29**	**14**	**3**	**110**
Morning Snack							
Peach, fresh	1 medium peach	1 Fruit	57	14	1	0	0
			57	**14**	**1**	**0**	**0**
Lunch							
Egg Drop Soup (page 64)	¾ cup	½ Carb, ½ Fat	61	5	5	2	541
Stir-fry made with:							
Chicken breast, meat only, cooked	3 ozs.	3 Very Lean Meat	140	0	26	3	63
Pepper, red, fresh cooked	½ cup	1 Vegetable	19	5	1	0	1
Onions, fresh cooked	½ cup	1 Vegetable	46	11	1	0	3
Pea pods (snow peas), fresh cooked	½ cup	1 Vegetable	34	6	3	0	3
Oil, sesame seed	1 tsp.	1 Fat	40	0	0	5	0
Oil, peanut	1 tsp.	1 Fat	40	0	0	5	0
Rice, brown, cooked	⅔ cup	2 Starch	145	30	3	1	7
Plum, fresh	1 plum	½ Fruit	30	8	0	0	0
			555	**63**	**40**	**16**	**618**
Dinner							
Tilapia fillet, cooked	4 ozs.	4 Very Lean Meat	149	0	30	3	41
Rotini (spiral pasta), cooked	⅔ cup	2 Starch	156	31	5	1	1
Asparagus, fresh cooked	½ cup	1 Vegetable	22	4	2	0	10
Roll, whole grain	1 small roll	1 Starch	88	16	2	1	170
Margarine, 67% oil (Smart Balance)	1 Tbsp.	2 Fat	85	0	0	9	90
			499	**51**	**39**	**15**	**313**
Evening Snack							
Yogurt, non-fat, vanilla	1 cup	1 Fat-Free Milk	89	15	7	0	119
Fruit, dried mixed	2 Tbsp.	1 Fruit	55	13	1	0	28
			144	**28**	**8**	**0**	**146**

Friday—Totals for the Day

Nutrient	Quantity	DRI Comparison	% of Day's Calories	Goals
Calories	1483			1450 to 1550
Fat	34 grams		21%	10 to 30 %
Saturated fat	8 grams		5%	0 to 10 %
Trans fatty acids, total	0 grams			
Polyunsaturated fat	10 grams		6%	
Monounsaturated fat	12 grams		7%	
Cholesterol	274 milligrams			0 to 300 mg
Sodium	1187 milligrams			0 to 2400 mg
Carbohydrate	194 grams		52%	40 to 55%
Dietary fiber	19 grams	Low		25 to 45 grams
Sugars	68 grams			
Protein	103 grams		27%	10 to 35 %
Calcium	733 milligrams	Low		More than 1000 mg
Carb (Breakfast)	37 grams			
Carb (AM Snack)	14 grams			
Carb (Lunch)	63 grams			
Carb (PM Snack)	0 grams			
Carb (Dinner)	51 grams			
Carb (EV Snack)	28 grams			
Iron	13 milligrams	Low		18 to 45 mg
Magnesium	331 milligrams			320 to 1280 mg
Phosphorus	1141 milligrams			More than 700 mg
Potassium	2926 milligrams	Low		More than 4700 mg
Vitamin A_RAE	483 micrograms	Low		700 to 2800 mcg
Vitamin C	191 milligrams			75 to 300 mg
Vitamin B12	4 micrograms			More than 2.4 mcg
Folate, total	376 micrograms	Low		More than 400 mcg
Thiamine	1 milligrams			More than 1.1 mg
Riboflavin	2 milligrams			More than 1 mg
Niacin	24 milligrams			More than 14 mg
Vitamin B6	2 milligrams			More than 1.3 mg

Saturday

Food Item	Serving Amount	Exchanges	Cal	Carb (g)	Prot (g)	Fat (g)	Sod (mg)
Breakfast							
Egg substitute	½ cup	2 Very Lean Meat	60	2	12	0	230
Bacon, fried, drained	1 slice	1 Fat	32	0	2	3	139
Toast, whole-wheat	2 slices	2 Starch	153	26	8	2	292
Milk, fat-free	1 cup	1 Fat-Free Milk	83	12	8	0	108
			329	**40**	**31**	**5**	**768**
Morning Snack							
Fresh fruit salad	¾ cup	1 Fruit	59	15	1	0	4
			59	**15**	**1**	**0**	**4**
Lunch							
Beef patty, ground, extra lean, pan broiled	3 ozs.	3 Medium-Fat Meat	197	0	21	12	67
Hamburger bun	1 small bun	2 Starch	120	21	4	2	206
Mustard	2 tsp.	Free Food	7	1	0	0	112
Tomato, raw	1 slice, medium	Free Food	4	1	0	0	1
Potato chips, baked	¾ oz.	1 Starch	82	17	1	1	112
Garden salad mix	2 cups	1 Vegetable	30	6	2	0	25
Salad dressing, balsamic vinaigrette	1 Tbsp.	½ Fat	38	2	0	3	145
			478	**48**	**29**	**17**	**669**
Dinner							
Pork loin chop, boneless, lean only, cooked	3 ozs.	3 Lean Meat	184	0	25	9	55
Golden Potato Casserole (page 152)	1 rectangle	2 Starch, ½ Fat	201	31	8	4	362
Broccoli, fresh cooked	½ cup	1 Vegetable	22	4	2	0	20
Milk, fat-free	1 cup	1 Fat-Free Milk	83	12	8	0	108
			490	**47**	**44**	**13**	**546**
Evening Snack							
Feta Bruschetta (page 14)	1 bruschetta	1 Starch, 1½ Fat	151	16	5	7	376
			151	**16**	**5**	**7**	**376**

Saturday—Totals for the Day

Nutrient	Quantity	DRI Comparison	% of Day's Calories	Goals
Calories	1506			1450 to 1550
Fat	44 grams		27%	10 to 30 %
Saturated fat	13 grams		8%	0 to 10 %
Trans fatty acids, total	1 grams			
Polyunsaturated fat	7 grams		4%	
Monounsaturated fat	18 grams		11%	
Cholesterol	169 milligrams			0 to 300 mg
Sodium	2362 milligrams			0 to 2400 mg
Carbohydrate	166 grams		44%	40 to 55%
Dietary fiber	18 grams	Low		25 to 45 grams
Sugars	55 grams			
Protein	109 grams		29%	10 to 35 %
Calcium	953 milligrams	Low		More than 1000 mg
Carb (Breakfast)	40 grams			
Carb (AM Snack)	15 grams			
Carb (Lunch)	48 grams			
Carb (PM Snack)	0 grams			
Carb (Dinner)	47 grams			
Carb (EV Snack)	16 grams			
Iron	12 milligrams	Low		18 to 45 mg
Magnesium	264 milligrams	Low		320 to 1280 mg
Phosphorus	1322 milligrams			More than 700 mg
Potassium	2970 milligrams	Low		More than 4700 mg
Vitamin A_RAE	643 micrograms	Low		700 to 2800 mcg
Vitamin C	144 milligrams			75 to 300 mg
Vitamin B12	6 micrograms			More than 2.4 mcg
Folate, total	337 micrograms	Low		More than 400 mcg
Thiamine	2 milligrams			More than 1.1 mg
Riboflavin	3 milligrams			More than 1 mg
Niacin	20 milligrams			More than 14 mg
Vitamin B6	2 milligrams			More than 1.3 mg

Averages—for the Week

Nutrient	Quantity	DRI Comparison	% of Day's Calories	Goals
Calories	1509			1450 to 1550
Fat	41 grams		24%	10 to 30 %
Saturated fat	11 grams		7%	0 to 10 %
Trans fatty acids, total	0 grams			
Polyunsaturated fat	9 grams		5%	
Monounsaturated fat	16 grams		10%	
Cholesterol	174 milligrams			0 to 300 mg
Sodium	1963 milligrams			0 to 2400 mg
Carbohydrate	197 grams		51%	40 to 55%
Dietary fiber	23 grams	Low		25 to 45 grams
Sugars	71 grams			
Protein	94 grams		24%	10 to 35 %
Calcium	860 milligrams	Low		More than 1000 mg
Carb (Breakfast)	42 grams			
Carb (AM Snack)	15 grams			
Carb (Lunch)	57 grams			
Carb (PM Snack)	0 grams			
Carb (Dinner)	58 grams			
Carb (EV Snack)	25 grams			
Iron	15 milligrams	Low		18 to 45 mg
Magnesium	318 milligrams	Low		320 to 1280 mg
Phosphorus	1312 milligrams			More than 700 mg
Potassium	3031 milligrams	Low		More than 4700 mg
Vitamin A_RAE	761 micrograms			700 to 2800 mcg
Vitamin C	169 milligrams			75 to 300 mg
Vitamin B12	7 micrograms			More than 2.4 mcg
Folate, total	446 micrograms			More than 400 mcg
Thiamine	2 milligrams			More than 1.1 mg
Riboflavin	2 milligrams			More than 1 mg
Niacin	24 milligrams			More than 14 mg
Vitamin B6	2 milligrams			More than 1.3 mg

10 Most Asked Questions about Diabetes

1. Can people with diabetes eat sugar?

Yes, they can. Sugar is just another carbohydrate to the body. All carbohydrates, whether they come from dessert, breads, or carrots, raise blood sugar. An equal serving of a brownie and of a baked potato raise your blood sugar the same amount. If you know that a rise in blood sugar is coming, it is wise to focus on the size of the serving.

The question of "how much sugar is too much?" has to be answered by each one of us. No one who wants to be healthy eats a lot of sugar.

2. Do people with diabetes have to eat a special diet?

No, they should eat the same foods that are healthy for everyone—whole grains, vegetables, fruit, and small portions of lean meat. Like everyone else, people with diabetes should eat breakfast, lunch, and dinner and not put off eating until dinnertime. By then, you are ravenous and will eat too much. This sends the blood sugar levels soaring in people with diabetes, and doesn't allow them to feel hungry for breakfast the next morning. Some people (with or without diabetes) do best when they eat five or six tiny meals or snacks a day.

3. What is diabetes?

Let's begin with insulin. It is a hormone that is produced in the pancreas, which is an organ located near your stomach. When you eat food, it is digested and broken down into glucose, a sugar. In this form it can travel around to feed all the cells in your body by way of the bloodstream. But the glucose cannot get into your cells unless insulin is there to open the door. Without insulin, the glucose stays in the bloodstream. And each time you eat, more glucose goes into your bloodstream. High levels of blood glucose or blood sugar is the sign that you have diabetes.

In type 1 diabetes, the body cannot produce insulin at all. Something has caused the body to destroy the cells in the pancreas that make insulin. People with type 1 diabetes must have insulin injections or use an insulin pump to stay alive.

In type 2 diabetes, the body is either not making enough insulin or not using it well. People can help their bodies use the insulin more effectively by losing weight and being active every day. Some people have to take diabetes pills or insulin to get their blood sugar levels back to normal.

4. What causes diabetes?

To start with, you need to have the gene for diabetes. Then there has to be something that triggers the gene. For many people who develop type 2 diabetes, the trigger is being overweight and sedentary. For others, it might be a stress on the body such as pregnancy or a serious accident requiring surgery.

For a child with type 1 diabetes, a virus may have confused the immune system into identifying the beta cells in the pancreas as part of the virus, and so the immune system destroyed the beta cells and stopped the production of insulin.

5. How many people have diabetes in the United States?

About 18 million people have diabetes in the U.S., but 8 million of those don't know it. There are 1 million new cases of diabetes diagnosed every year. The most distressing of these are the growing number of teens and older children who are developing type 2 diabetes—which usually occurs much later in life.

6. Why don't people know that they have diabetes?

The people who develop type 1 diabetes know because it comes on quickly and the symptoms are serious. But it affects only about 10 percent of the people with diabetes.

Type 2 accounts for the other 90 percent. Because it doesn't hurt and the symptoms come on gradually, people have usually had type 2 diabetes for 7 to 10 years when they get diagnosed.

7. Is there a cure for diabetes?

Not yet. Some people with type 2 diabetes may seem to have cured it by losing weight and getting regular daily exercise, because their blood sugar returns to normal levels and stays there. This may continue for years, but eventually the pancreas just wears out, and they will need medication to manage their blood sugar levels.

A small number of people with type 1 diabetes who have had a successful pancreas or islet cell transplant no longer have diabetes because their bodies are producing insulin again. However, they have to take powerful immunosuppressant drugs for the rest of their lives to prevent their bodies from rejecting the transplant.

8. Is there a type of diabetes that only happens when a woman is pregnant?

Yes, it is called gestational diabetes. After the baby is born, the woman no longer has diabetes, but she needs to take care to be active and to maintain a healthy weight or she might develop type 2 diabetes later on in life. During the last two months of her pregnancy, she will need to follow a meal plan to keep her blood sugar in normal ranges, or her baby may grow too big, causing problems for her and the baby during the birth process.

9. Does diabetes hurt?

High blood sugar can make you feel tired and irritable, but it comes on so gradually that you may not realize what is happening. It can blur your vision. That's on the outside. On the inside, constantly high blood sugar levels are silently damaging your blood vessels and nerves and can cause problems everywhere from your eyes to your feet, and especially to your heart. If diabetes starts hurting, damage has already been done.

10. Is there any way to avoid the damage that diabetes can do to the body?

Yes. We now know how to manage blood sugar levels, and persons with diabetes can learn what to do to keep healthy. Working with dietitians to develop a meal plan of foods that they like helps them get the nutrients their bodies need and not eat too much carbohydrate at any one meal or snack. Checking their blood sugar, in the morning or two hours after a meal for example, with a small glucose meter gives them and their health care providers information about how high their blood sugar is going and when, and about the effect of any diabetes medication they are taking.

A daily 30- to 45-minute walk is another simple but powerful way to lower blood sugar and to be healthier all over.

Learning to bring blood sugar levels back to normal every day is the key to preventing diabetes from doing any damage. We have extensive research to show that this is true. People can even prevent diabetes from developing at all by taking the same steps of eating healthy meals and getting daily exercise. These are also the tools that can reverse some of the damage that might have already been done.

Index

Recommended Reading List
(ADA is the American Diabetes Association.)

The American Diabetes Association Complete Guide to Diabetes, 4th ed.; ADA, 2005, 554 pages.

Diabetes Meal Planning Made Easy, 3nd ed., Hope S. Warshaw, MMSc, RD, CDE, BC-ADM; ADA, 2006, 302 pages.

Type 2 Diabetes for Beginners, Phyllis Barrier, MS, RD, CDE; ADA, 2005, 160 pages.

The "I Hate to Exercise" Book for People with Diabetes, 2nd ed., Charlotte Hayes, MMSc, MS, RD, CDE; ADA, 2006, 156 pages.

Dr. Buynak's 1-2-3 Diabetes Diet, Robert J. Buynak, MD, Gregory L. Guthrie; ADA, 2006, 196 pages.

The Official Pocket Guide to Diabetic Exchanges, 2nd ed., ADA, 2003, 64 pages.

Guide to Healthy Restaurant Eating, 3rd ed., Hope S. Warshaw, MMSc, RD, CDE, BC-ADM; ADA, 2005, 734 pages.

The Diabetes Carbohydrate & Fat Gram Guide, 3rd ed., Lea Ann Holzmeister, RD, CDE; ADA, 2005, 604 pages.

About the Author

Phyllis Pellman Good is a *New York Times* bestselling author whose books have sold nearly 10 million copies.

Good is the author of the *Fix-It and Enjoy-It* cookbook series for stove-top and oven cooking. In addition to this book, the series includes:

- **Fix-It and Enjoy-It Cookbook**
  All-Purpose, Welcome-Home Recipes

- **Fix-It and Enjoy-It Potluck Heaven**
  543 Stove-Top and Oven Dishes That Everyone Loves

- **Fix-It and Enjoy-It 5-Ingredient Recipes**
  Quick and Easy—for Stove-Top and Oven!

- **Fix-It and Enjoy-It Healthy Cookbook**
  400 Great Stove-Top and Oven Recipes
  (with nutritional expertise from Mayo Clinic)

Good is also the author of the nationally acclaimed *Fix-It and Forget-It* slow-cooker cookbooks, several of which have appeared on *The New York Times* bestseller list, as well as the bestseller lists of *USA Today*, *Publishers Weekly*, and *Book Sense*.

There are currently six books in that series:

- **Fix-It and Forget-It Cookbook (Revised and Updated)**
  700 Great Slow-Cooker Recipes

- **Fix-It and Forget-It Lightly (Revised and Updated)**
  600 Healthy, Low-Fat Recipes for Your Slow Cooker

- **Fix-It and Forget-It Christmas Cookbook**
  600 Slow Cooker Holiday Recipes

- **Fix-It and Forget-It 5-Ingredient Favorites**
  Comforting Slow-Cooker Recipes

- **Fix-It and Forget-It Diabetic Cookbook**
  Slow Cooker Favorites to Include Everyone
  (with the American Diabetes Association)

- **Fix-It and Forget-It Kids' Cookbook**
  50 Favorite Recipes to Make in a Slow Cooker

Among Good's other cookbooks are:

- **The Best of Amish Cooking**

- **"Fresh From Central Market" Cookbook**

Phyllis Pellman Good is Executive Editor at Good Books. (Good Books has published hundreds of titles by more than 135 authors.) She received her B.A. and M.A. in English from New York University. She and her husband, Merle, live in Lancaster, Pennsylvania. They are the parents of two young-adult daughters.

For a complete listing of books by Phyllis Pellman Good, as well as excerpts and reviews, visit www.Fix-ItandEnjoy-It.com or www.GoodBooks.com.

Fix-It and Enjoy-It Diabetic Cookbook: Stove-Top and Oven Recipes—for Everyone! is the second joint effort by Phyllis Pellman Good and the American Diabetes Association. Their first cooperative project was the very popular *Fix-It and Forget-It Diabetic Cookbook: Slow-Cooker Favorites—for Everyone!* The two books work well together—one is for slow cooker recipes, and the other features stove-top and oven cooking.